8th EDITION

AFRICA'S
TOP WILDLIFE COUNTRIES
Botswana, Kenya, Namibia, Rwanda, South Africa,
Tanzania, Uganda, Zambia & Zimbabwe
Also including Ethiopia, Malawi, Mozambique, R. Congo,
Mauritius and Seychelles Islands

MARK W. NOLTING

Africa's Top Wildlife Countries
(Eighth Edition, completely revised and updated)
Copyright: 2012 by Mark Nolting
ISBN: 978-093989515-1
Edited by: Sarah H. Taylor
Cover and Interior Design by: 1106 Design
Maps and Illustrations by Duncan Butchart
Published by: Global Travel Publishers, Inc.

Enquiries should be addressed to: Global Travel Publishers, Inc. 5353 N. Federal Highway, Suite 300, Ft. Lauderdale, FL 33308, U.S.A., Telephone (954) 491-8877 or (800) 882-9453, Facsimile (954) 491-9060. Email safaribooks@aol.com.

PUBLISHER'S NOTE: Although every effort has been made to ensure the correctness of the information in this book, the author, editor and publisher do not assume, and hereby disclaim, any liability to any party for any loss or damage caused by errors, omissions, misleading information or any potential travel problem caused by information in this guide, even if such errors or omission are a result of negligence, accident or any other cause.

Publisher's Cataloging-in-Publication
(Provided by Quality Books, Inc.)

Nolting, Mark, 1951–
    Africa's top wildlife countries : Botswana, Kenya,
Namibia, Rwanda, South Africa, Tanzania, Uganda, Zambia
& Zimbabwe : also including Ethiopia, Malawi,
Mozambique, R. Congo, Mauritius and Seychelles Islands /
Mark W. Nolting.—8th ed.
    Includes index.
    p. cm.
    ISBN 9780-939895-15-1
    ISBN 9780-939895-16-8

    1. Wildlife watching—Africa, Sub-Saharan—
Guidebooks. 2. Safaris—Africa, Sub-Saharan—
Guidebooks. 3. National parks and reserves—Africa,
Sub-Saharan—Guidebooks. 4. Africa, Sub-Saharan—
Guidebooks. I. Title.

QL337.S78N65 2012   916.704'3312
                           QBI12-200012

Printed in the United States of America
Distributed by Publishers Group West / Perseus Books

Printed on recycled paper

. . . .

Dear Safarier:

You are about to plan the adventure of a lifetime! If this is your first safari or your tenth, there is one thing I can guarantee — Africa will inspire you! It is impossible to not be touched in some way by the magic of Africa. The sights and sounds will leave you breathless and the people you'll encounter will leave an imprint on your spirit.

Over the past three decades I have had the privilege of exploring Africa on countless safaris. Having seen the need for an easy-to-use, comprehensive travel guide covering all the top wildlife regions, I authored this guidebook — now in its 8th edition and also available in an electronic version. Having spent hours of preparation for each of my earlier safaris, and carrying with me several heavy resource books on mammals, reptiles, birds and trees, as well as maps, phrase books and a diary, the idea of consolidating all this into one book was formed, and I authored the *African Safari Journal* — now available in it's 5th edition.

Why do so many people wish to go to Africa, and why do so many return time and time again after experiencing a well-planned safari? One of the main allures of Africa is that you can find adventure there. When you go on a game-viewing activity, you never know what you're going to see or what is going to happen. Every safari is exciting.

With so many changes taking place in the realm of travel, it is imperative to book your safari with a company whose expertise and passion are in sync with your own. From my very first safari I had a dream to establish a safari company unlike any other. From that dream, the Africa Adventure Company was born in 1986. For the past nine years I have been honored to have been selected as one of the top *Conde Nast Traveler's* Specialists for Africa in the World, and have been on *Travel & Leisure's* A-List for several years as well. As a company we have steered clear of the cookie cutter itineraries and focused on what we love the most, remote Africa. My passion has been to have people experience the "real Africa." If you have traveled on one of our trips you know what I am referring to; small out-of-the way camps, top notch guiding, incredible game viewing and memories to last a lifetime.

More and more of the continent's wildlife is becoming threatened. We may be the last generation to see Africa in its true glory — huge herds of wildlife and tribal cultures living unaffected lifestyles. Going on a photographic safari is a donation, in itself, toward conserving African wildlife and habitats. A safari could be the most enjoyable and rewarding environmental contribution you will ever make and there is no better time to venture to Africa than the present!

Sincerely,

Mark W. Nolting, President, Africa Adventure Company

A Personal Invitation from the Author

Before booking your trip to Africa, contact us at

The Africa Adventure Company

to discuss the many safari options we have to offer.
Call today — my expert staff and I would love to
assist you in planning your safari!

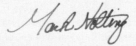

The Africa Adventure Company
5353 North Federal Highway, Suite 300
Ft. Lauderdale, FL 33308
Tel: 800-882-WILD (9453) • Tel: 954-491-8877 • Fax: 954-491-9060
Email: safari@AfricanAdventure.com
Website: www.AfricanAdventure.com

Table of Contents

Table of Contents

Call of the Wild

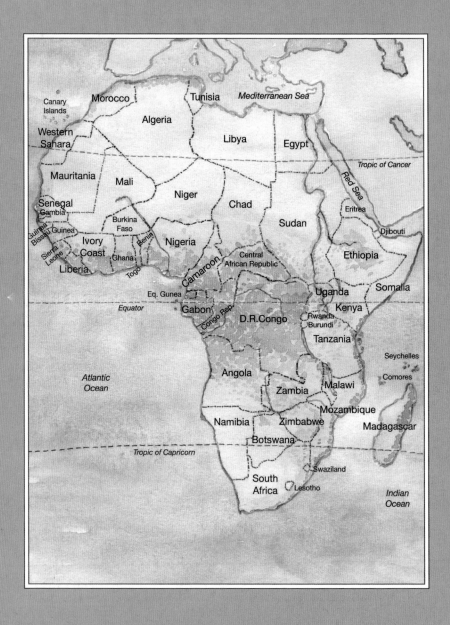

CALL OF THE WILD

A safari to Africa is like no other trip on earth. Most who have ventured to Africa rate it as the best travel experience of their lives. Why? A safari is a real adventure! Africa allows you to experience nature at its finest — almost devoid of human interference. The continent pulses to a natural rhythm of life that has remained basically unchanged since the beginning of time.

At our deepest roots, the African continent communicates with our souls. Travelers return home, not only with exciting stories and adventures to share with friends and family, but with a better understanding of nature, a feeling of accomplishment, increased self-confidence and broader horizons from having ventured where few have gone. Here's the kind of adventure about which many dream but few experience!

Having visited Africa once, you will want to return again and again to the peace, tranquility and adventure it has to offer. In this book, I invite you to explore the reasons for this ceaseless pull as we journey to some of the most fascinating places on earth.

Feature films like *The Serengeti* (Imax), *Out of Africa* and *Gorillas in the Mist,* television series like *The No. 1 Ladies' Detective Agency,* along with countless documentaries, have kindled in the hearts of many people the flame of desire for travel to Africa. Paging through oversized coffeetable books also makes the thought of traveling in Africa almost irresistible.

Most people travel to Africa to see the large and spectacular wildlife, unique to this fascinating continent, in its natural surroundings. In addition to lion, elephant, rhino, buffalo, hippo and giraffe, there is an amazing array of other large and small mammals, as well as spectacular birds and a tapestry of compelling cultures.

The finest safaris are not only those that provide the thrill of seeing the big mammals, but also explore the whole ecosystem and capture the true spirit of the African wilderness — making your visit an exciting and educational experience. The combination of unforgettable adventures, great food, service, accommodations and meeting interesting people is the perfect formula for the trip of a lifetime!

Africa has such a tremendous variety of attractions that most everyone can find something fascinating to do. In addition to fabulous wildlife, the continent boasts one of the world's largest waterfalls (Victoria Falls), the world's longest river (the Nile), the world's largest inland delta (the Okavango), the world's oldest desert (the Namib), the world's largest intact volcanic caldera (Ngorongoro), the world's highest mountain that is not part of a range (Mt. Kilimanjaro) and beautiful cities like Cape Town. Africa is also home to some of the world's last and largest animal migrations. Accommodations ranging from comfortable to opulent have made Africa extremely inviting to even the most discerning traveler and the adventurer as well.

Africa is huge. It is the second largest continent on earth, covering over 20% of the planet's land surface. More than 3 times the size of the United States, it is also larger than Europe, the United States and China combined. No wonder it has so much to offer!

The time to visit Africa is now. Despite a network of large wildlife reserves, Africa's growing population threatens natural habitats and the wildlife they contain, as people look for ways to get ahead. More and more water from the Mara River, Ruaha and Rufiji Rivers in East Africa, for instance, is being used for cultivation, leaving less for the wildlife and changing migration patterns. Some researchers fear that the Serengeti Migration, the greatest migration of large land mammals on earth with over 2 million wildebeest and zebra, is threatened.

Only viable ecotourism initiatives — where local communities reap benefits from foreign income generated by lodges and entry fees to parks — can provide an alternative to short-term poaching, the growing of subsistence crops on marginal land, or selling out to multinational companies that transform entire landscapes into sterile mono-cultures. Most of Africa's people cherish their rich cultural background, yet they also yearn for material development. The challenge is to make room for both. Many of the localities featured in this book will provide you with an opportunity to see wildlife in abundance and also to meet people whose ancestors have been coexisting with nature for thousands of years. But

Zebras are black animals with white stripes with a pattern unique to each individual

the pressure is on, and the time to go is now, while Africa can still deliver all that it promises — and more!

HOW TO USE THIS BOOK

Africa's Top Wildlife Countries highlights and compares wildlife reserves and other major attractions in the continent's best game viewing countries. *This book makes planning your adventure of a lifetime easy. It is based on over 30 years of my first-hand travel experience in Africa, on trip reports from my staff and literally thousands of clients we have sent on safari. This guidebook is designed to help you decide the best place or places to go in Africa, to do what personally interests you most, in a manner of travel that suits you!*

With so much conflicting information available on the Internet, many people become quickly confused. One of the most valuable elements of this book is that I have simplified the travel planning process by **rating the safari accommodations according to the quality of experience** they provide. I have focused on accommodations, parks and reserves that would be of greatest interest to international travelers.

Using the easy-to-read **When's The Best Time To Go For Game Viewing chart** (see inside front cover), you can conveniently choose the specific reserves and country(ies) that are best to visit during your vacation period. From the **What Wildlife Is Best Seen Where chart** (see page 1), you can easily locate the major reserves that have an abundance of the animals you wish to see most. From the **Safari Activities chart** (see page 2), you can choose the reserves that offer the safari options that interest you most. From the **Temperature and Rainfall charts** (see pages 70–71), you can decide how best to dress for safari and have an idea of what weather to expect.

Also included are **Safari Tips, Photography Tips, Packing Lists** and **What to Wear and Take**, and a **Visa/Vaccination chart** to better prepare you and to enhance your enjoyment while on safari.

The **Safari Glossary** (see pages 579–581) contains words commonly used on safari and defines words used throughout the book. English is the major language in most of the countries covered in this guide, so language is, in fact, not a problem for English-speaking visitors.

The **Safari Resource Directory** (see pages 569–592) provides a veritable gold mine of difficult-to-find information and sources on Africa. The **Suggested Reading List** (see pages 582–584) includes publications on the wildlife, cultures, landscapes and history of sub-Saharan Africa.

Want a quick snapshot of camps and lodges that offer the **best safari experience**? Turn to the "Country Highlights" page of each chapter.

The **9 top safari countries** are divided between Southern Africa and East and Central Africa, and, in general, appear in their order of desirability as safari destinations. The most important safari countries are **Botswana, Zimbabwe, Zambia, Namibia** and **South Africa** in Southern Africa and **Tanzania, Kenya, Uganda** and **Rwanda** in East Africa. Following the top wildlife countries in

Every day on safari holds unexpected delights

Southern Africa are chapters on **Mozambique** and **Malawi**, and following the East and Central Africa top countries are chapters on the **Republic of the Congo** and **Ethiopia**. Last but not least are the island paradise countries of the **Seychelles** and **Mauritius**.

To get the most out of this book, first read through this introduction ("Call of the Wild"). Next, in order to start picking the countries that interest you most, read the "**Country Highlights**" pages at the beginning of each chapter, and then the complete chapters on the countries that you feel offer the kind of experience you are looking for in Africa. Then call us at the Africa Adventure Company (toll-free 1-800-882-9453 in the United States and Canada or 954-491-8877 from other countries) or email us (safari@AfricanAdventure.com) to discuss your thoughts, or visit us on our website www.AfricanAdventure.com and complete a safari questionnaire. We will be happy to speak with you, and to match the experience you are looking for with fabulous safari program options — putting you on track to experience the safari of a lifetime!

WHAT IS A SAFARI LIKE?

What is a safari like? For one thing, exciting beyond words!

What is a typical day on safari? Most safaris are centered on guests participating in two or three activities per day, such as morning and afternoon game drives in four-wheel-drive (4wd) vehicles or minivans. A game drive consists of having your guide drive you around a park or reserve in search of wildlife. Your guide helps you to interpret and understand what you are seeing in the bush.

Most activities last 2 to 5 hours and are conducted when the wildlife is most active: early in the morning (often before breakfast), just after breakfast,

Rhinos are herbivores and are characterized by large keratin horn

in the late afternoon and at night (where allowed by park authorities). Midday activities might include spending time in a "hide" observing wildlife coming to a waterhole or river, visiting a local village or school, birdwatching or viewing game as it passes by your tent or lodge, writing about your experiences in your journal, lazing around the swimming pool or taking a siesta (nap). After an exhilarating day on safari, many guests return to revel in the day's adventures over exquisite European or Pan-African cuisine in lodges and camps that range from comfortable to extremely luxurious with private swimming pools and butler service.

The kind and quality of experience you may have on safari vary greatly from country to country, and even from park to park within the same country. For instance, going on safari in the top wildlife countries of East and Central Africa (Kenya, Tanzania, Uganda and Rwanda) is generally very different from going on safari in Southern Africa (Botswana, Zimbabwe, Zambia, Namibia and South Africa).

Simply watching wildlife from a vehicle anywhere in Africa is an experience in itself. However, a growing number of travelers prefer more from the safari than simply watching animals. How can that be accomplished? By choosing a safari that includes parks that allow you to participate in activities that make you a more integral part of the safari, like walking, boating, canoeing, horseback and elephant-back riding. Consider choosing smaller camps and lodges that are unfenced where wildlife is allowed to walk freely about the grounds.

Depending on the park or reserve, safari activities might include day game drives, night game drives, escorted walks, boating, canoeing, kayaking, white-water rafting, ballooning, hiking, mountain climbing, fishing, horseback riding, African elephant-back riding — the options are almost endless. See "Safari Activities" (pages 41–54) and the **Safari Activities Chart** (page 2).

In terms of the long-term future of Africa's wildlife reserves, it is important to consider selecting a destination from which local people benefit in tangible ways. To be guided by or to meet happy people from various cultures and to learn about their customs will greatly enhance your trip to Africa.

Another excellent way to get the most out of your adventure is to have a **private safari** arranged for you. Why? A private safari immediately becomes *your* safari. You do not have to bow to the wishes of the majority of the group or a set itinerary of group departures. With your guide, you are basically free to explore your own interests, spend as much time as you want photographing particular animals, and generally do things at a pace that suits you.

In some cases, for an extra charge you can book a private vehicle for your party when on a flying safari or on a group driving safari. I highly recommend this option as it allows you greater flexibility as to how you spend your time during the day.

To gain a better understanding of what you might experience on safari, I suggest you read the trip reports in **"Bush Tails"** (www.AfricanAdventure.com and see pages 585–592).

DISPELLING MYTHS ABOUT TRAVEL ON THE "DARK CONTINENT"

Many prospective travelers to Africa seem to think that they have to "rough it" on safari. Nothing could be further from the truth!

Almost all of the top parks and reserves covered in this guide have deluxe or first class (Class A+, A or A/B by our grading system) lodges or camps (all with en suite bathrooms) that serve excellent food, specifically designed to cater to the discerning traveler's needs. Going on safari can be a very comfortable, fun-filled adventure!

Many prospective travelers to Africa have voiced their fear of being overwhelmed by mosquitoes and other insects or the fear of encountering snakes on safari. Most travelers return pleasantly surprised, having found that insects or snakes are less of a problem on safari than in their own neighborhoods. For example, on my last several safaris I do not think I had one mosquito bite!

The fact is that most safaris do not take place in the jungle, but on open savannah during the dry season, when the insect populations are at a minimum. In addition, the best time to go on safari, for most of the countries, is during their winter, when insect levels are low and when many snakes hibernate. Also, many parks are located over 3,000 feet (915 m) in altitude, resulting in cool to cold nights, further reducing the presence of any pests. In any case, except for walking safaris, most all of your time in the bush will be spent in the safety of a vehicle or boat. Although some vaccinations are recommended, they are actually not required for travel to many of the top wildlife areas.

LANGUAGE

English is widely spoken in all the countries featured in this book except the Republic of the Congo, where French is the international language.

I recommend picking up a copy of the *African Safari Journal* (see pages 612–613) which has words and phrases in French, KiSwahili (Kenya, Tanzania), Shona (Zimbabwe), Setswana (Botswana) and Zulu (Southern Africa), along with illustrations of 311 mammals, birds, reptiles, insects and trees. Your guide will love it if you start naming the animals you spot in his native language. I suggest you take a copy with you on your safari!

GREEN TRAVEL

Travelers are becoming more and more interested in visiting properties that protect the environment as well as ensure that the local people benefit from their visits. So what does "Going Green" mean? Green travel has a very low impact on the environment. Travelers take photos and leave little more than footprints. True ecotourism ensures that the local people, who are living

Game viewing from an open vehicle

adjacent to parks and reserves, benefit directly from tourism in such a way that they have a positive incentive to preserve wildlife and the environment.

A safari that includes visits to the right camps and lodges is in itself a contribution toward the preservation of wildlife and wildlife areas and an economic benefit and incentive for the local people to protect their environment. This in turn helps ensure these areas will remain intact for generations to come. Taking the right safari could be one of the best donations to the "Green" movement you could make!

SECURITY

Concerns over security for the last several years have become less of an issue for most travelers. Finally, travelers are realizing that most of the top wildlife

The annual migration of bee-eaters in Chobe, Botswana

countries are huge (larger than the state of Texas), and that they need only be concerned with security in the areas in which they are traveling, not every crack and corner of the countries they are visiting.

The question should be "Is travel safe *for tourists* in the specific wildlife reserves and areas you wish to travel?" For instance, I consider the neighborhood I live in "safe." However, there are parts of my city not 2 miles away that I would not like to risk driving through at night. Please keep in mind that the people of these African countries covered in this guide welcome tourists with open arms!

Please also keep in mind that on many safaris, guests actually fly directly from one reserve to another, and the only people they encounter are other guests and the staff and guides in the safari camps and lodges at which they are staying. Driving safaris are most commonly using well-traveled roads, and the guides are in frequent contact with each other and their offices by radio and/or cell phone.

If you hear news of possible security issues, pay attention to where in the country there are concerns; the area of concern could be hundreds of miles from where you are visiting.

There is little to be worried about when it comes to terrorism while on safari. Safari camps and lodges cater to people from all over the world and are, in almost all cases, owned by non-American or non-British companies. One of the safest places in the world has to be in the African bush!

BESPOKE TRAVEL

"Bespoke Travel" is customized, tailor-made adventures. These elite adventures are for travelers who want to focus on unique and exclusive experiences. Many tour companies imply that they have "invented" this level of travel, however, this has been our (Africa Adventure Company) specialty for over 25 years. We call upon our own expertise and valuable contacts in Africa to make those once-in-a-lifetime dreams come true!

CHOOSING ACCOMMODATIONS

The type of accommodation included in a tour of Africa will have a major influence on the type of experience and adventures you will have on safari.

There is a great variety of styles and levels of comfort in accommodation available in the major cities and while on safari varying in range from simple bungalows to extravagant suites with private swimming pools. Options include hotels, lodges, small camps with chalets or bungalows, houseboats, villas, permanent tented camps, seasonal mobile tented camps and private mobile tented camps.

An important factor to consider when choosing accommodations or a tour is the size of the lodges or camps. In general, guests receive more personal attention at smaller camps and lodges than at larger ones. Large properties tend to stick to a set schedule, while smaller properties are often more willing to amend their schedules according to the preferences of their guests. However, larger accommodations tend to be less expensive, which makes tours using the larger ones more affordable.

Many larger lodges and permanent tented camps (especially in East Africa) are surrounded by electrical fences, allowing guests to move about more as they please with little chance of bumping into elephant and other dangerous wildlife. Travelers (including myself) who enjoy having wildlife roaming about camp should seek properties that are not fenced; these lodges and camps are best for travelers who want to experience nature at close quarters.

I feel that the most important element in choosing accommodations for a safari is *location, location, location*. If wildlife is your main focus, then the question should be: "What accommodations are located in areas that will provide the best game viewing — and even more specifically — game viewing of the species you wish to see most, and offer the activities (day and night game drives, walks, motor boat excursions, canoe safaris, etc.) that interest you most?"

Game viewing can be dramatically better (or worse) from one property to the next — from properties that may be literally just a few miles (kilometers) apart. Permanent tented camps in Botswana's Okavango Delta and lodges in the private reserves near Kruger National Park (South Africa) are prime examples of this.

Through personal experience and having read literally thousands of trip reports from past clients, one area can have several times the wildlife concentrations of another area nearby. However, if you look up these properties on the Internet, they all boast to having spectacular game! This is why I suggest booking your safari with a true African expert who has visited the reserves and

5-star luxury at Kings Pool in the Linyanti Reserve, Botswana *(top)*, Seasonal mobile tented camps such as Dunia in Tanzania have their own charm *(bottom)*

receives *frequent and recent* reports from visitors to camps and lodges, as they will know the properties that offer the best game experience and that offer the food, service and accommodation level that would best suit you.

Great photographers can make any camp or lodge look extremely appealing in brochures and on websites. But what is the property really like? How well do the management and staff treat their guests? Is the food really as good as they boast? Again, this is where an African expert can best assist with first-hand experience.

The web is also full of sites where guests boast or complain about properties they have visited. I frankly suggest taking these reports as a tip that you should look further into the situation but do not take them as "gospel," as it is just too easy for lodge, hotel and property owners and staff to write up bogus "outstanding" reports, or, on the other hand, too easy for guests to blow their negative experiences out of proportion. In any case, the reports may be "old news" if new management or owners have been put in place and have turned a property around.

Descriptions of most properties are easy to find on the Web. The discerning reader, however, should look for sites where independent **experts** have written up the hotels, safari camps and lodges — and not the properties themselves. I invite you to visit our website www.AfricanAdventure.com and check out our clients' trip reports with their own unbiased descriptions of their safaris, the accommodations and game viewing experiences.

Hotels and Hotel Classifications

Many African cities have 4- and 5-star (first class and deluxe) hotels that are comparable to lodging anywhere in the world, with air-conditioning, swimming pools, one or more excellent restaurants and bars, and superb service.

Hotels in this book have been categorized as Deluxe, First Class, Tourist Class, and Basic. We have included "Basic" properties only in areas where they are the best or only choice — such as in some remote locations in Ethiopia. **All properties have en suite bathrooms with hot and cold running water showers and flush toilets unless stated in the respective descriptions.**

DELUXE: An excellent hotel, rooms with air-conditioning, one or more restaurants that serve very good food, and that feature a swimming pool, bars, lounges, room service — all the amenities of a four- or five-star international hotel.

FIRST CLASS: A very comfortable hotel, with air-conditioning, at least one restaurant and bar, and most with a swimming pool.

TOURIST CLASS: A comfortable hotel with simple rooms, most with air-conditioning, a restaurant and bar, and most with a swimming pool.

BASIC: A simple property that is the only or the best option in a remote area.

Lodges and Camps

Properties that range from comfortable to deluxe (many have swimming pools) are located in or near most parks and reserves. Many lodges and camps are located in wildlife areas 3,000 feet (915 m) or more above sea level, so air-conditioning often is not necessary.

Lodges are simply "hotels in the bush." Most lodges are constructed with concrete and mortar and are fenced, thus resulting in the sense of being removed from the bush.

There is often confusion over the term "**camp**." A camp can refer to chalets, bungalows or tents found in a remote location. Camps range from very basic to extremely plush. Deluxe camps often have better service and food, and most offer a truer safari atmosphere than large lodges and hotels, and the night sounds can be heard through the canvas walls — an experience, I feel, that should not be missed!

Permanent tented camps (sometimes also called "fixed tented camps") are camps that are not moved. Aside from generally having better food and service than lodges, guests of permanent tented camps have more of a "safari" experience. They are less isolated from the environment than those who stay in a lodge. Tents are normally very large, with lovely en suite bathrooms, and set on raised decks.

Seasonal mobile tented camps are generally located in an area for a few months and then moved to another location, according to seasonal wildlife movements. The tents are usually set on the ground, and have en suite flush toilets and safari (bucket) showers. Seasonal camps are not marked on the maps in this guide as their locations change.

Mobile tented camps are discussed under "Types of Safaris" below.

Lodge and Camp Classifications

Lodges and tented camps are classified as Class A+ to C. In previous editions, I graded accommodations primarily based on facilities, food and service.

However, in this edition, I have taken into account the overall experience, including general quality of game viewing (location, location, location), guides and management. For instance, a lodge that might be rated "A" for accommodations but is in just a fair game-viewing area, or have a reputation for having poor guiding or management, might be rated "A/B" or "B." Alternatively, a property that provides a fabulous overall safari experience might receive a higher rating than the accommodations alone might dictate.

Singita Lebombo features exciting game viewing and upscale accommodations

In general, I have listed the accommodations in order of preference, within each category. There are so many accommodations from which to choose, I have taken a lot of the guess work out of the process for you. Some of the properties included, I feel, are seriously overrated, and have graded them accordingly. You have been warned! Please keep in mind that **a lower-grade accommodation may be preferable over a higher-class** one if the lower-grade option offers better guides and management, a better location (better wildlife) and activities that are of greater interest to you. This is why I list on the "Country Highlights" page of each chapter, properties that provide the **"Best Safari Experience."** As you often spend very little time in your room or tent, I suggest you focus more on the "experience" you wish to have — and not just the facilities.

Please note that, as with hotels, all accommodations have en suite flush toilets and hot and cold running water showers, unless stated otherwise.

CLASS A+: An extremely luxurious lodge or permanent tented camp (five-star) with superb cuisine and excellent service, with swimming pools, and many with private "plunge" pools (small swimming pools) for each chalet or tent. Lodges and chalets are air-conditioned, while the tents may be air-conditioned or fan-cooled.

CLASS A: A deluxe lodge or tented camp, almost all with swimming pools, excellent food and service, large nicely appointed rooms or tents with comfortable beds and tasteful decor; most of the lodges have air-conditioning and the tents are usually fan-cooled.

CLASS A/B: A lodge or tented camp with very good food and service, and many have swimming pools. The rooms/tents are of good size but perhaps not as large as "Class A" properties. Facilities could be "Class A," but located in a sub-standard game viewing area.

CLASS B: A comfortable lodge or camp with good food and service, most with fan-cooled rooms, and many have swimming pools.

CLASS B/C: Most often, a "Class B" property is one that is very rustic or somewhat inconsistent in the quality of accommodation, food and service, or offer a substandard wildlife experience.

CLASS C: A basic lodge or tented camp with fair food and service, or a "Class B" or "B/C" structure with fair to poor food or service, or located in a poor wildlife area.

FOOD ON SAFARI

Excellent cuisine, along with interesting local dishes, is served in the top hotels, lodges, camps and restaurants. Many of the more expensive lodges now produce a combination of "Pan-African cuisine" — innovative recipes and ingredients from across the continent, and international fare. Restaurants serving cuisine from all over the world may be found in the larger cities in Africa.

Most international travelers are impressed with the quality of the food and drink served on their safari. The most common "complaint" I hear on safari is "the food was so good I gained weight!" The fresh air will give you a healthy appetite. Typical meals include:

A private bush dinner complete with delicious cuisine and South African wines

Breakfast — Usually fruit and cereal, eggs, bacon and sausage, toast and preserves, juices, tea and coffee.

Lunch — Assorted cold meats and salads with cheeses and bread, and perhaps a warm dish (i.e. quiche).

Dinner — Normally three courses, with an appetizer or soup, main entree and vegetables, and a dessert. Class A+ (and some Class A) lodges and camps usually serve four or more courses.

Some safari camps and lodges will provide a light breakfast of tea, coffee, rusks (hard biscuits traditionally served in southern Africa), and cereal in the early morning. Brunch is served at about 11:00 a.m. and follows a game drive or other activity. Tea, coffee, cake and biscuits (cookies) are served at about 3:30 p.m. Following the afternoon game activity, guests return to the lodge for a delicious dinner.

TYPES OF SAFARIS

Flying Safaris

Flying safaris are safaris in which guests are flown within or near the wildlife reserves that are to be visited. They are then usually picked up at the airport or airstrip upon arrival and driven to their camp or lodge — which is often a game drive in itself.

Guides and vehicles are based at the camps and lodges at which guests will be staying. Guests join others staying at the property on "shared" game activities, or, most often for a surcharge, they may book a private vehicle and guide. A real advantage is that the resident guides should have intimate knowledge of the area because they are usually based in the same camp for the season.

This type of safari is very popular in Botswana, Zimbabwe, Zambia, Namibia, South Africa, Kenya and Tanzania. Time that would normally be spent on the road driving between the parks and reserves may instead be spent game viewing — the primary reason why most people travel to Africa in the first place!

Flying safaris are popular in both Southern and Eastern Africa

Guided Driving or Mobile Safaris

Driving safaris are simply safaris in which guests are driven by their driver/ guide from reserve to reserve. You generally have the same guide throughout the safari, who should have very good knowledge of all the parks and reserves to be visited.

Driving safaris are usually less expensive than flying safaris. However, travelers should take into account the amount of time it takes to get from reserve to reserve, the quality of the roads and whether or not there will be something enroute that will be of interest to them, and compare that to the cost of doing some or all flying on their safari. Some driving safaris make good sense as the parks and reserves are close to each other, or there are other things of interest to see enroute, such as schools or villages that the travelers wish to visit.

Fly/Drive Safaris

As the name implies, these safaris are a combination of some driving and some flying. The general idea is to fly over areas that are not interesting to drive or that you have already covered on the ground, and drive through the areas that have the most to offer. This is an excellent option in northern Tanzania, for instance, where safariers may be driven from Arusha to Tarangire, Lake Manyara, Ngorongoro Crater and the Serengeti, and then fly back to Arusha instead of driving the same route back. Other popular fly/drive options are available in northern Botswana (small group mobile safaris), Kenya and Uganda.

Self-Drive Safaris

In Africa, self-drive safaris are a viable option for general sightseeing in countries such as South Africa and possibly Namibia that have excellent road systems. However, self-drive safaris into wildlife parks and reserves are, in general, not a good idea for several reasons.

One major disadvantage of a self-drive safari is that you miss the information and experience that a professional driver/guide can provide. A good guide is also an excellent wildlife spotter and knows when and where to look for the animals you want to see most. In many cases, he or she can communicate with other guides to find out where the wildlife has most recently been seen. This also leaves you free to concentrate on photography and game viewing instead of worrying about the road, and it eliminates the anxiety of the possibility of getting lost.

Self-drive safaris, especially ones requiring 4wd vehicles, are most often more expensive than joining a group safari. Gas (petrol) is generally a lot more expensive than it is in North America. Vehicle rental costs are also high, and the driving is often on the left side of the road.

Finally, self-drive safaris by people without extensive experience in the bush can be dangerous. Lack of knowledge about wildlife and the bush can result in life-threatening situations.

An International Driver's License is required by some of the countries covered in this book. Contact the tourist offices, consulates, or embassies of the countries in which you wish to drive for any additional requirements.

Overland Safaris

Overland safaris may cover several countries and last from around six weeks to nine months. Participants take care of all the chores and sleep in small pup tents. In addition to the initial cost of the trip, travelers must contribute to a "food kitty." The trip leader is generally hired for his mechanical skills and often knows little if anything about wildlife. In any case these safaris are primarily about getting from point A to point B, and have little wildlife orientation. Because many of these safaris originate in Europe, where they load up with supplies, only a small amount of the money spent for the safari reaches the local people. A lack of local infusion of funds places this type of safari very low on the ecotourism scale.

Lodge and Permanent Tented Camp Safaris

Lodge safaris are simply safaris that use lodges or permanent tented camps as accommodations. Some safaris mix lodges with tented camps or camps with chalets or bungalows, providing a greater range of experiences for their guests.

Mobile Tented Camp Safaris

Private and group mobile tented camp safaris are, in my opinion, one of the best ways to experience the bush and a great way of getting off the beaten track. Tents are set up in a campsite for a party of guests and then taken down after they leave. Tanzania, Zimbabwe and Botswana are excellent countries for mobile tented safaris; Kenya, Zambia and Namibia are also good destinations for this type of safari.

Mobile tented safaris range from deluxe to first class, midrange, limited participation and participation safaris. You may join a group departure or have a private safari, depending on your interests and budget. **Warning:** some tour operators advertise their mobile tented camp safaris as "luxury" when they actually operate them on a first class or even a midrange level (i.e. small tents with shower and toilet tents separate from the sleeping tents). Be sure to be perfectly clear as to what services they provide!

Tanzania has perfected deluxe mobile camping safaris

Another factor to consider is that the guides on higher-level mobile safaris are generally better than the ones on lower-level safaris.

Deluxe mobile tented camp safaris are the epitome of an African safari. The sleeping tents are large (approx. 12-by-16 ft./4-by-5 m in floor area or larger) and have en suite safari or bush (bucket) showers and safari (bush) toilets. Food and service are excellent. Camp attendants take care of everything, including the delivery of hot water for your shower. Campsites are private and usually set in remote areas of parks and reserves, providing a true *Out of Africa* experience. For a party of 4, the cost generally ranges from $650 to $1,200 per person per day.

First Class mobile tented safaris are similar to deluxe safaris except that the tents are a little smaller (approx. 8-by-12 ft./2.5-by-3.5 m), yet very comfortable; less expensive cutlery and crockery may be used, there are not quite as many staff, and there is usually a safari shower (hot water) and safari toilet tent attached to the back of each sleeping tent. The food and service is still very good, and private campsites are used. For a party of 4, the cost is around $500 to $600 per person per day, depending on the country and season.

Less expensive **midrange mobile tented safaris** are available in a number of countries. Like deluxe and first class mobile tented safaris, a camp staff takes care of all the chores. The difference is that the tents are smaller (approx.

8-by-8 ft./2.5-by-2.5 m) but are still high enough in which to stand. The food and service are good, and guests from one to three sleeping tents may share one separate toilet tent and one separate shower tent (with hot water). Private or group campsites may be used. For a party of 4, the cost is usually around $350 to $450 per person per day.

On **Limited Participation mobile tented safaris**, the guide usually has one camp attendant to do the heavy work, while guests are expected to assist in some camp chores. Bow-type nylon tents (approx. 8-by-8 ft./2.5-by-2.5 m) are often used, and you usually camp in public campsites. Rates typically range from $250 to $300 per person per day.

On full **participation mobile tented safaris**, participants are required to help with all of the camp chores. Group campsites with basic (if any) facilities are often used.

The only advantage is price. Participation camping safaris are almost always less expensive than lodge safaris. However, these are recommended for only hardy travelers with previous camping experience or with a sense of adventure. Many operators have minimum and maximum age limits for their safaris. Hot showers are usually available most nights, but not all. The cost is usually under $175 per person per day. The problem with these low-end safaris is that the guiding is often marginal at best, greatly compromising the quality of the experience.

Group Safaris

Group safaris are, in many cases, a more cost-effective way of experiencing the bush than private safaris (see below). Group safaris usually have scheduled departure dates. The key for group safaris in Africa is to be sure the group size is small. Group size should be limited, in my opinion, to 12 or fewer guests, whereas a maximum of 6 to 8 is preferable.

It never ceases to amaze me the number of tour operators that tout that their maximum group size is limited to *only* 16, 24 or 30 members. With such large groups, passengers in the lead vehicle see game, while those in the vehicles that follow eat dust. Each group usually has one head guide, who is followed by junior guides. A great deal of time is wasted getting under way and time schedules are very inflexible. Large group tours may be fine for Europe or Asia, but they have no place in the African bush!

Private Safaris

For those who wish to avoid groups, a private safari is highly recommended for several reasons.

An itinerary can be specially designed according to the kind of experience YOU want, visiting the parks and reserves YOU wish to see most, and traveling on dates that suit YOU best.

You may spend your time doing what you want to do rather than having to compromise with the group. If you wish, you may socialize with other travelers at mealtimes and still have the flexibility to do what you want on your game activities.

For instance, if you find a leopard up a tree with a kill, you may stay a few minutes or a few hours at that location — it's up to you!

What few people realize is that, in many cases, a private safari need not cost more than one with a large group. In fact, I have sent many couples and small groups on private safaris for not much more (and often less) than the cost of group safaris from other tour operators who offer the same or often inferior itineraries. If you find that difficult to believe, call, email or write us with what you have in mind, and we'll be happy to send you some sample itineraries (see pages 615 through inside back cover).

Specialist Guided Safaris

A specialist guide is a seasoned naturalist with extensive experience and excellent communication skills — one of the top guides in the region.

How significant is your guide on safari? There is a maxim in the Safari Industry that "a very good guide will take your safari to the next level, and make it 'spectacular.'" Using enthusiasm, insight, knowledge, and patience, an expert guide will make your vacation not just a safari, but also an unparalleled trip of a lifetime. The additional experience gained by having one of the top guides in Africa lead your safari is almost priceless.

Author Mark Nolting's wife and son, Alison and Nicholas, on a walking safari in Mana Pools, Zimbabwe, with specialist guide, Nick Murray

Your safari guide will spend anywhere from 8 to 15 hours with you per day, basically every waking moment. He or she will become your protector, teacher, fireside storyteller, and most of all, friend. It is very easy for any guide to point out the animals, however an outstanding guide will reveal to you the extraordinary spirit of Africa and what it has to offer.

Some specialist guides are great overall naturalists, while others may be experts in particular subjects, such as elephants, predators, birds, botany, nature photography, anthropology, archaeology, etc.

I feel it is a great idea (budget permitting) for a specialist guide to accompany travelers, especially on flying safaris (from one safari camp to another), as it adds continuity of a consistent high level of guiding throughout the safari; they are generally much more experienced than guides that are based at the safari camps and lodges themselves, and are in most cases very entertaining as well. We at the Africa Adventure Company in fact offer this upgrade option to many of our clients!

Honeymoon Safaris

There is no more romantic setting for a honeymoon than an African safari. Most honeymooners begin with a few days to relax and recover from the wedding in a five-star hotel or beach resort — then it's off on safari!

Honeymoon safaris, like all safaris, can include as plush or rustic accommodations, as you wish. Most camps and small lodges have a "honeymoon tent" or "honeymoon suite" on the premises to ensure maximum privacy. Please keep in mind that some tented camps and small lodges have two single beds in most of their rooms or tents, so be sure to let them know you are indeed honeymooners.

The epitome of a honeymoon safari, in my opinion, is to have a private vehicle and guide, and preferably spend at least a few nights in a tented camp. Tenting is truly the *Out of Africa* experience! A few nights tenting could be combined with time in more luxurious permanent tented camps and/or lodges — according to the honeymooner's tastes. What an exciting way to begin a life together!

Family Safaris

More and more parents and grandparents are taking their children and grandchildren on safari. Seeing nature in all its abundance as a child is an experience that cannot be underestimated. As of this writing, our son Miles is 18 years old, and has been on 12 safaris, and our son Nicholas is 15 and has been on ten safaris. We have thoroughly enjoyed experiencing Africa through their eyes. The kids have had numerous life-changing moments filled with exploration and adventure!

In most cases, the best option for families is a private safari with your own vehicle(s) and guide(s). You may travel at your own pace and choose camps and lodges that offer amenities, like swimming pools, that will provide the kids with

A special moment with African wild dog during a family safari in Mana Pools

some playtime as well as help them burn off some of that endless energy they seem to possess. In addition, visits to local schools and villages can provide insights into how children of their own age live in the countries you are visiting — and will hopefully make them more thankful for what they have!

Most guides, camp and lodge staff love to have children visit, and they go out of their way to make kids and the parents feel welcome. Be sure to plan into your trips some activities that your children enjoy.

Many camps and lodges have special children's programs where they are cared for and taken on their own adventures — allowing the parents to go on game drives alone or giving the children the opportunity to participate in other activities. On a recent trip our 2 boys had the time of their lives as they were taken out target practicing and were taught how to drive a land rover!

Many of the smaller camps and lodges in Africa have minimum age restrictions (usually ranging from 7 to 16 years of age), while most of the larger camps and lodges have no restrictions at all. Some camps and lodges have minimum age restrictions (12 or 16 years old) for activities offered, such as walks in the bush with professional guides and canoeing. However, if, for instance, your family or group takes over the entire lodge, camp or canoe safari departure, or if you do a private mobile safari, you can, in many instances, get around the minimum age

Why we like Africa

Our family vacations in Africa at least every other year. We started taking the kids when they were between 4½ and 5 years old. Before we get back from one trip we are already planning our next. What beckons us to keep on returning?

Madeline, who is almost 15 says, "I love going on game drives and spotting animals. I'm always scanning the trees and the tall grasses for leopards, cheetahs and lions. Taking pictures has now become a big thing for me. I always have my camera out and am ready to go. I love waking up every morning listening to the calls of the various birds of Africa. The fresh air and the beautiful sunrises are also great bonuses to waking up in the wilderness."

For Jack who is now age 13, "The flat plains and the fresh air are what make me want to come back. I love the open vehicles and the variety of animals. My favorite animal is the leopard, but I also like snakes and lizards. I also love using my big binoculars to spot all different kinds of game animals from far away."

Sean who is now 12 says, "I love seeing our guide Nic." (We all do.) "Besides going on game drives and photographing animals, I love to hang out at camp and play games. I also enjoy sitting by the fire and talking about our day and then eating a delicious meal. I even love all the noises in Africa, especially the grunting of hippos."

We traveled to Africa several times before kids and loved the adventure and seeing what life is like with little human intervention. Being in Africa makes us realize that there is an entirely different, peaceful world out there and it's important for the kids to see life outside our little suburb. We try to visit new places every time we go to Africa but there are some spots in which we long to return.

Madeline, Jack, Sean, Wendy and Mike Malloon

The Malloon's in Victoria Falls, Zimbabwe

requirements. As some safari camps and lodges cater to a maximum of 6 to 20 guests, taking over a camp may be easier than you think. Just try to book your safari well in advance to ensure availability.

For anyone wishing to travel only in malarial-free areas with their children, some reserves to consider are Madikwe, Kwandwe, Shamwari or Addo Elephant National Park in South Africa. Please keep in mind that malarial prophylaxes (pills or syrup) are available for children and adults alike.

Voluntourism Safaris

Voluntourism is the forefront of adventure travel and is seeing incredible growth across Africa. The opportunity to expand one's horizons beyond a traditional safari experience and work hand-in-hand with local conservationists and communities is unforgettable!

Voluntourism is commonly defined as the practice of individuals going on a non-paid working holiday for the purpose of volunteering themselves to worthy causes. Programs can vary widely from assisting in schools, orphanages and clinics to assisting environmentalists on game counts in a reserve. Programs can vary in length from a few days to several months. Many travelers book a traditional safari and then add on 3 days to 3 weeks on a worthwhile voluntourism program. For examples of interesting and exciting voluntourism programs, please see "The Mother Africa Trust on page 160 and go to www.AfricanAdventure.com.

Cultural Safaris

As the world becomes more modernized, the opportunity to go "back in time" visiting remote tribes is becoming rarer by the day.

Some of the safaris I personally treasure the most are ones I have taken "off the map" — visiting remote, "primitive" tribes that have had little interaction with the western world.

You can focus your entire trip on culture, or you can include cultural visits and interaction ranging from a few hours to several days to a wildlife safari.

Tall, slim and slender, the **Maasai** (Kenya and Tanzania) and **Samburu (Kenya)** are nomadic cattle and goat herders, and for them cattle is the most important social, economic, and political factor. Cattle are a sign of wealth and social standing, as well as a food source from a mixture of milk and blood tapped from a cow's jugular vein. The **Maasai** traditional homeland is southern Kenya and northern Tanzania in an area that has the most visited game parks and reserves, and are therefore the most frequently encountered by visiting tourists. Considering this exposure to western tourists, they still maintain remarkable facets of their original cultural identity.

The **Samburu** are closely related to the Maasai, speaking the same language *(Maa)* and follow many similar traditions. With their traditional homeland around Maralal in north central Kenya, the majority of their population is well away from the main areas of tourist and government influence. Like the Maasai, their morani (warriors) prefer red blankets and use red ochre to decorate their heads,

Cultural adventures include visiting the remote tribes of the Omo River Valley, Ethiopia

and the women wear beaded jewelry. They also tend cattle and goats, but it is cattle which is the center of Samburu social, political, and economic life. The Samburu are still nomadic people and when pasture becomes scarce in this semi-arid land, they pack up their manyattas (small settlements) on camels and move to better pastures.

The **Gabbra** are a remote, striking tribe located in northern Kenya. With no written language the continued existence of these tribal customs is a tribute to these hardy and resilient people who live very much beyond the confines of the modern world in possibly the harshest desert environment on the continent.

Located in southern Ethiopia, Omo River Valley is home to some of the most primitive tribes on earth. **Mursi** and Surma women practice some of the most profound forms of body adornment in the world today — inserting a seven inch diameter clay plate into their lower lips. Unmarried men practice the "Donga," or "stick fighting." Both men and women of the agro-pastoralist **Hamar Koke** tribe are stunningly beautiful with their long braided hair. The **Karo** are known for their exceptional face and body painting and for their dances and ceremonies. The **Dassanech** are pastoralists, and also practice flood retreat cultivation on the vast expanses of the Omo Delta in southern Ethiopia. Many of the Dassanech men are spectacularly scarified — depicting the number of enemies killed in battle.

Bushmen (Tanzania, Botswana and Namibia) are short in stature and of a yellowish/brown color, often living a hunter gathering lifestyle. Their language contains a variety of distinct clicks. These are the very earliest of cultures of Africa, responsible for the ancient rock paintings found in the Kalahari and south. Although simplistic in explanation, Bushmen are genetically more similar to Scientific Adam than any group elsewhere on the planet.

The **Himba** inhabit the Kaokoland area of Namibia. They are truly striking people to look at, as both men and women cover their bodies with a mixture of rancid butter, ash and ochre to protect them from the sun and give them their "signature" deep red color.

If this cultural element of travel interests you, my advice is to go now — as this type of experience is vanishing quickly!

Sole Use Accommodation (Villa) Safaris

Villa rentals are common-place in Europe and are often favored by travelers who look for a bit more independence and exclusivity on their vacation. The idea has expanded in Africa and now you can find villas or sole-use small safari camps and lodges that can be taken over on an exclusive basis in some of the most pristine game viewing regions in East and southern Africa. A private guide and vehicle, butler, chef and the privacy and freedom to dictate each day are just some of the reasons why this is the perfect answer for family and friends traveling together.

A customized safari could include stays at a number of sole-use properties in different reserves. South Africa, Kenya and Tanzania have the most villas from which to choose. Some of the top lodges and small camps to consider include:

- BOTSWANA: Little Mombo (Moremi GR) and Zarafa (Linyanti)
- ZAMBIA: Luangwa House and Robin's House (South Luangwa NP), Chongwe River House (Lower Zambezi NP), Kapinga Camp (Kafue NP) and Chuma Houses (Mosi-Oa-Tunya National Park)
- NAMIBIA: Little Ongava (Ongava GR)
- SOUTH AFRICA: Singita Castleton (Sabi Sands GR), Royal Malewane Royal and Malewane Suites (Thornybush GR), Uplands Homestead and Melton Manor (Kwandwe), Mount Anderson Ranch, Royal Madikwe (Madikwe GR), Tarkuni (Tswalu Kalahari Reserve), The Homestead and Zuka Lodge (Phinda GR)
- TANZANIA: Serengeti House (Grumeti Reserves), Bailey's Banda and Kiba Point (Selous)
- KENYA: The Sanctuary at Ol Lentille, Loisaba House and Loisaba Cottage, Laragai House and Ol Malo House (Laikipia), Ngarie Niti (Lewa Downs), Kanzi House (Tsavo/Amboseli) and Alfajiri (the coast)

- RWANDA: Jack Hanna's Guesthouse (Parc des Volcans)
- ZIMBABWE: Pamushana (Malilangwe Private Reserve), Little Vundu (Mana Pools), Acacia Camp (Hwange)

SAFARI ACTIVITIES

Africa can be experienced in many exciting ways. What follows are a number of types of safari activities. For additional information, refer to the country or countries mentioned.

Game Drives

The type of vehicle used on game drives varies from country to country.

Open vehicles usually have 2 or 3 rows of elevated seats behind the driver's seat. There are no side or rear windows or permanent roof, which provides you with unobstructed views in all directions and a feeling of being part of the environment instead of on the outside looking in. This is the type of vehicle most often used for viewing wildlife by safari camps in southern Africa. Open vehicles are used in Botswana, Zambia, Zimbabwe, Mozambique, Republic of the Congo and in private reserves in South Africa.

Open sided vehicles are open vehicles with roofs — often made of canvas, and are used in camps in southern Tanzania, and some

Safariers in a pop-top vehicle observing tree-climbing lions in Tanzania

camps that cater to flying safaris in northern Tanzania, Kenya, and Namibia. Open sided vehicles are not allowed in Kenya and Tanzania on driving safaris where you are driving from park to park.

In 4wd vehicles with **roof hatches or pop-top roofs**, riders may look through the windows or stand up through the roof for game viewing and photography. Ensuring that window seats are guaranteed for every passenger (a maximum of 6 or 7 passengers) is imperative. These vehicles are primarily used in Kenya, Tanzania and Uganda. Roof-hatch vehicles in these countries are generally more

Walking safaris are an exciting way to explore the bush

practical than open vehicles, because reserves in these countries usually get some rainfall 12 months of the year. On driving safaris in eastern and southern Africa, roof-hatch vehicles are often preferred because they offer more protection from rain, sun, wind and dust.

Wildlife viewing, and especially photography, is more difficult where **closed vehicles** are required (i.e. in national parks in South Africa).

Night Game Drives

Many African animals, including most of the big cats, are more active after dark, and night game drives open up a whole new world of adventure. Much of the actual hunting by lion and leopard happens after nightfall; therefore, night drives probably provide your best chance to observe these powerful cats feeding or even making a kill. Vehicles are typically driven by your guide, and an assistant (tracker) handles a powerful spotlight. By driving slowly and shining the beam into the surrounding bush, the eyes of animals are reflected back, and it is then possible to stop and take a closer look. When an infra-red filter is used on the beam, most animals behave in

A leopard is spotted during a night drive

a completely natural manner (providing the occupants of the vehicle keep quiet and still) and marvelous scenes can unfold.

Leopard, lion, hyena, bushbabies, porcupine, aardvark, genets, civets and honey badgers would be among the highlights of a night game drive, with nocturnal birds, such as owls and nightjars, adding to the experience. Night drives are conducted in national parks in Zimbabwe, Zambia and Malawi, and in private concessions or private reserves in Botswana, Zimbabwe, Kenya, Namibia, Tanzania, and South Africa.

Walking Safaris

Walking safaris put you in closest touch with nature. Suddenly your senses come alive — every sight, sound and smell becomes intensely meaningful. Could that flash of bronze in the dense brush ahead be a lion? I wonder how long ago these rhino tracks were made? Can that herd of elephant ahead see or smell us approaching?

Accompanied by an armed wildlife expert or Professional Guide, walking safaris last anywhere from a few hours to several days. The bush can be examined up close and at a slower pace, allowing for more attention to its fascinating detail than a safari solely by vehicle. Participants can often approach game quite closely, depending on the direction of the wind and the cover available.

The excitement of tracking rhino and lion on foot, crawling among a pack of African wild dog or being mock-charged by a young bull elephant is beyond words. Guides do not usually bring guests closer to wildlife than is comfortable for them. Zimbabwe, followed by Zambia are the best countries to visit for those looking for this type of adventure. Walking is also available in some parts of Botswana, Namibia, Mozambique, Malawi, Tanzania, Kenya, Uganda, Rwanda and South Africa.

Boat/Canoe/Kayak/Mokoro Safaris

Wildlife viewing by boat, canoe, kayak or mokoro from rivers or lakes often allows you to approach wildlife as close or even closer than by vehicle. **Game viewing** and birdwatching **by boat** is available in:

- BOTSWANA: Chobe National Park, Linyanti, Selinda, Kwando and the Okavango Delta
- ZIMBABWE: Along the shores of Lake Kariba including Matusadona National Park, and on the Zambezi River upstream from Victoria Falls and downstream from the Kariba Dam, including areas adjacent to Mana Pools National Park
- ZAMBIA: Upstream from Victoria Falls, along Lower Zambezi National Park and Kafue National Park
- MALAWI: Liwonde National Park
- SOUTH AFRICA: Phinda and iSimangaliso
- TANZANIA: On the Rufiji River, Ruaha River, and some lakes in the Selous Game Reserve
- UGANDA: On the Kazinga Channel in Queen Elizabeth National Park, on the Victoria Nile in Murchison Falls National Park and on Lake Mburo in Lake Mburo National Park

Canoe safaris are, in my opinion, one of the most exciting ways of experiencing the bush. Paddling or silently drifting past herds of elephant frolicking on the river's edge, and watching herds of buffalo and other game cross the river channels in front of you are a few examples of what you may encounter.

Canoe safaris from 3 to 9 days are operated along the Zambezi River below Kariba Dam on both the Zimbabwe and Zambia sides of the river. Wildlife is best in the area along Mana Pools National Park (Zimbabwe) and Lower Zambezi National Park (Zambia). Of all African adventures, this is definitely one of my favorites. Motorboats are not allowed along Mana Pools National Park; however, they are allowed along the Lower Zambezi National Park. Mana Pools is, in my opinion, by far the best place in Africa (if not the world) for canoe safaris. Excursions can last from a few hours to 3 days are available.

Canoeing adventure on the Zambezi River in Mana Pools, Zimbabwe

Short excursions are also available upstream from Victoria Falls (Zimbabwe and Zambia), along Matusadona National Park (Zimbabwe) and Kafue National Park (Zambia). One- to 3-day **kayak** safaris are operated along Zambezi River in Zambezi National Park upstream from Victoria Falls, Zimbabwe. Canoeing is also available on the Savuti Channel (Linyanti Concession), the Selinda Spillway (Selinda Concession) in Botswana, Phinda (South Africa) and Niassa (Mozambique).

Mokoro safaris from a few hours to several days in length are available in the Okavango Delta (Botswana). A mokoro is a flat-bottomed, dugout canoe used in the watery wilderness of the Okavango Delta. Although these craft may appear unstable, there is no better way to experience the beauty and tranquility of this spectacular wetland. Experienced polers pilot the mokoro through channels of papyrus and floating fields of water lilies, each with 1 or 2 passengers aboard.

Photographic (Photo) Safaris

The term "photo safari" generally means any kind of safari except where hunting is involved.

In its strictest sense, a photo safari is a safari during which you are escorted by a professional wildlife photographer. These safaris are mainly about learning wildlife photography and getting the best photos possible. These are recommended only for the serious shutterbug.

The best option by far for the serious photographer is to have a private vehicle and guide (see "Private Safaris" pages 33–34). Group safaris generally move too quickly from place to place, allowing insufficient time to get the best shots.

Balloon Safaris

At 5:30 in the morning, we were awakened by steaming hot coffee and tea brought to our bedsides by our private tent keeper. We were off at 6:00 for a short night game drive to where the hot-air balloons were being filled. Moments later, we lifted above the plains of the Serengeti Plains for the ride of a lifetime.

Silently viewing game from the perfect vantage point, we brushed the tops of giant acacia trees for close-up views of birds' nests and baboons.

A balloon safari over the Mara River in the Maasai Mara, Kenya

Most animals took little notice, but somehow the hippos knew we were there. Maybe it was our shadow or the occasional firing of the burners necessary to keep us aloft.

Our pilot was entertaining and knowledgeable of the ecosystem we flew over, and pointed out a variety of large birds flying alongside us and plains game, as well as a cheetah. We had the opportunity to see part of the Great Serengeti Migration from the air — an awesome sight indeed!

Our return to earth was an event in itself. About an hour after lift-off, our pilot made a perfect crash landing. By the way, most landings are "crash landings," so just follow your pilot's instructions and join in the fun.

Minutes later, a champagne breakfast appeared on the open savannah within clear view of herds of wildebeest, buffalo and zebra. Our return to camp was another exciting game drive, only a little bumpier than the trip out.

Hot-air balloon safaris are available in Kenya in the Maasai Mara Game Reserve and at Taita Hills near Tsavo West National Park, in Serengeti National Park (Seronera area, the Western Corridor and seasonally in the south), Tarangire National Park in Tanzania, near Namib-Naukluft National Park in Namibia, and in Pilanesberg Nature Reserve and Hazyview in Mpumalanga (South Africa).

Gorilla Safaris

Gorilla trekking is one of the most exciting adventures you can have on the "dark continent" and is certainly one of the most exciting experiences of my life.

Mountain gorillas now number about 700 individuals that live in the cool, forested heights of the Virunga Volcanoes, which straddle three countries — Rwanda, Uganda and the Democratic Republic of the Congo. This is the region in which renowned but controversial primatologist Dian Fossey undertook her studies.

Because the respective governments of Rwanda and Uganda do value the great apes for the foreign currency that they attract, efforts to conserve the remaining gorillas and provide opportunities to view them are extremely good. Correspondingly, security for tourists traveling to these areas is superb.

About 19 miles (30 km) to the north of the Virunga Mountains is Uganda's Bwindi Impenetrable National Park, which provides a refuge for an additional 300+ mountain gorillas.

Gorillas are perhaps the most charismatic of all animals, and a close encounter with a free-ranging family in their forest home will never be forgotten. A typical experience involves an uphill hike through thick vegetation in the company of a park ranger, trackers, porters and two armed guards. Habituated family groups are located, and you'll watch for an hour as they feed and go about their business.

Due to the threat of gorillas contracting potentially fatal human diseases, visitors are encouraged to keep a fair distance from them. The maximum group size is limited to 8 trekkers and gorilla visits are limited to 60 minutes.

Rare mountain gorilla twins in Rwanda's Volcanoes National Park

Given the physical exertion required, gorilla trekking is recommended only for safariers in reasonably good hiking condition. Stretchers are in fact available at some lodges to carry elderly or handicapped individuals that could not make the trek on their own. A large and growing number of people have been inspired to visit these peaceful relatives of mankind, and permits are at a premium in terms of both cost and availability.

Mountain gorillas are currently best seen in Bwindi Impenetrable Forest (Uganda) and Volcanoes National Park in Rwanda, and lowland gorillas in Odzala-Kokoua National Park (Republic of the Congo). At the time of this writing, gorilla trekking in the Democratic Republic of the Congo is not recommended, due to lack of security, however, security does appear to be improving. Permit fees, which provides funds for conservation, are as of this writing $750.00 per visit at Volcanoes National Park. The minimum age for trekking is 15. Permits for gorilla trekking are limited and gorilla safaris should be booked very far (a year if possible) in advance!

Chimpanzee Trekking

Chimpanzee trekking, like gorilla trekking, can be exciting beyond words. Chimp trekking is best in Mahale Mountains National Park and Gombe Stream

Chimp trekking is best in Mahale (Tanzania) and Kibale (Uganda)

National Park (Tanzania), Kibale Forest National Park (Uganda) and Nyungwe Forest Reserve (Rwanda). Watching the interactions of members of a troop of chimpanzees around you at close quarters is very entertaining!

White-Water Rafting

For white-water enthusiasts and newcomers alike, the Zambezi River (Zambia/Zimbabwe) below Victoria Falls is one of the most challenging rivers in the world. Some rapids are "Class Five" — the highest class runable. Zambia and Zimbabwe offer half-day and full-day trips, with Zambia also offering 2- and 3-day trips and Zimbabwe offering 2- to 6-day trips. Jinja (Uganda) also has Class Five white-water rafting and kayaking on the River Nile. The minimum age to participate is 15. No previous experience is required. Just hang on and have the time of your life! Half-day rafting and boogie boarding combinations are also offered on the Zambezi River (Zimbabwe).

White water rafting on the Zambezi River, Zambia and Zimbabwe *(top)*, An elephant-back safari in Victoria Falls, Zimbabwe *(middle)*, Horseback riding at ol Donyo Lodge, Kenya *(bottom)*

Elephant-Back Safaris

Elephant-back is a fabulous way to explore the bush. Guests ride well-trained African elephants, which are much larger than Indian elephants. Getting "up close and personal" with these amazingly intelligent mammals is both heartwarming and exciting!

Elephant-back safaris are offered at Abu's Camp in the Okavango Delta (Botswana), the Kapama Game Reserve (South Africa), near Victoria Falls (Zimbabwe) and Livingstone (Zambia).

Horseback Safaris

Game viewing by horseback is yet another intriguing way to experience the bush. Horseback safaris for the avid horseman from 5 to 10 days in length are conducted in the Okavango Delta (Botswana), for several days in length in the Tuli Block (Botswana) and at ol Donyo Lodge, and on the Mara plains (Kenya). These safaris are for only serious riders who can canter and who would enjoy spending 6 or more hours in the saddle each day.

Half and full-day safaris for the amateur or serious rider with less time are available at Victoria Falls (Zambia and Zimbabwe), the Tuli Block (Botswana), ol Donyo Lodge, Ol Lentille, Loisaba and Borana (Kenya), the Grumeti Reserves (Tanzania), Maputaland Coastal Forest Reserve, and the Waterberg region and Cape Town (South Africa).

Camel Safaris

Camel safaris allow access to remote desert areas which in many cases are difficult for 4wd vehicles to reach. Guests do some riding but primarily walking on multi-day trips escorted by Samburu or other tribesmen, with overnights in fly camps. This is a fabulous family safari as families can spend quality bonding time together. Camel excursions for a few hours in length are available from a number of safari camps and lodges in the Laikipia and Samburu areas of northern Kenya.

Train Safaris

Two of the most luxurious trains in the world — Rovos Rail and the Blue Train, offer excursions primarily in South Africa but also to Namibia, Zimbabwe and Tanzania. See the chapter on South Africa for details.

Quad Biking Safaris

Quad bike safaris are a fabulous way to explore primarily the desert regions of Africa. Riding up and down 600 foot (183 m) sand dunes in the Namib Desert near Swakopmund and visiting remote Himba tribes along the Kunene River and exploring the surrounding deserts in the Kaokoland and near Namib-Naukluft National Park in Namibia are high on my list, as well as exploring the Makgadikgadi Pans in Botswana.

Mountain Biking

Ever thought of game viewing by mountain bike? Well then pack your bags and head for Mashatu Game Reserve in eastern Botswana, where your guide rides ahead of you with a rifle strapped on his back and leads you through the bush were you may see elephant and lots of other big game. Mountain biking in the bush is also available from Tafika Lodge (South Luangwa, Zambia), some camps

A mountain biking adventure in Damaraland, Namibia

near Tarangire National Park and near Lake Manyara National Park (Tanzania), and some properties in Laikipia (Kenya).

Mountain Climbing

Africa has mountains to challenge the tenderfoot and the expert alike. Mt. Kilimanjaro (Tanzania), 19,340 feet (5,895 m) in altitude, is the highest mountain in Africa, followed by Mt. Kenya at 17,058 feet (5,199 m). The Ruwenzoris, or "Mountains of the Moon" (Uganda), are the highest mountain chain in Africa, rising to 16,762 feet (5,109 m). All of these mountains lie within a few degrees of the equator yet are usually snowcapped year-round. Hiking through fascinating and unique Afro-alpine vegetation found on all of these mountains gives you the feeling of being on another planet. With over 30,000 climbers a year, Mt. Kilimanjaro is by far the most popular of the three.

Scuba Diving and Snorkeling

Kenya, Tanzania, South Africa, Mozambique, Mauritius and the Seychelles offer excellent coral reef diving in the warm waters of the Indian Ocean. Lake Malawi and Lake Tanganyika offer a fascinating freshwater dive experience.

The Malindi-Watamu Marine National Reserve is probably the best choice in Kenya, and Pemba and Mnemba islands in Tanzania. The Quirimbas Archipelago and the Bazaruto Archipelago in Mozambique are fabulous, as is the whale shark diving along the coast.

The northern Natal coast of South Africa has excellent coral reefs, while the Southern Cape offers the ultimate underwater thrill of cage diving with great white sharks! Mauritius and the Seychelles feature numerous coral reefs and a variety of fabulous dive options.

Fishing

Africa has some very fine fishing to offer — from excellent deep-sea fishing off the east coast of the continent to great inland lakes that boast some of the largest freshwater fish in the world.

The best areas for **deep-sea fishing** are found off the coast of Kenya and Tanzania and in the Mozambique Channel, where blue, black & striped marlin, yellowfin tuna, sailfish, wahoo, kingfish, barracuda and other species may be caught by day and broadbill swordfish by night.

The best fishing season for the coast of Kenya and northern Tanzania is October to March, when the pelagic fish are biting. **Sailfish** are good all year round — just keep in mind that the ocean can be rough April to August. Sailfish are the most often caught of the billfish, and are especially challenging when fished on fly tackle. **Black marlin** come close to shore and are often encountered in very shallow water, while **striped marlin** tend to run offshore in cleaner water. Fighting a jumping **blue marlin** is possibly the ultimate thrill. **Broadbill swordfish**, possibly the strongest fighter in the ocean, are fished on overnight expeditions where the sea floor plunges to depths between 1,500 and 2,000 feet (460–610 m). **Tiger, mako,** and **hammerhead sharks** species are often caught; other species include **bull sharks** and **white-tip sharks**.

The Seychelles and Mauritius also offer very good fishing. The Seychelles, in fact, is considered one of the top bonefishing destinations in the world.

Freshwater fishing for tigerfish (great fighters) or Nile Perch (sometimes weighing over 100 lbs./45 kg) as well as other species across the continent can be very exciting. While fishing, you may watch elephant cross a channel, listen to hippo grunting and watch a variety of kingfishers and herons fly by — adding another dimension to the sport that can be found nowhere else in the world! **Nile Perch**, the largest freshwater species in Africa, can attain a weight of well over 200 pounds (90 kg). These giants, like huge bass, are fished for in a similar way and fight in a similar style. They will jump, run and fight in the most spectacular manner. Most anglers fish with a 40-pound rig and large "crankbaits," and some have even caught them on fly. Nile Perch have been introduced to many large lakes in Central and East Africa, including Lake Victoria, Lake Turkana, Lake Tanganyika and Murchison Falls National Park (Uganda).

Possibly the best freshwater fighting fish in the world, the **tigerfish**, comes in two varieties: the regular tigerfish and the goliath tigerfish. Many different methods are used to catch this fearsome toothed, aggressive fish, ranging from cast and retrieve of spinners and lures, trawling spinners and lures, drifting with live bait, drifting with fish fillets and fly-fishing. Possibly the most exciting thing about tigerfishing is the high-speed strike and the manner in which they leap and jump out of the water when hooked. Classic places for tigerfishing (and game viewing at the same time) are on the mighty Zambezi River along Lower Zambezi National Park (Zambia) and Mana Pools National Park (Zimbabwe) on the mighty Zambezi River, and Matusadona National Park (Zimbabwe) on Lake Kariba. Other great spots include the Okavango Delta and the Chobe River in Botswana.

Goliath tigerfish occur farther north on the Congo River and many of the lakes in that region, including Lake Tanganyika. Tigerfish attain a weight of up to 25 pounds (11 kg), though this is rare and one can expect more around the 5 to 10 pound (2.3 to 4.5 kg) mark, while the goliath tigerfish can get well over 100 pounds (45 kg), but is a lot harder to catch.

There are no natural trout in Africa; however, many dams, lakes and rivers have been stocked over the years and can provide some very entertaining fishing. The best areas in Africa for trout are the Drakensberg foothills and high-altitude grasslands east of Johannesburg in South Africa, and the Kenyan Highlands where they are fished with many of the classic British flies.

Most often, tackle will be provided, which saves you the trouble of carrying the stuff halfway around the world only to find it unsuitable. The exception to this is fly-fishing, where you probably will need to bring your own equipment. Most freshwater fishing requires a license, which can usually be obtained from your hotel, lodge or camp for a small fee.

Birdwatching

If you are not already a keen birdwatcher, there is a good chance that you will be converted before the end of your safari. Birdwatching in Africa is almost beyond belief. Some countries have recorded over 1,000 different species and some reserves over 500. The strident, sometimes beautiful calls of many birds

The bateleur eagle is found throughout sub-Sahara Africa

will form a continual "soundtrack" to your African safari, add to the atmosphere and provide lasting memories.

The wonderful thing about birds is that they are present just about everywhere, all the time. The surroundings of camps and lodges are always good localities for bird-watching because a variety of species have become used to the presence of people, and many birds will appear on the scene if you simply sit quietly on your veranda. Game drives are constantly punctuated by views of large or colorful birds, and, if you take the time, numerous less-dramatic species.

Most reserves in Africa are simply heaven for birdwatchers. The best times for birdwatching are often the opposite of the best times for big game viewing. Birdwatching, however, is good year-round in many regions. For illustrations of many of the birds as well as mammals you are likely to see on safari I suggest you pick up a copy of the *African Safari Journal* (Global Travel Publishers) to take with you on safari.

Star Gazing

Breathtaking views of the night sky are a typical feature of clear nights in African wilderness areas. A cloudless night provides a glorious opportunity to become familiar with several interesting constellations and noteworthy stars, as well as up to five planets. One or more of the planets Venus, Jupiter or Mars will be visible at any given time. The Milky Way is quite astounding when viewed through binoculars! Stargazing apps are available for the I-Pad and other tablets — be sure to bring yours along!

Other Safari Activities

Additional options for the special-interest traveler include anthropology, archaeology, art and backpacking.

COMBINING EAST AND SOUTHERN AFRICA WITH OTHER WORLD DESTINATIONS

There are many areas in the world that interest travelers and many of these different destinations combine well with an Africa safari. All the different air connections make combining an Africa safari with another destination a simple matter. Many travelers stop off in Europe either before or after a safari, as there are so many flights to Africa via London, Amsterdam, etc.

A great combination is **Egypt** or Egypt and **Jordan** — especially in the cooler months of November to May, with east Africa or even southern Africa as there are daily flights out of Cairo heading south. We send many guests on trips visiting the pyramids, Sphinx and other attractions in Cairo and on Nile cruises, as well as to Jordan to see Petra and other sites (see www.AfricanAdventure.com). **Dubai** is also becoming very popular as a stopover before or after a safari.

If you have time, consider combining **Australia** and/or **New Zealand** with Africa, as you can conveniently fly from Johannesburg (South Africa) directly into Perth or Sydney (Australia). From Sydney and Perth there are direct flights into Auckland in New Zealand. I recommend you contact the DownUnder Adventure Company (800-882-9453; 954-491-8877, www.safaridownunder.com); please see page 614 for additional details.

For those planning on visiting both Africa and **India**, there are direct flights from Nairobi (Kenya), Addis Ababa (Ethiopia) and Johannesburg (South Africa) to Mumbai (India).

Combining **South America** with Africa also works well as there are flights from Sao Paulo (Brazil) to Johannesburg and from Buenos Aires (Argentina) to Johannesburg (South Africa).

COST OF A SAFARI

When first-time travelers to Africa start looking at safari programs, they often feel that safaris are "expensive." What they soon realize is that most safari programs include all meals and game activities while in the safari camps and lodges, road and charter flight transfers, taxes, park fees and in some cases, laundry and drinks. I like to compare this to a ski vacation, where the accommodation and flights are booked in advance and may seem quite reasonable — but after you add up the credit card bills that follow for the ski lift tickets, rental car, ski rentals and all your meals, you then have a fair comparison with the relative cost of a safari.

The cost per day is most dependent upon how comfortably you wish to travel (the level of accommodation), the remoteness of the safari, type of transportation used, the quality of the guides, whether you're on a private safari or on a group tour, and the countries involved. Deluxe accommodations and transportation are normally more expensive in countries off the beaten track than in the more popular tourism spots.

For example, deluxe (Class A) safari camps in Botswana are often more expensive that Class A lodges in Kenya or Tanzania. Camps in Botswana, Zambia, Namibia and Zimbabwe cater to smaller groups and are generally situated in more remote locations, and charter aircraft are often used to reach them — making safaris to these areas more expensive than a driving safari using lodges.

Sunset on the Makgadikgadi Pans, Botswana

As in Europe and other parts of the world, general-interest tours cost less than tours with more unique itineraries. Getting off the beaten track may dip a bit more into the wallet, but many travelers find the expense well worth it!

When comparing safaris, it is important to note what is included and not included. Some companies use what I consider a sales ploy by listing a relatively attractive price for a safari in their brochures or on the Internet, and then separately listing charter flight costs and park fees — which can increase the overall cost of the safari by another 30%; let the buyer beware! Most often, if you add up all those costs, you may find that they are in fact not offering value for money compared to safaris offered by other companies.

Some tour companies market "bare-bones" trips at attractive prices, but then charge extra for many "activities," drinks, laundry, breakfast and other meals, etc. The idea is to "hook" prospective safariers on the cheap price, and then try to "upsell" them on add-ons — most of which should have been included in the cost of the safari in the first place!

Be sure to note if taxes and breakfast are included when comparing costs for hotels — as most rates advertised on the Internet do not include either. This again can easily make a difference of 20 to 35% on the price. Also keep in mind that the advertised cost of accommodations at some safari camps or lodges often does not include game drives and other activities and park fees — only room and board, while others may be more comprehensive in what they include.

To obtain a good idea of the cost of safaris, I suggest you visit the website www.AfricanAdventure.com.

HOW TO CHOOSE A SAFARI COMPANY

When choosing a safari company to book your safari, there are a number of issues that should be considered:

- Does the person or persons working for the company with which you are speaking have extensive personal experience traveling in the areas you intend visiting? For instance, someone who knows South Africa may not be well qualified to give advice on Kenya or Tanzania, or vice-versa.
- Does the company offer the "type" of safari that best fits what you are looking for? Many tour companies cater to "niche" markets. Even though the company may come highly recommended to you, it may not be the best company for the experience for which you are looking.
- Does the company own their own safari camps and thus have a vested interest in promoting and booking you there even if it does not match your game viewing desires? Keep in mind that we do not own any properties in Africa so we are free to speak our minds and find you the ideal camp or lodge for your budget and safari dreams!
- Where is the company based? If it is based in Africa, the challenge is that if you encounter

A large lion takes to the water in Kafue, Zambia

problems on safari and seek refunds, you have no recourse. For instance, a couple I met in Rwanda booked not 1 but 2 safaris direct with African-based companies, and there was no one there when they arrived!

- Are the safari camps, lodges and hotels and the tour operators they use minimizing their impact on the environment and working toward the preservation of wildlife?

- Are real benefits received by the local communities in which they operate — giving the local people an economic incentive to preserve wildlife and the environment?
- If you are considering a group tour, how large is the group? I am still amazed at companies that boast that they offer tours limited to "only" 16 or 24 or 30 travelers. In my opinion, any group over 12 is ridiculously large for Africa (6 to 8 is preferable) unless it is a private group of family or friends. With large groups there are constant delays having to wait for the slow ones in the party, and this along with incompatibility among other issues can reach a boiling point after several days. Smaller groups are much more flexible — and fun!
- Does the tour operator have an in-house air department? Air schedules within Africa change, and having the same company book your land and your air arrangements is the safest way to go. If there are any changes in your air schedule, the operator is notified and they can then assist in getting you back on track. If your air is purchased elsewhere, then that company probably has little obligation or interest in helping you — and you may very well be left to fend for yourself.
- Does the company offer tours to Africa only, or do they offer tours to other destinations, as well? I suggest you look more seriously at companies that either offer Africa only, or for which Africa is their primary destination. Go with a company that focuses its attention and resources on the continent you wish to visit.
- Will the operator provide you with references of clients who have recently traveled with them? This may give you a better idea of the quality of the operation, and also may give you some insight into the experience you might have on a similar safari.
- Are you enjoying working with the tour operator? Planning a safari should be enlightening, educational and fun!
- How qualified are the guides they use on safari? A good guide is absolutely crucial to the success of your African experience.
- Is the tour company you have contracted providing you with a number of safari destinations and accommodation options from which to choose? Companies offering just a few set programs often try to convince people that one of their limited offerings is just perfect for the traveler, when in fact they are just trying to sell them on the program. Most people that love their African adventures rave about the fact that experience matched or exceeded their expectations.
- How long has the company been in business? Companies for instance that have been in business since 1990 have weathered two Gulf Wars, September 11th and other events that have bankrupted a number of companies. This says a lot for the financial stability of a company — as well as the expertise of the management and long-standing staff members.

- Does the company take credit cards for deposits as well as final payments on land and air arrangements? I am still amazed at the number of companies (some quite well-known) that do not take credit cards.
- Does the company have liability insurance (i.e. at least $2,000,000). Many small tour operators do not have insurance. The costs of defending against a single lawsuit could put an uninsured company into bankruptcy — and you could lose whatever you paid them for your trip.

I cannot tell you the number of distraught people that call our offices yearly, asking us if we can quickly put together a safari for them because they have bought non-refundable air tickets and their tour operator with whom they booked direct within Africa has "disappeared" with their money and will not return emails or calls.

Another issue to consider is reliability and safety. For instance, many companies based in Africa offering tours to international travelers are not licensed and have no insurance. What does this mean to you? As they are not licensed, they do not have to have

Cocktail time with friends in Hwange National Park, Zimbabwe

their vehicles inspected and are generally using the oldest vehicles available to keep their costs down — resulting in more breakdowns (perhaps with little or no backup), and making travel in their vehicles downright dangerous. They fear little or no recourse if they do not perform as contracted. So if you encounter a problem on a safari — good luck getting a refund! The temptation may be lower price. The old adage, "If it is too good to be true, then it probably is" — can certainly apply here. So why take the risk?

A safari is all about experiencing Africa — and it is quality people assisting you by booking the right safari for you and quality people maximizing that experience on the ground that counts.

SAFARI TIPS

While on safari, you will enjoy the attention and input of one or more guides whose job is to make sure that you have a safe, fun and enlightening experience. Although you will be in capable hands, the more you know before setting off, the more you will get out of your adventure.

- Background reading is perhaps the most important, although speaking to somebody who has been to the area you intend to visit can be invaluable. The *African Safari Journal* (see pages 612–613) is aimed at providing you with an advance overview, as well as being a guide and field book to record your observations. As such, it should be a constant companion on your travels.

- Your desire to visit Africa may well have been triggered by *National Geographic* documentaries or *Animal Planet*. This is all very well, but you should not expect to see everything in the way in which these films depict. The best wildlife films take years to create, and involve weeks or months of waiting for action to happen. Part of enjoying your safari is having a realistic expectation, and you should always remember that wildlife is just that, it's wild! With the exception of the most common birds and herbivorous mammals, nothing can be guaranteed on safari — and that, really, is the thrill of it. It is the anticipation and chance that makes getting up early each morning, and driving around each bend in the road, so enthralling.

- It is vital to develop a good relationship with your guide from the outset. Bear in mind that he or she will not only know the area and its wildlife, but also the best ways to reveal this to you. Make sure that you state your expectations clearly from the word go, and don't be shy to get involved in each day's routine. If you have seen enough lions for one day, for example, let your guide know that you would like to focus on seeing other species.

- Rather than spending your whole safari charging about looking only for big game, aim to get an understanding and appreciation for the whole ecosystem, of which termites and fig trees play as big a role as elephants and lions. Developing an interest in birds, reptiles and trees means that you'll have a captivating experience at all times.

- Sensitivity toward wildlife is paramount. Your guide will know the correct distance to approach each individual species without causing stress, but in the rare instances where this may not be so, it is up to you to dictate the distance. The most enthralling wildlife encounters are often those in which the animals that you are viewing are unaware or unafraid.

- Being on safari generally puts you at less risk than you would be when traveling on busy roads in your own neighborhood, but many animals are potentially dangerous and some simple precautions are advisable. A good guide will naturally avert any risky situations, but as already mentioned,

A pack of wild dog scares off opportunistic vultures

respecting animals' space by not attempting to get too close is paramount. Almost all large mammals are frightened of humans, and generally run or move off when confronted with the upright form of a person. This can never be taken for granted, however, and you should not be tempted to leave the safety of a safari vehicle to approach an animal. It is equally important to remain seated while in open safari vehicles, because lions, for example, appear to regard safari vehicles as one entity, rather than a collection of edible primates! Many of the best wildlife lodges are not fenced and allow free movement of all wildlife, so you can expect to be escorted to and from your room or tent after dinner by an armed guard. Most large mammals may explore lodge surroundings after dark, but typically keep well clear during daylight hours. Exceptions include elephant, impala, bushbuck and some other herbivores which realize that the lodge offers protection from predators. Opportunistic vervet monkeys, and sometimes baboons, frequently raid kitchens and table fruit. Monkeys can become aggressive once they are accustomed to handouts, so the golden rule is to never feed them, or any other animal.

- Naturally, most people will want a record of their safari, so tips on photography follow (see pages 64–65).
- Read the "Safari Glossary" to become familiar with the terminology used in the bush. Once on safari, you will notice that when you ask people what animals they saw on their game drive, they might reply, "elephant, lion, leopard and oryx," when in fact they saw several members of each species. This use of the singular form, when more than one of that species was seen, is common. However, one exception to this rule is saying *crocs for crocodile*. This form of "Safariese" will be used throughout this guide to help separate you from the amateur.
- Carry your valuables with you or put them in a room safe or safety deposit box at your lodge or hotel.
- Do not call out to a person, signaling with an index finger. This is insulting to most Africans. Instead, use four fingers with your palm facing downward.
- During daytime game viewing activities, wear colors that blend in with your surroundings (brown, tan, light green or khaki). Do not wear perfume or cologne while game viewing. Wildlife can detect unnatural smells for miles and unnatural colors for hundreds of yards (meters), making close approaches difficult.

- The very few tourists who get hurt on safari are almost always those travelers who ignore the laws of nature and most probably the advice and warnings of their guides. Common sense is the rule.
- Do not wade or swim in rivers, lakes or streams unless you know for certain they are free of crocodiles, hippos and bilharzia (a snail-borne disease). Fast-moving areas of rivers are often free of bilharzia, but can still be a bit risky. Bilharzia, fortunately, is not the dreaded disease that it once was; if detected early it can be easily cured.
- Do not walk along the banks of rivers near dawn, dusk or at night. Those who do so may inadvertently cut off a hippo's path to its waterhole, and the hippo may charge.
- Do not walk close to the edge of a river or lake due to the danger of crocodiles.
- Malaria is present in almost all the parks and reserves covered in this guide. Malarial prophylaxis (pills) should be taken and must be prescribed by a physician in the USA but are available without prescription in many countries. Because most malaria-carrying mosquitoes come out from dusk until dawn, during this period you should use

mosquito repellent and wear long pants and a long-sleeve shirt or blouse, shoes (not sandals) and socks. For further information see the section on "Health" in the "Resource Directory" section of this book.

- Because of the abundance of thorns and sharp twigs, wear closed-toed shoes or boots at night and also during the day if venturing out into the bush. Bring a flashlight and always have it with you at night.
- Don't venture out of your lodge or camp without your guide, especially at night, dawn or dusk. Remember that wildlife is not confined to the parks and reserves in many countries, and, in fact, roams freely in and around many camps and lodges.
- Resist the temptation to jog or walk alone in national parks, reserves or other areas where wildlife exists. To lion and other carnivores, we are just "meat on the hoof" like any other animal — only much slower and less capable of defending ourselves.

Leopards have very sharp eyesight and can spot prey at a distance of nearly a mile (1.5 km)

PHOTOGRAPHIC TIPS

There are **2 basic kinds of digital camera** (as there are conventional film cameras). One kind with a built-in lens (comparable to the old "instamatic") and the other kind with detachable lens. For photographing wildlife, it is important to be able to zoom close to your subject, so you'll need a minimum of 10x "optical zoom," or — in the case of digital SLR — a lens of at least 300mm. Larger magnifications will be required for photographing birds. Most quality equipment has "image stabilization" technology and this is very valuable when shooting on safari.

As with digital cameras, the variety of **camcorders** on the market is not only bewildering, but constantly changing as technology advances. Many

Ship wrecks and ancient whale bones scatter the Skeleton Coast, Namibia

camcorders have optical zoom of 20x or more which is ideal for shooting wildlife, but don't be fooled by high "digital zoom" statistics as these exaggerated magnifications produce images that are highly pixelated (broken up into small squares) and unsatisfactory. Some digital camcorders are also able to take still photographs.

The quality of any still photograph (or movie clip) is dependent upon **lighting**. For this reason, the best wildlife photographs are taken in the early morning or late afternoon when sunlight comes at an angle. In the middle of the day, sunlight comes from directly overhead which creates hard black shadows on and around your subject matter.

Choosing where to place your subject in the viewfinder of your camera is known as **composition**. This is a vital aspect of photography and separates great images from ordinary ones. Things to avoid are chopping off part of your subject (for example, feet), zooming in too tightly or placing your subject in the very center of your frame. It is much more pleasing on the eye if an animal is pictured off center and thus "looking in" to a space. Likewise, placing the horizon of your landscape pictures in the bottom or top third of the frame (depending on whether the sky or foreground is of more interest), rather than in the very center, will create a more interesting perspective.

As already mentioned, many cameras have "image stabilization" technology. Blurred photographs are caused mostly by **camera shake**, which is the result of not holding the camera firmly, or not selecting the correct exposure options and thus using long shutter speeds. The use of a tripod is hard to beat but this is not very practical on a safari. Some travelers will extend one leg of a tripod or use a monopod. Alternately, use a soft "beanbag." Simply pack a small cloth bag in your travel kit and then fill it with dry beans (or rice) when you get to Africa. This will then provide you with a flexible yet solid support for your camera. In the absence of a tripod or beanbag, a rolled-up jacket or sweater placed on a window ledge or vehicle rooftop will provide decent support.

Vehicle vibrations are a major cause of blurred images, so ask your guide to turn off the vehicle engine for special shots.

It is obviously necessary to have all the required battery chargers for your equipment when you travel. An electrical adaptor will also be important for connecting to local power supplies. Even the most remote safari camps usually have a generator capable of charging batteries. Consider taking two batteries for each camera, so that you always have a backup.

Take two or three cards and consider copying the data (i.e. your images) onto a backup device. Some travelers now carry iPods, or even a laptop for copying image files onto; these instruments also allow you to better preview and edit photographs or video clips on the spot. It is wise to store cameras and lenses in plastic ziplock bags to protect them from dust and humidity.

SUGGESTED PACKING LIST

WOMEN'S CLOTHING

- ❏ Sandals or lightweight shoes
- ❏ Walking shoes or lightweight hiking shoes (not white for walking safaris)
- ❏ Wide-brimmed hat and a cap
- ❏ Windbreaker
- ❏ Sweater or fleece
- ❏ 2–3 pr. safari* pants
- ❏ 2–3 pr. safari* shorts
- ❏ 5 pr. safari/sports socks
- ❏ 3 short-sleeve safari* shirts
- ❏ 3 long-sleeve safari* shirts
- ❏ Swimsuit/cover-up
- ❏ 1 pr. casual slacks or skirt
- ❏ 1 or 2 blouses
- ❏ Belts
- ❏ 6 pr. underwear
- ❏ 3 bras
- ❏ 1 sports bra (for rough roads)
- ❏ pajamas

Optional (for dining at a top restaurant or on a luxury train)
- ❏ 1 cocktail dress
- ❏ 1 pr. dress shoes and nylons/panty hose

MEN'S CLOTHING

- ❏ Sandals or lightweight shoes
- ❏ Walking shoes or lightweight hiking shoes (not white for walking safaris)
- ❏ Wide-brimmed hat and cap
- ❏ Windbreaker
- ❏ Sweater or fleece
- ❏ 2–3 pr. safari* pants
- ❏ 2–3 pr. safari* shorts
- ❏ 5 pr. safari/sports socks
- ❏ 3 short-sleeve safari* shirts
- ❏ 3 long-sleeve safari* shirts
- ❏ Swim trunks
- ❏ 1 pr. casual slacks
- ❏ 1 sports shirt
- ❏ 6 pr. underwear
- ❏ Belts
- ❏ pajamas
- ❏ Large handkerchief

Optional (for dining at a top restaurant or on a luxury train)
- ❏ 1 pr. dress slacks, shoes and dress socks
- ❏ 1 dress shirt/jacket/tie

* Any comfortable cotton clothing for safari should be neutral in color *(tan, brown, light green, khaki)*. Evening wear can be any color you like!

COLD WEATHER ADDITIONS

- ❏ For travel in Southern Africa May to August, temperatures may drop below 40°F (5°C)
- ❏ warm pajamas or thermal underwear to sleep in
- ❏ warm ski hat covering the ears
- ❏ scarf
- ❏ gloves
- ❏ additional sweater or fleece

TOILETRIES AND FIRST AID

- ❑ Anti-malaria pills (prescription)
- ❑ Vitamins
- ❑ Aspirin/Tylenol/Advil
- ❑ Motion sickness pills
- ❑ Decongestant
- ❑ Throat lozenges
- ❑ Laxative
- ❑ Anti-diarrhea medicine
- ❑ Antacid
- ❑ Antibiotic
- ❑ Cortisone cream
- ❑ Antibiotic ointment
- ❑ Anti-fungal cream or powder
- ❑ Prescription drugs
- ❑ Medical summary from your doctor (if needed)
- ❑ Medical alert bracelet or necklace
- ❑ Band-Aids (plasters)
- ❑ Thermometer
- ❑ Insect repellent
- ❑ Sunscreen/sun block
- ❑ Shampoo (small container)
- ❑ Conditioner (small container)
- ❑ Deodorant
- ❑ Toothpaste (small tube)
- ❑ Toothbrush
- ❑ Hairbrush/comb
- ❑ Razor
- ❑ Q-tips/cotton balls
- ❑ Nail clipper
- ❑ Emery boards
- ❑ Makeup
- ❑ Tweezers

SUNDRIES

- ❑ Passport (with visas, if needed)
- ❑ International Certificate of Vaccination
- ❑ Air tickets/vouchers
- ❑ Money pouch
- ❑ Credit cards
- ❑ Personal checks
- ❑ Insurance cards
- ❑ Cellphone
- ❑ Sunglasses/guard
- ❑ Spare prescription glasses/contacts
- ❑ Copy of prescription(s)
- ❑ Eyeglass case
- ❑ Travel alarm clock
- ❑ Small flashlight (torch) and extra batteries
- ❑ Binoculars
- ❑ Sewing kit
- ❑ Small scissors
- ❑ Tissues (travel packs)
- ❑ Handiwipes (individual)
- ❑ Anti-bacterial soap
- ❑ Laundry soap (for washing delicates)
- ❑ Large waterproof bags for damp laundry
- ❑ Copy of the *African Safari Journal*
- ❑ Maps
- ❑ Business cards
- ❑ Pens
- ❑ Deck of cards
- ❑ Reading materials
- ❑ Decaffeinated coffee/ herbal tea
- ❑ Sugar substitute

CAMERA EQUIPMENT

- ❑ Lenses
- ❑ Digital memory cards/Film
- ❑ Camera bag or backpack
- ❑ Lens cleaning fluid
- ❑ Lens tissue/brush
- ❑ Extra camera batteries
- ❑ Flash
- ❑ Flash batteries
- ❑ Battery charger and adapters
- ❑ Waterproof bags for lenses and camera body
- ❑ Beanbag, small tripod or monopod
- ❑ Extra video camera batteries
- ❑ Video charger
- ❑ Outlet adapters (3-prong square and round plugs)
- ❑ Cigarette lighter charger (optional)

GIFTS & TRADES

- ❑ T-shirts
- ❑ Pens
- ❑ Inexpensive watches
- ❑ Postcards from your area/state
- ❑ Children's magazines and books
- ❑ Small acrylic mirrors
- ❑ Balloons
- ❑ School supplies

When's The Best Time To Go?

The **When's The Best Time To Go For Game Viewing** chart (see the inside front cover) shows, at a glance, when you should go to see the greatest numbers or concentration of large mammals in the countries, parks and reserves of your choice. Alternatively, the chart shows the best places to go in the month(s) in which you are planning to take your vacation. In other words, how to be in the right place at the right time!

For example, your vacation is in February and your primary interest is game viewing on a photographic safari. Find the countries on the chart in which game viewing is "excellent" or "good" in February. Turn to the respective country chapters for additional information and choose the ones that intrigue you the most. In this example, for instance, northern Tanzania would be an excellent choice. Use this chart as a general guideline because conditions vary from year to year. Timing can make a world of difference!

In most cases, the best game viewing, as exhibited on the chart, also corresponds to the dry season. Wildlife concentrates around waterholes and rivers, and the vegetation is less dense than in the wet season, making game easier to find.

Generally speaking, wildlife is best seen (game is most concentrated) in Kenya, Tanzania, Uganda, Rwanda and the Congo mid-December to March and June to mid-November, while the best game viewing in Zimbabwe, Zambia, Namibia, Malawi, Mozambique and South Africa is June to October. Good game viewing in Botswana, top private reserves in South Africa, northern Tanzania and parts of Kenya can be found year-round.

An elephant bull walks unnoticed past a male lion in South Luangwa, Zambia

There are, however, parks and reserves that are actually better outside of the dry season. In Botswana, the Central Kalahari Game Reserve, Magadikgadi Pans National Park and Nxai Pan National Park as well as several concession areas in the Okavango Delta are better in the green season, November to April. In the Okavango Delta, water levels have most often receded by November, exposing large floodplains of fresh grass that attracts antelope from the surrounding woodlands — that in turn attract lion, leopard and other carnivores out into the open. And as Okavango Delta camp rates at this time are significantly lower than during high season, there is an additional attraction for visitors who cannot afford or prefer not paying not high season rates — or who simply prefer being able to stay longer in the bush. Many travelers are now, in fact, discovering that traveling during low season actually fits their interests better than in high season. During the green season, the land is often luxuriously green and the air clear. The rainy season for the top wildlife countries usually involves occasional thundershowers followed by clear skies — not continuous downpours for days on end. People interested in scenery or who have dust allergies may want to plan their visits shortly after the rains are predicted to have started or soon after the rains are predicted to have stopped. Game may be a bit more difficult to find, but there are usually fewer travelers in the parks and reserves, which adds to the overall quality of the safari.

Many camps and lodges offer low-season rates, making travel during those times economically attractive. The low season in Kenya and Tanzania for most camps and lodges is April and May (except for Easter), while in Botswana the "Green Season" (offering the lowest rates) is generally December to March (except for the Christmas/New Year's period) and the low season is April through May or June. South Africa's high season is October to April for hotels and many safari camps and lodges as that is the time many Europeans travel to get out of the cold winter. Interestingly enough, December through March is the rainy season in the Kruger National Park area where most of the top lodges and camps are located, yet rates are often higher than in the dry season when game viewing is better!

Another advantage of traveling during the low season, especially if you visit the more popular parks and reserves in Kenya and Tanzania, is that there will be fewer tourists. In fact, one of my favorite times to visit this part of Africa is in November.

The best "Green Season" parks and reserves to visit in southern Africa (December to March) are the Okavango Delta, Moremi, Savute, Central Kalahari, Makgadikgadi, Nxai Pans (Botswana), Hwange (Zimbabwe), all regions of Namibia (except Etosha), and the private reserves near Kruger NP and the Cape Provinces in South Africa, and for East Africa (April, May and November) the Serengeti, and Ngorongoro Crater (Tanzania) and the Maasi Mara (Kenya).

In summary, the best time for you to go may be a combination of the best time to see the wildlife that interests you most (large mammals vs. birds), the relative costs involved (low or high season), and when you can get vacation time.

The **Temperature and Rainfall Charts** (see pages 70–71) give average high and low temperatures and average rainfall for each month of the year for a number of locations. Keep in mind that these are average temperatures; you should expect variations of at least 7 to 10°F (5 to 7°C) from the averages listed on the chart. Also keep in mind that at higher altitudes you should expect cooler temperatures. This is why many parks and reserves in Africa can be warm during the day and cool to cold at night. The most common packing mistake safariers make is not bringing enough warm layers of clothing!

Even though mid-day temperatures may be high, humidity levels are usually low as most reserves are located in semi-arid regions and/or at altitudes over 3,300 feet (1,000 m) above sea level.

AVERAGE MONTHLY TEMPERATURES
MIN/MAX IN FAHRENHEIT

CITY	JAN	FEB	MAR	APR	MAY	JUN	JUL	AUG	SEP	OCT	NOV	DEC
EAST AFRICA												
Dar-Es-Salaam	77/88	76/87	76/89	74/87	72/85	68/85	66/84	66/84	68/84	68/86	73/87	76/88
Dodoma	66/86	66/85	64/84	64/84	62/83	57/82	57/79	57/81	59/85	63/88	64/89	65/88
Kigoma	67/81	68/82	68/82	67/82	68/83	67/82	63/83	65/85	67/86	69/85	68/81	67/80
Nairobi	55/78	56/80	58/78	58/76	56/73	54/70	51/70	52/71	53/76	55/77	56/74	55/75
Mombasa	75/88	76/88	77/89	76/87	75/84	74/83	71/81	71/81	72/83	74/85	75/86	76/87
Kampala	65/84	65/83	64/82	61/81	63/79	63/78	63/78	62/78	63/81	63/82	62/81	62/81
Kabale	49/76	50/76	50/75	51/74	51/73	50/73	48/75	49/75	50/76	51/75	50/73	50/73
Kigali	43/68	48/68	46/68	43/68	41/68	37/68	41/68	39/70	37/70	48/68	37/68	39/68
Bujumbura	66/83	66/83	66/83	66/83	66/83	65/85	64/85	65/87	67/89	68/87	67/83	67/83
SOUTHERN AFRICA												
Harare	61/79	61/79	59/79	56/78	50/75	45/71	45/71	47/75	54/80	58/84	60/82	61/79
Victoria Falls	65/85	64/85	62/85	57/84	49/81	43/76	42/77	47/82	55/89	62/91	64/90	64/86
Hwange	64/85	64/84	62/85	57/84	47/80	42/76	40/76	45/81	54/88	61/90	64/89	64/85
Kariba	71/88	71/88	69/88	65/87	58/84	53/80	52/79	57/84	67/91	74/95	74/93	72/89
Mana Pools	71/89	71/89	70/89	67/88	62/85	57/81	56/81	59/86	66/92	73/97	74/95	72/91
Bulawayo	61/82	61/81	60/80	57/80	50/75	46/70	46/71	49/75	55/82	59/86	61/85	61/83
Maun	66/90	66/88	64/88	57/88	48/82	43/77	43/77	48/82	54/91	64/95	66/93	66/90
Lusaka	63/78	63/79	62/79	59/79	55/78	50/73	49/73	53/77	59/84	64/88	64/85	63/81
S. Luangwa	68/90	68/88	66/90	64/90	66/88	54/86	52/84	54/86	59/95	68/104	72/99	72/91
Windhoek	63/86	63/84	59/81	55/77	48/72	45/68	45/68	46/73	54/79	57/84	61/84	63/88
Swakopmund	54/77	54/73	54/73	59/77	59/77	64/82	54/77	54/77	54/77	54/77	54/77	54/77
Johannesburg	59/79	57/77	55/75	52/72	46/66	41/61	41/61	45/66	48/72	54/75	55/77	57/77
Durban	70/82	70/82	68/82	63/79	55/75	50/73	50/73	54/73	59/73	63/75	64/77	68/81
Cape Town	61/79	59/79	57/77	54/73	50/68	46/64	45/63	45/64	46/66	50/70	55/75	59/77

AVERAGE MONTHLY TEMPERATURES
MIN/MAX IN CENTIGRADE

CITY	JAN	FEB	MAR	APR	MAY	JUN	JUL	AUG	SEP	OCT	NOV	DEC
EAST AFRICA												
Dar-Es-Salaam	25/3	25/32	24/32	23/31	22/29	20/29	19/28	19/28	19/28	21/29	23/31	24/31
Dodoma	18/29	18/29	18/28	18/28	16/28	15/27	13/27	14/27	15/29	17/31	18/31	18/31
Kigoma	19/27	20/27	20/27	19/27	19/28	18/29	17/28	18/29	19/30	21/29	20/27	19/26
Nairobi	12/25	13/26	14/25	14/24	13/22	12/21	11/21	11/21	11/24	14/25	13/24	13/24
Mombasa	24/32	24/32	25/32	24/31	23/28	23/28	22/27	22/27	22/28	23/29	24/29	24/30
Kampala	18/28	18/28	18/27	18/26	17/25	18/26	18/26	17/26	17/27	17/27	17/27	17/27
Kabale	9/24	11/24	11/24	11/24	11/23	10/23	9/23	10/23	11/24	11/24	11/24	10/24
Kigali	6/20	9/20	8/20	6/20	6/20	3/20	5/20	4/20	3/21	9/20	3/20	4/20
Bujumbura	19/28	19/28	19/28	19/28	19/28	18/29	18/29	18/31	19/32	20/31	19/29	19/29
SOUTHERN AFRICA												
Harare	17/27	17/27	15/27	13/27	10/24	8/22	7/22	8/24	12/27	14/29	16/28	16/27
Victoria Falls	18/29	17/29	17/29	14/29	9/27	5/24	7/27	12/31	16/32	18/32	18/31	18/30
Hwange	18/29	18/29	17/29	14/29	9/27	5/24	5/25	7/27	12/31	16/32	18/32	18/30
Kariba	22/31	21/31	21/31	19/31	15/29	12/27	11/26	14/29	19/33	23/35	24/34	22/32
Mana Pools	22/32	21/32	21/32	20/31	17/29	14/27	13/27	15/30	19/34	23/36	23/35	22/33
Bulawayo	17/28	17/28	16/27	14/27	10/24	8/22	8/22	10/24	12/28	15/30	16/31	16/29
Maun	19/32	19/31	18/31	14/31	9/28	6/25	6/25	9/28	13/33	18/35	19/34	19/34
Lusaka	17/26	17/26	17/26	15/26	13/25	10/24	10/23	12/25	15/30	18/31	18/30	18/28
S. Luangwa	20/32	20/31	19/32	18/32	19/31	12/30	11/29	12/30	15/35	20/40	22/37	22/33
Windhoek	17/30	17/29	15/27	13/25	9/22	7/20	7/20	8/23	12/26	14/29	16/29	17/31
Swakopmund	12/25	12/23	12/23	15/25	15/25	18/28	15/28	15/28	12/25	12/25	12/25	12/25
Johannesburg	15/26	14/25	13/24	11/22	8/19	5/16	5/16	7/19	9/22	12/24	13/25	14/25
Durban	21/28	21/28	20/28	17/26	13/24	10/23	10/23	12/23	15/23	17/24	18/25	20/27
Cape Town	16/26	15/26	14/25	12/23	10/20	8/18	7/17	7/18	8/19	10/21	13/24	15/25

AVERAGE MONTHLY RAINFALL IN INCHES

CITY	JAN	FEB	MAR	APR	MAY	JUN	JUL	AUG	SEP	OCT	NOV	DEC
EAST AFRICA												
Dar-Es-Salaam	2.6	2.6	5.1	11.4	7.4	1.3	1.2	1.0	1.2	1.6	2.9	3.6
Dodoma	6.0	4.3	5.4	1.9	0.2	0	0	0	0	0.2	0.9	3.6
Kigoma	4.8	5.0	5.9	5.1	1.7	0.2	0.1	0.2	0.7	1.9	5.6	5.3
Nairobi	1.5	2.5	4.9	8.3	6.2	1.8	0.7	0.9	1.3	2.2	4.3	3.4
Mombasa	1.1	0.8	2.4	7.7	12.7	4.7	3.5	2.6	2.6	3.4	3.8	2.4
Kampala	1.8	2.4	5.1	6.9	5.8	2.9	1.8	3.4	3.6	3.8	4.8	3.9
Kabale	2.4	3.8	5.2	4.9	3.6	1.2	0.8	2.4	3.7	3.9	4.4	3.4
Kigali	3.5	3.5	4.1	6.5	4.9	1.0	.3	.8	2.4	3.9	3.9	3.5
Bujumbura	3.7	4.4	4.8	4.9	2.3	0.4	0.3	0.4	1.5	2.5	3.9	4.4
SOUTHERN AFRICA												
Harare	7.7	7.1	4.5	1.2	0.5	0.2	0	0.1	0.3	1.2	3.8	6.4
Victoria Falls	6.6	5	2.8	1.0	0.1	0	0	0	0.7	1.1	2.5	6.8
Hwange	5.7	5.1	2.3	0.8	0.1	0	0	0	0.1	0.8	2.2	5.0
Kariba	7.5	6.2	4.4	1.2	0.2	0	0	0	0	0.7	2.9	6.9
Mana Pools	8.7	7.1	4.2	1.0	0.2	0	0	0	0	0.5	2.3	9.1
Bulawayo	5.6	4.4	3.3	0.8	0.4	0.1	0	0	0.2	0.8	3.3	4.9
Maun	4.3	3.2	2.8	1.0	0.3	0.1	0	0	0	1.2	2.0	3.8
Lusaka	9.1	76	5.7	0.7	0.2	0	0	0	0	0.4	3.6	5.9
S. Luangwa	7.7	11.3	5.6	3.6	0	0	0	0	0	2.0	4.3	4.3
Windhoek	1.7	2.0	2.2	1.1	0.2	0.1	0.1	0.1	0.1	0.4	0.9	1.0
Swakopmund	0.5	0.5	0.5	0.4	0.4	0.4	0.3	0.4	0.4	0.6	0.6	0.4
Johannesburg	4.5	3.8	2.9	2.5	0.9	0.3	0.3	0.2	0.1	2.7	4.6	4.3
Durban	5.1	4.5	5.3	4.2	2.0	1.2	1.4	1.7	2.4	3.9	4.5	4.6
Cape Town	0.6	0.7	0.7	2.0	3.5	3.3	3.5	3.1	2.0	1.4	0.5	0.6

AVERAGE MONTHLY RAINFALL IN MILLIMETERS

CITY	JAN	FEB	MAR	APR	MAY	JUN	JUL	AUG	SEP	OCT	NOV	DEC
EAST AFRICA												
Dar-Es-Salaam	66	66	130	292	188	33	33	26	31	42	74	91
Dodoma	152	110	138	49	5	0	0	0	0	5	24	92
Kigoma	123	128	150	130	44	5	3	5	19	28	143	135
Nairobi	39	65	125	211	158	47	15	24	32	53	110	87
Mombasa	25	19	65	197	320	120	90	65	65	87	98	62
Kampala	47	61	130	175	148	73	45	85	90	96	122	99
Kabale	58	97	130	125	92	28	20	58	98	99	110	87
Kigali	90	90	105	165	125	25	7	20	60	100	100	90
Bujumbura	95	110	121	125	56	11	5	11	37	65	100	115
SOUTHERN AFRICA												
Harare	196	179	118	28	14	3	0	3	5	28	97	163
Victoria Falls	168	126	70	24	3	1	0	0	2	27	64	174
Hwange	145	129	57	20	3	0	0	0	2	21	56	127
Kariba	192	158	113	30	4	1	1	0	1	18	74	175
Mana Pools	221	181	107	26	4	0	0	0	1	13	59	231
Bulawayo	143	110	85	19	10	3	0	0	5	20	81	123
Maun	110	80	70	25	7	3	0	0	0	30	50	95
Lusaka	232	192	144	18	3	0	0	0	0	11	92	150
S. Luangwa	195	287	141	91	0	0	0	0	0	50	108	110
Windhoek	43	53	56	28	5	3	3	3	3	10	23	26
Swakopmund	12	15	12	10	10	10	7	9	11	15	16	11
Johannesburg	112	96	74	61	23	8	8	5	3	69	117	109
Durban	130	114	135	107	54	31	36	43	61	99	114	117
Cape Town	15	18	18	50	90	85	90	80	50	36	13	15

AFRICAN ECOSYSTEMS

Africa is a continent of incredible diversity. Straddling the equator, and stretching beyond both the tropic of Cancer and Capricorn, almost every conceivable landscape and climate is present on the giant landmass. From snow-capped peaks to parched deserts, and from dripping rainforests to expansive savannahs, each habitat has its own particular community of plants and animals. No other parts of the world contain as much unaltered habitat, and nowhere are large mammals still so numerous and widespread. All African countries have extensive networks of protected areas and — in many cases — these are actually increasing in size as nature-based tourism becomes an ever more important component of local economies. Nevertheless, Africa's wild places face innumerable threats and challenges as human populations increase, and development goes unchecked. The impact of man-induced climate change is of growing concern here, as it is around the world.

Cheetah hunt by vision rather than by scent

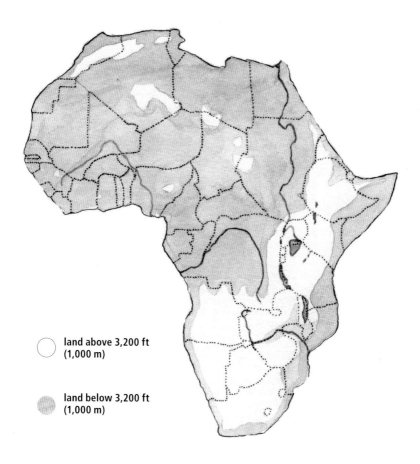

land above 3,200 ft
(1,000 m)

land below 3,200 ft
(1,000 m)

Altitude above sea level is a major factor in terms of Africa's climate, as it determines the vegetation types and distribution of wildlife, as well as the patterns of human settlement. The continent can be divided into "high" and "low" regions, with the land above 3,200 feet being more temperate even on the equator. European colonists chose to establish settlements on the higher plateaus, where wheat, tea and livestock such as cattle and sheep were able to thrive. Malaria and most livestock diseases are prolific in hot lowlands, so these areas were spared from much development and still contain some extensive wilderness areas. The Congo Basin and most of west Africa is a steamy wet lowland, while the majority of countries of east and southern Africa enjoy the benefits of both temperate and tropical or subtropical climates. The southern African highveld plateau experiences bitterly cold night temperatures during winter (May to

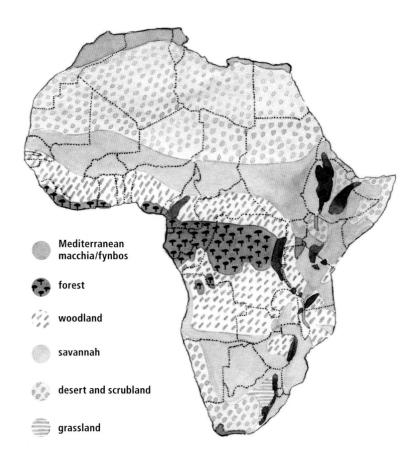

Mediterranean
macchia/fynbos

forest

woodland

savannah

desert and scrubland

grassland

August), while towns that are at high altitude such as Nairobi experience cool
nights throughout much of the year.

Africa can be divided into several broad categories of landscape that are
a result of climate (particularly rainfall), altitude, topography and soils, all of
which are interlinked. Geographers refer to these landscapes as vegetation zones
(or biomes), and they include well-known types such as forest, desert and grassland. In most cases, these and other vegetation zones do not have well defined
boundaries but merge into adjacent habitats to create zones of transition. On the
following pages, the more conspicuous vegetation types, and their characteristic
wildlife, are briefly described.

A well-rounded safari includes visits to several types of habitats and parks,
which gives the visitor an overall picture of wildlife and ecosystems.

Savannah

The African landscape so often depicted in films — and imagined by travelers — is a park-like vista of grassland dotted with flat-topped trees. This is the savannah, a mosaic of woodland and grassland. The ratio of trees to grass, and the dominant species of trees is determined by rainfall and soil type. This is the dominant habitat in most of the large wildlife reserves in East and southern Africa, with thorny acacia trees being conspicuous. Seasonal grass fires are an important mechanism in the maintenance of savannah ecosystems, as they

encourage grass growth and limit the spread of woody plants. Large herbivores including giraffe, elephant, zebra, buffalo and wildebeest favor the savannah, which also supports the highest density of lions and other large predators. Bird diversity is great with eagles, vultures, bustards, rollers, hornbills, larks, shrikes, starlings and weavers among the conspicuous families.

Woodland

Woodland generally occurs in higher rainfall areas but often merges with savannah. Trees are taller and more closely spaced, sometimes with their canopies touching. Much of southern Tanzania, Zambia and Zimbabwe is blanketed in moist *miombo woodland,* while swathes of dry *mopane woodland* occur in northern Botswana and the low-lying parts of Zimbabwe and northeastern South Africa. Browsing herbivores such as kudu live in woodlands, while roan and sable favor grassy clearings. African elephant may be seasonally abundant in mopane woodland. Birds such as woodpeckers, cuckoos, turacos, tits, orioles, warblers and sunbirds are well represented in woodlands.

Scrublands and Semidesert

In low rainfall areas such as the Kalahari and northern Kenya, short thorny trees and shrubs (particularly acacia and commiphora) are interspersed with hardy grasses. Termite mounds may be a conspicuous feature of these landscapes. Bands of taller trees occur along seasonal streams (drainage lines) where they typically tap into an underground water supply. Aloes, euphorbias and other succulents may occur on well-drained slopes. These landscapes are transformed after good rainfall and typically explode with life for short periods. Gazelles, oryx, cheetah, bat-eared fox and black-backed jackal are often resident, while gerbils and other rodents can be seasonally abundant. Bustards, sandgrouse and larks are typical birds, while eagles, goshawks, falcons and other raptors are often conspicuous.

Desert

Africa has two true deserts. The Sahara is undoubtedly the world's most famous but it is not known for its wildlife and is not dealt with here. In contrast, the Namib Desert (after which the country of Namibia is named) is an extraordinary wilderness with a host of unique arid-adapted plants and animals. Deserts are characterized by extremely low annual rainfall, although brief periods of bounty follow uncharacteristic thunderstorms. Large mammals are few and mostly nomadic, but a variety of interesting arid-adapted birds and reptiles are present.

Forest

Forest may be defined as an area with total tree cover where tree canopies interlock. There are several kinds of forest in Africa, ranging from equatorial/lowland rain forest, coastal forest, temperate montane forest and bands of riverine forest in savannah habitats. The temperate montane forests of Rwanda and Uganda are home to mountain gorillas, while chimpanzees and various other primates occur in forest pockets of Uganda and Tanzania. African elephant, buffalo and various species of duiker are typical forest mammals. A large number of bird species are restricted to forests of one kind or another throughout Africa; some are canopy feeders while others skulk on the forest floor. The Congo Basin is the second largest rainforest on the planet, after the Amazon. Lowland forests contain hardwood trees attractive to loggers and extensive areas have been cleared or are currently under threat.

High Altitude Grassland

On the highveld plateau of South Africa, a prairie-like grassland once dominated the landscape but intensive agriculture and coal mining have now reduced this to a fragment of its former extent and many grassland specialist species are now endangered. Indigenous trees are largely absent due to winter frosts and regular fires, but hardy alien species such as eucalyptus and weeping willow are now conspicuous. The upland regions of Ethiopia, Kenya, Malawi and Tanzania have smaller but usually more pristine areas of high altitude grassland. Large mammals are few but birds are abundant and conspicuous.

Rivers, Lakes and Wetlands

Africa has several major rivers, including the north-flowing Nile — the world's longest — which empties into the Mediterranean. The Congo River is second only to the Amazon in terms of volume as it drains west into the Atlantic. The Zambezi, Limpopo, Ruvuma, Rufiji, Galana and Tana are the major river systems draining southern and eastern Africa into the Indian Ocean. These rivers are all fed by smaller tributaries, many of which are seasonal. All of these waterbodies are essential for people and wildlife but many are threatened by inappropriate agriculture, deforestation and erosion of catchments and the impacts of global warming. A chain of great lakes occurs in the two arms of the Rift Valley, and the world's third largest — Lake Victoria — is sandwiched in between. Botswana's Okavango Delta is formed by the river of the same name spilling out into the Kalahari Basin; the Rufiji and Zambezi Deltas are important coastal wetlands. Hippo are restricted to rivers and wetlands, while elephant, buffalo and many other large mammals are water dependent. A vast array of birds including pelicans, flamingos, storks, herons, ducks, geese, cormorants, kingfishers, jacanas, plovers and migratory sandpipers inhabit wetlands of various types.

Coast and Reefs

The shore and seas off Africa's coast support diverse wildlife communities in habitats ranging from kelp beds and coral reefs, to mangroves and pristine beaches. The deep pelagic waters beyond the continental shelf are home to whales, dolphins, sea turtles and great white sharks, as well as birds such as albatrosses, petrels and shearwaters.

There is a vast difference between the east and west coasts of the continent. The cold Benguela current sweeps north from the Antarctic to bring cool, nutrient-rich water to the western Cape and Namibia, with large numbers of fur seals and gannets thriving in the productive waters that are, however, threatened by commercial fishing fleets. In contrast, the Indian Ocean is warmed by equatorial waters, with coral reefs off the Kenyan, Tanzanian and Mozambican coasts, and palm-fringed islands such as Zanzibar and Seychelles. Fish and other wildlife have been heavily harvested along this tropical coast, which has been exploited and fought over by traders, settlers and locals for centuries. Fortunately, marine reserves in Kenya, Tanzania and South Africa protect extensive areas.

A few days on an island or beach is a perfect way to end an African safari, with the splendor of a healthy coral reef surpassing most terrestrial habitats in terms of diversity and color.

Use the **What Wildlife Is Best Seen Where** chart (page 1) as a guide in finding the major parks and reserves that are most likely to have the animals you are most interested in seeing on safari.

CONSERVATION IN AFRICA

Africa is blessed with some of the most extensive wilderness areas on planet Earth — the Serengeti, Okavango and Congo Basin are among the most spectacular. A look at any map will show that a large proportion of land has been set aside as national parks or game reserves in many countries, with Botswana (39%) and Tanzania (15%) among those with the greatest percentage of land devoted to wildlife.

In most cases, these national parks were founded by colonial governments prior to 1960; although there are some notable exceptions such as in Uganda where three new national parks were established in 1993. Many of the national parks were initially set aside as hunting reserves for settlers. Rural people, most of whom were dependent upon wildlife for their sustenance, were deliberately excluded. It was because wildlife was primarily seen as something to pursue, hunt and kill that the word "game" (as in "fair game") came into use, and that is why wildlife reserves are still today known as game reserves (even though hunting is prohibited). In time, hunting came to an end in the national parks, because the wildlife resource was seen to be finite, and a "conservation" ethic took root.

In most cases, the early national parks were run along military lines, and local people who attempted to capture "game" were regarded as the enemy — poachers

Gorilla permit fees help fund conservation efforts in Uganda and Rwanda

to be punished and jailed. This approach to national parks undoubtedly safe-guarded large areas of wild land (for which modern-day conservationists can be grateful), but, at the same time, it alienated local communities who came to regard the reserves — and sometimes even the animals themselves — as symbols of repression.

In the 1990s, conservation philosophy in Africa swung toward initiatives that brought communities and wildlife closer together. Two things had become obvious. First, even the largest national parks contained only portions of eco-systems; many species extended their range beyond the boundaries. Second, a protectionist approach dictated to local people by governments or enthusiastic foreign environmentalists would have very little chance of succeeding in the absence of any real incentives.

While the borders of most national parks remain intact, innovative community-based programs encourage local people to develop sustainable resource utilization in adjoining areas. This concept serves to maintain natural ecosystems beyond the borders of protected areas, as opposed to the establishment of marginal farming activities that generally destroy or displace all wildlife.

Non-consumptive utilization, such as ecotourism, provides jobs and financial returns to communities, while the harvesting of thatching grass, honey, wood and wildlife, such as antelope and fish, provides direct sustenance. In essence, these programs set out to restore ownership and responsibility for wildlife to the local people. In areas of low seasonal rainfall (much of East and southern Africa) the financial returns from wildlife have proven to exceed most forms of agriculture or livestock farming.

Perhaps the most interesting development in recent years are the so-called transfrontier initiatives, such as Peace Parks, which link existing protected areas across national boundaries. These potentially massive areas not only allow for greater expansion of wildlife but also provide developing countries with growth points for ecotourism and stimulate greater economic cooperation between neighbors.

There can be little doubt that ecotourism has made a significant contribution to the conservation of wildlife in Africa, through job creation and the stimula-tion of local economies. Another important benefit is that many young African people have been reconnected to the wildlife that their grandparents interacted with and depended upon, because they have become skilled and articulate guides, hosts and hostesses.

There is much to be positive about for the future of African wildlife. As many governments recognize the value of ecotourism, many rural people are deriv-ing real benefits from sustainable resource use, and protected areas are actually increasing in size. But conservation is not just about elephants and other large mammals — it is about the land itself. Much still has to be achieved outside of Africa's savannah biome, because rainforests, temperate grasslands and spe-cialized ecosystems, such as mangroves, shrink daily and rare, geographically isolated species face extinction. Taking a safari to Africa in itself is a significant donation to conserving wildlife!

African Facts at a Glance

Area: 11,635,000 square-miles (30,420,000-km²)

Approximate size: More than three times the size of the United States; larger than Europe, the United States and China combined; the second largest continent, covering 20% of the world's land surface

Population: 625,000,000 (approx.)

Largest waterfall: Victoria Falls (the world's largest waterfall by volume), twice the height of Niagara Falls and one-and-a-half times as wide

Longest river: Nile River (world's longest), 4,160 miles (6,710 km)

Largest crater: Ngorongoro Crater (largest intact caldera/crater in the world), 12 miles (19 km) wide with its rim rising 1,200 to 1,600 feet (366 to 488 m) off its expansive 102 square-mile (264-km²) floor

Highest mountain: Mt. Kilimanjaro (highest mountain in the world not part of a range), 19,340 feet (5,895 m)

Largest lake: Lake Victoria (world's third largest), 26,828 square-miles (69,485-km²)

Largest freshwater oasis: Okavango Delta (Botswana), over 6,000 square-miles (15,000-km²)

Largest desert: Sahara (world's largest), larger than the continental United States

Largest land mammal: Elephant (world's largest), over 15,000 pounds (6,800 kg)

Largest bird: Ostrich (world's largest), over 8 feet (2.5 m) tall

Deepest lake: Lake Tanganyika (world's second deepest), over 4,700 feet (1,433 m)

Longest lake: Lake Tanganyika (world's longest), 446 miles (714 km)

Longest rift valley: The Great Rift Valley, a 5,900 mile (9,500 km) gash from the Red Sea to Lake Malawi, with 30 active volcanoes

Most species of fish: Lake Malawi (500 species)

Tallest people: The Dinka of southern Sudan (world's tallest) generally reach on average 5'11" (180 cm)

Shortest people: The pygmies of the Congo (world's shortest) reach only 4'11" (125 cm)

Eastern and Southern Africa World Heritage Sites

The United Nations Educational, Scientific and Cultural Organization (UNESCO) has a focused goal to protect and embrace the past for future generations to enjoy. World Heritage sites are chosen based on their unique and diverse natural and cultural legacy. The preservation of these sites around the world is considered to be an outstanding value to humanity.

Below is a list of Eastern and Southern Africa World Heritage Sites:

Botswana
Tsodilo Hills

Ethiopia
Simien National Park
Rock-Hewn Churches, Lalibela
Fasil Ghebbi, Gondar Region
Aksum
Lower Valley of the Awash
Lower Valley of the Omo
Tiya
Harar Jugol, the Fortified Historic Town

Kenya
Lake Turkana National Park
Mt. Kenya National Park / Natural Forest
Lamu Old Town

Malawi
Lake Malawi National Park
Chongoni Rock Art Area

Mauritius
Aapravasi Ghat

Mozambique
Ilha de Mozambique

Namibia
Twyfelfontein

Seychelles
Aldabra Atoll
Vallee de Mai Nature Reserve

South Africa
Fossil Hominid Sites of Sterkfontein, Swartkrans, Kromdraai and Environs
Greater St. Lucia Wetland Park
Robben Island
uKhahlamba/Drakensberg Park
Mapungubwe Cultural Landscape
Cape Floral Region Protected Area
Vredefort Dome
Richtersveld Cultural and Botanical Landscape

Tanzania
Ngorongoro Conservation Area
Ruins of Kikwa Kisiwani and Ruins of Songo Mnara
Serengeti National Park
Selous Game Reserve
Kilimanjaro National Park
Stone Town of Zanzibar
Kondoa Rock-Art-Sites

Uganda
Bwindi Impenetrable National Park
Ruwenzori Mountains National Park
Tombs of Buganda Kings at Kasubi

Zambia
Mosi-oa-Tunya / Victoria Falls

Zimbabwe
Mana Pools National Park, Sapi and Chewore Safari Areas
Great Zimbabwe National Monument
Khami Ruins National Monument
Mosi-oa-Tunya / Victoria Falls
Matobo Hills

Botswana

Botswana

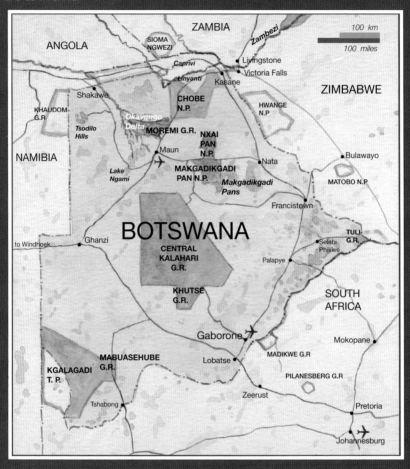

Botswana is dominated by the great Kalahari Desert which is actually a varied landscape of grasslands, bush scrub and savannah. In the far northwest, the Okavango River spills out onto the deep Kalahari sands to create the magical Okavango Delta — one of the continent's great wilderness regions. At some 224,606-square-miles (581,730-km²) Botswana is about the size of Texas (or France). The average elevation is around 3,200 feet (1,000 m) above sea level. Botswana's population numbers some 1.6 million, with the great majority living in the southeast, including the capital city of Gaborone. Setswana and English are the official languages. Currency is the Pula.

Botswana
Country Highlights

- Visit what is considered by many experts as one of the top wildlife countries in Africa for game viewing.
- Enjoy the exclusivity of private concession areas with very few guests and great game.
- Search for the big cats (leopard, cheetah and lion) surrounded by Botswana's epic scenery.
- Enjoy mokoro (canoe) and motorboat game viewing excursions through the crystal clear waterways of the Okavango Delta.
- Marvel at the mysteries of the Kalahari, from the famous Bushmen to spending time with habituated meerkats.
- Spend several nights (if not your whole safari) in some of Botswana's world-class luxury permanent tented or mobile tented camps.
- View elephant herds in Chobe and the Linyanti/Selinda/Kwando region, sometimes numbering over a hundred strong.

When's the Best Time to Go for Game Viewing

■ Excellent ■ Good □ Fair ■ Poor ■ Closed

Country	Park/Reserve	JAN	FEB	MAR	APR	MAY	JUN	JUL	AUG	SEP	OCT	NOV	DEC
Botswana	Moremi/Okavango												
	Linyanti/Selinda/Kwando/E. Makgadikgadi												
	Central Kalahari/Nxai Pan/W. Makgadikgadi												
	Savute (Southwestern Chobe)												
	Chobe												
	Tuli												

Best Safari Experience

Mombo and Little Mombo (Moremi), Zarafa, Selinda, DumaTau, and Savuti (Linyanti/Selinda region), Duba Plains, Vumbura Plains, Chitabe and Chitabe Lediba (Okavango Delta), deluxe mobile tenting in Moremi and Khwai (Okavango), Kalahari Plains (Central Kalahari), Jack's Camp (Makgadikgadi), Ngoma and Chobe Chilwero (Chobe), and Mashatu Main Camp and Tented Camp (Northern Tuli)

BOTSWANA

Botswana has earned a reputation as one of the finest if not <u>the</u> finest safari destination in Africa. Very little of the country has been developed in any way, and the small population of less than two million people is concentrated in the southeastern part of the country. The vast northern region of the Okavango Delta and the contiguous conservation areas of Moremi, Kwando, Linyanti, Selinda, Savute and Chobe, along with nearby Nxai Pan, Makgadikgadi Pans and the Central Kalahari Game Reserve, are some of the greatest wildernesses on the planet.

Alexander McCall Smith's best-selling book (and TV) series *The No. 1 Ladies' Detective Agency* (Random House), *The Cry of the Kalahari* by Mark and Delia Owens (Houghton Mifflin), the hilarious feature films, *The Gods Must Be Crazy*

Cape Buffalo, one of the "Big Five", is frequently seen in Botswana

(I and II), feature stories in National Geographic and numerous documentaries on television have all helped Botswana to gain international recognition as a top safari destination.

More than four-fifths of the country is covered by the sands of the Kalahari, scrub savannah and grasslands. The land is basically flat with a mean elevation of 3,280 feet (1,000 m).

The Kalahari Desert is not a barren desert of rolling sand dunes as one might imagine. It contains grass-

A malachite kingfisher strikes a graceful pose while fishing

lands, bush, shrub and tree savannah, dry riverbeds and occasional rocky outcrops.

The "Pula" is not only Botswana's unit of currency, but also the Setswana word for rain, which is so critical to this country's wealth and survival. The rainy season is December to March, with the heaviest rains usually occurring in January and February. Winter brings almost cloudless skies. January (summer) temperatures range from an average maximum of 92°F (33°C) to an average minimum of 64°F (18°C). July (winter) temperatures range from an average maximum of 72°F (22°C) to an average minimum of 42°F (6°C). Frost sometimes occurs in midwinter.

Batswana is also the term used for all citizens of Botswana, and they all speak the Setswana language. English is spoken by most of the people, especially the youth. Cattle are their most important symbol of wealth and prestige. Ancestor worship was the chief form of religion until missionaries arrived in 1816 and converted large numbers of Batswana to Christianity.

The San, Basarwa or bushmen, were the first inhabitants of the area and may have come to southern Africa 30,000 years ago. Bechuanaland became a protectorate of the British Empire on September 30, 1885, and became the independent country of Botswana on September 30, 1966.

Today, very few of the people dress in their traditional costume, except for special celebrations. However, for many Batswana, tribal customs are still important in day-to-day life.

Botswana has a multi-party democracy and is one of the most economically successful and politically stable countries on earth. Botswana's greatest foreign exchange earners are diamonds, tourism, cattle (there are three times as many cattle in Botswana as there are people) and copper-nickel matte.

🐾 WILDLIFE AND WILDLIFE AREAS

As far as the conservation of wildlife is concerned, Botswana is one of Africa's greatest success stories. It is not surprising, though, because the country has set aside nearly 40% of its land area for wildlife. National parks and game reserves cover 17% of the country's area — one of the highest percentages of any country in the world. In addition, another 22% of the country has been set aside as wildlife management areas. These wildlife management areas adjoin the national parks and game reserves and form the core around which the safari industry operates. Most of the 22% of the wildlife land is leased out by the authorities to safari companies. In turn, they have created wonderful, private reserves (or concession areas as they are known locally) that have incredible wildlife-viewing opportunities. These private reserves are what make Botswana's tourism what it is today. Visitors are able to get away from crowds, as numbers are strictly regulated, and guests are able to enjoy one of the highest ratios of wildlife acreage per visitor anywhere in Africa.

Botswana's combination of great game, uncrowded reserves, excellent small camps (most cater to 24 or fewer guests) and the use of open vehicles for day and night game viewing is difficult to beat.

The five main reserve areas most often visited by international tourists are all in the far northern reaches of the country. They are the Okavango Delta, Moremi Game Reserve (within the Okavango Delta), Linyanti/Selinda/Kwando region, the Savute (southwestern part of Chobe National Park), and the Chobe River region in the northeastern part of Chobe National Park near Kasane. Chobe National Park (northeastern section) is the only one of these regions that may be crowded.

The Linyanti/Selinda/Kwando region, and the majority of the Okavango Delta outside of Moremi Game Reserve, has been divided into private concession areas that feature camps that can be visited by a limited number of guests. Only guests staying at the camps within each respective concession are allowed in these areas, guaranteeing exclusivity. Night game drives and limited, off-road driving are allowed in most of these areas, because the rules governing these concession areas are not as restrictive as in the national parks and game reserves. Game viewing in many of these concessions is, in fact, as good or better than game viewing in some of the reserves themselves.

Because the regions are each distinct in character, if time allows, a well-rounded wildlife safari to Botswana should include two to three days each in three or more of these areas, along with a few days in the Makgadikgadi Pans, Nxai Pan or Central Kalahari Game Reserve.

Chobe National Park, Moremi Game Reserve, the Okavango Delta, and the Linyanti/Selinda/Kwando region rank among the best wildlife areas in Africa. The Okavango Delta is the largest inland delta in the world. This "water in the desert" phenomenon has created a unique and fascinating ecosystem that is well worth exploring.

Generally speaking, game viewing for the Okavango Delta, Moremi, Linyanti, Chobe and Savute is good all year, although large numbers of elephant

An iconic image of the Okavango Delta as elephants traverse the wetlands

Northern Botswana

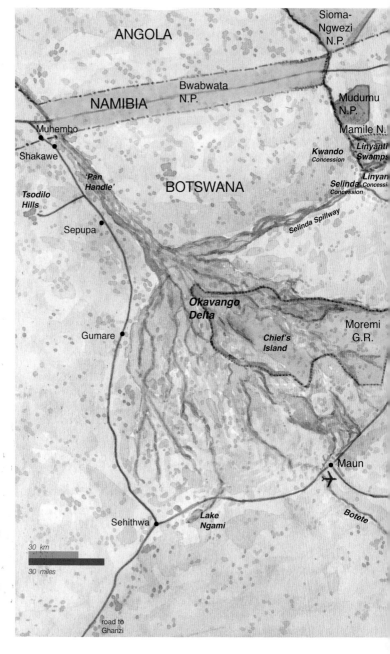

ANGOLA

Sioma-
Ngwezi
N.P.

Bwabwata
N.P.

NAMIBIA

Mudumu
N.P.

Mamile N.

Muhembo

Shakawe

Kwando
Concession

Linyanti
Swamps

'Pan
Handle'

BOTSWANA

Selinda Concessi
Concession

Linyan

Tsodilo
Hills

Selinda Spillway

Sepupa

Okavango
Delta

Moremi
G.R.

Gumare

Chief's
Island

Maun

Sehithwa

Lake
Ngami

Botete

30 km

30 miles

road to
Ghanzi

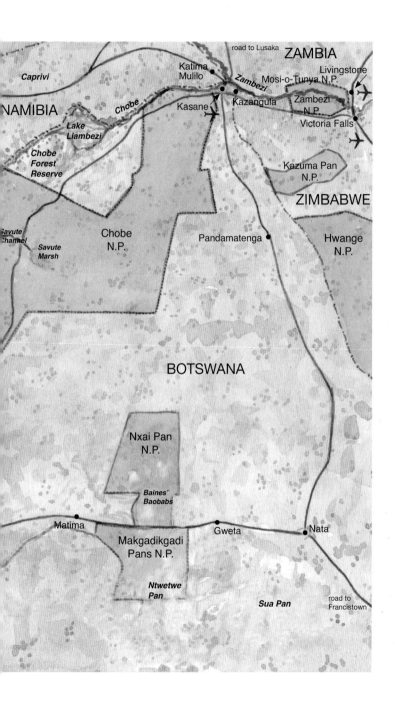

road to Lusaka

ZAMBIA

Katima Mulilo

Zambezi

Mosi-o-Tunya N.P.

Livingstone

Kasane

Kazangula

Zambezi N.P.

Caprivi

NAMIBIA

Chobe

Victoria Falls

Lake Liambezi

Chobe Forest Reserve

Kazuma Pan N.P.

ZIMBABWE

Savute Channel

Savute Marsh

Chobe N.P.

Pandamatenga

Hwange N.P.

BOTSWANA

Nxai Pan N.P.

Baines' Baobabs

Matima

Gweta

Nata

Makgadikgadi Pans N.P.

Ntwetwe Pan

Sua Pan

road to Francistown

concentrate around the waterways and marshlands in the dryer months of May through November.

The rainy season is predominantly December to March and usually consists of occasional short thundershowers. More and more travelers prefer to travel at this time of the year, as the bush is luxuriantly green and lush with little dust in the air. You may have to work a little harder at finding game in some areas, but there is still plenty to see, and as the safari camp and lodge rates are significantly lower than in high season, visitors can afford to stay a lot longer — easily making up the difference in game seen! Another advantage is that there are fewer travelers in most of the camps — allowing for more personal attention.

Many areas of Botswana including parts of the Okavango Delta, the Savute, Nxai Pan National Park, Makgadikgadi Pans National Park and the Central Kalahari Game Reserve are, in fact, better to visit during this period than in the dry (high) season. Game viewing in Nxai Pan is best in the wet summer season (November to April), and Makgadikgadi Pans and Central Kalahari Game Reserve are best December to April. Reserves in the south are, at times, excellent, but they are season dependent.

Calving season throughout the country is November to February, during the summer months. The abundance of young animals (babies) make for wonderful photographic opportunities from mid-November or December through March. The sight of warthog piglets and impala lambs, only a few days to a few months old, will charm even the most stoic safarier.

The rut, or season when impala males fight for dominance, provides plenty of action from April to May.

Fishing for tigerfish, bream, barbel and pike is very good, especially September to December. Fishing is not allowed in the Moremi Game Reserve and is not allowed anywhere in Botswana from January until the end of February.

Many camps are accessed only by small aircraft, which allows visitors to minimize the time spent on roads between reserves and maximize the time viewing wildlife and enjoying the variety of other activities the region has to offer. Game activities are conducted by resident guides in the camps. Specialist guides may be booked to travel with you — adding a consistent high level of guiding throughout your safari.

Most scheduled charter flights have baggage limits of 44 pounds (20 kg) per person (unless you decide to "purchase" an extra seat on the plane for your extra luggage), so bring only what you need, and pack it in only soft-sided bags. Free laundry service and amenities are available at all of the better camps.

Group and private luxury, first-class (full-service) and budget (participatory) mobile tented safaris are generally less expensive per day than flying safaris, and they are another excellent way to experience the reserves. I highly recommend small group and private luxury mobile camp safaris here, especially as the guides are generally excellent, and stay with you (as guides do with the other levels of mobile safaris) throughout the safari.

The Wildlife Department runs the parks. Driving in the parks is currently not allowed at night, but it is allowed in the private concession areas.

NORTH AND CENTRAL

Maun

Maun is the safari center of the country's most important tourist region. Many travelers fly into Maun to join their safari; others begin their safari at Victoria Falls (Zimbabwe), Livingstone (Zambia) or Kasane, Botswana, and end up in Maun. Very few international travelers actually stay in Maun; instead they fly in and connect directly to a safari camp.

ACCOMMODATION — TOURIST CLASS: • **Thamalakane River Lodge**, located on the Thamalakane River, features 10 comfortable stone-and-thatch chalets with private patios. • **Royal Tree Lodge**, situated on a 500-acre (200-hectare) farm just 10 miles (15 km) south of Maun airport on the western border of a farm on the Thamalakane River, consists of 7 large Meru-style tents plus 2 honeymoon suites, catering for a maximum of 18 guests. • **Island Safari Lodge** is located 9 miles (14 km) north of Maun on the western bank of the Thamalakane River and has brick-and-thatch bungalows, swimming pool, bar and restaurant.

Moremi Game Reserve

Moremi is the most diversified of all the Botswana parks, in terms of wildlife and scenery. Located in the northeastern part of the Okavango Delta, Moremi contains over 1,160-square-miles (3,000-km²) of permanent swamps, islands, flood plains, forests and dry land.

One of the reasons Moremi is so unique is that it (as well as some other parts of the northern Delta) receives the richest deposits of sediment from the annual floods. This produces the most nutritious grasses that attract large herds of antelope, which in turn attract large numbers of predators.

In the flood plains, reedbuck, common waterbuck, red lechwe, tsessebe, ostrich, sable and roan antelope, crocodile, hippo and otter can be found. In the riparian forest, you may spot elephant, greater kudu, southern giraffe, impala, buffalo and Burchell's zebra, along with such predators as lion, leopard, ratel (honey badger), spotted hyena and cheetah. Bat-eared fox, black-backed and side-striped jackals are often seen in the riparian forest, as well as in the flood plain. The reserve also has a good wild dog population, seldom-seen species include pangolin, aardvark, porcupine and hedgehog.

Game viewing is excellent during the drier months of May to November when the bush has thinned out, making wildlife sightings a bit easier. In parts of Moremi, game viewing is, in fact, excellent year-round — especially the northern end of Chief's Island.

During a visit in 2001, I was honored to witness four white rhino being released into the wild at Mombo Camp. The release was part of a grand, ongoing plan to repopulate both black and white rhino species into the wild in Botswana. As a

Moremi's most famous leopard, Lagadema

result of further introductions and a healthy breeding population, the national herd has grown to 60 white and black rhino. You now have a chance of seeing the "Big Five" (lion, leopard, elephant, buffalo and rhino) once more on safari in Botswana!

Elephant and buffalo are the only large animals that migrate. After the rains have begun, they move northward to the area between Moremi and the Kwando-Linyanti River systems. Other wildlife may move to the periphery of, or just outside, the reserve.

Moremi is also an ornithologist's delight. Fish eagles, kingfishers and bee-eaters abound. Other birds commonly seen include parrots, shrikes, egrets, jacanas, pelicans, bateleur eagles, hornbills, herons, saddle-billed storks, yellow-billed oxpeckers, wattled cranes, reed cormorants, spur-winged geese, long-tailed shrikes and flocks of thousands of red-billed quelea, which group together in the form of a sphere like a great spotted flying ball.

With the onset of the floods, generally in May or June, waterfowl follow the progression of the floodwaters as they flow through the region.

Moremi is open year-round; however, some areas may be temporarily closed due to heavy rains or floods. Four-wheel-drive vehicles are necessary. Night game drives and escorted walks are not permitted. This is an excellent reserve for mobile tenting. The South Gate is about 62 miles (100 km) north of Maun.

ACCOMMODATION IN MOREMI GAME RESERVE — CLASS A+: • **Little Mombo** and **Mombo Camp** are situated in the reserve near the northern tip of Chief's Island, where the savannah meets the Okavango, in what is considered by many to be the best game viewing area in southern Africa. Big game is plentiful year-round in this area. **Mombo** (9 tents) and **Little Mombo's** (3 tents) luxurious tents are built on raised decks each with a sala, verandah and lounge area overlooking the flood plains. Each camp has its own dining tent, lounge, plunge pool and connected by a raised walkway. They share a gym. Activities include day and early evening game drives (up to a half hour after sunset). Night game drives may be allowed in the future.

CLASS A: • **Chief's Camp**, located on the western side of Chief's Island (9 miles/15 km south of Mombo), has 12 tents set close together with private viewing decks, hammocks and loungers overlooking the seasonal flood plains, a swimming pool, beauty treatment room and zen garden. • **Camp Moremi** is a 22-bed tented camp located overlooking Xakanaxa Lagoon. Game drives are offered. • **Xigera Camp** is situated within the Moremi Game Reserve on a large island in the Delta. The camp has 10 luxury tented rooms on raised platforms. Activities include mokoro rides, walks outside the reserve, game viewing by vehicle (when water levels are low) and extended boat rides to the Chief's Island region.

Luxury mobile camping in Moremi *(top)*, A private sala at Little Mombo *(middle)*, Mombo Camp's classic lounge area *(bottom)*

CLASS A/B: • **Xakanaxa Camp** features 12 tents overlooking the Xakanaxa Lagoon. Game drives and boat trips are offered. • **Camp Okuti** has 5 unique curved chalets with private balconies and river views. This family-friendly camp welcomes children 7 and up. Game drives and boat rides are offered.

The Okavango Delta

The Okavango, covering over 6,000-square-miles (15,000-km^2), is a natural mosaic of palm-fringed islands, open savannah, flowing rivers, crystal-clear lagoons and flood plains sprinkled with water lilies, and gigantic baobab and jackalberry trees.

Okavango Delta and Moremi Game Reserve

Nxamaseri Camp

Vumbura Plains Cai

Little Vumi

Duba Plains

Nqoga

Jao

Thaoge

Okavango Delta

Mombo Camp
and Little Mombo

Kwetsani Camp

Tubu
Tree
Camp

Jacana Camp

Chief's Camp

Tsodilo Hills

Jao Camp

Boro

Gumare

Xigera
Camp

Abu's
Camp

Seba Camp

Matsibe

Xudum

Sandveld
Tongue

Xaranna Okava

Xudum Ol

20 km

20 miles

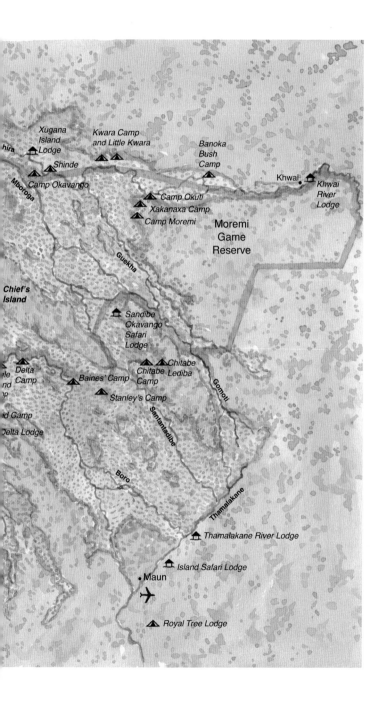

Xugana
Island
Lodge

hira

Shinde

Mboroga

Camp Okavango

Kwara Camp
and Little Kwara

Banoka
Bush
Camp

Khwai

Khwai
River
Lodge

Camp Okuti

Xakanaxa Camp

Camp Moremi

Moremi
Game
Reserve

Guekha

Chief's
Island

Sandibe
Okavango
Safari
Lodge

Delta
Camp

ile
nd
ip

Baines' Camp

Chitabe
Lediba

Chitabe
Camp

Stanley's Camp

d Camp

Delta Lodge

Gomoti

Santantadibe

Boro

Thamalakane

Thamalakane River Lodge

Island Safari Lodge

Maun

Royal Tree Lodge

Jacana Island in the heart of the Delta

The Okavango River originates in the central African highlands in Angola, which is about 600 miles (1,000 km) northwest of Botswana, then it fans out into the Kalahari Desert to create a vast system of thousands of waterways, separated by innumerable islands, and it eventually disappears into the Kalahari sands.

The wonder of this inland delta — the primordial silence, unusual flora, big game and superb bird life — make it well worth a visit.

Game viewing for the larger land mammal species is excellent in many parts of the Delta. Large herds of buffalo, elephant, giraffe and a variety of antelope are often seen. Lion, leopard, cheetah and other predators are also frequently encountered. The Okavango is an ornithologist's and botanist's dream come true.

Crocodiles are most heavily concentrated in the larger waterways and in the northern part of the Delta and the panhandle, where there is permanent, deep

A pride of lions at Duba Plains prepare to hunt

water. However, crocs are found throughout the Delta.

Mother Nature must have smiled on this region, for the waters are highest during the peak of the dry season. It takes six months for the rainy season floodwaters to travel from their source in the Angolan highlands to the Delta. Flying into the Delta gives you an overall perspective of the region and is an adventure in itself. Game can be easily spotted and photographed from the air.

A 150-mile- (240-km) long buffalo fence has been constructed along the southern and western edges of the Delta to keep cattle

Exploring the Okavango Delta in a mokoro

from moving into the pristine natural areas. The villages and their cattle are to the west and south of the fence; therefore, little game is found on the Maun (southern) side.

Calling the Okavango a "swamp" is a misnomer, since the waters are very clear and are continually moving. The clarity is mainly due to the fact that the waters carry little sediment. There is only about a 203 foot (63 m) drop in altitude over 150 miles (240 km) from the upper to the lower Delta. In addition, the larger stands of papyrus in both the panhandle and in the north act as a large filtration plant, filtering out impurities and helping to keep the waters crystal clear.

Activities in the Delta include mokoro (dugout canoe) and modern canoe excursions, motorized boat game safaris, day and night vehicle game drives, nature walks on islands, bird watching, and fishing on request. Motor boats allow you to visit more distant attractions, and must be used for fishing or where the water is too deep to pole a mokoro or canoe. Where there is access by land, a 4wd vehicle is necessary.

One of the most relaxing ways to experience the majesty of the Okavango Delta waterways is by mokoro. Traveling by mokoro allows you to become a part of the environment. Sitting inches from the waterline, thoughts of hippos or crocodiles overturning your boat cross your mind but soon pass with assurances from your guide and the peacefulness of the pristine environment.

Patterns of gold are created by the reflection of papyrus on the still waters of the narrow channels during early morning and late afternoon. You sometimes pass through channels that can appear to be narrower than the boat itself. Silence is broken only by the ngashi (boatman's pole) penetrating and leaving the water, by the cries of countless birds and by the movement of game along the Delta's banks. Tiny frogs chime to an unknown melody. At sunset, clouds reflect in the

Open-vehicle game drives bring you close to the action

waters and create the illusion of floating in the sky. Life slows to a regenerative pace.

Guided excursions, ranging in length from a few hours to a full day, using mekoro (plural for mokoro), canoes or small motor boats, are offered by many camps in the Delta. Canoes are larger and therefore a little more comfortable, but mekoro harmonize better with the natural surroundings. To minimize cutting the large trees in the Delta, camps use specially built fiberglass mekoro, which look and move like the real thing — without a cost to the woodlands. Mokoro trips for two or more days, during which you camp on remote islands in the Delta, are possible when booked in advance.

The islands in the Delta are created by many natural geological forces. Another of the causes for islands are termites, whose mounds have been built up over the eons. Because of the cement-like quality of termite mounds, the soil is sometimes dug up and used to build elevated paths in camps and even airstrips. Meanwhile, diamond prospectors inspect termite mounds closely. Since soil is brought up from quite a depth, it provides them with easily accessible core samples.

One of the real highlights of any safari is to sight African wild dogs, and the northern regions of Botswana are one of Africa's last refuges for this rare and endangered animal.

As might be expected of an inland delta, the Okavango is a haven for birds and a huge attraction for birdwatchers from around the world. There is a bewildering variety of aquatic and terrestrial species, and the Okavango boasts the highest concentration of African fish eagles on the continent. There are good numbers of the elusive and awe-inspiring Pel's fishing owl and the seasonally breeding African skimmers.

Large, mixed aggregations of waterfowl are common during the dry winter months, when the Angolan floodwaters fill up the seasonal wetlands. It is not uncommon to see five or six species of heron alongside four or five varieties of stork, with ducks, waders, cormorants and kingfishers — all gathered in the shallows or surrounding vegetation. The beautiful African pygmy goose, Pel's fishing owl, lesser jacana, slaty egret, wattled crane and the goliath heron are among the most sought-after birds.

It is not only waterfowl that populate the Okavango Delta, for the surrounding savannah and riverine woodlands provide ideal habitats for a host of hornbills, parrots, woodpeckers, rollers, shrikes, plovers, waxbills, weavers and bee-eaters, among others. Northern Botswana (and, indeed, the whole country) is renowned as a stronghold for birds of prey, with substantial populations of martial eagle, bateleur, tawny eagle, white-headed vulture, to name just a few.

Fishing is best in the northwestern part of the Delta. The best time of the year for catching tigerfish is September to November. For barbel, the best time is from the end of September through October, when the fish are running (a feeding frenzy). Overall, the best time for fishing is September to December.

Horseback safaris, possibly the finest in Africa, last from 5 to 10 days. Four to six hours a day are spent in the saddle. Afternoons are often spent walking, swimming, fishing or on mokoro trips. Only experienced riders are allowed, because they must be able to confidently canter alongside herds of game, including zebra, giraffe and antelope. Accommodations are usually in luxury or first class mobile tented camps.

An **elephant-back safari** (on an African elephant) is a unique way of experiencing the bush. Guests can fly to Abu's Camp, where they can ride on elephant back, joining the lead elephant along with several other adults and youngsters.

Male cheetahs are territorial and base their home range where several females reside and overlap

One of Vumbura Plains' luxurious suites *(top)*, Elephant-back safaris await at Abu's Camp *(middle)*, Duba Plains sits under a canopy of trees *(bottom)*

Another option is Stanley's and Baines' Camps, where guests may walk for a few hours with trained elephants.

If you wish to visit **Tsodilo Hills** (see page 107) to see the rock paintings, consider making reservations in advance. By booking in advance, you can fly from your camp in the Okavango to the Tsodilo Hills airstrip and then be driven to the hills.

ACCOMMODATION — CLASS A+:
• **Vumbura Plains Camp** is a premier luxury camp with 14 tents (divided into 2 separate camps of 7 tents) with private plunge pools and huge decks, linked by raised boardwalks to the dining, lounge and bar areas. The family suite features two separate rooms connected by a private deck. Vumbura Plains is located in the northern part of the Delta. Day and night game viewing by vehicle, mokoro excursions, limited walks, boat game drives, fishing and massages are offered.
• **Abu's Camp** is a luxury camp with 6 tents featuring private decks, stylish interiors and indoor-outdoor showers. There is a "star bed" allowing guests to sleep under the stars. Elephant-back safaris, mokoro rides, walks and vehicular game drives are offered. While elephant back riding is part of the experience, guests may walk with the elephants and interact with the researchers on-site. • **Jao Camp**, located in a private concession area west of the Moremi Game Reserve, has 9 large tented rooms (including 1 family tent) with lounge areas under thatched roofs. Each room has an outdoor shower and a "sala" with mattresses under thatch, for great midday siestas. Jao has two plunge pools, an exercise room and spa. Activities include day and night game drives, motor boat excursions (usually May to October, depending on water levels) and mokoro (dugout canoe) trips.

CLASS A: • **Duba Plains** accommodates a maximum of 12 guests in luxury tents in a remote region of the Delta. There is a thatched lounge, dining and bar area as well as a pool. Duba has a strong lion and buffalo population as well as other sought-after species. Game drives and walks are offered. • **Little Vumbura Camp**, located in the northern area of the Delta, offers 6 tented rooms (including 1 family tent), each with private decks. The main dining area has a decked lounge and a pool. It offers motorboat excursions, game viewing by mokoro, day and night game drives, and limited walks. • **Chitabe Camp**, located on a private concession bordered by the Moremi Game Reserve on 3 sides, has 8 luxury tents set on wooden decks. Day and night game drives and some walks are offered. • **Chitabe Lediba**, located in the same private concession area as Chitabe Camp, has 5 luxury tents including 2 family tents. Activities include day and night game drives and limited walks. • **Kwetsani Camp** located in the Jao Concession, is a 10-bed luxury tented camp raised on stilts beneath the shady canopy that overlooks the expansive plains. The 5 spacious tented "tree-house" chalets are built under thatch roofs. Day and night game drives, motorboat and mokoro excursions (water levels permitting) are offered. • **Tubu Tree Camp**, also situated in the Jao Concession, is a treehouse-style tented safari camp built on raised wooden platforms. The camp has 5 large, comfortable tents, each with small, private decks including an outdoor shower. Activities include day and night game drives. When the Okavango's annual flood is at its highest (normally May to late September), boating, fishing and mokoro trips are also offered. • **Sandibe Okavango Safari Lodge**, located on a private concession

Little Vumbura's expansive deck overlooks the Delta *(top)*, Kwetsani Camp features tree-house chalets *(bottom)*

surrounded by Moremi Game Reserve on three sides, has 8 thatched cottages with private decks and a swimming pool. Activities include day and night game drives, escorted walks, mokoro trips and motorboat excursions. • **Khwai River Lodge** overlooking the Khwai flood plains has 14 air-conditioned tents (28 beds) under thatch, mini-bars and private viewing decks with hammocks. The camp has a gym and spa facility plus swimming pool. Day and night game drives, guided walks along Khwai River and cultural visits to the village are offered. • **Xaranna Okavango Tented Camp** is located on the edge of the Okavango Delta and features 9 tents each with a sala and private plunge pool. Activities include boating, mekoros as well as morning and night game drives. • **Xudum Okavango Delta Lodge**, located in the same concession as Xaranna, offers 9 suites with large bathtubs, outdoor showers and private plunge pools. Activities include boating, mekoros as well as day and night game drives. • **Eagle Island Camp** is situated west of Chief's Island and has 11 air-conditioned luxury tents set on raised wooden decks with thatched roofs. April through October, activities include mokoro rides, motorized boats, and sundowner cruises; day and night game

Camp Okavango's thatched bar, dining room and fire pit

drives are offered year-round. • **Stanley's Camp**, located in the southern part of the Delta, consists of 8 tents raised up on a boardwalk and offers day and night game drives, guided walks and mokoro excursions (water levels permitting). For an additional fee, guests may spend time walking with trained elephants. • **Baines' Camp** is located in the same concession as Stanley's Camp and features 5 well appointed rooms set on elevated platforms, and a swimming pool. Activities include game drives, mokoro safaris, as well as walks with an armed guide. An educational elephant interaction offered at Stanley's Camp is available to guests at Baines'.

CLASS A/B: • **Camp Okavango** is a tented camp in the eastern Delta accommodating 24 guests in East-African-style tents each with a private sun deck. • **Jacana Camp** is a small camp featuring 5 tents, including a new family tent, set in the Jao Concession, and is primarily a water camp that offers mokoro and motorboat excursions. Day and night game drives are generally possible by vehicle September through May, when the water levels are lower. This is a family-friendly camp and children of all ages are welcome. • **Shinde**, located on a palm island on the edge of the Shinde Lagoon, has 8 tents and a multi-tiered lounge area is built under a canopy of ebony and mangosteen trees. Activities include mokoro trips, boat rides, fishing, walks and game drives. • **Seba Camp** is located in the Okavango on an island facing west. This family-friendly camp features 8 tents including 2 family suites. Children of all ages are welcome. Activities include limited game drives, night drives, boating, mokoros, walks and general birding around the camp. • **Xugana Island Lodge** has 8 reed chalets (16 beds) built on stilts and a swimming pool. Xugana offers boat rides, mokoro trips, walks and fishing. • **Little Kwara Camp** is next to Kwara Camp and has 5 tents and offers the same activities as Kwara Camp.

CLASS B: • **Banoka Bush Camp**, a raised camp overlooking a lagoon, has 10 tents including 2 family tents. Activities include game drives and mokoro rides (water level dependent). • **Kwara Camp**, situated just north of the reserve, has 8 tents (16 beds) and offers day and night game drives, walks, mokoro rides, fishing and evening boat cruises. • **Nxamaseri Camp**, located in the panhandle of the Delta, is one of the top fishing camps in the Okavango. Guests also enjoy boat and mokoro trips. • **Delta Camp** has 8 reed chalets. Walks and mokoro excursions are offered.

Tsodilo Hills

Over 2,700 Bushmen paintings are scattered through the rocky outcrops of Tsodilo Hills. The largest of the four hills rises 1,000 feet (305 m) above the surrounding plain. Archaeological evidence indicates that these hills may have been inhabited as long as 30,000 years ago.

Located west of the Okavango Delta, Tsodilo Hills is accessible by a flight from Maun (or from safari camps in northern Botswana) to the Tsodilo Hills airstrip, where a guide must be pre-arranged to drive you to the sites. The most convenient access is by helicopter from a safari camp in the Delta or Moremi. Alternatively, Tsodilo is a very long and rough day's ride from Maun by 4wd vehicle.

There are no facilities, so travelers must fly in just for the day, or be totally self-sufficient. Unfortunately, the bushman experience has become touristy, so don't expect to see Bushmen living as they did thousands of years ago. However, the rock paintings are worth a visit. Because water is scarce in this area, be sensitive and do not drink in the presence of Bushmen.

ACCOMMODATION: None.

Linyanti, Selinda and Kwando Concession Areas

The Linyanti, Selinda and Kwando concession areas, situated northeast of the Okavango Delta and northwest of the Savute marshes within Chobe National Park, are home to many crocodile, hippo, sitatunga, lechwe, southern giraffe,

(continued on page 110)

Linyanti, Selinda and Kwando Concession Areas

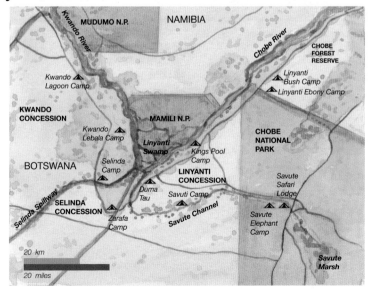

~ BOTSWANA'S SEASONAL WATER LEVELS ~

OKAVANGO DELTA

One issue to consider when visiting the Okavango Delta is the water levels and how they can affect the safari camps and the activities they may offer. Each year the Okavango presents a different scenario to its inhabitants and its visitors.

The annual "flood" usually begins to arrive in April or May and subsides in September or October. It is an eagerly awaited event as the levels of the incoming water have an enormous impact on the region. A safari camp, after a low flood, may be surrounded by huge, open grassland savannahs. The next year, that same camp may be surrounded by water as the result of an extremely high flood, and the game viewing areas will change. This is all part of the fun of traveling to the Okavango. It's a dynamic and constantly changing system!

Vehicles have a unique challenge with rising waters

When the seasonal floods arrive, much of the savannah is submerged — forcing the wildlife to concentrate on fewer and smaller islands. The area covered by game drives may be reduced; however, the drives are still productive. Safari camps have built numerous bridges to allow access to more dry areas (islands) during the height of the floods, thereby preserving the quality of the game viewing experience.

The level of the seasonal floods in the Okavango Delta are dependent on three main factors:

1) New flood waters arriving in the Delta via the Okavango River and its tributaries. This level is primarily dependent on the amount of rainfall that took place in the Angolan highlands approximately 6 months earlier.

2) Level of the water still present in the Delta from the previous year's rainfall and previous year's flood, and the level of the water table.

3) Level of rainfall in the current year's rainy season.

The distribution of the water within the Delta itself is also dynamic and is influenced by sediment deposition, wetland vegetation growth aligned to this deposition, large mammal movements and, to a lesser extent, localized tectonic activity.

The flood levels in the Delta usually begin rising in April, peak in June or July, and begin subsiding in September.

In a world where clean water is now a rarity and where biodiversity is so threatened, we must and should revel in the jewel that is the Okavango!

~ BOTSWANA'S SEASONAL WATER LEVELS ~

THE LINYANTI SWAMPS, SAVUTE CHANNEL, SELINDA SPILLWAY AND THE SAVUTI MARSH

Other important outcomes of the increase in water levels (or a return to the wet cycle) in Botswana are the return of major flows to the Savute Channel, which had been completely dry since 1982, the re-flooding of the Linyanti Swamps, the filling of Lake Liambezi in the Caprivi strip, and the flow of water into the Selinda Spillway and the Savuti Marsh.

It is important to note that these changes and cycles are massively important to the overall health and diversity of the entire ecosystem.

In the case of the **Savute Channel** and the adjacent **Linyanti Swamps**, the spatial distribution of elephants is hugely affected. The Linyanti region has been the center of some of the highest densities of African elephant during August, September and October each year. Now, with the onset of the "wet" cycle, the Savute Channel and nearby **Selinda Spillway** are both carrying major flows of water as they reach over hundreds of miles (hundreds of kms) through areas where there had not been water for over 20 years. Both these channels are enabling the previously concentrated elephants to spread out into other browse areas along those channels and have reduced the pressure on the vegetation along the Linyanti Swamps. This may have the effect

Lions adjust their hunting skills with the changing environment

of "resting" the area over the next couple of decades, allowing increases in some vegetation types which in turn may lead to species other than elephants benefitting for a time.

The flow in the Savute Channel into the **Savute Marsh** means fabulous game and bird viewing along that beautiful thread of water. During the "dry" years, there had been a considerable build up of hippo populations in the Linyanti marshes and associated waterways, and now many of these have moved into the Savute where some of the finest hippo viewing and interactions can be seen.

As part of a longer term cycle of approximately 20 years, we can expect this to become a trend over the next decade — always remembering that in any trend there may be an anomaly.

Written in association with Map Ives, Environmentalist for Wilderness Safaris

African wild dogs are the most successful hunters on the continent with 80% of their hunts ending with a kill

(continued from page 107)

elephant, buffalo, lion, wild dog (with good chances of seeing them) and spotted hyena. The region is, in essence, a mini "Okavango Delta" with a lot of big game. This is also big elephant country, with literally thousands in the region — especially in the dry season.

The Savute (Savuti) Channel, which had been dry for decades, as of this writing is flowing more than it has in over 25 years, bringing much needed water inland to this arid environment. The channel is now flowing all the way to the Savute Marsh in Chobe National Park!

The Kwando and Linyanti Rivers form the region's border with Namibia. The Kwando River flows southeast and then meets the southern end of the Great Rift Valley. This causes the river to flow northeast, and at this point its name changes to the Linyanti River and later to the Chobe River, which eventually meets the Zambezi River.

A juvenile leopard's spots help it blend in to its surroundings

This region is prolific in bird life. Big game is most concentrated in this region during the dry season (May to November). Game viewing for the rest of the year is also quite good. Most of the elephant used to migrate out of the area with the coming of the rains (November), however, now that the Savute River is flowing, there is less pressure during the dry season on the vegetation, and more are remaining in the area. Much of the rest of the game including the predators, remain in the region.

ACCOMMODATION — CLASS A+: • **Zarafa Camp**, located in the Selinda Concession, is a luxurious 8-bed tented camp, which can be booked on a private basis if it's a group of 6 guests with no surcharge applicable. The sumptuous 1,000-square-foot (93 m²) tents feature private plunge pools, outdoor showers and expansive decks overlooking the flood plains of the Zibadianja Lagoon. Unique to the camp, every tent is also equipped with a complimentary Canon digital camera and range of lenses that guests can use while on safari. Pictures are burnt to CD Rom at the end of the guest's stay to take with them. Day and night game drives and escorted walks are offered. Zarafa also has a houseboat used for birdwatching and sundowner cruises. • **Kings Pool Camp**, located on the Linyanti Concession overlooking a lagoon, has 9 luxurious tents set on raised decks with indoor-outdoor showers, a gym and a plunge pool. The camp is set on a small lagoon that is often full of hippo. Day and night vehicle game drives, boating on a double-decker "Queen Sylvia" houseboat in the luxury of old style colonial barge (water levels permitting), and walks are offered. There is a hide within the camp and also a number of hides in the bush.

CLASS A: • **Selinda Camp** is an 18-bed tented camp with unique open-air bathrooms that are fully screened and include large bathtubs. The private decks overlook the Selinda spillway. Activities include day and night game drives, boating (water levels permitting— usually July to October) and guided walks. The **Selinda Canoe Trail** is a 4 day/3 night canoe safari for up to 8 guests along the Selinda Spillway within the Selinda Concession. Trail camps are set up on remote islands. Top specialist guides lead set departures from mid-May to mid-October annually. Accommodations are in dome tents with separate shower and toilet tents for the party. • **DumaTau** is a 20-bed tented camp that has been rebuilt at a new site shaded by enormous trees with views of the Savute Channel. Day and night vehicle game drives, boat game viewing excursions and walks are offered. • **Savuti Camp**, located on the **Savute Channel** about 10 miles (17 km) from its source within the Linyanti Concession, has 7 standard tents including a family tent. A number of hides are located along the channel. Day and night game drives and canoeing on the Savute Channel are offered.

CLASS A/B: • **Kwando Lagoon Camp** is set on the banks of the Kwando River within the Kwando Concession and has 8 tents (16 beds) under thatch. Day and night vehicle game drives, boat excursions, walks and fishing are offered. • **Kwando Lebala Camp**, located in the Kwando Concession, is situated on vast open plains and has 8 luxury tents (16 beds) under thatch. Day and night game drives are offered. • **Linyanti Ebony Camp** overlooks the Linyanti marsh and has 4 raised tents with private decks and views of the marshes. Activities include day and night game drives, visits to hides, walks and mokoro rides (water levels permitting).

CLASS B: • **Linyanti Bush Camp** is a 12-bedded camp with Meru-style tents located in a concession area within the Chobe Forest Reserve. The main area is elevated on a wooden decking overlooking the Linyanti swamp. Activities include day and night game drives, walking, visits to hides, mokoro excursions and fishing (water levels permitting).

Zarafa's welcoming lounge *(top, left)*, Selinda Camp is a classic tented camp *(top, right)*, View from a tent at Savute Safari Lodge *(middle)*, Dumatau overlooks the Savute Channel *(bottom)*

Savute (Chobe National Park)

Savute is mainly an arid region located in the southern part of Chobe National Park. The landscape ranges from sandveld to mopane forest, acacia savannah, marshlands to rocky outcrops. The Savute Channel connects the grasslands or marshlands of the interior with the Linyanti River. The Savute River is flowing for the first time in many years, and has reached the park areas, and the marshlands are slowly filling.

The Savute, like the northern part of Chobe National Park, is famous for its lions and its bull elephant herds. The area is also home to eland, kudu, roan antelope, sable antelope, waterbuck, tsessebe, giraffe, wildebeest, impala and many other antelope, along with numerous predators, including leopard, cheetah, wild dog, spotted hyena, black-backed jackal and bat-eared fox.

Bird watching is best during the green season (November to April). Large flocks of dazzling carmine bee-eaters hawk insects, and large gatherings of white and Abdim's storks patrol the plains for grasshoppers. The world's heaviest flying bird — the kori bustard — is a common and conspicuous inhabitant of the area. Rollers, kestrels, plovers, sandgrouse, coursers, queleas and doves are among the other prominent groups.

A few bushmen paintings may be found in this region. Four-wheel-drive vehicles are necessary for the Savute. Night drives and walks are not permitted as this is part of Chobe National Park.

ACCOMMODATION — CLASS A/B: • **Savute Safari Lodge**, situated on the banks of the Savute Channel, has 12 Swedish-style wood-and-thatch chalets. The lounge, dining area and plunge pool overlook the channel. Day game drives are conducted. • **Savute Elephant Camp** has 12 luxury air-conditioned tents built on raised wooden decks overlooking the Savute Channel. The camp has a fireplace and lounge area, library and a swimming pool that overlooks a waterhole. Morning and afternoon game drives are offered.

Chobe National Park (Chobe River/Northern Region)

Famous for its large herds of elephant, Chobe National Park covers about 4,250-square-miles (11,000-km^2) and is situated only about 50 miles (80 km) from Victoria Falls (Zimbabwe and Zambia). The Chobe River forms its northern and northwestern boundaries, and across the river lays the Namibia's Caprivi Strip. Bird life is prolific, especially in the riverine areas.

The four main regions of the park are along the Chobe River in the northeast near Kasane, the Corridor around Ngwezumba and Nogatsaa, a portion of the Linyanti Swamps in the northwest, and the Savute (discussed above) in the west. This is the only park in Botswana that receives large numbers of tourists.

Northern Chobe is famous for its huge elephant and buffalo populations, which number in the thousands. Lion are seen fairly often. Game viewing by boat along the Chobe River can be spectacular, especially May to November in the dry season when large herds of elephant and a variety of other wildlife come down to the river to drink. On my last three visits we witnessed herds of 50 to

Chobe National Park

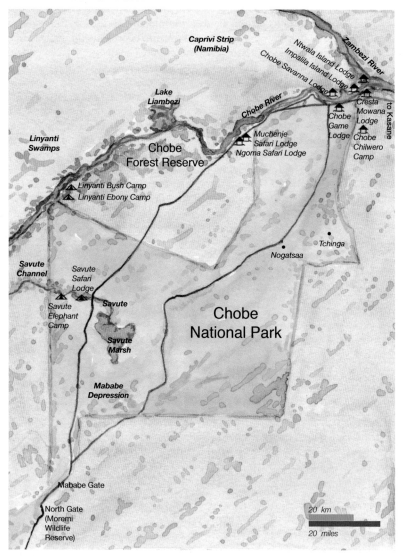

100 elephant swimming across the river at sunset. This is an excellent park for game viewing by boat!

Game viewing is actually very good during the midday at this park, as well as in the mornings and late afternoons. Animals can be seen making their way

Game viewing by boat on the Chobe River

to the river to drink and may be seen along the river's edge at close range by both boat and vehicle.

Along the River Road between the entrance gate from Kasane and Chobe Game Lodge, you are likely to see numerous hippo, red lechwe, puku, common waterbuck, warthog and guinea fowl. Driving from the lodge toward the old Serondela Campsite, you can usually see giraffe, impala, zebra and occasionally kudu and Chobe bushbuck. Large water monitor lizards are commonly seen.

The hot and dry Corridor (Ngwezumba to Nogatsaa) is one of the few areas in the country where oribi (a delicate long-necked antelope) is found. Gemsbok, eland, ostrich and steenbok are sometimes seen. Prevalent species include giraffe, elephant, and roan and sable antelope.

One of the great highlights of the Chobe River is the breeding colonies (with up to 1,000 birds per colony) of carmine bee-eaters, which are active during September and early October. These magnificent birds — dressed in pink and turquoise — provide a truly breathtaking spectacle. Other species found along the river are the rare rock pratincoles, African skimmer, white

Carmine bee-eaters in flight

fronted bee-eaters and large, mobile flocks of open-billed stork and spur-winged geese.

Four wheel drive vehicles are necessary for most of the park. Vehicles are restricted to the roads. Night drives and walks are not allowed. Some guests stay in accommodations across the Chobe River in Namibia.

ACCOMMODATION — NORTHERN CHOBE — CLASS A: • **Chobe Chilwero Camp** has 15 luxurious air-conditioned cottages with mini-bars, balcony and outdoor shower. The property has a wine cellar, business center, library, wood burning pizza oven and full-fledged spa. Located on an escarpment, the views extend all the way to Namibia's Caprivi Strip and the Chobe River. Game viewing is by vehicle and boat. • **Ngoma Safari Lodge**, located just outside the western boundary of Chobe, features 8 river facing suites with spacious interior and exterior living areas. The swimming pool, sundeck, dining and bar area have expansive views of the river. Activities include day and night game drives, walks, village visits and game viewing by boat. This area is not crowded, making it all the more attractive. • **The Zambezi Queen**, a luxury houseboat that cruises the Chobe River, features 14 suites with private balconies and upscale furnishings. Of the 14 suites, 4 are master suites, some with their own private outdoor area. Smaller boats enable guests to get up close to the game. Tiger and bream fishing are available in season. • **Ntwala Island Lodge** offers 4 suites with private plunge pools and viewing decks, outdoor baths and private salas. Access is by boat transfer from the Kasane area. Game viewing is by private boat.

Chobe Chilwero offers decadent cottages *(top)*, Zambezi Queen, a unique way to experience the Chobe River *(bottom)*

CLASS A/B: • **Muchenje Safari Lodge** is situated on an escarpment edge, located outside the western boundary (the Ngoma region) of Chobe National Park on the Chobe River. The camp consists of 11 thatched chalets, lounge/dining room, viewing deck overlooking the Chobe flood plain and swimming pool. Activities include morning and night game drives, boat trips, bush walks and cultural visits to a nearby village. This area is not crowded. • **Chobe Savanna Lodge**, located on the Namibian banks of the Chobe River, has 12 stone-and-thatch cottages with private decks, air-conditioning, mini bars and swimming pool. Activities include early morning or evening game drives, sunset cruises, fishing and guided nature walks. • **Chobe Game Lodge** is a Moorish-style lodge with 96 beds set on the banks of the Chobe River within the park. The lodge has a large swimming pool and spacious grounds. All rooms are air-conditioned and the 4 luxury suites have private plunge pools. Sundowner cruises and day game drives are offered. • **The Nguni Voyager** is a houseboat with 5 comfortable cabins, lounge, bar, jacuzzi and viewing decks. Each room has its own private tender boat and guide to enable exclusive water-based activities (no land based activities are offered).

CLASS B: • **Impalila Island Lodge**, situated on an island across from the park in Namibia, has 8 elevated chalets and a swimming pool. Access is by boat transfer from the Kasane area. Activities offered are mostly water based, including mokoro trips, boat game drives and fishing. • **Cresta Mowana Lodge** has 111 rooms and is located 5 miles (8 km) east of the park. Game drives by vehicle and boat are offered.

Kasane

Kasane is a small town adjacent to the northeastern border of Chobe National Park about an hour and a half drive from Victoria Falls (Zimbabwe) or Livingstone (Zambia). Many tourists are driven here from Victoria Falls and Livingstone to begin their Botswana safari.

ACCOMMODATION — See "Chobe National Park" above.

Nxai Pan National Park

Nxai Pan National Park, well known for its huge springbok population and healthy cheetah population, covers over 810-square-miles (2,100-km²) and is located north of the Maun-Nata road in Northern Botswana.

The Nxai Pan is a fossil lake bed about 15-square-miles (40-km²) in size; it is covered with grass during the rains. The landscape is dotted with baobab and acacia trees. Kgama-Kgama Pan is second to Nxai Pan in size.

In addition to springbok and cheetah, wildlife includes gemsbok, eland, greater kudu, southern giraffe, blue wildebeest, red hartebeest, springbok, steenbok, brown and spotted hyena, lion and other predators. During the rains, elephant and buffalo may also be seen. After the first rains have fallen, game viewing is often excellent (December through April). Bird life is excellent during the rains.

Baines' Baobabs, situated in the park not far from the Maun-Nata road, were immortalized by the famous painter Thomas Baines in 1862. His painting, titled "The Sleeping Five," is of five baobabs, one of which is growing on its side. Seldom are baobab trees found growing so closely together. Baines' Baobabs were later painted by Prince Charles.

This park is seldom visited by international travelers, and is well worth a visit from December to April. A 4wd vehicle is necessary. Night drives are not permitted.

ACCOMMODATION: CLASS A/B: • **Nxai Pan Camp**, built into a tree line, has 9 tents (including a family suite) with private viewing decks. Activities offered include game drives, guided walks with the bushmen and excursions to Baines' Baobabs.

Nxai Pan/Makgadikgadi

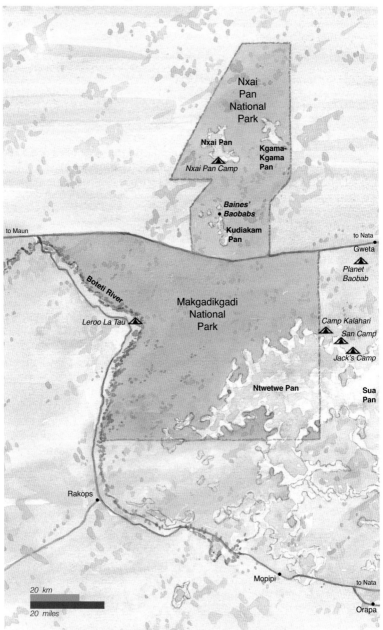

Makgadikgadi Pans National Park

Makgadikgadi Pans National Park includes a portion of the 4,600-square-mile (12,000-km²) Makgadikgadi Pans, which is the size of Portugal. The pans are nearly devoid of human habitation and give one a feeling of true isolation.

Once one of the world's largest prehistoric lakes, most of the Makgadikgadi Pans are now barren salt plains fringed with grasslands and isolated "land islands" of vegetation, baobab and palm trees. Scattered Stone Age tools have been found. Engravings left by explorers David Livingstone and Frederick Selous in the trunks of ancient baobab trees mark their passage through the region so many years ago.

The reserve itself covers about 1,550-square-miles (3,900-km²). It is located south of the Maun-Nata road in northern Botswana and borders Nxai Pan National Park to the north. Large herds of blue wildebeest, zebra, springbok, gemsbok and thousands of flamingos may be seen December to May. Other wildlife includes suricate and meerkat. This is one of the best places to see the nocturnal brown hyena.

A recent exciting change is that the **Boteti River**, which forms the western border of the park, is flowing for the first time in decades! As a result, general wildlife viewing has in fact improved year-round in parts of the reserve. In addition, rhino may now be seen on the western side of the reserve.

Quad bike excursions are offered during the dry season (usually May to November) and are a fun way to experience the vastness of these pans. On evening excursions deep into the pans, once you turn off the engines you may experience the most "deafening" silence and brightest stars imaginable.

A highlight for many visitors is spending time with a troop of habituated **meerkats** — voted by the British as the cutest animal species in the world. Guided by one of the researchers, you sit closely to them, and walk with them as they hunt for food. Don't be surprised if one climbs on you to get a better view!

Meerkats of the Makgadikgadi Pans

A 4wd vehicle is highly recommended.

ACCOMMODATION — CLASS A: • **Jack's Camp** is a classic camp (20 beds) in the '40s safari style. The pool has been built under a tent, guaranteeing a cool respite from the hot sun. Activities include day and night game drives, riding quad motorbikes on the pans (in the dry season), walks with bushmen trackers, visiting habituated troops of meerkats and lectures by resident researchers.

CLASS A/B: • **Leroo La Tau** overlooks the newly flowing Boteti River on the western border of the park, and consists of 12 thatched chalets on raised decks, bar, dining room and plunge pool . One of the main activities is watching the wildlife dramas that unfold right in front of the lodge. Activities include guided walks, day and night game drives and cultural excursions to the nearby village. • **San Camp**, a 12-bed tented camp set right on the edge of the pans, offers the same activities as Jack's Camp. The camp was completely rebuilt in 2011, with larger tents and day beds on the verandahs. The guides at both Jack's and San Camp have university degrees in zoology, biology, anthropology or similar subjects. Adventurous 5-night/6-day Kubu Island quad bike trips are also offered, which include 3 nights at San Camp and 2 nights fly camping at Kubu Island.

A magical sunset at San Camp

CLASS B: • **Camp Kalahari**, nestled among acacias and palms, features 10 canvas tents (including a family tent), a thatched library, lounge and dining area. Activities include visiting a family of meerkats and Chapmaan's Baobab, walking safaris with bushmen, quad biking and optional sleep-outs under the pans. A special horseback riding itinerary is offered with expert guide David Foot.

The Central Kalahari Game Reserve is home to black-maned lions

CLASS C: • **Planet Baobab** offers traditional painted mud huts, grass huts and campsites with shared facilities plus a pool for guests to enjoy. Cultural safaris and overnight fly camping to view fossil plates are offered. The Kalahari Surf Club offers a Pan experience — guests camp on the edge of the saltpans and take quad bike trips across the pans and escorted walks.

Central Kalahari Game Reserve

This 20,000-square-mile (52,000-km^2) reserve, one of the largest in the world, covers a portion of the Kalahari Desert. It is an area of enormity, epic landscapes, wooded dunes and petrified river valleys.

Wildlife is not abundant in the dry season, but the area becomes alive after brief rain showers and is at its peak from December through April as herbivores with their newborn young (followed by predators) gravitate into the petrified river systems. Game viewing in May and June is also quite good. This is one of the most underrated parks for visiting at this time period in Africa!

Central Kalahari Game Reserve

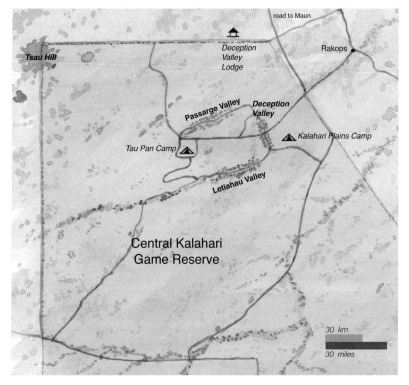

road to Maun

Deception
Valley
Lodge

Rakops

Tsau Hill

Passarge Valley

Deception
Valley

Kalahari Plains Camp

Tau Pan Camp

Letiahau Valley

Central Kalahari
Game Reserve

30 km

30 miles

Guided walk with a bushman

With arguably the best cheetah populations within Botswana, the Central Kalahari Game Reserve is also home to the black-maned lions, good populations of meerkats, brown hyena, caracal, leopard, African wild cat, Cape fox, bat-eared fox, black-backed jackals, eland, red hartebeest, eland, honey badger (which are easily sighted between April and November), steenbuck, oryx, springbuck and blue wildebeest. Even wild dogs are resident in the Kalahari, albeit at lower concentrations than the Okavango Delta and Linyanti.

Perhaps the best part of this gigantic reserve, from a visitor's perspective, is the **Deception Valley** area where American researchers Mark and Delia Owens were based during their work on the brown hyena. This drainage line is in a hauntingly remote location, populated with mostly nomadic wildlife and thin vegetation. Wildlife is attracted en masse to the Valley and surrounding pan systems — taking advantage of temporary highly nutritive grazing.

Travelers are encouraged to stay at camps within the park, as this is where the key experience is. Night drives are not permitted.

Sleep under the stars at Kalahari Plains Camp

ACCOMMODATION — CLASS A/B:
• **Kalahari Plains Camp** is located in the Okwa Valley — one of the most remote dry river systems in the park. A permanent waterhole and access to the interdunal system, including the pans provide a more annual game experience. The camp features 10 tents with unique sleep-out decks that enable guests to sleep under the stars, and a small plunge pool near the main lounge/dining area. Activities include guided walks with bushmen and game drives as well as access to the famous Deception Valley. • **Tau Pan Camp**, situated within the Central Kalahari Game Reserve, features 8 desert rooms under thatch with views of the Tau Pan waterhole. Walks with the bushmen and game drives are offered. • **Deception Valley Lodge**, located outside of the northern periphery of the reserve, has 5 large units. Walks with bushmen guides, afternoon and night drives are conducted outside the reserve.

THE SOUTH

Gaborone

Gaborone, phonetically pronounced "Hab oh roni," is the capital of Botswana. In the center of town is the main shopping and commercial center — the Mall. Other than some shopping, visiting some of the landmarks mentioned in *The No. 1 Ladies' Detective Agency* book and film series and the **National Museum**, there is little of interest for the international traveler.

ACCOMMODATION — FIRST CLASS: • **Grand Palm Hotel** has 152 air-conditioned rooms, 3 restaurants, outdoor heated pool, fitness center, lighted tennis courts and business center. • **The Gaborone Sun** is located 1.5 miles (2 km) from the city center. This 203-room, air-conditioned hotel has a swimming pool, tennis and squash courts and casino. • **The President Hotel** is an air-conditioned hotel centrally located in the Mall.

Northern Tuli Game Reserve

In the remote southeastern corner of Botswana, at the confluence of the Limpopo and Shashe Rivers, and at the junction of the borders of Botswana, South Africa and Zimbabwe, lies an area of approximately 180,000-acres (72,000-hectares).

The Tuli Enclave features a diverse topography

Game viewing at Mashatu Game Reserve

It is known historically as the Tuli enclave — a diverse wilderness of open grassland, mopane veld, riverine forest, semi-arid bush savannah, marshland, and sandstone outcrops.

A unique feature of this region is the history, both natural and culturally that dates back 80 million years. Dinosaur footprints and fossilized dinosaur skeletons compliment the cultural history of Mapungubwe and Mmamagwa, two African kingdoms that predate Great Zimbabwe and Tulamela. The formation of the Greater Mapungubwe Transfrontier Conservation area (formerly the Limpopo-Shashe TFCA) involving Botswana, South Africa and Zimbabwe with a focus on wildlife and cultural history is nearing completion and is set to be a tourism drawing card for those visitors seeking a more adventurous safari.

Because the properties within the reserve are privately owned, they are generally less restricted than the private concession areas, reserves and national parks in Botswana, and may conduct activities such as off-road driving, walking with armed rangers, night game drives, horseback riding and mountain biking. This is a great reserve for the active traveler!

The Tuli is home to large herds of elephant, as well as lion, cheetah, eland, impala, wildebeest, giraffe and zebra. Leopard, bat-eared fox, African wild cat, hyena, jackal and wild dog may be seen searching for prey.

This reserve has to be one of the best kept secrets in Africa for game viewing — a real "sleeper." This is one of the best game viewing spots on the continent!

The region is a 5.5-hour drive from Johannesburg and a 6-hour drive from Gaborone. Alternatively, a scheduled flight and air or road transfer can be arranged into the Limpopo Valley Airfield, which is situated within the Nothern Tuli Game Reserve. You may also take a scheduled flight from Johannesburg to Polokwane and then take a 2-hour road transfer to the reserve.

Mashatu Main Camp's upscale suite

ACCOMMODATION — CLASS A:
• **Mashatu Main Camp**, located on the Mashatu Game Reserve, the largest

and most diverse of the properties in the reserve with 70,000 acres (28,000 hectares) of privately owned land. Up to a maximum of 28 guests are comfortably accommodated in 14 air-conditioned suites featuring "his" and "her" bathrooms. The property has a floodlit waterhole and a swimming pool. Game viewing is conducted in open 4wd vehicles, on mountain bikes, on foot and on horseback. Fly camping is also offered.

CLASS A/B: • **Mashatu Tented Camp,** set in a remote northern area of the Mashatu Game Reserve, accommodates up to 16 guests in eight fan-cooled tents and there is a plunge pool. Guests explore the reserve in 4wd vehicles, on foot, with mountain bikes and on horseback. • **Tuli Safari Lodge**, situated on the banks of the Limpopo River, has 10 thatched chalets and a swimming pool.

The charm of Mashatu Tented Camp

Mabuasehube Game Reserve

Mabuasehube is an extremely remote reserve in southwestern Botswana. Mabuasehube is about 695-square-miles (1,800-km²) in size and shares its western border with Kgalagadi Transfrontier Park. The park has 6 large pans and sand dunes over 100 feet (30 m) high.

The best time to visit is during and just after the rainy season begins (December to April), when a variety of arid-adapted animals can be seen. Springbok are present in good numbers, while gemsbok, eland and red harte-beest are sparse, but are likely to be seen. This is an excellent locality for the elusive brown hyena, and impressive black-maned Kalahari lions are invariably present. Other interesting mammals seen here are the Cape fox, honey badger, aardwolf and aardvark.

Among the many interesting birds here are the secretary bird, kori bustard, black-breasted snake eagle, crimson-breasted shrike and the swallow-tailed bee-eater. The huge communal nests of the sociable weaver are a feature of this pristine landscape. At sunset the sandveld comes alive to the clicking sound of barking geckos, calling from their burrow entrances.

Mabuasehube is 333 miles (533 km) from Gaborone. A 4wd vehicle is needed, and the drive takes at least 11 hours. Quickest access is by private charter flight to Hukuntsi.

ACCOMMODATION: None.

Kgalagadi Transfronteir Park

See "Kgalagadi Transfrontier Park" in the chapter on South Africa for details.

Zimbabwe

Zimbabwe

Zimbabwe is a scenic land consisting of a central plateau that drops down to the Zambezi and Limpopo River valleys in the north and south respectively. The average altitude is about 3,300 feet (1,000 m) on the plateau, rising to 8,000 feet (2,440 m) in the Eastern Highlands. The plateau is dominated by brachystegia *(miombo)* woodland, with acacia and mopane savanna in the larger valleys. A mosaic of grassland and forest occurs in the Eastern Highlands. With an area of 150,872-square-miles (390,759-km²), Zimbabwe is about the size of California (or Great Britain). The population is estimated at 11.5 million, with the capital of Harare having some 2 million inhabitants. Shona, Ndebele and English are the main languages. Multi-currency system dominated by the US dollar.

Zimbabwe
Country Highlights

- This is the best country in Africa for walking and canoe safaris — providing the opportunity to really be "in the adventure" lead by professional guides ranked as the best on the continent.
- Experience some of Africa's best game viewing by vehicle as well, with opportunities to see prized species such as African wild (painted) dogs in Mana Pools, both black and white rhino in Malilangwe, along with huge herds of elephant in Hwange.
- Sit in one of the numerous hides to see wildlife from a totally different perspective.
- Visit Victoria Falls, not only to see the Falls, but to take an elephant back safari or try a day of white water rafting down the Zambezi River's up to Class 5 rapids — a wild ride!
- Experience landscapes of incredible natural beauty and amazing rock paintings in the Matobo Hills.
- Marvel at the immense and ancient ruins of Great Zimbabwe, the largest stone-built structures in Africa south of the Pyramids.

When's the Best Time to Go for Game Viewing

■ Excellent ■ Good ☐ Fair ■ Poor ■ Closed

Country	Park/Reserve	JAN	FEB	MAR	APR	MAY	JUN	JUL	AUG	SEP	OCT	NOV	DEC
Zimbabwe	Hwange (Main Camp & Sinamatella)												
	Hwange (Makalolo/Somalisa)												
	Matusadona												
	Mana Pools												
	Matobo Hills												
	Malilangwe												

Best Safari Experience

Vundu and mobile camping (Mana Pools), Pamushana (Malilangwe), Little Makalolo, Somalisa and Somalisa Acacia, Hwange Camp and Davison's (Hwange), Amalinda (Matobo Hills), and Elephant Camp (Victoria Falls)

ZIMBABWE

Thought by some to be the land of King Solomon's mines, Zimbabwe (previously called Southern Rhodesia) is a country blessed with beautiful and varied landscapes, and excellent game parks.

Most of Zimbabwe consists of a central plateau, 3,000 to 4,000 feet (915 to 1,220 m) above sea level. The highveld, or high plateau, stretches from southwest to northeast from 4,000 to 5,000 feet (1,220 to 1,525 m) with a mountainous region along the eastern border from 6,000 to 8,000 feet (1,830 to 2,440 m) in altitude.

The northern border is formed by the mighty Zambezi River, while the Limpopo River creates the division between Zimbabwe and South Africa in the south. The spectacular Victoria Falls were created by a fracture in the Zambezi Valley, which is an extension of the Great Rift Valley.

Zimbabwe is a land-locked country, but it is rich in biological diversity due to its proximity to the temperate south, tropical north and semi-arid west. Much

Using a tree limb to its fullest advantage, a leopard gazes
out across the plains in search of prey and predators

Mana Pools is one of the best places in Africa to see wild dog

of the country is a highland plateau at about 3,300 feet (1,000 m) above sea level on one of the world's oldest granite formations. In the north and south, the Zambezi and Limpopo River valleys, respectively, create hot lowlands as well as international boundaries. The granite shield forms the main watershed of the country, with numerous spectacular rock formations. This plateau is dominated by miombo woodland, but is also ideal farming country, so much of the natural vegetation has been replaced.

The so-called Eastern Highlands are a chain of sandstone and basalt mountains, characterized by a cooler, wetter climate. The highest peaks rise above 6,500 feet (2,000 m). Temperate forests occur in patches from Nyanga to Chimanimani, and sub-tropical forests are found in the humid lowlands of the Honde, Burma and Rusitu valleys, which enter Mozambique. In the western part of the country, on the border with Botswana, deep Kalahari sands dominate in places and create yet another unique environment for wildlife.

The climate is moderate on the central plateau, but hot in the low-lying Zambezi and Limpopo valleys in the summer. Seasons are reversed from the northern hemisphere. Winter days (May to August) are generally dry and sunny with day temperatures in Harare averaging 59 to 68°F (15 to 20°C). Summer daytime temperatures average 77 to 86°F (25 to 30°C), and October is the hottest month. The rainy season is December through March.

The major ethnic groups are the Mashona and AmaNdebele. About 50% of the population is syncretic (part Christian and part traditional beliefs), 25% Christian, 24% traditional and 1% Hindu and Muslim. Twenty-five percent of the population lives in urban areas, with half of that 25% residing in the cities of Harare and nearby Chitungwiza. English is understood by a majority of the population.

In the first century, the region was inhabited by hunters related to the San Bushmen. Cecil Rhodes and the British South Africa Company took control in 1890, and the area was named Southern Rhodesia, which became a British colony in 1923. Prime Minister Ian Smith and the white minority declared unilateral independence from Britain on November 11, 1965. After a decade long civil war, Zimbabwe officially became independent on April 18, 1980, with Robert Mugabe as president.

Main foreign exchange earners are minerals, tobacco, agriculture and tourism.

Zimbabwe has had more than its share of political and economic woes during the last decade. However, with the formation of the inclusive government and adoption of a multiple currency regime, the situation has greatly improved. The economy has stabilized, tourism has seen a large increase, and foreign investment is beginning to return. Most importantly, many tourists who have traveled there have been handsomely rewarded with excellent wildlife viewing and guiding in uncrowded parks. The fact that Zimbabwe and Zambia have been chosen to host the UN World Tourism Organization (UNWTO) General Assembly in 2013 is a testament in itself to the positive changes that have occurred.

By visiting the parks, tourists are supporting camps and lodges that in turn provide fuel and transportation for National Park anti-poaching units. Park fees paid by tourists go directly to the national parks to help fund them. In addition, tourists are providing jobs for Africans working in the camps, many of whom are supporting an average of over 8 family members living in villages. If there is one wildlife country in Africa where the people and the wildlife populations stand to benefit more from tourism — Zimbabwe is it!

My wife and I and our two children recently spent almost a month in Zimbabwe visiting all the top reserves and attractions, and must admit that it was the best family trip we have ever had. Many of the safari camps and lodges were full. When it comes to tourism, Zimbabwe is "back." Go now — while a safari there is still a great value and a fabulous experience!

🐾 WILDLIFE AND WILDLIFE AREAS

Adventurers wishing to do more than view wildlife from a vehicle should seriously consider a safari in Zimbabwe. It offers the greatest variety of methods of wildlife viewing in Africa, including day and night game drives in open vehicles, game viewing by motorboat, walking, canoeing, kayaking, rafting and travel by houseboat. This is in fact the best country in Africa for walking safaris and canoe safaris — and also one of the best for game viewing by vehicle.

Canoeing down the Zambezi River provides unique moments with wildlife

As mentioned earlier, the country is situated at the junction of three major climatic zones (temperate south, tropical northeast and semi-arid west), and there is a resultant diversity of wildlife. All of Africa's big-game species are here, as well as over 660 bird species and an amazing variety of reptiles, frogs and invertebrates. Plant life is equally impressive, from Afro-alpine proteas in the east to tropical baobabs in the hot valleys of the north and south. The distinctive miombo woodlands (dominated by *brachystegia* trees) are characterized by a unique variety of plants and associated wildlife.

Zimbabwe offers excellent and well-maintained parks and reserves. The country's three premier reserves, which also rate among the best in Africa, are Hwange and Mana Pools National Parks and Malilangwe Wildlife Reserve.

Hwange National Park is famous for its huge elephant population (about 28,000) and numerous large pans. During the dry season, Mana Pools on the Zambezi River has one of the highest concentrations of wildlife of any park on the continent, and is the best park in Africa for walking and canoe safaris, and for seeing African wild dog. Scenic Malilangwe Wildlife Reserve is teeming with wildlife, including rare and endangered species such as the roan and sable antelope, black and white rhino.

Many of the safari camps cater to only 8 to 20 guests and offer personalized service, comfortable accommodations and superb guiding. The professional guiding standards in Zimbabwe are, in fact, the highest of any country on the continent.

Instead of driving to the reserves, virtually all international visitors fly to the parks, taking advantage of scheduled charter flights. There are also private and group mobile tented safaris available in Hwange and Mana Pools.

Game viewing is by open vehicle, and walking is allowed with a licensed Professional Guide who carries a high-caliber rifle at all times for their client's protection. Night game drives are conducted in most of the reserves.

THE WEST

Victoria Falls National Park

Dr. David Livingstone became the first European man to see Victoria Falls on November 16, 1855, and named them after the British queen of his day. In his journal he wrote, "Scenes so lovely must have been gazed upon by angels in flight."

Victoria Falls is approximately 5,600 feet (1,700 m) wide, twice the height of Niagara Falls, and one and one-half times as wide. It is divided into five separate waterfalls: Devil's Cataract, Main Falls, Horseshoe Falls, Rainbow Falls and Eastern Cataract, ranging in height from 200 to 355 feet (61 to 108 m).

Peak floodwaters usually occur around mid-April when 150 million gallons (625 million liters) per minute crash onto the rocks below, spraying water up to 1,650 feet (500 m) in the air. During March and April, so much water is falling that the spray makes it difficult to see the falls. May to February is actually a better time to see them, but keep in mind that they are spectacular any time of the year.

Victoria Falls and the Zambezi River form the border between Zambia and Zimbabwe. The banks of the 1,675-mile- (2,700-km) long Zambezi River, the fourth largest river in Africa and the only major river in Africa to flow into the Indian Ocean, are lined with thick riverine forest.

A rainbow over the falls can often be seen during the day and a lunar rainbow within a 2- to 4-night period over a full moon.

Fortunately, the area around the falls has not been commercialized on the Zimbabwe side, and there are unobstructed views from many vantage points, which are connected by paved paths. An entry fee (currently US$30.00) is required. Be prepared to get wet as you walk through a luxuriant rain forest surrounding the falls, a result of the continuous spray. A path called the Chain Walk descends from near Livingstone's statue into the gorge of the Devil's Cataract, which provides an excellent vantage point.

Victoria Falls can also be viewed from Zambia. Zambian visas for day visits are generally available at the border for most nationalities (the border

Victoria Falls-Livingstone

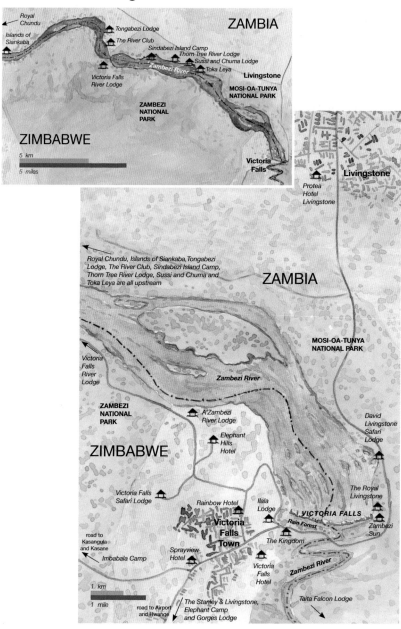

ZAMBIA

Royal Chundu

Islands of Siankaba

Tongabezi Lodge

The River Club

Sindabezi Island Camp

Thorn Tree River Lodge

Sussi and Chuma Lodge

Zambezi River

Toka Leya

Victoria Falls River Lodge

Livingstone

MOSI-OA-TUNYA NATIONAL PARK

ZAMBEZI NATIONAL PARK

ZIMBABWE

5 km

5 miles

Victoria Falls

Livingstone

Protea Hotel Livingstone

Royal Chundu, Islands of Siankaba, Tongabezi Lodge, The River Club, Sindabezi Island Camp, Thorn Tree River Lodge, Sussi and Chuma and Toka Leya are all upstream

ZAMBIA

MOSI-OA-TUNYA NATIONAL PARK

Victoria Falls River Lodge

Zambezi River

ZAMBEZI NATIONAL PARK

A'Zambezi River Lodge

Elephant Hills Hotel

David Livingstone Safari Lodge

ZIMBABWE

Victoria Falls Safari Lodge

Rainbow Hotel

Ilala Lodge

The Royal Livingstone

VICTORIA FALLS

Rain Forest

Zambezi Sun

Victoria Falls Town

road to Kasangula and Kasane

Imbabala Camp

Sprayview Hotel

The Kingdom

Victoria Falls Hotel

Zambezi River

1 km

1 mile

road to Airport and Hwange

The Stanley & Livingstone, Elephant Camp and Gorges Lodge

Taita Falcon Lodge

150 million gallons of water per minute crash over Victoria Falls during peak floodwaters in mid-April

crossing can take up to a few hours so please allow plenty of time). Generally speaking, the falls are more impressive on the Zimbabwean side— especially July to December.

Mammals that can be seen in close proximity to the falls include the beautifully marked bushbuck, vervet monkey and banded mongoose. Birds to look out for include the noisy trumpeter hornbill, green pigeon and Schalow's turaco, which feed on figs, and the rock pratincole, reed cormorant and giant kingfisher that may be found in the rapids above the falls. One of Africa's rarest birds of prey, the diminutive Taita falcon, is frequently seen on the cliffs below the falls, alongside peregrine falcon, augur buzzard and Verreaux's (black) eagle.

The **Zambezi Nature Sanctuary** has crocodiles up to 14 feet (4.3 m) in length and weighing close to 1,000 pounds (450 kg). Tribal dancing may also be seen at the Boma Restaurant near the Victoria Falls Safari Lodge, and at the "Jungle Juction" at the Victoria Falls Hotel. **Big Tree** is a giant baobab over 50 feet (15 m) in circumference, 65 feet (20 m) high and 1,000 to 1,500 years old.

Sundowner cruises operate above the falls, where hippo may be spotted and elephant and other wildlife may be seen coming to the shore to drink.

The "**Flight of Angels**," a flight over the falls by helicopter (best choice) or in a small plane, is highly recommended to acquire a feeling for the true majesty of the falls. Game-viewing flights, upstream from the falls along the Zambezi

River and over Victoria Falls National Park, are also available. It is best to reserve seats in advance. **Zambezi Spectacular** flights upstream from the falls along the Zambezi River and over gorge, are also available.

One of the world's highest commercially run **bungee jumps** (over 300 feet [100 m]) is operated on the bridge crossing the Zambezi River. Even more exciting is the **Gorge Swing**— a 200 foot (70 m) free-fall, ending in a swing across the Zambezi Gorge.

Canoeing and **kayaking** safaris are a great way to explore the upper Zambezi, from near Kazungula to just above Victoria Falls. Adventurers pass numerous hippo, crocs, elephant and other wildlife as they paddle two-man kayaks or canoes on safaris ranging from a half-day to four days in length. No previous kayaking or canoeing experience is necessary. Accommodation is in tents with separate bush shower and toilet facilities.

Half- and full-day **horseback rides** around the Victoria Falls area are available for novice and experienced riders, while multi-day horseback safaris are available only for experienced riders. Morning and afternoon **elephant back safaris** (African elephants) provide another interesting way to experience the

The gorge swing gives a thrilling 200 foot free-fall and swing across the Zambezi Gorge

Class 5 white water rapids guarantee the ride of a lifetime

bush — allowing an "up close and personal" interaction with these intelligent pacheoderms.

The upper Zambezi River offers one of the most exciting and challenging **white-water rafting** trips in the world. There are numerous fifth-class rapids, which are the highest class runable, and these can be experienced either with a professional oarsman at the helm or in a raft with everyone paddling. No experience is required; just hang on and enjoy the ride! The 1-day trip is rated as the wildest commercially run 1-day trip in the world. For some travelers, this is a highlight of their safari.

Around 8:30 a.m., rafters walk down into the gorge to the river's edge where the rafting safari begins. Rafts with up to 8 paddlers, or up to 8 riders and 1 oarsperson, disappear from sight as they drop into deep holes and crash into waves over 12 feet (3.5 m) high, and they are further dwarfed by sheer cliffs that often rise hundreds of feet on both sides of the canyon.

Each group is usually accompanied by a professional kayaker who helps "rescue" those who have fallen out of the rafts. At the end of the trip, rafters have to climb back out of the gorge to the top of the escarpment, about 700 feet (213 m) above. For most people, this is the most difficult part of the excursion. Two to six day trips are also offered. The trips are operated from approximately July to January, depending on water levels.

For the even more adventurous, there is **boogie boarding** on the rapids. This is often done in conjunction with a half or full day of white-water rafting.

ACCOMMODATION — DELUXE: • **Victoria Falls Hotel** has been refurbished and maintains much of its colonial elegance, including its graceful architecture, spacious terraces and colorful gardens, and it is only a 10-minute walk from Victoria Falls. The hotel has 161 air-conditioned rooms and suites, swimming pool and tennis courts. From the hotel you can see the bridge and the Zambezi Gorge. • **Victoria Falls Safari Lodge**, located a 5-minute drive from the falls, has 72 decorated air-conditioned rooms and suites. The lodge is built under thatch and overlooks a flood-lit waterhole where wildlife may be seen coming to drink. The open-air restaurant, bar and swimming pool all have views of the park. Optional excursions including nature trails, bird and game hides, and game walks with

The historic Victoria Falls Hotel

a professional guide are offered. A complimentary hourly shuttle service is available to Victoria Falls town and to the entrance to the falls.

FIRST CLASS: • **Ilala Lodge**, a 34-room thatched lodge with a swimming pool, is located within walking distance to the falls. • **Elephant Hills Hotel** is a large hotel located about 15 minutes out of town. It has a golf course and swimming pool.

TOURIST CLASS: • **The A-Zambezi River Lodge**, was refurbished in 2011 and features one of the largest buildings under traditional thatch on the continent. The lodge is located 1.5 miles (2.5 km) from town on the banks of the Zambezi River and has 83 air-conditioned rooms and swimming pool. Complimentary scheduled transfers to the town and the falls are offered. • **The Kingdom** is only a 10-minute walk from the falls and has 294 air-conditioned rooms that are separated in 2- and 3-story units, a casino, food court and swimming pool. This is a good hotel for families. • **Sprayview Hotel** is a budget hotel with rooms located a little more than a mile (2 km) from the falls. • **Rainbow Hotel** is located near Victoria Falls village and has 88 air-conditioned rooms and a swimming pool.

ACCOMMODATION NEAR VICTORIA FALLS — CLASS A: • **Elephant Camp**, located on a private concession bordering the Masuie River and Zambezi gorges, features 12 luxury tented suites each with private deck and plunge pool. Two complimentary transfers to town are included in your stay. Guests have an opportunity to meet the elephants at the onsite sanctuary.

CLASS A/B: • **The Stanley & Livingstone**, situated on a 6,075-acre (2,430-hectare) private estate a 10-minute drive from the falls, has 16 luxury suites. A raised patio overlooks nearby waterholes. • **Gorges Lodge**, located 15 miles (24 km) from Victoria Falls, overlooks the Zambezi Gorge and has 6 single and 4 double-story rooms and a swimming pool. • **Imbabala Camp**, located on private land on the banks

A suite at Elephant Camp

of the Zambezi River only a mile (2 km) from the Botswana border, has 8 individual chalets (1 family chalet sleeps 4 people) and a swimming pool. Day and night game drives by vehicle, boat game viewing excursions, birding walks and fishing are offered. Walking safaris are available with prior arrangements.

Zambezi National Park

Victoria Falls National Park includes Victoria Falls as well as the 216-square-mile (560-km²) Zambezi National Park. The park is located west of the falls and extends for 25 miles (40 km) along the Zambezi River upstream from the falls.

Zambezi National Park is well known for its sable antelope, among other species, such as elephant, zebra, eland, buffalo, giraffe, lion, kudu and waterbuck. Noteworthy birds include collared palm thrush, white-breasted cuckooshrike, racquet-tailed roller, African finfoot, Schalow's turaco, Pel's fishing owl and rock pratincole.

Day game drives, walks, canoeing and kayaking are offered from Victoria Falls. Fishing for tigerfish and tilapia is good. There are 30 sites along the river for picnicking and fishing (beware of crocodiles). Since the game reserve does not have all-weather roads, parts of it are usually closed during the rains from November 1 to May 1.

ACCOMMODATION — CLASS A: • **Victoria Falls River Lodge** is located in Zambezi National Park on the banks of the Zambezi River. The camp features 12 tents with private decks overlooking river, a swimming pool, bar and boma.

Hwange National Park

Hwange (previously called Wankie), Zimbabwe's largest national park, is famous for its large herds of elephant and buffalo. Other wildlife commonly seen includes giraffe, zebra, greater kudu, impala, wildebeest, tsessebe, black-backed jackal, lion and hyena. Leopard, African wildcat, bat-eared fox, serval, honey badger and civet, sable antelope, roan antelope and gemsbok may also be seen. Rhino is occasionally encountered — more often on walks than on game drives.

Hwange is slightly larger than the state of Connecticut, covering 5,656-square-miles (14,651-km²). The park is located in the northwest corner of the country, just west of the main road between Bulawayo and Victoria Falls. Hwange boasts over 100 species of mammals and 400 species of birds.

The park ranges from semi-desert in the south to a plateau in the north. The northern part of Hwange is mudstone and basalt, and the southern part is Kalahari sand veld. The park has an average altitude of 3,300 feet (1,000 m). Winter nights can drop to below freezing, and summer days can be over 100°F (38°C), while average temperatures range from 65° to 83°F (18° to 28°C).

There are no rivers and only a few streams in the east of the park, but water-holes (fed by wells) and springs provide sources of water year-round for wildlife. During the dry season, these permanent waterholes (pans) provide a spectacular stage for guests to view wildlife performing day-to-day scenes of survival.

Hwange National Park

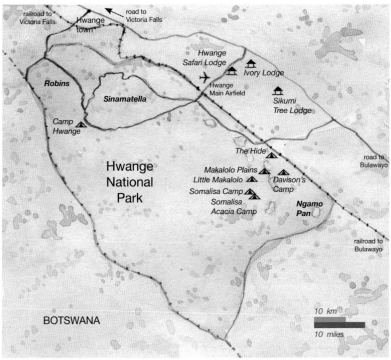

Generally, there are no seasonal animal migrations. The best time to see the highest concentrations of wildlife is during the dry season, from June to October, when the game concentrates around the waterholes. Game viewing is very good in May, November and December, and good January through April. During the "Green Season" from January to March, game is dispersed in the teak woodland in the east and the mopane woodland in the north. However, the Makalolo and Somalisa private concession areas within the park have good populations of wildlife year-round.

An estimated population of 28,000 elephants lives in Hwange, although these animals move freely to the north and west into Botswana. Birdwatching is excellent, and numerous Kalahari-sand specialists are present in good numbers. Kori bustard, Bradfield's hornbill, crimson-breasted bushshrike, swallow-tailed bee-eater and scaly-feathered finch are all abundant. Hwange is an important refuge for birds of prey, with bateleur, martial eagle and white-headed vulture among the species that enjoy sanctuary here. Endangered palm-nut vultures are occasionally seen.

The **wilderness area** of Hwange in the southeastern part of the park includes the **Makalolo** and **Somalisa concession areas**, and is ecologically

Author Mark Nolting with his family observe elephants during a walking safari in Hwange

diverse, including vast, open palm-fringed plains, acacia woodlands, flood-plains and teak forests. The vleis in this region are Zimbabwe's "Serengeti plains" — only with large herds of elephant and buffalo instead of big herds of wildebeest and zebra. In the rainy season these vleis become Zimbabwe's "Namaqualand" with endless fields of flowers. As the grass stays relatively short during the rainy season (December to March), the game remains easy to spot in these wide-open areas.

Lion are frequently seen in Hwange

A real plus is that only guests staying at camps in these private concession areas are allowed in the region — guaranteeing exclusivity with very few tourists. Safari camps in these concession areas include Makalolo, Little Makalolo, Davison's, Somalisa and Somalisa Acacia.

The wilderness area has the highest concentration of big game in the park — primarily because waterholes are pumped year-round. For instance, a recent 24-hour game count at the waterholes in the Makalolo concession yielded 5,519 elephant and 1,271 buffalo! The combination of great game and exclusivity make this the best region in Hwange for an overall wildlife experience.

The last time we visited, we sat in a hide and watched several elephant herds each numbering over 100 members come to the waterhole and drink and frolic. One baby elephant had a wonderful time running across the waterhole at full speed until it fell, making a big splash, and then it just got up and did it again and again. This was "bush TV" at its finest!

The **Main Camp** area is the only part of the park that may be crowded at times, as guests of a number of camps, campsites and lodges situated outside of the reserve use this as an entrance. Nearby is the Painted Dog Conservation Center — a very impressive complex where wild dogs that have been snared or otherwise injured are nursed back to health and released back into the wild if the researchers feel they have a good chance of surviving. Several hundred school children visit the centre every year. The organization funds unarmed anti-poaching units that remove snares from inside as well as on the fringes of the park.

The **Sinamatella** area differs from the southern areas as it is not on Kalahari sands but is a very hilly area with granite kopjes (outcrops), deep valleys, some

Summer rains bring lush vegetation and plentiful water

open grasslands, a number of natural springs and seasonal rivers. The predominant woodland is mopane with scattered open grassland.

During the dry season, elephants may be seen digging in the seasonal river beds for the water to percolate up through the sand so they can quench their thirst. This then becomes a source of water for all sizes of animals. To walk along these rivers with a professional guide and sit with these giants while they drink is a magnificent experience! This area is also an Intensive Protection Zone (IPZ) for the protection of endangered rhino that may be tracked on foot.

The elephant population in this area is very large and visitors may see huge herds at the waterholes. The lion populations are some of the largest and most stable in the park. Sable antelope, roan antelope, giraffe, impala, hippo, klipspringer, warthog, hyena and leopard may also be seen in the area.

The Sinametalla region has three main year-round water sources — Masuma Dam, Shumba and Manduvu Dam (the largest body of water in the park) — each with a thatched picnic area and hides. The natural springs in the area can only be accessed by foot, making walking in this area special, as you may start off going to investigate a spring and may end up following up a pride of lions or a herd of buffalo.

During our last visit we were driven to a spot overlooking a dry riverbed where we sat unnoticed as elephants drank from waterholes they had dug in the sand. On a morning drive we found fresh black rhino spoor and tracked it about 6 miles (10 km) but lost the tracks after it left a mud wallow, due to so many elephant spoor covering the tracks. Although we did not find the rhino this time, the tracking was very exciting as we encountered elephant, buffalo and other wildlife during the hike. Later we walked up to a kill and found six hyena on it. As we approached the hyena scattered and then the vultures moved in.

The **Bumbusi Ruins**, ancient stone buildings that were home to a king, are located 15 miles (24 km) northwest of Sinamatella Camp. The **Robins area** is very hilly with many little river courses, and is also a great walking area.

Open-vehicle game drive in Hwange

Hwange has approximately 300 miles (480 km) of roads, some of which are closed during the rainy season. All-weather roads run through most of the park. Some roads near the main camp are tarmac, which detracts a bit from the feeling of being in the bush.

Vehicles must keep to the roads (except in the private concession areas where limited off-road driving is allowed), and visitors are not allowed to leave their vehicles unless escorted by a licensed Professional

Guide, or in designated areas, such as hides, game-viewing platforms or at fenced-in picnic sites. Open vehicles are allowed only for licensed tour operators.

Airstrips for small aircraft are available at Makalolo, Somalisa and at Main Camp; large and small aircraft may land at Hwange Airport.

Mobile tented camp safaris to the Sinamatella and Robin's areas (the best location in the park for mobile tented camping) are available.

ACCOMMODATIONS — Makalolo Plains, Little Makalolo, Davison's Camp, Somalisa and Somalisa Acacia are located in exclusive areas within the park. Only guests of those camps are allowed in their respective regions. The Hide is located on the park border; guests enter the park through the Kennedy Pan entrance. Sikumi Tree Lodge and Hwange Safari Lodge are all located in 60,000-acre (24,000-hectare) Dete Vlei (private reserve), and Ivory Lodge is situated on a 6,000-acre (2,400-hectare) conservancy bordering Hwange National Park, a 30- to 60-minute drive from the Main Gate.

CLASS A: • **Little Makalolo** features 6 luxury tents, a plunge pool and "wood pile" hide overlooking the waterhole in front of camp. Day and night game drives and escorted walks, and visits to Ziga, Mpendo and other local schools are offered. Guests may participate in 24 hour wildlife counts that occur on platforms overlooking waterholes during a full moon. • **Somalisa Acacia Camp** has 4 luxury tents including a family tent, splash pool and dining room overlooking a waterhole. Activities include day and night game drives and guided walks.

CLASS A/B: • **Camp Hwange** is a new camp located on an exclusive private concession in the north of the park near Shumba — one of the largest open grassland areas in this region. The camp overlooks a waterhole and features 8 large tents under thatch with flush toilets and safari showers. Activities include day and night drives, guided walks and sitting in log hides. It is only a 3 hour drive from Victoria Falls. **Kazuma Trails** offers mobile tented safaris using large tents with flush toilets and safari showers. • **Somalisa Camp** is an authentic bush camp comprised of 6 comfortably furnished tents complete with flush toilets and safari showers under the stars. The main area and pool overlook a waterhole. Activities include guided walks, day and night game drives and game viewing from hides. • **Davison's Camp** features 9 tents with private verandahs and views over the vlei. The dining tent, bush bar and pool overlook an active waterhole. Day and night game drives, escorted walks, and visits to local schools are offered. • **Makalolo Plains** has 9 tents including a family tent, set on raised wooden platforms. Raised walkways connect the sleeping tents with the lounge/dining room area and plunge pool. There is a raised viewing deck and underground hide overlooking the waterhole • **The Hide** has 10 tents under thatch that overlook a waterhole. Activities include day and night game drives and walks. Two guests may overnight in the romantic Dove's Nest tree house. • **Ivory Lodge** is built on a 6,000-acre (2,400-hectare) conservancy boarding Hwange National Park. The 9 elevated tents are built in the tree tops of a teak forest with views of the floodlit waterhole. Activities offered are game drives on the concession and on the Dete Vlei, walking safaris, time in hides, and visits to local schools and villages. As it is used by the **Mother Africa Trust** (see page 160), guests can participate in wildlife research on voluntourism visits.

CLASS B/C: • **Hwange Safari Lodge** has 100 double rooms, a swimming pool, conference center and elevated game-viewing platform with a bar overlooking a waterhole.

CLASS C: • **Sikumi Tree Lodge** has 11 thatched tree houses and a swimming pool.

Little Makalolo provides luxury in a remote setting *(top, left)*, **Kazuma Trails** perfects mobile camping *(top, right)*, **Davison's Camp** offers comfortable canvas tents *(middle, left)*, **Somalisa's** open-air lounge and dining room *(middle, right)*, **Ivory Lodge** overlooks a waterhole *(bottom, left)*, The hide in front of **Camp Hwange** *(bottom, right)*

THE NORTH

Kariba (Town)

Kariba town is located on the eastern shore of Lake Kariba between Matusadona and Mana Pools National Parks. Some people fly to Lusaka (Zambia) and are then transferred by aircraft, boat or vehicle to one of the parks. Kariba Dam, one of the largest in Africa, is a short distance from town. Water sports (beware of crocodile and hippo) and cruises on the lake are available.

ACCOMMODATION — TOURIST CLASS: • **Caribbea Bay Resort**, located on the shores of Lake Kariba, is a Sardinian-style resort with 83 air-conditioned rooms. There are 2 swimming pools, a popular poolside bar, several restaurants and a casino.

Lake Kariba

Sunsets over the waters of island-dotted Lake Kariba are rated among the most spectacular in the world. One of the largest man-made lakes on earth, covering over 1,970-square-miles (5,100-km²), Kariba was formed in 1958 by damming the Zambezi River. The lake is 175 miles (280 km) long and up to 20 miles (32 km) in width and is surrounded, for the most part, by untouched wilderness.

When the dam was completed and the waters in the valley began to rise, animals were forced to higher ground, which temporarily became islands that were soon to be submerged under the new lake. To save these helpless animals, Operation Noah was organized by Rupert Fothergill. Over 5,000 animals, including 35 different mammal species, numerous elephant and 44 black rhino, were rescued and released in what are now Matusadona National Park and the Chete Safari Area.

Lights from commercial kapenta fishing boats are often seen on the lake at night. Fishing is excellent for tigerfish, giant vundu, bream, chessa and nkupi. October is the optimum month for tigerfishing (although very hot), and November to April for bream. Bird life, especially waterfowl, is prolific and superb viewing of African fish eagles is guaranteed. Cormorants and kingfishers are in abundance.

Matusadona National Park

Situated on the southern shore of Lake Kariba and bounded on the east by the dramatic Sanyati Gorge and the west by the Umi River, this scenic 543 square-mile (1,407-km²) park has elephant, lion, kudu, impala and buffalo. Other game includes sable antelope, roan antelope and waterbuck. Tracking black rhino on foot is popular. Part of Matusadona is, in fact, an IPZ (Intensive Protection Zone) for rhino. Leopard, cheetah and wild dog are occasionally spotted.

Matusadona National Park

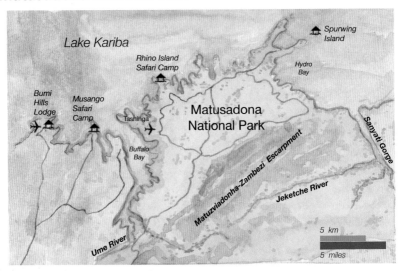

Wildlife viewing is best along the shoreline in the dry season (May to October) when the level of the lake is low. When the lake level is high, much of the foreshore is covered in water, making game viewing more difficult.

Game viewing by boat is a real attraction, and walking safaris are popular. This is a great park for **boating/walking excursions**: boat along the shoreline until you see something exciting, then go ashore and walk with your Professional Guide for a closer look!

Fishing is excellent, but beware of crocodiles. Private mobile tented safaris with Professional Guides are another great way to experience the bush. Motor yachts complete with captain, staff and Professional Guide provide private parties with great freedom and comfort in exploring the region.

ACCOMMODATION — CLASS A/B: • **Bumi Hills Lodge,** located on the western outskirts of the park on a hill overlooking the lake, has 20 well-appointed rooms with terraces or balconies, an infinity swimming pool and spa. Walks, game viewing by vehicle and by boat, fishing and village visits are offered.

ACCOMMODATION — CLASS B: • **Musango** has 8 tents under thatch including 2 honeymoon tents with private plunge pools and a swimming pool. Walks, vehicle and boat game drives, canoeing, fishing, birding, visits to dinosaur fossil sites, villages and the rhino orphanage are offered.

CLASS C: • **Rhino Island Safari Camp,** situated near Elephant Point, has 6 chalets and are set on wooden platforms with thatched roofs. Activities include game viewing drives, walks, and boat cruises along the Matusadona shoreline. • **Spurwing Island** is a 40-bed camp with tents, cabins and thatched chalets and a swimming pool. Walks, game drives by vehicle and by boat, and fishing are offered.

Tracking black rhino on foot is a highlight for visitors to Matusadona National Park

Mana Pools National Park

During the dry season, Mana Pools National Park has one of the highest concentrations of wildlife on the continent. This is in fact the best park in Africa for walking and canoe safaris. The park is situated on the southern side of the Lower Zambezi River downstream (northeast) of Lake Kariba and Victoria Falls.

This 845-square-mile (2,190-km²) park is uniquely characterized by fertile river terraces reaching inland for several miles from the Zambezi River. Small ponds and pools, such as Chine Pools and Long Pool, were formed as the river's course slowly drifted northward. Reeds, sandbanks and huge mahogany and acacia trees near the river give way to dense mopane woodland to the park's southern boundary along the steep Zambezi Escarpment.

Mana Pools National Park covers part of the Middle Zambezi Valley, which is home for 12,000 elephant and 16,000 buffalo (with herds of over 500 each).

Mana Pools is one of the best parks on the continent for seeing African wild dog. Species commonly seen in the park include elephant, leopard, buffalo, greater kudu, waterbuck, zebra, eland, impala, bushbuck, lion and crocodile. Large pods of hippo are often seen lying on the sandbanks, soaking up the morning sun. Occasionally spotted are cheetah, jackal, spotted hyena and the rare nyala. Large varieties of both woodland and water birds are present.

On our last visit with my wife and two sons, we spent a week in the park and did not want to leave. We had one wonderful day canoeing on the river that included paddling up close to a bull elephant that was crossing a river channel. Later we "bum-crawled" up to within about 15 feet (5 meters) of a pack of 11 dogs and sat with them for over an hour. Our game drives were very productive including spending time watching a very relaxed cheetah in a dry riverbed.

A pack of wild dogs is lead by an "alpha" female *(top)*, Cape buffalo on the shore of the Zambezi River *(bottom)*

Mana Pools National Park

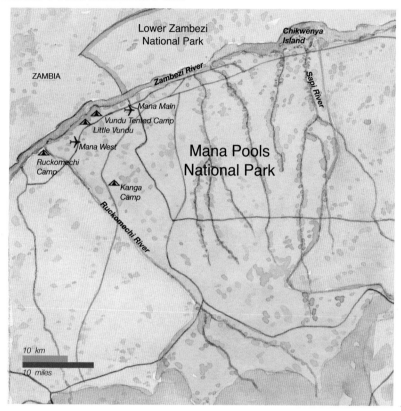

The highlight was spending time sitting under a tree with 3 bull elephants, one of which came within about 10 feet (3 meters) of us!

Walking Safaris

This is by far my favorite park in Africa for walking in the bush. I especially love what I call "**driving/walking**" excursions. You start off on a game drive, and once something of interest is found like fresh spoor (tracks) or animals a distance away from the road, you get out of the vehicle and track or walk up to wildlife with your Professional Guide.

Walking safaris like this one may sound a bit risky. They are, however, quite safe — as long as the safari is conducted by a fully licensed Professional Guide. Just follow the directions of your guide, use common sense and enjoy the adventure.

A walking safari with a Professional Guide can result in epic game viewing moments

Canoeing Safaris

For the adventurous traveler, canoeing safaris are one of the best ways to experience the African bush and is one of my favorite safaris on the entire continent. Traveling silently by canoe, you can paddle closely to wildlife that is wading in the river or has come to drink along the shore. Most importantly, you actively participate in the adventure!

Canoe safaris may be taken from a few hours to several days in length. Canoeing is fun in itself, but what I love about it is that it provides access to areas (river shoreline and islands) that cannot be reached by vehicle — providing opportunities for new adventures to unfold. If accompanied by a Professional Guide, this becomes a **canoeing/walking excursion**: you canoe until you see elephant, lion or other interesting game on or near the shoreline, you then pull into shore and walk up for a closer view. This is exciting beyond words!

Canoe safaris are lead by licensed canoe guides and last from 3 to 9 days, covering different stretches of the river. They are operated from Kariba Dam downstream for up to 159 miles (255 km) past Mana Pools National Park to Kanyemba near the Mozambique border.

The river is divided into four canoeing segments: 1) from below Kariba Dam through the Kariba Gorge to Chirundu, 2) from Chirundu to the border of Mana Pools, 3) along Mana Pools National Park and 4) downstream (east) of the park through the rugged Mupata Gorge to Kanyemba. The section (3) along Mana Pools National Park is by far the best section for wildlife viewing. In addition, no motorized boats are allowed on the Mana Pools side of this stretch of the river, making it all the more attractive (motorboats are allowed on the Zambian side of the river).

Three different "levels" of canoe safaris are available:

(1) Luxury (full-service) canoe safaris are led by a Professional Guide licensed to escort you on walks. These safaris have a cook and camp attendants who take care of all the chores, which allows guests to spend all their time exploring the area and enjoying the bush. The tents are larger than the other options, and each has an en suite bush shower and toilet.

(2) First Class (full-service) canoe safaris are also lead by a Professional Guide licensed to take guests on walks. Guests are accommodated in comfortable tents (large enough to stand but smaller than the luxury class) with cots with

Canoeing along the Zambezi River (Zambezi Escarpment is in the distance)

mattresses, sheets and blankets. Safari shower and bush toilet tents are usually separate from the sleeping tents, or in some cases, bush toilets may be en suite.

(3) Budget (participation) canoe safaris do not have a support vehicle on land — meaning you carry all the gear in the canoes. Camping is often done on islands in the Zambezi where there are no facilities. Participants sleep in sleeping bags in small pup tents or under mosquito nets, and everyone pitches their own tents and helps with the chores. They are not lead by a Professional Guide; walking inland is limited to 165 feet (50 m) from the riverbank. As you cannot take walking safaris into the bush, I do not recommend this level of canoe safari unless one cannot afford the other options.

Elephant are often seen swimming from the mainland to islands in the Zambezi in search of food. On most canoe safaris, guests see hundreds of hippo, buffalo, waterbuck, impala, countless elephant, crocodile, lion and many other species.

Although these canoe safaris are by no means marathons, participants paddle their own canoes — allowing them to be more involved in the adventure. Your guide will instruct you on safety precautions. Previous canoe experience is not necessary, however, spending at least a few hours in a canoe before your African safari will allow you to feel more comfortable canoeing in a foreign environment. If you like the idea of canoeing but prefer to do little or no paddling, I suggest you book a luxury canoe safari and request a paddler.

The best time to visit the park, for one of the finest exhibitions of wildlife on the continent, is at the end of the dry season (July to October) when large numbers of elephant, buffalo, waterbuck and impala come to the river to drink and graze on the lush grasses along its banks. Game viewing is also good in May, June and early November. During the rainy season (November to April), many large land mammals move away from the river toward the escarpment.

Because many roads within the park are closed during the rainy season, the camps are also closed. The best access to the park are with scheduled or private charter flights. Four-wheel-drive vehicles are recommended in the dry season and necessary in the rainy season.

Vundu Tented Camp is built under thatch along the Zambezi

ACCOMMODATION — CLASS A/B:
• **Vundu Tented Camp** is located right on the Zambezi River within the park and has 8 large tents (including a 2-bedroom, 2-bath family tent) with open-air bathrooms and unobstructed river views. The main lounge area is built in the tree canopy, an ideal vantage point to view the elephants and hippos below. From camp you may take day and night game drives, canoeing safaris ranging from a few hours to 3 days in length, and walks to explore and appreciate the rich flood plains and river channels. Two

and 3-day luxury canoe safaris are also offered. The owner is also a wild dog researcher for the Painted Dog Conservation Group. Voluntourism programs are offered such as recording wild dog data that is used for the research. • **Ruckomechi Camp**, built on the Zambezi River in the western boundary of the park, has 10 tents including a family tent. The main area features a lounge, dining room, library and swimming pool. Game drives, walks, motorboat excursions upstream of the park boundary, hides and canoeing are offered. • **Kanga Camp**, located about an hour's drive inland from the Zambezi River, has 6 Meru-style tents with flush toilets and safari showers. Game drives and walks are offered.

Ruckomechi Camp's pool area overlooks the river

CLASS B: • **Little Vundu**, a traditional tented camp located 2-miles (3-km) upstream from Vundu Camp, has 5 tents with open air bathrooms with flush toilets and safari showers. The dining area has a beautiful view of the Zambezi River and is accessed by a bridge over a small channel — a favorite place for nyala, elephant, buffalo, lion, hyena, leopard, wild dogs, waterbuck and impala to come to drink.

Harare

Harare is the capital and largest city in Zimbabwe. Points of interest include the **National Art Gallery**, **Botanical Garden**, **Houses of Parliament** and the **Tobacco Auction Floors**. **Mbare Msika Market** is good for shopping for curios from local vendors. Harare is a good place to shop for Shona carvings made of wood and soapstone, silverwork and paintings. A park adjacent to the Intercontinental Hotel features a large variety of brilliant flora. **Harare Botanical Gardens** has indigenous trees and herbs.

Harare's best restaurants include Amanzi, Emmanuels, and Victoria 22.

ACCOMMODATION — DELUXE: • **Meikles Hotel**, one of the "Leading Hotels of the World," has 306 rooms and suites with luxurious appointments, a swimming pool, sauna, gym and traditional Old World atmosphere.

FIRST CLASS: • **York Lodge**, located 15 minutes from the airport, is a luxury bed and breakfast featuring 8 suites. Each room opens out onto a verandah overlooking a lush garden and swimming pool. • **Imba Matombo**, located a 15-minute drive from Harare in the suburb of Glen Lorne, accommodates guests in rooms in a large home and chalets (20 beds total). The property has a tennis court, swimming pool and excellent restaurant. • **Rainbow Towers** (formerly the Sheraton Hotel) has 325 air-conditioned rooms and suites, a swimming pool, tennis courts, and a sauna and gym.

TOURIST CLASS: • **Wild Geese Lodge**, located 20 minutes by road from the city center and 30 minutes from the airport, is a private guesthouse set in beautiful gardens, with 10 rooms and suites. • **Holiday Inn** has 200 air-conditioned rooms and a swimming pool. • **Best Western Jameson Hotel** has 128 air-conditioned rooms and suites and a swimming pool.

THE SOUTH

Matobo (Matopos) National Park

Hundreds of kopjes supporting thousands of precariously balanced rocks give the 164-square-mile (424-km²) Matobo National Park one of the most unusual landscapes in Africa. A jewel of a park, it is a well-kept secret and is a highlight for many that venture there. The park is divided into two sections — a general recreational area with pony trails and a game reserve.

Matobo National Park has the highest concentration of eagles in the world, with black eagles, African hawk eagles, Wahlberg's eagles and crowned eagles known to exist within the reserve. Other birdlife includes purple-crested lourie, boulder chat, and both peregrine and lanner falcon.

Part of the park is an IPZ (Intensive Protection Zone) for black and white rhino. Leopard are plentiful but are seldom seen. Other wildlife includes sable antelope, giraffe, zebra, hippo, civet, genet, black-backed and side-striped jackal, caracal and porcupine.

Unique rock formations in Matobo National Park

The region has over 3,500 Bushman rock paintings — more than any other place in Africa. Some of the paintings are thought to be over 6,000 years old, while almost any that you will see will be at least 1,500 years old. The paintings were created as part of religious and spiritual ceremonies held by hunter-gatherers. **Nswatugi Cave** rock paintings include images of giraffe and antelope. For **Bambata Cave**, allow 1.5 hours for the hike that is well worth it to see the superb art that includes long processions of people. **White Rhino Shelter** rock paintings are also worth a visit. **Inanke Cave** is quite possibly the best painted site in Africa — but it's a hike to get there!

Cecil Rhodes was buried on a huge rock kopje called **"View of the World,"** from which there are sensational panoramas of the rugged countryside, especially at sunrise and sunset. A colony of dazzling platysaurus flat lizards may be seen at Rhode's gravesite; the colorful reptiles provide great photographic opportunities.

This is definitely one of the best areas to visit for a quality cultural experience. In addition to game viewing, we have visited rock painting sites, villages, a rural clinic, a primary and secondary school, orphanage, a church and an authentic African healer. The cooler and dryer months of June through September are probably the best time to visit, however, this is a great park and region to visit year-round.

ACCOMMODATION — CLASS A: • **Camp Amalinda**, attractively built into enormous kopjes, has 9 thatched chalets, open-air dining room and a magnificent natural rock pool. Activities include game drives, walks, horseback riding on a nearby property, visiting sites of Bushman paintings in the park and in nearby rural areas, visits to nearby villages, orphanages, schools, clinics, churches and African healers. Spa treatments can be arranged between activities. The owners operate the Mother Africa Trust, providing much needed assistance in the community and wonderful voluntourism opportunities for visitors. The camp is located about a 10-minute drive from the park.

Camp Amalinda is the ideal base when exploring this region

CLASS B: • **Matobo Hills Lodge**, located in a beautiful "amphitheater" of rock kopjes about a 10-minute drive from the park, has 17 thatched chalets (doubles) and a swimming pool creatively built into the rocks. Game drives, walks and visits to Bushman paintings and local villages are offered.

Interpreting Hunter-Gatherer Rock Art

When it comes to rock art, few regions on earth can match the cultural treasures of southern Africa. Painted by hunter-gatherers (often called 'Bushmen' or 'San') these images appear at thousands of sites across the region and show a wide variety of animals, people and abstract shapes in an array of scenes. Paintings are found wherever suitable surfaces exist, which in Zimbabwe means on the granite and sandstone outcrops dotted across the country. The art is thought to date back at least 13,000 years although it is possible painting started much earlier. Due to the natural forces of erosion and weathering as well as human interference, much of the art still visible on the rocks is unlikely to be more than 5,000 years old. What do we know about the people who painted them? Not nearly enough! Unlike in South Africa and Botswana, there are almost no ethnographic records relating directly to the ancient artists behind these Zimbabwean images, making it difficult to fully understand their meanings!

The rock art in the Inanke Cave depicts interactions with the spirit world

Rock art does more than just tell us about the achievements and activities of the people who painted it. In fact it's actually a significant aspect of their religion, conveying concepts and ideas about their interactions with the spirit world and their god. It's not just art — it's a code, part of a wider set of rituals (like dances, prayers and body art) that are lamentably unrecoverable today, but we are beginning to open that crack. It is clear that the creators of these paintings didn't just paint anything; they chose what to paint and how to paint it.

What else do we know about the originators of these paintings? Many experts contend that they were specialists among their people, often referred to as "shamans" or healers, or medicine men. (Academics are still arguing about whether these terms are appropriate, so for the sake of brevity I will use "shaman" in this article.) The art is thus interpreted as recollection or careful reinvention of the visions the shaman experienced while in an altered state of consciousness or "trance." Shamans would enter these states through strenuous dancing (the so-called Trance Dance) or perhaps even the use of certain herbs and plants. They would do this in order to contact

A giraffe painted in the Nswatugi Cave may have represented a concept of health and healing

the supernatural world, heal the sick, control animals (for hunting) and influence weather (most especially rainmaking). The paintings would be created as a way of expressing and emphasizing the extraordinary power behind these activities.

In the art the depictions of animals cannot be taken as literal. Animals represent metaphoric images in the same way that the lamb has a spiritual meaning in the Christian religion. In the rock art it is likely that these images represent human emotions, relationships and interpretations of their world. Different animals were imbued with wide-ranging symbolic meanings: the giraffe for example possibly being associated with concepts of health and healing; felines, especially lions, seem to represent danger or evil. The artists exaggerated certain characteristics of some animals and suppressed others. Likewise the human figures are much more than some ancient family photo album. Rather they conjure metaphoric human relationships, both with each other and the wider world in which these people lived. We are only just beginning to explore, let alone fully understand these themes.

By Paul Hubbard
Rock Art Guide, Archaeologist, Historian, and Author of numerous titles including *The Matopos: A Guide and Short History,* (2011, Bulawayo: Khami Press)

The Mother Africa Trust

The Mother Africa Trust was formed out of the requests from many of Amalinda Camp's (Matobo Hills) guests who were looking for efficient ways to assist its local communities.

Creating purpose-driven safaris, the Trust supports anyone who wishes to volunteer to work in southern Africa and who wants to "give

Volunteers share their knowledge with local children *(top and bottom)*, Volunteers from Minnesota give back to the Matobo Hills community *(middle)*

back" something to the wonderful communities and environments found there. The Trust has a wide range of objectives including reforestation, wildlife research, community development ranging from teaching assistance and infrastructure construction to simple repairs and maintenance. The projects are varied and meant to be stimulating, productive and long-lasting. For example, we have had people teaching art to underprivileged children, assisting in orphanages, tracking and counting rare waterfowl, feeding endangered vultures, de-snaring injured elephants and teaching orphans.

These voluntourism opportunities allow you to get deeply involved with so many aspects of African life, culture and wildlife in a way that transcends a normal vacation. And best of all, you have a chance to make a real and positive impact on the people and environment in a continent aching for assistance.

Paul Hubbard, Project Manager, The Mother Africa Trust, www.mother-africa.org

Bulawayo

Named after the royal city of the last Matabele King, Lobengula, Bulawayo is Zimbabwe's second largest city. It is home to more than a million people, although driving through the tiny city center you would think it was a sleepy little town. Dating from 1881, Bulawayo is Zimbabwe's oldest modern town and has a charm and attraction all of its own with its mixture of historical and modern buildings. The **Railway Museum** is interesting, and the **National Museum** is one of the best museums in southern Africa.

Some visitors to Matobo National Park fly in to Bulawayo Airport.

ACCOMMODATION — FIRST CLASS: • **Bulawayo Club**, founded in 1895 in downtown Bulawayo, has been restored to its previous glory. Rooms feature local artwork and the restaurant serves modern African cuisine.

TOURIST CLASS: • **Churchill Arms Hotel** is a modern Tudor-style hotel with 50 rooms, located 4 miles (6 km) from the city center. • **Holiday Inn Bulawayo** is located in the center of town and has 150 air-conditioned rooms. • **Nesbitt Castle**, built in 1906 by a Scottish architect, has 9 exclusive suites and is located a short distance from the city.

The Bulawayo Club is a colonial gem

Great Zimbabwe

These impressive stone ruins, a World Heritage Site, located 11 miles (18 km) from Masvingo, look distinctly out of place in sub-Saharan Africa, where almost all traditional structures have been built of mud, cow dung, straw and reeds. The origin of these ruins is rather confusing, but it is now certain that they represent an important ceremonial and residential center for former Zimbabwean rulers. Evidence of artifacts from the Far East indicates that the site was part of a trading center that involved the export of ivory and gold. Some historians believe it was an eleventh century Shona settlement.

In 1890, Fort Victoria (now Masvingo) became the first settlement of whites in what is now Zimbabwe. The settlers first discovered the Great Zimbabwe Ruins in 1887.

The city was at its prime from the twelfth to fourteenth centuries. The Acropolis or Hill Complex, traditionally the King's residence, is situated high on a granite hill overlooking the Great Enclosure (a walled enclosure) and the less-complete restoration of the Valley Complex.

ACCOMMODATION — TOURIST CLASS: • **Lodge of the Ancient City** has been attractively built in the style of the ruins, with comfortable rooms and a swimming pool. • **Great**

Zimbabwe Hotel is a country hotel, located a few minutes walk from the ruins, with a swimming pool and 56 rooms. • **The Inn on Great Zimbabwe**, located on a hillside minutes from Great Zimbabwe, has 8 rooms.

Malilangwe Wildlife Reserve

Malilangwe is one of Africa's best kept secrets, and is very possibly the best private reserve in Africa!

The reserve covers 148,000 acres (66,600 hectares) and is located in south-eastern Zimbabwe on the northern border of Gonarezhou National Park. This is one of the most scenic reserves on the continent as well, with a variety of ecosystems from open savannah areas with huge baobab trees and waterholes to hills and huge, rocky outcrops.

During our last visit we found the entire experience spectacular. On game drives we spotted a variety of species including leopard, cheetah, lion, greater kudu, duiker, klipspringer, blue wildebeest, sable antelope and roan antelope. We spent time at a hyena den with 3 pups that came right up to the vehicle. We tracked black rhino (of which there are many in the reserve) for about 2 hours but lost them in the thick grass. We followed a pack of wild dogs until they killed an impala not more than 50 yards (50 m) from our vehicle. Later, while having a "sundowner"

White rhino (pictured) as well as black rhino are plentiful on the Malilangwe Wildlife Reserve

at a waterhole, we were visited by not one, but a dozen white rhino. Between wildlife excursions our sons played tennis and went fishing on the lake.

There are over 100 rock painting sites that date back more than 2,000 years in the area.

Easiest access is by scheduled charter flight from Johannesburg on Mondays or Thursdays, or by private charter. Some travelers are transferred by vehicle from Bulawayo, stopping at the Great Zimbabwe Ruins enroute.

ACCOMMODATION — CLASS A+: • **Pamushana** is a luxury lodge consisting of six air-conditioned luxury suites (one, two and 3 bedroom) and one villa with indoor and outdoor showers, private plunge pool, double-sided fireplace, mini-bar and fridge, lounge, direct dial telephones and game viewing deck with Swarovski spotting scope, high-speed wireless Internet, satellite TV, fax facilities and US telephones. Guests enjoy 2 swimming pools (one is heated), sauna, 2 tennis courts and an extensive wine cellar. An open-air lounge, teak deck, dining room and library overlook the Malilangwe Dam

A giant baobab at Malilangwe *(top)*, Luxurious Pamushana is perched on a rock kopje *(bottom)*

Pamushana's main lounge area and pool

and sandstone hills. Activities include day and night game drives, walks, canoeing, bass and bream fishing, tennis (hard and clay courts), spa treatments, and visits to local schools and villages and to San Bushman paintings. Three is a 9-hole golf course located just 45 minutes away. Great Zimbabwe (World Heritage Site) and Gonarezhou National Park (including the Chilojo Cliffs) can be visited on day trips for an additional charge.

Gonarezhou National Park

The second largest park in Zimbabwe, Gonarezhou borders the country of Mozambique in southeastern Zimbabwe and covers over 1,950-square-miles (5,053-km²) of bush.

Gonarezhou means "the place of many elephants" and is definitely elephant country. Other species commonly seen are lion, buffalo, zebra, giraffe and a variety of antelope species. Nyala are regularly seen in riverine areas. Rarely seen are roan antelope and Liechtenstein's hartebeest.

The park is divided into two regions, the Chipinda Pools section, which includes the Runde and Save subregions, and the Mabalauta section. Game viewing is best in the Runde subregion.

Perhaps the most beautiful part of the reserve is the **Chilojo Cliffs** on the broad Runde River. These impressive cliffs are composed of oxide-rich sandstone, which is spectacularly colorful at sunset.

Much of the park is comprised of Mopane woodland and scrub. Visited mostly by the more adventurous, this park provides a true wilderness experience. Among the birds to be seen here are giant eagle owl, lappet-faced vulture, woolly-necked stork, Bohm's spinetail, red-billed helmetshrike and golden-breasted bunting.

The Frankfurt Zoological Society has been heavily involved with the park over the last several years, resulting in huge improvement in the quality of the wildlife experience there, as the wildlife we encountered was very relaxed and approachable, including a number of "big tuskers."

Gonarezhou National Park

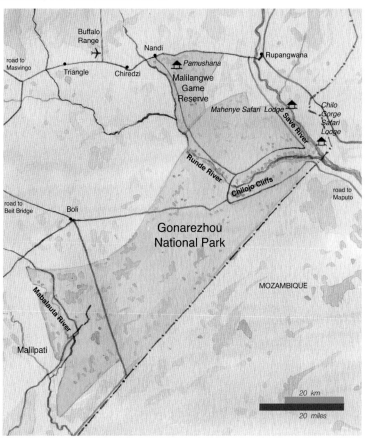

Gonarezhou has been earmarked for incorporation into the proposed Great Limpopo Transfrontier Conservation Area.

The park is usually only open in the dry season, May 1 to October 31. Winter temperatures are mild; however, summer temperatures can exceed 104°F (40°C).

From Masvingo, drive southwest to Chiredzi, then continue either 36 miles (58 km) to Chipinda Pools or 105 miles (170 km) to Mabalauta Camp. Four-wheel-drive vehicles are highly recommended. The nearest airstrip is Buffalo Range.

CLASS C: • **Chilo Gorge Safari Lodge**, set on the cliffs of the gorge overlooking the Save River, has 14 thatched chalets with private balconies. • **Mahenye Safari Lodge** is situated on the Save River bordering the reserve and consists of 8 thatched units with private balconies. Activities include walking safaris, game drives, visits to a local village and trips to the Chilojo Cliffs.

Zambia

Zambia

Zambia is one of Africa's least developed countries, with vast areas of wilderness and a comprehensive network of national parks protecting its wildlife. The landscape is an upland plateau ranging in altitude from 3,000 to 5,000 feet above sea level (915 to 1,525 m) with dry savannah and miombo woodland predominating. Zambia's economy is based on copper mining, agriculture and tourism. At 290,586-square-miles (752,614-km²), Zambia is larger than Texas (or France), but has a population of some 11 million. Lusaka is the capital city with 1.3 million inhabitants. English is the official language, with Bemba, Tonga, Ngoni and Lozi widely spoken. Currency is the Zambian Kwacha.

Zambia
Country Highlights

- Zambia's bush camps and small lodges (many of them owner-operated) are one of the last secret gems in southern Africa — offering personal attention that is often lacking in many larger lodges and camps.
- The country combines outstanding guides, beautiful scenery and excellent game viewing.
- There is nothing like a walking safari and Zambia is a top destination for them!
- A microlight over the Luangwa River (South Luangwa National Park), giving you truly a bird's eye view of the animals and crocs in the river.
- A hot air balloon ride at sunrise over the Busanga Plains (Kafue National Park) will take your breath away.
- Kafue National Park is two and half times the size of South Luangwa, it has more species of antelope than any park in Africa but almost no tourists!
- End your safari adventure with time in Livingstone in one of the luxury lodges along the Zambezi River, and gazing on Victoria Falls, the largest waterfall by volume in the world!

When's the Best Time to Go for Game Viewing

■ Excellent ■ Good □ Fair ■ Poor ■ Closed

Country	Park/Reserve	JAN	FEB	MAR	APR	MAY	JUN	JUL	AUG	SEP	OCT	NOV	DEC
Zambia	South Luangwa (Northern)												
	South Luangwa (Central & Southern)												
	Lower Zambezi												
	Kafue												

Best Safari Experience

Chiawa, Old Mondoro (Lower Zambezi), Tafika, Kiango, Puku Ridge, Chikoko, Crocodile and Mwanba (South Luangwa), Mwaleshi (North Luangwa), Busanga Bush Camp and Shumba (Kafue) and Toka Leya (Livingstone)

ZAMBIA

A country rich in wildlife, Zambia has gained a well-deserved heightened popularity over the last several years as a top safari destination. Extraordinary game viewing, outstanding guides and a variety of accommodations, Zambia attracts those looking for a remote, authentic safari experience.

Zambia was named after the mighty Zambezi River, which flows through western and southern Zambia. The Zambezi River is fed by its Kafue and Luangwa tributaries, and forms the boundary between Zambia and Zimbabwe before flowing through Mozambique — eventually emptying into the Indian Ocean. The three great lakes of Bangweulu, Mweru and Tanganyika are in northern Zambia, and Lake Kariba is found along the southeastern border adjacent to Zimbabwe.

The country is predominantly a high plateau ranging in altitude from 3,000 to 5,000 feet (915 to 1,525 m), which is why it has a subtropical rather than a tropical climate. April to August is cool and dry, September to October is hot and dry, and November to March is warm and wet. Winter temperatures are as cool as 43°F (6°C) and summer temperatures can exceed 100°F (38°C). The dry season, with clear sunny skies, is May to October.

The Zambian people are predominantly composed of Bantu ethnic groups who practice a combination of traditional and Christian beliefs. English is the official language and is widely spoken, in addition to 73 other languages and dialects. In contrast to most African countries, over 40% of the population lives in urban areas, due mainly to the copper mining industry.

Zambian people are renowned for their extremely friendly and laid back nature. Zambia is one of the least densely populated countries in Africa and large tracts of land remain undeveloped and wild.

In 1888, emissaries of Cecil Rhodes signed "treaties" with African chiefs ceding mineral rights of what was proclaimed Northern Rhodesia, which came under British influence. In 1953, Northern Rhodesia, Southern Rhodesia (now Zimbabwe) and Nyasaland (now Malawi) were consolidated into the Federation of Rhodesia and Nyasaland. The Federation was dissolved in 1963. Northern Rhodesia achieved its independence on October 24, 1964, as the Republic of Zambia. Since the elections in 1991, Zambia has a multiparty democratic political system.

Zambia's economy is based primarily on copper mined in the "Copper Belt" near the Congo border. Other major foreign exchange earners are agriculture (exporting fruit, coffee, sugar, flowers, vegetables) and the tourism industry.

🐾 WILDLIFE AND WILDLIFE AREAS

Zambia provides fabulous options for the wildlife adventurer, including both night and day game drives by open vehicle, walking safaris using remote bush camps or mobile tented camps, canoe safaris and white-water rafting.

Zambia boasts 20 gazetted national parks covering over 24,000-square-miles (60,000-km^2), and with the 34 game management areas adjacent to the parks, the country has set aside 32% of its land for the preservation of wildlife. However, some of the national parks and reserves are not open to the general public.

The country's 4 major parks are South Luangwa National Park, North Luangwa National Park, Lower Zambezi National Park and Kafue National Park. South Luangwa and the Lower Zambezi are the most popular of the 4, largely due to their large concentrations of game. Kafue National Park offers great game viewing with few tourists, and North Luangwa is the ultimate park for walking and the only park in Zambia where one can see black rhino.

Zambia is excellent for walking safaris, which are operated primarily in South Luangwa, North Luangwa, Lower Zambezi and Kafue National Parks. Virtually all of the camps offer morning walks and day and night game drives.

Canoeing on the Zambezi River in the Lower Zambezi National Park

Fishing is very good for tigerfish in Lake Kariba and the Zambezi River, and for tigerfish, goliath tigerfish, Nile perch and lake salmon in Lake Tanganyika.

Visitors who have their own vehicles must return to the camps by nightfall, and, therefore, cannot conduct night safaris on their own; neither may they leave the roads in search of game or walk in the park without the company of an armed wildlife guard and qualified guide.

More wildlife may be viewed June through October when the grass level is low and game is easier to see. Many of the rivers will have dried up and the game is concentrated around the lagoons and oxbow lakes — making game viewing all the more spectacular. Game viewing is still good in November, April and May, and the bush is certainly more lush and beautiful at that time! December to March is the hot and humid rainy season when foliage becomes thicker, making wildlife more difficult to spot. This is however a great time for birding, and for travelers who really prefer having the parks almost to themselves.

THE NORTH AND NORTHEAST

South Luangwa National Park

The natural beauty, variety and concentration of wildlife make this huge 3,494-square-mile (9,050-km²) park one of the finest in Africa. The Luangwa River dominates a beautiful flood plain. The river is totally unaffected by any commercial development and contains the highest concentrations of hippopotamus on earth.

South Luangwa is home to savannah, wetland and forest animals. The southern regions are predominantly woodland savannah with scattered grassy areas. Kudu and giraffe are numerous. To the north, the woodlands give way to scattered trees and open plains, where Cookson's wildebeest, Crawshay's zebra and other savannah animals dominate the scene.

Thornicroft's giraffe are indigenous to the park. Elephant, lion, leopard, hyena, buffalo, waterbuck, impala, kudu, puku, bushbuck and zebra are plentiful. There are also small herds of Cookson's wildebeest, unique to Luangwa, while African wild dog are present in small numbers and occasionally seen. The Luangwa Valley is in fact one of the best places in Africa to view leopard, which are most commonly sighted on night game drives from July to October!

November, with the onset of the rains, is a time of rebirth with the calving of impala, wildebeest and other species. Most of the Palearctic migrants have arrived, along with large flocks of Abdim's and white storks.

Hippo and crocs abound in the muddy Luangwa River, a tributary of the Zambezi, which runs along much of the park's eastern boundary and then traverses the southern part of the park.

Over 400 species of birds have been recorded, including sacred ibis, saddle-billed storks, yellow-billed storks, goliath herons, Egyptian geese, spur-winged geese, fish eagles (Zambia's national bird), crowned cranes, carmine bee-eaters (spectacular breeding colonies September through November), woodland king-fishers, lilac-breasted rollers, bateleur eagles, western banded snake eagle, Pel's fishing owl and Maeves' starlings. The best time for bird watching is November

South Luangwa

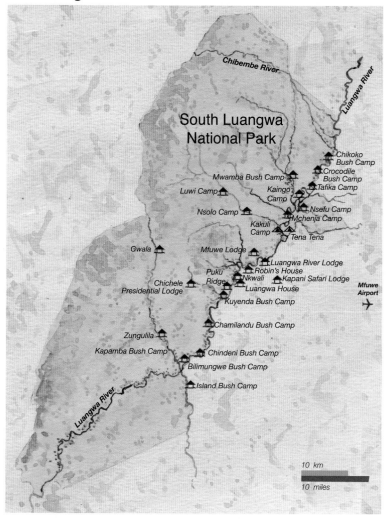

to April. There is a spectacular breeding colony of yellow billed storks close to Tafika Lodge (best viewed May to July each year). Large concentrations of crowned cranes are also remarkable in the Nsefu Sector late in the dry season.

A real advantage of this great park is that visitors can experience day and night game drives in open vehicles, as well as participate in walking safaris ranging in length from a few hours to 3 or more days.

South Luangwa is one of the best parks in Africa for **night drives**. Leopard, genet, civet and other nocturnal species are often seen.

Aerial view of the winding Luangwa River *(top)*, Walking safaris are a highlight in the South Luangwa *(bottom)*

Walking safaris were first pioneered in this park by Norman Carr, and are conducted by a licensed walking guide accompanied by an armed national parks game scout. Most lodges and camps offer morning and afternoon walks that often cover only 2 to 5 miles (3 to 8km) at a comfortable pace — allowing guests to experience nature up close.

Multi-day walks are also offered, during which guests hike 5 to 10 miles (8 to 16km) from bush camp to bush camp or from mobile camp to mobile camp. Walking safaris are only conducted from June to October during the dry season when the foliage has thinned out enough for safe walking. Children under the age of 12 are not allowed on walks.

Many lodges have their own smaller bush camps, catering to a maximum of 6 or 7 guests, set in remote regions of the park where walking is the main activity. However, bush camps are also excellent for those who do not want to do a lot of walking, but wish simply to experience isolation in the bush. In addition to walking, some bush camps also offer day and night game drives.

If you take a multi-day walking safari, I suggest you stay at least 2 additional nights in the park for day and night game drives by open vehicle; it will give you the opportunity to see many species that you might not have seen on your walking safari.

Over the years I have taken a number of **ultralight (microlight) flights** from Tafika Lodge over a wilderness region of the park, and must say that this is one of the most exciting adventures I have taken in Africa! I have seen huge herds of elephant and buffalo, large pods of hippo, a variety of antelope species and even lion. None of the wildlife even took note of us, except for crocs, which quickly fled to deep water. John Coppinger, my pilot, surmised that they must have thought we were a pterodactyl!

Another unique way of observing and photographing wildlife unnoticed is by spending time in **hides** or **blinds** on the Luangwa River. For instance, a wide network of blinds are set up each season by Kaingo Camp and Mwamba Bush

Camp, offering a truly unique perspective and close-up views of hippo, elephant, crocs, buffalo and colorful birdlife.

There are few all-weather roads in the park north of Mfuwe, so most of the northern camps are closed mid-November to April, and the camps that stay open during that period are usually reachable only by motorboat.

Mfuwe International Airport is about an hour flight from Lusaka. South Luangwa's main gate is 433 miles (700 km) from Lusaka; driving takes about 10 hours and is not recom-

Elephant are plentiful in the South Luangwa

mended. Some international visitors fly into Mfuwe from Lilongwe (Malawi) and Kariba (Zimbabwe).

ACCOMMODATION IN NORTHERN SOUTH LUANGWA — Because this region has few all-weather roads, the camps usually open in May and close at the end of October before the onset of the rains. This area is generally **less crowded** than Central Luangwa near Mfuwe.

CLASS A/B: • **Tafika Camp,** located on the eastern back of the Luangwa River, is owned and run by the Coppinger family who has lived in the Luangwa Valley for almost 30 years. Tafika has 4 large thatched chalets and 1 2-bedroom family chalet plus a honeymoon suite— all with panoramic views of the Luangwa River. Day and night game drives, walks, village visits, mountain biking, specialist painting safaris and exciting ultralight (microlight) flights are offered. Because this is the only northern camp open in November, guests of that period have the entire region virtually to themselves. • **Kaingo Camp,** located on the western bank of the Luangwa River, has been owned and operated by the Shenton family for decades. The camp has 6 recently renovated thatched chalets with outdoor bathtubs and private riverfront decks. Three daily game activities are offered including walks, day and night game drives, and photography from a great network of hides. • **Mchenja Camp,** set beneath a grove of ebony trees on the banks of the Luangwa River, has 5 stylish tents under thatch. There is a small pool and bar next to the dining area. Day and night game drives and walks are offered. • **Tena Tena** accommodates up to 10 guests in 5 tents under thatch overlooking a waterhole. Day and night game drives, morning walks, and community visits are offered as well as 6-day mobile tented walking safaris. • **Nsefu Camp,** located near the Luangwa River a 60- to 90-minute drive from Mfuwe Airport, has 6 brick and thatch rondavels (12 beds) with open-roofed bathrooms. Day and night game drives and morning walks are offered.

CLASS B: Chikoko and Crocodile are associated with Tafika Camp, Mwamba with Kaiango, and Nsolo, Luwi and Kakuli with Kapani Camp. Walking safaris from camp to camp are available from each group of camps and are usually limited to 6 guests. • **Chikoko Bush Camp** is located on the western bank of the Chikoko River in an area with no roads, so it is highly unlikely that you will see other tourists. The campsite is the original area that iconic guide and explorer, Norman Carr, selected

Tafika's thatched lounge area *(top)*, Mwamba's open-air dining room and bar *(middle, left)*, A chalet at Kaingo Camp *(middle, right)*, Chikoko Bush Camp *(bottom)*

for the first walking safari in the Luangwa Valley. Walking safaris provide abundant game sightings. There are 3 tree chalets on raised platforms 10 feet (3 m) above the ground. • **Crocodile Bush Camp** consists of 3 grass-and-pole chalets with open-air bathrooms built under a canopy of ebony trees. The camp is located within the park, 2.5 miles (4 km) upstream from Tafika, and caters to a maximum of 6 guests. Walking safaris are conducted between Tafika, Crocodile Camp and Chikoko Bush Camp. • **Mwamba Bush Camp**, located on the banks of the Mwamba River a 3-hour walk from Kaingo Camp, has 3 reed-and-thatch chalets with open-air bathrooms. The chalets are uniquely designed with large skylights (protected by mosquito netting) to give you the feeling that you are sleeping "under the stars." Walks, as well as day and night game drives, are offered. • **Nsolo Camp**, situated near a permanent waterhole, caters to a maximum of 8 guests in 4 chalets set on decks overlooking an open vlei. The fronts of the chalets are completely open during the day and are closed using tent material at night. There are some roads for game drives; however, walks are the most prominent activity. • **Luwi Camp** is located farther inland than Nsolo and has 4 bamboo huts accommodating a maximum of 8 guests. Walking safaris from camp are offered, and some guests walk from this camp to Nsolo Camp. • **Kakuli Camp**, set on a riverbank overlooking the confluence of the Luangwa and Luwi Rivers, accommodates a maximum of 8 guests in 4 tents. Day and night game drives as well as walks are offered.

ACCOMMODATION IN CENTRAL AND SOUTHERN SOUTH LUANGWA (this region of the park has many all-weather roads and is usually open year-round).

CLASS A: • **Puku Ridge Camp**, set on a secluded ridge, accommodates up to 12 guests in this tented camp. Day and night game drives and guided walks are offered. • **Chichele Presidential Lodge**, the former Presidential hideaway transformed into an "early-Victorian yet contemporary lodge," is set on a hill overlooking the surrounding plains. The lodge has a swimming pool and caters to 20 guests in cottages with air-conditioning, ceiling fans and inclusive mini-bar. Activities include day and night game drives and walks. Spa treatments can be done in the comfort of your room. • **Luangwa River Lodge**, located on the banks of the Luangwa River overlooking the Wafwa Oxbow Lagoon, has 5 chalets. Day and night game drives and walks are offered.

CLASS A/B: • **Kapamba Bush Camp** overlooks the Kapamba River and consists of 4 open-fronted stone chalets each with large sunken bathtub and double shower. Daily walks and day and night game drives are offered. • **Chamilandu Bush Camp** overlooks the Luangwa River and consists of 3 grass-and-thatch chalets, built on raised wooden decks. Walks and limited day and night game drives are offered. • **Chindeni Bush Camp** overlooks a permanent oxbow lagoon and has 4 luxury tents on raised wooden decks. Bush walks, as well as limited day and night game drives, are offered. • **Bilimungwe Bush Camp**, set on a permanent waterhole, has 4 large reed-and-thatch chalets. Walking safaris are the primary activity, but limited day and night game drives are offered. • **Nkwali Camp**, situated just outside the park on the eastern banks of the Luangwa River, is open year-round and has 6 chalets and a swimming pool. Day and night game drives and walks are offered. • **Luangwa House**, situated next to Nkwali, is a private luxury residence for up to 8 guests (in 4 bedrooms). The house offers private guides and vehicles for game drives and walks as well as a swimming pool, private chef and staff. • **Robin's House**, also on the same property as Nkwali, has 2 bedrooms with private bathrooms and is great for families. • **Kapani Safari Lodge** has 8 standard chalets and 1 suite, with small refrigerators and a large swimming pool. Kapani was operated by the late Norman Carr, who introduced walking safaris to Zambia. The camp offers day and night game drives and walks. • **Mfuwe Lodge**, set on two picturesque lagoons, has

18 chalets (including 2 suites) with private decks, a huge bar/dining/deck area and a large swimming pool. Day and night game drives are offered.

CLASS B: • **Kuyenda Bush Camp** has 4 grass chalets (preferred maximum of 6 guests), set on the banks of the Manzi River. Daily walks as well as day and night game drives are offered. • **Zungulila** has 4 tents erected on platforms all with sweeping views of the Kapamba River. Walking safaris are the primary activity in the morning and game drives in the afternoon/evening. • **Gwala** is located farther up the Kapamba River from Zungulila set in the heart of an ebony grove. Only walks are offered.

North Luangwa National Park

As the name implies, this largely undeveloped 1,780-square-mile (4,636-km²) park lies north of South Luangwa National Park in the upper Luangwa Valley.

Mark and Delia Owens, coauthors of *Eye of the Elephant* and *Cry of the Kalahari* (Houghton Mifflan), conducted wildlife research here and were successful in reducing poaching and creating an infrastructure to attract tourists.

The park lies between the 4,600-foot-high (1,400-m) Muchinga Escarpment on the west and the Luangwa River on the east, with altitudes ranging from 1,640 to 3,610 feet (500 to 1,100 m). Vegetation includes miombo woodland, scrubland and riverine forest.

Wildlife includes lion, leopard, elephant, buffalo, zebra, eland, kudu, Cookson's wildebeest (much larger populations than in South Luangwa), impala, bushbuck, hippo, crocodile and a large population of spotted hyena. Black-maned lion are seen here more often than in South Luangwa.

In 2010 the final translocation of 5 black rhinos was successfully completed as part of an ambitious program by Frankfurt Zoological Project to create a founder population of these endangered animals that used to flourish in the Luangwa Valley. There are now approximately 24 black rhino within the 77-square-mile (200-km²) Rhino Sanctuary. Currently, rhino are seldom seen, however, that may change if and when the southern fence is dropped.

Nearly 400 species of birds have been recorded, including species not usually seen in South Luangwa, such as the half-collared kingfisher, long-tailed wagtail, white-winged starling, yellow-throated longclaw and black-backed barbet.

Walking is by far the primary activity, however, there are now enough roads (about 60 mi./100 km) in the park for productive game drive/walk combinations and limited night drives.

This park is visited by very few tourists. It is in fact unlikely that you will encounter any other groups.

Guests staying several days in the park may have time to visit the **waterfalls** located near the foot of the Muchinga Escarpment. The excursion involves a long drive and a two-hour walk. The water at the falls is so clear that you may see hippo, crocs and fish swimming underwater. You can also swim (at your own risk) in some shallow pools nearby. Game seen enroute to the falls

North Luangwa

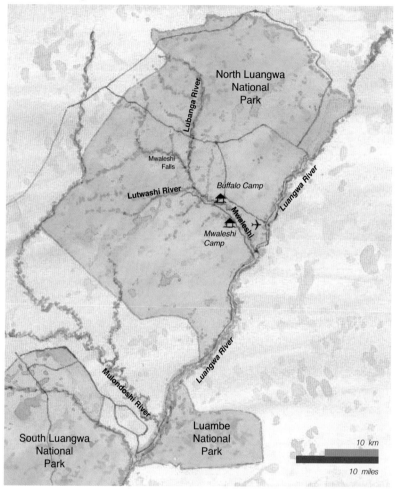

may include elephant, Lichtenstein's hartebeest, bushpig, roan antelope and Moloneys monkey.

The rainy season is November to March, and the best time to visit is June to October. Access to the park is best by a 45-minute or so charter flight from Mfuwe Airport; alternatively it is about a 6-hour drive. I suggest spending 6 or more nights divided between North and South Luangwa.

Mwaleshi Camp offers comfortable reed chalets

ACCOMMODATION — CLASS B:
• **Mwaleshi Camp** is a bush camp set on the banks of the Mwaleshi River with 4 reed-and-thatch chalets. Escorted walks, day and night game drives are offered. An early morning walk from camp is often followed by a bush breakfast and a game drive back to camp.

CLASS C: • **Buffalo Camp** is a rustic, 8-bed bush camp. Set on the north bank of the Mwaleshi River, it offers escorted walks and limited day and night drives.

THE SOUTH AND WEST

Lower Zambezi

Declared a national park only in 1983, this is Zambia's newest national park, and in a relatively short period of time has become one of Africa's finest.

Located along the Zambezi River across from Mana Pools National Park (Zimbabwe), the Lower Zambezi National Park extends 75 miles (120 km) along the Zambezi River between the Chongwe River on the west and nearly to the Luangwa River to the east, and approximately 20 miles (35 km) inland.

The varied scenery and habitats of Zambezi River with gigantic baobab trees and stands of huge winter thorn trees with the escarpment towering in the background help make this an attractive park to visit. Wildlife includes about 80 species of mammals and over 400 species of birds.

Lower Zambezi National Park

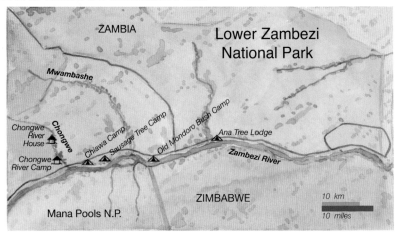

From escorted walks, day and night game drives, canoeing, river cruises and fishing for the world renowned tiger-fish, you may see elephant, hippos, buffalo, lion, leopard, warthogs, crocs and a variety of antelope. Concentrations of wildlife are highest during the dry season when prey and predator concentrate along the Zambezi River. Cheetah, rhino and giraffe are not found in the park.

Game viewing is best July to October and is good in May and June. The best fishing months are September, October, and the first 2 weeks of November.

ACCOMMODATION — CLASS A: • **Chiawa Camp**, located on the banks of the Zambezi River within the park, has 6 standard tents, 2 superior tents and 1 honeymoon tent (all 3 categories are perfect for honeymooners)

Boating and walking safaris from Chiawa Camp

A luxurious tent at Chiawa Camp *(top)*, Old Mondoro's chalets overlook the river *(middle)*, Chongwe River Camp *(bottom)*

and feature footed bathtubs, indoor-outdoor showers, king-size beds and elevated wooden platforms with day-beds to enjoy the expansive views. The charming thatched lounge/bar area has an upstairs observation deck and lounge, and there is a refreshing plunge pool. Day and night vehicle game drives, morning and afternoon river cruises, visits to the hide, fishing (it's excellent here), canoeing and walking are offered.

CLASS A/B: • **Old Mondoro Bush Camp** located on the banks of the Zambezi River within the park, has 4 reed-and-pole rooms with canvas roofs, wide verandahs and outdoor daybeds. The focus is on walking trails; day and night game drives, boat safaris and canoeing are also available. Many guests will spend a few nights here along with a few nights at Chiawa Camp, because they are located in different regions of the park and favor different activities. • **Sausage Tree Camp** has 8 Bedouin-style tents with open-air bathrooms. Day and night game drives, boat cruises, fishing, walking and canoeing are offered. • **Chongwe River Camp** is a comfortable "bush camp" located just outside the western border of the Park consisting of 10 double chalets with 1 honeymoon suite, each with open-air bathrooms. Activities include game drives in open vehicles, guided walks, canoeing, boating and fishing. • **Chongwe River House** is a private house accommodating up to 8 guests in 4 bedrooms. The activities offered are exclusive to guests and include game drives, boat cruises, walking and canoeing safaris and fishing. There is a swimming pool and private chef for guests' enjoyment. • **Ana Tree Lodge** is scheduled for complete renovation and will include 8 tents with open plan bedroom and lounge. A vast plain stretches from the lodge to the banks of the Zambezi River. Game drives, walking safaris, boating and fishing are offered.

Lusaka

Attractions in Lusaka, the capital of Zambia, include the Luburma Market and Chieftainess Mungule's Village. Woodcarvings made by local craftsmen can be seen at Kabwata Cultural Center. There is also a museum near the city center. The international airport is 16 miles (26 km) from the city.

ACCOMMODATION — FIRST CLASS: • **Protea Hotel Lusaka**, located within the Arcades Shopping and Entertainment Complex, features 100 rooms, restaurant, lounge and swimming pool. • **Taj Pamodzi Hotel** is a 192 room air-conditioned hotel, and has a restaurant, room service, a swimming pool and gym. • **Lusaka Inter-Continental Hotel** has 224 rooms, 24-hour room service, 3 restaurants, a casino, gym and a swimming pool. • **Southern Sun Ridgeway** is an air-conditioned 155-room hotel with 2 restaurants, bar and a swimming pool.

Kafue National Park

Kafue National Park, one of the largest in Africa, covers 8,687-square-miles (22,400-km²), making it 2.5 times the size of South Luangwa National Park and half the size of Switzerland.

Kafue has the largest number of different antelope species of any park in Africa. Many of the species, such as greater kudu and sable antelope, are said to be substantially larger than elsewhere in the country. Visitors usually see a greater variety of species in Kafue, although not the quantity of wildlife that they might see in South Luangwa. Kafue is, however, definitely a park for anyone wanting to get off the beaten track!

Antelope tense and alert, listening for predators in the morning dawn

Kafue National Park

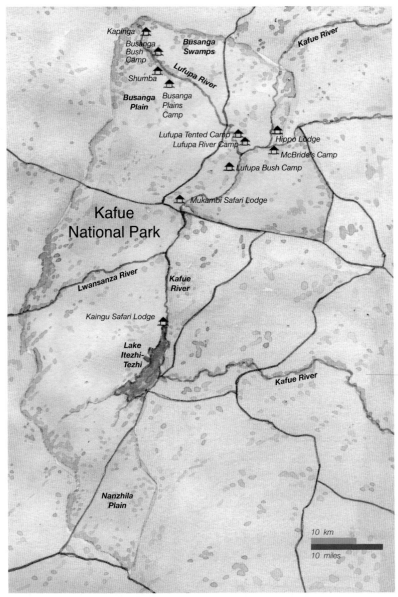

Game viewing in this park is sometimes a combination of riding in a vehicle, walking and boating on the rivers and swamp boats (great fun — operated by a few select camps) through the swamps, according to the wishes of the group.

The Busanga Plains and marshes in the north have a greater number and variety of wildlife species. Animals are easier to spot here than in the dense woodland savannah in the south. This region is predominantly miombo forest, which gives way to savannah grasslands, along with rock hills, marshes and riverine forests. The Kafue River runs through the northern part of the park and along its east central border.

Large herds of red lechwe may be seen on the Busanga Plains. Sitatunga may be found in the Busanga Swamps on the northern border of the park. Lion are often seen on day and night game drives. This is the best park in Zambia to see cheetah, which are being seen quite frequently. Leopard are occasionally seen. Also present on the plains are buffalo, elephant, puku, wildebeest, impala, roan antelope, sable antelope, greater kudu, Lichtenstein's hartebeest, waterbuck, wild dog and hyena. More than 400 species of birds have been recorded.

The Busanga Plains are truly an amazing sight. The 350-square-miles (900-km²) of plains are broken by numerous small palm "islands," and have a feel of the openness of the short grass plains of the southeastern Serengeti coupled with the presence of water and landscape similar to Botswana's Okavango Delta. Some of the camps are accessed by **helicopter** — a truly amazing way to see the plains!

Ballooning over the Busanga Plains is an experience not to be missed, and is available from select camps.

There is little to be seen on the 4-hour, 170-mile (275-km) drive from Lusaka; scheduled charter flights from Livingstone and Lusaka are available and are a better alternative. Game is especially difficult to spot in the rainy season. Most safari camps are open from May to December, with the best game viewing being from July to October.

Ballooning over the Busanga Plains

Cheetah are frequently seen on the Busanga Plains

ACCOMMODATION — Safari camps located on the Busanga Plains (and offering the best game viewing) include Shumba, Kapinga, Busanga Bush Camp and Busanga Plains Camp. Teetse flies are more prevalent in the camps that are not located on the Busanga Plains.

CLASS A: • **Shumba** has 6 luxury safari tents on raised platforms, dining and bar area with views of the surrounding plains. Day and night game drives, swamp boat rides, walking safaris and services of a masseuse are offered. Ballooning is offered August to October. • **Kapinga** blends into its surroundings with only 3 luxury safari tents and offers very personalized service. Day and night game drives, swamp boat rides, walking safaris and spa treatments are offered. The camp is scheduled to be rebuilt and to re-open in mid-2013.

CLASS A/B: • **Busanga Bush Camp** has 4 thatched huts with views over the grassy flood plains. Day and night game drives and walks are offered. Ballooning is offered August to October.

CLASS B: • **Mukambi Safari Lodge**, located at the entrance to Kafue National Park has 8 chalets, 1 luxury family unit and 7 traditional safari-style tents and 2 swimming pools.

Morning and night game drives, boat trips and walking safaris are offered.
• **Busanga Plains Camp,** sister camp to Mukambi Safari Lodge, has 4 safari tents and offers game drives and walking safaris.

CLASS C: • **Lufupa Tented Camp,** situated near the confluence of the Kafue and Lufupa Rivers, has 9 canvas Meru tents and offers day and night game drives, walks, fishing and game viewing by boat. • **Lufupa River Camp** has 7 twin Meru tents and 2 family tents. • **Lufupa Bush Camp,** a new camp on the Lufupa River, has 4 brick and thatch rondavels. Activities include game drives, guided walks and game viewing by boat. • **Hippo Lodge,** located in the northern sector of Kafue, has 4 rustic chalets and 2 tents with open-air bathrooms. • **Kaingu Safari Lodge** offers 4 safari tents under thatch and 1 family house built on raised platforms with views of the river. Walking safaris, canoeing and boating are offered. • **McBride's Camp,** located in the northeast section of the park, consists of 5 thatched chalets with private verandahs. The camp specializes in walking safaris.

Shumba's tents feature canopied beds *(top),* Busanga Bush Camp overlooks the flood plains *(bottom)*

Victoria Falls

Called Mosi-oa-Tunya, "the smoke that thunders," Victoria Falls is one of the seven natural wonders of the world. Visitors may walk along the **Knife Edge Bridge** for a good view of the Eastern Cataract and Boiling Pot.

A **sunset cruise** is a very pleasant experience; hippo and crocodile are often seen. Fixed-wing aircraft and helicopter **flights over the falls** are a great way to get a bird's eye view of Victoria Falls. A boat excursion to **Livingstone's Island** is highly recommended for great views of the falls. This only operates when the water flowing over the falls is its lowest, from August to November. Half-day **elephant back riding** excursions are offered and highly recommended as a way to spend up close and personal time with these intelligent creatures. **Canoe safaris** are conducted upstream of the falls. **Fishing** for tigerfish on the Zambezi River is best from June to October (September is best), before the rains muddy the water.

One of the world's highest commercially run **bungee jumps** is operated on the bridge crossing the Zambezi River. After falling over 300 feet (100 m), a member of the bungee staff is lowered to the jumper and connects a cable to his harness. The jumper is winched into the upright position and then winched back up onto the bridge.

Livingstone/Victoria Falls

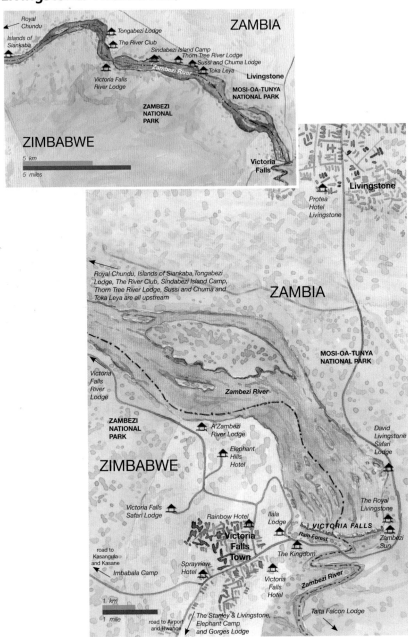

ZAMBIA

Royal Chundu

Islands of Siankaba

Tongabezi Lodge

The River Club

Sindabezi Island Camp

Thorn Tree River Lodge

Sussi and Chuma Lodge

Toka Leya

Zambezi River

Livingstone

Victoria Falls River Lodge

MOSI-OA-TUNYA NATIONAL PARK

ZAMBEZI NATIONAL PARK

ZIMBABWE

5 km

5 miles

Victoria Falls

Livingstone

Protea Hotel Livingstone

Royal Chundu, Islands of Siankaba, Tongabezi Lodge, The River Club, Sindabezi Island Camp, Thorn Tree River Lodge, Sussi and Chuma and Toka Leya are all upstream

ZAMBIA

MOSI-OA-TUNYA NATIONAL PARK

Victoria Falls River Lodge

Zambezi River

ZAMBEZI NATIONAL PARK

A'Zambezi River Lodge

ZIMBABWE

Elephant Hills Hotel

David Livingstone Safari Lodge

Victoria Falls Safari Lodge

Rainbow Hotel

Ilala Lodge

The Royal Livingstone

VICTORIA FALLS

Rain Forest

Zambezi Sun

road to Kasangula and Kasane

Victoria Falls Town

The Kingdom

Sprayview Hotel

Imbabala Camp

Victoria Falls Hotel

Zambezi River

1 km

1 mile

road to Airport and Hwange

The Stanley & Livingstone, Elephant Camp and Gorges Lodge

Taita Falcon Lodge

A thrilling microlight ride over Victoria Falls

The Zambezi River below Victoria Falls is one of the most exciting **white-water rafting** experiences in the world. Numerous fifth-class rapids (the highest class runable) make this one of the most challenging rivers on earth. Trips are operated on the Zambezi River below Victoria Falls from the Zambia and Zimbabwe side of the Zambezi River. See the description of white-water rafting in the "Victoria Falls" section of the chapter on Zimbabwe for further details.

The falls are located about 3 miles (5 km) from Livingstone. See the chapter on Zimbabwe for a detailed description of the falls.

Mosi-oa-Tunya (Smoke That Thunders) National Park

Much of the area around the Victoria Falls on the Zambian side is positioned within the 4-square-mile (10-km²) Mosi-oa-Tunya National Park. Only a small section is fenced off into a game park that has a small population of sable, eland, warthog, giraffe, zebra, buffalo and elephant. There are 2 monuments within the park — one where the pioneers used to cross the river, and the other at the old cemetery. There are no large predators in the park.

ACCOMMODATION WITHIN THE PARK — CLASS A: • **Toka Leya Camp** is situated on the banks of the Zambezi River in the eastern sector of the Mosi-oa-Tunya National Park. Accommodations consist of 12 safari-style tents (including 2 family tents), each with a small air-conditioner over the bed and view of the Zambezi River and surrounding

Sundowner cruises on the Zambezi are a popular activity *(top)*, Toka Leya's riverfront pool and deck *(bottom)*

islands. There is a swimming pool and spa for guests to enjoy on hot African days. Activities include a tour of the falls on the Zambian side, game drives, river cruises and guided walks. • **Sussi and Chuma Lodge**, located on the Zambezi River just a 10-minute drive above Victoria Falls, consists of 12 luxury rooms with air-conditioning, and private decks. There is a swimming pool, spa and sundowner deck. The camps offer tours to the falls, Livingstone Museum visits, and a cultural village tour as well as game drives and guided walking safaris within Mosi-oa-Tunya National Park. • **Chuma Houses** are 2 exclusive properties featuring 2 bedrooms (1 double and 1 twin room). There is a spacious lounge and dining room area, kitchen, outdoor verandah, barbeque area and private swimming pool. Guests have their own private chef, butler and a private guide, vehicles and boat. • **Royal Chundu**, located 31 miles (50 km) from the Livingstone Airport, features 2 lodges, River Lodge with 10 riverfront suites and Island Lodge with 4 villas on the private Katambora Island. There is a floating spa, infinity pool and dinner is served in the open-air boma.

CLASS B: • **Thorn Tree River Lodge**, located in Mosi-oa-Tunya, has 7 stone rooms under thatch and 2 wood suites under thatch with private verandahs with views of the river and bush. Activities include river cruises, tours of the Victoria Falls area, game drives and elephant back safaris are conducted from camp.

Livingstone

Livingstone is a city of over 100,000 inhabitants, 5 miles (8 km) from the town of Victoria Falls. Driving from Lusaka takes 5 to 6 hours (295 miles/470 km) and flying takes a little over an hour.

The **Livingstone Museum** is the National Museum of Zambia and is renowned for its collection of Dr. Livingstone's memoirs. Other exhibits cover the art and culture of Zambia. The **Railway Museum** has steam engines and trains from the late 1800s and 1900s.

Livingstone Zoological Park is a small, fenced park near Livingstone covering 25-square-miles (65-km²). It is stocked with giraffe, buffalo, impala and other wildlife. The best time to visit is from June to October.

ACCOMMODATION — DELUXE: • **The Royal Livingstone** has a total of 173 rooms including 3 standard suites, 1 presidential suite and 2 paraplegic (handicapped) rooms, restaurant and bar. All rooms have air-conditioning, satellite television, mini-bar, safe and private balconies and terraces that offer views of the Zambezi River.

FIRST CLASS: • **The David Livingstone Safari Lodge and Spa**, set on the banks of the Zambezi River, is a colonial-style property with 72 luxury rooms and 5 loft suites. There is also a spa, tropical infinity swimming pool, restaurant and bar. • **Protea Hotel Livingstone** consists of 80 deluxe rooms with satellite TV. The hotel is situated next to a shopping and entertainment center enroute from the falls to Livingstone town.

TOURIST CLASS: • **Zambezi Sun** has a total of 212 rooms with private balconies and satellite TV including 4 suites and 2 paraplegic rooms, and a restaurant and bar focused around the central swimming pool.

ACCOMMODATION NEAR LIVINGSTONE — CLASS A: • **The River Club** is located 12 miles (20 km) upstream from Victoria Falls and has a distinct Edwardian flavor with 10 luxury chalets overlooking the Zambezi River. Visits to the falls and other local attractions, river cruises and village visits are offered. • **Tongabezi Lodge**, situated on the Zambezi River 12 miles (20 km) upstream from Victoria Falls, has recently been refurbished and sleeps 22 guests in 5 thatched river cottages, 4 spacious stone-and-thatched houses, 1 enclosed house with private plunge pool and 1 Garden Cottage with 2 bedrooms set away from the river. Guests enjoy the swimming pool and activities such as canoeing, boat excursions, fishing, croquet, and flights over the falls are offered.

The charm of the River Club *(top)*, One of Tongabezi Lodge's intimate cottages *(middle)*, Sindabezi Island Camp *(bottom)*

CLASS A/B: • **Sindabezi Island Camp**, located on an exclusive island in the Zambezi River 2 miles (3 km) downstream from Tongabezi Camp, has 5 romantic thatched cottages lit only by candles and lanterns with private verandahs. • **The Islands of Siankaba**, consisting of two islands in the Zambezi River, 24 miles (38 km) upstream from Victoria Falls, has 7 teak-and-canvas chalets on raised platforms with facilities and a swimming pool. The two islands are linked by a series of suspension bridges and overhead walkways. Activities include guided walks on the main island, village/school tour, mokoro trips, and sunset river cruises, as well as trips to Victoria Falls.

CLASS B/C: • **Taita Falcon Lodge**, located 5 miles (7 km) downstream from the falls, overlooking the spectacular Batoka Gorge and the Zambezi River, has 6 chalets with verandahs.

Namibia

Namibia

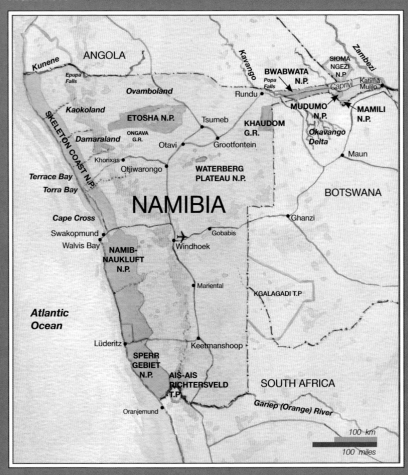

Namibia is one of Africa's driest countries, with the Namib and Kalahari Deserts dominating the landscape. Elevation ranges from sea level on the Atlantic seaboard to some 5,410 feet (1,650 m) at Windhoek on the central plateau. In the far north, the permanent water of the Kunene and Okavango Rivers allows for productive agriculture and it is here that most of the population live. Just over two million people inhabit the 318,250-square-miles (824,268-km²) of Namibia, which is about the size of Texas and Oklahoma combined. Windhoek is the capital city. English is the official language. Currency is the Namibian Dollar.

Namibia
Country Highlights

- Seeing sunrise over the highest sand dunes in the world at Sossusvlei.
- Flying in a small charter plane or hot-air balloon over the unmistakable, epic scenery of Namibia.
- Visiting UNESCO World Heritage Site at Twyfelfontein to see the ancient rock engravings.
- Tracking desert elephant and black rhino in Damaraland.
- Viewing seal colonies, whale bones and shipwrecks on the Skeleton Coast.
- Watching the pecking order of game around Etosha's and Ongava's waterholes.
- Accompanying San bushmen on a traditional hunt.
- Visiting the Himba, taking a boat cruise on the Kunene River and quad biking in Kaokoland.

When's the Best Time to Go for Game Viewing

■ Excellent ■ Good □ Fair ■ Poor ■ Closed

Country	Park/Reserve	JAN	FEB	MAR	APR	MAY	JUN	JUL	AUG	SEP	OCT	NOV	DEC
Namibia	Etosha/Ongava												
	Namib-Naukluft												
	Skeleton Coast												
	Damaraland												

Best Safari Experience

Little Kulala and Kulala Desert Lodge (Namib Naukluft), Wolwedans Boulders Camp and Private Camp (Wolwedans), Damaraland Camp (Damaraland), Little Ongava, Ongava Tented Camp, Ongava Lodge (Ongava/Etosha), Serra Cafema (Kaokoland), Hoanib Skeleton Coast Camp (Skeleton Coast)

NAMIBIA

In addition to wildlife, Namibia has some of the most spectacular desert ecosystems in the world. A geologist's and naturalist's paradise, Namibia is famous for its stark beauty and diversity of tribes.

Essentially a desert land, Namibia is one of the most interesting and unusual of African countries. The Namib, in fact, is considered to be the oldest desert in the world. It may seem inhospitable in its dryness, but an astonishing variety of wildlife exists there, including unique, desert-adapted species, together with the big game of the savannah. Namibia has a sparse population just over 2 million, the majority of which live in Windhoek (the capital city) or in the far northern regions of Ovamboland.

Namibia is situated in the subtropics, and flanked by the cold Atlantic Ocean. The cold Benguela current, which drifts northward from Antarctica, has a massive influence on the climate. Cool, dry air is pushed inland, creating a temperate coastline, and the extreme desert conditions of the Namib. Most of the country receives less than 10 inches (250 mm) of rain (the entire coastal region has less than 1 inch/25 mm); 80% of this rain falls between October and April.

Namibia has a subtropical climate. Inland summer (October to April) days are warm to hot with cool nights. From May to September (winter), days are warm with clear skies but the nights can become quite cold. Summer (December to March) is the "rainy" season, and most rainfall occurs in the north and northeast.

There are five perennial (permanent) rivers in Namibia, all forming a border with neighboring countries. The Gariep (Orange) River is in the south and divides Namibia from South Africa while the Kunene, in the far north, forms a natural border with Angola. The Kavango, Kwando, Linyanti and Chobe Rivers separate the country from Botswana, while the mighty Zambezi separates it from Zambia and Zimbabwe. All other rivers in the country are ephemeral, running only when good rains are received in their catchment areas.

Namibia is one of the world's most sparsely populated countries. Its population is 86% black, 7% white and 7% colored (of mixed descent). The Owambo tribe represents at

Zebra gather at a waterhole in Ongava

least half of all the black Namibians, while other tribes include Damara, Herero, Kavango, Nama, Caprivian, San (Bushmen), Rehoboth Baster, Himba, Topnaar and Tswana. Herero women, colorfully dressed in red and black, continue to wear conservative, impractical and extremely hot attire that was fashioned for them by puritanical, nineteenth century missionaries. Most people live in the northern part of the country where there is more water.

In 1884 much of the coast became German South West Africa until 1915, when South Africa took control during World War I. In 1920 the Union of South Africa received a mandate by the League of Nations to govern the region as if it were part of South Africa. The United Nations retracted the mandate in 1966 and renamed the country Namibia. The country became independent on March 21, 1990.

Namibia is one of the world's largest producers of diamonds and has the world's second largest uranium mine. Tsumeb is the only known mine to have produced over 200 different minerals. Other major industries include fishing, agriculture and the burgeoning tourism industry.

The epic scenery of Namibia's Skeleton Coast

WILDLIFE AND WILDLIFE AREAS

Namibia has set aside about 14% of its surface area as proclaimed national parks. Etosha is the most famous, and it offers game viewing on par with other top reserves in southern Africa.

The Namib-Naukluft and Skeleton Coast parks protect unique desert ecosystems, and are an attraction for smaller life forms and landscapes, as well as low concentrations of desert-adapted big game. Lion have returned to the Skeleton Coast, and elephant may be seen there as well. Other key areas to consider visiting are Kaokoland for spectacular scenery and to visit the Himba, and Bushmanland to visit the San Bushmen.

Game viewing in Etosha and Ongava is best during the dry season May to November. Due to Namibia's unique desert, game viewing in the desert areas is great all year round.

A few selected tour operators and lodges may use open-sided vehicles in Etosha National Park, however, self-drive travelers are only allowed in Etosha in closed vehicles. Open-sided vehicles are allowed in all other parks. Walking is allowed in all parks and reserves, except Etosha. However, walking is not recommended unless you are accompanied by an experienced guide.

THE NORTH AND WEST

Windhoek

Windhoek is the capital and administrative, commercial and educational center of Namibia, situated in the center of the country at 5,410 feet (1650 m) above sea level. Windhoek is also the starting point for most Namibian safaris. Eros Airport serves as the gateway for most charter flights departing for the safari camps.

The capital has been influenced greatly by German architecture from the early colonial days. Three castles were built between 1913 and 1918, and are located close together in what is now the fashionable suburb of Klein Windhoek. The **Heinitzburg** is now one of Windhoek's finest hotels, while Italy's ambassador to Namibia resides in the **Schwerinsburg**, and the **Sanderburg** has become a private dwelling. The **State Museum**, dating from the end of the nineteenth century, is housed in the **Alte Feste** (Old Fort), and is closer to the city center.

Other places of interest include Windhoek's **Botanical Gardens**, the **National Art Gallery**, **Post Street Mall** with its impressive collection of meteorite rocks, the **Supreme Court** building and **Heroes Acre** — a burial place reserved for Namibia's most revered freedom fighters — a few kilometers out of town on the B1 road, toward Rehoboth.

Joe's Beerhouse is an iconic "watering hole," with a popular bar and restaurant known for its informal atmosphere. The NICE restaurant (Namibian Institute of Culinary Excellence) and bar is one of the city's hippest and most sophisticated new spots. It offers international cuisine infusing Namibian classics such as exquisite game dishes with Asian or Italian, along with traditional dishes. Am Weinberg serves wholesome and healthy Namibian haute cuisine, and offers a great outdoor venue. Leo's at the Heinitzburg Hotel has varied cuisine ranging from international to French a la carte; the atmosphere is extremely formal. Luigi & The Fish is known for good seafood, has a pool table and is popular (especially among the young). Restaurants offering a great African vibe include La Marmite, offering some fabulous West African cooking.

On a day trip from Windhoek you can visit the historic Elegant Farmstead at Ovitoto where you can meet the colorful Herero people.

The Olive Exclusive Boutique Hotel

ACCOMMODATION — FIRST CLASS: • **The Olive Exclusive Boutique Hotel** has 7 suites individually decorated, each with a lounge area, fireplace and spacious decks. The restaurant offers a seasonal menu. • **Heinitzburg Hotel**, the only member of the Relais and Chateaux group of excellence in Namibia, is an old castle with 16 air-conditioned rooms. • **The Olive Grove** offers 10 air-conditioned rooms and 1 executive suite in a location close to the city center. The verandah offers al fresco dining and there is a tranquil garden and pool. • **Windhoek Country Club Resort and Casino**, located several kilometers from the city, has 152 air-conditioned rooms, tennis courts, an 18-hole golf course and a swimming pool. A complimentary shuttle takes guests to and from the city center. • **The Safari Court** (4-star) and **Hotel Safari** (3-star) are located 2 miles (3 km) from the city center; The Safari Court has 257 rooms and Hotel Safari has 192 (all air-conditioned). The complex includes several restaurants, bars, swimming pools and free transport to and from Windhoek. • **Kalahari Sands Hotel and Casino**, located in the center of town, has 173 air-conditioned rooms and suites. There is a rooftop swimming pool and fitness center.

TOURIST CLASS: • **Elegant Guest House** offers 6 rooms with air-conditioning, television and complimentary coffee-tea. • **Villa Verdi**, a small guest lodge located a few minutes walk from downtown, has 13 standard rooms, 3 apartments and 1 luxury suite and a swimming pool. • **Hotel Thüringerhof** has 80 air-conditioned rooms and a beer garden.

Namib-Naukluft Park

The consolidation of the Namib Desert Park and the Naukluft Mountain Zebra Park along with the incorporation of other adjacent lands, including most of what was called "Diamond Area #2," created the largest park in Namibia and

Namib-Naukluft Park

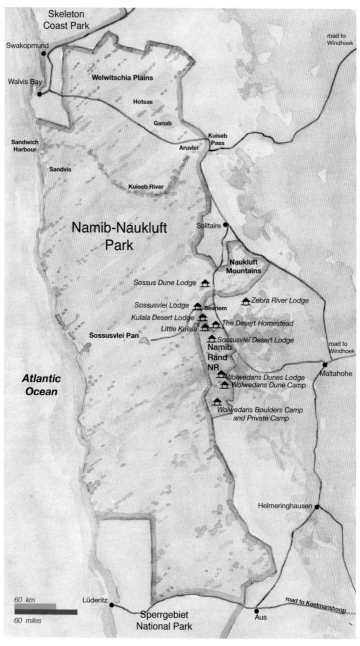

Skeleton
Coast Park

Swakopmund

road to
Windhoek

Walvis Bay

Welwitschia Plains

Hotsas

Ganab

Sandwich
Harbour

Aruvlei

Kuiseb
Pass

Sandvis

Kuiseb River

Namib-Naukluft
Park

Solitaire

Naukluft
Mountains

Sossus Dune Lodge

Zebra River Lodge

Sossusvlei Lodge
Kulala Desert Lodge
Little Kulala

Sesriem

The Desert Homestead

Sossusvlei Pan

Sossusvlei Desert Lodge

Namib
Rand
NR

road to
Windhoek

Atlantic
Ocean

Wolwedans Dunes Lodge
Wolwedans Dune Camp

Maltahohe

Wolwedans Boulders Camp
and Private Camp

Helmeringhausen

60 km

60 miles

Lüderitz

Sperrgebiet
National Park

Aus

road to Keetmanshoop

one of the largest in the world. Namib-Naukluft Park covers 19,215-square-miles (49,768-km²) of desert savannah grasslands, gypsum and quartz plains, granite mountains, an estuarine lagoon and wetlands, a canyon and huge, drifting apricot-colored dunes.

The Kuiseb River runs through the center of the park from east to west and acts as a natural boundary separating the northern grayish-white gravel plains from the southern deserts.

Herds of gemsbok (oryx), springbok, mountain zebra and flocks of ostrich roam the region.

Many small, fascinating creatures have uniquely adapted to this environment and help make this one of the most interesting deserts in the world. The dunes are home to numerous unique creatures, such as the translucent Palmato gecko, shovel-nosed lizard and Namib golden mole.

The 5 main regions of the park are the Namib, Sandwich Bay, Naukluft, Sesriem and Sossusvlei areas.

It is generally acknowledged that the **Namib** is the world's oldest desert. The Namib is known as the "living desert" because of the diversity of life existing

Ostrich descend the sand dunes of Sossusvlei

in seemingly inhospitable conditions. In this dry place, an intriguing array of desert-adapted animals and plants are nourished by condensation from the sea mists off the distant Atlantic Ocean.

The Welwitschia Flats is located on a dirt road about 22 miles (35 km) south of the Swakopmund-Windhoek Road and is one of the best areas to see

the prehistoric *Welwitschia mirabilis* plants. Actually classified as trees, many *welwitschia* are thousands of years old and are perfect examples of adaptation to an extremely hostile environment. The waterholes at Hotsas and Ganab are good locations to spot game; Ganab and Aruvlei are known for mountain zebra.

If you plan to deviate from the two main roads through the park, a permit is required and is obtainable weekdays only at the Environment and Tourism Office in Swakopmund, Windhoek or every day at Sesriem.

The **Sandvis** area includes **Sandwich Harbor**, 26 miles (42 km) south of Walvis Bay, and is acces-

The prehistoric *Welwitschia mirabilis* plants

sible only by 4wd vehicles. Fresh water seeps from under the dunes into the saltwater lagoon, resulting in a unique environment. Bird watching is excellent September through March. Only day trips are allowed to the harbor. Permits are required and may be obtained from the Ministry of Environment and Tourism in Swakopmund and Walvis Bay.

The **Naukluft** region is an important watershed that is characterized by dolomitic mountains over 6,445 feet (1,965 m) in height with massive picturesque rock formations and thickly foliated riverbeds. Large numbers of mountain zebra, along with springbok, kudu, klipspringer, rock hyrax, baboon and black eagles are frequently sighted. Also present are cheetah and leopard.

There are several hiking trails from which to choose. One of the more interesting trails is the Naukluft Trail, 10.5 miles (17 km) in length, requiring 6 to 7 hours of hiking. A 75-mile (120-km) trail, which takes 8 days, may also be hiked April to October, with prior permission.

Sesriem Canyon is about 0.6 mile (1 km) long and is as narrow as 6 feet (2 m), with walls about 100 feet (30 m) high. In some places the canyon takes on a cave or tunnel-like appearance.

Sossusvlei has the highest sand dunes in the world, exceeding 1,000 feet (300 m). The base of the second highest sand dune in the world (Big Daddy) can be closely approached by vehicle. If you can only visit the country for a few days and want to see the most impressive desert scenery, Sossusvlei is the place to visit!

The hike along the knife-edge rim to the top of "Big Daddy" is strenuous, requiring 60 to 90 minutes of taking 2 steps up and sliding 1 step down. The view from the top into other valleys and of the mountains beyond is marvelous. Even up there, colorful beetles, ants and other desert critters roam about.

Sunrise on these magnificent and colorful dunes is spectacular. On my last visit we enjoyed photographing gemsbok as they walked through the desert.

Sunset is also spectacular, and as most people visit the dunes in the morning, you will pretty well have the dunes to yourself if you visit at that time.

Balloon safaris offer unbelievable views at sunrise, and can be accessed from most lodges in the area.

Sossusvlei is located 55 miles from the Sesriem (Main) Entrance to the park. For those staying in accommodations outside of the reserve who must use the main gate entrance, please be aware that there could be a line of up to 100 cars to get into the reserve — delaying your entrance (and possibly missing sunrise on the dunes). Staying at properties that have private access to the reserve or at one within the park is highly recommended.

ACCOMMODATION — CLASS A+:
• **Little Kulala** has 11 thatch-and-canvas chalets or "Kulalas" (Oshiwambo word "to sleep") set on wooden platforms with private plunge pools. Guests may also sleep under the stars on the roof of their chalet — a private stargazing platform! Little Kulala and Kulala Desert Lodge are located on the scenic, 52,000-acre (21,000-hectare) Kulala Wilderness Reserve, which is on the boundary of the park. A private entrance gate provides quick access into the park. Activities include day visits to the Sossusvlei dunes, desert breakfasts under the camel-thorn acacia trees, visit to Sesriem Canyon,

Ballooning along the dunes of Namib-Naukluft National Park *(top)*, Little Kulala's bright and airy design *(middle and bottom)*

drives into the desert, ballooning, walking trails, horseback riding, quad biking and visits to the private reserve.

Kulala Desert Lodge

CLASS A/B: • **Kulala Desert Lodge**, situated on the Kulala Wilderness Reserve, has 16 stylish thatched and canvas "kulalas." A rooftop sleeping area allows guests to enjoy a night under the spectacular desert sky. All the activities offered by Little Kulala are also available at Kulala Desert Lodge.
• **Sossusvlei Desert Lodge** has 10 spacious air-conditioned stone-and-glass suites. Activities include guided nature walks, quad bike excursions, ballooning; scenic drives to Sossusvlei and the Sesriem Canyon are only possible with an additional night at the lodge. The lodge is too far from Sossusvlei to reach it at sunrise.

CLASS B: • **Sossus Dune Lodge** is located within the park, which enables guests to reach Sossusvlei before sunrise and stay after dark. The lodge is built to resemble an "afro-village" with canvas and thatch tents, each with private decks to enjoy the views.
• **The Desert Homestead** offers 20 chalets situated 20 miles (32 km) from Sesriem, and has horse riding facilities including overnight trails. • **Zebra River Lodge** is located in the Tsaris Mountains and has 13 rooms. Swimming, nature drives and hikes to 5 natural springs are offered on the farm.

CLASS C: • **Sossusvlei Lodge**, located at the gate to the Sesriem area and about 37 miles (60 km) from Sossusvlei, has 45 rooms and an adventure center.

Namib Rand Nature Reserve

The 463-square-mile (1,200-km²) Namib Rand Nature Reserve, situated in the pristine Namib Desert just east of Namib Naukluft Park, is the largest private

Wolwedans Boulders Camp features only 4 tented chalets

nature reserve in southern Africa. It is a world of wind-sculpted orange dunes and jagged mountains. There is plenty of opportunity here to experience true solitude in the desert, as the reserve is so huge compared to the number of guests hosted at any one time.

While this is not a game-rich area, you will find springbok, gemsbok, zebra, baboon, ostrich and more, which eke out their existence under the arid desert conditions. Across this diverse canvas of contrasting landscapes traverse an exciting variety of large and small desert creatures — as wild and ancient as their habitat, including bat eared fox, yellow mongoose, Rupell's korhaan.

CLASS A: • **Wolwedans Dunes Lodge** has 9 chalets with private balconies built on wooden platforms. • **Wolwedans Boulders Camp**, located 28 miles (45 km) from Wolwedans Dunes Lodge, is an intimate camp with just 4 guest tents, dining and lounge tent, deck and open fireplace. • **Private Camp** (an extension of Boulders Camp) is an idyllic retreat for honeymooners and those looking for privacy. • **Mountain View Suite** is walking distance from Dunes Lodge and features a spacious bedroom with king size bed, private shaded patio, lounge and dining area. The main verandah has a star gazing bed to sleep outside.

CLASS B: • **Wolwedans Dune Camp**, set on the 463-square-mile (1200-km²) Namib Rand Nature Reserve, has 6 tents. Activities include desert drives, game viewing and walking trails.

Swakopmund and Walvis Bay

The resort town of Swakopmund, located on the coast and surrounded by the Namib Desert, has many fine examples of German colonial architecture.

The coastal strip south of Swakopmund to Walvis Bay (a distance of about 20 mi./30 km) has the highest density of shorebirds in southern Africa and perhaps on the whole continent. In excess of 13,000 birds of more than 30 species feed on the nutrient-rich beaches. The majority are palearctic waders, including knot, Curlew sandpiper, turnstone and grey plover (present only between September and April). The threatened Damara tern and black oystercatcher may also be seen.

Walvis Bay plays an important role in Namibia's economy, with its international seaport and airport that are the entry points for many visitors who embark on one of the many desert adventures the country has to offer. Another fun adventure is **quad biking** into the dunes just outside of Swakopmund.

Some travelers base themselves at Swakopmund and take day trips to the many attractions in the area. Some of the more interesting excursions include a visit to **Walvis Bay Lagoon**, home to the greater and lesser flamingos, a visit to the **Moon Valley** and the **Swakop River Canyon**, home to the world's oldest living fossil plant — the

White pelican in Walvis Bay *(top)*, Popular seal cruise in Walvis Bay *(bottom)*

Welwitschia mirabilis — and the largest, man-made, offshore Guano Island, home to flocks of cormorants and Cape gulls, as well as pelicans. On the **Dolphin & Seal Cruise** you can enjoy champagne and oysters while having a very good chance of observing Heaviside and bottlenose dolphins as they swim alongside the boat, turtles, and the huge seal colony at Pelican Point. On my last two visits, a Cape fur seal jumped right into our boat!

The Tug is the best restaurant in town. Kucki's Pub and the Swakopmund Brauhaus also serve good food.

The best time to visit the coast for sunbathing, fishing and surfing is from December to February; June to July is cold with some rain.

A bungalow at The Stiltz

ACCOMMODATION — FIRST CLASS: • **Swakopmund Hotel & Entertainment Centre** has 90 rooms, a swimming pool, tennis courts and a gym. Guests have use of the Rossmund Golf Course, 1 of only 4 desert golf courses in the world. • **The Hansa Hotel** is an attractive hotel with 58 rooms. • **The Sams Giardino House**, situated with a view of the dunes of the Namib Desert and within walking distance of the city center, has 9 rooms and a wine cellar. • **The Stiltz** is set on the Swakop riverbed overlooking the sand dunes and bird rich lagoon at the river mouth. There are 10 very comfortable wooden bungalows, all of which are built on stilts and interlinked by wooden walkways to the main dining bungalow. A luxury villa, sleeping 6, is available for families.

TOURIST CLASS: • The **Villa Margarita Guesthouse** has 7 rooms and is decorated with some pretty funky art. • **Hotel Schweizerhaus** has 24 rooms (some with sea views). Café Anton, part of the same premises, is famed for its pastries, cakes and refreshments.

Cape Cross Seal Reserve

Cape Cross Seal Reserve, home to the largest breeding seal colony in the southern hemisphere (approximately 200,000 seals), is open daily from 9:00 a.m. to 5:00 p.m.

ACCOMMODATION — CLASS B: • **Cape Cross Lodge**, located 75 miles (120 km) north of Swakopmund, has 30 rooms with superb views of the ocean, and a restaurant and wine cellar.

Skeleton Coast Park

Skeletons of shipwrecks and whales may be seen on the treacherous coast of this park, which stretches along the seashore and covers over 2,000-square-miles (5,000-km²) of wind-sculpted dunes, canyons and jagged peaks of the Namib. This coastal stretch is without doubt inhospitable in the extreme. The San (Bushmen) who once lived in the area dubbed it "The land God made in anger!"

The freezing Benguela Current of the Atlantic flows from Antarctica northward along the Namibian coastline and meets the hot, dry air of the Namib Desert, forming a thick fog bank that often penetrates inland for more than 20 miles (32 km) almost every

The Skeleton Coast

day and often lingers until the desert sun burns it off between 9:00 and 10:00 a.m. It is this very fog that brings life and sustenance to every living thing in the Namib. Yet when there is the occasional easterly wind instead of fog, there is sunshine.

The park is divided into southern and northern sections. The **southern section** is more accessible and lies between the Ugab and Hoanib Rivers. Permits and reservations (paid in advance) must be made with Namibia Wildlife Resorts (NWR) for stays at either Torra Bay or Terrace Bay.

Ancient shipwrecks scatter the coastline

This Cape Frio Seal Colony has an estimated 40,000 seals

The **northern part** of the park has been designated as wilderness area and can be visited only with fly-in safaris.

The northern region has many unusual and fascinating attractions. One such attraction is the **Cape Frio Seal Colony**, which has grown to about 40,000 individuals.

A walk down the **roaring dunes** will give you the surprise of your life. Suddenly, everyone is looking up to spot the B-52 bomber that must be overhead. Apparently, the sand is just the right diameter and consistency to create a loud noise when millions of its granules slide down the steep dune. Incredible!

Driving through **Hoarusib Canyon**, you will witness striking contrasts of dark-green grasses against verdite canyon walls and near-vertical white dunes.

Big game is present in surprisingly large numbers for a desert environment and includes desert elephant, cheetah, leopard and baboon. Brown hyena are plentiful but rarely seen. Black-backed jackal, springbok and gemsbok are often sighted. The big news is that lion, after decades of absence, have returned to the Skeleton Coast! They have been seen on the beaches, and will, like the hyena and jackal, hunt seals.

Birds may be sparse, but are interesting. Small flocks of Gray's lark forage off the gravel plains, while Ludwig's bustard, tractrac chat and bokmakierie are among the species likely to be seen near camps and on walks.

The east wind brings detritus (small bits of plant matter) providing much-needed compost for plants and food for lizards and beetles. The west wind brings the moisture on which most life depends in this desert — one that is almost completely devoid of water. The ancient "fossil" plant, *Welwitschia mirabilis,* is also found in the region.

The park supports some of the most harsh yet tranquil, inhospitable yet fragile environments in the world. Every participant in this unique ecosystem was carefully and cleverly designed for its role, be it the fog-gathering lichens or the water-independent gemsbok.

A visit to the Skeleton Coast may include seeing the Himba

The nomadic and very tribal Himba people, bedecked in ritualistic jewelry and ochre skins, may be visited on the outskirts of the park. Also visit the Cape Frio Seal Colony where 40,000 lumps of fur and fat lie basking on the beach, the "Clay Castles" and an amethyst mine.

The Skeleton Coast is at its finest from January through March, however, this is an excellent reserve to visit any time of the year.

ACCOMMODATION NEAR THE SKELETON COAST — CLASS A: • **Hoanib Skeleton Coast Camp,** located next to the wildlife-rich Hoanib River, is a new camp with 8 standard tents and 1 family tent. Activities include game drives, trips into the Skeleton Coast Park, and escorted walks. Game in this area includes elephant, giraffe, lion, zebra, oryx and springbok.

CLASS A/B: • **Okahirongo Elephant Lodge** has 7 luxury chalets (including a 2-bedroom Presidential suite) with large bathrooms complete with tub, indoor-outdoor showers and private gazebo.

CLASS C: • **Kuidas Camp, Purros Camp** and **Kunene Camp** accommodate guests in basic igloo huts with chemical toilets and separate bucket showers. Guests normally fly from camp to camp and go on walks and nature drives from the camps.

Damaraland

Damaraland is a large region with many attractions and is located east of Skeleton Coast National Park and southwest of Etosha National Park. This is an arid, mountainous region of spectacularly rugged scenery. Damara herders can be seen throughout this region.

The **Brandberg** is a massive mountain covering an area of 19-by-14 miles (23-by-30 km) and rises 6,500 feet (1,980 m) above the surrounding plains to 8,440 feet (2,573 m) above sea level. Its special attraction is that it harbors thousands of rock paintings, including one of the most famous in the region — "**The White Lady.**"

Twyfelfontein was declared a UNESCO World Heritage Site in June 2007. The geology of the area consists of great Etjo sandstone formations rising from the Huab River valley, providing the "canvases" for the age-old art found there. Twyfelfontein or /Ui-//aes ("place among packed stones") boasts one of the

Damaraland

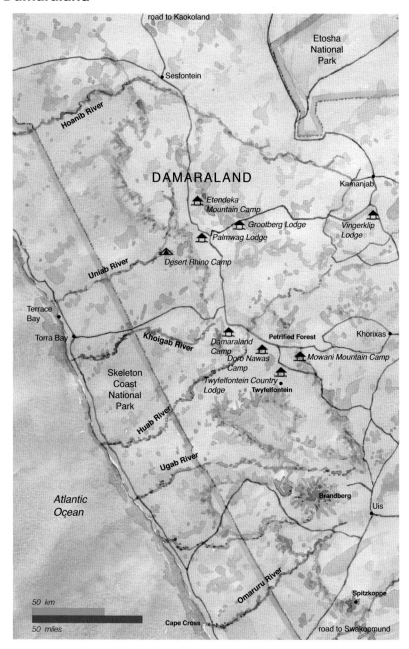

Giraffe and lion are depicted in ancient rock engravings at Twyfeltontein

largest concentrations of rock petroglyphs (engravings) on the African continent. Most of these well-preserved engravings represent rhinoceros, elephant,
ostrich and giraffe, as well as drawings of human and animal footprints. The
site also includes 6 painted rock shelters with motifs of human figures in red
ochre. Twyfelfontein forms an extensive and high-quality record of ritual practices relating to hunter-gatherer communities (the San Bushmen) in this part of
southern Africa over the last 2,000 or more years. The Petrified Forest has many
broken, petrified tree trunks up to about 100 feet (30 m) in length. *Welwitschia*
plants may also be seen here.

Burnt Mountain, a colorful mountain composed of many shades of purple
and red, glows as if on fire when it is struck by the rays of the setting sun.

The **Spitzkoppe**, known also as "The Matterhorn of Namibia," peaks at
5,853 feet (1,784 m) above sea level. These huge granite peaks stand out starkly
against the surrounding gravel plains and provide some serious, high-quality
rock climbing.

Vingerklip (Finger Rock), a massive limestone monolith, spearing 115 feet
(35 m) into the sky, is the last remnant of a plateau formed 15 million years ago.

Wildlife is sparse, however, desert elephant are often seen. Other wildlife
that has adapted to a near-waterless environment includes desert black rhino,
lion, oryx, Hartman's mountain zebra (smaller body with bigger ears than the

Desert black rhino in Damaraland

common zebra), black-backed jackal, and a subspecies of southern giraffe that does not drink water at all. Wildlife migrates east and west along the dry river-beds in search of food and water.

Among the interesting birds of the region are Ludwig's bustard, Ruppell's korhaan and rosy-faced lovebird.

Damaraland is interesting to visit year-round, with the best time to see big game being April through December.

Damaraland Camp's lounge area

ACCOMMODATION — CLASS A:
• **Damaraland Camp**, a luxury 20-bed tented camp with a pool, is situated in the Huab River valley where desert-adapted elephants are often seen and desert rhino may also be seen. Activities consist of guided walks and nature drives in open vehicles. Visits to Twyfelfontein are offered to guests staying three or more nights. • **Mowani Mountain Camp** has 12 luxury tented suites each with private wooden decks, and 1 suite with private butler, dining and lounge area. Activities include guided nature drives and visits to Twyfelfontein.

CLASS A/B: • **Desert Rhino Camp** has eight canvas tents elevated on wood decking with private verandahs. The lounge and dining tent have uninterrupted views of desert and mountains. Primary activity is rhino tracking by vehicle or foot. The rhino tracking runs in conjunction with the "Save the Rhino Trust," which gives guests an opportunity to see conservation in action and to raise funds for the endangered black rhino.• **Doro Nawas Camp** is a 16-room lodge built on a rugged, rocky knoll in the middle of a plain adjacent to the Aba-Huab River. Activities revolve around game and bird viewing and visits to Twyfelfontein (offered daily). The camp is well placed to search for desert elephant.

CLASS B: • **Palmwag Lodge** offers 3 types of accommodations. The lodge has 2- and 4-bed thatched bungalows and the camp has 8 large Meru-style tents. A campsite is also available. Activities include hiking and guided tours into their massive 1,737-square-mile (4,500-km²) private reserve that has one of the largest populations of black rhino in Africa. • **Vingerklip Lodge** has 22 comfortable bungalows, each with a view across the valley, and a swimming pool. • **Grootberg Lodge** was completely funded by the European Union (EU) and donated to the local community of the #Khoadi //Hoas Conservancy. Grootberg has 12 rooms and is located on the very edge of the Grootberg Plateau with

Doros Nawas has epic views from every tent *(top)*, Visitors have a chance to see desert elephant *(bottom)*

stunning views overlooking the Klip River valley. Activities here include guided scenic walks and drives, elephant and rhino tracking and horse trails.

CLASS C: • **Etendeka Mountain Camp** is a tented camp (20 beds) with open air bathrooms with bucket showers. Exploring the region by open 4wd vehicle and walks is offered. • **Twyfelfontein Country Lodge**, which is the nearest accommodation to the World Heritage Site, has 56 rooms, restaurant and bar area plus a swimming pool.

Kaokoland

This region of rugged mountain ranges interspersed with wide valleys is north of Damaraland and bordered on the west by Skeleton Coast National Park. Wildlife is sparse but includes elephant, giraffe, gemsbok, ostrich, some black rhino and lion. Himba tribes may be seen in the region. Kaokoland, or the

Kaokoland

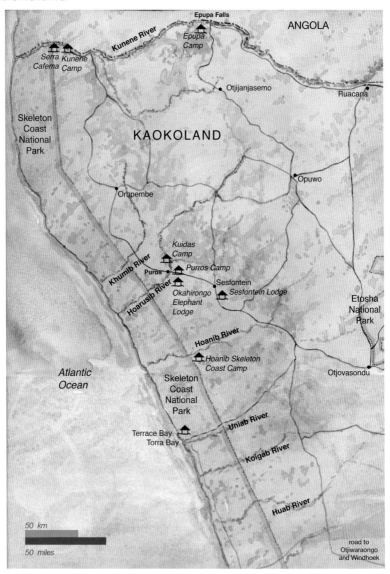

Kaokoveld as it is sometimes known, is generally acknowledged as being one of the last true wilderness areas remaining on Earth.

If you wish to visit a Himba village, it is customary to wait a distance from the village until someone comes and invites you in. If you come across a village that is deserted, please do not take anything that you may find lying around. Due to their nomadic lifestyle, the Himba often leave possessions behind because they know they will return.

The best time to visit is May to December. A minimum of 2 fully self-contained 4wd vehicles per party is required, and a professional guide is highly recommended. There is no fuel in the western region. You will in most instances need to be totally self-sufficient; please respect this extremely fragile area, carry out all that you take in, leaving just footprints behind!

ACCOMMODATION — CLASS A+: • **Serra Cafema**, one of the most remote camps in all of southern Africa, is located on the Kunene River in an area of incredible beauty. The camp offers 8 spacious canvas-and-thatch chalets. Activities include walks, nature drives, boating and visits to local Himba tribes. Access is by air charter.

CLASS B: • **Sesfontein Lodge**, located between Skeleton Coast Park and Etosha National Park, is an old fort with rooms and suites arranged around a swimming pool and central oasis-garden.

CLASS C: • **Epupa Camp** is located on the Kunene River near Epupa Falls and opposite the Angolan border. There are 9 safari-style tents.

Kaokoland's dramatic scenery *(top)*, Activities at Serra Cafema include boating on the Kunene River *(middle)*, Thatched chalets at Serra Cafema *(bottom)*

Etosha National Park

Etosha — the "great white place" or "place of emptiness" — is one of Africa's greatest parks in both size and variety of wildlife species. The park covers 8,569-square-miles (22,200-km²) in the northern part of the country and lies 3,280 to 4,920 feet (1,000 to 1,500 m) above sea level.

Although still ranking as one of the biggest game reserves in Africa, it originally was several times larger and, in fact, the largest reserve in the world.

The park's vegetation is mainly mixed scrub, mopane savannah and dry woodland that surround the huge Etosha (Salt) Pan. The pan is a silvery white, shallow depression, dry except during the rainy season. Mirages and dust devils play across what was once a lake fed by a river that long ago changed course.

Apart from evaporation, water present in the pan from time to time will also seep through to the impermeable clay floor of the area, thus producing plentiful springs, particularly in the southern parts of the pan. The water here might have twice the salinity of seawater. Along the edge of the pan are springs that attract wildlife during the dry winter season.

The eastern areas of the park experience the most rainfall and have denser bush than the northwestern region, which is mainly open grasslands. About 40 waterholes spread out along 500 miles (800 km) of roads provide many vantage points from which to watch game. The rainy season here coincides with the summer months and visitors should bear in mind that, after any good rainfall that might occur in the period between November and April, animals will no longer have the need to visit the waterholes along the tourist road network, so game viewing in these months might prove to be less rewarding.

Surrounded by antelope and zebra, an elephant cools off in an Etosha waterhole

Etosha

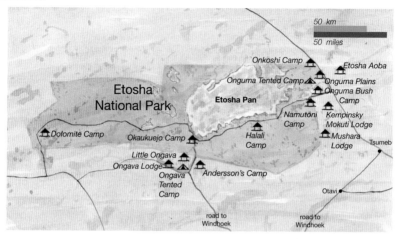

Etosha is famous for its huge elephant population, which is most visible July to September in the center of the park. Large numbers of elephant may also be seen in May, June and October. When the rains begin in January, some elephant herds migrate north to Angola and west to Kaokoland and begin returning in March. Large populations of zebra, blue wildebeest, springbok and gemsbok migrate westward from the Namutoni area in October and November to the west and northwest of Okaukuejo Camp, where they stay until around March to May. From June to August they migrate eastward again, past Okaukuejo and Halali Camps, to the Namutoni plains where there is water year-round. The calving season (which attracts predators) for a number of antelope species is November through April. The park is totally fenced, although this does not always stop the elephant from going where they please.

Lion are commonly seen, and zebra are often sighted way out on the barren pan where lions have no cover from which to launch an attack. Black-faced impala and Damara dikdik, one of Africa's smallest antelopes, are two distinctive species of this area. Black rhino occur throughout the park, with the best viewing opportunities at Okaukuejo. Leopard are seen fairly often.

A real attraction to photographers is that it is, in fact, common to see from five to eight or more mammal species at a waterhole at the same time.

Bird life is prolific, and 340 species have been recorded. The main pan is of importance as a regional breeding site for lesser and greater flamingos, as well as white pelicans. Over one million flamingos may gather to breed in the saline shallows of the salt pan, when conditions are suitable, but tourists are not given access to the breeding colonies of these sensitive birds. Birds of prey are particularly well-represented, with martial eagle, black-breasted snake eagle, bateleur, pale chanting goshawk, pygmy falcon and red-necked falcon among the most arresting. Other frequently seen species are red-billed teal, Namaqua sandgrouse, Burchell's sandgrouse, kori bustard, purple roller and crimson-breasted shrike.

Roads run along the eastern, southern and western borders of the Etosha Pan. The area around Namutoni Camp, in the eastern part of the park, receives more rain than the other regions of the park. Eland, kudu and Damara dikdik are often seen in the area. A good spot to see elephant is at Olifantsbad, a waterhole between Halali and Okaukuejo Camps.

From Okaukuejo you can drive along the southwestern edge of the pan to Okondeka and west to the Haunted Forest, a dense concentration of eerie-looking African moringa trees. Etosha is a 5-hour drive on good, paved roads or a 1-hour charter flight from Windhoek.

Travel on all roads inside the National Park is restricted to the hours between sunrise and sunset, all resort gates being closed and locked outside these times. During the year sunrise occurs between 6:00 and 7:00, and sunset between 5:30 and 7:30 in the evening, depending on the season.

ACCOMMODATION — CLASS A+: see "Ongava Game Reserve" below.

CLASS A: • **Onguma Plains** is situated on the 50,000-acre (20,000-hectare) Onguma Private Nature Reserve near von Lindequist Gate (eastern side of the park). The lodge has 11 air-conditioned mini-suites and 1 maxi-suite each with a music system, mini-bar, telephone and computer/Internet facilities, an outside shower and wooden verandahs. • **Onguma Tented Camp** overlooks a floodlit waterhole and has 7 tents with both an indoor and outdoor shower. Unfortunately no children under the age of 12 are permitted.

CLASS A/B: • **Mushara Lodge**, located on the eastern boundary of Etosha, has 10 chalets, 1 family unit and 2 single rooms, all with air-conditioning, mini-bar and telephones. • **Andersson's Camp** is situated only 2.8 miles (4.5 km) from Andersson's Gate at the southern entrance into Etosha. The resurrected former farmstead has 20 tented units on raised decks for enhanced views of the waterhole.• **Kempinski Mokuti Lodge**, located 550 yards (500 m) from the von Lindequist Gate, has 106 air-conditioned thatched bungalows, a swimming pool and an airstrip.

CLASS B: • **Onguma Bush Camp** is a rustic camp with 6 air-conditioned bunga-lows, and 1 family room. The camp is most used by self-drive tourists and families. • **Onkoshi Camp** features 15 chalets with raised decks, thatched roofs, retractable doors and panoramic views over the Etosha pan. Activities include morning and afternoon game drives and star gazing. Between activities guests enjoy the swim-ming pool, bar and restaurant. • **Dolomite Camp** is located in western Etosha near the Dolomietpunt waterhole. The camp has 20 chalets with western views (ideal for sunsets). There is a dining room, bar, swimming pool and laundry facilities. Guided game drives are offered.

CLASS C: • **Etosha Aoba** accommodates up to 18 guests in thatched cottages and is located 7 miles (12 km) from the von Lindequist Gate.

CLASS B, B/C & C: There are 3 **National Park camps**, all operated by Namibia Wildlife Resorts (NWR), a para statal and the only company allowed to build and operate tour-ist establishments in Etosha. These are situated at Namutoni, Halali and Okaukuejo respectively. The 3 camps have lodge accommodations, trailer (caravan) and camping sites, swimming pool, floodlit waterhole, restaurant, store, petrol station and landing strip. The camps are fenced for the visitors' protection. • **Namutoni Camp**, situated 7 miles (11 km) from the eastern von Lindequist Gate, features an attractive fortress built in 1904 and converted into a restaurant, with a viewing platform on the upper ramparts. • **Halali Camp** lies halfway between Namutoni and Okaukuejo Camps at the foot of a dolomite hill. • **Okaukuejo Camp**, situated 11 miles (18 km) from the Andersson Gate entrance, has some delightful chalets, especially those closest to the waterhole.

Ongava Game Reserve

Ongava Game Reserve is a 115-square-mile (300-km²) private reserve along the southern boundary of Etosha near Andersson Gate. The reserve is the top privately-owned rhino breeding area in the country, currently with 10 black and 19 white rhino, along with high concentrations of a variety of game.

Night game drives and walks, which are not allowed in Etosha, are allowed on the reserve. Guests staying on the reserve usually take morning game drives in Etosha and take afternoon game drives or walks and night game drives in the reserve. Birdwatching is good. Some of the key Namibian "specials" to be seen here include Hartlaub's francolin, white-tailed shrike, Monteiro's hornbill and bare-cheeked babbler.

ACCOMMODATION — CLASS A+: • **Little Ongava** offers 3 spacious luxury suites each with its own plunge pool, a "sala," an additional outdoor shower and a view of the waterhole in front of the lodge. Guests at Little Ongava share a dedicated guide and 4wd vehicle ensuring the optimum nature experience.

CLASS A: • **Ongava Tented Camp** has 9 large tents and a private waterhole. Both Ongava Lodge and Ongava Tented Camp offer day and night game drives and walks on the reserve and day game drives in open-sided vehicles into Etosha. • **Ongava Lodge** has 14 luxury

Viewing rhino on a game drive *(top)*, Little Ongava's suites include plunge pools *(middle)*, Ongava Tented Camp *(bottom)*

air-conditioned rock-and-thatch chalets. The camp overlooks a flood-lit waterhole and has a swimming pool and a hide.

Bushmanland

Tsumkwe, the unofficial capital of Bushmanland and home to the Bushmen (San) people, borders Botswana and is situated south of Khaudom and east of Grootfontein.

A bushman prepares to hunt

The Ju/'hoansi people were the last independent hunters and gatherers in southern Africa, planting no crops and domesticating no animals until 1920. The 2000 or so Ju/'hoansi are now permanently settled in approximately 30 villages where they continue to hunt and gather within n!oresi — areas of 115 to 230 square miles (300 to 600 km²) where different bands have rights to the natural resources. They also keep cattle and earn income through tourism and by selling traditional crafts. They speak the central of three dialects of !Kung — the language spoken by the northern Bushmen.

The Nyae Nyae Conservancy was formed in 1998 and gives the Ju/'hoansi the right to benefit from wildlife and tourism activities in the area. A 4wd vehicle is required to explore the area.

ACCOMMODATION — CLASS B/C: • **Tsumkwe Lodge** can accommodate up to 12 people in 6 thatched rooms. From here, the Nyae Nyae (Bushman) area and the Khaudum Game Reserve 30 miles (50 km) to the north can be explored. • Guests at **Nhoma Camp**, located 50 miles (80 km) west of Tsumkwe, are introduced to the cultures and traditions of the Ju/'hoansi San. The Ju/'hoansi show guests how they gather food and introduce them to many of their customs and beliefs. You see the San just as they really exist in their traditional villages. Access to the camp is by road and air charter.

Waterberg Plateau Park

Situated south of Etosha National Park and east of the town of Otjiwarongo, this 156-square-mile (400-km²) park is the home of several scarce and endangered species, including black rhino, white rhino, roan antelope and sable antelope. Other species include brown hyena, eland, tsessebe, kudu, gemsbok, giraffe, impala, klipspringer and dikdik. Leopard are sometimes seen on the top of the plateau.

This is a prime area for seeing many of Namibia's near-endemic bird species, and a Mecca for birdwatchers from across the world. Hartlaub's francolin, Ruppell's parrot, white-tailed shrike, Monteiro's hornbill, rockrunner, bare-cheeked babbler and Bradfield's swift are all resident.

Waterberg Plateau Park also contains unique flora, along with rock paintings and engravings. Three trails lead up to the top of the sandstone plateau, which rises over 820 feet (300 m) above the surrounding plains, and one runs across the top. Walking on the plateau is restricted to organized, guided walking trails.

ACCOMMODATION — CLASS B: • **The Waterberg Camp**, operated by NWR, accommodates guests in comfortable premier bush chalets, and 2- and 4-bed bush chalets and double rooms, all nestled along the base of the Waterberg Plateau cliffs. There is a swimming pool, and a restaurant and bar in the restored Rasthaus, built in 1908. • **Mount Etjo Safari Lodge** has comfortably furnished rooms. The main lodge area overlooks a waterhole.

ACCOMMODATION NEAR WATERBERG — CLASS A/B: • **Okonjima Lodge** is family-run and located on a private game reserve and has 10 comfortable rooms. The farm is the home of the AfriCat Foundation, which is committed to the long-term conservation of large carnivores, particularly cheetah and leopard. Their **Bush Camp** has 8 luxury, thatched African-style chalets, while the **Bush Suite** (CLASS A) privately caters for 4. All 3 lodges have their own pools. Activities include walks and watching orphaned wild animals, adopted by the family, roam freely about the farm. • **African Wilderness Trails** is a farmstead with 5 rooms, swimming pool and sauna. Game drives, hikes, and trips to the Waterberg Plateau Park and The Cheetah Conservation Fund project are offered.

CLASS B: • **Waterberg Guest Farm** is a 103,784-acre (42,000-hectare) estate with 4 double guest rooms and 2 luxury bush bungalows, a pool and a floodlit waterhole.

THE SOUTH

Lüderitz

Lüderitz is a small town and harbor on Namibia's southern coastline and is where the Namibian diamond rush began in 1908.

Halifax Island, Mercury Island, Ichaboe Island and the Possession Islands support 95% of the Namibian population of African penguins, the country's entire population of Cape Gannets and 80% of the world's bank cormorants and 25% of the world's crowned cormorants. Consider taking a boat trip to Halifax Island to see African penguins, as well as Heaviside dolphin, cape fur seals and a variety of bird life.

Sand has swallowed a building in Kolmanskop

Lüderitz Yacht Club, located on the scenic harbor, is open to the public, and is a great place to meet locals. Restaurants in Lüderitz rightly boast about serving some of the best oysters in the world, as well as fabulous lobster and fish.

From Lüderitz you may take a guided tour to the picturesque ghost town of **Kolmanskop** — abandoned between 1938 and 1956. The town was slowly covered in sand, with the sand drifts around the houses and in the rooms making unusual photographic subjects. Kolmanskop is in fact high on the list for many professional and semi-professional photographers. The museum is very interesting as well.

A population of 150 to 200 desert-dwelling **feral horses** live west of Aus. They are smaller than conventional horses and can go without water for several days at a time.

Quickest access to Lüderitz is by scheduled flights from Windhoek and from Cape Town.

Kolmanskop looks like a ghost town *(top)*, Lüderitz Nest Hotel *(bottom)*

ACCOMMODATIONS — TOURIST CLASS: • **Lüderitz Nest Hotel** has 73 ocean view rooms with a children's playground, restaurant and a pool.

Sperrgebiet National Park

The Sperrgebiet, Namibia's newest national park (proclaimed in 2008), covers over 10,000-square miles (26,000-km²) and extends from south of Lüderitz to the Orange River bordering South Africa. This is a restricted diamond mining area controlled by De Beers, who is in the process of relinquishing control of the region.

The old **Elizabeth Bay** mine is another ghost town located in the **Sperrgebiet National Park**, south of Lüderitz. Large seal colonies may be seen in Elizabeth Bay as it hosts 40% of the worlds cape fur seals. Further south into the Sperrgebiet is the **Bogenfels**, the largest coastal rock arch in Southern Africa, at 180 feet (55 m) in height. The ghost town of **Pomona** has the highest average wind speeds in southern Africa.

Entry to the park is only allowed with Ministry of Environment and Tourism concessionaires.

ACCOMMODATIONS: see "Lüderitz."

Ai-Ais/Richtersveld Transfrontier Park

In the south, August 2003 saw Namibia's Ai-Ais Hot Springs Resort and Fish River Canyon areas combine with South Africa's Richtersveld area to become the Ai-Ais / Richtersveld Transfrontier Park.

Second in size only to the Grand Canyon, **Fish River Canyon** is 100 miles (161 km) in length, up to 17 miles (27 km) in width and up to 1,800 feet (550 m) deep. The Fish River cuts its way through the canyon to the Orange River, which empties into the Atlantic Ocean.

The vegetation and wildlife are very interesting. Many red aloes make the area appear like you might imagine the planet Mars. Baboons, mountain zebra, rock hyrax, ground squirrel and klipspringer are often seen, while kudu and leopard remain elusive. The river water is cold and deep enough to swim in some areas.

There is a well-marked path into the canyon in the north of the park where the 4-day hike begins. The main hiking trail is 53 miles (86 km) in length; due to possibly extreme summer temperatures and the risk of flash flooding, the hike is only open from the beginning of May until mid-September. It is also only recommended for those who are extremely fit, and you must have a doctor's certificate of fitness in order to obtain your permit. Advance bookings are necessary, and there must be a minimum of 3 per group. The going is tough because much of the walking is on the sandy, rock-strewn floor of the canyon. No facilities whatsoever exist en route, so this hike is not for the tenderfoot. Water is readily available (but do take purification tablets) from the many pools that join up to become a river during the rainy summers, but you must carry your own food supplies. Hot sulphur springs are located at Palm Springs, about halfway along the trail. The hike does represent a challenge to participants, but also a wonderful experience in the most remote nature imaginable.

ACCOMMODATION — CLASS A/B: • **Gondwana Canon Lodge,** located just 12 miles (20 km) from the main Canyon viewpoint at Hobas, has 28 thatched bungalows, blending beautifully into their surroundings of massive granite boulders.

CLASS B: • **Vogelstrausskluft Lodge** is situated on the western rim of the Canyon, and offers 4 luxury suites as well as 20 twin rooms.

CLASS C: • **Canon Roadhouse** offers 9 rooms, swimming pool and filling station. • **The Ai-Ais Hot Springs Resort**, operated by NWR, is located at the southern end of the canyon at the end of the hiking trail and boasts a large thermally-heated swimming pool and mineral baths.

South Africa

South Africa

At the southern end of the continent, South Africa is an extremely diverse country with temperate highlands, subtropical savannah, alpine-like mountains, semi-desert and unique Mediterranean-like shrub lands known as "fynbos." Much of the country is a high plateau averaging some 4,800 feet (1,500 m) above sea level, with the Drakensberg rising to 11,400 feet (3,450 m). The country is flanked by the cool Atlantic and warm Indian Oceans, each of which has a strong bearing on the climate. South Africa is the most industrialized nation on the continent but still has large protected areas including the famous Kruger National Park and surrounding areas which occupy most of the lowveld. Covering some 471,445-square-miles (1.2 million-km²), South Africa is twice the size of Texas. English is the official language, with Zulu, Tswana, Xhosa, Sotho and Afrikaans all widely spoken. The population is estimated at around 45 million. Pretoria and Cape Town are the capital cities but Johannesburg is the business hub. Currency is the Rand (ZAR).

South Africa
Country Highlights

- Visit one or more lodges in the Sabi Sand, Timbavati or Thornybush Private Game Reserves (near Kruger) that South Africa is so famous for. You'll have the opportunity to possibly see the "Big Five" on your first game drive! Bring a good camera and get ready for epic leopard shots!
- Spend time in Cape Town, one of the world's most beautiful cities.
- Travel up the Garden Route, stopping in charming towns like Plettenberg Bay, as well as up South Africa's diverse coast for whale watching and perhaps for a glimpse at a great white shark.
- Take a five-star trip back in history and travel in style aboard the Blue Train or Rovos Rail.
- Experience the finest wines and cuisine available on the continent.

When's the Best Time to Go for Game Viewing

■ Excellent   ■ Good   □ Fair   ■ Poor   ■ Closed

Country	Park/Reserve	JAN	FEB	MAR	APR	MAY	JUN	JUL	AUG	SEP	OCT	NOV	DEC
South Africa	Kruger N.P.												
	Pvt. Reserves near and within Kruger												
	Kwandwe/Shamwari												
	Phinda												

Best Safari Experience

Singita Lebombo Lodge, Singita Sweni Lodge (Kruger area), Singita Boulders Lodge, Singita Ebony Lodge, MalaMala Main Camp, MalaMala Sable Camp, MalaMala Rattray's, Tanda Tula, Cheetah Plains (Sabi Sand); The Motse and Tarkuni (Tswalu); Grootbos Garden and Grootbos Forest Lodges (Grootbos); Phinda Vlei and Phinda Forest (Phinda Game Reserve)

SOUTH AFRICA

South Africa is commonly promoted as "The Rainbow Nation" and "A World In One Country" and with two oceans, subtropical savannah, arid scrub-land, deserts, and the impressive Drakensberg Mountains, this is hard to deny. This large country is rich in natural beauty and wildlife diversity and covers about 4% of the continent's land surface. The southwestern corner (Cape Town and surroundings) is climatically and botanically unique. The country consists of a high-altitude central plateau surrounded by a rim of mountains, which are particularly impressive in the KwaZulu-Natal Drakensberg. Think of an inverted soup bowl, and you will have a rough idea of the country's landscape.

The plateau is temperate in climate, and it is there that most people live and where agriculture is most developed. In the south, the coastal plain is very narrow or non-existent, with cliffs often plunging directly into the sea. In the east, the lowlands are more extensive, most notably in the warm lowveld with the Kruger National Park and its rich wildlife. The country's largest river is the Orange, which rises in Lesotho and meanders some 1,400 miles (2,200 km) west to spill out into the Atlantic Ocean. A number of large rivers drain to the east into the Indian Ocean, predominantly the Limpopo, Olifants, Sabie, Komati, Umfolozi, Tugela and Kei.

There are three distinct climatic zones within South Africa. The entire central plateau and eastern parts (including the lowveld) experience summer rainfall (October to March). It is warm to hot (depending upon altitude) in summer and cool to warm during winter (May to August). Nights can be cold, even at lower altitudes, in mid-winter. The southwestern corner, including Cape Town, experiences dry, warm summers and cool, wet winters — a Mediterranean climate not unlike California or southern France. The region east of the southwestern Cape, extending along the coast to East London, experiences rainfall throughout the year, but is prone to drought conditions.

Seventy percent of the population belongs to four ethnic groups: Zulu (the largest), Xhosa, Tswana and Bapedi. Fifteen percent of the population is white, of which 60% is Afrikaner. English and Afrikaans are spoken throughout the country.

In 1488 Portuguese navigator Bartholomew Dias discovered the Cape of Good Hope. The first Dutch settlers arrived in 1652 and the first British settlers in 1820. To escape British rule, Boer (which means farmer) Voortrekkers (forward marchers) moved from Cape Town to the north and east, establishing the independent Republic of the Transvaal and Orange Free State.

Two very big economic breakthroughs were the discovery of diamonds in 1869 and, even more importantly, the discovery of gold in Transvaal shortly thereafter. Conflict between the British and Boers resulted in two separate Anglo-Boer Wars beginning in 1899 and the ultimate British victory in 1902.

In 1910 the Union of South Africa was formed and remained a member of the British Commonwealth until May 31, 1961, when the Republic of South Africa was formed outside the British Commonwealth. On April 27, 1994, a national election open to all races was held and was won by the African National Congress (ANC) under the charismatic leadership of Nelson Mandela.

🐾 WILDLIFE AND WILDLIFE AREAS

In line with its numerous distinct geographic, altitudinal and climatic zones, South Africa supports a great diversity of wildlife and plants. In fact, well over 10% of all the world's plants and flowers occur in South Africa. Virtually all of Africa's great land mammals are to be found (mostly in the eastern lowlands), as well as whales, dolphins and other marine species in the surrounding oceans. In many places, large mammals have been reintroduced to locations where they were once hunted to extinction, with the white rhinoceros being perhaps the biggest success story.

Birdlife is outstanding throughout the country, with some 600 breeding species and close to 800 overall, including Eurasian migrants and seabirds. A good number of bird species are endemic (restricted) to South Africa, particularly in the Karoo, highveld grasslands and Cape fynbos regions, making this a highly popular destination among international birdwatchers.

Reptiles, frogs and other life forms are equally well represented. The Cape fynbos region is home to an astonishing 8,500 plant species and is considered to be one of the world's eight Floristic Regions. The plants in this winter rainfall area are characterized by relatively small leaves and include many varieties of erica and protea. The Karoo is a semi-arid scrubland, but it is a botanist's dream because of its astonishing number of hardy and succulent plants. The

A big tusker in the Sabi Sand Game Reserve

The mesmerizing gaze of a leopard in the Sabi Sand Game Reserve

much-celebrated Namaqualand region is renowned for its springtime (late August to early September) displays of colorful flowers. True forests are sparse in South Africa, with only small patches on the southern coast near Knysna and Transkei, and along the Northern KwaZulu-Natal coast and in the eastern escarpment. Acacia, combretum and mopane dominate the sub-tropical lowlands, with taller evergreen trees along rivers and watercourses.

South Africa has a good network of protected areas, with over 700 publicly owned reserves (including 19 national parks), which cover about 6% of the land surface. In addition to that, there are about 200 private game and wildlife reserves. The Kruger National Park is the largest park, and together with the second largest (Kgalagadi Transfrontier Park), accounts for about 40% of the total protected area. The great majority of the other parks and sanctuaries are quite small.

In recent years, South Africa has been the primary catalyst for a number of proposed Transfrontier Conservation Areas (TFCAs), which link protected areas across national boundaries and form "corridors" to link separated parks. The idea is to have multi-use areas, which incorporate the needs of local people while safeguarding the natural resources over a larger area. The first of these areas to be formally promulgated was the Kgalagadi National Park. Other TFCAs are in various stages of negotiation and development in Mozambique, Swaziland, Namibia and Zimbabwe.

The Kruger and other national parks are frankly not well suited to international visitors with limited vacation time. They are ideally suited to self-drive visitors on tight budgets with lots of time, and are most popular with South African holiday-makers and larger coach-tour (40+ tourists) groups. Open vehicles are generally not allowed, although a few local companies are now allowed open sided and canvas-roofed vehicles. Visitors are required to stick to a designated road and track network.

Accommodation is mostly at large rest camps, although there are some smaller bush camps. Most campsites have ablution blocks (communal bathrooms) with hot and cold water, and many sites even have laundry facilities. Generally speaking, the major roads in the parks are tarred and the minor roads are constructed of good quality gravel, allowing for comfortable riding — and mass tourism.

In contrast, a number of **private reserves** offer premier accommodation, superb food, day and night game drives in open vehicles and escorted walks. Leopard, lion and other animals have become accustomed to game viewing vehicles at many of these comparatively small reserves, and local guides often know the territories or whereabouts of particular animals, which ensures more predictable and intimate encounters. Trained guides and trackers interpret the wildlife and ecosystem for guests. In a move toward partial privatization, the Kruger has allocated sites within the park for experienced operators to set up and manage more exclusive camps and lodges.

GAUTENG

Johannesburg

Johannesburg began as a mining town when the largest deposits of gold in the world were discovered in the Witwatersrand in 1886. Since the Middle Ages, one-third of the gold mined in the world has come from the Witwatersrand field.

This "City of Gold," locally known as "Egoli," is now the country's largest commercial center and city and the country's main gateway for overseas visitors. The city itself has a population of approximately 2 million, while the total urban area including **Soweto** (South Western Townships) has a population of approximately 4 million.

The **Apartheid Museum** is a museum complex dedicated to illustrating Apartheid and the twentieth century history of South Africa. Other atractions include the **Museum Africa**, the **Gold Mine Museum** and **Gold Reef City**, a reconstruction of Johannesburg at the turn of the century, "**Cradle of Mankind**" anthropological excursions, and the **De Wildt Cheetah Centre**.

ACCOMMODATION — DELUXE: • **The Saxon Boutique Hotel, Villas and Spa**, located in the Sandhurst suburb of Sandton, makes a world-class statement of ethnic African elegance. Set in 6 acres (2.5 hectares) of lush landscaped gardens, there are 24 luxurious suites overlooking the gardens. For those looking in the ultimate retreat, there

An Egoli Suite at the Saxon Hotel *(top)*, Intercontinental Johannesburg Airport Sun *(middle)*, African Rock *(bottom)*

are 3 new villas each with its own terrace and plunge pool. • **The Michelangelo**, located on Nelson Mandela Square has 242 rooms, restaurant and lounge, a heated swimming pool, steam bath, fitness center, business center and direct access to one of South Africa's best malls. • **The Westcliff Hotel**, set on a hilltop overlooking the city and zoo, has 115 rooms and suites, a business center, spa facility and a swimming pool. Some of the suites have private swimming pools. • **Davinci Hotel & Suites**, adjacent to Nelson Mandela Square, features 220 rooms, an infinity pool, health spa, gym, restaurant and bar. • **InterContinental Johannesburg Airport Sun** is located right across from arrivals and departures at the airport, and it features a restaurant, bar, fitness center and indoor pool. • **InterContinental Sandton Sun & Towers** is located adjacent to one of the country's finest shopping malls. The hotel has 231 air-conditioned rooms, a health club, swimming pool and five restaurants. • **Palazzo-Montecasino**, located in the heart of the Montecasino entertainment complex in the northern suburb of Fourways, has 246 rooms, several restaurants, bars and a gym.

FIRST CLASS: • **African Rock**, located in a quiet suburb near the airport, has 9 rooms with air-conditioning, mini-bar and satellite television. There is a garden, swimming pool, lounge, bar and dining area. • **The Fairlawns Boutique Hotel & Spa**, located in the suburbs, consists of 19 suites and offers a fully equipped gym, Balinese spa, restaurant and a bar. • **Athol Place**, a boutique hotel in northern Johannesburg, features 10 luxury air-conditioned suites. There is a library with fireplace, large outdoor pool, patio area and the lounge. Complimentary pre-dinner drinks and canapés are served daily. • **D'Oreale Grand Hotel**, located a 5-minute drive from Johannesburg International Airport, has 196 air-conditioned rooms in palatial-style buildings, with a health spa, tennis courts, swimming pool, bars and restaurants. • **Southern Sun O.R. Tambo International Airport** has 366 air-conditioned rooms, a popular restaurant, wine bar and swimming pool.

TOURIST CLASS: • **Metcourt Laurel** has 80 air-conditioned rooms. Guests may use the facilities at The Emperor Mondior • **City Lodge O.R. Tambo International Airport** have simple rooms. • **The Airport Grand**, just three miles from the international airport has 149 air-conditioned rooms, restaurant, bar and guest swimming pool.

Pretoria

Pretoria is an attractive city and the administrative capital of South Africa. Points of interest include **Paul Kruger's house**, **Voortrekker Monument**, **Natural History (Transvaal) Museum**, **Union Buildings**, the **State Opera House** and **Church Square**.

ACCOMMODATION — DELUXE: • **131 Herbert Baker Boutique Hotel** features 7 luxury rooms with private balconies and air-conditioning. An elegant restaurant serves full breakfasts and dinner. • **Kievits Kroon Country Estate**, located 10 minutes north of Pretoria, is a Cape-Dutch themed hotel with 142 rooms, 2 restaurants, swimming pool and conference facilities. The Wellness Centre has a heated pool, jacuzzis, sauna, steam bath, gym and health bar. • **Sheraton Pretoria Hotel & Towers**, set opposite the Union Buildings in Pretoria, has 175 rooms and suites. There is a restaurant, lounge and bar on site. • **Illyria House** is a privately owned residence in an exclusive suburb of Pretoria with 6 luxurious suites. The hotel is 5 minutes from the train station (ideal for Rovos Rail or Blue Train trips).

FIRST CLASS: • **Rozenhof Guest House** is an elegant property in a suburb of Pretoria. It features 7 luxury bedrooms, all individually decorated. There is a lounge with fireplace, dining room, swimming pool and verandah. • **Court Classique**, located in Arcadia (Pretoria), has rooms ranging from studios to 2-bedroom suites with kitchenettes.

TOURIST CLASS: • **Southern Sun Pretoria** has 242 rooms and suites, a restaurant and swimming pool.

The Blue Train

The world-renowned luxurious Blue Train offers an experience that has all but disappeared in modern times. The train is promoted as "A Five-Star Hotel on Wheels," and that it is.

Two Blue Trains were built in South Africa and put into service in 1972. The suites have individual air-conditioning controls, television, radio and en suite bathrooms with shower or bathtub. The luxury compartments are only about 3 feet (1 m) wider than the deluxe cabins and also contain CD and video players. A staff of 34 is onboard to take care of guests.

The lounge on the Blue Train

Five-star meals (two sittings for lunch and dinner) are served in the beautifully appointed dining car, which features exquisite table settings. Dress for lunch is "smart casual," and for dinner a jacket and tie are required for men and elegant dress for ladies.

The train runs overnight from Cape Town to Pretoria on average 3 times a week, and vice versa, year-round, and periodically there are special routings (such as Pretoria to Durban). Book well in advance because reservations are often difficult to obtain.

Rovos Rail

Rovos Rail has 5 restored luxury steam trains, each with 20 coaches accommodating up to 72 passengers, 2 dining cars and an observation car. Please note that the journeys are not all "steam-hauled." Every effort is made to use steam for at least a portion of the trip, usually arriving or departing Pretoria. The Deluxe Suites have en suite showers, while the Royal Suites have en suite showers and Victorian baths. Royal Suites are about 50% larger than Deluxe Suites. Rovos Rail recently introduced Pullman Suites to its range of accommodations. These are significantly smaller than the Deluxe Suites, however, they are a lot more affordable. Jacket and tie are required for men and elegant dress for ladies at dinner.

Rovos Rail scenic trip from Pretoria to Cape Town

You have the choice of a 2-night trip from Pretoria to Cape Town with a sightseeing stop in the old mining town of Kimberley and in the quaint village of Matjiesfontein; a 2-night trip from Pretoria to see Victoria Falls; a 2-night trip from Pretoria via Ladysmith (game drive in Nambiti Private Game Reserve), escorted tour of the Zulu battlefields and ending in Durban; an annual 8-night safari from Pretoria to Kimberley, Upington, Sossusvlei, Etosha and Swakopmund (Namibia); and a once-a-year, 13-night safari from Cape Town to Dar es Salaam (Tanzania), and vice versa. Another annual favorite is the 8-night African

A deluxe suite on Rovos Rail

Collage linking some of South Africa's scenic highlights between Pretoria and Cape Town including Kruger National Park, Swaziland, Durban, the Drakensberg Mountains and the lovely Garden Route.

MPUMALANGA AND LIMPOPO PROVINCES

Kruger and The Private Reserves

The most popular area in the country for wildlife safaris for international visitors is the private reserves that lie along Kruger National Park's western border.

There is a tremendous difference in the variety and quality of experience between visiting Kruger National Park and staying in the National Park rest camps versus visiting the adjacent private reserves. In Kruger, which has over 900,000 tourists each year, only closed vehicles are allowed, and off-road driving is not allowed. Park rangers in open park vehicles conduct night game drives, but driving after dark in private vehicles is not allowed. Facilities are fair but too basic for most international travelers.

In the adjacent private reserves, day and night game viewing is conducted in open vehicles, walking is allowed and facilities are excellent. In other words, visitors have a greater opportunity to experience the bush in the private reserves than in Kruger. A safari to Kruger National Park using national park camps is considerably less expensive than a safari of the same length in the private reserves, however, you generally see much less game — and the game you encounter could be hundreds of yards (meters) from the road.

The best game viewing in Kruger National Park is May to October, during the sunny, dry winter season, when the grass has been grazed down and the deciduous plants have lost their leaves. Game viewing in the private reserves is actually good year-round, because the guides are in radio contact with other vehicles (they can direct each other to the best sightings) and can drive off-road in search of game. Calving season is in early summer (November and December) for most game species.

Winter days (June to August) are usually warm, with an average maximum temperature of 73°F (23°C) and clear skies. Late afternoons are cool, while temperatures at night and in the early morning sometimes drop below freezing. The rainy season is from November to March, with December, January and February receiving the heaviest downpours. Temperatures from October to February sometimes rise to over 100°F (38°C). March and April are cooler as the rains begin to diminish.

The best time to look for over 450 bird species in this region is October to March — just the opposite of the best game viewing periods. However, bird watching is good year-round because less than half the bird population is composed of seasonal migrants.

To get to the area from Johannesburg, many people take about an hour's flight to Mpumalanga, Hoedspruit, or an air charter directly to their camp. Alternatively, the drive from Johannesburg to Kruger (Skukuza) is about 310 miles (500 km) northeast on good, tarred roads and takes 5 to 6 hours.

Kruger National Park

Kruger is the largest South African park and has more species of wildlife than any other game sanctuary in Africa — 130 species of mammals, 114 species of reptiles, 48 species of fish, 33 species of amphibians and 468 species of birds.

The park is home to large populations of elephant (over 8,000), buffalo (over 25,000), Burchell's zebra (over 25,000), greater kudu, giraffe, impala, white rhino, black rhino, hippopotamus, lion, leopard, cheetah, wild dog and spotted hyena, among others.

Kruger's 7,523-square-miles (19,485-km²) make it nearly the size of the state of Massachusetts. The park is 55 miles (88 km) wide at its widest point and 220 miles (355 km) long. The fences separating the park and the Timbavati and Sabi Sand Reserves were taken down years ago, effectively increasing the size of the conservation area by 15% and allowing the wildlife greater freedom of movement. However, the annual winter migration routes of antelope, zebra and various other species in search of water and better grazing are still cut off by fences. Several hundred windmills and artificial waterholes have been constructed to provide the water that is so desperately needed in the dry season.

The park can be divided into three major regions: northern, central/south-eastern and southwestern. Altitude varies from 650 feet (200 m) in the east to 2,950 feet (900 m) at Pretoriuskop in the southwest.

The northern region from the Letaba River to the Limpopo River is the driest. Mopane trees dominate the landscape, with the unique baobab (upside-down) trees becoming increasingly numerous toward Pafuri and the Limpopo River. From Letaba to Punda Maria is the best region for spotting elephant, tsessebe and sable and roan antelope. Elephant prefer this area since it

Kruger National Park

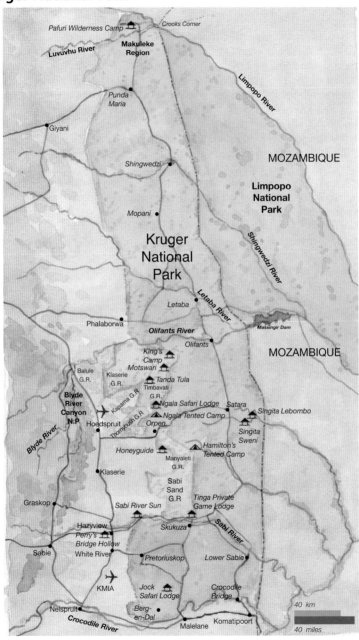

is less developed than the other regions, making it easier to congregate away from roads and traffic, and mopane trees (their preferred source of food) are prevalent.

The central/southeastern region is situated south of Letaba to Orpen Gate and also includes the eastern part of the park from Satara southward, covering Nwanedzi, Lower Sabie and Crocodile Bridge. Grassy plains and scattered knobthorn, leadwood, and marula trees dominate the landscape. Lion inhabit most areas of the park but are most prevalent in this region, where there is also an abundance of zebra and wildebeest — their favorite prey. Cheetah and black-backed jackal are best spotted on the plains. Wild dogs are mainly scattered through flatter areas, with possibly a better chance of finding them in the Letaba-Malopene River area, Skukuza, and northwest of Malelane.

The southwestern part of the park, including a wide strip along the western boundary from Skukuza to Orpen Gate, is more densely forested with thorny thickets, knobthorn, marula and red bush-willow. This is the most difficult region in which to spot game — especially during the rainy season. Many of the park's 600 white rhino prefer this area.

Black rhino are scattered throughout the southern and central areas, often feeding on low-lying acacia trees. Although common, mostly nocturnal leopard

Open-vehicle game drives bring you close to the action

are rarely seen. Buffalo roam throughout the park, while hippos prefer to inhabit the deeper parts of Kruger's many rivers by day.

Among the most conspicuous of Kruger's birds are the raptors. Commonly encountered throughout the year are the tawny eagle, bateleur, brown snake eagle and martial eagle, while the migratory Wahlberg's eagle is present in large numbers between September and March. A hundred or more white-backed vultures commonly show up at carcasses of large mammals, with lappet-faced, white-headed and hooded vultures in smaller numbers. Even without a prior interest in birds, you'll soon become captivated by the abundant lilac-breasted rollers, yellow-billed hornbills, greater blue-eared starlings, long-tailed shrikes and fork-tailed drongos. Several species of francolin can be seen crossing roads, particularly in the late afternoon, and red-billed oxpecker are always found pecking ticks from the coats of antelope, rhino and giraffe. In the wet season, carmine bee-eater, woodland kingfisher and European roller are conspicuous roadside birds. Some of the best bird watching is in the rest camps and picnic spots where you have a chance to walk around and listen. When out on the roads, it is advisable to switch off the vehicle motor on a regular basis to just listen and wait — you'll soon be rewarded with sightings of a variety of birds.

A juvenile lion pauses for a drink

During the South African school holidays and long weekends, the number of day visitors to the park is limited and accommodations are almost impossible to obtain. Be sure to reserve in advance.

ACCOMMODATION IN PRIVATE CONCESSION AREAS WITHIN KRUGER NATIONAL PARK — CLASS A+: • Singita Lebombo Lodge and Singita Sweni Lodge are located on a 37,500-acre (15,000-hectare) private concession area within Kruger National Park. Both camps offer day and night game drives and escorted walks. • **Singita Lebombo**, overlooking the confluence of the Nwanetsi and Sweni Rivers, has 15 luxurious air-conditioned suites with private plunge pools, a heath spa, gym and main swimming pool. • **Singita Sweni Lodge**, the smallest of the Singita lodges, has 6 luxurious suites

The pool at Singita Lebombo overlooks the treetops *(top)*, Pafuri Wilderness Camp's open-air lounge *(bottom)*

built on stilts and tucked away among the trees. Each suite features floor-to-ceiling glass walls, private viewing decks and open-air living area along the Sweni River. • **Tinga Private Game Lodge**, located on the banks of the Sabie River, features 2 luxury lodges, Narina and Legends. Each has 9 suites with private deck and plunge pool. Activities include game drives, bush walks and birdwatching.

CLASS A/B: • **Ngala Lodge** has 20 air-conditioned thatched cottages with separate lounge and shaded decks. There is a swimming pool. Day and night game drives, walks, and three-day walking safaris are offered in a luxury mobile tented camp. • **Ngala Tented Safari Camp** has 6 spacious tents set on wooden platforms overlooking the seasonal Timbavati River. There is an infinity swimming pool. • **Pafuri Wilderness Camp** lies within the 61,776-acre (24,000-hectare) Makuleke Concession in northern Kruger National Park where the borders of South Africa, Zimbabwe and Mozambique meet. The camp is located on the northern bank of the Luvuvhu River shaded by large ebony trees and consists of 20 East African style Meru tents — 6 of which can be used as family units. • **Pafuri Wilderness Trails** accommodates a maximum of 8 guests in thatch-and-canvas tents raised on low platforms. The focus is on walking trails led by an armed guide and tracker. • **Jock Safari Lodge**, located on a private concession area within the southern part of Kruger, has 15 luxury suites with private salas (outdoor lounges) and a swimming pool. Day and night game drives are conducted. • **Hamilton's Tented Camp** offers 6 "Out of Africa" styled canvas tents complete with teak floors and private decks. The main lodge is connected by raised walkways. Game drives, guided walks and Nomadic African spa treatments are offered.

ACCOMMODATION NEAR KRUGER NATIONAL PARK — CLASS B: • **Perry's Bridge Hollow Boutique Hotel** is only minutes from Kruger National Park and accessible to the Panorama Route. There are 30 air-conditioned rooms and family suites. • **Sabi River Sun**, located next to the Sabie River, offers 60 rooms, a restaurant and a variety of activities such as fishing, mountain biking, 18-hole golf course and 5 swimming pools.

Private Reserves adjacent to Kruger

A number of privately owned wildlife reserves are found along the western border of Kruger. Associations of ranchers have fenced the western boundary of their reserves but have not placed fences between their individual properties, allowing game to roam throughout the reserves and Kruger National Park. The private reserves, in general, have exceptionally high standards of accommodation, food and service.

Sabi Sand Game Reserve

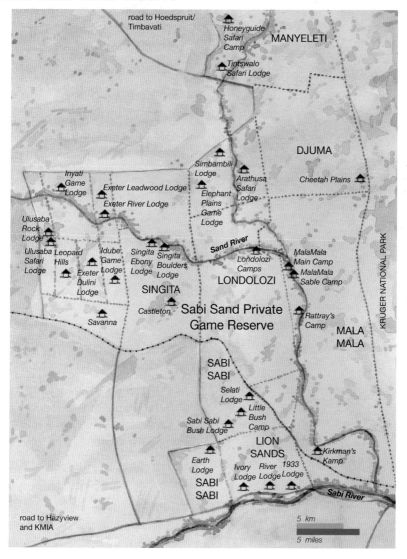

A rhino mother and calve add to the thrill of Big Five game viewing

A very important advantage private reserves have over national parks is that private reserves use open vehicles, which give not only a better view but also a much better feel of the bush. At most reserves, a game tracker sits on the hood or the back of each vehicle. Drivers are in radio contact with each other, greatly increasing the chances of finding those species that guests want to see most.

Singita Private Game Reserve

Vehicles may leave the road to pursue game through the bush. Night drives, which are only allowed in national park vehicles in Kruger, provide an opportunity to spot nocturnal animals rarely seen during the day. Walking safaris with an armed tracker are available at some camps and lodges.

Over the years I have had the privilege of staying at virtually all of the lodges in this region, and I am happy to report that the great majority of them consistently offer good food, service and accommodations that range from comfortable to opulent.

ACCOMMODATION — SABI SAND PRIVATE GAME RESERVE: Sabi Sand Private Game Reserve is situated about a 5-hour drive or 1-hour by scheduled air service from Johannesburg. There is also scheduled air service from nearby Kruger Mpumalanga International Airport located about 87 miles (140 km) from the reserve. All the lodges have airstrips for scheduled and private air charters. Lodges in the reserve include Singita (Boulders and Ebony camps), MalaMala (MalaMala Main Camp, Rattray's and Sable camps), Londolozi (Granite, Tree, Pioneer, Founders and Varty), Ulusaba (Rock and Safari Lodge), Cheetah Plains, Sabi Sabi (Earth, Bush, Selati and Little Bush Camp), Simbambili, Exeter, Inyati and Idube reserves. All of the camps offer day and night game drives, and most offer walks.

CLASS A+: Singita has been rated by *Condé Nast Traveler Magazine* and *Travel & Leisure* as one of the top lodges in the world for many years. • **Singita Boulders Lodge** has 12 air-conditioned suites built around the rocks and feature sheer glass walls, fireplace, wrap-around views, private deck and plunge pool. • **Singita Ebony Lodge** features 12 air-conditioned suites, (including 2 family suites) decorated with colonial-inspired furnishings, fireplace, deck, private plunge pool and indoor-outdoor showers. The 2 Ebony Lewis Suites (Class A) offer the same luxurious Singita experience at a lower rate. Boulders and Ebony share a gym and spa center. • **Singita Castleton Camp** is an exclusive villa accommodating 12 guests with a private chef, guide and staff. Activities include game drives, mountain biking, archery and visits to a local village. • **Rattray's on MalaMala** offers 8 comfortable suites, each overlooking the Sand River, with private heated plunge pools and secluded verandahs. The camp offers a maximum of 4 guests per safari vehicle. • **Lion Sands Ivory Lodge** has 6 luxurious air-conditioned, thatched suites with private plunge pools and decks, gym and health spa, and 2 hides.

CLASS A: • **MalaMala Sable Camp**, adjacent to MalaMala Main Camp, caters to up to 14 guests in 7 luxurious suites. The camp has a swimming pool, boma, cozy bar, and lounge/dining room. The viewing deck provides a magnificent view over the Sand River. This camp may be reserved exclusively for a private party or individual guests. • **MalaMala Main Camp** is a luxurious camp with 18 air-conditioned, spacious thatched rondavels (each with separate "his" and "hers" bathrooms) and a swimming pool. Families with children are welcome. • **Ulusaba Rock Lodge** has 10 air-conditioned suites situated on top of an 800-foot (244 m) hilly outcrop, each with a private deck overlooking the savannah below. The lodge has a swimming pool surrounded by a natural waterfall, two tennis courts and a masseuse.

• **Earth Lodge** (Sabi Sabi Reserve) has 13 air-conditioned suites, including a presidential suite, each with their own plunge pools and patios. The lodge has a wine cellar, health spa, library and swimming pool. • **Londolozi Private Granite Suites** features 3 suites suspended over the Sand River. The suites share a private swimming pool, ranger and game viewing vehicle. • **Londolozi Tree Camp** has 6 suites each with its own plunge pool and a private sala. The camp has a boma, swimming pool and lounge deck. • **Londolozi Pioneer Camp** has 3 suites with private plunge pools. The suites are decorated to reflect the 1920s.

MalaMala Main Camp's inviting lounge area

Singita Boulders Lodge *(top)* and Singita Ebony Lodge *(bottom)* offers the ultimate in luxury. A suite at Lion Sands Ivory Lodge *(middle, left)*, Rattrays on the world famous MalaMala Game Reserve *(middle, right)*

CLASS A/B: • **Cheetah Plains** offers 8 comfortable air-conditioned thatched-roof rondavels, a pool, bar and viewing deck, which overlooks the waterhole. • **Arathusa Safari Lodge**, located in the northern region of the reserve, has 10 thatched luxury suites with indoor-outdoor showers, mini-bar and tea/coffee making facilities. • **Elephant Plains Game Lodge** is family owned and run and features six luxury suites with outdoor shower and private viewing deck. Visits to a local village can be arranged. • **Simbambili Lodge**, located in the northern part of the reserve, has 8 air-conditioned, thatched chalets with private plunge pools and salas. • **Sabi Sabi Bush Lodge** overlooks a waterhole and has 25 air-conditioned thatched suites, including a spacious presidential suite, and a swimming pool. • **Selati Lodge** (Sabi Sabi) has 8 air-conditioned chalets (including a presidential suite with private vehicle/guide). The thatched lounge and swimming pool overlook the bushveld. • **Little Bush Camp** (Sabi Sabi) offers 6 air-conditioned suites with indoor-outdoor showers, private viewing decks and thatched roof. • **Leopard Hills**, located in the western part of Sabi Sand, is built on a hill overlooking a waterhole and has 8 air-conditioned suites with private plunge pools and swimming pool. • **Ulusaba Safari Lodge**, situated on the banks of the Mabrak River,

A canopied bed at Cheetah Plains

has 10 luxurious "tree" chalets. A spa treatment center and tennis courts are shared with guests from Ulusaba Rock Lodge. • **Savanna** overlooks a series of 4 waterholes and offers seven fully air-conditioned tented suites with private decks. Several of the suites have private plunge pools. • **Exeter** features 3 lodges, (Leadwood Lodge, River Lodge and Dulini Lodge), each offering elegant air-conditioned suites set on the banks of the Sand River with private plunge pools and decks. • **Kirkman's Kamp** overlooks the Sand River and has 18 air-conditioned rooms with private terraces and a swimming pool. • **Lion Sands River Lodge** is located in the southern part of the reserve with 6 miles (10 km) of river frontage on the Sabi River. The lodge has 18 air-conditioned, thatched rooms, gym and heath spa, swimming pool, sala and 4 hides. • **Idube Game Lodge** has 10 air-conditioned chalets and a swimming pool. • **Inyati Game Lodge** has 10 thatched chalets (doubles) with expansive decks and a swimming pool. • **Londolozi Varty Camp** is comprised of 8 chalets and 2 superior suites (Class A) that are all air-conditioned. Children and families are welcome. • **Londolozi Founders Camp** is a family-friendly camp and offers 10 chalets (3 superior and 7 standard chalets).

ACCOMMODATION — MANYELETI GAME RESERVE: Guests fly to Hoedspruit or by charter aircraft directly to their respective camps. CLASS A/B: • **Tintswalo Safari Lodge**, located along the seasonal Nwaswitsontso River, features 7 suites. There is a Clarins Spa with a variety of treatments offered. Activities include game drives, bush walks and lectures. • **Honeyguide Safari Camp** consists of 2 camps, Mantobeni and Khoya Moya, each consisting of 12 tents and caters to a maximum of 48 guests. Daily walking trails and night game drives are offered.

Timbavati, Manyeleti, Thornybush and Kapama Game Reserves

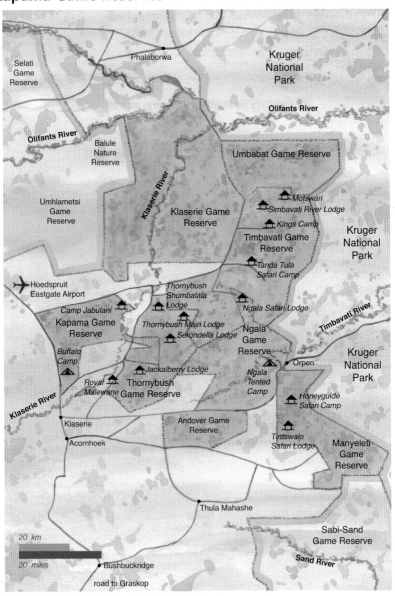

Selati Game Reserve

Phalaborwa

Kruger National Park

Olifants River

Olifants River

Balule Nature Reserve

Umbabat Game Reserve

Klaserie River

Umhlametsi Game Reserve

Klaserie Game Reserve

Motswari
Simbavati River Lodge

Kings Camp

Timbavati Game Reserve

Kruger National Park

Tanda Tula Safari Camp

Hoedspruit Eastgate Airport

Thornybush Shumbalala Lodge

Camp Jabulani

Kapama Game Reserve

Thornybush Main Lodge
Serondella Lodge

Ngala Safari Lodge

Timbavati River

Ngala Game Reserve

Kruger National Park

Buffalo Camp

Jackalberry Lodge

Royal Malewane
Thornybush Game Reserve

Ngala Tented Camp

Orpen

Honeyguide Safari Camp

Klaserie River

Klaserie

Acornhoek

Andover Game Reserve

Tintswalo Safari Lodge

Manyeleti Game Reserve

Thula Mahashe

Sabi-Sand Game Reserve

20 km

20 miles

Bushbuckridge

Sand River

road to Graskop

246

ACCOMMODATION — TIMBAVATI GAME RESERVE: Guests of the camps listed below fly to Hoedspruit or by charter aircraft directly to their respective camps. Day and night game drives and walks are offered. CLASS A/B: • **Motswari** has 15 air-conditioned rondavels with private decking and views of the bush. The camp has 2 bars, a swimming pool and open-air boma. • **Simbavati River Lodge** consists of 8 luxury and three 2-bedroom thatched chalets (ideal for families).

ACCOMMODATION — THORNYBUSH GAME RESERVE — CLASS A: • **Tanda Tula Safari Camp** features 12 tents with private deck, comfortable

Tanda Tula's deck is the perfect place to watch the sunset

loungers, Victorian bathtub and outdoor shower. There is a large lounge, bar and infinity pool overlooking a waterhole. Dinner is served in the open air boma. In addition to morning and night game drives and guided walks, spending the night on the "star beds" can be arranged. • **Kings Camp** has 11 thatched colonial suites each with air-conditioning, romantic Victorian bathtubs, indoor-outdoor showers, mini-bars, and a swimming pool. • **Royal Malewane**, situated near Hoedspruit and adjacent to the Kruger National Park, has 6 luxurious suites, plus the Royal Suite and the Malewane Suite (Class A+) — each accommodating 4 guests in 2 bedrooms with private vehicle, chef, butler and guide. **Africa House** (Class A) is Royal Malewane's exclusive family-friendly bush villa for 12 people with all the private amenities of a vehicle, guide and chef.

CLASS A/B: • **Thornybush Main Lodge**, located in the Thornybush Game Reserve adjacent to Kruger, has 20 glass-fronted air-conditioned suites including two family units with decks overlooking a waterhole, and a swimming pool. • **Thornybush Shumbalala Lodge** is an intimate camp with 5 suites including a 2-bedroom Presidential suite. Walks are offered for the more adventurous.

CLASS B: • **Serondella Lodge** is an 8-bed camp offering delightful thatched suites overlooking a waterhole. • **Jackalberry Lodge** is a rustic 10-bedded camp and offers views of the Drakensberg Mountains. Morning and night game drives as well as walking safaris are offered.

ACCOMMODATION — KAPAMA GAME RESERVE — CLASS A: • **Camp Jabulani** is located near Hoedspruit in the Limpopo Province, and is only 25 miles (40 km) from the Kruger National Park. The camp has just 6 secluded rondavel suites, each with a private splash pool, fireplace, air-conditioning, indoor-outside shower. Activities include day and night elephant-back safaris, morning and evening game drives, bush walks, bird

A decadent suite at Camp Jabulani

Highlights of your stay at Camp Jabulani are the elephant-back safaris

watching and a visit to the Hoedspruit Endangered Species Center where they have a facility for cheetah conservation.

CLASS A/B: • **Buffalo Camp** accommodates guests in 8 canvas tents built on raised wooden decks. Walkways connect the tents to the main lounge where the thatched bar, dining room, pool and campfire are located.

Blyde River Canyon, Pilgrim's Rest and Bourke's Luck Potholes

West of the Kruger National Park, the landscape rises abruptly in altitude. This dramatic escarpment, which separates lowveld from highveld, is formed by the imposing Drakensberg range. The best way to appreciate this area is by driving from Hoedspruit, up and through the Strydom Tunnel, to Graskop and then south to the town of Sabie. The Blyde River Canyon is an area of great scenic beauty, with the impressive red sandstone gorge rising half a mile (1 km) above the river below. Three isolated rock pinnacles, each capped with vegetation, have the appearance of traditional African huts and are known as the **Three Rondavels**. This is a good lookout point for birds such as Alpine swift, jackal buzzard and red-winged starling.

South of the Three Rondavels lookout are the astonishing **Bourke's Luck Potholes**. There, the sandstone bedrock has been carved out at the confluence of the Treur and Blyde Rivers, to form a series of whirlpool-eroded potholes. Nearby, a number of beautiful waterfalls occur during the summer rainy season, and there are numerous lookout points and short walking trails. For the fit and enthusiastic, there are back-packing trails into the **Blyde River Canyon** itself.

The little village of **Graskop**, frequently covered in mist, is famous for its crafts and coffee shops. The grasslands fringing the village are home to a few surviving pairs of South Africa's rarest bird — the blue swallow. To the west of Graskop is the picturesque village of **Pilgrim's Rest**, a living museum. This was the site of major alluvial gold panning and digging between 1873 and 1876. Some of the original buildings remain standing, while many others have been meticulously restored. There is certainly great Old World charm about the tin-and-wood buildings— now shops, bars or guesthouses. Explore the unusual and quaint shops, take a drive in a horse-drawn carriage through the village, play golf, fish for trout or go horseback riding. The small village nature reserve supports a number of oribi and birds, such as bush blackcap and chorister robin.

South of Pilgrim's Rest is the town of **Sabie**, the center of the region's timber industry. This is the gateway to the winding **Long Tom Pass** — a smooth tarmac road meandering through highland meadows to the trout fishing havens of **Lydenburg** and **Dullstroom**. The modern road is set upon a wagon route that was charted in 1871, which allowed access to the lowveld and Indian Ocean for the isolated Boer Republic. The name of the pass is derived from a large field gun used by the Boers in a skirmish with the British in 1900.

ACCOMMODATION IN THE REGION — DELUXE: • **Cybele Forest Lodge** (White River) is a lovely lodge with luxuriously appointed rooms and cottages and a swimming pool. This forested area is great for walks, horseback riding, and trout fishing. The Spa in the Forest offers a range of health and beauty treatments. • **Highgrove House** is a renovated colonial farmstead featuring 8 decorated garden suites. Each includes overhead fans, open fireplaces and secluded verandahs with views of the forest or valley and avocado orchards. To maintain an atmosphere of fine dining, dress code for dinner is smart.

Cybele Forest Lodge

FIRST CLASS: • **Kings Walden Garden Manor** (Tzaneen) has 6 rooms each with fireplace and king bed. The swimming pool and expansive lawn have views of the Drakensberg Mountains. • **Oliver's Restaurant and Lodge**, located on the White River Country Estate, has 12 luxury rooms and your stay there includes entrance to the White River Country Club.

TOURIST CLASS: • **Rissington Inn** is an affordable country lodge in the heart of the lowveld.

ACCOMMODATION BETWEEN THE REGION AND JOHANNESBURG — DELUXE: • **Mount Anderson Ranch** is an exclusive 20,000-acre (8,000-hectare) property with 3 rooms in a large ranch house. Trout fishing, horseback riding, nature drives and walks are offered. The lodge is booked out to one private party at a time. • **Walkersons Country Manor** resembles a Scottish highland estate because it is surrounded by lakes and rivers. The suites have log fireplaces and mountain walks and trout fishing are the main attraction. • **Critchley Hackle** is a rustic stone-built complex.

NORTH WEST PROVINCE

Pilanesberg Nature Reserve

This beautiful reserve was opened in 1979 and covers 212-square-miles (550-km²). It is located within a 17-mile- (27-km) wide volcanic bowl that rises over the surrounding plains, and it offers good game viewing in a beautiful, hilly setting. Both white and black rhino are fairly common; elephant, eland, red hartebeest and sable antelope are frequently seen. Lion, cheetah and leopard occur in reasonable numbers, and the elusive brown hyena occurs alongside its more gregarious relative, the spotted hyena. Close to 400 species of birds have been recorded, with crimson-breasted shrike, grey hornbill, pearl-spotted owl and golden-breasted bunting among the characteristic residents. Day and night game drives and hot-air balloon safaris are conducted in the reserve. Some visitors stay at accommodations in Sun City and take day trips to the reserve.

ACCOMMODATION — CLASS A: • **Ivory Tree Game Lodge**, located in the northeastern region of the Pilanesberg Game Reserve, offers 60 air-conditioned suites, pool, bar, dining room and open-air boma. Custom 10-seater vehicles are used for game viewing.

CLASS B: • **Bakubung** overlooks a hippo pool and has 76 air-conditioned rooms and 66 self-catering cabanas, conference center, restaurant, swimming pool and children's playground. Guests may take a 10-minute shuttle to Sun City. • **Kwa Maritane** has 90 comfortable rooms and a swimming pool. • **Tshukudu** offers 6 luxury air-conditioned cottages each with elevated views of the surrounding reserve.

Sun City

Sun City is a large entertainment vacation complex with numerous restaurants, Las Vegas-style floor shows, casinos, tennis and a variety of water sports. The Lost City Golf Course is an 18-hole Gary Player-designed course with desert style on the front 9 holes and African bushveld on the back 9 holes. The Gary Player Golf Course is an 18-hole bushveld course and is home of the annual Nedbank Golf Challenge. Sun City is a 2-hour drive (116 mi./187 km) or a short flight from Johannesburg. Excursions to Pilanesberg Nature Reserve are offered by some of the hotels.

ACCOMMODATION — DELUXE: • **The Palace Hotel of the Lost City** has been constructed as a royal residence from an ancient civilization and is set in 62-acres (25-hectares) of lush gardens. The property has 338 rooms and four suites, a pool with 6-foot (2-m) surfing waves and water chutes, several restaurants and bars and 2 world-class Gary Player golf courses.

FIRST CLASS: • **The Cascades**, landscaped with lush gardens, waterfalls and a swimming pool, has 243 rooms with views over the gardens and golf course. • **Sun City Hotel** has 340 rooms with tropical landscaping and a large swimming pool.

TOURIST CLASS: • **Sun City Cabanas** is the most informal of the Sun City hotels and has 380 cabanas.

Madikwe Game Reserve

An area of plains, interrupted in places by inselberg rock outcrops, Madikwe is dominated by acacias and sweet grasses. "Operation Phoenix" translocated some 8,000 animals from other parks in South Africa, Namibia and Zimbabwe to begin stocking the reserve.

A few packs of the endangered wild dog occur in the 465-square-mile (750-km²) reserve, and this is one of the best places to see them in South Africa. In addition there are healthy populations of lion, cheetah and leopard. Black and white rhino and a wide range of antelope are numerous.

Birdlife is outstanding, with numerous species characteristic of the Kalahari, such as violet-eared waxbill, swallow-tailed bee-eater and pied babbler.

A plus for some travelers is that the area is malaria free.

Madikwe Game Reserve

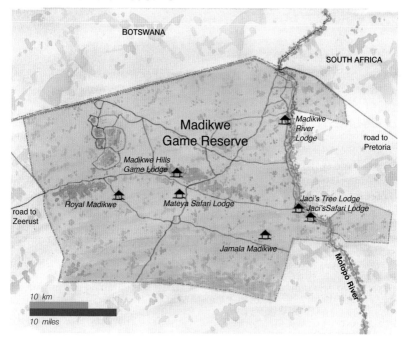

Visitors to Madikwe Game Reserve have an excellent chance of seeing wild dog

ACCOMMODATION — CLASS A: • **Mateya Safari Lodge** consists of 5 air-conditioned thatched suites including a sala, plunge pool and outdoor shower. There is a restaurant, lounge and an 8,000 bottle wine cellar. Game viewing activities include day and night game drives in open vehicles (with a maximum of four people per vehicle) as well as bush walks. • **Royal Madikwe** is a luxury residence accommodating up to 10 people on an exclusive basis. The main lodge houses the fireplace, dining room with open designer kitchen, lounge and viewing deck with hot tub. A private safari guide and vehicle are available throughout your stay.

CLASS A/B: • **Jaci's Safari Lodge** has 8 thatched chalets overlooking a small stream where the animals come to drink (there is a 2-bedroom suite with private pool). • **Jaci's Tree Lodge** has 8 "tree houses" built on stilts with large private decks. The main building includes an open-air dining room, lounge, swimming pool and 4-sided fireplace. Both of Jaci's lodges offer day and night game drives and are very family friendly. • **Madikwe River Lodge** offers 16 split-level thatched chalets with private decks set in a riverine forest. There is a main dining area, lounge, boma and swimming pool. Day and night game drives and walks are offered. • **Madikwe Hills Game Lodge** consists of 10 glass-fronted suites with private plunge pools, air-conditioning, overhead fans and fireplaces during the cooler months. Day and night game drives and bush dinners are highlights of your stay. • **Jamala Madikwe** features 5 freestanding villas with individual pools and salas, private decks and outdoor showers. Day and night game drives are offered.

THE CAPE PROVINCES

Kgalagadi Transfrontier Park

In May 2000 Kalahari Gemsbok National Park was officially merged with Botswana's Gemsbok National Park to form the Kgalagadi Transfrontier Park. The park is located in the northwest corner of South Africa and the southwest corner of Botswana, bordering Namibia to the west. This huge 13,900-square-mile (36,000-km²) park is predominantly semi-desert and open savannah. Scattered thorn trees and grasses lie between red Kalahari sand dunes. San Bushmen inhabited the area as far back as 25,000 years ago.

The most interesting (and productive from an animal-viewing perspective) habitat in the park is the fossil riverbeds. Tens of thousands of years ago, in a wetter era, the Auob and Nossob Rivers flowed into the Orange River, but today they are no more than furrowed drainage lines. They do, however, hold underground water, and once in a decade or so, they flow briefly after particularly heavy downpours. It is in the Auob and Nossob drainage lines that the largest camel thorn acacias grow, providing shade, nutrition and nesting sites for a host of creatures. Grasses grow taller and sweeter here, too. The two main roads in the park follow the Nossob and Auob (they are linked by the so-called "Dune Road") where a much higher concentration of animals are seen than in the surrounding dunes.

The park is famous for the majestic gemsbok (oryx), which occur in abundance. This is also one of the best places to see and photograph the gazelle-like springbok, the national sporting emblem of South Africa. Blue wildebeest occur in small numbers — a mere remnant of a migratory population that may have once rivaled the famed Serengeti herds. Predator viewing is often quite good, with lion, leopard and particularly cheetah, seen with frequency. The Kalahari lions are among the most handsome in Africa, for there is little dense bush to scratch or damage their coats and manes. The elusive, mostly nocturnal, brown hyena may be encountered in the early mornings or late afternoon. This park also offers wonderful opportunities to see less common creatures such as honey badger, aardwolf, bat-eared fox and African wild cat, which, though primarily nocturnal, are often active during the day, especially in the cooler winter months.

Birdwatchers will not be disappointed, for the Kalahari supports a wide variety of species not commonly seen elsewhere. The gigantic thatched nests of sociable weavers are unmistakable wonders of avian architecture. Built by the small, sparrow-sized weavers, the huge structures commonly grow to a size that breaks the branches of the tree in which they are built. Birds of prey thrive in the Kalahari, with pale chanting goshawk, gabar goshawk, bateleur, secretarybird, lanner falcon and the tiny pygmy falcon all very common. Giant eagle owls are regularly seen at their daytime roosts, while white-faced and pearl-spotted owls hunt about the rest camps after dark. Three species of sandgrouse can be seen quenching their thirst at waterholes, while the world's heaviest flying bird, the kori bustard, is extremely common.

Kgalagadi Transfrontier Park

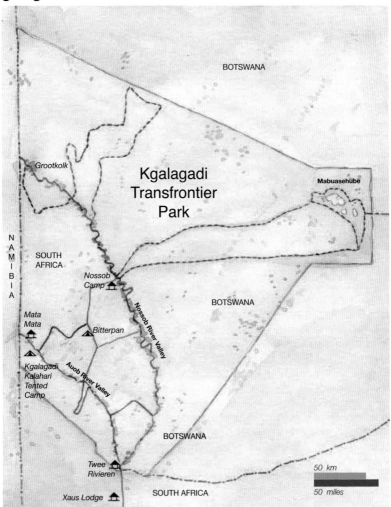

Summer temperatures can exceed 104°F (40°C). Winter days are pleasant, but temperatures can drop below freezing at night. The animals have adapted to desert conditions by eating plants with high water content, such as wild cucumber and tsamma melon.

The southern entrance to the park is about 255 miles (411 km) north of Upington, which has scheduled air service from other major cities in the country.

The park can be accessed from Namibia at the Mata Mata Gate by bona-fide tourists only who are required to book a minimum of two nights stay.

ACCOMMODATION — CLASS B: • **Kgalagadi Kalahari Tented Camp**, set on a red sand dune overlooking a waterhole, has 15 tents, including 4 family units and a swimming pool. • **Bitterpan**, located a 3-hour drive (4wd only) from Nossob, has 4 chalets on stilts with shared cooking facilities.

CLASS C: There are three rest camps with self-contained cottages with kitchens, huts with and without bathrooms, camping sites, stores, gas (petrol) and diesel. • **Twee Rivieren** is located at the southern entrance to the park. The camp has a restaurant, swimming pool and a landing strip for small aircraft. • **Nossob**, located in the north-eastern part of the park near the Botswana border, has bungalows with bathrooms kitchens, as well as huts with separate facilities and communal kitchens. The camp has an information center for the plant and animal life in the park and has a landing strip for small aircraft. • **Mata Mata**, located on the western border of the park, has simple cottages with kitchens and huts (some with separate facilities) and a communal kitchen.

ACCOMMODATION NEAR THE PARK — CLASS C: • **Xaus Lodge**, located 10 miles outside the park, has 12 individual chalets with private decks overlooking the salt pan and waterhole.

Tswalu Kalahari Reserve

Tswalu Kalahari Reserve is the largest privately owned game reserve in South Africa, covering 290-square-miles (900-km²). Black rhino, roan and sable antelope may be seen, as well as up to 30 species of plains game.

This reserve has been made famous by the filming of "Meerkat Manor." Spending time with these habituated meerkats, possibly the cutest animals on earth, is not to be missed.

Other activities include morning and night game drives, guided walks, horseback riding, archery, star gazing, sundowners, and special activities for children. Ballooning and massage treatments are available but must be pre-booked.

The reserve is located west of Kuruman. Transfers are available from Kimberley or Upington; quickest access is by air charter from Johannesburg or Cape Town.

Habituated meerkats at Tswalu *(top)*, Tswalu's family-friendly Motse Lodge *(bottom)*

ACCOMMODATION — CLASS A+: • **The Motse** consists of 8 *legae* (a Tswana word for small house/suite), 2 of which are family units accommodating 4 people. Each legae includes a bedroom, indoor and outdoor walk-in shower, open fireplace and private sun deck overlooking a waterhole. The main lodge has an outdoor heated swimming pool, terrace, boma, wine cellar, a gift shop and children's play room. • **Tarkuni** is available for exclusive use for families and small groups of up to 10 guests. Accommodation includes 5 luxury bedrooms, lounge and dining room, library, covered patio and heated swimming pool. For children, 2 sets of bunk beds and separate nanny quarters with 2 single beds and a bathroom are available. Private guide and game viewing vehicles as well as a dedicated chef are included.

Kimberley

Kimberley is the "diamond city," where one of the world's biggest diamond strikes occurred in 1868. Visit the open-air museum and the "Big Hole," where over 3 tons of diamonds were removed from the largest hole dug by man on earth.

ACCOMMODATION — FIRST CLASS: • **Kimberley Club** offers 21 bedrooms with an ambience of a bygone era.

TOURIST CLASS: • **Garden Court Kimberley** has 135 rooms and a swimming pool.

Cape Town

Sir Francis Drake once said of the Cape Town area, "The fairest cape we saw in the whole circumference of the globe." Today, Cape Town is still thought by many well-traveled people to be one of the most beautiful settings in the world. The Cape reminds me of the California coast — stark, natural beauty and a laid-back atmosphere.

Cape Town's dramatic Table Mountain

An afternoon **Champagne Cruise** past islands with hundreds of seals, and featuring rocky cliffs and sandy beaches, allows a delightful perspective of the area.

The **Victoria & Alfred Waterfront (V & A)** has a variety of shops, historical buildings, museums, waterfront walks, restaurants, nightclubs, luxury and first class hotels, three micro breweries, theater, boat trips, helicopter rides and the **Two Oceans Aquarium**, which exhibits species from both the Atlantic and the Indian Oceans.

Tours to **Robben Island**, where Nelson Mandela was held as a political prisoner for so many years, depart from the Nelson Mandela Gateway situated at the Clock Tower at the Victoria & Alfred Harbor. The boat transfer to the island takes about 30 minutes. An hour tour of the island includes a visit to Mandela's

Cape Town & Environs

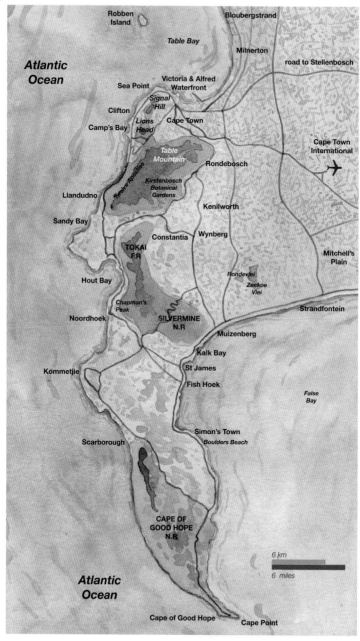

Robben Island

Bloubergstrand

Table Bay

Milnerton

Atlantic Ocean

road to Stellenbosch

Victoria & Alfred Waterfront

Sea Point

Signal Hill

Clifton

Lions Head

Cape Town

Camp's Bay

Cape Town International

Table Mountain

Rondebosch

Twelve Apostles

Kirstenbosch Botanical Gardens

Llandudno

Kenilworth

Sandy Bay

Constantia

Wynberg

TOKAI F.R

Mitchell's Plain

Rondevlei

Zeekoe Vlei

Hout Bay

Chapman's Peak

Noordhoek

SILVERMINE N.R

Strandfontein

Muizenberg

Kalk Bay

St James

Kommetjie

Fish Hoek

False Bay

Simon's Town

Boulders Beach

Scarborough

6 km

6 miles

Atlantic Ocean

CAPE OF GOOD HOPE N.R

Cape of Good Hope

Cape Point

The Cape Peninsula is a "must see" for visitors to Cape Town

cell, a stone quarry, an old village and a drive around the island, where you may see African (jackass) penguins and have great views of the city.

The one-day excursion down the Cape Peninsula to the **Cape of Good Hope Nature Reserve** and **Cape Point** is one of the finest drives on the continent. The reserve has lovely picnic sites, a population of bontebok and a variety of beautiful wildflowers. Some people say this is where the Atlantic meets the Indian Ocean, but that actually happens at **Cape Agulhas**, the southernmost point of Africa. Be sure to stop in **Simon's Town** en route to visit the wonderful **African penguin colony** (formally called jackass penguins).

Whale watching in the Atlantic seaboard, Hout Bay and False Bay is good July and August and best September and October. **Kirstenbosch National Botanical Gardens**, one of the finest gardens in the world, has 9,000 of the 21,000 flowering plants of southern Africa.

The **Cableway** (or 3-hour hike) up **Table Mountain**, with breathtaking views, is a must. The cable car can take 65 passengers at a time and does a full rotation on the way up. There is a good restaurant on the top of the mountain. Bring warm clothing because it is usually much cooler and windier on top. Table Mountain also offers the highest commercial abseiling or rappelling in the world.

A more active way to discover the area is by **kayaking** in single or double kayaks. Trips are available around Cape Point, from Table Bay to Clifton, in Hout Bay, in the Langebaan Lagoon and at Rietvlei (for bird watching), and from Simons Town to **Boulders Beach** to see the penguin colony. **Horseback riding** on beaches at Hout Bay, on the beaches, dunes and lagoons at Noordhoek Valley, or in the winelands is another great option. **Mountain biking** off Table Mountain to the Cape of Good Hope Nature Reserve and in the winelands is popular. From the Victoria & Alfred Waterfront, you may go

An African penguin

Ocean rafting in rubberducks (Zodiacs), which reach speeds in excess of 80 mph (120km/hr). Wet bikes and jet skis may be rented in Blouberg and Muizenberg. **Quad bikes** may be rented in Melkbos, 30 minutes from central Cape Town. **Sand boarding** is offered on some of the biggest sand dunes in the Cape, about an hour's drive out of Cape Town, either in Atlantis or Betty's Bay. Thunder City offers 1-hour flights in fighter jets — with just you and the pilot!

The Atlantic Ocean and False Bay offer good angling and **deep-sea fishing**. Maasbanker and mackerel are numerous in the warmer waters in Table Bay in summer, while False Bay is one of the top angling areas with Gordon's Bay harbor as an entry point to the ocean. The fishing harbors of Kalk Bay and Hout Bay are excellent, particularly at the peak of the season around June and July. Simon's Town is the principle harbor for tuna boats, and there is a club for tuna fishermen that offers boats for charter. At the Cape of Good Hope Nature Reserve, fishing is particularly good from the rocky vantage points on both sides of the peninsula. The west coast offers good fishing at many points along the coast. At Bloubergstrand, fishing off the rocks is good. Fishing charters depart from the V & A Waterfront, Hout Bay, Simon's Town and Gordon's Bay and range from four hours to a full day.

Some of the finer **restaurants** include the Atlantic Grill, Baia and Emily's (Victoria & Alfred Waterfront), Buitenverwachting, Constantia Uitsig, La Colombe and The Greenhouse (Constantia); Blue Danube (Tamboerskloof); Planet Restaurant (Mt. Nelson, Gardens); the Gold Restaurant, Aubergine, Caveau Wine Bar and Deli, Fork, 95 Keerom St, Five Flies, Signal at the Cape Grace and The Roundhouse (Camps Bay), Harbour House (Kalk Bay); and Beluga (Green Point), and Salt at The Ambassador where one can enjoy sundowners before dinner.

Signal Restaurant at the Cape Grace

Cape Town has many fabulous **shopping** areas, including The Victoria & Alfred Waterfront (small shops offering excellent quality and variety), Greenmarket Square (local stalls featuring African crafts, textiles and handmade goods, Monday to Saturday only), Cape of Good Hope Fine Wine Exporters (will arrange to ship cases of wine home — you will probably have to pay duty), The Collector (Church Street — a small downtown gallery), Jewel Africa (City Centre — manufactures jewelery, enormous variety of precious and semi-precious stones, also curios and craftwork), Uwe Koetter (manufacturing jewelery), Cape Gallery and Pan African Market (Church Street), Waterkant Street area (home furnishings and accessories) Long Street Arcade (variety of antique and collectable dealers in one arcade) and La Cotte Wineshop (Franschhoek — noted for its extensive selection of older wines, shipping arranged).

February through April is the best time to visit the Cape because there is very little wind; October to January is warm and windy and is also a good time to visit. May to August can be rainy and cool. However, this is one of the most beautiful cities in the world to visit any time of the year.

ACCOMMODATION — DELUXE: • **Ellerman House** is a grand old home with 11 rooms and suites, a swimming pool and fabulous spa. It is a historical landmark situated in the suburb of Bantry Bay within walking distance of the famous Clifton Beach. • **Cape Grace** is an elegant hotel located in the Victoria & Alfred Waterfront on its own quay, and offers 120 rooms and suites with views of Table Mountain or the harbor, a gourmet restaurant, lounge, spa, "Bascule" whiskey bar and a swimming pool. • **Mount Nelson Hotel** is a colonial gem set on nine landscaped acres near the base of Table Mountain and has luxurious rooms, several gourmet restaurants, two swimming pools, tennis courts and a spa. • **One&Only Cape Town**, located on the V & A Waterfront, features 131 rooms and suites with views of the marina, sea or Table Mountain. There are several upscale restaurants, a bar, infinity pool and luxury spa. • **Taj Cape Town** is located in the heart of the historic district near the St. George's Mall and features 177 rooms with city or Table Mountain views. There are several dining options including a champagne and oyster bar. • **Cape Royale Luxury Hotel and Residence** consists of 95 suites with fully-equipped kitchen, floor-to-ceiling windows and views of the V & A Waterfront and Table Mountain. • **Table Bay** is a 329-room hotel located in the Victoria & Alfred Waterfront with satellite television, a restaurant, conference facilities and a swimming pool, spa and health club. • **15 on Orange Hotel** is located in the Gardens suburb at the foot of Table Mountain

Waterfront views at the Radisson Blu *(top)*, The Cape Grace is located on the V & A Waterfront *(middle)*, Kensington Place *(bottom, left)*, Ellerman House's elegant pool area *(bottom, right)*

A sea-facing room at the Twelve Apostles *(top)*, Welgelegen Guesthouse *(far left)*, Steenberg Hotel's traditional garden *(middle, right)*, The library at O on Kloof *(bottom, right)*

and offers 129 rooms and suites, fine dining restaurant, 2 bars, coffee shop, spa and pool deck with views of Table Mountain.

FIRST CLASS: • **Radisson Blu Hotel Waterfront**, located a few minutes walk or complimentary hotel shuttle to the Victoria & Alfred Waterfront, has 181 rooms, two restaurants and a pool. Rooms either overlook the ocean in front or Table Mountain behind. • **Village & Life's Waterfront Village**, located in the V & A Waterfront and walking distance from shops and restaurants, offers fully-serviced 1- and 2-bedroom apartments with open lounge and dining areas. There is a concierge and daily housekeeping. • **Queen Victoria Hotel** features 34 rooms and suites, a designer spa, gym, pool and pool bar, upscale restaurant — all located in the heart of the V & A Waterfront. • **Manna Bay** has five suites, restaurant, bar and swimming pool. The hotel has cell phones available during your stay that are pre-loaded with numbers for local attractions and recommended restaurants. • **Victoria & Alfred Hotel**, located in the Victoria & Alfred Waterfront, has 94 air-conditioned rooms and suites with views of the ocean or Table Mountain. There is a gourmet restaurant with harbor views. • **The Townhouse Hotel** is a 12-story hotel close to the historic Parliament Buildings, with 106 air-conditioned rooms. • **The Cullinan Inn**, located walking distance to the Victoria & Alfred Waterfront, has 410 rooms with great views of Cape Town, a bar, swimming pool, gym and restaurant.

TOURIST CLASS: • **Portswood Hotel**, located a five-minute walk to the Victoria & Alfred Waterfront, has 103 air-conditioned rooms.

GUESTHOUSES: • **Kensington Place** is located within walking distance to Cape Town's trendy Kloof Street, with its diverse eating and shopping establishments. It has 8 suites with private balconies overlooking the bay and Table Mountain, and a swimming pool. • **Clarendon House** is an elegant guesthouse with 7 rooms situated in Fresnaye, one of Cape Town's prime residential seafront suburbs. • **Welgelegen**, a beautiful double-story Victorian home in the popular suburb of Gardens within walking distance of Kloof Street, has 12 air-conditioned bedrooms and a swimming pool. • **Four Rosmead** consists of 8 bedrooms (including the Bellegables Suite) in an exclusive guesthouse situated on the slopes of Table Mountain in the residential suburb of Oranjezicht. • **Cape Cadogan** has 12 bedrooms and the Owner's Villa that are decorated with an eclectic mix of contemporary and antique furniture using dramatic fabrics to maximum effect.

ACCOMMODATION IN THE CAPE AREA — DELUXE: • **Steenberg Hotel**, located in the Constantia valley, is a restored Cape house that includes 24 rooms with private patios with views of the vineyard or golf course. There is a pool, 18-hole golf course and spa. • **The Cellars-Hohenort Hotel** is comprised of 2 luxury country houses with a swimming pool and is situated in the beautiful Constantia Valley, a 15-minute drive from Cape Town. The rooms and suites are surrounded by lush gardens. • **The Bay Hotel**, located opposite the beach at Camps Bay, a 10-minute drive out of Cape Town, has 72 rooms and 6 suites and a swimming pool. • **Twelve Apostles Hotel** has 70 rooms, with sea or mountain views, swimming pool and restaurant. • **Colona Castle** is a spectacular villa with 3 standard suites and 5 full suites, each decorated with sumptuous furnishings and antiques. The hotel is located on the False Bay coastline and offers views of Table Mountain, the peninsula and the winelands. Guests can enjoy a gourmet restaurant and swimming pool, and spa treatments are available upon request. • **The Vineyard Hotel & Spa** is a 175-room hotel situated in the suburb of Newlands on 6 acres, a 15-minute drive from the City Center and the Victoria & Alfred Waterfront, and within easy walking distance of the up-market Cavendish Shopping Centre. It has 3 restaurants, a health and fitness center, spa and swimming pool.

FIRST CLASS: • **Greenways**, located near Kirstenbosch Botanical Gardens, is a magnificent mansion with 8 rooms and 6 suites, a swimming pool and a croquet lawn.

The Winelands

From humble beginnings as an experimental vineyard below Table Mountain by the Dutch East India Company during the seventeenth century, the wine industry in South Africa today has spread over a large and diverse area. Grapes are grown in nearly 60 officially declared appellations covering over 250,000-acres (100,000-hectares).

There are 6 important wine producing areas within a 2-hour drive of Cape Town, offering an amazing array of different wine styles from the many estates, private wine cellars and cooperatives. A superb marine- and mountain-influenced climate, coupled with stunning scenery, makes this an attractive area to visit. Hundreds of restaurants serve interesting regional cuisine matched to the local wines, which helps to drive the continuing Cape wine renaissance. The areas close to Cape Town are 1) Constantia, 2) Durbanville, 3) Paarl, Wellington and Franschhoek, 4) Stellenbosch, 5) Swartland, and 6) Walker Bay. **Constantia** is sometimes referred to as the cradle of wine making in the Cape; Simon vander Stel was granted land here in 1685. Constantia is a leafy zone on the southeast of the Cape Peninsula facing the Atlantic Ocean. It is cooled by sea breezes from two sides, southeasterly from False Bay, and northerly gusts over the Constantiaberg mountain spine. Red and white wines are produced, but the area is recognized for whites, especially sauvignon blanc.

Durbanville is an area in transition from rustic tradition to modern development. The area of rolling hills north of the city gets cooling nighttime mists and influences from both Table and False Bays. Wine farming dates from 1716, and the area was originally known for bulk wine production, but is now recognized for sauvignon blanc and merlot. **Paarl**, **Wellington** and **Franschhoek** have a variety of microclimates, soil types and grape varieties, with German and Huguenot heritage as well as the Dutch dating from the seventeenth century. Paarl is noted for shiraz, and more recently viognier, while Franschhoek has become a center for food and wine appreciation. The area is better known for white wine styles, especially chenin and semillon, but some wonderful shiraz and "bordeaux style" red blends are also being produced.

Stellenbosch is known to most as the red wine producing area in South Africa. However, the local estates produce great sparkling, white and fortified wines, as well. Cooler mountain slopes and cooling sea breezes from False Bay help moderate summer temperatures. The Simonsberg and Helderberg mountain areas fall within the Stellenbosch region. The area is recognized for cabernet, pinotage, shiraz and sparkling wines.

Swartland is the wheat and tobacco farming area north of Cape Town, and it is traditionally associated with big red wines. Swartland is now producing very good white wines — especially in the Groenekloof area that provides cooling

La Residence is nestled in the heart of Franschhoek

Atlantic Ocean breezes. Swartland, along with the Malmesbury and Tulbagh areas, is recognized for pinotage, shiraz and sauvignon blanc.

The age-old adage that the best wine is grown within sight of the ocean is true for **Walker Bay**. Famous also for the winter whale watching, the area, which includes Elgin, is recognized for pinot noir, chardonnay and pinotage.

The main towns of the Cape Winelands are Stellenbosch, Paarl and Franschhoek. **Stellenbosch** is known for its unique Cape Dutch architectural heritage and the Stellenbosch (Maties) University. The town is also home to the Bergkelder wine complex, the Village Museum, and many galleries, specialty and antique shops. **Paarl** is the home of the Afrikaans Language Museum and the Taal Language Monument, and the KWV wine complex located in the Berg River Valley between the dramatic mountain scenery of the Paarlberg and the Klein Drakenstein Mountains. **Franschhoek**, nestled in the Valley of the Huguenots among spectacular mountains, is a charming village with many galleries, shops, cafés and fine restaurants and is also home to the Huguenot Monument and Museum.

There are 4 popular wine routes through the beautiful wine country northeast of Cape Town. The Stellenbosch Route covers 55 private

Lanzerac Manor's traditional Cape Dutch architecture

265

cellars and cooperative wineries, including the Bergkelder, Blaauwklippen and Delheim, and the Van Ryn Brandy Cellar. The Paarl Route covers 26 cooperative wineries and estates, including Nederburg Estate and KWV Cooperative. The Franschhoek Route covers 24 cooperative wineries and private wine estates, includ-

ing Bellingham and Boschendal. The Worcester Route has 20 cooperative wineries and estates.

There are a number of excellent restaurants in the region, including 96 Winery Road, Overture, Terroir and Rust en Vrede (Stellenbosch), Bosman's (Paarl) and La Petite Ferme, Haute Cabriere and the Tasting Room at Le Quartier Francais (Franschhoek).

ACCOMMODATION — DELUXE: • **Le Quartier Francais**, a lovely country inn located in Franschhoek, has 15 deluxe rooms and 2 luxurious suites and the "Four Quarters" which consists of 4 exclusive suites with fireplaces, an excellent restaurant and swimming pool. • **Babylonstoren**, one of the oldest Cape Dutch farms, offers twelve 1- and 2-bedroom cottages with modern amenities. The wine and fruit farm date back 300 years and the fresh produce is featured in the seasonal menu in the restaurant. There is a spa, sauna and indoor plunge pool. • **La Residence** is a 30-acre working farm in Franschhoek and offers 11 luxurious suites. There is an infinity pool, full service spa, complimentary transfers

A bedroom at Majeka House *(top)*, Le Quartier Francais' rooms are built around a courtyard *(middle)*, Delaire Graff Estate is in the heart of the winelands *(bottom)*

into town and gourmet dining. • **Grande Provence Estate**, located on a 74-acre (30-hectare) vineyard in Franschhoek, features 5 suites, each uniquely decorated. Guests enjoy the swimming pool, spa, wine cellar tours and tastings and a chic gourmet restaurant. • **Delaire Graff Estate**, a boutique hotel situated between Stellenbosch and Franschhoek, features 10 individual lodges each with a private pool. There is a spa, gym and gourmet restaurant serving the estate's wine. • **Grand Roche**, a luxury estate hotel located in Paarl, has 34 rooms and suites with terraces overlooking the gardens. There is a swimming pool, fitness center and tennis courts. The gourmet restaurant, Bosman's is one of the finest in the country. • **Majeka House** is 5 minutes from the village Stellenbosch and has 15 lavish rooms with garden or pool views. A small restaurant and spa are available. • **Lanzerac Manor & Winery** has 48 luxurious bedrooms and suites, authentic Cape Dutch architecture, restaurant, bar, lounge with a cigar bar, and 3 outdoor swimming pools.

FIRST CLASS: • **Franschhoek Country House and Villas** features 39 rooms and suites with decadent bathrooms and amenities. The award winning Monneaux Restaurant serves contemporary cuisine. • **D'Ouwe Werf**, located in Stellenbosch, is a beautiful old inn with 32 rooms and suites, tennis courts, restaurant, vine-covered terrace, garden and swimming pool. • **Roggeland Country House** is a stately Cape Dutch farmhouse located near Paarl, with 10 bedrooms and a swimming pool. • **Auberge Rozendal Farm Country House**, a 140-year-old homestead located near Stellenbosch, has Victorian-style cottages and a swimming pool. • **Mont Rochelle**, surrounded by the estates vineyards high on a mountain overlooking the Franschhoek Manor, has 22 rooms, a restaurant, swimming pool and sauna. • **River Manor**, a 2-minute stroll from the charming village center of Stellenbosch, has 16 rooms, a swimming pool and spa. • **La Petit Ferme** has 5 private cottages set among the vineyards, each with private patio and plunge pool. Spacious bedrooms have fireplaces

La Petit Ferme is a favorite among visitors to the winelands

and bathrooms with large tubs and showers. • **Le Franschhoek Hotel and Spa** offers 63 rooms with views of the gardens, a wellness spa, tennis and bicycling to wine farms in the surrounding vineyards, and a restaurant.

GUEST HOUSES: • **Rusthof Franschhoek** is an exclusive country house in Franschhoek with 8 air-conditioned rooms and swimming pool. • **Residence Klein Oliphants Hoek**, is located in Franschhoek and has 8 spacious rooms, a swimming pool and extensive gardens.

North of Cape Town

This region has attractions that easily rival those on the more well-known Garden Route. Fabulous mountain scenery, whale and bird watching along the stark Atlantic Coastline and the magnificent proliferation of flowers in August and September make this a region well worth visiting. The **West Coast Ostrich Farm** is located 20 minutes north of Cape Town on the way to the West Coast National Park.

West Coast National Park

West Coast National Park covers 107-square-miles (276-km²) along the Atlantic Ocean about an hour's drive north of Cape Town and includes the Langebaan Lagoon, several islands and coastal areas. Whales can be seen from the park's shoreline between July and November.

Langebaan Lagoon, a wetland of internationally recognized importance, often has populations of over 50,000 birds comprised of 23 resident species and dozens of migrants from northern Europe and Asia. In total, over 250 different species have been recorded. Bird hides allow close viewing of the thousands of waders that migrate here in the summer months. Langebaan is also the site of a fossil footprint approximately 117,000 years old. Strandloper is an open-air restaurant on the beach serving a BBQ of the seafood caught in the area.

During spring, the land is in full flower. The **Postberg Nature Reserve** section of the park is open for visitors to enjoy from mid-August until the end of September. Bontebok, Cape mountain zebra, eland and Cape grysbok can be seen. A special bird is the black harrier. At Geelbek there is a historic farm and national monument with a country-style restaurant. It also serves as National Park Headquarters.

Another attraction in the area is the **West Coast Fossil Park**, located in Langebaanweg. The park has a visitor center with fossil displays, laboratory and lecture room, coffee shop and tea garden.

ACCOMMODATION IN THE REGION — FIRST CLASS: • **Bartholomeus Klip Farmhouse**, located in the Swartland region, is a restored Victorian farmhouse with 5 bedrooms, set on a historic wheat and sheep farm combined with thousands of acres (hectares) of private nature reserve. Walks, mountain biking, and water sports at the dam are offered along with game drives to look for wildlife such as the Cape mountain zebra, and explore unique fynbos of the reserve. The lodge is located about a 75-minute drive from West Coast National Park and a 3-hour drive from Lambert's Bay.

ACCOMMODATION — GUESTHOUSES: • **Farmhouse Hotel**, located on a hill in Langebaan, has 18 rooms and a restaurant serving traditional Cape cuisine. • **Kersefontein Guest House**, located on a working farm on the Berg River, has 6 rooms and is a national monument.

Lambert's Bay

Lambert's Bay is famous for the crayfish and fish industry. Bird Island (now more a peninsula than an island) is found near the entrance of the harbor and is the breeding ground of thousands of Cape gannets, cormorants, penguins and other seabirds. There is a new information center, restaurant and truly sensational bird hide that offers outstanding photographic opportunities.

Muisbosskerm is an open-air seafood restaurant on the beach. Meals are prepared on open fires behind a hedge of thorny shrubs that are traditionally used for building sheep pens. The west coast crayfish is excellent.

ACCOMMODATION — see "The Cederberg" (following page).

The Cederberg

This rugged, mountainous 502-square-mile (1,300-km²) wilderness area dotted with interesting rock formations created by erosion, also features waterfalls, clear mountain pools, rock paintings and beautiful fynbos flora.

This is a fabulous area (along with Namaqualand to the north) in which to see millions of flowers blooming in the spring and is part of the "Wildflower Route." The best time to see wildflowers in the Cederberg is August to early September.

There are over 250 marked hiking trails in the Cederberg.

From the Cederberg consider taking a day trip to Lamberts Bay to visit the gannet colony and see the whales in season.

The area is also known for the cultivation of unique products such as Rooibos Tea. There are a number of vineyards in the region, and tobacco is also cultivated, especially around the Rhenish Mission Station at Wupperthal. The nearby **Biedouw Valley** is famous for the profusion of wild flowers in spring (August and September) and the large variety of colorful vygies *(mesembryanthemums)* reaching right up to the mountains.

Cederberg is the part of the "wildflower route"

Bushmans Kloof Lodge *(top)*, Activities at Bushmans Kloof include visiting ancient cave paintings *(bottom)*

Clanwilliam, located 150 miles (240 km) from Cape Town, is the gateway to the Cederberg, via the Packhuis Pass, and much of the Karoo and the Maskam areas. It is famous for the Clanwilliam Dam (recreational water sports), the Ramskop Flower Reserve, Rooibos Tea factory and the many restored historic buildings.

ACCOMMODATION — CLASS A: • **Koro Lodge**, situated 1.5 miles (2 kms) away from the main lodge, is a renovated farmhouse that has been transformed into a stunning private villa consisting of 2 luxury bedrooms and a loft large enough to accommodate 4 children. The villa comes equipped with its own chef, game ranger and vehicle. Besides the guided game drives, guests can go on guided rock art walks (more than 125 rock art sites, some dating back 10,000 years), botanical tours, mountain biking, nature hikes, abseiling, canoeing, archery, croquet, fly fishing and swimming in crystal clear rock pools. • **Bushmans Kloof Lodge**, a Relais & Chateaux property and a South African Natural Heritage site, is located on the 19,275-acre (7800-hectare) Bushmans Kloof Wilderness Reserve and provides a sanctuary for indigenous wildlife, birdlife and 755 species of plants. Wildlife on the reserve includes bontebok, red hartebeest, black wildebeest, Cape mountain zebra, Burchell's zebra, eland and springbok, however, the game is often difficult to approach closely. The lodge has 14 rooms and 3 suites.

CLASS B: • **Saint Du Barry's Country Lodge**, located in Clanwilliam, has 4 rooms and 1 family unit with a plunge pool.

Namaqualand

Namaqualand is located north of the mouth of the Olifants River and south of the Orange River, and it is a place of rare and exquisite beauty, with vivid contrasts between vast expanses of space and brilliant displays of flowers in spring (August to early September). The area is largely semi-desert with warm dry temperatures year-round, and it has about 4,000 species of plants.

The flora of this region is unique. After a good rainy season there are not only carpets of annual flowers, but also a wide variety of geophytes (plants with bulbs, corms and tubers), dwarf shrubs and succulents that vary from creepers to large-stem succulents like the chubby kokerboom *(Aloe dichtoma),* a tree-succulent.

The reason for this unique flora is the region's low and sporadic winter rainfall, which gives rise to plant adaptations for survival during moist winters and to dry and very hot summers. In winter and spring the plant cover is high with perennials and many annuals, but in the summer Namaqualand becomes a barren scene. This winter-summer transformation is almost unimaginable and must be seen to be believed.

There are many towns in this region that are famous for their flowers. Nieuwoudtville is home to many of the geophytes; Van Rhynsdorp features many of the succulents in the area; and Garies, Kamieskroon and Springbok become carpeted with wildflowers such as daisies, herbs, succulents and lilies in the springtime.

ACCOMMODATION — TOURIST CLASS: • **O'Kiep Country Hotel**, located in O'Kiep, 5 miles (8 km) north of Springbok, is a comfortable country hotel with 18 air-conditioned rooms, restaurant and bar. • **Kamieskroon Hotel**, located in the heart of Namaqualand, has 24 rooms, lounge, restaurant and bar. • **Karoo Lodge Guest House** located in the center of Springbok, has 26 air-conditioned rooms, restaurant and bar. • **Annie's Cottage**, a beautifully restored manor house situated in the heart of Springbok, has 11 rooms (all individually decorated) and a very relaxing garden and pool area. • **Mountain View Guest House** in Springbok has 10 air-conditioned suites with mini-bars.

East of Cape Town
Hermanus, Gansbaai and De Kelders

This beautiful region is located less than a 2-hour drive from Cape Town or Franschhoek (The Winelands). Explore this charming seaside town, walk in the **Fernkloof Reserve** with magnificent views over scenic Walker Bay, stroll along the cliff paths, and visit the Saturday Craft Market. The Hamilton Russell and Bouchard & Finlayson wineries have tasting facilities not far from Hermanus. There are specialist wine shops in Hermanus that offer wine tasting to showcase the local wine estates in the Hermanus area.

Hermanus and the Walker Bay area, which encompasses Gansbaai, are some of the best land-based **whale-watching** sights in the world. The whales come into these waters from the Antarctic Convergence between July and November.

The southern right whale is eight times as big as a large bull elephant, and it reaches over 50 feet (15 m) in length and 50 tons in weight. It is so aware of its exact position that it is able to pass under, or next to your boat with its tail fluke curved around you. Breaching is an incredible sight and can only be likened to a missile being launched from a submarine.

The coastline along Hermanus provides epic scenery and frequent whale sightings

Boat trips to Walker Bay and Gansbaai for whale watching, and to nearby Dyer Island to view Cape fur seals, African (jackass) penguins, thousands of cormorants and other seabirds, and to great white shark dive (see description under "Scuba Diving in the Southern Cape") are highly recommended. A visit to Grootbos Nature Reserve is also recommended (see the description that follows).

ACCOMMODATION HERMANUS — DELUXE: • **The Marine**, situated in Hermanus on a cliff overlooking Walker Bay, is a Relais & Chateaux hotel with 42 rooms and suites, 2 restaurants, a swimming pool and a heli-pad. Golf, tennis, bowls and squash are available at a nearby Country Club. • **The Western Cape Hotel and Spa** has 145 rooms and suites, golf courses, swimming pool, and Acquabella Spa and Wellness Centre. • **Birkenhead House**, perched high on the cliffs of Hermanus overlooking the whale watchers paradise of Walker Bay, has 11 luxurious rooms with mountain or sea views. There is a spa, pool and gym as well as complimentary transfers to town. The property has an exclusive villa which is a child-friendly alternative with 5 suites.

Auberge Burgundy

GUEST HOUSES: • **Auberge Burgundy Guest House**, situated on Walker Bay, has 18 rooms and suites with sea, garden or pool views. The Burgundy

Restaurant offers outstanding cuisine, featuring fresh local seafood. • **Sandbaai Country House**, located on the beachfront, has 11 rooms. • **De Kelders Bed and Breakfast**, located near Gansbaai overlooking the cliffs of De Kelders and the sea, has 5 rooms. • **Blue Gum Country Estate** is located outside of Stanford, 12 miles (20 kms) beyond Hermanus. The lodge features 10 suites, decorated in English country or African style. Guests enjoy the swimming pool and exclusive access to a boat on the Stanford River. Morning and evening cruises are offered.

ACCOMMODATION NEAR HERMANUS — DELUXE: • **Mosaic Farm Lagoon Lodge**, located on the Hermanus Lagoon, features 5 safari-style suites with large sunken tubs, private patio with views of the mountains and lagoon. Beach excursions, kayaking and guided nature walks are included in your stay. Optional activities such as quad biking or wine tasting are available for additional cost.

Grootbos Nature Reserve

Grootbos is a private fynbos reserve located between Hermanus and Gansbaai about a 2-hour drive from Cape Town. This is an excellent place to stay if you plan to whale watch, take boat excursions to see seal colonies and dive with great white sharks.

Grootbos Nature Reserve has a diversity of fynbos vegetation with over 740 plant species and over 100 bird species. Activities available at Grootbos

Pristine beaches near Grootbos Nature Reserve

include nature drives, horseback rides, and walks along the 20 miles (30 km) of beaches.

The deck at Grootbos Garden Lodge

ACCOMMODATION — CLASS A: • **Grootbos** has 2 lodges, the **Garden Lodge** (11 suites) and the **Forest Lodge** (16 suites). Each suite includes a separate lounge with fireplace, large bedroom, mini-bar and sweeping views. Grootbos features 2 restaurants with central fireplace, intimate bars and lounge areas with wooden deck overlooking Walker Bay, wine cellar, library and gift shop, large swimming pool, ecological interpretation and research center and Leica spotting scopes for whale watching. From the deck, you may have a vista all the way to Cape Point. Garden Lodge is "family friendly" and children are welcome.

Scuba Diving in the Southern Cape

The world's two great oceans, the cold south Atlantic and the warm Indio-Pacific, rub brawny shoulders along the southernmost curve of Africa. This contrast of temperatures produces two extremes in underwater habitats and at least three unique opportunities for the adventurous diver: the Southern Cape, Southern Natal Coast (Durban area) and Northern Natal Coast (near Sodwana Bay and Rocktail Bay).

An airborne great white shark off Dyer Island

For those seeking the ultimate underwater thrill, the Southern Cape offers the magnificent cold-water predator — the great white shark. South Africa is one of the few places in the world where divers can encounter this formidable creature from the safety of a shark cage. The great white shark is a protected species in South Africa and reaches heroic proportions in these rich waters.

Dyer Island is believed to be one of the best places in the world to view the great white shark. The island is 6 nautical miles from Gansbaai and is a bird sanctuary and a breeding site of the African penguin. Adjoining the island is a smaller rocky island called Geyser Rock, which supports a large seal population. Separating Geyser and Dyer Island is a channel named "Shark Alley" where the boats anchor hoping to sight these magnificent predators.

There have been a few licenses granted to commercial shark diver companies in the Southern Cape area, and all operations have experienced skippers and divers on board who supply all the necessary equipment required to enter the cages. You do not need a diving qualification to enter the cage. Non-divers can see the sharks from the boat because they come very close to the surface. The best time to see the great white sharks is between May and October. The probability of seeing a shark during January, February and March is about 50%.

The boats go out to sea between 7:00 and 9:00 a.m. and, depending on weather conditions, they reach the anchoring spot in about 20 to 25 minutes. The anchor is put down, the cage goes into the water and a scent trail is begun. Once final preparations for the dive are made, you settle down to spend the rest of the time watching, diving and enjoying the day. A light lunch and drinks are available on the boat, and there is a toilet on board.

The water temperature can be anywhere between 54° and 61°F (12° and 16°C). Visibility is usually 20 to 26 feet (6 to 8 m), but it can go up to 40 to 50 feet (12 to 15 m) on a good day and down to 7 to 10 feet (2 to 3 m) on a bad day.

Diving facilities, equipment and training in South Africa are generally excellent.

The Garden Route

One of the most beautiful drives on the continent, the Garden Route is lined with Indian Ocean coastal scenery, beautiful beaches, lakes, forests and mountains, with small country hotel accommodations and large resort hotels. The Garden Route runs between Mossel Bay (east of Cape Town) and Storms River (west of Port Elizabeth).

A number of tours and self-drive options are available from Cape Town to Port Elizabeth (or vice versa) for a minimum of 2 nights/3 days. These programs visit a variety of areas and attractions. The **coastal route** from Cape Town passes through the winelands, Hermanus, Mossel Bay and the coastal areas of Wilderness, Knysna and Plettenberg Bay to Port Elizabeth. The **mountainous route** from Cape Town passes through the winelands,

The Plettenberg perched high on a cliff *(top)*, Water views rooms at the The Plettenberg *(bottom)*

Garden Route

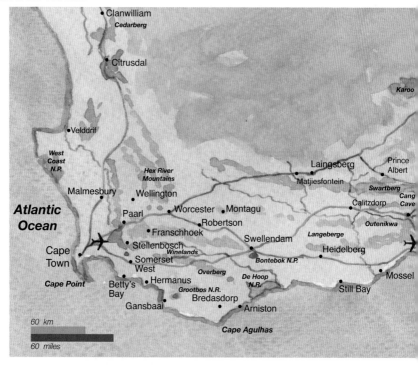

Caledon, Swellendam, over magnificent Tradouw Pass to Barrydale and Calitzdorp, and then to Oudtshoorn. Continue over the Outeniqua Mountains to Wilderness and through the coastal areas to Port Elizabeth. The **northern route** from Cape Town passes through the winelands, Matjiesfontein, and Prince Albert to Oudtshoorn. From there you can join the coastal areas route to Port Elizabeth.

Departing Cape Town, the better way to begin the **coastal route** is to drive to Somerset West, turn toward the coast at The Strand, and continue along False Bay passing Gordon's Bay, Betty's Bay (where there is a mainland colony of African penguins) and onward to Hermanus. The road down to the coast yields fine views of the rugged coastline. The southernmost vineyards in Africa are located nearby.

Southern right whales usually start arriving in **Walker Bay** (Hermanus) in June or July and usually depart by December, with the peak season being August and September. The best time for whale watching in general along the Garden Route is also August and September.

You may continue to **Cape Agulhas**, the southernmost tip of Africa, where the Atlantic and Indian Oceans meet, and to **Waenhuiskrans** (Arniston), a 200-year-old fishing village. An interesting day visit from Arniston is the **De Hoop Nature**

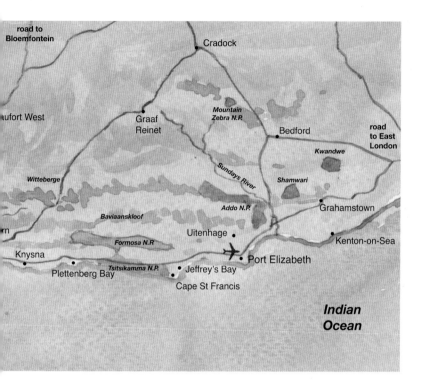

Reserve, which is a pristine reserve with magnificent, unspoiled beaches. It is the breeding ground of the African black oystercatcher and has a colony of Cape vultures. Other species seen include bontebok, eland and Cape mountain zebra.

Continue to the town of **Mossel Bay** and then drive north to **Oudtshoorn** where you can ride an ostrich — or at least watch them race — and tour an ostrich farm. Located about 16 miles (26 km) north of Oudtshoorn are the **Cango Caves**, the largest limestone caves in Africa, with colorful stalactites and stalagmites.

Return to the coast via **George**, an Old World town with oak-tree-lined streets set at the foot of the Outeniqua Mountains. A narrow-gauge steam train runs in the morning from George across the **Knysna Lagoon** to Knysna and back to George that same afternoon.

Continue east to the **Wilderness Area**, which encompasses a number of interlinking lakes, and onward to Knysna, a small coastal town with a beautiful lagoon excellent for boating. The Knysna Forest and the Tsitsikamma Forest together form South Africa's largest indigenous high forest.

Farther east lies **Plettenberg Bay**, the Garden Route's most sophisticated resort area. The boardwalk complex has many shops, restaurants and a casino. Whale-watching boat trips depart from the beach.

Nearby is **Tsitsikamma National Park** — a lushly vegetated 50 mile (80 km) strip along the coast. Wildlife includes the Cape clawless otter, grysbok, bushbuck and blue duiker. Over 275 species of birds have been recorded. The park has hiking trails, including the famous **Otter Trail**, and underwater trails for both snorkelers and scuba divers. At **Bloukrans Bridge**, about 25 miles (40 km) from Plettenberg Bay, is the highest **bungee jump** in the world — 708 feet (216 m)!

The northern route passes the Paarl winelands area through a portion of the Great Karoo (semi desert) to **Matjiesfontein**, a charming little town where the buildings and railway station have been preserved in their original Victorian style. From there the route runs southeast through Prince Albert to Oudtshoorn, where it meets the southern route.

From Plettenberg Bay you may continue to St. Francis Bay, Jeffrey's Bay (famous for surfing) and to Port Elizabeth.

ACCOMMODATION — SOUTHWEST TO NORTHEAST:

WAENHUISKRANS — FIRST CLASS: • **The Arniston** has 31 rooms and a swimming pool. Whales are often seen May to October.

SWELLENDAM — FIRST CLASS: • **Klippe Rivier Country House** is a Cape Dutch homestead in which the old wine house and stables have been converted into 6 luxury bedrooms and 1 honeymoon cottage.

OUDTSHOORN — FIRST CLASS: • **Rosenhof Country Lodge** has 12 rooms, 2 executive suites and a swimming pool.

GUEST HOUSE: • **Altes Landhaus**, cradled in the Schoemanshoek Valley, is a Cape Dutch-style homestead offering all suites.

TOURIST CLASS: • **De Opstal Farm**, a working ostrich farm located between Oudtshoorn and the Cango Caves, has air-conditioned rooms and a swimming pool. • **Queens Hotel** has 40 rooms and is located in downtown Oudtshoorn.

PRINCE ALBERT — TOURIST CLASS: • **The Swartberg Hotel**, located north of Outdshoorn, is a charming hotel with 14 rooms in the main house and 5 cottages that are ideal for families.

GEORGE — DELUXE: • **The Fancourt Hotel & Country Club Estate** is an elegant hotel (a National Monument) with 115 rooms and suites, several restaurants, 3 championship golf courses, swimming pool, tennis and a spa.

FIRST CLASS: • **Hoogekraal Country House**, an eighteenth century coastal estate, has 8 basic rooms.

WILDERNESS — DELUXE: • **Views Boutique Hotel & Spa**, located directly on the ocean, features 18 suites with modern furnishings and large glass windows. There are 2 restaurants, rooftop pool deck and sun terrace, cocktail lounge and fully serviced spa.

TOURIST CLASS: • **Wilderness Beach Hotel and Spa** is situated on the ocean and the lagoon and has 149 rooms. There is an outdoor swimming pool, restaurant and wellness center.

GUEST HOUSE: • **Wilderness Manor** is situated on Wilderness Lagoon within walking distance of the beaches and village shops. The manor is known for its 4 elegant rooms decorated in Afro-colonial style.

BETWEEN WILDERNESS AND KNYSNA — DELUXE: • **Lake Pleasant Hotel**, a converted 1840 manor house situated within a bird sanctuary on a natural freshwater lake, has 20 air-conditioned self-contained suites and 6 villas, a restaurant, beautifully restored bar, wine cellar, indoor swimming pool, spa (wellness center), steam room, sauna and tennis courts.

KNYSNA — DELUXE: • **Pezula Resort Hotel and Spa** is a retreat overlooking Knysna Lagoon, with suites with private balconies, health spa and 18-hole champion golf course. • **St. James Club** is located on the shores of the Knysna Lagoon, with 15 suites, a swimming pool and floodlit tennis courts. • **Phantom Forest Lodge**, located on the Phantom Forest Eco Reserve, is situated on the Knysna River and offers guests a unique bio-diversity of Afro-montane forest, estuarine wetland and Cape coastal fynbos. The lodge has 12 tree suites that are comprised of a sitting room, bedroom with private forest bathroom and an outside deck area. Activities include walking trails, canoeing and bird watching. • **Turbine Boutique Hotel** is comprised of 24 rooms and suites. The pool deck overlooks the canal and there are 2 restaurants, a bar and spa.

FIRST CLASS: • **Belvidere Manor** fronts the Knysna Lagoon and has a variety of guest cottages, swimming pool and charming gardens.

TOURIST CLASS: • **Kanonkop Guest House** is a boutique property 5 minutes from Knysna. The rooms are individually decorated with views of the forest and lagoon. • **Yellowwood Lodge**, a restored Victorian house, has 11 rooms. • **Point Lodge**, set on the water's edge, has 9 rooms and a swimming pool.

PLETTENBERG BAY — DELUXE: • **The Plettenberg** is a 5-star Relais & Chateaux Hotel built on a rocky headland with breathtaking vistas of the sea with 37 air-conditioned luxury rooms and suites, and 2 swimming pools. The adjoining Beach House has its own pool and is ideal for a family or small group of friends. • **Tsala Treetop Lodge** has 10 secluded suites built with natural stone, wood and glass set at the top of the canopy of the trees about 20 feet (6 m) above the forest floor. Each suite has an indoor-outdoor shower and a plunge pool. • **Kurland**, a luxury country hotel established in old Cape Dutch tradition surrounded by polo fields, has 12 large and beautifully furnished suites situated around the swimming pool. There is a health spa with fully equipped gymnasium, sauna and steam bath. • **Hunter's Country House** has elegantly decorated thatched cottages and a charming restaurant with a wine cellar.

FIRST CLASS: • **Hog Hollow**, set on the edge of the forest with great views of the Tsitsikamma Mountains, has 12 suites (chalets) with private decks and fireplaces.

TOURIST CLASS: • **Country Crescent Hotel**, located just outside of Plettenberg Bay, has 39 rooms and a swimming pool. • **Lairds Lodge Country Estate**, a Cape Dutch homestead, is located between Knysna and Plettenberg. Accommodations include 10 rooms and suites.

STORMS RIVER — TOURIST CLASS: • **Protea Hotel Tsitsikamma Village Inn** has 49 Swiss-style chalets.

ST. FRANCIS BAY — FIRST CLASS: • **Jyllinge Lodge**, located on the beach in a charming coastal resort town, has 8 rooms. • **Thatchwood Country Lodge** overlooks St. Francis Links golf course and offers simple, comfortable accommodations.

PORT ELIZABETH — DELUXE: • **Shamwari Townhouse**, located 100 meters from the beach, features 7 suites with private terraces. South African cuisine is served in the Jazz Room. • **Hacklewood Hill Country House**, built in 1898, is an elegant residence located in a suburb, with 8 rooms, a swimming pool and tennis courts. • **Radisson Blu Hotel Port Elizabeth** has panoramic views of Algoa Bay and features 173 guest rooms, a gourmet restaurant, an Irish inspired lounge, outdoor pool and fitness center.

FIRST CLASS: • **Protea Hotel Marine Hotel**, located near the beach, has 114 rooms and a swimming pool. • **Singa Lodge** has 11 individually designed suites. There is an outdoor bar, pool and restaurant. • **The Windemere**, walking distance from the beach, offers 9 spacious bedrooms and swimming pool.

TOURIST CLASS: • **Protea Hotel Edward**, a historical landmark, has 97 rooms and a swimming pool.

MATJIESFONTEIN (NORTHERN ROUTE) — TOURIST CLASS: • **The Lord Milner** is located just off the Cape Town-Johannesburg Road (N1).

Shamwari Private Game Reserve

Shamwari is a 35,000-acre (14,000-hectare), malaria-free private game reserve located 47 miles (75 km) northeast of Port Elizabeth.

Wildlife on the reserve includes white rhino, black rhino, elephant, buffalo, lion, hippo and 17 species of antelope. Day and night game drives and walks are offered.

ACCOMMODATION — CLASS A: • **Eagles Crag Lodge** features 9 superior suites each with private deck and pool, as well as, indoor-outdoor showers. The lodge has a spa, dining room, library, lounge and cocktail bar. • **Long Lee Manor** is an Edwardian mansion with 18 air-conditioned rooms and suites. There are 2 swimming pools and the lodge overlooks a waterhole. • **Lobengula Lodge** has 5 air-conditioned suites built into the bushveld. • **Riverdene**, a restored settler's home, is family-friendly and accommodates 18 guests. There is an infinity pool, playroom and open-air boma. • **Bushman River Lodge** is also a restored settler's home, with 4 suites, swimming pool, boma and lounge area. • **Bayethe Lodge** offers 9 tents nestled along the bed of the river, camouflaged under trees. Each tent is air-conditioned and has a private plunge pool and viewing deck. • **Sarili Lodge**, ideal for families, accommodates a maximum of 10 people and features a child-friendly swimming pool, barbeque area and has a special children's menu.

Addo Elephant National Park

This 29,000-acre (11,718-hectare) park, located in a malaria-free area about 45 miles (72 km) north of Port Elizabeth, was formed to protect the last of the elephant and Cape buffalo in the Eastern Cape. Other wildlife in the park includes black rhino, greater kudu, eland, red hartebeest and bushbuck. By far the main attraction of the park is the opportunity for close encounters with elephants.

ACCOMMODATION — CLASS A: • **Gorah Elephant Camp**, set on a private concession area in the park, has 11 luxurious tents with private decks and views of the savannah. Gorah House, the main lodge building, was built in 1856 and has been restored to its colonial style.

FIRST CLASS: • **RiverBend Lodge**, located on a private game farm adjacent to the park, has 8 suites, a spa and a swimming pool. Walks on the farm and horseback riding are offered. • **Kuzuko Lodge** adjoins Addo Elephant National Park and has 24 air-conditioned chalets. Day and night game drives are offered with access into the national park. • **Elephant House**, set in the Sundays River Valley and minutes from

Addo Elephant National Park, features 9 rooms opening out onto the courtyard.
• **Woodall Country House and Spa** has rooms and suites with private verandahs and outdoor showers.

Kwandwe

Kwandwe is a 62,000-acre (25,000-hectare) private reserve of rolling hills and savannah located in the malaria-free Eastern Cape, about 20 minutes by road from Grahamstown and 2 hours from Port Elizabeth. The reserve includes 19 miles (30 km) of river frontage on the Great Fish River. Over 7,000 head of game was reintroduced into the reserve, including both black and white rhino, lion, elephant, cheetah, Cape buffalo and a variety of antelope.

ACCOMMODATION — CLASS A:
• **Kwandwe Great Fish River Lodge** overlooks the Great Fish River and has 9 air-conditioned suites with bathrooms, indoor-outdoor showers, private plunge pools and salas, a swimming pool and wine cellar. Activities include day and night game drives, walks, fishing, rhino tracking, overnight fly-camping and visits to historical Grahamstown. • **Uplands Homestead** is a private safari villa with 3 bedrooms, a private game ranger, chef and butler. The restored farmhouse is ideal for families and private parties.
• **Kwandwe Ecca Lodge** features 6 intimate suites, each with a large verandah and private plunge pool. Main guest areas include a dining room and bar area, interactive kitchen, and lap pool.
• **Melton Manor**, is a sole-use safari villa with 4 spacious bedrooms, an interactive kitchen, private butler, ranger and chef.

Kwandwe has reintroduced both white and black rhinos on the game reserve *(top)*, Kwandwe Fish River Lounge *(middle)*, Kwandwe's Melton Manor *(bottom)*

KWAZULU-NATAL

KwaZulu-Natal is located in eastern South Africa along the Indian Ocean. The Drakensberg Mountains rise to 11,420 feet (3,482 m) and run roughly north and south along its western border, which it shares with Lesotho.

KwaZulu-Natal is the home of the Zulu and several small yet interesting reserves. Hiking in the Drakensberg Mountains is popular.

KwaZulu-Natal

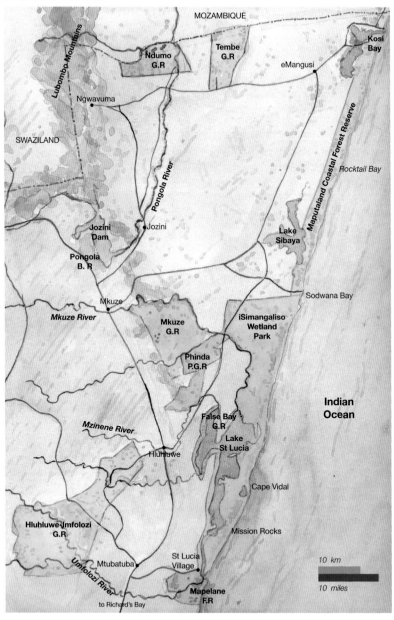

MOZAMBIQUE

Kosi
Bay

Tembe
G.R

Ndumo
G.R

eMangusi

Lubombo Mountains

Ngwavuma

SWAZILAND

Maputaland Coastal Forest Reserve

Rocktail Bay

Pongola River

Jozini
Dam

Jozini

Lake
Sibaya

Pongola
B. R

Mkuze

Sodwana Bay

Mkuze River

Mkuze
G.R

iSimangaliso
Wetland
Park

Phinda
P.G.R

Indian
Ocean

Mzinene River

False Bay
G.R

Lake
St Lucia

Hluhluwe

Cape Vidal

Hluhluwe-Imfolozi
G.R

Mission Rocks

Umfolozi River

Mtubatuba

St Lucia
Village

10 km

10 miles

to Richard's Bay

Mapelane
F.R

Durban

The largest city in KwaZulu-Natal, Durban has a beachfront called The Golden Mile that features amusement parks, amphitheater, colorful markets and aquarium (Sea World). Rickshaws, with drivers in traditional Zulu costume, are available along the beachfront. The Victoria Market and Grey Street Mosque are evidence of the strong Indian influence in this area.

ACCOMMODATION — FIRST CLASS: • **Suncoast Hotel and Towers** features 128 contemporary rooms in the main hotel or 37 luxury rooms in the tower wing. There is a restaurant, bar, spa and is part of the Suncoast Casino complex. • **Quarters Hotel**, set in a trendy suburb of Durban, consists of 4 restored Victorian homes and features 23 bedrooms. There is a restaurant and bar on site. • **Hilton Durban**, a business hotel located next to the International Convention Centre, has a restaurant, 3 bars and swimming pool.

TOURIST CLASS: • **Protea Edward Hotel**, a hotel with Old World charm and located on the beachfront, has 101 rooms, restaurant and a swimming pool. • **The Royal Hotel**, located in the city center, has 204 rooms and suites and swimming pool. • **Garden Court Marine Parade** has 346 sea-facing rooms and suites and a swimming pool. • **Southern Sun North Beach** has 285 rooms and suites, 2 restaurants and a swimming pool.

ACCOMMODATION NEAR DURBAN — DELUXE: • **Fairmont Zimbali Lodge**, located 26 miles (42 km) north of Durban, has been built in a forest and is surrounded by a championship 18-hole Tom Weiskopf golf course. The lodge has 76 rooms, colonial-style restaurant with views over the Indian Ocean, tennis courts, a private beach, outdoor pool, a health spa, conference facilities, golf club and pro shop. Nearby attractions include the traditional Zulu village of Shakaland, Crocodile Creek, Zulu Battlefields, Chaka's Rock and Hluhluwe Game Reserve. • **Oyster Box Hotel** features 86 luxurious rooms and suites located on the ocean's edge. There are several dining options, a bar, fitness room, swimming pool and spa. • **Beverly Hills**, located north of Durban on the beach at Umhlanga Rocks, has 88 rooms and suites, 24-hour room service, restaurant, bar and a swimming pool. • **Selbourne Lodge and Golf Resort** is an English manor-style resort set close to the Indian Ocean, with 72 rooms and suites. Facilities include an 18-hole golf course, restaurant, private beach club, tennis courts and swimming pool.

Zululand

This is the most tropical part of South Africa, with many plant and animal species typical of East Africa, extending south along what is a broad coastal plain. It is not surprising that Zululand also has the greatest concentration of wildlife areas and game ranches in the country. This is also the land of scenic hills and valleys, dotted with Zulu homesteads, many still in the traditional "beehive" style.

ACCOMMODATION — CLASS A/B: • **Protea Hotel Shakaland**, a resort built on the movie set for the films *Shaka Zulu* and *John Ross,* offers a look into the Zulu culture. Take a walk through a typical Zulu village where you may be shown the art of bead making, spear throwing and beer brewing, visit the Sangoma (witch doctor) and enjoy a display of Zulu dancing. Guests are accommodated in 55 traditional beehive huts. There is a restaurant, bar and swimming pool.

Drakensberg Mountains

Referred to as uKhahlamba — "Barrier of Spears," this 120 mile (200 km) long mountain range rises on the eastern escarpment of South Africa and borders the mountain Kingdom of Lesotho. This region was witness to much of the early history of South Africa such as the Stone Age occupation, the San hunter-gatherers referred to as "Bushmen," migrating chiefdoms from the Great Lakes of Central Africa in the 1300s, and the ox wagons of Boer settlers negotiated the pass in the 1830s and 1840s. Now a World Heritage Site, the mountain flora and fauna are complimented by the 35,000 San rock art images.

ACCOMMODATION — CLASS A/B: • **Cleopatra Mountain Farmhouse** is located at the foot of the Drakensberg Mountains. Accommodations include 11 standard rooms, suites and private cottages. Activities include hiking on mountain trails, horseback riding, fishing, birding and swimming in mountain pools. • **Cathedral Peak's** accommodation range from inter-leading family rooms to private rondavels and exclusive honeymoon suites. Guests can enjoy daily horseback riding, squash, tennis, swimming pool, boule, badminton, volleyball, croquet, lawn chess, mini golf, gym, sauna, mountain bike trails, trout fishing and a challenging 9-hole golf course. • **Fordoun Hotel and Spa**, located in the Midlands, has 17 suites with private verandahs, a spa and a bio-energy specialist. Fly-fishing is available.

Midlands — Rorke's Drift

There are numerous Zulu War and Anglo-Boer War battle sites in the region, including Isandlwana and Rorke's Drift. Tour guides who are superb storytellers make the history of that day come alive, and long, family associations with the area and its people allow you some unique Zulu perspectives on the battles fought with the British soldiers.

Overlooking the Battlefield of Isandlwana, the 6,250-acre (2,500-hectare) **Fugitives' Drift Game Reserve** is 5 miles (8 km) from Rorke's Drift on the Buffalo River in KwaZulu-Natal. Diverse and abundant wildlife includes giraffe, zebra, kudu, hartebeest and a host of smaller antelope, as well as 275 recorded bird species. The **Buffalo George** is a Natural Heritage Site where spectacular walks can be enjoyed.

ACCOMMODATION — CLASS A: • **Isandlwana Lodge** is carved into the iNyoni rock overlooking Mt. Isandlwana and offers 12 luxury rooms and a swimming pool.

CLASS B: • **Fugitives' Drift Lodge** consists of 8 colonial-style cottages with private verandahs and views of the plains. Most people who stay here are interested in tours of the Anglo/Zulu battlefields. • **Zulu Wings Game Lodge** is located close to Isandlwana, Rorke's Drift and Blood River Battlefield sites and offers 6 cozy rooms, a lounge, pool table and swimming pool. • **Three Tree Hill Lodge** specializes in the second Anglo-Boer War (1899–1902) and overlooks The Battle of Spioenkop. There are 6 cottages, swimming pool and library. Tours of the battlefield are given.

Hluhluwe-Imfolozi Park

The Hluhluwe and Imfolozi Reserves, the oldest reserves in Africa (proclaimed in 1895), were combined to form Hluhluwe-Imfolozi Park — now the third largest reserve in South Africa. As there are no roads directly connecting

Hluhluwe and Imfolozi, each section of the park must be visited separately. The best time to visit is during the dry winter months (May to September). Game drives by open vehicle and walks with national park guides are available.

The Imfolozi section of the park is located about 165 miles (265 km) north of Durban. This 185-square-mile (478-km^2) reserve of open grassland and savannah woodland is best known for having the world's largest concentration of white rhino — approximately 1,900. Other species include black rhino, elephant, nyala, greater kudu, waterbuck, zebra, wildebeest, buffalo, giraffe, black-backed jackal, lion and cheetah. Over 400 species of birds have been recorded.

The 90-square-miles (231-km^2) of grassland, forest and woodland of the Hluhluwe section of the park is host to a variety of wildlife, including large numbers of white rhino, along with black rhino, elephant, buffalo, southern giraffe, wildebeest, Burchell's zebra, kudu, lion, cheetah, Samango monkeys, hippo and crocs. This is one of the best parks in Africa to see the splendid nyala antelope. Over 425 bird species have been recorded, with narina trogon, cinnamon dove and Natal robin among the more interesting species.

The Hluhluwe section of the park is located about 18 miles (29 km) from St. Lucia and 175 miles (282 km) from Durban. The park contains walking trails.

ACCOMMODATION — CLASS B: • **Hilltop Camp**, an attractive camp in the Hluhluwe section run by the park, has simple chalets and a restaurant.

ACCOMMODATION NEAR THE PARK — CLASS A/B: • **Zululand Tree Lodge**, located on the Ubizane Game Reserve near the Hluhluwe entrance, has 24 fan-cooled treehouse-style chalets with large sliding glass doors and a swimming pool. Game drives to Hluhluwe Umfolozi and Mkuzi Game Reserves, walks, horseback riding, local community visits and cruises on Lake St. Lucia are offered.

Phinda Private Game Reserve

Phinda covers 85-square-miles (220-km^2) of landscape, much of it reclaimed from former livestock and pineapple farms. The habitats are extremely diverse, with acacia and broad-leafed savannah, riverine woodland, marshes and rocky hillsides. Groves of unique sand-forest exist on ancient dunes, and this remarkable dry forest is home to rare plants and mammals such as suni, bushpig and nyala, and unusual birds, including African broadbill, Neergaard's sunbird and pink-throated twinspot.

Wildlife at Phinda includes white rhino, giraffe, elephant, hippo, zebra and buffalo, as well as the big carnivores — all reintroduced since 1991 and thriving in this reborn wilderness. This is one of the best reserves in southern Africa for seeing cheetah. Bird watching is outstanding; among the more interesting species are crested guineafowl, gorgeous bushshrike, pygmy kingfisher, lemon-breasted canary and Eastern Nicator.

Phinda operates along the lines of private reserves bordering Kruger, with day and night drives in open 4wd vehicles, bush walks and boma dinners. Additional experiences offered include boat cruises and canoeing on the Mzinene River,

excursions to the nearby Indian Ocean, and flights to enjoy an aerial perspective of the region. Loggerhead turtles, bottlenose dolphins, whale sharks and rays are among the marine animals often seen from the air. Three-day walking safaris with overnights in a luxury mobile tented camp, and a Bush Skills Academy are also offered.

The rights to the land itself were recently returned to the community.

ACCOMMODATION — A+: • **The Homestead** is a luxurious private villa on Phinda Private Game Reserve situated in the west of the Reserve. The villa includes 4 spacious suites and a private butler, chef, guide and 4wd safari vehicle for exclusive use of the guests. • **Phinda Rock Lodge** has 6 air-conditioned suites nestled on the edge of a rocky cliff, each with indoor-outdoor showers and plunge pool. • **Phinda Vlei Lodge** has 6 air-conditioned suites on stilts, each with their own plunge pool.

CLASS A: • **Phinda Forest Lodge** has 16 air-conditioned chalets, surrounded on three sides by glass and built on stilts between the forest floor and the towering torchwood trees, and a swimming pool. The windows open up to the canopy beyond.

Phinda Private Game Reserve *(top)*, A suite at Phinda Mountain Lodge *(middle)*, Phinda Rock Lodge *(bottom)*

• **Phinda Mountain Lodge** has 25 spacious air-conditioned chalets with views of the Ubombo mountain range, private plunge pool and outdoor shower. • **Phinda Zuka Lodge** offers 4 thatched Zululand bush cottages with private verandahs overlooking the waterhole. Private guide/host, butler and chef are exclusive to the camp.

iSimangaliso and Maputaland Marine Reserves

These two reserves combined to form Africa's largest marine conservation area, covering 342-square-miles (885-km²). The reserve runs along the coastline from 0.6 mile (1 km) south of Cape Vidal to the Mozambique border and 3.5 miles (5.6 km) out into the Indian Ocean.

Several species of turtles, including loggerhead and the endangered leatherback, lay their eggs on the northern beaches. iSimangaliso includes the southernmost coral reefs in the world and is the only breeding spot for pink-backed pelicans in South Africa. Flamingos migrate to the reserve, depending upon the salinity levels in the lakes and lagoons. Boat tours are available from the village of St. Lucia.

ACCOMMODATION — CLASS B: • **Makakatana Bay Lodge**, located within the iSimangaliso Wetland Park Reserve, has 5 air-conditioned suites and 1 honeymoon suite, swimming pool, restaurant and bar.

Maputaland Coastal Forest Reserve

The Maputaland Coastal Forest Reserve is a remote reserve containing very possibly the highest forested sand dunes in the world. No construction is allowed on the ocean side of these huge dunes. The beach is, in fact, rated as one of the most beautiful and pristine beaches in the world!

Maputaland is one of the best areas for scuba diving in southern Africa. The Indian Ocean "Big Five"— humpback whales, whale sharks, huge leather back turtles, bottlenosed dolphins and ragged-tooth sharks — can be seen on dives.

Wildlife includes large spotted genet, water mongoose, hippos and turtles (in season). KwaZulu locals are often seen collecting mussels and catching reef fish in the reserve.

A deserted beach along the Maputaland Coastal Forest Reserve

This region offers some of the best scuba diving in South Africa

Beach walking, snorkeling, surf casting and fly-fishing, and exploring the unique flora and bird life of this region provide visitors with plenty to do. Black Rock, a large sandstone protrusion into the Indian Ocean about 4 miles (6.7 km) from Rocktail Bay, is one of the few places in the world where pelagics may be fished from shore. Lala Neck, located south of Rocktail Bay, is very good for snorkeling. Lake Sibaya, the largest freshwater lake in South Africa, is separated from the Indian Ocean by only the coastal dunes.

Rocktail Beach Camp

ACCOMMODATION — CLASS A/B:
• **Rocktail Beach Camp** lies within the coastal forest, 765 yards (700 m) inland from the warm Indian Ocean. Its 12 chalets (including 3 family rooms) are tucked away in the indigenous forest, each with private verandah (some with ocean views). A fully accredited dive center provides scuba diving and snorkeling activities offshore. Other activities include surf fishing, quad biking, birding, horseback riding guided drives to various sites and the local village. • **Thonga Beach Lodge**, on the shores of the Maputuland coast,

has luxury thatched suites with private balconies with sea or dune views. Snorkeling and off shore scuba diving are offered.

Sodwana Bay National Park

Fishing (especially for marlin) and scuba diving are the main attractions of this 1.6-square-mile (4.1-km²) reserve.

ACCOMMODATION — CLASS B/C: • **Sodwana Bay Lodge** has chalets with air-conditioning, ceiling fan and satellite television. Activities offered include scuba diving and big-game fishing.

Scuba Diving — Natal Coast

In the transition zone between Sodwana and Rocktail Bay's coral reefs and the Cape's kelp forests is the city of Durban and the southern Natal Coast. Aliwal Shoal, Lander's Reef and the Produce wreck are the diving focal points of the region.

Escorted boat dives to these rocky reefs are opportunities to view a wide variety of southern Africa's marine animals, including potato bass (a large grouper), eels, rays, turtles and myriad reef fish.

The best time to see Aliwal's famed "ragged tooth sharks" is June and July. A group of huge resident bridle bass (jewfish) and schools of dagger salmon make the nearby wreck of the Produce their home.

Zululand's semitropical coast has South Africa's warmest and clearest waters — ideal for scuba diving and snorkeling. Because the coral reefs are home to both warm- and cold-water fishes, there are more fish families to be found on the reefs off shore of Rocktail Bay and Sodwana Bay than in the whole of the Great Barrier Reef. Escorted boat dives are offered from Sodwana Bay and Rocktail Bay (see above).

Africa's most southern coral reefs are composed of hard and soft reefs. Named according to their distance from the Sodwana launch site, these reefs are called Quarter-, Two-, Three-, Four-, Seven- and Nine-Mile reefs. The reefs are home to many species of colorful Indian Ocean tropical fish, rock cods (groupers), kingfish (a large jack), barracudas and moray eels. Dolphins are sometimes sighted on the way to dive sites, and humpback whales migrate through the area in February and September. "Ragged tooth" sharks and enormous whale sharks (the world's biggest fish) are sometimes seen by divers in January and February. Manta rays and pelagics are also part of the fish mix. Loggerhead, green and leatherback sea turtles use the undeveloped coastline for nesting from December to March. Night drives and walks to see turtles nesting can be arranged.

Diving is possible year-round, with the best conditions between February and June. Visibility ranges from 20 to 100+ feet (6 to 30+ m), depending on sea conditions, with an average of 65 feet (20 m). Water temperature ranges from 70 to 80°F (21 to 27°C). Most diving is conducted from 25 to 125 feet (8 to 38 m) below the surface.

Mozambique

Mozambique

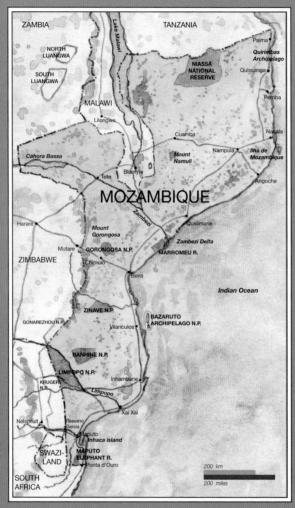

Mozambique is a huge country of about 308,640-square-miles (799,380-km²), which is larger than either Texas or France. Maputo is the capital city, and more than 80% of the population lives on or near the Indian Ocean. Much of the country is a low-lying coastal plain, drained by the Zambezi and Limpopo river systems. The climate is warm to hot, and frost free, with rainfall between October and March. Moist miombo woodland is the dominant habitat of the interior, with semiarid acacia and mopane woodland-savannah along the low-lying drainage systems. Much of the coastal vegetation has been replaced by sugarcane and other forms of agriculture, but the coast and offshore islands are spectacularly beautiful. A colony of Portugal until 1976, Portuguese is still widely spoken and forms a common language among the many ethnic groups. The currency is the meticais.

Mozambique
Country Highlights

- Explore Ilha de Mozambique — the old capital of Mozambique.
- Safari to Gorongosa National Park, a huge diversity of eco-zones with the most viable game viewing area in Mozambique.
- The Niassa Reserve is twice the size of Kruger National Park and offers spectacular scenery.
- Travel to the Quirimbas Archipelago featuring remote islands with exclusive lodges, white sandy beaches, blue sea, great fishing and amazing diving.
- Swim with the whale sharks off Mozambique's coast.
- Visit Ibo Island, a slave travel island, for a true cultural experience.

When's the Best Time to Go for Game Viewing

▨ Excellent ▩ Good ☐ Fair ■ Poor ▥ Closed

Country	Park/Reserve	JAN	FEB	MAR	APR	MAY	JUN	JUL	AUG	SEP	OCT	NOV	DEC
Mozambique	Gorongosa												
	Niassa												
	Diving in Quirimbas and Bazaruto												
	Whale Sharks (Tofo area)												

Best Safari Experience

Explore Gorongosa (Gorongosa National Park) and Lugenda Wilderness Camp (Niassa Reserve)

MOZAMBIQUE

Mozambique's greatest attractions to the international traveler are its remote wildlife reserves and pristine beaches — especially on the idyllic islands off its 1,550 mile (2,500 km) coastline with properties offering barefoot luxury at its finest.

In addition to enjoying beautiful white sandy beaches, adventure activities including diving, snorkeling and fishing are world class. A visit to the coast of this country can be the perfect beginning or ending to a safari in eastern or southern Africa.

The country is ideal for the true adventurer seeking a remote bush experience in seldom visited wildlife reserves, and for travelers wishing to explore new territory well off the beaten path.

Mozambique is bordered on the southwest by South Africa and Swaziland, on the west by Zimbabwe, Zambia and Malawi, and on the north by Tanzania. The country encompasses nearly 309,000-square-miles (800,000-km^2) and is three times the size of the United Kingdom.

Most of the country is comprised of coastal lowlands that are wide in the south and narrow as one travels northward, where the plains rise to plateaus and mountains along the borders of Zimbabwe, Zambia and Malawi. The highest point in the country is Binga Peak (7,993 ft./2,436 m) on the Zimbabwean border. The Zambezi River's flood plains are the dominant feature in the center of the country, with the river flowing from the Cahora Bassa Dam near the Zimbabwe border to the 62-mile wide (100 km) Zambezi Delta and emptying into the Indian Ocean. The far north is characterized by striking inselbergs (tall granite outcrops). The other main rivers transecting the country are the Rio Limpopo in the south, the Rio Save in the center and the Rio Rovuma, which serves as a border with Tanzania in the north.

As Mozambique lies primarily in the tropics, the climate is warm to hot and humid. Generally, the rainy season is from November to March. However, the weather patterns are not as consistent as they were a few decades ago. Cyclone season is February to March, with the "cyclone belt" covering just the south of the country.

Bantu-speaking tribes migrated to the area around the first century A.D. Small chiefdoms formed and many consolidated into larger kingdoms. Arab traders arrived by ship around the eighth century A.D. Vasco da Gamma "discovered" Mozambique by landing on Ilha de Mozambique in 1497. The Portuguese quickly gained control of a number of islands along the coast in a quest to control the gold trade and later the ivory and slave trades from the mainland. The Portuguese

A dhow sails off Mozambique's 1550 miles (2500 km) of coastline

signed a treaty with Britain in 1891 that set the boundaries of Portuguese East Africa. The country became independent on June 25, 1975 with Samora Machel as president. A long civil war decimated much of the country and ended with a peace agreement in 1992. The country has recovered well since that time.

Mozambique has an approximate population of 23 million, nearly half of which are under the age of 14. About 30% of people live in towns and cities, and almost 80% are subsistence farmers. Of the major tribal groups, the Makua-Lomwe is the largest representing nearly half of the population, followed by the Tsonga, Shona, Sena, Nyungwe, Chuabo, Sena and Yao.

There are over 60 languages and dialects spoken. About a quarter of the people speak Portuguese, with English being spoken in the major cities, as well as in most of the hotels, safari camps and beach resorts attracting international guests.

The country is a melting pot of African, Portuguese, Arabic and Indian cultures. About 52% are Christian (most are Roman Catholics), 28% Muslim and the majority of the rest follow traditional religions (ancestor worship and animism) or are agnostic. Due to the multi-cultural influence the food is interesting and the seafood is, in fact, spectacular. Be sure to try the *piri piri* prawns!

🐾 WILDLIFE AND WILDLIFE AREAS

Much of Mozambique's wildlife was decimated during the civil war that ended in the early 1990s. However, the wildlife populations have greatly improved through innovative conservation efforts. Some parks have, in fact, been restocked with indigenous species. The major wildlife reserves to consider visiting on the mainland are Reserva do Niassa (Niassa Reserve), Parque Nacional da Gorongosa (Gorongosa National Park) and the Parque Nacional do Limpopo (Limpopo Transfrontier Reserve) bordering Kruger National Park (South Africa). The wildlife is not as concentrated as the better reserves in Zambia, Botswana and South Africa. However, a real plus is that you will virtually have the parks to yourself. Birding is amazing, with over 600 species recorded.

These parks draw adventurers looking for pristine bush experiences and ones looking for new frontiers. A visit to one or more reserves can be combined with a wonderful beach holiday!

Marine Life

Some of Mozambique's greatest wildlife attractions lie below sea level. The coast and the islands support an amazing variety of fish, coral, marine mammals and plants. Around two thousand species of fish representing over 80% of the families of the Indo-Pacific region occur here. Among the most interesting is the whale shark, the largest fish in the world growing up to 50 feet in length. Whale sharks are often sited by divers and boaters especially from October to February.

Humpback whales are frequently seen from June to October

Other sea life includes the dugong (similar to the manatee), several species of dolphin (bottlenose, striped, spinner and humpback), humpback whales, turtles (leatherback, loggerhead, hawksbill and green) and manta rays. Mozambique is certainly one of the best-kept secrets for divers.

The best sightings of humpback whales in the south is during the late winter (June to October) and may also be seen in the north in the Pemba area July to November. Water temperatures range from 82°F/28C in summer (and up to 86°F/30C December to February) to 72°F (22C) during the winter months (May to July).

Marine parks include Parque Nacional de Querimbas (Quirimbas National Park) and Parque Nacional de Bazaruto (Bazaruto National Park).

THE NORTH

Pemba

Pemba is the capital of the province of Cabo Delgado and the major city in the north of the country. The town is situated on the Bay of Pemba, a huge, natural deep-water bay.

Formerly known as Porto Amelia, this traditional Mozambique fishing port features interesting Portuguese-colonial architecture, and offers scuba diving and world-class blue water fishing close by. The coral reefs lie close to the shore and within reach are the abundant fishing waters at St. Lazarus Banks.

Pemba can be accessed by scheduled or private air service from Maputo, Johannesburg (South Africa), Nairobi (Kenya) and Dar-es-Salaam (Tanzania). Some visitors stay at this quaint coastal town and enjoy the beaches and diving, while others use it as a waypoint and connect to the more exclusive islands in the Quirimbas Archipelago, or to the Niassa Reserve.

ACCOMMODATION — TOURIST CLASS:
• **Pemba Beach Hotel and Spa** has Arabian-influenced architecture with 100 rooms comprising of standard and luxury room types, self-catering villas and 5 suites, 2 restaurants, 2 bars, gym, 2 saltwater pools, a spa and beach club.
• **Londo Lodge**, situated on a peninsula just south of the Quirimbas National Park, has only 6 private villas (5 Beach View and 1 Executive), infinity swimming pool and massage facilities.

Quirimbas Archipelago

The Quirimbas Archipelago consists of 32 tropical coral islands and stretches for 62 miles (100 km) along the coast from Pemba to the Tanzanian border.

It contains one of the world's richest reefs and most bio-diverse marine areas in the world, with dugongs, fish eagles and turtles. Humpback whales pass through the islands on their annual migration and can be seen during the months of July to November. Humpback and spinner dolphins may be seen year round. The area has very little development, making it all the more attractive to international visitors.

Pemba Beach Hotel and Spa *(top)*, The turquoise waters of the Quirimbas Archipelago *(bottom)*

The impressive marine area of **Quirimbas National Park** covers 580-square-miles (1,500-km²) and includes 11 coral islands. These islands feature phenomenal vertical drop-offs, some up to 1,300 feet (400 m). These walls are abundant with coral covered caves and tropical fish and game fish. The park is also home to a wide variety of bird species such as mangrove fish eagles, herons, flamingos, kingfishers, plovers and coucals.

ACCOMMODATION — DELUXE: • **Guludo Beach Lodge**, located 50 miles (80 km) north of Pemba, features individual bandas with thatched porches and canopied beds. The beachfront resort offers scuba diving, sunset sailing trip, whale watching, island excursions and village visits.

Vamizi Island (Ilha Vamizi)

Vamizi Island is an 8-mile (12-km) crescent-shaped idyllic tropical island situated a short charter flight from Pemba.

Activities offered at the lodge include world-class scuba diving and snorkeling in the pristine coral reefs, deep sea, fly or shore fishing, kayaking, cruising by dhow and being pampered in the spa. Guided walks and a day trip to nearby Rongui Island are available.

ACCOMMODATION — DELUXE: • **Vamizi**, the only lodge on the island, offers 10 spacious sea-facing beach villas nestled under trees. The palm-thatched villas have expansive verandas and Swahili daybeds and marble bathrooms. Access is via a short charter flight from Pemba.

A candlelit dinner on Vamizi Island

Quilálea Island

Quilálea Island, situated in the southern region of the Quirimbas Archipelago, is a unique island marine sanctuary, fringed with pristine beaches and surrounded by the tropical Indian Ocean. The island is only 88 acres (35 hectares) in size and offers the ultimate in seclusion and privacy as the only residents are the hotel guests and staff.

ACCOMMODATION — DELUXE: • **Quilálea** is a private retreat accommodating up to 18 guests in 9 luxury air-conditioned villas, with secluded verandas with panoramic sea views. Each villa was constructed entirely with indigenous materials. Scuba diving, snorkeling, fishing, and excursions on their 38 foot sailing yacht are available. Access is via a short charter flight from Pemba.

Matemo Island

Matemo Island is located approximately 20 minutes flying time north of Pemba. Palm groves, lush vegetation, white beaches and an azure sea provide an idyllic setting for this exotic Quirimbas island destination. Ideal for honeymooners or families, Matemo offers a wide range of marine activities plus a fascinating insight into local culture.

ACCOMMODATION — DELUXE: • **Matemo Island** accommodates a maximum of 46 guests in 23 luxury air-conditioned chalets, each located just yards (meters) from the beach, with private patios with a hammock, indoor-outdoor showers and panoramic ocean views. Spa treatments, diving, snorkeling, fishing and cultural island excursions to Ibo Island are offered.

Medjumbe Private Island

This romantic and exclusive island getaway of endless white sand and translucent sea mesmerizes all who visit, while the untouched marine environment allows for constant new discoveries, whether your passion is diving, fishing, snorkeling, or simply exploring the spectacular beaches.

This small island of unspoiled beaches surrounded by translucent waters is just 875 × 380 yards (800 × 350 m) in size and offers total exclusivity and privacy, as the only human inhabitants being guests and staff. The diving off the island is world class, and the first of many exquisite sites can be found just 1.5 miles (2 km) from shore. Snorkeling and fishing, waterskiing, sailing, kayaking and sunset cruises are also offered.

Matemo Island features white sand beaches *(top)*, Matemo's main lodge *(middle)*, A charming room at Medjumbe Private Island *(bottom)*

ACCOMMODATION — DELUXE: • **Medjumbe Private Island** accommodates just 24 guests in 12 secluded luxury air-conditioned chalets each with panoramic sea views, their own plunge pool, deck, patio and sala.

Ibo Island (Ilha Do Ibo)

Ibo Island lies within Quirimbas National Park and is historically the most interesting island in the archipelago, and has been nominated for World Heritage status. For 500 years it was a prominent trading post on the East African coast, and had, in fact, become the most important town in Mozambique by the late eighteenth century. The island has three forts, an old catholic church and other historic buildings, and is virtually untouched by large commercial developments. Visiting here is like going back in time.

ACCOMMODATION —FIRST CLASS: • **Ibo Island Lodge** is located on the waterfront and incorporates three mansions each over a century old with walls a yard (1 m) thick, with 12 air-conditioned rooms with either sea or garden views. The restaurant serves dinner on the rooftop terrace highlighting the freshest seafood. The dhow sailing excursion is popular and an opportunity to visit neighboring islands.

Niassa Reserve (Reserva Do Niassa)

This 16,200-square-mile (42,000-km^2) park is set on the southern border of Tanzania, and is about twice the size of Kruger National Park (South Africa). The scenery is incredible, with giant inselbergs, baobab trees and palms reaching

The Niassa Reserve is the largest in Mozambique

out to the sky from what is one of the largest protected areas of miombo *(bra-chystegia)* woodland on the continent.

This is the largest reserve in Mozambique and has the highest concentration of game of any reserve as well. Due to its remoteness, the wildlife populations here were much less affected by the civil war than the country's other reserves. As this is a reserve and not a national park, there are a number of people living within it's borders.

Wildlife includes approximately 12,000 elephant, 9,000 sable antelope, 5,000 buffalo and 200 wild dog, along with good populations of lion, leopard, eland, Lichtenstein's hartebeest, kudu, bushbuck, impala, wildebeest, zebra, waterbuck and hippo. The elephant are famous for their large tusks. Three subspecies endemic to the park include Boehm's zebra, Niassa wildebeest and Johnston's impala.

Over 370 bird species have been recorded including Pel's fishing owl, Taita falcon, Bohm's bee-eater, African skimmer, Stierling's woodpecker and the African pitta.

ACCOMMODATION — CLASS A/B:
• **Lugenda Wilderness Camp**, located on the Lugenda River, has 8 fan-cooled luxury tents with large verandahs, a boma, and a swimming pool. Game drives, canoeing and escorted walks are offered. Access is by scheduled air charter from Pemba. The camp is open from June 1st until December 15th. Children under the age of 12 are not allowed.

Lugenda Wilderness Camp

CENTRAL

Gorongosa National Park (Parque Nacional da Gorongosa)

Gorongosa National Park covers approximately 1,455-square-miles (3,770-km²) of the floor of the Great East African Rift Valley and is considered to be the

Wildlife within Gorongosa is best viewed from May to November

Gorongosa National Park

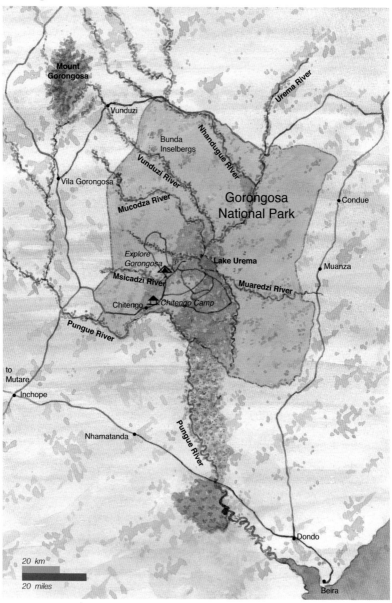

country's most biologically diverse reserve. Habitats include lowland miombo woodland, mopane woodland, rainforests, extensive grasslands and swamps.

The park was named after 6,107 foot (1,862 m) Gorongosa Mountain, which dominates the landscape. Many rivers formed on its slopes flow into Lake Urema, which is centrally located in the park.

Wildlife populations here have increased greatly over the past several years. The Carr Foundation has been restocking buffalo, wildebeest and zebra. Other wildlife that may be seen includes lion, elephant, hippo, crocodile, kudu and waterbuck, eland, sable, hartebeest, oribi, nyala, two species of bushbaby, and with luck, leopard, lion, and wild dog.

The diversity of soil types in the valley support an astonishing number of plant species that in turn support many different species of reptiles, frogs, and fish; more than 400 bird species, including the endemic green-headed oriole on Mount Gorongosa, Pel's fishing owl, collared palm thrush, green malkoha, lesser seedcracker, anchieta's tchagra, moustached grass warbler, spotted creeper, cabanis bunting and arnot's chat.

Attractions within the park include the Lake Urema wetlands, the limestone gorges of the Cheringoma Plateau and Murombodzi Waterfall.

There are approximately 93 miles (150 km) of game viewing roads in the park. The best time to visit is during the dry season May to November. During the rainy season (January to April) the park is closed. The best access is by a 30-minute charter flight, or a three and a half hour long drive from Beira.

ACCOMMODATION — CLASS A/B:
• **Explore Gorongosa** is the only private tourism camp in Gorongosa National Park and is a true authentic safari camp. The eco-camp features 6 tents with solar power and eco-toilets. Activities include escorted walks and day and night game drives within the park.

CLASS C: • **Chitengo Camp** is run by the national parks department and has 15 air-conditioned cabanas with a restaurant and pool.

Elephants wade through the wetlands *(top)*, A tent at Explore Gorongosa *(bottom)*

SOUTH

Limpopo Transfrontier Reserve (Parque Nacional do Limpopo)
Located along the South African border, much of the wildlife in this reserve was killed off during the civil war that ended in 1992. Wildlife populations are fortunately recovering.

The 75,000-acre (30,000-hectare) "Sanctuary" area, located within the reserve borders Kruger National Park, has the best game viewing, and is where most of the game is being trans-located in an effort to help restock the park.

Easiest access is by 4wd vehicle from Kruger National Park. Alternatively, you can fly by private charter from Maputo.

ACCOMMODATIONS — CLASS C: **Machampane Wilderness Camp** is located in the Sanctuary Area and has 5 tents on raised decks overlooking the Machampane River.

Vilanculos
Vilanculos is the gateway coastal city to the Bazaruto Archipelago, 435 miles (700 km) north of Maputo, directly opposite the islands of the Bazaruto Archipelago in the tropical Inhambane province.

Bazaruto Archipelago
Bazaruto and Benguerra Islands are the two largest islands off the Mozambican coast and feature beautiful white-sand beaches, world-class scuba diving and snorkeling, magnificent high sand dunes, coastal bush and green fresh-water lakes inhabited by crocodiles. Bird "specials" include the blue-throated sunbird and Rudd's apalis.

For the avid angler, the Bazaruto Archipelago is ranked as the best marlin-angling destination in the eastern Indian Ocean. The best time for marlin fishing is from mid-September until the end of December and for sailfish fishing is from April to August, with smaller game fish available year-round.

Bazaruto National Park includes Bazaruto, Benguerra, Magaruque, Santa Carolina and Bangue Islands, all of which are located 6 to 9 miles (10 to 15 km) off the coast just north of Vilanculos.

There are accommodations ranging from comfortable to deluxe from which to choose on Bazaruto Island (Indigo Bay and Bazaruto Lodge) and on Benguerra Island (Azura, Marlin Lodge and Benguerra Lodge).

Dolphin are visible through the crystal clear water

One of the pristine beaches within the Bazaruto Archipelago

Benguerra Island

Benguerra Island is the second largest island in the chain, covering approximately 21-square-miles (55-km^2) of magnificent beaches and surrounded by coral reefs. The island was declared a National Park in 1971, and includes forest, savannah, dunes and wetlands including freshwater lakes.

ACCOMMODATION — DELUXE: • **Azura**, Mozambique's first luxury eco-boutique retreat, was built entirely by hand in partnership with the local community. Azura has just 15 villas including 3 Luxury Beach Villas, 11 Infinity Beach Villas and the Presidential Villa. Each beachfront villa has an indoor-outdoor shower, pool, air-conditioning, private sun deck, minibar, and butler service. Activities include snorkeling and scuba diving, big game fishing (marlin, sailfish, tuna), dhow trips,

The luxurious and eco-friendly Azura Lodge

cruises to remote beaches and island walks. • **Benguerra Lodge** is set within Benguerra Bay on the protected northwest side of the island in an ideal location. There are 4 types of accommodations: Bungalows, Cabanas, Casitas and the Villa — all with direct beach access. Activities include wind surfing, snorkeling and scuba diving, hobie cat sailing, dhow rides and deep-sea and saltwater fishing.

ACCOMMODATION — FIRST CLASS: • **Marlin Lodge**, located on Benguerra Island, accommodates 34 guests in 14 luxury Beach Chalets and 3 Executive Beach Suites constructed from local hardwoods and elevated on stilts with deck platforms. Each is air-conditioned and has an indoor and an outdoor shower, and a private, thatch-covered deck with sea facing views and direct beach access. There is a swimming pool with beach gazebo and serviced pool bar. The lodge welcomes children 14 years and older. Activities include wind-surfing, catamaran sailing, kite-flying and ocean ski paddling, waterskiing, snorkeling, scuba diving and sunset cruises on a dhow.

Deep sea fishing is popular from Indigo Bay Island Resort *(top)*, A suite at Indigo Bay *(bottom)*

Bazaruto Island (Ilha do Bazaruto)

Bazaruto is 23 miles (37 km) long and 4 miles (7 km) wide, making it by far the largest of the islands in the archipelago. Savannah grassland dominates the western part of the island while large sand dunes dominate the eastern part of the island.

ACCOMMODATION — DELUXE: • **Indigo Bay Island Resort and Spa**, on the southwestern shore of Bazaruto Island, offers guests a variety of accommodations including 29 Beach Chalets, 1 Honeymoon Chalet, 12 Luxury Bay View Villas, 1 Executive Suite and a Presidential Villa. Each chalet and villa is air-conditioned and has a mini-bar and private balcony. The Bay View Villas and Honeymoon Chalet also feature private plunge pools. Facilities include two swimming pools and a pool bar, beach snack bar, modern gym and the Sanctuary Spa. Activities available include scuba diving, snorkeling, hobie cat sailing, horseback riding, sundowner cruises, dune boarding, land rover safaris, golf, catamaran island hopping and saltwater fly-fishing.

TOURIST CLASS: • **Bazaruto Lodge** has 25 A-frame thatch-roofed bungalows

(12 standard, 11 superior and 1 honeymoon) set in lush tropical gardens. All units are air-conditioned with ceiling fans.

Maputo

Maputo, formerly known as Lorenzo Marques, is the capital of Mozambique. The city is a hodgepodge of new and old buildings with wide streets lined with jacaranda and palm trees, and is humming with activity.

The **Museu de Historia Natural** (Natural History Museum) is worth a visit, if only to see what may be the world's largest collection of elephant foetuses. The **Museu Nacional de Art** (National Art Museum) features the works of many of Mozambique's best contemporary artists. The nineteenth century **Fortaleza** (Fort) has a small museum. The **Mercado Municipal** will give you an insight into the life of the people and the variety of local produce available. **FEIMA** (art's and crafts market) is located across from the Polana Serena Hotel and is open daily. The CCFM (Centro Cultural Franco Moçambicano-French/Mozambican Cultural Centre) has a number of bands performing in the evenings.

One of the most unusual buildings in Africa is the **Iron House of Maputo**, located near the city center. This house was made entirely of iron and was designed by Gustave Eiffel. Built in the late nineteenth century to be the governor's home, it proved to be far too hot for residence. **Inhaca Island** is a densely wooded island off Maputo, 10 minutes by small aircraft and two hours by ferry boat.

Be sure to try a few local restaurants and enjoy the local beers and a plate of *piri piri* prawns. **Piri Piri**, opposite the Polana Shopping Centre, serves sumptuous *piri piri* chicken, fantastic prawns and long glasses of cold local beer in "Giraffe" glasses. **Gianni's**, on the other side of the Polana Shopping Centre serves fresh ice cream made with local fruit and served with waffles and pancakes. **Costa do Sol**, located at the end of the Marginal coast road, is famous for its shellfish.

ACCOMMODATIONS — DELUXE: • **The Polana Serena Hotel** is situated ten minutes away from the city center and the airport. This majestic colonial building offers 164 air-conditioned rooms and 23 suites. The hotel overlooks the Bay of Maputo and offers landscaped gardens, a swimming pool and several restaurants and bars.

ACCOMMODATIONS — FIRST CLASS: • **Southern Sun Maputo**, located 5 miles (7 km) from the international airport, is the only beachfront hotel in the city of Maputo. Facilities include a swimming pool, sea view restaurant, bar and fitness center, and free Internet access in all guest rooms.

ACCOMMODATION — TOURIST CLASS: • **Cardoso** has 114 air-conditioned standard rooms, 4 luxury suites and 12 executive rooms, gymnasium, swimming pool and wireless Internet throughout the hotel.

Malawi

Malawi

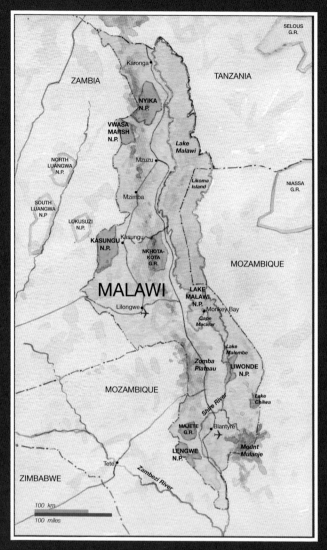

Known to many as the "Warm Heart of Africa" Malawi is a beautiful country dominated by the great lake of the same name. The altitude varies from 120 feet (37 m) in the Shire Valley to 9,847 feet (3,002 m) on the summit of Mount Mulanje. Brachystegia (miombo) woodland prevails over most of the country, with open grassland and moorland on higher ground. The population of Malawi is around 12 million, with about 500,000 in the capital of Lilongwe. The majority of the population are subsistence farmers. Chichewa and English are the official languages. Currency is the Malawian Kwacha.

Malawi
Country Highlights

- Interact with some of Africa's friendliest people!
- Boat, kayak, sail or have a beach holiday on beautiful Lake Malawi — the third largest lake in Africa.
- Take a night boat ride on the Shire River looking for monster crocodiles, and sleep out on a starbed platform on the flood plains of the Shire River in Liwonde National Park.
- Walk in the eerie montane forests of the high Nyika Plateau and look for leopard and serval on night drives.
- Visit remote Likoma Island for snorkeling, scuba diving, swimming, sailing and exploring the local villages.

When's the Best Time to Go for Game Viewing

■ Excellent   ■ Good   ☐ Fair   ■ Poor   ■ Closed

Country	Park/Reserve	JAN	FEB	MAR	APR	MAY	JUN	JUL	AUG	SEP	OCT	NOV	DEC
Malawi	Liwonde												
	Majete												
	Nyika												

Best Safari Experience

Chelinda Lodge (Nyika), Kaya Mawa Lodge (Likoma Island), Mumbo Island Camp (Lake Malawi), Mvuu Wilderness Lodge (Liwonde National Park)

MALAWI

Malawi, the warm heart of Africa, is a beautiful country with a variety of holiday attractions, interesting cultures and a few wildlife reserves of interest to the international traveler. Lake Malawi is a popular beach destination for travelers who have been on safari in Zambia, Zimbabwe, or other southern African countries.

Geographically, the country is dominated by Lake Malawi, which stretches along the spine of the country. It is often referred to as the "calendar lake" because its surface dimensions are 365 miles (568 km) long and 52 miles (84 km) wide.

This freshwater lake, the southernmost in the Rift Valley chain, is the third largest in Africa. It is also one of the deepest of the Great Rift Valley lakes (2,296 feet/700 m deep), with its deepest point 755 feet (230 m) below sea level. Lake Malawi has over 400 species of freshwater fish and the largest number of cichlid fish species in the world.

Malawi is bordered by Zambia to the west, Tanzania to the north and Mozambique to the east, southwest and south. From north to south, Malawi is about 560 miles (900 km) long. The dominant geographical features in the south of the country are the Shire River and the high plateau of Dedza, Zomba and the Kirk Mountain Range, reaching an altitude from 5,050 feet (1,540 m) to 8,000 feet (2,440 m) above sea level.

As a whole, the country ranges in altitude from 120 feet (37 m) in the lower Shire Valley in the south to a height of 9,847 feet (3,002 m) at Mount Mulanje, also in the south. The northern lakeshore and adjacent low country rise steeply to the west. Several areas, the Misuku Hills, the Nyika Plateau (Nganda Point is the highest peak on the plateau at 8,551 feet/2,607 m) and the Viphya Plateau, dominate the areas of higher ground.

The dominant vegetation of Malawi is *brachystegia* or miombo woodlands. Malawi has a tropical climate with a rainy season extending from November to March in the south and November to April in the north. Its climate is influenced locally by the lake and by altitude. Temperatures vary considerably, from a maximum of 104°F (40°C) in the low-lying Shire Valley (pronounced shirry) to below freezing on the plateaus, where frost may occur.

In the early fifteenth century, the area was inhabited by the Maravi people (a derivation of the word Malawi), who moved in from the west of the continent around the twelfth century. Arab slave traders were well established in the area by 1870 and were handling more than 20,000 slaves per year. David Livingstone first visited the area in 1859, and on his subsequent visits brought many British missionaries.

Nyasaland became a protectorate of the British Empire in 1891 and in 1953 joined the Federation of Northern (now Zambia) and Southern (now Zimbabwe) Rhodesia. Malawi became independent in 1964.

Chichewa is the national language, but English is the official language and is widely spoken. The most popular beer is Carlsberg, brewed according to Danish traditions. You may want to try some Malawi Gin, and do not miss out on Malawian cashew nuts, peanut butter and Mulanje Gold, an admirable substitute for Kahlua.

The country's economy is based on agriculture; 90% of its population is rural, and agriculture accounts for 40% of the gross domestic product and 90% of its export revenues. Almost 70% of agricultural produce comes from small land holding farmers, whose principal crops are maize, tobacco, tea, sugarcane, groundnuts and coffee. With a population in excess of 12 million, almost every available piece of arable land is cultivated.

🐾 WILDLIFE AND WILDLIFE AREAS

Great importance has been attached to the protection of Malawi's natural heritage, which is reflected in the number of national parks and reserves within the country. Despite the burdens of overpopulation, almost 20% of Malawi's land area is set aside as either national park, game reserve or forest reserve.

Malawi's primary wildlife attractions are Liwonde National Park, Nyika National Park and Lake Malawi itself. Zambia is an excellent country to combine with Malawi, because South Luangwa National Park (Zambia) is easily accessible by air from Lilongwe.

Nyika National Park

The Nyika Plateau is a wild, remote and spectacular area of rolling montane grasslands interspersed with pockets of evergreen forest. The upland area of the Nyika (which means "wilderness" in the local Tumbuka language) Plateau was designated as Malawi's first national park in 1966. Today it is the country's largest park, encompassing a total area of 1,210-square-miles (3,134 km²).

Game on the plateau is plentiful; reedbuck, common duiker and roan antelope are the dominant animals, along with eland and Burchell's zebra. Leopard, hyena and bushpig may be seen on evening drives.

A night game drive in Nyika National Park

The stunning views from the Nyika Plateau

The flower-filled, rolling grasslands of the Nyika are home to wattled crane, Denham's bustard, churring and black-lored cisticolas, common quail, rufous-naped lark, red-tufted malachite sunbird and mountain nightjar. The evergreen forest pockets, often beginning in valley heads and following drainage lines, are sanctuary to the large chequered elephant shrew, bushpig and forest duiker. They are also home for a number of forest-dwelling birds such as moustached green tinkerbird, Fulleborn's black boubou, Sharpe's akalat, olive-flanked alethe, scaly francolin, white-tailed flycatcher and bar-tailed trogon.

The best time to visit the park for botanists (for wildflowers and orchids) is September to January. For birders, September to March is best, although the heavy rains in January through April can restrict access and activities in the park. Wildlife viewing is good throughout the year.

A network of dirt roads meanders across the plateau. Access to the park is via Thazima Gate, 34 miles (55 km) from Rumphi and 81 miles (130 km) from Mzuzu. From Thazima Gate, it is about 37 miles (59 km) to the Malawian Parks Board Camp of Chelinda.

Chelinda Lodge

Lake Malawi

Magnificent Lake Malawi is the country's largest tourist attraction. The huge lake supplies a seemingly endless number of protein-rich fish to the local people. Chambo, a sought after tilapia (freshwater bream), is a good-eating fish.

On the lake you will see fishermen in their bwatus (dugout canoes) fishing either with nets or with lines. Sometimes at night you will see the twinkling of lights on the lake from bwatus and boats with small outboard motors.

The mostly clear waters of the lake make this an inviting environment for recreational activities. The southern lakeshore hotels are best equipped for watersports, and offer boardsailing, waterskiing, sailing, snorkeling and scuba diving.

Lake Malawi offers some of the best inland sailing in Africa. Although rough waters can suddenly develop with the onset of strong winds, there are no tides or currents in the lake. The prevailing wind is southeasterly, and the lake is generally at its calmest around March to June and is roughest in July and August. However, the lake can be rough at any time.

Likoma Island

Likoma Island is located in the north of Lake Malawi on the east side of the lake very close to the Mozambique coastline. To visit the island is to step back in time. Just 7-square-miles (17-km²) in size with one small dirt road and a few vehicles, the local people survive largely by fishing, and rice and cassava farming. The island has hundreds of huge baobab trees and a number of glorious sandy beaches and rocky coves. The waters are crystal clear throughout the year and the diving and snorkeling is among the best in Lake Malawi.

Likoma Island on Lake Malawi

Kaya Mawa Lodge is located on the southern tip of Likoma Island

ACCOMMODATION — FIRST CLASS: • **Kaya Mawa Lodge** is situated on the southwestern tip of the island at the head of a crescent-shaped bay, surrounded by mango trees and ancient baobabs. It consists of 10 stone and teak-framed thatched cottages each with a shower, sunken bathtub, a "loo with a view," and private terrace with direct water access. The Honeymoon Room is tucked away on its own private island and offers incredible views. Activities include snorkeling, scuba diving (additional fee), swimming, sailing and visits to the local villages. Day trips to Mozambique can be arranged.

TOURIST CLASS: • **Chintheche Inn**, situated on a sandy beach just south of Nkhata Bay on the western shore of the lake, has 10 fan-cooled rooms, restaurant, and swimming pool.

Lake Malawi National Park

Lake Malawi National Park is the first national park to provide protection to the freshwater life of a deep-water

A thatched cottage at Kaya Mawa Lodge

Rift Valley lake. The 34-square-mile (88-km²) park is located in the southern part of the lake and includes 12 islands and most of the Nankhumba Peninsula. Its crystal clear waters and myriad of colorful cichlid fish darting among the rocky shoreline entice one to don a mask and snorkel and join the fish in their daily activities.

Wildlife that may be seen includes bushbuck, klipspringer, crocs and hippos. Bird life includes fish eagles, trumpeter hornbill, white-breasted cuckooshrike, crowned and black eagles, golden-backed pytilia and mocking chat.

ACCOMMODATION ON THE SOUTHERN LAKESHORE — CLASS A/B: • **Pumulani** is located on the shore of Lake Malawi and features 10 individual villas, each with a large bedroom, living area and private deck with lake views. Activities include snorkeling, fishing, sailing, dhow cruises, nature walks and kayaking. Optional activities for an additional charge are waterskiing, scuba diving, wake boarding and tube rides. • **Club Makakola**, set on a sandy beach on the shores of Lake Malawi, has cottages and 55 rooms, 2 swimming pools, tennis courts, squash court, 9-hole Mlambe Golf Course and a conference center. Fishing, parasailing, diving and excursions to the Cape Maclear area are offered.

CLASS B: • **Livingstonia Beach Hotel** has 18 rooms and 8 rondavels, all fancooled, a restaurant and swimming pool. Sailboards, kayaks and boats are available for hire. • **Nkopola Lodge** is set on a hillside on the shore of Lake Malawi about 12 miles (20 km) north of the town of Mangochi. The lodge has 55 air-conditioned rooms and a restaurant.

ACCOMMODATION ON MUMBO ISLAND — CLASS B: • **Mumbo Island Camp**, located on a pristine tropical island on Lake Malawi set off the Cape Maclear Peninsula, consists of five double tents and one four-bed family unit, each with a shady deck and hammock. The island

Mumbo Island Camp offers total privacy and seclusion

offers total privacy and isolation from the mainland. There is a dining area, bar and water sport gazebo. Activities include swimming, sea kayaking, snorkeling, diving and exploring the local islands and lakeshore.

Lilongwe

Lilongwe became the capital in 1975 and features Old Town and New Town. **Old Town** hustles and bustles with markets and buildings close together, and the **New Town** (also known as the Garden City) offers modern architecture, open pedestrian precincts and parklands.

A visit to the market in the Old Town is a worthwhile experience. There, one can buy anything from live chickens to used motorcar parts. The air is ripe with the aroma of dried fish, spices and fresh vegetables.

For 6 months of each year (April to September) the **Tobacco Auction Floors** in Lilongwe and Limbe are hives of activity as buyers gather from around the world. Those thinking of visiting the floors should call in advance.

The **Lilongwe Nature Sanctuary**, located between the old and new towns, is a good place for seeing small mammals, such as porcupine, civet and vervet monkeys. It is also a good place for spotting birds, such as red-throated twinspot and perhaps African finfoot.

ACCOMMODATION — FIRST CLASS: • **Capital Hotel** is located in the New Town, adjacent to the commercial and diplomatic areas. The hotel has 185 air-conditioned rooms, 2 restaurants and a swimming pool.

TOURIST CLASS: • **Heuglin's Lodge** is an exclusive guesthouse with 6 bedrooms and a large swimming pool set in a quiet area of the Garden Suburbs of New Town. • **Lilongwe Hotel**, situated on 3 acres of landscaped gardens in the heart of the Old Town, has 91 air-conditioned rooms, 2 restaurants and a swimming pool. • **Kumbali Lodge**, situated on a farm on the outskirts of town, has 16 tastefully furnished rooms and is set in expansive gardens.

Downtown Lilongwe *(top)*, Heuglin's Lodge *(bottom)*

Blantyre

Blantyre, named after the birthplace of the great explorer David Livingstone, began as a mission station in 1876. Its position in the agriculturally rich highlands, which has a more temperate climate, made it attractive to the first commercial traders.

Today, Blantyre is the largest city in the country and is also the commercial and industrial center of Malawi. Historical sites include the **Blantyre Mission**, the beautiful church of **St. Michael's and All Angels**, and the **Mandala House**, the oldest building in the country (erected in 1882).

Blantyre's market is more modern and does not have quite the same appeal as that of Lilongwe.

ACCOMMODATION — FIRST CLASS: • **Ryall's Hotel Blantyre**, situated in the middle of town, is the oldest established hotel and offers 120 comfortably appointed rooms, a swimming pool and gym. • **Sunbird Mt. Soche Hotel**, located very close to the city center, has 132 air-conditioned rooms, 2 restaurants and a swimming pool.

Liwonde National Park

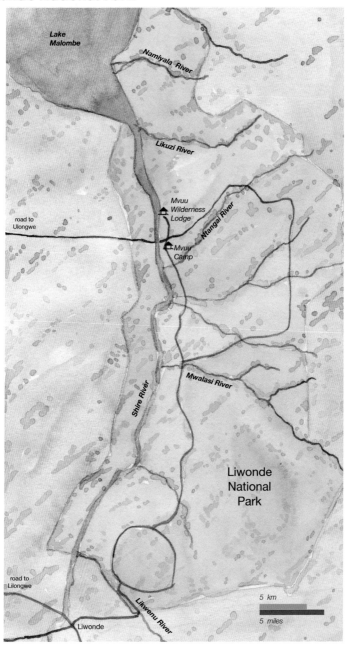

Lake
Malombe

Namiyala River

Likuzi River

Mvuu
Wilderness
Lodge

Ntangai River

road to
Ulongwe

Mvuu
Camp

Mwalasi River

Shire River

Liwonde
National
Park

road to
Lilongwe

Likwenu River

Liwonde

5 km

5 miles

Liwonde National Park

Established in 1973, the 212-square-mile (548-km²) Liwonde National Park was created to protect the important riverine vegetation and mopane woodland of the upper Shire Valley and is now Malawi's showpiece park.

A major feature of the park is the Shire River, which provides one of the last refuges in the country for hippo and Nile crocodile. The river flows out of

Lake Malawi and forms the western boundary of the park. It forges its way southward over tumultuous rapids and falls to join the Zambezi River beyond Malawi's borders.

In Liwonde you have a good chance of seeing good numbers of impala, sable antelope, common waterbuck, warthog, hippo, elephant and crocodile. Lion are also seen. This is a birder's paradise

Game viewing in Liwonde National Park is best from May to October

with over 400 species recorded, including Boehm's bee-eater, Lilian's lovebird, brown-breasted barbet, Pel's fishing owl, white-backed night heron and marsh tchagra.

The best time for game viewing is during the dry season, May to October. Birding is best November to April, but is very good year-round.

Liwonde National Park lies 75 miles (120 km) from Blantyre and 152 miles (245 km) from Lilongwe, via the town of Liwonde.

ACCOMMODATION — CLASS A: • **Mvuu Wilderness Lodge**, set on a quiet backwater area of the Shire River, offers splendid views of the mighty river from its bar/dining deck. The lodge has 8 luxury units, and offers day and night game drives in open vehicles, boating excursions and escorted walks.

CLASS C: • **Mvuu Camp** is a 36-bedded camp with stone chalets split into double chalets and specially designed 2-room family units.

The Shire River *(top)*, Mvuu Wilderness Lodge *(bottom)*

Majete Wildlife Reserve

Majete Wildlife Reserve, proclaimed in 1955, was heavily poached in the '80s and '90s. Since 2003 it has been under the management of the African Parks — a not-for-profit organization that takes on total responsibility for the rehabilitation and long-term management of national parks and other protected areas, in public and private partnerships with African Governments.

Wildlife in this 173,000-acre (70,000-hectare) fenced reserve includes spotted hyena, leopard, elephant, black rhino, buffalo, eland, zebra, sable, nyala, bushbuck, kudu, Lichtenstein's hartebeest, waterbuck, impala, and warthog. Birding is typical of species found in a Miombo woodland region, with 250 species having been recorded.

Majete is located about 50 miles (80 kms) south of Blantyre in the Lower Shire Valley, and is reached by a drive down the Chikwawa Escarpment.

ACCOMMODATION — CLASS A/B: • **Mkulumadzi Lodge**, located at the junction of the Shire and Mkulumadzi Rivers, is new lodge with 4 well-appointed stone-and-canvas chalets overlooking the Shire River, a pool, bar and curio shop. Activities include walks, game drives and boat trips.

Tanzania

Tanzania

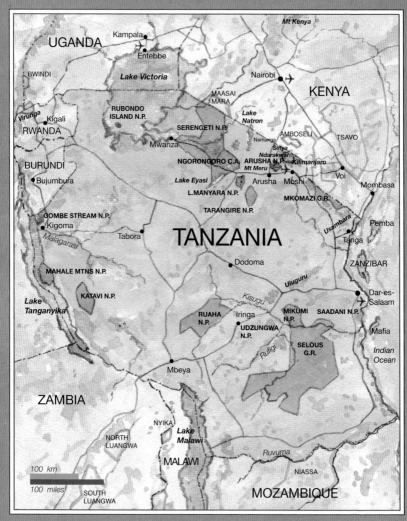

Set between the tropical Indian Ocean and the two arms of the Rift Valley, Tanzania is one of Africa's most scenically beautiful countries. It also has some of the most extensive protected areas including the fabled Serengeti. The landscape rises from sea level to 19,000 feet (5,894 m) at the summit of Mt. Kilimanjaro. Covering 365,000-square-miles (945,000-km²), Tanzania is about the same size as Texas and Oklahoma combined. The population numbers some 36 million, with Dodoma as the administrative capital. The famous port city of Dar es Salaam has been a key trading center for centuries. KiSwahili is the most widely spoken language, but English is also commonly used. Currency is the Tanzanian Shilling.

Tanzania
Country Highlights

- Tanzania is considered by many experts as one of the two top wildlife countries on the continent (along with Botswana).
- Have front row seats to the spectacle known as the Great Migration of the Wildebeest across the majestic Serengeti plains.
- Experience world-class luxury mobile camping in Tarangire the Grumeti Reserves and the Serengeti.
- Descend into the Ngorongoro Crater, the largest caldera in the world, for a day of game viewing and opportunity to see the "Big Five"
- Climb Mt. Kilimanjaro – the highest peak in Africa.
- Spend time with the Hadzabe Bushmen, the Datoga and the Maasai.
- Fly to the Selous and experience guided walking safaris and game viewing by boat.
- Trek chimpanzees at Mahale or Gombe, and visit remote Katavi to see big game with very few tourists.
- Finish your safari adventure with a stay on Zanzibar or one of the charming outer islands offering barefoot luxury.

When's the Best Time to Go for Game Viewing

■ Excellent ■ Good ☐ Fair ■ Poor ■ Closed

Country	Park/Reserve	JAN	FEB	MAR	APR	MAY	JUN	JUL	AUG	SEP	OCT	NOV	DEC
Tanzania	Lake Manyara												
	Ngorongoro												
	Serengeti (Southeastern)	*	*	*	*								*
	Serengeti (Western) and Grumeti					*	*	*					
	Serengeti (Northern)								*	*	*	*	
	Tarangire												
	Selous/Ruaha												
	Mahale/Gombe/Katavi												

*Great Serengeti Migration

Best Safari Experience

Ndarakwai Ranch, Oliver's Camp (Tarangire); Manyara Ranch; Kisima Ngeda (Lake Eyasi); Sayari (Serengeti), Serengeti Explorer and Ubuntu Seasonal Camps (Serengeti); Faru Faru, Sabora Plains and Singita Explore (Grumeti Reserves); Greystoke (Mahale); Jongomero (Ruaha), Beho Beho, and Selous Safari Camp (Selous)

TANZANIA

Between Africa's highest mountain (Kilimanjaro) and Africa's largest lake (Victoria) lies one of the best game viewing areas on the continent. This region also includes the world's largest unflooded intact volcanic caldera (Ngorongoro) and the most famous wildlife park (the Serengeti). There is great chimpanzee trekking at Mahale in the west, and to the southeast lies one of the world's largest game reserves — the Selous.

Volcanic highlands dominate the north, giving way southward to a plateau, then semidesert in the center of the country and highlands in the south. The coastal lowlands are hot and humid with lush vegetation. One branch of the Great Rift Valley passes through Lake Natron and Lake Manyara in northern Tanzania to Lake Malawi (Lake Nyasa), while the other branch passes through Lakes Rukwa and Tanganyika in the west.

The "long rains" usually occur in April and May, however, this does not mean it rains all the time, as the thundershowers will come and go. Lighter rains often occur in late October and November. Altitude has a great effect on temperature. At Arusha (4,600 ft./1,390 m), the Southern Highlands (6,700 ft./2,030 m) and the top of Ngorongoro Crater (7,500 ft./2,285 m), nights and early mornings are especially cool. Tanzania's highest temperatures occur December to March and are lowest in July.

Some scientists debate that East Africa was the cradle of mankind. Some of the earliest known humanoid footprints, estimated to be 3.5 million years old, were discovered at Laetoli by Dr. Mary Leakey in 1979. Dr. Leakey also found the estimated 1.7-million-year-old skull Zinjanthropus boisei at Oldupai (formerly Olduvai) Gorge in 1957.

From as far back as the tenth century, Arabs, Persians, Egyptians, Indians and Chinese were involved in heavy trading on the coast. The slave trade began in the mid-1600s and was abolished in 1873.

British explorers Richard Burton and John Speke crossed Tanzania in 1857 to Lake Tanganyika. The German East Africa Company gained control of the mainland (then called German East Africa) in 1885, and the German government held it from 1891 until World War I, when it was mandated to Britain by

Leopards are known for their climbing skills and spend much of their days lounging on tree branches

the League of Nations. Tanganyika gained its independence from Britain in 1961, and Zanzibar gained its independence in December 1963. Zanzibar, once the center of the East African slave trade, was ruled by sultans until they were overthrown in January 1964. Three months later, Zanzibar formed a union with Tanganyika — the United Republic of Tanzania.

There are 120 tribes in Tanzania. Bantu languages and dialects are spoken by 95% of the population, with KiSwahili the official and national language. Over 75% of the people are peasant farmers. Export of coffee, cotton, sisal, tea, cloves and cashews bring 70% of the country's foreign exchange. Tourism is now one of the country's top foreign exchange earners.

The Great Migration is located in the northern Serengeti near the Mara River from August through October

🐾 WILDLIFE AND WILDLIFE AREAS

Reserves cover over 100,000-square-miles (259,000-km²); only a few countries on earth can boast having a greater amount of land devoted to parks and reserves. The 15 national parks, 17 game reserves and 1 conservation area comprise over 15% of the country's land area. In total, over 25% of the country has been set aside for wildlife conservation. Tanzania's great variety of wildlife can be at least partially attributed to its great diversity of landscapes, with altitudes ranging from sea level to 19,340 feet (5,895 m).

Tanzania is one of the best wildlife countries in Africa for mobile and seasonal tented camp safaris. Vehicles with roof hatches or pop-tops are used on driving safaris. Safari camps and lodges that have guides and vehicles based at them may in many cases use open-sided vehicles — similar to those used in many reserves in Southern Africa.

If accompanied by a national park guide, walking is allowed in Arusha, Mt. Kilimanjaro, Gombe Stream, Mahale Mountains, Katavi National Park,

Ruaha National Park, Rubondo Island National Park, Selous Game Reserve and Loliondo Game Reserve (bordering the eastern side of the Serengeti National Park). Areas for walking have recently been designated in Tarangire National Park and in the northern part of Serengeti National Park. Walking is also allowed in the Ngorongoro Conservation area (but not within the Ngorongoro Crater itself) if accompanied by a conservation ranger.

The best weather for viewing game in northern Tanzania is June through March. Late December to February and July and August are the busiest periods. April and May is traditionally the rainy season and travel in 4wd vehicles is highly recommended, however, as the seasons are not as pronounced as they were a few decades ago, travelers during that period may in fact encounter little rain. Advantages of traveling in April and May include lower rates, fewer tourists, and great game viewing in some parks, such as the Serengeti and Ngorongoro Crater. This is a great time to drive through the Great Serengeti Migration, with possibly no other vehicles in sight!

Light rains usually fall late October to early December, but little negative effect on game viewing in some reserves. November is in fact one of my favorite times for northern Tanzania; a little rain is nice because it helps drop the dust out of the air, and the bush turns from brown to green. In southern Tanzania the best months for game viewing are June to November due to the longer 6 month dry season compared to the north.

The country contains 35 species of antelope and over 1.5 million wildebeest — over 80% of the population of this species in Africa. The calving season for wildebeest is from mid-January to mid-March.

THE NORTH

This region, from Mt. Kilimanjaro in the east to Serengeti National Park in the west, is the area most visited by tourists and boasts many of the country's most famous parks.

Some visitors reach Arusha, gateway to the area, by flying directly into Kilimanjaro International Airport. Others fly into Nairobi (Kenya) and then take a 1-hour flight to Kilimanjaro or a 5-hour drive via Namanga to Arusha, or they fly into Dar es Salaam and then take an hour's flight to Kilimanjaro or Arusha airports. Kilimanjaro International Airport is located 34 miles (54 km) east of Arusha and 22 miles (35 km) west of Moshi, and has a bank, bar, shops and a restaurant.

The traditional "**Northern Circuit**" includes Arusha National Park, Tarangire National Park, Lake Manyara National Park, Ngorongoro Conservation Area, Oldupai Gorge and the Serengeti National Park. Other areas of interest in the north include Ndarakwai Ranch, Sinya, and Lake Eyasi (opportunities for great cultural experiences), Manyara Ranch Conservancy, Grumeti Reserves, Mt. Meru and Mt. Kilimanjaro.

From Arusha the Northern Circuit runs 45 miles (73 km) west on a good tarmac road, across the gently rolling Maasai plains with scattered acacia trees, to

Northern Tanzania and Southern Kenya

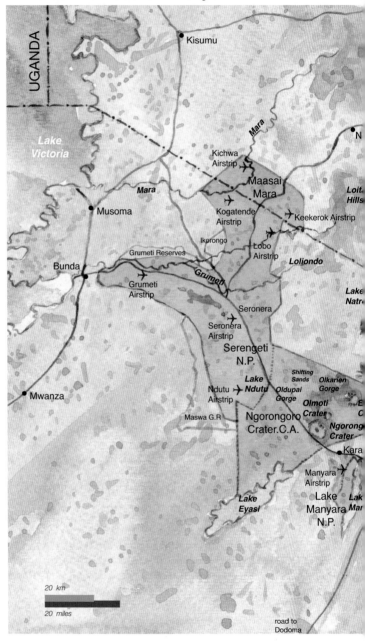

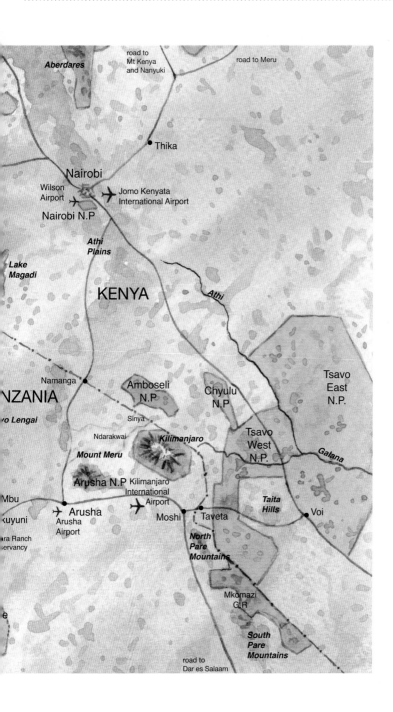

Aberdares

road to
Mt Kenya
and Nanyuki

road to Meru

● Thika

Nairobi

Wilson
Airport

Jomo Kenyata
International Airport

Nairobi N.P

*Athi
Plains*

*Lake
Magadi*

KENYA

Athi

Namanga ●

NZANIA

Amboseli
N.P

Chyulu
N.P

Tsavo
East
N.P.

o Lengai

Sinya

Kilimanjaro

Tsavo
West
N.P.

Galana

Ndarakwai

Mount Meru

Arusha N.P

Kilimanjaro
International
Airport

*Taita
Hills*

Mbu

✈ Arusha

Arusha
Airport

Moshi

Taveta

Voi

Kuyuni

*North
Pare
Mountains*

a Ranch
ervancy

e

Mkomazi
G.R

*South
Pare
Mountains*

road to
Dar es Salaam

Traditional Maasai boma *(top)*, Children attend a local "open air" classroom *(bottom)*

Makuyuni. You can then either continue on the main road toward Dodoma for another 20 miles (32 km) to Tarangire National Park or turn right (northwest) to Mto wa Mbu (Mosquito Creek) on a paved road.

En route you pass many Maasai bomas (villages) and Maasai in their colorful traditional dress walking on the roadside, riding bicycles, herding their cattle and driving overloaded donkey carts.

Maasai Morani completing the circumcision ritual are sometimes seen clad in black with white paint on their faces. They leave the village as children for a period of training and instruction by elders and return as men.

Mto wa Mbu is a village with a market filled with wood carvings and other local crafts for sale. Be sure to bargain. If you take a few minutes to walk into the village behind the stands, you will get a more realistic (and less touristy) view of village life.

Continuing west, you soon pass the entrance to Lake Manyara National Park. The road then climbs up the Rift Valley escarpment past huge baobab trees and numerous baboons looking for handouts (please do not feed any wild animals). Fabulous views of the valley and Lake Manyara Park below can be seen. Next you pass through beautiful cultivated uplands, the village of Karatu and other small villages, past the turnoff to Lake Eyasi, and on up the slopes of the Crater Highlands to the Ngorongoro Crater. The road then follows the southern rim of the crater and finally descends the western side to Oldupai Gorge and Serengeti National Park and the Grumeti Reserves, and Lake Victoria.

The Northern Circuit is thought by some travelers to be "crowded." If your driver/guide sticks to the main roads and tracks, as many do, then the park will certainly seem full of tourists. You can avoid most of the crowds by booking a safari with a company that uses top guides, 4wd drive vehicles and no limitations to the distance (kilometers) they may drive. Many guides who are restricted by the number of kilometers they may drive, are penalized financially for driving over their limit, and are rewarded financially for driving under the limit. For instance, I once met a group in the central Serengeti that were very upset because their guides refused to drive them to see the "migration" because the distance was too great and they would have exceeded their kilometer limit! Driver/guides who really know the park will then be happy to take you to lower utilized areas off the beaten track for a real safari.

Arusha

This town is the center of tourism for northern Tanzania and is situated in the foothills of rugged Mt. Meru. Named after a sub-tribe of the Maasai, the Wa-Arusha, it is located on the Great North Road midway between Cairo and Cape Town. Makonde carvings and other souvenirs are available in the numerous craft shops at the center of town. Walking around the Arusha Market, located down the road from the clock tower, is an interesting way to spend a few hours. Consider visiting a school or clinic to better experience the local culture.

ACCOMMODATION — DELUXE: • **Arusha Coffee Lodge**, located near the Arusha Airport on a coffee plantation, is comprised of 18 standard suites and 12 Plantation suites, each with private decks. There is a swimming pool and 24-hour room service. • **Lake Duluti Lodge** is based in an old coffee estate and has 18 suites and a swimming pool. • **Onsea House**, located outside Arusha, features 5 rooms with private terraces and views of the gardens. There is a restaurant, swimming pool, lawn bar and garden.

FIRST CLASS: • **Shangazi House**, located near Arusha National Park, is set in beautiful gardens with 6 cottages with private verandahs and a swimming pool. • **Arumeru River Lodge** offers 21 rooms with ceiling fans, mosquito netting and private terraces. There is a lush garden, swimming pool and an organic vegetable garden. • **Serena Mountain Village, Arusha** has thatched rondavels, swimming pool and conference center. The lodge is set in lovely gardens and is located 6 miles (10 km) east of Arusha overlooking Lake Duluti. • **Hatari Lodge** has 9 bungalows (doubles) with open fireplace, designed in a classic retro style. The lounge and deck have views of Mt. Kilimanjaro. • **Arusha Safari Lodge**, situated in a valley between Mt. Kilimanjaro and Mt. Meru, offers comfortable guest cottages, fitness center, sauna, steam room, jacuzzi, and swimming pool. Polo matches are often played on the grounds. • **Moivaro Lodge**, situated outside of Arusha on a coffee plantation, has 40 double (or triple) cottages and

Arusha Coffee Lodge *(top)*, Plantation Suite at Arusha Coffee Lodge *(middle)*, Serena Mountain Village *(bottom)*

a swimming pool. • **Ngare Sero Mountain Lodge** is a farmhouse situated on the slopes of Mt. Meru with 10 rooms. • **Mount Meru Game Lodge** is located in 33 acres of gardens bordered by the Usa River and the animal sanctuary. The lodge consists of 15 rooms and 2 suites.

TOURIST CLASS: • **Olasiti Lodge** features 24 rooms, a swimming pool and a bar with views of Mt. Meru. • **Snow Crest Hotel**, 10 minutes from Arusha, has 83 rooms, swimming pool, sundeck, restaurant and lounge. • **Kibo Palace Hotel**, in Arusha's Town Center, has 65 rooms, fitness center, massage room, and swimming pool.

Arusha National Park

This highly underrated park is predominantly inhabited by forest animals, while in the other northern parks, savannah animals are more prevalent. Arusha National Park is the best place in northern Tanzania to spot black-and-white colobus monkeys and bushbuck and to photograph larger species with Mt. Kilimanjaro or Mt. Meru in the background. Early mornings are best for this because Mt. Kilimanjaro is less likely to be covered with clouds. Travelers should consider spending at least half a day here as this park is so different from the other parks and reserves on the "Northern Circuit."

This 53-square-mile (137-km²) park is actually the merger of three regions: Meru Crater National Park, Momela Lakes and Ngurdoto Crater National Park. The wide range of habitats, from highland rain forest to acacia woodlands and

Arusha and Arusha National Park

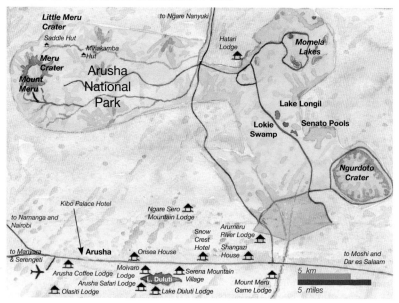

crater lakes, hosts a variety of wild-life. Armed park guides are required to accompany you for walks in the western part of the park or for climb-ing Mt. Meru; guides are available at Park Headquarters at Momela Gate.

On the open grassland near the entrance to the park, Burchell's zebra are often seen. High in the forest can-opy of the Ngurdoto Forest is a good place to find blue monkeys and black-and-white colobus monkeys. Olive baboons are common and red duiker are sometimes seen.

A submerged hippo in the Momella Lakes

Walking is not allowed in the 2 mile (3 km) wide **Ngurdoto Crater**, which is, in essence, a reserve within a reserve. However, there can be good views (especially in the early morning) of the crater, Momela Lakes and Mt. Kilimanjaro.

Driving north from Ngurdoto, you pass Ngongongare Spring, the Senato Pools (sometimes dry) and Lokie Swamp and are likely to see common water-buck and maybe Bohor reedbuck and the rare red duiker. Buffalo are often seen around Lake Longil.

As you continue past Kambi Ya Fisi (hyena's camp), the landscape becomes more open, and elephant and giraffe can be seen. Hippo and a variety of water-fowl can be seen at the shallow, alkaline **Momela Lakes**, where **canoe safaris** are offered.

Driving west from Momela, you may encounter black-and-white colobus monkey and red duiker enroute to the **Arched Fig Tree** — large enough to drive a vehicle through.

From Kitoto, a 4wd vehicle is needed to reach **Meru Crater**. The sheer cliff rises about 4,920 feet (1,500 m) and is one of the highest in the world.

At the base of Mt. Meru, you may encounter elephant and buffalo. Kirk's dikdik, banded mongoose and klipspringer can also be seen in the park. The best time to visit for game viewing is June through March.

Over 400 species of birds have been recorded, with Hartlaub's turaco, red-fronted parrot and brown-breasted barbet among the species not easily found elsewhere in northern Tanzania.

Mt. Meru (14,977 ft./4,566 m) is an impressive mountain that is classified as a dormant volcano; its last eruption was just over 100 years ago.

Mt. Meru is best climbed in 4 days. As a bonus you have a chance to see some wildlife such as giraffe and buffalo. The 3 nights are spent in the national park mountain huts. These huts have bunk beds in rooms that sleep 4 to 8 people and a communal dining area. Food and equipment is carried by porters and meals are prepared by your cook.

Arusha National Park is an excellent place to see black-and-white colobus monkeys

On Day 1 (5-6 hours walking), you start from Momela Gate 4,920 feet (1,500 m) in late morning. You steadily climb past open grasslands and motane forest to Fig Tree Arch. The route continues through less dense forest to **Miriakamba Hut** (8,245 ft./2,514 m), situated in a grassy glade

On Day 2 (3-6 hours walking), hike from Miriakamba Hut to the saddle below Little Meru is steep all the way. Elephant Ridge, the half-way point, has excellent views of the summit ridge and across most of the crater floor. Continue uphill through giant heather and other moorland vegetation to **Saddle Hut** (11,710 ft./3,570 m), After lunch, some trekkers summit **Little Meru Crater** (12,530 ft./3,820 m) and return to camp before sunset

On Day 3 (10-12 hours walking), you begin your summit attempt at around 2 a.m. – climbing the steep path to Rhino Point (12,650 ft./3,800 m), and then continue along a ridge of ash and rock to reach Cobra Point (14,270 ft./4,350 m) around sunrise. The views of the cliffs of the Crater rim and the Ash Cone rising from the Crater floor, of Mt. Kilimanjaro to the east, and the surrounding Rift Valley are spectacular if the weather is clear. Hike another hour or more to the summit of Socialist Peak (14,975 ft./4,566 m). The route back to Rhino Point is on a dramatic, narrow ridge with sheer drops. After a rest, continue to Saddle Hut for brunch before and onward to **Miriakamba**

Hut (2,514 m). For anyone suffering from vertigo, it is not recommended that they climb past Rhino Point.

On Day 4 (2–3 hours walking, you hike to Momela Gate through grassland and mixed forest with good chances of seeing some wildlife.

The best months to climb are June to October and late December to February. Bring all your own gear and make your reservations in advance.

The turnoff to the park entrance is 13 miles (21 km) east of Arusha and 36 miles (58 km) west of Moshi. Continue another 7 miles (11 km) to Ngurdoto Gate. Walking is allowed in the western part of this park where there are a number of hikes and picnic sites to enjoy when accompanied by a park ranger.

ACCOMMODATION NEAR THE RESERVE — See Accommodations: Arusha

Ndarakwai Ranch

Ndarakwai is an 11,019 acre (4,460-hectare) private wildlife reserve located on the northwest slopes of Mt. Kilimanjaro. Flood plains, hills, acacia woodland and views of Mt. Kilimanjaro and Mt. Meru make this one of the most beautiful, pristine, wild areas of northern Tanzania.

There is permanent water on the ranch — a key element in making it a haven for wildlife — especially in the dry season. Wildlife includes a recorded 63 species of mammals and more than 340 species of birds.

Activities include day and night game drives (off-road driving allowed) in open vehicles, half-day or full-day escorted walks with armed guides and cultural visits with neighboring Maasai communities. An optional activity offered is the elephant interaction to meet the ranch's two habituated elephants. This exclusive activity is limited to two guests in the morning and afternoon, and must be booked in advance. This is one of the best places for a quality visit to Maasai villages that are far off the tourist track. Voluntourism programs are also available and highly recommended.

Ndarakwai Ranch

ACCOMMODATION — CLASS A/B: • **Ndarakwai Ranch** is family-owned and has 15 large tents on platforms under thatch. The ranch is located about an hour and a half drive from Kilimanjaro International Airport or Arusha, and is a great place to begin your safari. The ranch's **tree house** is a favorite among guests where, during the dry seasons, you are likely to gaze down at a herd of sixty or more elephants at the waterhole. In the evening, the tree house is the ideal location for sundowners.

Sinya

The Sinya region is Maasailand bordering the southwestern corner of Amboseli National Park in Kenya. Mt. Meru lies to the southwest and Mt. Kilimanjaro to the southeast. This area is know for its hills and acacia woodland.

Unlike at Amboseli National Reserve in Kenya, one seldom if ever encounters other tourists on the Tanzania side of the border.

There is no permanent water in the area except for a few boreholes used by the Maasai for their livestock. In addition to seeing resident game, wildlife can be seen traversing the area, moving to and from permanent water in Amboseli National Reserve to permanent water on the slopes of Mt. Kilimanjaro.

Game viewing in Sinya is good; however, its major attraction may be that it offers very good opportunities for a non-touristy, cultural experience with the Maasai.

Sinya is about an hour and a half drive from Namanga and about a two-hour drive from Arusha.

ACCOMMODATION — CLASS A/B: • **Kambi ya Tembo** has 20 tents with private verandahs. Activities include game drives, sundowners and Maasai visits.

Tarangire National Park

Large numbers of baobab trees dotting the landscape of this 1,003-square-mile (2,600-km^2) park make it one of the most scenic reserves in Africa — and one of my favorites. Tarangire is the best park on the northern circuit to see lions in trees and large numbers of elephant.

Fewer tourists visit this park than Manyara, Ngorongoro and Serengeti, however, this park should not be missed. Wildlife viewing is excellent, especially from July to November, when many animals concentrate near the only permanent water source in the area — the Tarangire River and its tributaries.

At the beginning of the short rainy season (November), some herds of migratory species including wildebeest and zebra, soon followed by elephant, buffalo, Grant's gazelle, Thomson's gazelle and oryx, begin migrating out of the park. The creation of the Manyara Ranch Conservancy has helped open up the migration route from Tarangire to Lake Manyara National Park. However, as some migration routes have been cut off from the expansion of man's presence, many of these animals are remaining in the park and few are migrating out of the park or far beyond the park's borders. December to February is also a good time to visit.

Tarangire

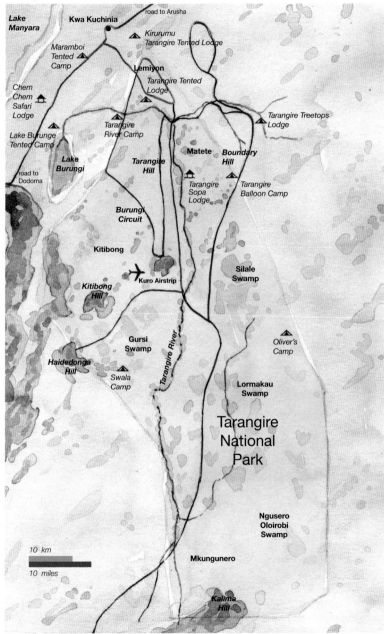

Lake Manyara

Kwa Kuchinia

road to Arusha

Kirurumu Tarangire Tented Lodge

Maramboi Tented Camp

Lemiyon

Tarangire Tented Lodge

Chem Chem Safari Lodge

Lake Burunge Tented Camp

Tarangire River Camp

Tarangire Treetops Lodge

Lake Burungi

road to Dodoma

Tarangire Hill

Matete

Boundary Hill

Tarangire Sopa Lodge

Tarangire Balloon Camp

Burungi Circuit

Kitibong

Silale Swamp

Kitibong Hill

Kuro Airstrip

Gursi Swamp

Tarangire River

Oliver's Camp

Haidedonga Hill

Swala Camp

Lormakau Swamp

Tarangire National Park

Ngusero Oloirobi Swamp

10 km

10 miles

Mkungunero

Kalima Hill

Giraffe, waterbuck, lesser kudu and other resident species remain in the park. The migratory animals that do manage to leave the park usually return at the end of the long rains in June.

On a recent two-day visit during November we saw more than 600 elephant, several prides of lion, leopard in a tree with an impala kill, eland, oryx, along with a variety of other antelope. The game viewing was excellent!

Tarangire wildlife populations include approximately 30,000 zebra, 25,000 wildebeest, 5,000 elephant, 5,000 buffalo, 5,000 eland, 2,500 Maasai giraffe and 1,000 oryx. Other prominent species include Grant's and Thomson's gazelle, hartebeest, impala, lesser and greater kudu, reedbuck and gerenuk. Lion and leopard are frequently seen. Cheetah and spotted hyena are also present, as are the banded, slender, dwarf and marsh mongoose. African wild dog may also be seen.

An ancient baobab tree *(top)*, Walking safaris are offered by some Tarangire camps *(bottom)*

Approximately 550 bird species have been recorded. Specialties include the northern pied babbler, Eastern chanting goshawk, black-faced sandgrouse, slender-tailed nightjar, coqui francolin, magpie shrike and D'Arnaud's barbet. Lappet-faced vulture, yellow-necked spurfowl, Fischer's lovebird, white-bellied go-away bird, rosy-patched bushshrike and ashy starling are among the characteristic species. Bird watching is best December through May.

The **Lemiyon region**, the northernmost region of the park, is characterized by large numbers of majestic baobab trees. This unique landscape is also dotted by umbrella acacia trees, as well as some open grasslands and wooded areas. Elephant, wildebeest and zebra are often seen. Visitors with little time for game viewing may want to concentrate on the Matete and the Lemiyon areas, including the Tarangire River.

The **Matete region** covers the northeastern part of the park and is characterized by open grasslands with scattered umbrella acacia and baobab trees and the Tarangire River. Lion, fringe-eared oryx and klipspringer are seen quite often. Bat-eared fox are also present.

On the 50-mile (80-km) **Burungi Circuit**, you pass through acacia parklands and woodlands. You are likely to see a number of species, including elephant, eland and bushbuck.

The eastern side of the **Kitibong area** is a good place to find large herds of buffalo. The eastern side is mainly acacia parklands, and the western side is thicker woodlands.

The **Gursi section** is similar to the Kitibong area with the addition of rainy season wetlands, which are home to large populations of water birds.

The **Larmakau region**, located in the central eastern part of the park, has extensive swamps, and is not visited by many travelers. **Nguselororobi**, in the south of the park, is predominantly swamp with some woodlands and plains. The **Mkungunero section** has a few freshwater pools and a variety of bird life.

During the heavy rainy season (March to May), some roads become impassable. There is an open market every Sunday not far from the entrance of the park.

ACCOMMODATION IN THE RESERVE — CLASS A: • **Oliver's Camp**, located inside the southern region of the reserve and sitting on an elevated ridge overlooking a flood plain, has 10 tents each with private verandahs. Day game drives, night game drives and walking safaris are offered. • **Swala Camp** is a permanent tented camp, located on the western side of the park, with 12 recently refurbished tents and a swimming pool. Morning and afternoon game drives and walking safaris are offered.

CLASS A/B: • **Tarangire Balloon Camp** has 6 luxury safari tents with butler service. The camp is located near Boundary Hill and features balloon safaris.

CLASS B: • **Tarangire Sopa Lodge** has 75 rooms each with 2 queen size beds, sitting area and private terrace, and a swimming pool.

CLASS B/C: **Tarangire Tented Lodge** is set on a high ridge overlooking the Tarangire River, and has 35 tents (doubles) and 6 bungalows (triples) and a large swimming pool.

ACCOMMODATION ON THE PERIPHERY OF THE PARK — CLASS A: • **Tarangire Treetops Lodge** is set in

Guests at Oliver's Camp have views of the flood plains from their beds

A guest tent at Swala Camp *(top)*, Tarangire Treetops Lodge is elevated in baobab trees *(bottom)*

a private game reserve adjacent to the park, about a 45-minute drive from the park entrance. Each of the 20 luxurious tents is built around one of the baobab treetops and has a private deck. Activities offered outside the park include walking, hilltop sunset cocktails and night game drives.

CLASS A/B: • **Chem Chem Safari Lodge**, located northwest of Tarangire in the Tarangire/Lake Manyara Corridor on a private game concession, has 8 luxury tents with private wooden decks. There is a dining room, lounge, library, sundeck, swimming pool and spa. Game drives in open vehicles are offered.

CLASS B: • **Kirurumu Tarangire Tented Lodge**, located on a private concession near the main entrance, has 10 tents, 2 honeymoon suites and 2 family suites. Activities include guided bush walks, mountain biking and game drives in Tarangire National Park. • **Lake Burunge Tented Camp**, built on the western shores of Lake Burunge just northwest of the park, features 20 tents and 10 lodge rooms with a central dining and bar area connected by walkway. Activities include guided walks, canoeing and cultural interactions with Maasai and Datoga tribes. • **Maramboi Tented Camp**, located 10 miles (17km) from Tarangire in the migratory corridor to Lake Manyara, has 20 tents and 10 lodge rooms with private verandahs and a swimming pool. Activities include game drives, guided walks, bird watching and Maasai village visits. • **Tarangire River Camp**, located in a private concession near the main entrance, has 20 tents with views of Mt. Meru. Activities include game drives, guided walks and cultural visits to the local Maasai and Datoga tribes.

The Tarangire/Lake Manyara Corridor

The Kwakuchinja Corridor, or migration route between Tarangire National Park and Lake Manyara National Park, had become severely restricted until the Tanzania Land Conservation Trust got involved and the Manyara Ranch was created. The migration of wildlife between these two parks, which are only 25-miles (40-km) apart, has become much improved.

Resident wildlife includes groups of large bull elephants, giraffe, oryx eland, lesser kudu, wildebeest, zebra, gazelle, along with lion, cheetah, leopard, bat-eared fox, and wild dog.

Day and night game drives (off-road driving allowed), escorted walks, viewing from hides, visits to local villages, fly camping and horseback riding are available on this 35,000-acre (14,175-hectare) property. Day trips to Lake Manyara and Tarangire national parks are also offered.

A stay at Manyara Ranch Conservancy includes open-vehicle game viewing *(top)* and comfortable tents *(bottom)*

ACCOMMODATION — CLASS A: • **Manyara Ranch Conservancy** is a tourism initiative developed in partnership with local Maasai and African Wildlife Foundation. To help sustain the conservancy a luxury camp has been built and features 6 deluxe tents with private viewing decks.

Lake Manyara National Park

This 125-square-mile (325-km^2) park has the Great Rift Valley Escarpment for a dramatic backdrop and was once one of the most popular hunting areas of Tanzania. Two-thirds of the park is covered by alkaline Lake Manyara, which is situated at an altitude of 3,150 feet (960 m).

Lake Manyara

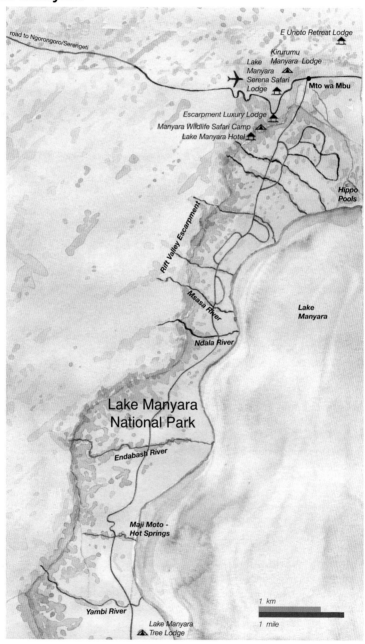

road to Ngorongoro/Serengeti

E Unoto Retreat Lodge

Kirurumu
Manyara Lodge
Lake
Manyara
Serena Safari
Lodge

Mto wa Mbu

Escarpment Luxury Lodge
Manyara Wildlife Safari Camp
Lake Manyara Hotel

Hippo
Pools

Rift Valley Escarpment

Msasa River

Lake
Manyara

Ndala River

Lake Manyara
National Park

Endabash River

Maji Moto -
Hot Springs

Yambi River

1 km

1 mile

Lake Manyara
Tree Lodge

The turnoff to Lake Manyara is past Mto wa Mbu on the road from Makuyuni to Ngorongoro Crater, about 75 miles (120 km) west of Arusha.

Despite its comparatively small size, the park has five distinct vegetation zones and a remarkable diversity of wildlife. From the crest of the Rift Valley to the shores of the lake, the varied topography and soils support characteristic plants and animals. The first zone reached from the park entrance is groundwater forest that is fed by water seeping from the Great Rift Wall, with wild fig, sausage, tamarind and mahogany trees. Elephant prefer these dense forests, as well as marshy glades. The other zones include the marshlands along the edge of the lake, scrub on the Rift Valley Wall, open areas with scattered acacia, and open grasslands.

Manyara, like Tarangire National Park (Tanzania) and Ishasha in Queen Elizabeth National Park (Uganda), is well known for its tree-climbing lions, which may occasionally be found lazing on branches of acacia trees. Some people believe that lions climb trees in Manyara and Tarangire to avoid tsetse flies and the dense undergrowth while they remain in the cool shade. They also believe that lions of the Ruwenzori National Park in Uganda climb trees to gain a hunting advantage. Finding lion in the trees in Lake Manyara is rare, so don't set your heart on it — look at it as an unexpected bonus.

Manyara features large concentrations of elephant and buffalo. Other wildlife includes common waterbuck, Maasai giraffe, zebra, impala, baboons and blue monkeys.

Some 450 species of birds — including an astonishing total of over 40 varieties of birds of prey — have been recorded, which makes Manyara one of Tanzania's best bird watching localities and one of the world's most impressive raptor havens. Among the exciting birds regularly seen are saddle-billed stork, crowned eagle, southern ground hornbill, silvery-cheeked hornbill, grey-hooded kingfisher, long-tailed fiscal, spotted morning thrush and black-winged red bishop.

The level of the lake fluctuates with rainfall. When the lake is high, the fish population increases and pelicans and storks flourish. At lower levels, the salinity of the water increases, and vast flocks of lesser and greater flamingo feed on brine shrimp and algae in the shallows.

The northern part of the park can be crowded, but as the southern part has very few visitors, consider packing a breakfast and/or a picnic lunch and spend most of a day exploring the south.

Tree climbing lion in Lake Manyara National Park

Much of the wildlife is resident year-round, making this a good park to visit any time. The best time to visit is December to March, followed by June to October. A 4wd vehicle is recommended for travel in April and May.

Other activities offered in and near the park include night game drives (with bush dinner), walking on the edge of the escarpment and mountain biking.

Roads in the northern part of the park are good year-round and 4wd is not needed, although in the rainy season some side tracks may be temporarily closed. Four-wheel-drive vehicles are sometimes necessary and highly recommended for travel in the more remote southern part of Lake Manyara. There is an open market every Thursday at Mto wa Mbu village.

ACCOMMODATION — CLASS A: • **Lake Manyara Tree Lodge**, located in the remote southwestern area of the park in a mahogany forest, has 10 luxury treehouse suites and a swimming pool. A 2-night stay is recommended as it takes at least 2 hours to drive from the park gate to the lodge.

CLASS A/B: • **Escarpment Luxury Lodge**, perched on the rim overlooking Lake Manyara, has 16 chalets with private decks from which to enjoy the view. A cycling tour to nearby village of Mto wa Mbu can be arranged. • **Lake Manyara Serena Safari Lodge**, set on the Rift Valley Escarpment overlooking the park and the Rift Valley 1,000 feet (300 m) below, has 67 rooms and a swimming pool. The hotel offers walks along the Rift Valley Escarpment and to Mto wa Mbu village.

CLASS B: • **Kirurumu Manyara Lodge**, set on the escarpment overlooking the Rift Valley, has 27 tents covered by thatched roofs. Short nature walks around the area as well as hikes down the escarpment to Mto wa Mbu village are offered.

CLASS C: • **Manyara Wildlife Safari Camp** overlooks Lake Manyara and the national park. It features 10 tented chalets with private balconies. • **E Unoto Retreat Lodge** is a totally Maasai inspired and owned lodge with 25 bungalows overlooking a natural

The Escarpment Luxury Lodge overlooks Lake Manyara

spring outside the park. Mountain biking, nature walks and exclusive visits to their nearby village are offered. • **Lake Manyara Hotel**, set on the escarpment overlooking the park, has 100 rooms and a swimming pool.

Lake Eyasi

Lake Eyasi lies on the southern border of the Ngorongoro Conservation area and is Tanzania's largest soda lake. The remote region is seldom visited by travelers and is home for the Hadzabe Bushmen and the Datoga (also called the Barabaig or Mang'ati) tribe. Here you can have a much truer picture of tribal life than in the more touristy areas.

Hadzabe Bushmen are traditional hunter-gatherers who speak a "click" language similar to the Bushmen of southern Africa. The men hunt in the early mornings and afternoons with bows and arrows. Poison arrows are used for large game and non-poison arrows for birds and small game. The women gather wild fruits, roots and tubers. The **Mang'ati** (also called the **Datoga**) is a tribe similar to the Maasai that herd cattle and goats. Their diet primarily consists of meat, milk, and blood.

Hunting with the Bushmen is one of the most exciting cultural experiences you can have in Africa. Recently my wife and I and our 2 children spent 2 days at Lake Eyasi and enjoyed every minute of it. We left the lodge before sunrise

Remote Lake Eyasi is off the traditional safari route

and with the assistance of a local guide found a bushman encampment that had apparently been deserted just a few days earlier.

After about 45 minutes of searching, we located their new camp, and shortly thereafter set off with 5 hunters armed with traditional bows and arrows (they gave our boys bows and arrows as well). Their first mission was to find a dikdik that they had shot the night before that had escaped. My son Nicolas became the "hero" of the day by finding the lost metal arrowhead on the pathway, as arrowheads require a relatively high price in the form of trade with the local blacksmith. We never found the dikdik, but they did shoot a bushbaby, and quickly made a fire the traditional way, cooked and ate it. We returned to their camp, where we were invited to dance with them and to take target practice. Shooting those bows is harder than you might think!

Later that day we visited the local blacksmith, and spent a few hours with the Datoga (Mang'ati) tribe. The women invited our children to dance (jump) with them, and we spent some time in huts, seeing how they lived. What made the experience with the bushmen and the Datoga even more special is that we had them to ourselves — just our family and our guide.

Only travelers with a keen interest in culture should venture here. If you visit the area, please do your part in helping them maintain their culture by not giving the Bushmen or the Mang'ati any clothing or other western articles. Your guide will know what is appropriate. Lake Eyasi is a perfect family destination as children are welcome to get involved in all the activities.

Lake Eyasi is about a 3-hour drive from the Karatu — Ngorongoro Crater road.

Hadzabe bushmen giving hunting tips to Miles and Nicholas Nolting *(top)*, Kisima Ngeda Camp *(bottom)*

ACCOMMODATION — CLASS A/B: • **Kisima Ngeda Camp** is located on the eastern shore of Lake Eyasi and has 6 permanent tents built under a thatched structure. The camp is managed by Chris Schmelling, who grew up in the area and knows the tribe quite well.

CLASS B: • **Tindiga Tented Lodge** is located a mile from Lake Eyasi and has 10 canvas and thatched tents.

The Karatu Area — Bordering the Ngorongoro Conservation Area

This is a highland area of rich farmland near the town of Karatu, located between the Rift Valley Escarpment overlooking Lake Manyara National Park and the Ngorongoro Conservation Area. Many visitors stay in comfortable accommodations here and take day trips into the Ngorongoro Crater and to Lake Manyara. There is an open market in Karatu on the seventh of each month.

The **Iraqw Cultural Center** allows visitors the opportunity to learn more about the local Iraqw tribe, who have inhabited the immediate Ngorongoro highlands for over 200 years. Guests may tour a traditional Iraqw home and observe a biogas plant used for producing cooking and lighting gas from animal dung for a home — eliminating the need for firewood or charcoal and thereby helping to minimize the effects of deforestation. Our kids particularly enjoyed trying their hand at throwing the traditional spears.

ACCOMMODATION — CLASS A: • **The Manor at Ngorongoro** is set on an extensive country estate with 18 luxurious cottages and a 3-bedroom family house, each with a fireplace and butler service. Activities include horseback riding, guided walks of the estate, swimming pool and spa. • **Gibb's Farm** has 18 Farm Cottages (Class A) and 2 Standard Cottages (Class B) set in the gardens. Walks to nearby waterfalls, hikes to the Ngorongoro Crater rim, mountain biking and village visits can be arranged. • **Exploreans Ngorongoro Lodge**, located near the conservation gate, has 20 private log cabins each with a fireplace, living room and private terrace. There is a restaurant, bar, swimming pool and spa.

CLASS A/B: • **Kitela Lodge** is an exclusive lodge with 20 chalets with a heated pool and spa. • **Plantation Lodge**, set in lovely gardens on a coffee farm near Karatu, has 14 rooms and a swimming pool.

CLASS B: • **Ngorongoro Farmhouse** is located 2.5 miles (4 km) from the Ngorongoro park gate and has 50 rooms with colonial charm and private verandahs. Walks are available in the surrounding area. • **Tloma Lodge** offers 36 rooms. The lodge is located close to the Tloma Primary School where guests can visit and meet the children.

The Manor at Ngorongoro *(top)*, Gibb's Farm *(bottom)*

Ngorongoro Crater Conservation Area

Ngorongoro Crater is the largest unflooded, intact caldera (collapsed cone of a volcano) in the world. Known as the eighth Wonder of the World, its vastness and beauty are truly overwhelming, and it is believed by some to have been the proverbial Garden of Eden. Many scientists suggest that before its eruption, this volcano was larger than Mt. Kilimanjaro.

Ngorongoro contains possibly the largest permanent concentration of wildlife in Africa, with an estimated average of 30,000 large mammals. In addition, this is one of the best reserves in Africa in which to see black rhino.

Large concentrations of wildlife make Ngorongoro Crater their permanent home. Game viewing is good year-round. Because there is a permanent source of fresh water, there's no reason for much of the wildlife to migrate as it must do in the Serengeti.

Ngorongoro Crater itself is but a small portion of the 3,200-square-mile (8,288-km²) Ngorongoro Conservation Area, a World Heritage Site that is characterized by a highland plateau with volcanic mountains as well as several craters, extensive savannah and forests. Altitudes range from 4,430 to 11,800 feet (1,350 to 3,600 m).

Ngorongoro Crater Conservation Area

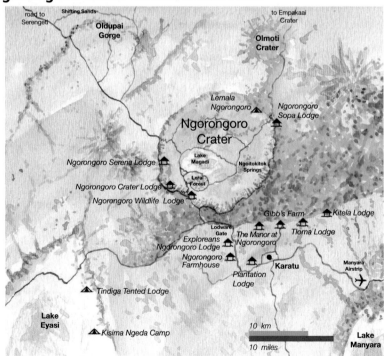

The Ngorongoro Crater, a World Heritage Site

Ngorongoro Crater is about 12 miles (19 km) wide and its rim rises 1,200 to 1,600 feet (365 to 490 m) off of its expansive 102-square-mile (265-km²) floor. From the crater rim, elephant appear as small dark specks on the grasslands.

The steep descent into the crater along winding roads takes 25 to 35 minutes from the crater rim. The crater floor is predominantly grasslands (making game easy to spot) with two swamps fed by streams, and the Lerai Forest. The walls of the crater are lightly forested. You may descend on a road beginning on the western rim or on the eastern rim. Once on the floor, most guests are driven clockwise or counter-clockwise around the crater floor.

Lake Magadi, also called Crater Lake and Lake Makat, is a shallow soda lake near the western rim entry point of the crater that attracts thousands of flamingos and other water birds.

The dirt road continues past Mandusi Swamp. Game viewing is especially good in this area during the dry season (July to October) because some wildlife migrate to the fresh water. Hippo, elephant and reedbuck, among many other species, can usually be found here.

You then come to Round Table Hill, which provides a good view and excellent vantage point to get your bearings. The circular route continues over the Munge River, the source of which is in the Olmoti Crater north of Ngorongoro Crater, to Ngoitokitok Springs. From there, you journey past Gorigor Swamp, fed by the Lonyokie River, to the Hippo Pool, which is probably the best place to see hippo.

The Lerai Forest, primarily composed of fever trees (a type of acacia), is a good place to spot elephant and waterbuck and, if you are very lucky, leopard. There are 2 picnic areas here with long-drop toilets and running water. The "exit only" road climbs the wall of the

Game viewing on the crater floor

crater behind the forest. The road from the eastern rim can be used as both a down and up road into the crater.

On a recent visit we spent a morning and afternoon on the crater floor spending time looking for the elusive rhino! Even though we ran into more vehicle traffic than on the rest of our trip we still have to appreciate that 5 or more vehicles at a sighting is not huge when you consider how many travelers around the world have their heart set on seeing one of the Natural Wonders of the World! We in

Lake Magadi attracts thousands of flamingos

fact never had more than 2 other vehicles at our sightings as our naturalist guide knew that we wished to avoid other vehicles when possible. If you are concerned about the "crowds" in the Crater, I suggest you book a private vehicle and guide.

Some tour companies tell prospective clients that the Ngorongoro Crater is not worth a visit. I disagree, and feel that they are just trying to avoid the expensive

The highlight of a visit to the Ngorongoro Crater — black rhino!

entry fees in order to make their tours less expensive. That's like saying that if you go to Delhi it's not worth going to see the Taj Mahal!

Close to 400 bird species have been recorded in and around the Ngorongoro Crater. Birds commonly encountered on the crater floor are kori bustard, northern anteater chat, rufous-naped lark, rosy-breasted longclaw, superb starling and rufous-tailed weaver, as well as a host of waterfowl and waders. Different bird life thrives on the forested crater rim and misty highlands, with augur buzzard, golden-winged sunbird, malachite sunbird, tacazze sunbird, Schalow's turaco, white-eyed slaty flycatcher and streaky seedeater all being common.

At the picnic sites, vervet monkeys are very aggressive in getting at your food. Black and yellow-billed kites (predatory birds) habitually make swooping dives at lunch plates out in the open, and it is advisable to eat inside your vehicle! Camping has not been allowed on the crater floor since 1992.

Since this is classified as a conservation area and not a national park, wildlife, human beings and livestock exist together. Ground cultivation is not allowed. The Maasai are allowed to bring in their cattle for the salts and permanent water available on the crater floor, but they must leave the crater at night.

Ngorongoro Crater is about 112 miles (180 km) west of Arusha. An airstrip is located farther along the crater rim, but it is not used for scheduled charter flights as fog often keeps it closed in the mornings. Four-wheel-drive vehicles are required for game drives into the crater, and guests must be accompanied by a licensed guide or ranger.

Olmoti Crater, located about an hour's drive from where the eastern ascent/decent road intersects with the Ngorongoro Crater rim, is the perfect excursion for travelers who would like to explore more of the Crater Highlands and to possibly encounter Maasai going about their daily lives. From the Maasai village of

Nainokanoka at the base of the crater, you hike with a ranger from Ngorongoro Conservation Area Authority for about an hour to the top of the 10,165 foot (3,099 m) crater rim.

Another interesting excursion — for the adventurous and hardy only — is to take the beautifully scenic drive past Olmoti Crater through Maasailand to the 10,700 foot- (3,260 m) high **Empakaai Crater**, situated 20 miles (32 km) northwest of Ngorongoro Crater on a road that is difficult (and sometimes impossible) to negotiate, even with a 4wd vehicle. The crater is 5 miles (8 km) in diameter and is absolutely beautiful.

The 1,000 foot (300 m) decent to the floor of Empakaai Crater takes less than an hour to hike and is amazing. Maasai are often encountered on the drive as well as on the hike in and out of the crater. Flamingos and a variety of other bird life are often found lining the shores of Lake Empakaai. Allow a very long day for this excursion, or camp on the rim of the crater if you can stand the cold!

Ol Doinyo Lengai (10,600 ft./3,231 m) — an active volcano and holy mountain of the Maasai, **Lake Natron** and possibly even Mt. Kilimanjaro may be seen from the crater's rim.

About 30 miles (50 km) west of Ngorongoro Crater and a few miles off the road to the Serengeti is **Oldupai Gorge**, site of many archaeological discoveries, including the estimated 1.7-million-year-old *Zinjanthropus boisei* fossil. The fossil is housed in the National Museum in Dar es Salaam. A small

Oldupai Gorge

museum overlooks the gorge itself, and a guide there will tell you the story of the Leakeys' research and findings. Due to efforts in conserving the area, trips into the gorge where the *Zinjanthropus boisei* fossil was found are only allowed by special permit.

On one of our family's safaris, the drive to Oldupai Gorge brought us into contact with "the old" with a visit to Richard Leakey's Museum & Archaeological Site, and "the present" with further interaction with the Maasai people living near the Gorge. My older son especially enjoyed listening to the museum guide talk about man's predecessors, and having his picture taken next to the marker where the famous fossil was discovered.

We then drove to the **Shifting Sands**, located 4 miles (6 km) northwest of Oldupai Gorge. These crescent-shaped sand dunes, called "barchans," are about 100 yards (100 m) long and about 30 feet (9 m) high, and were formed by volcanic ash spewed from the active volcano Ol Doinyo Lengai. The strong prevailing winds move the dunes an average of 55 feet (17 m) per year. En route to the Shifting Sands you can see signs that have been posted over the years showing the dune's "progress." This is one of the few places in the world where these dunes exist. While climbing a dune we were joined by 3 Maasai boys who spent some time playing with our children.

The vast flat plains around Oldupai Gorge and west toward Ndutu and the Naabi Hills are underlain with volcanic ash, which promotes the growth of highly

The Shifting Sands is a fun place to stretch your legs en route to the Serengeti

nutritious annual grasses. These plains are the principle breeding grounds of the one and a half million wildebeest, which drop their calves in January or February and feed on the lush but short-lived grasses. When the rains come to an end, the wildebeest move north and the plains bake under the relentless sun.

To the north of Oldupai are the **Gol Mountains**, a range of jagged hills and deep valleys. A great number of vultures nest in the **OlKerian Gorge**, and the elusive striped hyena may sometimes be seen. At the western end of the Gols, the huge monolith of **Nasera Rock** is a striking landmark and — if you have the energy to climb to the top — allows for breathtaking views across the endless wilderness. These areas, along with the Shifting Sands, are great areas to visit for those who want more adventure in their safaris and wish to get off-the-beaten path.

The western part of the conservation area is covered by the Serengeti Plains. Game viewing in this region bordering the Serengeti National Park is best between December and March, when the Serengeti migration is usually in the area.

ACCOMMODATION — CLASS A+: • **Ngorongoro Crater Lodge**, set on the southwestern rim of the crater, has 3 separate camps: North and South Camp, each with 12 suites, and Tree Camp with 6 suites. Each stilted suite is elegantly furnished with claw-foot bathtubs and has butler service.

CLASS A/B: • **Ngorongoro Serena Safari Lodge**, situated on the western rim of the crater, has 75 rooms and suites, recently refurbished with private balconies. The dining room, bar and central fireplace overlook the crater.

CLASS B: • **Ngorongoro Sopa Lodge**, located on the eastern rim of the crater, has 96 rooms and a swimming pool all overlooking the crater floor. There is an exclusive down-and-up access road into the crater nearby.

CLASS B/C: • **Ngorongoro Wildlife Lodge**, a 75-room hotel, has a wonderful view of the crater.

SEASONAL CAMP: • **Lemala Ngorongoro**, located just below the crater rim 2 miles (3 km) from the Ngorongoro Sopa Lodge, has 9 heated tents and a tented dining room.

Serengeti National Park

The Serengeti is Tanzania's most famous park, and it has the largest concentration of migratory game animals in the world. It is also famous for its huge lion population and is one of the best places on the continent to see them.

Serengeti is derived from the Maasai language and appropriately means "endless plain." The park's 5,700-square-miles (14,763-km²) makes it larger than the state of Connecticut. Altitude varies from 3,120 to 6,070 feet (950 to 1,850 m).

The park, a World Heritage Site, comprises most of the Serengeti ecosystem, which is the primary migration route of the wildebeest. The Serengeti ecosystem also includes Kenya's Maasai Mara National Reserve, bordering on the north; the Loliondo Controlled Area, bordering on the northeast; the Ngorongoro Conservation Area, bordering on the southeast; the Maswa Game Reserve, bordering on the southwest; and the Grumeti Reserves and the Ikorongo Controlled Areas, bordering on the northwest. The "western corridor" of the park comes within 5 miles (8 km) of Lake Victoria.

Serengeti

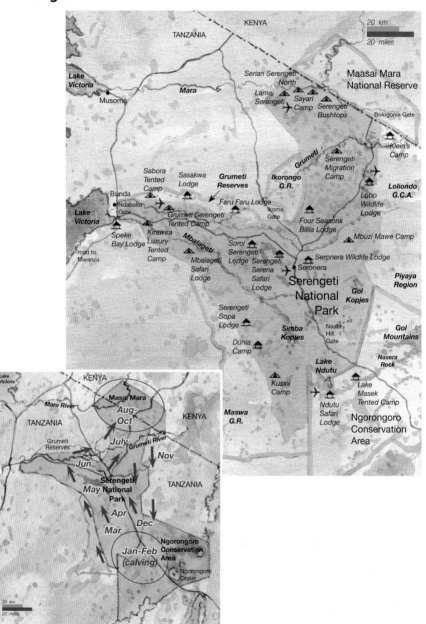

Nearly 500 species of birds and 35 species of large plains animals can be found in the Serengeti. The park may contain as many as 1.5 million wildebeest, 500,000 zebra, 300,000 Grant's gazelle, 250,000 Thomson's gazelle, 120,000 impala, 70,000 topi, 20,000 buffalo, 9,000 eland, 8,000 giraffe, 1,000 lion and 800 elephant.

Most of the Serengeti is a vast, open plain broken by rocky outcrops (kopjes). There is also acacia savannah, savannah woodland, riverine forests, some swamps and small lakes.

The north is hillier, with thick scrub and forests lining the Mara River, where leopards are sometimes spotted sleeping in the trees. Acacia savannah dominates the central region, with short- and long-grass open plains in the southeast and woodland plains and hills in the western corridor.

The Serengeti is home to over 800 elephant

It is impossible to predict the exact time of the famous Serengeti migration of approximately 1.3 million wildebeest, 200,000 zebra and 250,000 Thomson's gazelle, which covers a circuit of about 500 miles (800 km).

The key element in understanding "The Greatest Wildlife Show on Earth" is that it follows the general "rainfall gradient" across the ecosystem, with lower rainfall in the southeast (short-grass plains) and higher rainfall in the northwest. The migration moves from Kenya back to the short-grass plains of the Serengeti and Ngorongoro Conservation Area once the short rains have begun (usually in late October into November), and after the short-grass plains have dried out (usually in April or May), the migration moves northwest to higher rainfall areas and areas of permanent water — and fresh grass.

From December to April wildebeest, zebra, eland and Thomson's gazelle usually concentrate on the treeless short-grass plains in the extreme southeastern Serengeti

Leopard *(top)* and cheetah *(bottom)* are frequently seen on the Serengeti plains

and western Ngorongoro Conservation Area near Lake Ndutu in search of short grass, which they prefer over the longer dry-stemmed variety. In April and May, the height of the rainy season, a 4wd vehicle is highly recommended.

Other species common to the area during this period are Grant's gazelle, eland, hartebeest, topi and a host of predators including lion, cheetah, spotted hyena, honey badger and black-backed jackal. Kori bustard, secretarybird, yellow-throated sandgrouse and rufous-naped lark are resident birds of the open plains, which attract large numbers of migratory Montagu's and pallid harriers (from Europe) between September and March.

During the long rainy season (April and May) nomadic lions and hyena move to the eastern part of the Serengeti. The migration, mainly of wildebeest and zebra, begins in May or June. Once the dry season begins, wildebeest and zebra must migrate from the area. There is no permanent water, and both of these species must drink on a regular basis.

The rut for wildebeest is concentrated over a three-week period and generally occurs at the end of April, May or early June. After a gestation period of eight and one-half months, approximately 90% of the pregnant cows will give birth on the short-grass plains within a six-week period between the mid/end of January and February. Zebra calving season is spread out over most of the year, with a slightly higher birth rate

December through March. The best time to see wildebeest and zebra crossing the Grumeti River is in June/early July and November, and the best time to see them crossing the Mara River is from July to November.

Wildebeest move about 6 to 10 abreast in columns several miles long toward the western corridor. Zebra do not move in columns but in family units.

As a general rule, by June the migration has progressed west of Seronera. The migration then splits into three separate migrations: one west through the corridor toward permanent water and Lake Victoria and then northeast; the second due north, reaching the Maasai Mara of Kenya around mid-July; and the third northward between the other two to a region west of Lobo Lodge, where the group disperses.

During July through October, the highest concentration of the migration in the Serengeti is in the extreme north. The first and second groups meet and usually begin returning to the Serengeti National Park in late October; the migration then reaches the central or southern Serengeti by December.

A unique way to experience the Serengeti is by **hot air balloon**. Your pilot may fly you, at times, over 1,000 feet off the ground for panoramic views, and at other times at a very low altitudes (a few yards/meters off the ground) for great game viewing and photographic opportunities. The flight lasts about an hour, depending on wind conditions. After landing, guests enjoy a champagne breakfast. There are balloon launch sites in the central Serengeti and in the western corridor, and a seasonal one in the Southeastern Serengeti. There are no launch sites in the northern Serengeti. Balloon safaris are not accessible from all camps and lodges.

Ballooning over the Serengeti

There has been much international concern about a proposed highway through the Serengeti. The initial proposed routing was to pass across the northern part of the Serengeti, however, there are other proposed routes to the south of the park. As of this writing, the issue is still unresolved. This is just another possible reason that you should travel to Tanzania sooner than later!

Southern Serengeti — Short Grass Plains

Short-grass plains dominate the part of the Ngorongoro Conservation Area bordering the Serengeti. As you move northwest into the park, the plains change to medium-grass plains and then into long-grass plains around **Simba Kopjes** north of Naabi Hill Gate. Topi, elephant, Thomson's and Grant's gazelle, bat-eared fox and warthog are often seen here.

There are two saline lakes in the south of the park, **Lake Masek** and **Lake Lagaja**, known mainly for their populations of lesser and greater flamingos.

Seronera

The **Seronera Valley** is located in the center of the park and is characterized by large umbrella thorn trees — the archetypal image of the African savannah. Game is plentiful, and the area is famous for lion and leopard. Other wildlife includes hyena, jackal, topi, Maasai giraffe and Thomson's gazelle. This is the best area of the park to find cheetah, especially in the dry season. In the wet season, many cheetah are found in the short-grass plains. They are, however, found throughout the park.

Banagi Hill, 11 miles (17 km) north of Seronera on the road to Lobo, is a good area for Maasai giraffe, buffalo and impala. Four miles (6 km) from Banagi on the Orangi River is a hippo pool.

Lobo

From Banagi northward to Lobo and the Bologonja Gate are rolling uplands with open plains, bush, woodlands and magnificent kopjes. This is the best area of the park to see elephant. Forests of large mahogany and fig trees are found along the rivers where kingfishers, fish eagles and turacos can be seen. Other wildlife found in the Lobo area includes grey bush duikers and mountain reedbuck. Large numbers of Maasai giraffe are permanent residents.

Extreme Northern Serengeti & the Lemai Wedge

This part of the park has great game viewing year-round, however, from around mid-July to October, when the migration is generally in the area, the game viewing here is spectacular! Thousands of wildebeest and zebra gather along the Mara River to cross either north toward Kenya or south toward the central Serengeti.

The **Lemai Wedge**, a wedge-shaped piece of land consisting of a mixture of acacia forest, small valleys and large open plains bordered to the north by the Maasai Mara Reserve (Kenyan border) and to the south by the Mara River, is a very special place in the Serengeti. Escorted game walks allowed, making it all the more attractive.

From late July to October, when one arm of the migration is usually in the Maasai Mara in Kenya, consider focusing your time in the northern Serengeti. You will have a very good chance of seeing the migration, with only a fraction of the tourists that you would probably encounter game viewing in the Maasai Mara. Having those expansive Serengeti Plains almost to yourself is a priceless experience for travelers who are looking for more out of a safari than just seeing animals.

The Great Migration crossing the Mara River in the northern Serengeti

The hilly escarpment along the river is a key rhino breeding ground, and the rock kopjes are home to huge prides of lion. This is also a one of the best areas in Tanzania to see cheetah!

Western Corridor

The western corridor road begins 3 miles (5 km) north of Seronera and passes over the Grumeti River and beyond to a central range of hills. Eighteen miles (29 km) before Ndabaka Gate is an extensive area of black cotton soil, which makes rainy season travel difficult. This area is best visited June to March for its fabulous resident game. For the migration, it is best visited June, July and late October to early December. Do keep in mind that as there is permanent water in this area, game viewing is good year-round. Colobus monkeys may be found in the riverine areas. Other wildlife includes eland, topi, impala, dikdik, hippo and crocodile.

The area is known for its huge crocodiles, which reach 20 feet in length. There is a swinging bridge across the Grumeti River that provides a great viewpoint down the river.

The granite kopjes or rocky outcrops that dot the plains are home to rock hyrax, Kirk's dikdik and klipspringer. Banded, dwarf and slender mongoose are occasionally seen nearby. Verreaux's eagle are sometimes sighted near the Moru Kopjes.

Three species of jackal live in the Serengeti: black-backed, side-striped and golden. Side-striped jackal are rare, golden jackal are usually found in the short grass plains and black-backed jackal are quite common. The 6 species of vultures found in the park are white-backed, white-headed, hooded, lappet-faced, Ruppell's and Egyptian.

At the time of this writing, there are daily scheduled charter flights between the northern Serengeti and the Maasai Mara in Kenya. There is a dry-weather road (often impassable in the rainy season) from Mwanza and Musoma (Lake Victoria) to the west through Ndabaka Gate. The main road from the Ngorongoro Conservation Area via Naabi Hill Gate is open year-round.

Travel in the park is allowed only from 6:00 a.m. until 7:00 p.m. Visitors may get out of the vehicle in open areas if no animals are present. Do stay close to the vehicle, and keep a careful lookout. Night game drives are not allowed.

The Serengeti is so large, I recommend spending at least 2 or 3 days in each of 2 regions. Many travelers spend 5 to 7 days in this great park. On our last visit, our family spent 10 days and did not want to leave!

Park Headquarters are located at Seronera, while the park staff housing is located at Ft. Ikoma, outside of the park.

ACCOMMODATION — CLASS A+: • **Sayari Camp**, an extraordinary permanent tented camp located in the northern Serengeti close to the bridge to the Lemai Wedge, is divided into 2 wings of 6 and 9 luxury tents with private verandahs. Each wing enjoys its own bar, dining room and lounge with a shared swimming pool. There is good resident game year-round, peaking during the Migration crossings that occur usually from July through early November. Activities include open vehicle game drives and walking safaris. • **Serengeti Bushtops**, located 15 miles from the Mara River, has 12 tents with private decks, hot tub, personal telescopes and 24-hour butler service.

CLASS A: • **Kusini Camp**, located in the southern Serengeti, has been rebuilt and refurbished with 12 tents scattered around a rock formation. The camp is ideally located for the calving season of the wildebeest, which takes place in this area around February of each year. Game viewing is at its best from December through March. The camp supports the Cheetah Watch Program. • **Serengeti Migration Camp**, located 14 miles (22 km) west of the Lobo airstrip, has 20 luxurious tents all with expansive decks. The main lodge overlooks the swimming pool and a water hole. • **Lamai Serengeti**, located in the northern Serengeti, features 12 tents split between two separate camps. Each luxury tent has a step-down shower and tub area and an outdoor shower on the deck, and an expansive private deck. • **Four Seasons Bilila Lodge**, located in the central/ northern Serengeti, features 74 rooms, suites and villas, restaurant, lobby lounge, bar, boma, wine cellar, infinity swimming pool and Anantara spa. The Corner Suites and Private Villas have private plunge pools and large teak decks. • **Soroi Serengeti Lodge**, located in the western corridor, features 25 thatched chalets with hardwood floors, Turkish baths, outdoor showers, and private decks with spectacular views. The main lounge and dining room are built around large rock kopjes and acacia trees. Between game drives enjoy swimming in the infinity pool or have a spa treatment on your private patio. • **Kirawira Luxury Tented Camp**, located in the western corridor approximately 55 miles (90 km) west of Seronera and 6 miles (10 km) east of the Kirawira Ranger Post, has a classic Victorian atmosphere, with 25 luxury tents and a

Serengeti Migration Camp *(top, left)*, Sayari Camp *(top, right)*, Mbuzi Mawe Camp *(middle, left)*, Kusini Camp *(middle, right)*, Sayari Camp's pool area overlooks the Serengeti plains *(bottom)*

Serengeti Serena Safari Lodge *(top)*, Dunia Camp *(middle, left)*, Lake Masek Tented Camp *(middle, right)*, Serengeti Explorer Camp — luxury mobile camping at its best! *(bottom)*

swimming pool. • **Grumeti Serengeti Tented Camp**, located in the western corridor 53 miles (85 km) west of Seronera Lodge and 31 miles (50 km) east of Lake Victoria, has 10 spacious tents.

CLASS A/B: • **Mbuzi Mawe Camp**, located on a kopje between Seronera and Lobo, consists of 16 tents. • **Serengeti Serena Safari Lodge**, set on a hill overlooking the Serengeti Plains about 18 miles (29 km) northwest of Seronera Lodge, has 66 rooms and a swimming pool. Walking safaris and hikes with sundowners can be arranged. • **Mbalageti Safari Lodge** is a permanent tented camp located in western Serengeti overlooking the Mbalageti River Valley, consisting of 24 tented chalets, each with a private verandah.

CLASS B: • **Lobo Wildlife Lodge**, located in the north of the park 43 miles north of Seronera, has 75 rooms uniquely designed around huge boulders. • **Serengeti Sopa Lodge**, located 25 miles (40 km) southwest of Seronera Lodge and 60 miles (96 km) from Naabi Hill Gate, has 69 rooms each with 2 queen size beds, private balconies and a swimming pool.

CLASS C: • **Seronera Wildlife Lodge**, situated in the center of the park 90 miles (145 km) from Ngorongoro Crater, has 57 double rooms.

ACCOMMODATION ON THE PERIPHERY OF THE PARK — CLASS A/B: • **Kleins Camp**, situated in a 25,000-acre (10,000-hectare) private reserve bordered on the west by Serengeti National Park, has 10 thatched cottages made from local rocks. Day and night game drives, guided bush walks and visits to local Maasai are offered. • **Lake Masek Tented Camp** overlooks the shores of Lake Masek. The camp has 20 tents, a comfortable lounge, restaurant and expansive deck with views over the lake. It is located in the Ngorongoro Conservation Area bordering Serengeti National Park.

CLASS B/C: • **Lukuba Island Resort**, situated in Lake Victoria approximately 9 miles (15 km) from Musoma town, has 5 stone and thatch bungalows. • **Speke Bay Lodge**, located on the southeastern shore of Lake Victoria, 9 miles (15 km) from the Serengeti National Park, has 8 thatched bungalows on the lakeshore. Fishing, boat excursions and mountain biking are offered.

CLASS C: • **Ndutu Safari Lodge** is a rustic lodge with 34 rooms located on the edge of the park in the Ngorongoro Conservation Area.

SEASONAL MOBILE CAMPS — LUXURY: • **Serengeti Explorer Camp** has 10 luxury tents and periodically moves location within the Serengeti according to migration game movements and weather conditions. The focus of the camp is a large dining tent with a shaded lounge area and a campfire every evening, around which guests can share the day's adventures with like-minded souls. • **Dunia Camp**, located in the Nyareboro area, north of the Moru Kopjes, has 8 large tent, and is seasonally opened for peak game viewing (closed April to May). • **Serian Serengeti North**, located close to the Mara River in the northern Serengeti, features 6 tents and is open from July to mid-November. • **Serengeti Under Canvas** has 8 Bedouin-style tents. • **Olakira Camp** features 8 large tents with an intimate dining tent, lounge tent and fireplace.

FIRST CLASS: • **Ubuntu Camp** is a seasonal camp located in the northern Serengeti near the Mara River. With just 6 tents, the camp is an intimate base for game viewing. • **Nduara Loliondo** is situated in a private conservation area in Loliondo immediately bordering the northeastern Serengeti. Day and night game drives, walking, and Maasai visits are offered. • **Simiyu Mobile Camp** moves 3 times a year as it follows the migration across the Serengeti and features 8 tents with private verandahs.

MID-RANGE: • **Kati Kati Tented Camp** is a mobile camp located in the central Serengeti. There are 15 mobile tents, dining tent and drinks served around a camp fire.

Grumeti Reserves

Grumeti Reserves is located adjacent to the western corridor of the Serengeti, bordering the national park, and encompasses over 350,000-acres (40,000-hectares) of unrivaled wilderness. The area forms part of the famous migratory route, which is traveled by hundreds of thousands of animals every year.

The real advantage of this private reserve is that guests can enjoy the splendor of the Serengeti Plains and it's spectacular wildlife with only a few other vehicles ever in sight.

Sasakwa Lodge, Sabora Tented Camp and Faru Faru are three of the best properties in Africa — with Sasakwa providing true elegance in the wilderness. Our family had a fabulous time here on a recent visit. We saw the migration in all its glory with endless wildebeest columns moving through the area. As the reserve is so large, we hardly encountered another vehicle on our game drives. While staying at Sasakwa, my wife Alison went horseback riding while our boys Miles, Nicholas and I tried our hand at archery, played some tennis and went for a swim to get some much appreciated exercise.

Game drives and walks are enjoyed with resident professional guides. Other activities include archery, lawn croquet, mountain biking, equestrian pursuits, and hot air ballooning.

The Grumeti Reserves offers luxurious accommodations in a remote setting

ACCOMMODATION — CLASS A+:
• **Sasakwa Lodge** offers 9 individually air-conditioned cottages (ranging in size from 1 to 4 bedrooms) that have been positioned in the garden for complete privacy, each with its own heated infinity pool, a comfortable lounge area, elegantly appointed bathrooms and generous sized bedroom with a four-poster bed. More experienced riders can enjoy rides onto the Serengeti plains.
• **Sabora Tented Camp** accommodates 18 guests in 9 luxurious tents reminiscent of Hemingway, Blixen and Roosevelt. The spacious air-conditioned tents are decorated in rich fabrics, antiques and Persian rugs. • **Faru Faru Lodge** accommodates 22 guests in luxurious comfort. Offering fantastic views across the Grumeti River, the lodge is built with barefoot elegance with huge windows where guests can watch the constant stream of game to the camp's waterhole next to the heated swimming pool. • **Serengeti House** is an exclusive private villa with 2 suites in the main house and 2 garden suites, a swimming pool and tennis court.

SEASONAL MOBILE CAMPS — LUXURY:
• **Singita Explore** is a private luxury mobile camp exclusive for up to 12 guests. The theme is modern, robust and stylish.

Faru Faru Lodge *(top)*, Private mobile camping at Singita Explore *(bottom)*

Lake Natron Region

Located between the Ngorongoro Conservation Area and the Kenya border, **Lake Natron** is a shallow, alkaline lake approximately 38 miles long and 15 miles wide (60 by 25 km). This remote lake is one of East Africa's largest breeding areas for both lesser and greater flamingos.

This is a remote wilderness with limited wildlife, a few scattered Maasai settlements and rugged sand tracks. You may encounter Maasai tribesmen as they tend their herds of cattle, visit the waterfalls and see the inland cliffs that are home to thousands of Ruppell's vultures.

South of Lake Natron is **Ol Doinyo Lengai**, the only active carbonatite volcano in the world and holy mountain of the Maasai. This steep mountain takes about 10 hours to climb and return to its base. The climb starts at midnight, due to the extremely high midday temperatures and to allow the opportunity to enjoy the beauty of the volcano at night.

ACCOMMODATION — CLASS B: • **Ngare Sero Lake Natron Camp** offers 8 self-contained tents. Activities include bird and nature walks and climbs on Ol Doinyo Lengai.

CLASS C: • **Moivaro Lake Natron Tented Camp** can arrange climbs on the mountain.

Rubondo Island National Park

Located in the southwestern part of Lake Victoria, the main attractions of this 93-square-mile (240-km²) island are sitatunga (indigenous) and small groups of chimpanzees. Walking is allowed and the wildlife that may be seen includes black-and-white colobus monkey, giraffe, bushbuck and otters. There are no large predators. Nearly 400 species of birds have been recorded, including storks, herons, ibises, kingfishers, bee-eaters, flycatchers and an abundance of fish eagles.

In addition to the main island, there are about a dozen small islands that make up the park. Habitats include papyrus swamps, savannah, open woodlands and dense evergreen forests. Visitors, accompanied by a guide who is usually armed, may walk along forested trails in search of wildlife or wait patiently at a number of hides. The best time to visit is November to February. A few boats are available for hire.

Flying by air charter is the only easy way to get to the park. An airstrip is located at Park Headquarters.

ACCOMMODATION — CLASS A/B: • **Rubondo Island Camp** has 10 tents under thatch and a swimming pool. Activities include fishing, walks in search of chimpanzees and other wildlife, and birdwatching.

Mt. Kilimanjaro National Park

Known to many through Ernest Hemingway's book *The Snows of Kilimanjaro* (Arrow), Mt. Kilimanjaro is the highest mountain in the world that is not part of a mountain range, and it is definitely one of the world's most impressive mountains. Kilimanjaro means "shining mountain"; it rises from an average altitude of about 3,300 feet (1,000 m) on the dry plains to 19,340 feet (5,895 m), truly a world-class mountain. On clear days, the mountain can be seen from over 200 miles (320 km) away.

The Mawenzi Peak rises in the distance

The mountain consists of three major volcanic centers: Kibo (19,340 ft./5,895 m), Shira (13,650 ft./4,162 m) to the west and Mawenzi (16,893 ft./5,150 m) to the east.

The base of the mountain is 37 miles (60 km) long and 25 miles (40 km) wide. The park is a World Heritage Site and covers 292-square-miles (756-km²) of the mountain above 8,856 feet (2,700 m). The park also has six corridors that climbers may use to trek through the Forest Reserve.

Hikers pass through zones of forest, alpine and semidesert to its snow-capped peak, situated only three degrees south of the equator. It was once thought to be an extinct volcano, but due to recent rumblings, it is now classified as dormant.

Climbing Mt. Kilimanjaro was definitely a highlight of my travels. For the struggle to reach its highest peak I was handsomely rewarded with a feeling of accomplishment, fabulous views of the African plains, and many exciting memories of the climb. In fact, with over 30,000 climbers a year, Kilimanjaro is second only to the Everest and Annapurnas areas in Nepal in popularity as a trekking destination outside of Europe.

The early stages of a Kili climb

Kilimanjaro may, in fact, be the easiest mountain in the world for a climber to ascend to such heights. But it is still a struggle for even fit adventurers. On the other hand, it can be climbed by people from all walks of life that are in good condition and have a strong will. Mind you, reaching the top is by no means necessary; the flora, fauna and magnificent views seen enroute are fabulous.

A Christian missionary, Johann Rebmann, reported his discovery of this snow-capped mountain, but the Europeans didn't believe him. Hans Meyer was the first European to climb Kilimanjaro, doing so in 1889.

The most unique animal in this park is the Abbot's duiker, which is found in only a few mountain forests in northern Tanzania. Other wildlife includes elephant, buffalo, eland, leopard, hyrax, and black-and-white colobus monkeys. However, very little large game is seen.

Bird life is sparse but interesting, with bronze sunbird, red-tufted malachite sunbird, alpine chat and streaky seedeater not uncommon. You might see augur buzzard and white-necked raven soaring above you, and you may even be lucky enough to see the rare bearded vulture.

A guide welcomes climbers to the Rongai One Camp *(top)*, Porters carry all equipment and food *(middle)*, Clouds roll in at Kibo Camp as climbers prepare for the summit *(bottom)*

The best time to climb is mid-December to mid-March and June to October during the drier seasons when the skies are fairly clear. The temperatures in July and August can be quite cool. April and May should be avoided because of heavy rains and overcast skies.

From April to May, during the long rainy season, the summit is often covered in clouds, with snow falling at higher altitudes and rain at lower altitudes. The short rains (November) bring afternoon thunderstorms, but evenings and mornings are often clear.

Many routes to the summit require no mountaineering skills.

Mountaineers wishing to ascend by technical routes may wish to get a copy of *Guide to Mt. Kenya and Kilimanjaro* (Mountain Club of Kenya), edited by Iain Allan.

The Park Headquarters is located in Marangu, about a 7-hour drive from Nairobi, or 2 hours from Arusha. Children under 10 years of age are not allowed over 9,843 feet (3,000 m).

Travelers wishing to see Mt. Kilimanjaro, but who do not wish to climb it, may do so (provided the weather is clear) from Arusha National Park or Amboseli National Park (Kenya). Day trips and treks to the first camp only are also available as an option.

Zones

Mt. Kilimanjaro can be divided into five zones by altitude: 1) cultivated lower slopes, 2) forest, 3) heath and moorland/lower alpine, 4) highland desert/alpine and 5) summit. Each zone spans approximately 3,300 feet (1,000 m) in altitude. As the altitude increases, rainfall and temperature decrease; this has a direct effect on the vegetation each zone supports.

The rich volcanic soils of the **lower slopes** of the mountain around Moshi and Marangu up to the park gate (6,000 ft./1,830 m) are intensely cultivated, mostly with coffee and bananas.

The **forest** zone (5,900–9,185 ft./1,800–2,800 m) receives the highest rainfall of the zones, with about 80 inches (2,000 mm) on the southern slopes and about half that amount on the northern and western slopes. The upper half of this zone is often covered with clouds, and humidity is high, with day temperatures ranging from 60 to 70°F (15 to 21°C). Don't be surprised if it rains while walking through this zone; in fact, expect it.

The challenge of the Kili trek is forgotten once reaching the summit

In the lower forest, there are palms, sycamore figs, bearded lichen and mosses hanging from tree limbs, tree ferns growing to 20 feet (6 m) in height, and giant lobelia which grow to over 30 feet (9 m). In the upper forest zone, giant groundsels appear. Unlike many East African volcanic mountains, no bamboo belt surrounds Kilimanjaro.

Black-and-white colobus and blue monkey, olive baboon and bushbuck may be seen. Elephant, eland, giraffe, buffalo and suni may be seen on the northern and western slopes. Also present but seldom seen are bushpig, civet, genet, bush duiker, Abbot's duiker and red duiker.

Zone three, a lower alpine zone ranging from 9,185 to 13,120 feet (2,800 to 4,000 m), is predominantly **heath** followed by moorlands. Rainfall decreases with altitude from about 50 inches to 20 inches (1,250 to 500 mm) per year. Giant heather (10 to 30 feet/3 to 9 m high), grasslands with scattered bushes and beautiful flowers, including "everlasting" flowers, protea and colorful red-hot pokers, characterize the lower part of this zone.

You then enter the **moorlands** with tussock grasses and groups of giant senecios and lobelias — weird, prehistoric-looking Afro-alpine vegetation that would provide a great setting for a science fiction movie. With a lot of luck, you may spot eland, elephant, buffalo or klipspringer.

The **highland desert/alpine zone** is from around 13,120 to 16,400 feet (4,000 to 5,000 m) and receives only about 10 inches (250 mm) of rain per year. Vegetation is very thin and includes tussock grasses, "everlasting" flowers, moss balls and lichens. The thin air makes flying too difficult for most birds, and the very few larger mammals that may be seen do not make this region their home. What this zone lacks in wildlife is compensated for by the fabulous views. Temperatures can range from below freezing to very hot, so be prepared.

The **summit** experiences arctic conditions and receives less than 4 inches (100 mm) of rain per year, usually in the form of snow. It is almost completely devoid of vegetation.

Kibo's northern summit is covered by the Great Northern Glacier. On Kibo there is an outer caldera about 1.5 miles (2.5 km) in diameter. Uhuru peak is the highest point on the outer caldera and also the highest point on the mountain. Kilimanjaro's glaciers have been shrinking with global warming, and it has lost most of its ice peak in the last decade.

Within the outer caldera is an inner cone that contains the Inner or Reusch Crater, which is about .5 mile (1 km) in diameter. Vents (fumaroles) spewing steam and sulfurous gasses are located at the Terrace and the base of the crater. Within the Inner Crater is an ash cone with an ash pit about 1,100 feet (335 m) across and about 400 feet (120 m) deep.

Routes

In regard to routes, Kilimanjaro is divided into two halves by a line running north/south between Barafu Camp and Kibo Hut. All climbers who ascend on the Machame, Shira, Lemosho, and Umbwe routes must descend on the Mweka route.

Kilimanjaro Routes

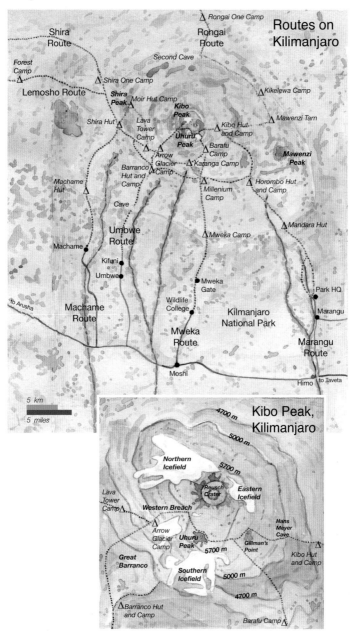

All climbers who ascend on the Rongai and Marangu Routes must descend on the Marangu Route. The Marangu Route is the only two-way route; all other routes are one way only. Climbers from the Rongai and Marangu routes only meet climbers from the other routes on the Kibo Crater rim. This system is effective in reducing the impact of large numbers of climbers on all routes, except for the Marangu Route.

Climbers on the Machame, Shira, Lemosho, and Umbwe Routes may approach the summit via the Western Breach or may skirt around to Barafu and climb up to Stella Point.

Climbing Kilimanjaro to the summit, Uhuru Peak, via the routes described below requires no mountaineering skills. The Marangu and the Machame Routes are the most popular, carrying 85% of all climbers, while the Shira, Lemosho, Rongai and Umbwe routes are much less used. Climbers stay in basic mountain huts on the Marangu Route and camp on all other routes. Climbs booked with a professional climb operator are full service climbs, meaning that all the climbers have to do is hike. The chief guide, assisted by a team consisting of a cook, assistant guides and porters take care of everything else.

The park has rescue teams based at the Park Headquarters, on the eastern edge of the Shira Plateau, and rangers at various points spread over the mountain.

At the end of your climb you receive a diploma certifying your accomplishment at Park Headquarters. Many climbers then spend the night in a hotel in Marangu or Arusha and have the pleasure of sharing their experiences with unwary visitors planning to begin their Kilimanjaro adventure the following day.

The nights before and after the climb are often spent in a lodge or hotel in or near Arusha or Marangu.

For the quality of your experience to be the best possible on this busy mountain I recommend a 6 day-Rongai Route or an 8 day-Shira Route climb. These 2 routes allow you to visit some of the quieter areas of Kilimanjaro, are scenically interesting and the itineraries are structured to give the best chance to reach the summit.

Rongai Route

The Rongai route starts just south of the Kenya-Tanzania border. It is as easy as the main Marangu trail and more attractive as it travels from the northern side of the mountain right across it to the southern slopes. The route has extensive views and spends one night at Mawenzi Tarn, the mountain's most beautiful campsite.

DAY 1: RONGAI GATE (6,398 ft./1,950 m) to RONGAI ONE CAMP (8,530 ft./2,600 m) — 3–4 HOURS. ALTITUDE GAIN 2,133 ft. (650 m).
Drive for 2.5 hours from your hotel in Marangu to Rongai Gate and start the climb through the forest where there is a good chance of seeing colobus monkeys. As the forest starts to thin, you cross a small stream and reach Rongai One Camp.

DAY 2: RONGAI ONE CAMP to KIKELEWA CAMP (11,811 ft./3,600 m) — 6–7 HOURS. ALTITUDE GAIN 3,281 ft. (1,000 m).
A steady climb all morning brings you to Second Cave, where there is a break for lunch. After lunch, depart toward Mawenzi Peak. The Kikelewa Camp will be reached in late afternoon.

DAY 3: KIKELEWA CAMP to MAWENZI TARN (14,104 ft./4,300 m) — 3–5 HOURS. ALTITUDE GAIN 2,293 ft. (700 m).

A short, steep climb, leaving all vegetation behind, brings you closer to Mawenzi Peak and after topping a small rise you enter the striking Tarn valley. After lunch in camp, take an acclimation walk.

DAY 4: MAWENZI TARN to KIBO CAMP (15,420 ft./4,700 m) — 3–4 HOURS. ALTITUDE GAIN 1,316 ft. (400 m).

Cross the saddle between the Mawenzi and the main summit, Kibo. This area is very desert-like. Arrive at the Kibo Camp for a late lunch. The afternoon is spent preparing for the summit push.

DAY 5: KIBO CAMP to UHURU PEAK (19,344 ft./5,896 m) AND DOWN TO HOROMBO CAMP (12,139 ft./3,700 m) — 10–15 HOURS.

Wake up around midnight and start the climb by flashlight (headlamps are better), plodding slowly up the switchbacks to pass Hans Meyer Cave and Jamaica Rocks and reach Gilmans Point. Upon reaching the crater rim there is a real sense of achievement. After a short rest those strong enough can continue for another 1.5 hours to the very top, Uhuru Peak (19,344 ft./5,896 m). The descent to Kibo Camp is surprisingly fast, and after a small rest and some food, the descent continues down to Horombo Camp.

DAY 6: HOROMBO CAMP to MARANGU MAIN GATE — 5–6 HOURS.

A steady descent takes you down into the forest and on through rich forest to the main park gate at Marangu (6,070 ft./1,850 m).

Shira Route

This route is from the west and is planned to give the best acclimation, while views are not as extensive as on Rongai, they are constantly changing as you traverse the mountain which is quite interesting.

DAY 1: SHIRA BARRIER (10,800 ft./3,300m) to SHIRA ONE CAMP (11,650 ft./3,550 m) — 2–3 HOURS. ALTITUDE GAIN 985 ft (300 m).

Drive 2.5 hours from Arusha to Londorossi Gate, register and drive up to the edge of the Shira Plateau within the park to start the walk. The trail climbs up to the Shira Plateau and then heads along a small path into the middle of the Shira Plateau and reaches Shira One Camp.

DAY 2: SHIRA ONE CAMP to SHIRA HUT CAMP (12,598 ft./3,840 m) — 5 HOURS. ALTITUDE GAIN 1,115 ft (340 m).

Walk south across the plateau to its rim, there is a chance to get to the top of the Shira Cathedral (12,303 ft./3,750 m) before following the old crater rim around and up to the Shira Hut Camp.

DAY 3: SHIRA HUT CAMP to MOIR HUT CAMP (13,120 ft./4,000 m) — 4–7 HOURS WALKING (INCLUDING AFTERNOON WALK FROM CAMP). ALTITUDE GAIN 525 ft. (160m).

A short morning walk through the moorlands brings you to Moir Hut Camp (13,780 ft./4,200m). After having lunch at the camp, there is time to acclimatize with an ascent of the nearby Lent Hills (14,350 ft/ 4,375m).

DAY 4: MOIR HUT CAMP to LAVA TOWER CAMP (14,925 ft./4,550 m). — 4–5 HOURS.

Another morning walk which traverses the side of Kibo to reach Lava Tower Camp (14,925 ft./4,550 m). In the afternoon there is a chance to acclimatize by following a trail up toward Arrow Glacier, reaching a height of 15,420 ft. (4,700 m) before returning to camp.

DAY 5: LAVA TOWER CAMP to KARANGA CAMP (13,123 ft./4,000 m) — 5–7 HOURS.
From Lava Tower you drop down to the Barranco Valley and then climb up steeply on the Barranco Wall. An undulating trail that continues and eventually drops into the Karanga Valley, the last water source on the way to the summit. After crossing the stream, a steep climb up the other side of the U-shaped valley leads to Karanga Camp.

DAY 6: KARANGA CAMP to BARAFU CAMP (15,092 ft./4,600 m) — 4–5 HOURS. ALTITUDE GAIN 1,969 ft (600 m).
Today you will walk across the compacted scree and rocks onto the Barafu Ridge and on to the Barafu Camp for lunch. There is a short acclimation walk in the afternoon.

DAY 7: BARAFU CAMP to UHURU PEAK (19,344 ft./5,896 m) AND DOWN TO MILLENNIUM CAMP (13,123 ft./4,000m) — 10–15 HOURS.
Midnight you will wake up and head off to the summit over the rocky ridge behind camp and then switchback up the main slopes to reach Stella Point on the crater rim. It is another 45 minutes to the very top, Uhuru Peak. The descent back to Barafu Camp is rapid and after a rest and some food, continue your descent to Millennium Camp.

DAY 8: MILLENNIUM CAMP to MWEKA GATE (5,413 ft./1,650 m) — 4–6 HOURS.
The route heads straight off Kilimanjaro through the lush rainforest to reach Mweka Gate.

Marangu Route

The Marangu Route is the least expensive route to climb and is second in popularity only to the Machame Route. Marangu has hut accommodations with separate long-drop toilets, and is the second easiest (most gradual) route to the summit (Rongai is the easiest).

This route may be completed in 5 days, but it's best to take 6 days, spending an extra day at Horombo Hut to allow more time to acclimatize to the altitude. The huts are dormitory-style with common areas for cooking and eating. As bunk space is limited in the huts, I suggest you plan on starting your treks early and arrive early.

DAY 1: MARANGU (6,004 ft./1,830 m) to MANDARA HUT (8,856 ft./2,700 m) — 4–5 HOURS. ALTITUDE GAIN: 2,854 ft. (870 m).
An hour or so is spent at Park Headquarters at Marangu Gate handling registration and arranging the loads for the porters. Try to leave in the morning to allow a leisurely pace and to avoid afternoon showers. The trail leads through the forest and is often muddy.
Mandara has a number of small wooden A-frame huts that sleep 8 persons each, 4 to a room, and a main cabin with a dormitory upstairs and dining room downstairs, for a total of 60 beds. Kerosene lamps, stoves and mattresses are provided.

DAY 2: MANDARA to HOROMBO HUT (12,205 ft./3,720 m) — 5–7 HOURS. ALTITUDE GAIN: 3,346 ft. (1,020 m).
On day 2, you pass through the upper part of the rain forest to tussock grassland and fascinating Afro-alpine vegetation of giant groundsels and giant lobelias to the moorlands. Once out of the forest, you begin to get great views of the town of Moshi and Mawenzi Peak (16,893 ft./5,149 m). If you can spare an extra day for acclimatizing,

Horombo is the best hut for this. There are some nice day hikes that will help you further acclimatize. Kibo is too high to allow a good night's sleep. Horombo has 120 beds and is similar to but more crowded than Mandara.

DAY 3: HOROMBO HUT to KIBO HUT (15,430 ft./4,703 m) — 5–6 HOURS. ALTITUDE GAIN: 3,225 ft. (983 m).

On the morning of day 3, the vegetation begins to thin out to open grasslands. You pass "Last Water" (be sure to fill your water bottles because this is the last source of water). The landscape becomes more barren as you reach "The Saddle," a wide desert between Kibo and Mawenzi Peak. Kibo Hut does not come in to view until just before you reach it. Kibo Hut has 58 beds and is located on the east side of Kibo Peak.

With the wind-chill factor, it can be very cold, so dress warmly. This is the day many hikers feel the effects of the altitude and may begin to experience some altitude sickness. Most people find it impossible to sleep at this height because of the lack of oxygen and the bitter cold, not to mention the possibility of altitude sickness. Get as much rest as you can.

DAY 4: KIBO HUT to GILLMAN'S POINT (18,635 ft./5,680 m) and UHURU PEAK (19,340 ft./5,895 m) AND DOWN TO HOROMBO HUT — 10–12 HOURS.

Your guide will wake you shortly after midnight for your ascent, which should begin around 1:00 a.m. Be sure not to delay the start; it is vital that you reach the summit by sunrise. The sun quickly melts the frozen scree, making the ascent all the more difficult.

The steep ascent to Gillman's Point on the edge of the caldera is a grueling 4- to 5-hour slog up scree. Hans Meyer Cave is a good place to rest before climbing seemingly unending switchbacks past Johannes Notch to Gillman's Point.

From Gillman's Point, Uhuru Peak is a fairly gradual climb of 705 feet (215 m). It will take another hour to hour and a half. Uhuru Peak is well marked, and there is a book in which you may sign your name.

If you are still feeling strong, ask your guide to take you down into the caldera to the inner crater, which has some steam vents. You return to Gillman's Point by a different route.

Standing over 16,000 feet (4,900 m) above the surrounding plains, the view was breathtaking in every direction. Sunrise over Mawenzi is a beautiful sight. You truly feel that you're on the top of the world!

Shortly after sunrise, you begin the long walk down the mountain to Kibo Hut for a short rest, then continue onward to Horombo Hut. Provided you are not completely exhausted, the walk down is long but pretty easy going. From Gillman's Point to Horombo takes about 4 hours and from Uhuru Peak, about 5.

DAY 5: HOROMBO HUT to MARANGU

Another long day of hiking as you descend past Mandara Hut to Park Headquarters.

Machame Route

This is the most popular and one of the most beautiful routes up the mountain. It is also one of the steepest routes. The park gate is located a few miles above Machame village. Hike 4 to 6 hours through rain forest to Machame Huts (9,843 ft./3,000 m).

The following day you hike 5 to 7 hours to the defunct Shira Hut (12,467 ft./3,800 m) on the Shira Plateau (see Shira Plateau Route for description of the area). Continue hiking about 4 hours to Lava Tower Camp. From Lava Tower Camp there had been 2 choices to reach Uhuru Peak. The route via the Western Breach with an overnight at Arrow Glacier (15,744 ft./4,800 m) before reaching the Inner Crater has been closed due to concerns about the possibility of falling ice chunks from the glacier. The route now used continues along the Southern Summit Circuit path to Barranco and Barafu before climbing to Uhuru via Stella Point (18,811 ft./5,735 m).

Lemosho Route

Next to the Umbwe Route, this is the least-used route and requires a minimum of 7 days. As with the Shira Plateau Route above, drive to the Londorossi Gate. Then drive to Lemosho Glades and hike through the rain forest to Forest Camp (8,000 ft./2,440 m). On the second day, take a full day's hike into the Shira Caldera, a high grassy plateau, to Shira One Campsite (11,500 ft./3,500 m). On day three, trek for 3 to 4 hours across the Shira Plateau to Shira 2 Campsite (12,200 ft./3,700 m). Those who feel strong can take an acclimatizing trek to Shira Cathedral. On Day 4, hike 7 hours down the Barranco Valley over 15,000 feet (4,570 m). This is great for acclimatization. Next go to the camp at Barranco Wall (12,900 ft./3,940 m). On day 5, climb up Barranco Wall (14,000 ft./4,270 m). On Day 6 trek to Barafu Camp (16,000 ft./4,600 m). On Day 7, begin trekking up the scree slopes just after midnight to Stella Point on the rim and onward to Uhuru Peak. Return to Barafu Camp and continue your descent to Mweka Hut (10,170 ft./3,100 m). On Day 8, hike to Mweka Gate.

Umbwe Route

The Umbwe Route is very steep and strenuous. The route begins at Umbwe (about 4,600 ft./1,400 m), a village 10 miles (16 km) from Moshi. Walk two miles to Kifuni village and into the forest. Follow the path for another 3.5 miles (5km) and then branch left into a mist-covered forest until you reach the forest cave (Bivouac #1) at 9,515 feet (2,900 m), 6 to 7 hours from Umbwe. Overhanging ledges extending about 5 feet (1.5 m) from the cliff provide reasonable protection for about 6 people; however, it is recommended you use your own tents. Water is available, but not close by.

Continue through moorlands and along a narrow ridge with deep valleys on either side. The thick mist and vegetation covered with "Old Man's Beard" moss creates an eerie atmosphere. The second caves at 11,483 feet (3,500 m) are still another 2- to 3-hour hike from Bivouac #1. The vegetation thins out, and you branch right shortly before arriving at Barranco Hut (12,795 ft./3,900 m) about 2 hours later.

From Barranco you can backtrack to the fork and turn right (north) and hike for 3 hours to where Lava Tower Camp (15,092 ft./4,600 m) used to stand. From there, the climb is up steep scree and blocks of rock to the floor of the crater and Uhuru Peak via the Great Western Breach. The climb from Lava Tower Camp to the caldera takes about 9 hours. An alternative from Barranco Hut is to traverse the mountain eastward and follow the Summit Circuit path to Barafu Camp. Descend via the Mweka Route, regardless of the summit routes used.

Equipment Checklist

The better equipped you are for climbing Mt. Kilimanjaro, the higher your chances of making the summit. When it comes to clothing, the "layered effect" works best. Bring a duffel bag to pack your gear in for the climb. Wrap your clothes in heavy garbage bags to keep them dry. Keep the weight under the porter's maximum load of 33 pounds (15 kg). Here's a suggested checklist of items to consider bringing:

CLOTHING

- ☐ Gortex (or other breathable-type) jacket (with hood) and pants, and a light raincoat
- ☐ polypropylene long underwear — tops and bottoms, medium and heavy weight
- ☐ wool sweater and/or heavy fleece (one or two)
- ☐ Gortex gaiters (to keep the scree/ rocks out of your boots at higher altitudes)
- ☐ tennis shoes or ultralight hiking boots (for lower altitudes)
- ☐ medium-weight insulated hiking boots for warmth and to help dig into the scree during the final ascent
- ☐ heavy wool or down mittens with Gortex outer shell and glove liners
- ☐ several pairs of wool socks and polypropylene liner socks
- ☐ several pairs of underwear
- ☐ track or warm-up suit (to relax and sleep in)
- ☐ long trousers or knickers (wool or synthetic) 3 pairs
- ☐ light, loose-fitting cotton trousers
- ☐ shorts (with pockets) one pair only
- ☐ wool long sleeve and cotton long sleeve shirts
- ☐ T-shirts or short sleeve shirts
- ☐ turtleneck shirt
- ☐ down vest
- ☐ balaclava (wool or synthetic)
- ☐ wide-brimmed hat or cap for protection from the sun
- ☐ bandana which serves as a dust mask (2 are highly recommend)
- ☐ wool hat
- ☐ sleeping pad (for all routes except the Marangu Route) — can be rented

MISCELLANEOUS

- [ ] day pack large enough to carry extra clothing, rain gear, two plastic water bottles (1 liter/quart each), camera and lunch
- [ ] Hydration system such as Camelbak or Platypus system (be sure you get the insulated version)
- [ ] sleeping bag (rated at least 0° F [–18° C])
- [ ] pocket flask for summit climb
- [ ] flashlight and a head lamp
- [ ] extra batteries for all electronic equipment
- [ ] light towel
- [ ] sunglasses and mountaineering glasses
- [ ] camera and extra memory card
- [ ] strong sunblock
- [ ] protective lip balm, such as Chapstick brand
- [ ] body lotion (otherwise skin may get dry and itchy) and hand soap
- [ ] water purifiers (tablets and/or UV water purifier)
- [ ] duffle bag
- [ ] half-dozen heavy garbage bags in which to wrap clothes
- [ ] toilet paper
- [ ] moist towelettes
- [ ] Multi-tool with pocket knife and scissors
- [ ] granola bars, trail mix and sweets that travel well
- [ ] powered drink mix
- [ ] envelopes for tipping: Lead guide, assistant guides, cook and porters
- [ ] earplugs for sleeping
- [ ] small thermometer
- [ ] Handheld GPS (not essential)
- [ ] Mobile phone and spare batteries — there is reception on the mountain. Check with phone carrier prior to use about overseas charges. Can use local SIM card if your phone is set up that way

BASIC FIRST AID KIT

- [ ] malaria pills
- [ ] moleskin and second skin
- [ ] plastic bandage strips, such as Band-Aid brand
- [ ] elastic bandages
- [ ] gauze pads (4" × 4")
- [ ] diuretics (diamox) — by prescription from your doctor
- [ ] broad-spectrum antibiotics (pills) — as above
- [ ] laxative
- [ ] Finger pulse oxymeter (not essential)
- [ ] toothbrush & toothpaste
- [ ] antihistamine tablets
- [ ] antibiotic cream
- [ ] antidiarrheal preparation — i.e. Imodium or Lomotil
- [ ] iodine
- [ ] aspirin or acetaminophen for headache/muscle pain (Ibuprofen)
- [ ] throat and cough lozenges
- [ ] decongestant (can be found in combination with antihistamine tablets)

Please note that it requires more time to boil water at higher altitudes to successfully kill the parasites that cause illness.

Climbing Tips

There are a number of ways to increase your chances of making it to the top. One of the most important things to remember is to take your time. *Pole pole* is Swahili for "slowly, slowly" which is definitely the way to go. There is no prize for being the first to the camp or hut, or first to the top.

Pace yourself so that you are never completely out of breath. Exaggerate your breathing, taking deeper and more frequent breaths than you feel you actually need. This will help you acclimatize and help keep you from exhausting yourself prematurely, and it will help lower the chances of developing pulmonary or cerebral edema.

Ski poles make good walking sticks; they can be rented from your tour operator or at Park Headquarters and are highly recommended. Bring a small backpack to carry the items to which you wish to have quick access along the trail, such as a water bottle, snacks and a camera. Most importantly, listen to what your body is telling you. Don't overdo it! A few people die each year on the mountain because they don't listen or pay attention to the signs and keep pushing themselves. Stop and enjoy the view from time to time and watch your footing while you climb.

On steep portions of the hike, use the "lock step" method to conserve energy. Take a step and lock the knee of your uphill leg. This puts your weight on the leg bone, using less muscle strength. Pause for a few seconds, letting your other leg rest without any weight on it, and breathe deeply. Then repeat. This technique will save vital energy that you may very well need in your quest for the top.

Some climbers take the prescription drug Diamox, a diuretic which usually reduces the symptoms of altitude sickness; but, there are side effects from taking the drug, including increased urination. You should discuss the use of Diamox with your doctor prior to leaving home.

Drink a lot more water than you feel you need. High-altitude hiking is very dehydrating, and a dehydrated body weakens quickly. Climbers should obtain 4 to 6 quarts (4 to 6 liters) of fluid daily from their food and drinks. Consume foods such as soups, oatmeal porridge, and fresh fruits to supplement water and other liquids. Climbers should drink until the color of their urine is clear. Most importantly, always convey the truth about how you are feeling to your guides so they can accurately assess your condition.

Most hikers find it difficult to sleep at high altitude. Once you reach the hut each afternoon, rest a bit, then hike to a spot a few hundred feet in altitude above the hut and relax for a while. Acclimatizing even for a short time at a higher altitude will help you get a more restful night's sleep. Remember, "Climb high, sleep low!"

Consume at least 4,000 calories per day on the climb. This can be a problem. Most climbers lose their appetite at high altitude. Bring along trail mix (mixed nuts and dried fruit), chocolate, and other goodies that you enjoy, to supplement the meals prepared for you.

Forget about drinking alcoholic beverages on the climb. Altitude greatly enhances the affects of alcohol. Plus, alcohol causes dehydration. A headache caused by altitude sickness can be bad enough without having a hangover on top of it.

As the entire descent is made in two days, your knees take a hard pounding; you may want to wrap your knees with elastic bandages or use elastic knee supports.

Most travelers who climb Kilimanjaro do so in conjunction with a safari. I am often asked if it is better to do the climb first or the safari first. There is no definitive answer, however, there are a few things to take into consideration: elevation and jet lag.

Some travelers tell me they want to "get the climb over with" and then go on safari. If you live at high altitude (i.e. over 5,000 feet/1500m), then you will already be acclimated to close to the base altitude of the mountain, and climbing first might not be a big problem for you. I do strongly recommend at least two nights in Africa before you start the climb, to allow some time to rehydrate from the long flight and to adjust to the time difference.

If you live at low altitudes, I suggest you take your safari first, as most of the reserves you will visit range from 3,000–7,500 feet (900–2,300 m) above sea level — allowing you time to become acclimated to close to the base altitude of the mountain. This also gives you more time to rehydrate and to recover from jet lag. In any case, I prefer going on safari first as I feel it helps maximize your chances of reaching the summit and the enjoyment of the climb as well.

Park Headquarters is located in Marangu, 29 miles (47 km) from Moshi, 63 miles (101 km) from Kilimanjaro Airport and 75 miles (120 km) from Arusha.

Equipment is available for rent from your tour operator (best choice), Park Headquarters and Kibo and Marangu Hotels; but it may not be of top quality. If possible, I recommend that you bring as much of your own gear as possible, except for collapsible walking poles and pads, and a heavy duty jacket or sleeping bag if you do not have one. However, if you are over 6 ft. 2 in. in height (188 cm) then bring your own sleeping bag, as extra length bags are usually not available for rent.

ACCOMMODATION MARANGU — FIRST CLASS: • **Kilimanjaro Mountain Resort**, situated 1.75 miles (3 km) from the center of Marangu, has 42 rooms with mini-bar, flat screen TV, swimming pool and gardens to relax in before and after the climb.

TOURIST CLASS: • **Springlands Hotel**, located near Moshi Town, is an ideal base for Kili climbs and features comfortable rooms with simple furnishings. • **Marangu Hotel**, located 1.5 miles (2.4 km) from Marangu village, is a rustic lodge with 29 double rooms.

THE WEST

The Western Circuit includes Mahale National Park, Gombe Stream National Park and Katavi National Park, and is the most remote and least visited of the "Circuits" covered in this book. For those wishing to get off the beaten path — read on!

Mahale Mountains National Park

The main attraction of this remote park, which was only gazetted in 1985, is to be able to walk among large populations of chimpanzees. The chimps have been studied by Japanese researchers for more than 35 years, and now many chimps have been habituated to humans.

Located about 95 miles (150 km) south of Kigoma, this 609-square-mile (1,577-km^2) park is situated on the eastern shores of Lake Tanganyika. The Mahale Mountains, featuring deep ravines, permanent streams and waterfalls, run through the center of the park, forming the eastern wall of the Great Rift Valley — with altitudes up to 8,075 feet (2,462 m) above sea level. The western side of the mountains, where the chimp trekking occurs, is primarily composed of semitropical rain forest with *brachystygia* (semi-deciduous) woodland on the ridges and montane forest at higher altitudes.

Trekking in the park occurs in the range of the M Group, which as of this writing consists of in excess of 60 individuals that have been habituated to human presence. Once found, trekkers can watch them naturally go about their normal daily activities from up to 10 yards (9 meters) away. When close to the chimps, trekkers are asked to wear masks, to avoid any transmission of diseases.

In addition to over 1,000 chimpanzees, the park is also home to 8 other species of primates, including red colobus monkey and Angolan black-and-white

Over 1,000 chimpanzees live in Mahale Mountains National Park

colobus monkey. Other wildlife includes bushbuck, otters, banded mongoose, Sharpe's grysbok and blue duiker.

Seasons are fairly predictable. The main dry season usually runs from mid-May to mid-October, with mid-December to mid-February also being quite dry. Rainy seasons are usually mid-October to mid-December and mid-February to mid-May. Nights are often cool and rainfall ranges from 60 to 100 inches (1,500 to 2,500 mm) per year. The best time to visit is during the two dry seasons mentioned above.

There are scheduled charter flights operating a few times a week from Arusha to Mahale, which will also pick up passengers at Lake Manyara, the Grumeti Reserves and the Serengeti. Otherwise, a private charter is required.

ACCOMMODATION — CLASS A: • **Greystoke Mahale** is located on the eastern shores of the lake and features 6 open-fronted bandas. Hikes to see chimpanzees, sailing by dhow, dugout canoeing, snorkeling and fishing are offered. The camp is open early June to the end of March.

CLASS B: • **Kungwe Beach Lodge** is set on the shores of Lake Tanganyika and has 10 comfortable tents. Chimpanzee tracking, fishing, bird watching, forest walks, kayaking, boat rides on Lake Tanganyika and snorkeling are offered.

Greystoke Mahale is reached by boat *(top)*, A thatched banda at Greystoke Mahale *(bottom)*

Gombe Stream National Park

Gombe Stream is the setting for Jane Goodall's chimpanzee studies and her films and books, including *In the Shadow of Man* (Houghton Mifflin). The remote 20-square-mile (52-km²) park is situated along the eastern shores of Lake Tanganyika 10 miles (16 km) north of Kigoma in remote northwestern Tanzania.

This tiny park covers a thin strip of land 3 miles (5 km) wide and stretches for 10 miles (16 km) along Lake Tanganyika. A mountain range ascends steeply from the lake at an altitude of 2,235 feet (681 m) to form part of the eastern wall of the western branch of the Great Rift Valley, rising to 5,000 feet (4,524 m).

Thick gallery forests are found along Gombe Stream and many other permanent streams in the valley and lower slopes of the mountains. Higher up the slopes are woodlands with some grasslands near the upper ridges.

The experience of seeing chimpanzees in the wild is by far the major attraction of this park. Other primates include red colobus monkey, blue monkey and baboon. Other wildlife of note includes buffalo, Defassa waterbuck and leopard.

Chimpanzees can usually be found around the research station and are quite habituated to humans. Two-hour morning and afternoon hikes into the forest searching for chimps can be arranged. The Kakombe Waterfall is worth a visit. There is also a nice walk along the lake shore northward from the guest house.

You can reach the park by water taxi (about 3 hours) from Ujiji or Kigoma.

ACCOMMODATION — CLASS B: • **Gombe Forest Lodge** is the only tented camp in the park and has 7 comfortable tents. Transfers from Kigoma to Gombe are by way of boat and take you past fishing villages and scenic hills.

Katavi National Park

Katavi offers incredible game viewing and remains virtually unvisited by travelers due to its remoteness. This undeveloped 1,545-square-mile (4,000-km^2) park is located between the towns of Mpanda and Sumbawanga on the main road running through western Tanzania from north to south.

Lake Katavi and its extensive floodplains are in the north of this park, which is about 2,950 feet (900 m) above sea level. To the southeast is Lake Chada, which is

An aerial view of Katavi National Park

Game viewing in Katavi *(top)*, A comfortable tent at Chada Katavi *(bottom)*

connected with Lake Katavi by the Katuma River and its extensive swampland. Miombo woodlands dominate most of the dry areas, except for acacia woodlands near Lake Chada.

Wildlife includes hippo, crocs, elephant, zebra, lion, leopard, eland, puku, roan antelope and sable antelope. Herds of several thousand buffalo are sometimes seen. Over 400 species of birds have been recorded.

The long rains are March to May. The best time to visit is July to October. Scheduled charter flights to the park are available at least twice a week from Arusha, and guests often can be picked up from other airstrips on the "Northern Circuit."

ACCOMMODATIONS — CLASS A/B: • **Chada Katavi** is located in the heart of Katavi National Park with views over the wide Chada Plain. Accommodations include 6 spacious safari tents with safari showers (hot water) and eco-flush toilets. Activities include game drives, walks and optional fly-camping. • **Katavi Wildlife Camp** offers 8 spacious tents with solar heated showers and eco-flush toilets. The tents are set on wooden platforms with verandahs overlooking the Katisunga plain. Activities include game drives, walks, and fly-camping.

CLASS B: • **Katuma Bush Lodge** has 10 tents and offers game drives in open sided vehicles and walking safaris.

Kigoma

Kigoma is the country's major port on huge Lake Tanganyika. From there you can catch a steamer to Burundi or Zambia. Kigoma is the closest town to Gombe Stream National Park and many travelers stay there while in transit to and from the park. Kigoma can be reached by air, by road or by a 2.5-day train ride (the train schedules are not dependable) from Dar es Salaam.

Ujiji, a small town 6 miles (10 km) south of Kigoma, is where the line, "Dr. Livingstone, I presume?" was spoken by Stanley in 1872. Buses run there regularly from the Kigoma Rail Station.

ACCOMMODATION — FIRST CLASS: • **Kigoma Hilltop Hotel**, located just outside Kigoma on the edge of Lake Victoria, has 30 air-conditioned cottages.

Lake Tanganyika

Lake Tanganyika forms much of the western border of Tanzania and is indeed an "inland sea." Located at the southern end of the Western Rift Valley, the lake is divided among four countries—Burundi, Democratic Republic of Congo (DRC), Zambia and Tanzania.

This is the world's longest lake (446 mi./714 km) and the world's second deepest lake (over 4,700 ft./1,433 m). Only Lake Baikal in Russia is deeper, at over 5,700 feet (1,738 m). The water flows into the Congo River system and ultimately into the Atlantic Ocean. During the slave trading period, Lake Tanganyika was a major transshipment route for slavers. More than 400 species of fish inhabit the lake's clear waters.

ACCOMMODATION — CLASS A: • **Lupita Island Lodge** is an all-inclusive luxurious resort set on a 110-acre (44-hectare) island with 12 standard suites and 2 executive suites, each with private plunge pools and lake views. There is a swimming pool, spa and gym. Activities include lake cruises, snorkeling, biking, hiking, bird watching, fishing and sun-downer cruises. Access is by private charter flight.

THE SOUTH

The "Southern Circuit" of wildlife reserves includes Ruaha National Park, Mikumi National Park and the Selous Game Reserve. The Selous and Ruaha are less visited than the northern Tanzania parks and offer a great opportunity to explore wild and unspoiled bush. Mikumi is seldomly visited by international travelers. Daily scheduled charter flights link the Selous and Ruaha with Dar es Salaam and Zanzibar.

Ruaha National Park

Ruaha is now the largest national park in Tanzania. Known for its great populations of elephant, buffalo, greater and lesser kudu, hippo, crocs, it is also one of the country's best national parks, and because of its location, it is one of the least visited.

Ruaha's scenery is spectacular. The landscape is characterized by miombo woodland with rocky hills on a plateau over 3,300 feet (1,000 m) in altitude. Park elevation ranges from 2,460 feet (750 m) in the Ruaha Valley to the 6,230 foot (1,900 m) Ikingu Mountain in the west of the park.

Once referred to by the early explorers as the Garden of Eden, Ruaha was originally part of the Saba Game Reserve formed in 1910 before becoming part of the Rungwe Game Reserve that was established in 1946. The Ruaha National

Ruaha

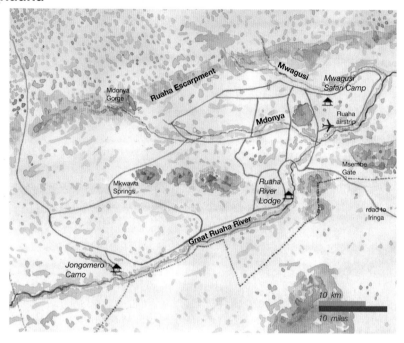

Park was gazetted as a park in 1964 when all hunting was prohibited. In 2008 it was extended from 5,000-square-miles (12,950-km²) in area to 8,500 square-miles (22,000-km²) by incorporating the former Usangu Wildlife Management Area.

One of the most important aspects of this is the overlapping of East African and southern African species of plants, trees, birds and mammals.

The Great Ruaha River, with its impressive gorges, deep pools and rapids, runs for 100 miles (160 km), close to the park's southern boundary, and it is home to many hippo and crocodiles. Black riverbed rocks are contrasted against golden grasses and baobab trees that line the riverbank, creating a unique and beautiful sight.

The dry season, June to October, is the best time to visit the park, when game is concentrated along the Ruaha River. Large numbers of greater and lesser kudu, elephant and impala can be seen, along with eland, sable antelope, roan antelope, buffalo, Defassa waterbuck, ostrich and giraffe. Lion, leopard, spotted and striped hyena, black-backed jackal, bat-eared fox and African wild dog are also present in significant numbers. Black rhino are present but seldom seen. Over 573 species of birds have been recorded.

In addition to morning and afternoon excursions, midday game viewing in this park can also be very productive because wildlife can be seen walking to and from the river.

Elephant frequent the Ruaha River

This is also one of the best parks in East Africa for escorted wildlife walks. The scenery and wildlife, especially along the Ruaha River, is exceptional in the dry season.

During the wet months of December to March, wildlife is scattered, but viewing is still good. Game viewing from February to June is difficult due to high grass.

The park is about a 2.5-hour charter flight from Dar es Salaam, or a 2-hour drive from Iringa. Park Headquarters is located at Msembe, 70-miles (112-km) from Iringa and 385 miles (615 km) from Dar es Salaam.

ACCOMMODATION — CLASS A:
• **Jongomero Camp**, located on the banks of the Jongomero Sand River in the southwestern section of Ruaha, has 8 classic luxury tents with double vanity and solar-heated showers. The camp offers game drives in open vehicles, escorted walks with armed professional guides, bush breakfasts and bush dinners. As the camp is in a remote part of the park, other travelers are seldom if ever seen.
• **Mwagusi Safari Camp**, located on the seasonal Mwagusi River, has 10 large

Jongomero Camp

tents with hot-cold running water showers and comfortable lounge areas under thatch. Game drives in open vehicles and walks are offered. Elephant may often be seen digging for water in the dry riverbed right in front of camp.

CLASS B: • **Ruaha River Lodge** is located on the banks of the Ruaha River and offers stunning views. The spacious 29 stone-and-thatch bandas are located in prime positions on the river bank, each with a private patio. There are two dining areas, one on the river's edge and another on a hill overlooking the river. Game drives are offered.

Mikumi National Park

Mikumi is the closest park to Dar es Salaam (180 miles/288 km), and it takes about 4 hours to drive on tarmac from Dar es Salaam via Morogoro. The park covers 1,247-square-miles (3,230-km^2) and borders the Selous Game Reserve to the south along the Tazara Railroad line, which runs down to Zambia and divides the park.

The park is dominated by the Mkata River flood plain, with swamps and grasslands dotted with baobab trees and miombo woodlands at an average altitude of 1,800 feet (550 m) above sea level. Elephant, buffalo, lion, hippo, zebra, wildebeest and Maasai giraffe are prevalent. Sable antelope, common waterbuck, Lichtenstein's hartebeest, eland, Bohor reedbuck and impala may also be seen. Black-and-white colobus monkey are frequently seen in the south of the park.

The long rains are from March to May and the short rains from November to December. Rainfall within the park ranges from 20 to 40 inches (510 to 1,070 mm) yearly.

It is difficult to say when the best time is to visit Mikumi. Unlike most parks, wildlife concentrates in this park during the wet season, when the vegetation is the thickest, making game viewing more difficult. Fewer animals are present in the dry season, but the ones present are easier to spot. Lion and elephant are two mammals that are more likely to be seen in the dry season. Considering this, the best time to visit is June through February.

This park is open all year, although some roads are closed during the rainy season. There is an airstrip at Park Headquarters.

ACCOMMODATION — CLASS A/B: • **Vuma Hill Tented Camp** has luxury tents under thatch and set on platforms and a swimming pool. Day trips to the Udzungwa Mountains are available. • **Stanley Kopjes Camp** *(formerly Foxes Safari Camp)* offers 8 custom-designed tents raised on wooden platforms and located around the rock kopje overlooking the Mkata flood plain and Mwangambogo waterhole. Day trips to the Udzungwa Mountains are available.

Selous Game Reserve

This little-known reserve happens to be the second largest game reserve in Africa, and it is a World Heritage Site. Over 21,000-square-miles (55,000-km^2) in area, the Selous is more than half the size of the state of Ohio, twice the area of Denmark and 3.75 times larger than Serengeti National Park. Unexploited and

Selous Game Reserve

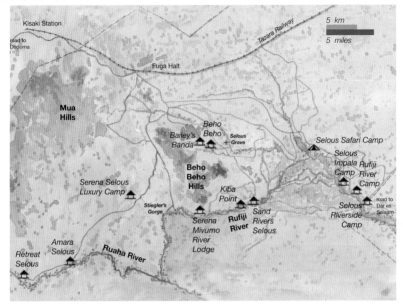

largely unexplored, no human habitation is allowed in this virgin bush, except at limited tourist facilities.

The Selous is a stronghold for over 50,000 elephant, 150,000 buffalo (herds often exceed 1,000), and large populations of lion, leopard, Lichtenstein's hartebeest, greater kudu, hippo, crocodiles, and numerous other species, including giraffe, zebra, wildebeest, waterbuck, African wild dog, impala and a small number of black rhino. Colobus monkey can be found in the forests along the Rufiji River. Over one million large animals live within its borders. Over 350 species of birds and 2,000 plant species have been recorded.

Almost 75% of this low-lying reserve (360 to 4,100 ft./110 to 1,250 m) is composed of miombo woodlands, with a balance of grasslands, floodplains, marshes and dense forests.

Morning walks accompanied by an armed ranger and guide are popular and are conducted by some of the camps. Fly-camping for a few nights is also available from select camps.

This reserve can give you the feeling of exploring the bush for the first time, because you will encounter relatively few other visitors during your safari.

The Rufiji River, the largest river in East Africa, roughly bisects the park as it flows from the southwest to the northeast. The Rufiji and its tributaries, including Great Ruaha and Luwego, have high concentrations of hippo and crocs. Fish eagles are numerous.

The remote Selous is the 2nd largest game reserve in Africa

Exploring the Rufiji River and its channels and lakes by boat is another great way to view game and experience the reserve. You should consider adding the Selous onto a northern Tanzania itinerary, because game viewing by boat is not possible in the Serengeti, Ngorongoro, Lake Manyara or Tarangire. Fishing is also popular.

On a recent walk we encountered 3 female elephant as we tried crossing a dry river bed. We backtracked to another crossing point but as we went down the path we met these same elephants walking up it. Our guide had us quickly move back down the path we had come.

All photographic safari activities are restricted to the northern 20% of the reserve. The best time to visit the reserve is during the dry season, June to November. Game viewing from December to February is good, although it is quite hot during that period. During the rainy season, many of the roads are impassable and wildlife is scattered. The reserve is usually closed from mid- to end of March to the end of May.

Camps feature boat rides on the Rufiji River

Most visitors fly to the Selous by scheduled or private air charter from Dar es Salaam, while others take advantage of scheduled and charter flights from Arusha, Zanzibar or other parks. Access by road is difficult and only possible in the dry season. A novel way to experience the vastness of the Selous is to arrive from Dar via the Selous Safari Train (check operational schedule). The train journey takes about 5 hours and allows travelers to enjoy the scenery enroute.

ACCOMMODATION — The camps are located about 160 to 235 miles (260 to 380 km) from Dar es Salaam, requiring a 4.5 to 9 hour drive in a 4wd vehicle. All camps have private airstrips and flying is highly recommended.

CLASS A: • **Beho Beho** has been completely refurbished and the 10 luxury stone cottages have a light, breezy feel and offer panoramic views over the Rufiji River flood plain. Game drives, boating on Lake Tagalala and superb walking are offered. There is a swimming pool to enjoy between game drives. • **Bailey's Banda**, a new private villa, features 2 bedrooms, private pool and deck. Guests enjoy exclusive vehicle, guide and staff. • **Selous Safari Camp**, a luxury tented camp set on the shores of Lake Nzerakera, is comprised of 2 intimate camps (one with 7 tents, the other with 6) each with its own bar, dining room and swimming pool. The camp also has a "dungo," a large elevated platform overlooking Lake Nzerakera for relaxing and watching game and bird life during the midday. Game drives, escorted walks, boat safaris, fishing, fly camping and multiday walking safaris are offered. • **Sand Rivers Selous** is situated on the banks of the Rufiji River and has 8 open-fronted chalets (5 standard rooms, 2 suites and 1 Honeymoon cottage) looking out over

Walking safaris are offered in the Selous *(top)*, Beho Beho *(bottom)*

the river. The 2 suites have plunge pools and a lounge area and the Honeymoon Cottage (known as The Rhino House) has its own plunge pool, lounge/dining area and private guide and vehicle. Game drives, walks, boat safaris, fishing, multi-day walking safaris

Selous Safari Camp *(top)*, Rufiji River Camp *(bottom)*

with fly-camping are offered. • **Kiba Point**, downstream from Sand Rivers Selous, is a private camp featuring 4 large open-fronted rooms and a private plunge pool. This 8-bedded camp is booked on a totally exclusive basis only and includes game drives, walks, fly-camping, boating and fishing. • **Amara Selous** is located on the Great Ruaha River and features 12 deluxe air-conditioned tents with large wooden decks and private plunge pools. Activities include open-vehicle game drives, walking safaris and boating on the river (water levels permitting). • **Serena Mivumo River Lodge** is built on the Rufiji River and has 12 thatched air-conditioned rooms and one suite. Game viewing by open vehicles and by motorboat, and spa treatments are offered.

CLASS A/B: • **Rufiji River Camp**, a comfortable tented camp with 20 tents, offers game drives, fishing, and boat safaris. • **Selous Riverside Camp**, overlooking the Rufiji River, consists of 10 large tented chalets overlooking the Rufiji River. • **Serena Selous Luxury Camp**, located away from the river, has 12 well-appointed tents and offers game drives and game viewing by boat. • **Retreat Selous**, located in the extreme western part of the reserve, has a selection of hillside, riverside and private riverside tents. Open vehicle game drives and boat excursions are carried out on the Ruaha River (water levels permitting).

CLASS B: • **Selous Impala Camp** is located on the banks of the Rufiji River. There are 6 tents with views of the river with private verandahs and swimming pool. The camp offers game drives, walking safaris and boat rides on the Rufiji River.

THE COAST

Dar Es Salaam

Dar es Salaam, which means "haven of peace" in Arabic, is the functional capital, largest city and commercial center of Tanzania. Many safaris to the southern parks begin here. Among the more interesting sights are the harbor, **National Museum**, **Village Museum** and the **Kariakoo Market**. Ask at your hotel about traditional dancing troops that may be performing during your stay.

Once the German capital, hub of the slave trade and end point of the slave route from the interior, **Bagamoyo** is an old seaport 46 miles (75 km) north of Dar es Salaam. Fourteenth century ruins, stone pens and shackles that held the slaves can be seen.

ACCOMMODATION — FIRST CLASS:
• **The Oyster Bay** is 4 miles (6 km) from town, located directly on the coast and has been recently renovated. The 8 suites have ocean views, air-conditioning and private balconies. • **The Hyatt Regency Dar es Salaam Kilimanjaro Hotel** is a 180 room air-conditioned hotel with a swimming pool, several restaurants and lounges and a fabulous view of the harbor. • **Dar es Salaam Serena Hotel** has 250 air-conditioned rooms with 2 restaurants, a bar, swimming pool and health club. • **Holiday Inn**, located in the city center, has 154 rooms, 2 restaurants and cocktail lounge • **Hotel Sea Cliff** features 114 rooms with ocean views, 2 restaurants, 2 lounges and a swimming pool.

TOURIST CLASS: • **The New Africa Hotel**, situated in the heart of Dar es Salaam's shopping and banking district, has 126 air-conditioned rooms and 7 suites, 2 restaurants, 2 bars, a casino and business center.

ACCOMMODATION NEAR DAR ES SALAAM — LUXURY: • **Amani Beach Club**, situated on the coast south of Dar es Salaam, has 12 luxury air-conditioned cottages, each with garden terrace and hammock overlooking the Indian Ocean, and swimming pool.

The Oyster Bay's pool area *(top)*, Ras Kutani Beach Resort *(bottom)*

FIRST CLASS: • **Ras Kutani Beach Resort**, located on a beautiful, remote beach 17 miles (28 km) south of Dar es Salaam, has 9 spacious cottages and 4 suites. Wind surfing, sailing, snorkeling, deep sea fishing and horseback riding are offered. Humpback whales can sometimes be seen from shore. Access is by a 10-minute charter flight or 1 hour road transfer from Dar es Salaam.

Lazy Lagoon Island

Lazy Lagoon Island is a private island retreat 44 miles (70 km) north of Dar es Salaam in the Zanzibar channel. It is approximately 4 miles (6 km) off shore from the historic slave town of Bagamoyo. The island is protected by coral and the delicate ecosystem still attracts suni antelope, duiker, and Galago bushbabies.

ACCOMMODATION — TOURIST CLASS: • **Lazy Lagoon Island Lodge** is the only lodge on the island and offers 12 individual beach cottages, each opening out on the white sand beach. Activities include sailing, windsurfing, kayaking and snorkeling as well as a guided tour around the Kaole ruins and Bagamoyo Slave Town.

Zanzibar

Zanzibar (known to the locals as Unguja) and its sister island, Pemba, grow 75% of the world's cloves. A beautiful island, Zanzibar is only 22 miles (35 km) from the mainland — a 20-minute, scheduled or charter flight from Dar es Salaam or a 90-minute hydrofoil ride. There are also several scheduled flights from Arusha taking about 60 minutes.

The narrow streets and Arabic architecture of historical Zanzibar City are exceptionally mystical and beautiful on a moonlit night. Main attractions include the **Zanzibar Museum**, former British Consulate, **Arab Old Fort**, the **Anglican Cathedral** built on the site of the former slave market, **Sultan's Palace**, town market and Indian bazaar. Livingstone's and Burton's houses are near the picturesque old Dhow Harbour, where traditional dhows are repaired and built. Antique shops stocked with Arab clocks, kettles, brass trays, Zanzibar beds, carved doors and frames have special atmospheres all their own.

The **Spice Tour** travels north of Stone Town and includes a visit to one or more spice gardens and farms. Various spices and plants, including cinnamon, cloves, nutmeg, vanilla, ginger and black pepper, along with fruits such as tamarind, guava, rose-apple and several types of mango and bananas, may be seen, touched, smelled and purchased. The **Dolphin Experience** offered from the southern end of the island is also worth considering.

Good restaurants include Mecury's, the Zanzibar Serena Inn, and The Archipelago located next to the Tembo Hotel in Stone Town. Just outside of town, Mtoni Marine also has a good restaurant. At 236 Hurumzi (formerly *Emerson &*

Zanzibar's colorful market

Zanzibar

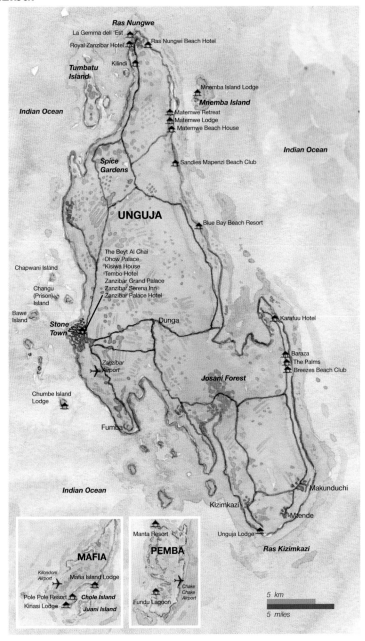

Ras Nungwe
La Gemma dell 'Est
Royal Zanzibar Hotel
Ras Nungwi Beach Hotel
Kilindi
Tumbatu Island

Mnemba Island Lodge
Mnemba Island
Matemwe Retreat
Matemwe Lodge
Matemwe Beach House

Indian Ocean

Sandies Mapenzi Beach Club

Indian Ocean

Spice Gardens

UNGUJA

Blue Bay Beach Resort

The Beyt Al Chai
Dhow Palace
Kisiwa House
Tembo Hotel
Zanzibar Grand Palace
Zanzibar Serena Inn
Zanzibar Palace Hotel

Chapwani Island

Changu (Prison) Island

Bawe Island

Stone Town

Dunga

Karafuu Hotel

Baraza
The Palms
Breezes Beach Club

Zanzibar Airport

Chumbe Island Lodge

Josani Forest

Fumba

Indian Ocean

Makunduchi

Kizimkazi

Mtende

Unguja Lodge

Ras Kizimkazi

Manta Resort

MAFIA

Kilondoni Airport
Mafia Island Lodge

Pole Pole Resort **Chole Island**
Kinasi Lodge   **Juani Island**

PEMBA

Chake Chake Airport

Fundu Lagoon

5 km

5 miles

A dhow sails along the coast *(top)*,
Luxurious Baraza *(middle)*, Matemwe
Retreat *(bottom)*

Green) the Tower Top Restaurant serves a limited seating for dinner each night and is quite popular.

The more pristine coral reefs off Zanzibar offer a superb diving or snorkeling experience. In addition to a mind-boggling diversity of brightly colored reef fish, dolphins, green turtles and the largest of all fishes— the harmless whale shark— are fairly numerous in the waters around Zanzibar.

For a taste of what Zanzibar was like prior to the arrival of the traders, sultans and farmers, a visit to **Jozani Forest** is highly recommended. This small patch of remaining forest — mostly palm, pandanus and mahogany trees— is home to the unique Zanzibar red colobus, one of Africa's rarest and most endangered primates. Among birds, the equally rare Fischer's turaco may also be seen at Jozani, along with paradise flycatcher, banded wattle-eye and numerous other species.

The roads in Zanzibar are good and it is approximately a 1 to 1.5 hour drive to reach your beach resort from the Zanzibar Airport.

ACCOMMODATION IN ZANZIBAR STONE TOWN — FIRST CLASS: • **The Beyt Al Chai** — Stone House Inn, located on the famous Kelele Square, has 5 air-conditioned suites. • **Zanzibar Serena Inn**, located on the waterfront in Stone Town, has 51 rooms (most with private balconies), seafront restaurant, bar and swimming pool. Guests have access to a beautiful private beach at the Mangapwani Caves.

TOURIST CLASS: • **Zanzibar Palace Hotel** has 9 rooms (2 of which are suites). The hotel is located in the heart of Stone Town. • **Kisiwa House** is a luxurious hotel in Stone Town. Located on a quiet street in the heart of the historical town, the hotel provides modern amenities in an intimate atmosphere. Burdani (deluxe) rooms, Junior and Senior Suites are all decorated in sumptuous Swahili and include en suite bathrooms, flat screen televisions, air-conditioning, in-room safe, hairdryer, mini-bar and upscale toiletries. Enjoy dining at the Darini Restaurant which is a delightful fusion of traditional and continental specialties or the Courtyard Lounge which serves teas, coffee and freshly baked pastries. • **Zanzibar Grand Palace**, a new property built to replicate a historic building, offers 32 deluxe rooms and 2 suites. There is a rooftop restaurant and dock café. • **Dhow Palace**, located in the heart of Stone Town about 300 yards (300m) from the waterfront and has 30 tastefully decorated fan-cooled rooms and rooftop restaurant (no alcoholic beverages served), with panoramic views of Stone Town. • **Tembo Hotel** has 40 air-conditioned rooms, restaurant (no alcoholic beverages served), and a swimming pool. From its waterfront location, ships are constantly seen, passing enroute to and from the harbor.

ACCOMMODATION ON THE BEACH — DELUXE: • **Baraza** is a "6-star" property located on a fabulous beach with 33 very spacious 1- and 2-bedroom villas with private plunge pools, several restaurants, swimming pool, and one of the top spas in East Africa. • **Matemwe Retreat** is a private section to Matemwe (see below in First Class) which features 4 exclusive 2-story suites with air-conditioned bedrooms on the first floor and a private sun terrace with plunge pool on the second. I love the 15 minute or so drive on the sand road along the coast through a fishing village to get to the property. This really sets the scene for the remote beach holiday! • **Kilindi** is located on a pristine section of beach and has 15 luxury pavilions – each with private plunge pools (some units with 2 pools). The eco-resort uses solar power and state-of-the-art water treatment and recycling. Guests enjoy regional cuisine, an infinity pool, superb spa and lush tropical gardens. Extensive water sports and excursions are available. This is a great property for honeymooners and others wishing for privacy. • **The Palms** is situated along a pristine white beach on the east coast of the island and consists of 6 villas featuring a bedroom, living room, Jacuzzi and private terrace overlooking the Indian Ocean. There is a swimming pool, dining room, evening bar and pool bar and massage facilities.

FIRST CLASS: • **Matemwe Lodge**, perched on the cliffs overlooking the northeast coast, has 12 bungalows with private verandahs with hammocks to enjoy the sea views. There are 2 swimming pools, restaurant, dive center and a variety of optional

The crystal blue water off Matemwe *(top)*,
A luxury pavilion at Kilindi *(bottom)*

excursions that can be booked. • **Matemwe Beach House**, a private 3-bedroom villa set right on the beach, has a swimming pool and is rented on an exclusive basis. Ideal for families, the house has a dedicated butler and chef. • **Blue Bay Beach Resort** is situated on a fine, white sand beach on the east coast of Zanzibar. This 25-acre (10 hectare) property has 112 air-conditioned rooms and suites in 2-story bungalows, 2 restaurants, 2 bars and a large swimming pool. Scuba diving and water sports are offered. • **Karafuu Hotel**, located on the east coast of Zanzibar about a 90-minute drive from the airport or Stone Town, has 89 air-conditioned rooms in bungalows, 5 restaurants, 2 bars, sports and entertainment facilities, spa and swimming pool. • **Breezes Beach Club**, located on the east coast near the village of Bwejuu, has 70 bedrooms in 2-story bungalows set on an unspoiled beach, 2 restaurants, 2 bars, conference facility, fitness center, flood-lit tennis court, disco and scuba diving center. • **Ras Nungwi Beach Hotel**, located about 36 miles (60 km) north of Zanzibar airport on the northern tip of the island, has 32 rooms, 2 restaurants, bar, swimming pool, PADI dive center, deep-sea fishing, water skiing and windsurfing. • **La Gemma dell 'Est** is located on the Northwest coast of Zanzibar on a magnificent stretch of beach where you are able to swim during low and high tide. The resort has 138 rooms including 41 suites, and a massive swimming pool with a sunken bar, restaurant, full water sports centre, big game fishing facility, full PADI certified dive school, diving, snorkeling, waterskiing, windsurfing, kayaking, and dhow cruises. • **Royal Zanzibar Hotel** is located on the northern tip of the island with a great beach, with 100 rooms and suites.

TOURIST CLASS: • **Sandies Mapenzi Beach Club**, located on a beautiful beach on the east coast 28 miles (45 km) from the airport, has 87 spacious rooms (all with air-conditioning), 2 restaurants, 3 bars, tennis courts and a swimming pool. Activities include mountain biking, archery, snorkeling, beach volleyball, table tennis, wind surfing, canoeing and deep-sea fishing. • **Unguja Lodge**, located at the southern tip of Zanzibar, has 11 self-contained villas (8 with sea views, the others with lush gardens terraces). There is a restaurant, bar, pool, library and PADI certified dive center.

Chumbe Island Coral Park

Located 6 miles (10 km) by boat from Stone Town, this nature reserve offers forest and marine nature trails, over half a mile (1 km) of protected reef, great bird watching and snorkeling. Over 40 species of birds, including the endangered roseate tern have been recorded on the island, and 370 families of fish have been identified on the colorful reefs that drop off to about 50 feet (16 m).

ACCOMMODATION — TOURIST CLASS: • **Chumbe Island Lodge** offers 7 palm-thatched bungalows set in the forest and facing the ocean. Each bungalow has solar-powered lights and is equipped to catch, filter and solar-heat its own water for warm showers.

Mnemba Island

Mnemba is an exclusive island located 2 miles (3 km) northeast of the Zanzibar mainland. The island is only 1 mile (1.5 km) in circumference and is idyllic for anyone who wants to truly get away from it all.

Mnemba's reefs are among the best around Zanzibar, and, along with a bewildering variety of spectacular reef fish, encounters with green turtles and whale sharks are fairly common. Humpback whales pass through the straits between Mnemba and the mainland, and pods of common dolphins are seen almost daily. The huge coconut crab is an occasional visitor and the charming little ghost crabs are abundant on the pearly white beach. A variety of birds roost on Mnemba's secure sandbanks, including crab plovers, dimorphic egret, lesser crested tern and a host of Eurasian migratory waders.

ACCOMMODATION — DELUXE: • **Mnemba Island Lodge** is an exclusive island getaway with 10 thatched beachside cottages. Wind surfing, fly-fishing, kayaking, sundowner dhow cruises, snorkeling and scuba diving are available. The lodge is an hour by road, followed by 20 minutes by boat from Stone Town.

Pemba Island

Pemba is located 16 miles (25 km) north of Zanzibar Island near the Kenyan border and offers some of the best scuba diving and deep-sea fishing in all of sub-Saharan Africa. The Pemba Channel runs between Pemba and the mainland with depths up to 2,625 feet (800 m). Sheer underwater walls drop 150 to 600 feet (45 to 183 m) just off the coastline. Divers often see eagle ray, grouper, tuna and a variety of tropical fish.

Access to the island is by boat transfer to Pemba Harbor (Mkoani) or by a 20-minute scheduled or private charter flight.

ACCOMMODATION — FIRST CLASS: • **Fundu Lagoon**, set on 3 miles (4.5 km) of private beach, has 18 bungalows (some on the beach and some on the ridge), a restaurant, 2 bars and a PADI dive center. Activities include snorkeling, scuba diving, sailing, fishing, water skiing and kayaking.

TOURIST CLASS: • **Manta Resort** has 15 comfortable rustic cabins, completely open in the front and built on raised platforms. There is a dive shop and scuba diving and snorkeling excursions are offered.

Mafia Island

A 40-minute flight south from Dar es Salaam or Zanzibar, this island offers some of the best big-game fishing in the world. Species caught include marlin, sailfish, tuna and shark. The diving is also very good.

ACCOMMODATION — FIRST CLASS: • **Kinasi Lodge** has 14 private chalets and is set on a hillside overlooking Chole Bay. Scuba diving, snorkeling, sport fishing, sailing and wind surfing are offered. Other activities include excursions to historic sites, villages, forests, secluded beaches and bays. • **Pole Pole Resort** offers 7 luxury bungalows. Built into its natural surroundings with traditional makuti roofing, the resort offers a variety of different activities including scuba diving, snorkeling and fishing.

TOURIST CLASS: • **Mafia Island Lodge**, located on Chole Bay, has 40 rooms. Scuba diving, snorkeling, deep-sea fishing, water skiing, sailing and motor boating are offered.

Kenya

Kenya

From the warm tropical waters of the Indian Ocean, to the icy heights of Mount Kenya at 17,058 feet (5,199 m), this is truly "a world in one country." Desert and arid savannah prevails in the northern frontier and southeast, while remnant forests extend over the high country and wetter west. Covering 225,000-square-miles (582,750-km²), Kenya is about the same size as Texas or France. The population numbers some 33 million, with over 2.5 million in the capital city of Nairobi. KiSwahili and English are the official languages. Currency is the Kenyan shilling.

Kenya
Country Highlights

- See the Great Serengeti Migration and game view at Kenya's most popular reserve — the Maasai Mara.
- Sunrise balloon safari across the Maasai Mara.
- Checking off the "Big Five" game viewing.
- Sundowners in Amboseli or at ol Donyo Lodge or Campi ya Kanzi with Mt. Kilimanjaro in the background.
- Nature walks with Maasai or Samburu guides.
- Get up close and personal with a baby elephant at Daphne Sheldrick Elephant Orphanage in Nairobi.

When's the Best Time to Go for Game Viewing

Excellent · Good · Fair · Poor · Closed

Country	Park/Reserve	JAN	FEB	MAR	APR	MAY	JUN	JUL	AUG	SEP	OCT	NOV	DEC
Kenya	Amboseli/ol Donyo/Campi ya Kanzi												
	Tsavo												
	Maasai Mara							*	*	*	*		
	Aberderes/Meru												
	Samburu												
	Laikipia Reserves												

*Great Serengeti Migration

Best Safari Experience

Tortilis Camp and Tawi Lodge (Amboseli); ol Donyo Lodge (Chyulu Hills/Tsavo region); Mara Plains, Sala's Camp, Mara Explorer, Rekero, Little Governors, Serian (Maasai Mara); SaSaab (Samburu); Loisaba, Segera and Solio (Laikipia); and Elsa's Kopje (Meru)

KENYA

The word "safari" is Swahili for "journey," and Kenya is where it all began. Hemingway immortalized the safari experience, although he was a sport and trophy hunter rather than a naturalist or photographer.

Joy Adamson was among the group of expatriates, in the 1960s and 1970s, whose endeavors to conserve African wildlife captured the world's attention. The writings of Karen Blixen, and the adaptation of her classic book *Out of Africa* into a motion picture starring Robert Redford and Meryl Streep, helped establish Kenya as a great safari destination in the modern era. Michael Poliza's new oversized coffee table book *Kenya* (te Neues) is a fabulous photographic treatise of the variety this country has to offer.

Visitors to Kenya can enjoy fabulous game viewing, birdwatching, hot-air ballooning, horseback riding, scenic flights, mountaineering, scuba diving, freshwater and deep-sea fishing, and numerous other activities.

Kenya is well known for the magnificent Serengeti Migration (shared with Tanzania) of more than one million wildebeest and zebra in the Maasai Mara and for the colorful Maasai, Samburu and other tribes that contribute so much to making this an attractive safari destination.

Kenya has one of the most diverse and majestic landscapes on the continent. The Great Rift Valley, with the steep-walled valley floor dropping as much as

Ballooning over the Maasai Mara and the Great Migration

A mother cheetah and her juvenile cub watch for prey and predators from a termite mound

2,000 to 3,000 feet (610 to 915 m) from the surrounding countryside, is more breathtakingly dramatic here than anywhere else in Africa.

The eastern and northern regions of the country are arid. Most of the population and economic production are in the south, which is characterized by a plateau that ranges in altitude from 3,000 to 10,000 feet (915 to 3,050 m), sloping down to Lake Victoria in the west and to a coastal strip to the east.

Over half the country is Christian, although many people still retain their indigenous beliefs. There is a Muslim population concentrated along the coast. The Maasai are found mainly to the south of Nairobi, the Kikuyu in the highlands around Nairobi, the Samburu in the arid north, and the Luo around Lake Victoria.

Bantu and Nilotic peoples moved into the area before Arab traders, who arrived on the Kenyan coast by the first century A.D. The Swahili language was created out of a mixture of Bantu and Arabic and became the universal trading language.

The Portuguese arrived in 1498 and took command of the coast, followed by the Omani in the 1600s and the British in the late nineteenth century. Kenya gained its independence within the British Commonwealth on December 12, 1963. Key foreign exchange-earners are tourism, coffee, tea and horticulture (flowers and vegetables exported to Europe, especially in the European winter).

🐾 WILDLIFE AND WILDLIFE AREAS

Kenya is one of the best countries on the continent for seeing large amounts of wildlife. In addition, lodge safaris, where guests are driven from park to park, are generally less expensive here than in Tanzania, Botswana or Zambia. Prices are even more attractive in Kenya's low season (April, May and November). Game viewing is still good in the low season due to the excellent visibility of the open plains of the Maasai Mara and other reserves.

Kenya's well-known parks have the reputation of being crowded in high season, and compared to less popular reserves, they are. However, I feel this should be put into perspective. There are very few reserves in Africa that have such great sightings of the wildlife species many safariers want to see most (leopard, lion, cheetah) than in reserves like the Maasai Mara and Samburu, so having several other vehicles on some sightings is perhaps not a bad tradeoff.

Booking a safari with a private vehicle and guide is a great way to maximize the quality of your game viewing experience. If a few vehicles show up on your sighting, if you wish, you can simply search for another game viewing opportunity perhaps further off the beaten path. In other words, you have much more control of your experience in the bush.

It is possible to get totally away from the crowds in some of the splendid private conservancies or the less popular national parks. Many private conservancies cater to a maximum of 12 to 24 guests in luxury accommodations and offer activities not allowed within the parks, such as night game drives and escorted walks. ol Donyo Lodge and Campi ya Kanzi, for instance, each cover at least 250,000-acres (100,000-hectares) and cater to no more than 16 guests. You can also visit the major reserves at times other than during peak seasons.

The Kenya Wildlife Services, formed to manage and conserve Kenya's national parks and reserves has enhanced security that has reduced poaching.

The Maasai Mara is the most popular reserve in Kenya for wildlife viewing and should, if at all possible, be included in your itinerary, unless you will be touring the Serengeti National Park in Tanzania at the time of the year when the Serengeti Migration is more concentrated in Tanzania (November to July).

In general, game viewing is best during the dry seasons, mid-December to March and July to October. Wildlife is easiest to spot in the Maasai Mara and Amboseli National Parks, which have vast wide-open plains. Samburu is the country's best northern reserve, and there are a number of excellent private reserves in the Laikipia region that offer day and night game drives, escorted walks and interesting tribal visits.

The country is an ornithologist's paradise, with over 1,000 species of birds recorded within its borders. Greater and lesser flamingos migrate along the Rift

Valley and prefer the alkaline lakes of Magadi, Elmenteita, Nakuru, Bogoria or Turkana. Lakes Naivasha and Baringo are freshwater lakes. Birdwatching is good year-round, but is perhaps best between September and March when many species of Eurasian migratory birds are present alongside the breeding residents.

Flying safaris are popular in Kenya as the country has an excellent network of scheduled flights to all the major reserves. Unique camel safaris are operated in the north, where guests spend time riding these "ships of the desert" and walking down dry riverbeds.

To give you the greatest variety of experiences on a safari in Kenya, I highly recommend combining visits to some of Kenya's top parks with stays in some private reserves.

THE SOUTH

Nairobi

Nairobi, situated at an altitude of about 6,000 feet (1,830 m), means "place of cool waters" in the Maasai language.

The **National Museum** features the Leakey family's paleo-anthropological discoveries, botanical drawings and the original tribal paintings of Joy Adamson. Studying the taxidermy displays of birds and wild animals will help you identify the live game while on safari. Across from the museum is the **Snake Park**, exhibiting over 200 species of the "well-loved" reptilian family. At the **Municipal Market** in the center of town on Muindi Mbingu Street, vendors sell and produce unusual and beautiful curios (be sure to bargain). The **Railroad Museum** will be of interest to railroad enthusiasts, and tells the compelling story of the "Man Eaters of Tsavo" — lions that killed hundreds of workers while the railroad was under construction. The **Nairobi Race Course** has horse racing on Sunday afternoons (in season); the track is an excellent place for people to watch and meet a diverse cross section of Nairobians.

One of the more popular dining and disco spots is the Carnivore, famous for its tasty selection of meats cooked on giant open grills. The Tamarind is known for excellent seafood. The Haandi and Haveli are possibly the finest of Kenya's great Indian restaurants. The Talisman in Karen, the Osteria del Chinati on Lenana Road and the Mediteraneo at the Junction are the best restaurants in Nairobi and its suburbs. Other excellent restaurants include Alan Bobbies' Bistro and 'Thai Chi' at The Stanley Hotel. The Thorn Tree Cafe is a renowned meeting place for overland travelers who leave messages on a bulletin board. The most happening disco in Nairobi these days is The Pavement in Westlands.

Other attractions include the **Bomas of Kenya**, which features regular performances of ethnic dances and 16 varying styles of Kenyan homesteads. At the **Giraffe Centre**, guests can learn more about the Rothschild's giraffes and even feed them from an elevated platform. The **Karen Blixen Museum** is also an interesting attraction, featuring many of this famous author's personal possessions on display in her restored home. The trained team at the **Daphne**

Feeding time at the Daphne Sheldrick Elephant Orphanage

Sheldrick Elephant Orphanage have reared sick and abandoned elephants back to health and released them into the wild at Tsavo East National Park. Using a milk formula she created, Daphne was the first person to successfully bottle-raise an orphaned milk-dependent elephant.

ACCOMMODATION IN NAIROBI — DELUXE: • **The Sankara Nairobi** is a premier hotel with sleek, modern rooms with floor to ceiling windows. The hotel is located in Westlands and features several dining options, a rooftop pool and full service spa. The hotel is ideal for business travelers. • **Nairobi Serena**, located a few minutes drive from town, is a member of the "Leading Hotels of the World," and has been completely remodeled with 183 air-conditioned rooms and suites, business center, conference facilities, Maisha Spa and a large swimming pool. • **Fairmont Norfolk Hotel**, a landmark in Nairobi, has a traditional safari atmosphere, a swimming pool, the fabulous Ibis Grill, and an open-air bar that is especially popular on Friday nights. The hotel was recently renovated, and all rooms are air-conditioned.

FIRST CLASS: • **Ole Sereni Hotel** overlooks Nairobi National Park and is located between the airport and city center. There are 134 air-conditioned rooms and a waterhole is visible from the restaurants, bar and swimming pool. • **The Stanley Hotel**, located in the center of town, has 240 air-conditioned rooms. • **Nairobi Safari Club** is an air-conditioned, all-suite hotel (146 rooms) with a health club and swimming pool.

TOURIST CLASS: • **Hilton International** is centrally located and has comfortable air-conditioned rooms and a swimming pool. • **Sarova PanAfric** features 164 air-conditioned rooms and restaurant. • **Intercontinental Nairobi** is located near the convention center and offers 376 rooms and suites, restaurant, bar, spa and gym.

ACCOMMODATION OUTSIDE OF NAIROBI — DELUXE: • **Giraffe Manor**, located in the suburb of Karen/Langata, was built in the 1930s and reflects Kenya's colonial heritage. The Manor is famous for having Rothschild's giraffes roaming about the property, often sticking their heads through open windows looking for handouts. This unique lodge has recently been remodeled and features 10 bedrooms with views overlooking the 140 acre sanctuary. • **Hogmead** is a new boutique hotel located in a suburb near Nairobi's domestic airport. The hotel features six spacious rooms overlooking lovely gardens, and 7 day rooms. The main lounge has a fireplace, verandah and bar. • **House of Waine**, situated in the suburb of Karen, is set on 2.5 acres and offers 11 bedrooms, each with a large marble bathroom. Meals are served in various locations on the property and there are two bars exclusively for hotel guests. • **The Tribe Hotel** is a boutique hotel located next to the Village Market, featuring over 150 shops and restaurants. The hotel offers 142 rooms and suites, an eclectic restaurant serving contemporary cuisine and a full service spa.

FIRST CLASS: • **Karen Blixen Cottages**, situated 20 miles (32 km) from Nairobi and a half mile (1 km) from the Karen Blixen Museum, has comfortable cottages and suites, restaurant, bar and swimming pool. • **Macushla House**, a private guesthouse located near Giraffe Manor, which is just a 20-minute drive from downtown Nairobi, caters to a maximum of 10 guests and features a swimming pool. • **Safari Park Hotel**, located 7 miles (11 km) from the city center in a quiet, country setting, has 228 rooms, a huge

Giraffe Manor *(top)*, Breakfast at the Giraffe Manor is a special thrill *(middle)*, The grounds of the Hogmead *(bottom)*

swimming pool, tennis and squash courts and several restaurants — all in a lush garden setting.

Nairobi National Park

Nairobi National Park, located only 8 miles (13 km) south of Nairobi, covers 45-square-miles (117-km²) and has a variety of game including several types of antelope, hippo, black rhino, and even the occasional lion and cheetah — a bit of everything except elephant. The park has one of the highest concentrations of black rhino in Africa, with a current population of over 60.

Nairobi National Park is a linking corridor to the Athi-Kapiti Plains and Kitengela for a wildlife migration to Amboseli National Reserve. Most of the park is open plains with areas of scattered acacia bush.

The permanent Athi River is fringed by yellow-barked fever trees, and there is a small patch of highland forest dominated by crotons. An impressive list of birds has been recorded, but occurrence is seasonal for many species. Among the characteristic varieties are ostrich, secretary bird, black-headed heron, augur buzzard, little bee-eater and Jackson's widowbird.

There is something very strange about being in the midst of wild game while still within sight of a city skyline. Altitude ranges from 4,950 to 5,850 feet (1,500 to 1,785 m) above sea level.

The David Sheldrick Trust manages a small animal orphanage near the main park entrance, caring for hurt, sick or stray animals. The side of the park facing Nairobi is fenced. A 4wd vehicle is recommended in the rainy season.

ACCOMMODATION WITHIN THE PARK — Class B • **Nairobi Tented Camp** is located in Nairobi National Park, 40 minutes drive from Nairobi International Airport and 20 minutes drive from the Wilson airport. Eight tents feature bucket showers. Easy access for game drives in the Nairobi National Park.

Amboseli National Reserve

Set on the Tanzanian border, Amboseli is in one of the most scenic settings in Africa: Every vista is dominated by the majestic, snow-capped peak of Mt. Kilimanjaro in neighboring Tanzania. The grandeur of this imposing feature provides a superb backdrop for photographing and viewing big game.

Amboseli is perhaps best-known for its abundant (over 1,000) and approachable elephants — the subject of several documentary films and researcher Cynthia Moss' classic book *Elephant Memories* (University of Chicago Press).

Amboseli National Reserve covers 150-square-miles (390-km²) and averages about 3,900 feet (1,190 m) in altitude. Elephant and giraffe are easily found, and many visitors enjoy photographing them as they pass in front of majestic Mt. Kilimanjaro. The mountain seems so close, but it is actually located in Tanzania, more than 30 miles (48 km) from the park.

The reserve lies in the rain shadow of Mt. Kilimanjaro and receives, on average, just 12 inches (300 mm) of rain per year. Interestingly, however, subterranean

Amboseli National Reserve

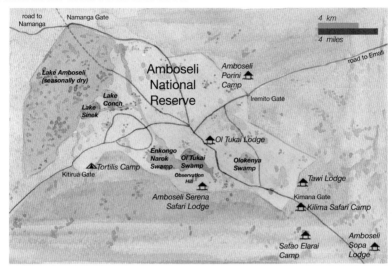

water draining off the northern slopes of Mt. Kilimanjaro surfaces in Amboseli in the form of freshwater springs. These springs are a major draw for wildlife, and the surrounding papyrus beds are an attractive habitat for wetland species. The dominant habitat is acacia-commiphora scrub or woodland, much of it on rocky, lava-strewn plains.

A dry and ancient lakebed occupies the western part of the reserve, but when it fills after heavy rains it can be a huge attraction for birds. Over 400 bird species have been recorded here, including three varieties of sandgrouse, rosy-patched bushshrike, Taveta golden weaver and purple grenadier. In addition to the plain's game typical of East Africa, the arid-adapted gerenuk, lesser kudu and fringe-eared oryx may be seen.

From Nairobi, travel south across the Athi Plains inhabited by the Maasai pastoralists. Visitors enter the reserve on a road that is most often badly corrugated from Namanga and pass Lake Amboseli (a salt pan), which is bone dry except in the rainy seasons, eastward across sparsely vegetated chalk flats to Ol Tukai. Mirages are common under the midday sun.

Approaching the center of the reserve, the barren landscape turns refreshingly green from springs and swamps fed by underground runoff from the overshadowing Mt. Kilimanjaro. These swamps give life to an otherwise parched land, providing water for nearby grasslands and acacia woodlands and attracting a profusion of game and waterfowl. Superb starling, red-and-yellow barbet and silverbird are among the bush birds in residence.

Large herds of elephant and buffalo are often seen around the swamps, especially at **Enkongo Narok Swamp**, where it is easy to obtain photos of animals

Scenic Amboseli National Park with Mt. Kilimanjaro in the background

(especially elephant) in the foreground and Mt. Kilimanjaro in the background. Early morning is best, before Mt. Kilimanjaro is covered in clouds; the clouds may partially clear in late afternoon.

Observation Hill is a good location from which to get an overview of the reserve. There is a pretty good chance of spotting cheetah, giraffe and impala, but oryx and gerenuk are less likely to be seen. Game viewing is best from mid-December to March (also the best views of Mt. Kilimanjaro) and from July to October, and due to the open terrain, is actually good year-round except for possibly April and May when it can be quite wet.

To limit destruction to the environment, driving off the roads is forbidden, and heavy fines are being levied against those who break the rules. Please do not ask your driver to leave the road for a closer look at wildlife. The park is about 140 miles (225 km) from Nairobi.

ACCOMMODATION — CLASS A: • **Tortilis Camp** is located just outside the reserve and has 16 luxury tents and two family units (each with two bedrooms and private dining areas). Day game drives within the park, bush breakfasts, guided walks, cultural visits, massage and beauty treatments are available as well as a swimming pool. • **Tawi Lodge** is located on a 6,000 acre conservancy 5 minutes from the Amboseli National Park. The lodge features 12 cottages each with views of Mt. Kilimanjaro. Day and night game drives in open vehicles are offered. There is a swimming pool, bush bar and spa treatments are offered. • **Satao Elerai Camp** is located on a private conservation area, 7 miles (12 km) southeast of Amboseli. There are 9 tents and 5 large lodge-style suites each with verandahs. Activities include day and night game drives and guided walks.

CLASS A/B: • **Ol Tukai Lodge**, which has recently been refurbished, offers 80 rooms with private patios with views of Mt. Kilimanjaro. Activities include game drives, bird walks and evening lectures. • **Amboseli Serena Safari Lodge** has 92 rooms including five family rooms and one suite. The lodge has recently been completely remodeled and refurbished and features a swimming pool.

CLASS B: • **Kilima Safari Camp** is located near the Kimana Gate Park entrance to Amboseli. The camp has 72 tents with private balconies and views of Mt. Kilimanjaro. • **Amboseli Sopa Lodge**, facing Mt. Kilimanjaro, offers 84 cottage-style rooms and suites with private verandas, a pool and dining room.

CLASS C: • **Amboseli Porini Camp**, located in the Selenkay Conservation Area just north of Amboseli, has six tents. Activities include day and night game drives and walks led by Maasai warriors.

Tortilis Camp *(top)*, A bungalow at Tawi Lodge *(bottom)*

ol Donyo Lodge

ol Donyo Lodge is set on a 270,000-acre (125,000-hectare) Maasai owned Mbirikani Group Ranch (part of the Amboseli ecosystem) in the foothills of the Chyulu Range, between Tsavo West, Amboseli National Park and Chyulu National Park. Guests of the lodge have panoramic views of Mt. Kilimanjaro and exclusive access to the ranch.

On game drives during my last visit we saw Maasai giraffe, oryx, Grant's gazelle, eland, bush duiker, dikdik, Coke's hartebeest, black-backed jackal and serval, among other game. Lion, cheetah and elephant may also be seen. Massive elephant bulls with close to 100 pound tusks are a feature and are resident at the waterhole right below the lodge. It is one of the few areas in Kenya outside of a National Park where lion concentrations are increasing, due mainly to Richard Bonham's innovative predator compensation scheme that is now reaping rewards.

Game viewing from ol Donyo Lodge's hide

On horseback we cantered among herds of zebra and wildebeest and came fairly close to giraffe, oryx and eland. This is certainly one of the best places for horseback riding in East Africa.

Easiest access is by air on the daily 50-minute scheduled flights from Nairobi's Wilson Airport.

A decadent pool cottage at ol Donyo Lodge

ACCOMMODATION — CLASS A+: • **ol Donyo Lodge** accommodates guests in eight thatched luxury cottages (configured for couples, families & multi-generational groups) with open fireplaces, verandahs, and 6 have private pools. Day and night game drives in open vehicles and escorted walks with excellent resident guides. Visits to the log-pile hide, Maasai visits, horseback rides ranging from an hour's ride to multi-day safaris, and mountain biking are offered. This is an ideal venue for families with children who enjoy private game drives. Sleep outs under the stars are possible on the cottage's roof top decks. Fly-camping is available. The camp has been a leader in preserving wildlife and simultaneously providing benefit to the local communities.

Ride Kenya is a sister organization to ol Donyo Lodge that offers superb 7-night horseback safaris with guaranteed departures nine months out of every year. Each night is spent in luxury mobile tented camps (arguably some of the finest in all of Kenya). One itinerary even ends in the marshes of Amboseli. Custom departures are also available.

Campi ya Kanzi

Campi ya Kanzi is located on a 280,000-acre (115,000-hectare) Maasai Group Ranch surrounded by Chyulu, Tsavo and Amboseli National Parks, and stretching to the foothills of Mt. Kilimanjaro. The landscape is quite varied from lush forests to riverine forest and savannah grasslands, as the altitude ranges from 3,000 to 6,900 feet (900 to 2,100 m). Wildlife includes elephant, lion, cheetah, leopard, lesser kudu, giraffe, fringe-eared oryx, gerenuk, zebra, wildebeest, hartebeest and mountain reedbuck. Over 400 species of birds have been recorded. Easiest access is by a 55-minute scheduled flight from Nairobi.

ACCOMMODATION — CLASS A: • **Campi ya Kanzi** has six luxury tents and two suites under thatch, set on raised wooden decks with private verandahs. Activities at this family-run lodge include day and night game drives, escorted walks with the Maasai trackers, Maasai cultural visits, and excursions to Tsavo West, Chyulu and Amboseli National Parks. There are lovely views of Mt. Kilimanjaro from the camp. The camp is one of the most eco-awarded lodges in East Africa. • **Kanzi House**, with room for up to 10 guests, is an exclusive property offering private game drives, private dining with a dedicated chef, and a swimming pool/jacuzzi.

Tsavo West National Park

Halfway between Nairobi and Mombasa lie Tsavo **West** and Tsavo East **National Parks**, which together with **Chyulu Hills National Park** cover over 8,217-square-miles (21,283-km²). Large herds of over 100 elephant are part of the massive population of over 15,000 in the Tsavo conservation area. The park has large prides of lion and a good leopard population and over 60 rhino found mainly within the Rhino valley and in the Rhino Sanctuary, the latter established to protect the remnant populations after the horrendous poaching in the 70s. Also present are caracal, giraffe, zebra and a variety of antelope.

Acacia and Commiphora woodland dominates the landscape, with ribbons of taller trees along the Galana, Tsavo and other rivers. The graceful doum palm, with its forked trunk, is prevalent along river beds. The many enormous baobab trees provide plenty of breeding cavities for barbets, starlings, parrots, rollers, kestrels and owls.

While big game is less concentrated here than in Amboseli National Park, the park's rugged terrain and landscape is quite impressive in itself.

Tsavo West National Park is predominantly semi-arid plains punctuated by occasional granite outcrops. The **Shetani Lava Fields**, covering 3-square miles (8-km²) are located near Kilaguni Lodge. The volcanic cones and lava

Tsavo National Park

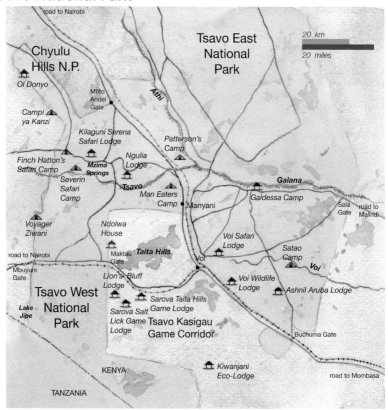

spread presents the best place to spot the klipspringer, a small antelope with hooves adapted to rock climbing. Altitudes range from 1,000 feet (305 m) to nearly 6,000 feet (1,830 m) in the Ngulia Mountains located in the northern region of the park.

From the **Mzima Springs** underwater viewing platform, located just south of Kilaguni Serena Safari Lodge, visitors may be lucky enough to watch hippo swim in the clear waters among the crocs and fish. Otters also inhabit these waters. The best viewing is early in the morning. Kilaguni Serena Safari Lodge is about 180 miles (290 km) from Nairobi.

Near Mzima Springs is the **Poachers Lookout.** Take a drive up this volcanic cone through dense acacia thornveld for breath-taking views of the surrounding plains.

The southern sector of Tsavo West National Park has more open plains than the northern areas. **Lake Jipe** is an ornithological paradise for water birds.

ACCOMMODATION — CLASS A:
• **Ndolwa House** is a small, luxury lodge set on a 10,000-acre (4,000-hectare) private ranch. The lodge consists of five stone cottages, dining room and bar area. Day and night game drives and bush walks are offered.
• **Finch Hattons Safari Camp** overlooks a hippo pool and has 35 raised tents with private decks and a swimming pool. Breakfast and lunch are served outside on the terrace overlooking the hippos and 6-course dinners are served in the elegant dining room.

CLASS A/B: • **Severin Safari Camp** has 27 unique octagonal tents overlooking a waterhole and Mt. Kilimanjaro beyond. • **Kilaguni Serena Safari Lodge** has 52 rooms and a swimming pool. • **Ngulia Lodge** has 56 rooms and a swimming pool.

CLASS B: • **Lions Bluff Lodge** is located on a 125,000-acre (50,000-hectare) private game conservancy and features 12 rondavels with private verandahs. Activities include day and night game drives, bush walks, cultural visits and World War I battlefield tours.

CLASS C: • **Voyager Ziwani**, situated just outside the southwestern boundary of the park, overlooks a freshwater dam and has 25 tents with attached showers and long-drop toilets. Day and night game drives, walks and excursions to the volcanic Lake Chala and walks among the World War I battlefields along the Tanzanian border are offered.

Finch Hattons Safari Camp *(top and bottom)*

Tsavo East National Park

Tsavo East is mostly arid bush dotted with rocky outcrops that are traversed by permanent and seasonal riverbeds lined with riverine forest. Tsavo East is generally hotter and drier, as it lies at a lower altitude (about 1,000 ft./305 m) than its western counterpart. The 3,000-square-miles (7,770-km²) south of the Galana River is more frequented by the public while the northern area is designated for low impact tourism. The 180-mile (290-km) long Yatta Plateau is one of the world's longest plateaus, and parallel to it meanders the Galana River.

Tsavo East holds the largest numbers of elephants in the country, sizeable prides of lion, cheetah, Maasai giraffe, lesser kudu, as well as a small population of highly endangered hirola (Hunter's hartebeest), which were relocated here in

1996 and seem to be holding their own. Among the interesting dryland birds are vulturine guineafowl, orange-bellied parrot, white-bellied go-away bird and golden-breasted starlings.

A game drive along the seasonal **Voi River** to the **Aruba Dam** is often quite productive. **Mundanda Rock**, an isolated hill located just north of Voi in a water catchment area, is a good place to look for elephant and buffalo. The scenic drive along the **Galana River** often produces sightings of hippo and crocs.

Voi is about 210 miles (340 km) from Nairobi.

ACCOMMODATION — CLASS B: • **Man Eaters Camp**, located on the banks of the Tsavo River, less than a mile (1.2 km) from the main highway and is within easy reach of both Tsavo East and West National Parks, and has 30 tents, restaurant, bar and swimming pool.

CLASS B/C: • **Galdessa Camp**, situated on the banks of the Galana River, has 11 rustic tented bandas in Main Camp and 3 in Private Camp, all under thatch. Activities include day and night game drives. Black rhino have been relocated into the park. • **Satao Camp** has 20 tents with views of the waterhole. • **Voi Safari Lodge**, in the hills above the town of Voi, has 52 rooms, a swimming pool and photographic hide. • **Voi Wildlife Lodge**, situated just outside the main gate, offers 72 rooms, several bars, a restaurant, health club and swimming pool. • **Ashnil Aruba Lodge** features 40 deluxe tents, restaurant, lounge and swimming pool. Day game drives and nature walks are offered.

CLASS C: • **Patterson's Camp**, set along the banks of the Athi River, has 20 basic tents.

Within The Tsavo Ecosystem

The **Tsavo Kasigau Wildlife Corridor** is a wildlife conservancy encompassing an enormous 380,000-acre (152,000-hectare) stretch of unspoiled private wilderness that is nestled between Tsavo East and West. This area hosts a large population of almost 1,000 elephant and forms a vital corridor route for wildlife as it disperses between the Galana River in Tsavo East and south to Lake Jipe in Tsavo West.

Located within this ecosystem is Camp Tsavo, dedicated to the environmental education of foreigners and Kenyans alike through their participation in a variety of community service programs. It is also the motivating epicenter for the testing and establishment of a variety of environmentally based micro-enterprises including aquaculture, apiculture,

Kiwanjani Eco-Lodge overlooks a waterhole

Sarova Salt Lick Lodge's unique design ensures great views from all rooms

sericulture and many more. Volunteers from around the world are accommodated at nearby Kiwanjani Eco-Lodge. This is a great program to consider if you are looking to do some short- or long-term volunteer work in Africa!

ACCOMMODATION — CLASS A: • **Sarova Salt Lick Game Lodge** and **Sarova Taita Hills Game Lodge** (Class B) are situated on the 28,000 acre privately managed Taita Hills Wildlife Sanctuary between the southern extensions of Tsavo East and West parks, about 240 miles (390 km) from Nairobi and 125 miles (200 km) from Mombasa. • **Sarova Salt Lick Game Lodge**, built on stilts to enhance viewing of wildlife visiting the salt lick, has 96 rooms and a photographic hide.

CLASS B: • **Sarova Taita Hills Game Lodge** has 60 rooms and a swimming pool. Night game drives and trips to nearby Lake Jipe can be arranged. • **Kiwanjani Eco-Lodge**, located between East and West Tsavo, features thatched cottages with private veran-dahs overlooking a waterhole.

Maasai Mara National Reserve

This is undoubtedly the finest wildlife area in Kenya for seeing big game. The reserve is also the stage of the famous BBC Television show "**The Big Cat Diary**" following the lives of the big cats living in and around the reserve. The reserve is famous for the **Great Migration**, which reputedly is one of the most impressive natural events in the world.

Unlike many reserves in Africa that are seasonal, game viewing here is in fact fabulous year-round. Restricted off-road game viewing is allowed, making it all the more attractive.

Maasai Mara National Reserve

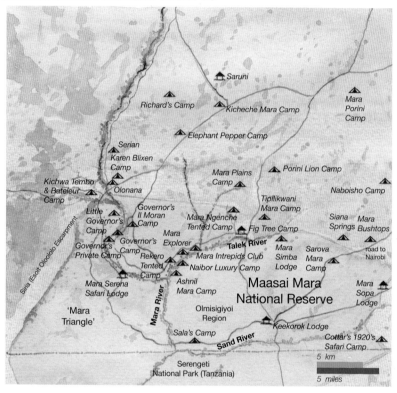

All of the big game is here: elephant, lion (prides of up to 40 or more), leopard, cheetah and buffalo are prevalent, along with a small population of black rhino. Other commonly sighted species include zebra, wildebeest, Thomson's gazelle, Defassa waterbuck, eland and Maasai giraffe. This is the only place in Kenya where topi are common.

Maasai Mara National Reserve, a northern extension of the Serengeti Plains (Tanzania), is located southwest of Nairobi and covers 590-square-miles (1,530-km²) of open plains, acacia woodlands and riverine forest along the banks on the Mara and Talek Rivers, which are home for many hippo, crocs and waterfowl.

Bordering the reserve, primarily to the north, are a number of conservancies — each with a number of camps and reserves. Most of the properties offer night game drives and escorted walks — activities not allowed in the Maasai Mara National Reserve itself. Some travelers choose to spend a few nights inside the reserve (especially for quicker access to possible wildebeest and zebra river crossings) and a few nights in a conservancy for the additional activities offered. An added bonus of most conservancies is that they are much less crowded than

Leopards are successful hunters using their spotted coat as camouflage until they make their deadly pounce

the Mara proper, as only guests of the camps on the conservancies are allowed to be on the respective properties.

The Maasai Mara National Reserve is bounded by the Siria (Esoit Oloololo) Escarpment rising about 1,000 feet (305 m) above the plains to the west, and by the Tanzanian border to the south.

The western part of the Mara is less crowded than the eastern part of the reserve. Most adventurers visiting the camps in the western part of the reserve fly into the Mara, while most people visiting the lodges and camps in the eastern Mara are driven into the reserve.

Lion are distributed throughout the park. Cheetah are most often seen on the short-grass plains. Black rhino are most concentrated in the Olmisigiyoi Region in the center of the park, in the northwest and in the extreme eastern parts of the park.

The best time to see the migration is from approximately mid-July to early November when great herds of wildebeest (1.4 million) and zebra (250,000) reside in the Mara region and northern Tanzania before returning to Serengeti National Park. From the southern Serengeti of Tanzania, a major portion of the migration moves northwest toward Lake Victoria, then north across the Mara River

Young Maasai warriors *(top)*, Game viewing on the Maasai Mara *(middle)*, A wildebeest makes the plunge into the Mara River *(bottom)*

into Kenya in search of grass, usually returning to Tanzania in late October or early November. The best time to witness large numbers of wildebeest and zebra crossing the Mara River is from late July to late October.

As the park teems with resident wildlife, game viewing is good year-round. There is a real advantage in visiting the reserve November to June as there are fewer travelers at that time. During one visit we saw lion, cheetah, thousands of wildebeest and zebra, and the unforgettable experience of witnessing part of the migration crossing the Mara River! We patiently sat at the river's edge for four hours and were handsomely rewarded for our patience.

The Mara is a paradise for birds and birdwatchers. Over 400 species have been recorded, with grassland and wetland birds especially well represented. Martial eagle, long-crested eagle and bateleur are common, while large numbers of vultures follow the great migration of wildebeest and zebra, feeding on the remains of those that die of exhaustion, old age or predator attacks. The Mara River and some of its tributaries are forested along their banks, providing ideal habitat for exciting birds such as Ross's turaco, black-and-white-casqued hornbill, blue flycatcher and the narina trogon.

Balloon safaris are very popular and certainly a unique way of experiencing Africa. In fact, this has to be one

A "coalition" of male cheetah search for prey across the grassy plains

of the very best places on earth for ballooning. On my last balloon safari we flew over part of the great migration and saw a variety of wildlife. The pilot was extremely entertaining as well as knowledgeable of the flora and fauna enroute. The champagne breakfast that followed was great fun for the entire group.

If you are looking for a great location to relax before flying home or if you enjoy fishing, consider flying from the Mara to **Mfangano Island** or **Rusinga Island** on Lake Victoria (book in advance).

In the northwestern part of the park, 4wd vehicles are recommended. There are at least two scheduled flights a day from Nairobi that serve the park. Keekorok Lodge is located about 170 miles (275 km) and the Mara Serena Safari Lodge about 210 miles (340 km) from Nairobi.

ACCOMMODATION — All lodges and camps listed below either conduct hot-air balloon safaris or will take you to where one is being offered; be sure to book well in advance. Many guests fly into the Mara (highly recommended) and are taken game viewing in 4wd vehicles (preferably) or minivans. Most camps and lodges are a five- to six-hour drive from Nairobi, so flying there is highly recommended.

Mara Explorer *(top, left)*, Sala's Camp *(top, right)*, Rekero Tented Camp *(middle)*, Rekero's dining room *(bottom, left)*, Little Governor's Camp *(bottom, right)*

ACCOMMODATION IN THE RESERVE — CLASS A+: • **Governor's Il Moran Camp** is located within the reserve, and has 10 huge tents lining the winding banks of the Mara River. Morning and afternoon game drives and walks on the periphery of the reserve are offered. • **Mara Explorer**, situated on the Talek River in the middle of the Mara, has 10 luxurious tents (each with private outdoor Victorian bathtubs). Activities include game drives, walking safaris outside the reserve, private bush meals and visits to Maasai communities.

CLASS A: • **Sala's Camp** is located on the banks of the Sand River in a private and secluded corner of the Mara, offering views across the plains toward Tanzania (and the Serengeti). The camp has six double tents and one honeymoon tent. Activities include morning and afternoon game drives, bush breakfasts and optional balloon safari or visit to a Maasai village. • **Mara Ngeche Tented Camp** is located at the confluence of the Mara and Talek Rivers. The camp features 6 tents with 4-poster beds and private verandahs. • **Naibor Luxury Camp** is located within the Mara Reserve and has 9 spacious, classic safari tents with flush toilets and safari showers. Morning and afternoon game drives, walks in nearby game concession, and visits to the Maasai village are offered. • **Rekero Tented Camp** is located very close to the confluence of the Mara and Talek Rivers. The camp has 6 tents and a large dining tent. Game drives, walks and bush picnics are offered. • **Little Governor's Camp**, located in the northwest part of the park on the Mara River, has 17 tents positioned around a waterhole. Guests reach the camp by crossing the Mara River by boat. Walks are offered outside the reserve. • **Governor's Camp**, located a few miles from Little Governor's Camp on the Mara River, has 37 tents including 6 family tents. Walks outside the reserve are offered. • **Mara Intrepids Club** is situated on the Talek River and has 30 tents with four-poster beds, 2 unique family tents and a swimming pool. Game drives are offered three times a day as well as walks in the adjacent Maasai land. There is an "Adventurers Club" for guests ages 4 to 12 and "Young Rangers" for 13 to 17.

CLASS A/B: • **Mara Serena Safari Lodge**, set on a hill in the central western part of the park, has 76 rooms and a swimming pool. Because it is set far from any other camps or lodges, guests encounter very few other vehicles. The view from the lodge of the expansive plains below is spectacular.

CLASS B: • **Governor's Private Camp** caters to private parties of up to 16 guests in 8 tents on wooden platforms with verandas, flush toilets and safari (bucket) showers. • **Mara Simba Lodge** has 36 rooms with private verandahs overlooking the Talek River and a swimming pool. • **Keekorok Lodge** is an old-style lodge with 72 rooms and 12 cottages and a swimming pool. • **Sarova Mara Camp** has 75 tents and a swimming pool. • **Ashnil Mara Camp** is located near the Mara River and offers 40 tents overlooking the Mara plains.

ACCOMMODATION OUTSIDE OF THE RESERVE — CLASS A+: • **Mara Plains Camp**, located only 1.5 miles (2 km) from the northern border of the reserve in the predator-dense and exclusive 30,000-acre Olare Orok Conservancy, has 7 deluxe tents, including 2 family tents, and offers game drives, walking and access to more private land conservancy (Olare Orok of 30,000 acres and Mara North of 80,000 acres) than any other camp in the Mara region. • **Mara Bushtops** (formerly Bush Tops) is located in the Mara Siana Wildlife Conservancy and features 12 tents which are open on 3 sides, providing outstanding panoramic views. Each features a large private terrace, hot tub, telescope for game viewing, and 24-hour butler.

CLASS A: • **Naboisho Camp** is a new camp located in the 50,000-acre Naboisho Conservancy, a 50,000 acre game concession east of the Mara/Serengeti eco-system. The region is host to a variety of animals including the big cats, elephants, giraffe, plains animals and rare wild dogs. The exclusive camp features 8 luxury tents with

A game drive based at Olonana Camp *(top)*, Mara Plains *(middle, left)*, Naboisho *(middle, right)*, Olonana *(bottom, left)*, Tipilikwani *(bottom, right)*

private verandahs with expansive views. Activities include game drives, walking safaris, night game drives, off-roading, cultural tourism and fly camping. • **Serian** is an exclusive wilderness camp set close to the Siria Escarpment, with 8 marquee tents, each with a private butler. The camp operates from June until the end of March and offers game drives as well as escorted walks and fly camping. • **Olonana**, set on the banks of the Mara River, has 14 luxury tents built on wooden platforms, each overlooking the river. The camp has a swimming pool and mini-spa. Activities include game drives, walking safaris and tour of a local village. • **Bateleur Camp** at Kichwa Tembo, situated on the western border of the Mara, is actually two camps, each with nine luxuriously furnished tents. Morning and afternoon game drives, night game drives on a private concession, guided walks and Maasai visits are offered. • **Cottar's 1920s Safari Camp**, set outside the eastern border of the reserve on a 250,000-acre (100,000-hectare) private concession within the Olderekesi concession, accommodates up to 12 clients in spacious tents, incorporating original safari antiques from the '20s. Four adjoining tents share their own dining tent and are perfect for families. Day game drives are conducted in the reserve while both day and night game drives are provided on the concession along with walking and fishing. There is a swimming pool and massage treatments are offered. For those looking for an exclusive experience there is the new **Cottar's Private House** which accommodates 10 guests with dining room, living room and dedicated staff of 8 people. • **Karen Blixen Camp** features 22 large canvas tents built on wooden platforms with spacious verandahs and cushioned daybeds. The tents, wellness center, open lounge and dining room overlook the Mara River. • **Kicheche Mara Camp**, located in the Mara North Conservancy, features 8 tents overlooking the Olare Orok stream. Activities include morning and afternoon game drives. Local village tours can be arranged for minimal cost. • **Saruni**, located north of the reserve, has 6 deluxe cottages and offers game drives, walking and spa services.

Class A/B: • **Elephant Pepper Camp** is a seasonal permanent tented eco-friendly camp situated on the northern edge of the Maasai Mara reserve. The 9 tents (including one honeymoon/family tent) have solar lighting and verandahs. Activities include extended game drives in 4wd vehicles, guided bush walks with Maasai, cultural visits, night game drives, picnics and sun-downers. • **Richard's Camp** is an eco-friendly camp and offers 8 tents. • **Tipilikwani Mara Camp** sits on the banks of the Talek River and includes 20 tents with private verandahs. Activities include game drives, bush walks, bush breakfast and optional night game drives.

CLASS B: • **Siana Springs** has 38 tents and a swimming pool. Walks and day and night game drives are offered. • **Kichwa Tembo** has 28 standard (Class A/B) and 12 luxury tents (Class A) and two thatched rondavels and a swimming pool. Escorted walks, Maasai village visits, day and night game drives in a private concession area are offered. • **Mara Sopa Lodge**, located on the eastern border of the park high on a ridge with views across the Mara near Ololaimutiek Gate, has 82 cottage-style rooms and suites with verandahs, and a swimming pool.

CLASS C: • **Mara Porini Camp** offers 6 tents and is situated in the Ol Kinyei Game Conserancy northeast of the Mara. • **Fig Tree Camp**, located on the Talek River, has 30 basic chalets and 30 tents and a swimming pool.

THE WEST

Lake Victoria

Lake Victoria is the largest lake in Africa and the second largest freshwater lake in the world (Lake Superior is the largest). The lake is approximately

26,650-square-miles (69,000-km²) in size and is bordered by Kenya, Tanzania and Uganda.

Fishing for the giant Nile perch is excellent; the largest one taken from the lake was reported to weigh 520 pounds (236 kg)! Nile perch weighing in excess of 100 pounds (45 kg) are sometimes caught.

Unfortunately, the Nile perch is not native to Lake Victoria. It was introduced in the 1950s and is a major predator of indigenous fish, some of which have become extinct. In recent years, the gigantic lake has also been plagued by the rapidly spreading water hyacinth, an aquatic plant from tropical America that has blanketed much of the water surface and starved it of oxygen. This has had grave consequences for aquatic wildlife as well as for local fishing communities.

Over 100 species of birds have been recorded on the islands. Spotted necked otters may also be seen.

Easiest access to the island camps in the lake is by air charter from the Maasai Mara or from Nairobi.

ACCOMMODATION — CLASS A: • **Rusinga Island Lodge** has 7 cottages (8 bedrooms) including a two-bedroom family unit. Fishing, boating, birdwatching, water skiing, wind surfing, pre-historic fossil digs, visits to nearby Ruma National Park, health spa, and mountain biking are offered.

CLASS A/B: • **Mfangano Island Camp**, just a 40-minute charter flight and 15-minute boat ride from the Maasai Mara, has 6 cottages. Fishing, boating, birdwatching and visits to Luo fishing villages are offered.

Kakamega Forest

The Kakamega Forest encompasses approximately 90-square-miles (230-km²) and is the eastern-most remnant of the great West African rain forests that once stretched the width of Africa. The Kakamega National Reserve is 44 Km Sq and there are 4 miles (7 km) of walking trails through a forest that includes some of Africa's greatest hard and soft woods, including Elgon Teak, red and white stink woods, and several varieties of Croton.

Kakamega is an ornithologist's dream, alive with different species of birds — some are found only in this part of Kenya. Avifauna specialties include great blue turaco, African gray parrot, blue-headed bee-eater, black-and-white casqued hornbill, emerald cuckoo, black-billed and Vieillot's black weavers, Chubb's cisticola, Turner's eremomella, joyfull greenbul, Luhder's bushshrike, honeyguide greenbul, Uganda woodland warbler, yellow-bellied wattle-eye and chestnut wattle-eye. The forest is also home to 350 species of trees, 400 species of butterflies and 7 species of primates including the endangered DeBrazza monkey, potto monkey, black-and-white colobus monkey, blue monkey and red-tailed monkey.

ACCOMMODATION — CLASS B: • **Rondo Retreat** has 15 double rooms plus 3 more that share a large bathroom in the main house (originally built in the 1920s).

THE RIFT VALLEY LAKES

Stretching some 4,000 miles (6,500 km) from the Red Sea to the Zambezi River, the Rift Valley is one of the most distinctive ruptures on the Earth's surface, and one of the few geological features that can be seen from the moon. The Rift Valley is thought to have begun to form some 40 million years ago, at a time when mankind's ancestors emerged onto the African savannahs. The slow rending apart of the Earth's crust also led to the formation and eruption of many volcanic mountains along or adjacent to the Rift Valley.

The Rift Valley is split into two arms: the Eastern Arm, which cuts through the center of Kenya, and the Western Arm, which forms the border between Uganda and the Democratic Republic of the Congo. A chain of beautiful lakes have formed along the length of the Rift Valley, and when combined with sheer cliffs and acacia flats, they make for breathtaking scenery.

Lake Naivasha

Lake Naivasha, located just 55 miles (89 km) northwest of Nairobi, is one of the most beautiful of Kenya's Rift Valley lakes, and features fringing papyrus beds, secluded lagoons and the picturesque Crescent Island. It is a favorite spot for picnics and water sports for Nairobi residents, and it is a birdwatcher's paradise. African fish eagles are abundant. Waterfowl, plovers, sandpipers, avocet, terns, kingfishers, storks and ibis are plentiful. This is a freshwater lake with a suspected underground outlet, so it is less attractive to flamingos, which prefer soda lakes.

Take a boat ride to **Crescent Island** and walk around this game-and-bird sanctuary, which is host to zebra, giraffe, waterbuck, several antelope species and a few camels.

ACCOMMODATION — CLASS A:
• **Loldia House**, a cattle ranch located on the northern side of Lake Naivasha, accommodates up to 10 guests in rooms at the main house and a cottage. • **Chui Lodge** is located on the Oserian Wildlife Sanctuary and has 8 individual cottages, each with a

The lush surroundings of Loldia House *(top and bottom)*

verandah, and a heated swimming pool. Activities include game drives and bush walks.
• **Kiangzai House,** also located on Oserian Wildlife Sanctuary, has 5 luxury bedrooms in the renovated homestead house, and a swimming pool.

CLASS A/B: • **Lake Naivasha Sopa Lodge** has 84 rooms in 2-storey cottages, all with terraces or verandahs. The hotel has panoramic views of the southern shores of the lake, a swimming pool, poolside pizzeria, hippo observation area and a fitness center. Nature walks and boat rides are offered. • **The Great Rift Valley Lodge and Golf Resort** is perched on the Eburu Escarpment overlooking Lake Naivasha. The resort offers 30 rooms with private balconies, as well as 40 three-bedroom Longonot villas. Activities include Adventurers Club for children, birding, nature walks and horseback riding safaris as well as golf on the championship course (additional fee).

CLASS C: • **Lake Naivasha Country Club** was built during the colonial era and is located on the lake shore with 51 rooms and a swimming pool. Sunset cruises are offered and a special Sunday afternoon tea is served.

Lake Elmenteita

Lake Elmenteita is a shallow, alkaline lake located between Lakes Naivasha and Nakuru. The lake only holds surface water for a brief period after heavy rain, and it rapidly evaporates. A white soda crust covers much of the lake. A number of

hot springs feed permanent lagoons on the fringes of the lake— very attractive to a host of birds.

Up to 50,000 lesser flamingos may feed here, and the uncommon great white pelican, avocet and chestnut-banded plover are breeding residents. The sparse, open bushland surrounding the lake is home to Grant's and Thomson's gazelle, as well as Rothchild's giraffe.

Lake Elmenteita Serena Camp

ACCOMMODATION — CLASS A: • **Lake Elmenteita Serena Camp** is located on the shores of Lake Elmenteita and is only 20 miles (30 km) from Lake Nakuru National Park. The camp offers 25 luxury tents with small verandahs.
• **Sleeping Warrior Lodge** has 10 bungalows, and is located in the Soysambu Conservancy with views of Lake Elmenteita and the Rift Valley • **Mbweha Camp,** situated on the 6400-acre (2560-hectare) private Congreve Conservancy, features 10 thatched cottages. Activities include morning and night game drives, bush walks and picnic lunches.

CLASS C: • **Lake Elementaita Lodge** has 33 rondavels. Nature walks and ox-wagon rides to the lakeshore are offered.

Lake Nakuru National Park

Lake Nakuru National Park encompasses the alkaline lake of the same name and is frequently visited by hundreds of thousands (sometimes more than a million) of greater and lesser flamingos, providing an amazing bird spectacle. More than 400 bird species in all have been recorded.

Located 100 miles (160 km) northwest of Nairobi on a fair road, the park covers 73-square-miles (188-km^2) — most of which is the lake itself.

Nakuru has been declared a **black rhino sanctuary** and has a fair number of these endangered animals. A small population of white rhino has been reintroduced from South Africa. Other wildlife includes lion, leopard, Rothschild's giraffe (introduced), waterbuck, reedbuck, hippo, baboon, pelican, and cormorant. The lake is an important stopover for thousands of migratory wading birds that head to and from Europe each year.

ACCOMMODATION — CLASS B: • **Sarova Lion Hill Lodge** is located in the park and has air-conditioned cottages (150 beds total) and a swimming pool.

CLASS C: • **Flamingo Hill Camp** offers 25 tents with canopy beds. Game drives, sundowners and massages (additional fee) are available for guests. • **Lake Nakuru Lodge** has rooms and cottages (120 beds) and a swimming pool. Horseback riding just outside the park and nature walks within the park are offered.

ACCOMMODATION NEAR LAKE NAKURU — CLASS A: • **Deloraine** is an old, colonial home set on a 5,000-acre (2,000-hectare) farm, and offers 6 rooms, tennis court and swimming pool. Horseback riding is available.

Lake Bogoria National Reserve

Lake Bogoria National Reserve, located north of Nakuru, has numerous hot springs and geysers along the lakeshore. Thousands of flamingos frequent this alkaline lake, as do greater kudu on the steep slopes of the lake's eastern and southern shores.

ACCOMMODATION — CLASS C: • **Lake Bogoria Lodge** has 45 rooms.

Lake Baringo

Lake Baringo, a freshwater lake located 20 miles (32 km) north of Lake Bogoria, is a haven for a colorful and mixed variety of bird life (over 400 species recorded). There is a sporting center for waterskiing, fishing and boating — beware of the hippos and crocodiles!

ACCOMMODATION — CLASS A/B: • **Samatian Island Lodge** is located on an island in the middle of Lake Baringo and offers 5 thatched chalets with lake views. The camp has a large pool and provides a variety of water-based activities like fishing, boating and bird watching.

CLASS B: • **Island Camp** is located in the center of Lake Baringo on Ol Kokwa Island. Take a walk and you may see a few waterbuck and meet the Njemps tribespeople who also inhabit the island. Boat safaris and water sports are available. • **Lake Baringo Club** has 52 rooms and a swimming pool. Boat and fishing trips are offered.

Lake Turkana

Sometimes referred to as the Jade Sea because of its deep green color, Lake Turkana is a huge inland lake surrounded by semi-desert near the Ethiopian border. It can be reached in 3 days of hard driving over rough terrain or a few hours by air charter from Nairobi.

Formerly named Lake Rudolf, this huge lake, which is over 175 miles (280 km) long and 10 to 30 miles (16 to 48 km) wide, is set in a lunar-like landscape of lava rocks, dried-up river beds and scattered oases.

The brown Omo River flows from the Ethiopian Highlands into the northern part of the lake, where the water is fairly fresh but becomes increasingly

Lake Turkana is over 175 miles long

saline farther south due to intense evaporation. The presence of puffer fish implies that the lake was at one time connected to the Mediterranean Sea by the River Nile.

One of the continent's largest populations of crocodile is found here. Because the bitter alkaline waters render their skins useless for commercial trade, crocodile are not hunted and grow to abnormally large sizes. Although the water is very tempting in such a hot, dry climate, swim only at your own risk!

Forty-seven species of fish live in the brackish waters, seven of which are found nowhere else. This is a very worthwhile location for keen birders, as aquatic birds abound. Expect to see pink-backed pelican, greater flamingo, spur-winged plover and African skimmer. Up to 100,000 little stint winter here on their annual migration from northern Europe. In the dry scrublands,

Members of the colorful Turkana tribe

birds that are absent or seldom seen elsewhere in Kenya include the swallow-tailed kite, fox kestrel, Abyssinian roller, star-spotted nightjar and Jackson's hornbill.

Fishing is a major attraction at Lake Turkana. Nile perch, the world's largest freshwater fish, can exceed 400 pounds (180 kg). Tigerfish, however, put up a more exciting fight. The El Molo tribe, the smallest tribe in Kenya (about 500 members), can be found near Loiyangalani.

Central Island National Park, a 2-square-mile (5-km^2) island containing three volcanic cones, is the most highly concentrated breeding ground of crocodile in Africa. Excursions to **South Island National Park**, also volcanic and full of crocodile, are available from the Oasis Lodge.

Easiest access to the park is by small aircraft. Four-wheel-drive vehicles are necessary. Loiyangalani is about 415 miles (665 km) and Ferguson's Gulf is about 500 miles (805 km) north of Nairobi.

ACCOMMODATION — CLASS C: • **Oasis Lodge**, located on the southeastern shore of the lake at Loiyangalani, has 24 basic cottages, 2 swimming pools, fishing boats and equipment for hire. Excursions to South Island National Park are available.

THE NORTH

Aberdare National Park

This 296-square-mile (767-km^2) park of luxuriant forest includes much of the Aberdare (renamed Nyandarua) Range of mountains.

The park can be divided by altitude into two sections. A high plateau of undulating moorlands with tussock grasses and giant heather lies between Ol Doinyo Lasatima (13,120 ft./3,999 m) and Kinangop (12,816 ft./3,906 m). This region affords excellent views of Mt. Kenya and the Rift Valley. Black rhino, lion, hyena, buffalo, elephant, eland, reedbuck, suni and bushpig may be seen.

On the eastern slopes below lie the forested hills and valleys of the **Salient**, home to black rhino, leopard, elephant, buffalo, waterbuck, bushbuck, giant forest hog, and black-and-white colobus monkey.

The park is also rich in bird life, including many species not easily seen elsewhere. The moorlands and montane forest are home to Jackson's and Moorland francolins, Aberdare cisticola and Cape eagle owl, as well as various eagles and buzzards. Several species of dazzling sunbirds, the ecological equivalents of the American hummingbirds, occur on the mountains and are frequently seen in the gardens of the various camps and lodges.

Night temperatures range from cool to freezing, as most of the park lies above 9,800 feet (2,988 m). A 4wd vehicle is required for travel within the park. The Ark and Treetops are about 110 miles (175 km) from Nairobi.

ACCOMMODATION — Guests of two tree hotels, **Treetops** and the **Ark**, are entertained by a variety of wildlife visiting their waterholes and salt licks.

CLASS B/C: • **The Ark**, a "tree hotel" overlooking a waterhole, has been refurbished and consists of small rooms, a glass-enclosed main viewing lounge, outside verandahs on each level (floodlit for all-night game viewing) and ground-level photo hide. The area near the Ark is a rhino reserve. Game drives in the Salient are offered. Guests

usually have lunch at the Aberdare Country Club before transferring to the Ark and are transferred back to the Aberdare Country Club by 9:00 the following morning to depart to their next safari destination. Children under seven are not allowed.
• **Treetops**, the first of the "tree hotels" (on stilts), is closed for 2012 and is being completely remodeled and refurbished. All rooms will have en suite facilities and enhanced views of the waterhole. Guests usually have a buffet lunch at the Outspan Hotel before transferring to Treetops and are returned to the Outspan by 9:00 the following morning to continue their safari. Children under seven are not allowed.

ACCOMMODATION NEAR THE PARK — CLASS B/C: • **Sangare Tented Camp** is located on a 6,500-acre (2,630-hectare) private ranch and has 12 tents. Game drives, bird-watching and horseback riding are offered.

Mt. Kenya National Park

Kenya's highest mountain and the second highest on the continent, Mt. Kenya lies just below the equator, yet it has several permanent glaciers.

Mt. Kenya's 2 highest peaks, **Batian** (17,058 ft./5,199 m) and **Nelion** (17,023 ft./5,188 m), are accessible by about 25 routes and should be attempted only by experienced rock climbers. **Point Lenana** (16,355 ft./4,985 m) is a non-technical climb that is accessible to hikers in good condition and is best climbed in the dry seasons. January to February is the best time to go, when views are the clearest and temperatures are warmer on top; July to October is also dry but colder. Vegetation changes are similar to those described for the Ruwenzori Mountains (see The Congo) and Mt. Kilimanjaro (see Tanzania).

Rock-climbing routes on the south side of the mountain are in best condition from late December to mid-March, while routes on the north side are best climbed from late June to mid-October. Ice routes are best attempted during the same periods but on opposite sides of the mountain. Howell Hut (17,023 ft./5,188 m), located on the summit of Nelion, sleeps 2.

Although rarely seen, climbers should be on the lookout for buffalo and elephant. Other wildlife that may be encountered includes leopard, duiker, bushbuck, giant forest hog, Syke's monkey and colobus monkey.

Because climbers can ascend to high altitudes very quickly, Mt. Kenya claims more than half of the world's deaths from pulmonary edema. My climbing partner had symptoms of pulmonary edema after reaching Austrian Hut (15,715 ft./4,790 m), and we had to abandon our attempt of Batian Peak and return to lower altitudes. Therefore, a slow, sensible approach is recommended.

The world's highest altitude scuba diving record was shattered at Two Tarn Lake (14,720 ft./4,488 m), one of more than 30 lakes on the mountain. In addition, climbers are occasionally seen ice skating on the Curling Pond below the Lewis Glacier.

The **Naro Moru Route** is a steep, quick route up the mountain, and is the one most commonly used. The climb to Point Lenana normally takes 2 or 3 days up and 1 or 2 down. The first night is often spent at Naro Moru Lodge or, better yet, at the Met — Meteorological Station — (10,000 ft./3,050 m) to assist altitude acclimatization.

The eastern wall of the Great Rift Valley

From Nairobi, drive 105 miles (168 km) to Naro Moru, then 10 miles (16 km) on a dirt road to the park gate (7,874 ft./2,400 m). You may be able to drive to the **Met Station**, unless the rains have washed out the road.

From the park gate, it is a 3.5 hour (6 mi./10 km) hike through conifer, hardwood and bamboo forests to the Met Station. Beware of buffalo en route. The Met Station has self-service bandas with mattresses, cooking facilities, long-drop toilets and water. To help you acclimatize, consider hiking for about an hour up to the tree line (10,500 ft./3,200 m) in the afternoon, returning well before dark.

From the Met Station, hike through the **Vertical Bog**, a series of muddy hills with patches of tussock grass. To keep your boots dry, you may want to wear tennis shoes through the bog. Cross the Naro Moru River and continue to **Teleki Valley**, where Mt. Kenya's peaks finally come into clear view (if it's not cloudy). After leaving the tree line, vegetation will change to tussock grass and heather moorlands with everlasting flowers, giant groundsel and giant lobelia that sometimes exceed 30 feet (9 m) in height.

From the Met Station, it takes about 6 hours to reach **Mackinder's Camp** (13,778 ft./4,200 m), which has a brick lodge and campsites. **American Camp** (14,173 ft./4,320 m), a camping spot one hour from Mackinder's Camp, is used by some campers who bring their own tents. Water is available from a nearby stream.

Austrian Hut (15,715 ft./4,790 m) is a 3- to 4-hour hike from Mackinder's Camp. Another hour is usually required to gain the additional 640 feet (195 m) in altitude needed to reach Point Lenana, only a half-mile away.

Austrian Hut is bitterly cold at night and is most often used by technical rock climbers attempting Nelion or Batian Peaks. Many climbers wishing to conquer Point Lenana begin from their camps in the **Teleki Valley** (Mackinder's) long before sunrise, reaching Point Lenana shortly after sunrise and return to Teleki Valley for the night. The view from Point Lenana is the clearest and one of the most magnificent panoramas I've seen from any mountain — and well worth the effort!

ACCOMMODATION NEAR THE PARK — CLASS A: • **The Fairmont Safari Club** (formerly the Mt. Kenya Safari Club) is located on the slopes of Mt. Kenya, outside the national park near Nanyuki, about 140 miles (224 km) from Nairobi. It was partially owned by actor William Holden and became one of the most famous "country clubs" in Africa. Facilities include swimming pool, Irish Pub, 9-hole golf course, and rooms, suites and luxury cottages with fireplaces (264 beds total). The Animal Orphanage contains a number of rare species, such as zebra duiker and bongo. Game drives are *not* conducted on the property.

CLASS B: • **Mountain Serena Lodge**, about 110 miles (177 km) north of Nairobi, is a "tree hotel" set in a forest reserve near the park overlooking a waterhole and salt lick, similar to Treetops and the Ark (see "Aberdare National Park"). All 42 double rooms face the waterhole. • **Lake Rutundu Cottages** is a rustic yet comfortable fishing lodge set on a small tarn (mountain lake) at 10,200 feet (3,100 m) altitude. Guests are accommodated in two cedar cabins with a hot tub. The lodge is self-catering, but most tour companies will provide full-service catering. The trout fishing is some of the finest in the world! Best access is by charter flight to Africa's highest airstrip, at 11,000 feet (3,355 m).

CLASS C: • **Naro Moru River Lodge**, located below the entrance to the park, has chalets and rustic, self-service cabins. Trout fishing is good.

LAIKIPIA REGION

Laikipia, located north of the Aberdares and northwest of Mt. Kenya, is a wild and sparsely populated region considered to be the gateway to Kenya's Northern frontier.

Much of Laikipia is composed of large, privately owned ranches that cover a wide range of landscapes from high plains to low forested valleys. On most ranches, cattle share the land with free-ranging wildlife. Some sanctuaries were created by local communities, which have combined small farms and grazing land into large group ranches — some of which are active in significant conservation programs. These community ranches are great places to learn about traditional cultures. A visit to one of these private ranches is highly recommended as a way to get off the beaten path.

Laikipia and Environs

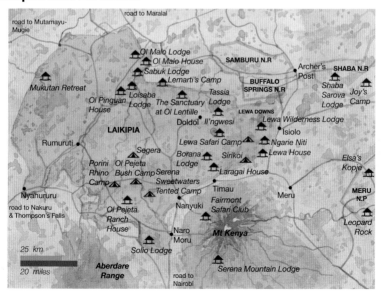

In this section I have included some properties that are technically not located in Laikipia, as they are in the same region and offer similar experiences.

Segera

The 50,000-acre (20,000-hectare) Segera is centrally located on the Laikipia Plateau with views of snow-capped Mt. Kenya. Segera is pivotal in the conservation strategy for the greater Laikipia and it forms a corridor between east and west that would otherwise prevent seasonal movement in the area's wildlife population. Flat topped acacia woodland and open grasslands host herds of elephant, buffalo, plains zebra, Grevy's zebra and reticulated giraffe as well as gazelle and predator species such as lion, leopard, spotted hyena and even the rare wild dog. Segera is also the flagship project of the Zeitz Foundation, which engages with surrounding communities in developing sustainable livelihood strategies as well as education and health facilities.

ACCOMMODATION — CLASS A: • **Segera**, located overlooking the seasonal Suguroi River with views toward Mt. Kenya, has seven luxury 2-story guest retreats (6 one-bedroom and 1 2-bedroom) with private decks and jacuzzis, as well as a swimming pool, art gallery, library and wellness center. Activities include day and night game drives and bush walks. Helicopter trips may be arranged.

Solio Ranch and Wildlife Sanctuary

This private 18,000-acre (7,200-hectare) rhino sanctuary has approximately 140 black rhino and white rhino. On my last visit I watched a black rhino with the largest horns I think I have ever seen!

Incredible rhino sightings at Solio Ranch

Other wildlife includes lion, leopard, cheetah, hippo, reticulated giraffe, oryx, and a variety of plain's wildlife and bird life. The reserve is situated near Aberdare National Reserve, a 3-hour drive from Nairobi or a 20-minute private air charter from Nanyuki.

ACCOMMODATION — CLASS A+:
• **Solio Lodge** is nestled in the valley between Mt. Kenya and the Aberdare Mountains. The lodge has six luxurious rooms with private lounge area and fireplace, as well as large bathrooms with a bath and shower. Activities include day and night game drives, horseback riding, guided walks and fishing trips.

Solio Lodge's main lounge area

Loisaba

Loisaba is a 65,000-acre (26,000-hectare) private wildlife conservancy located on the northern edge of the Laikipia Plateau. Day and night game drives, escorted walks, fly camping, horseback riding, helicopter rides and hot air balloon safaris are offered. I highly recommend spending a night in one of the star-bed camps. Set on an elevated platform, your bed is rolled out from under the roof and you spend the night looking up at thousands of stars.

ACCOMMODATION — CLASS A: • **Loisaba Lodge**, perched on the edge of a cliff overlooking Mt. Kenya in the distance, has 7 chalets with private verandahs, star-beds, a swimming pool and tennis court. There is also a separate two-bedroom Loisaba House and Cottage that provide private staff and guide for those guests.

CLASS B: **Loisaba Star Beds** offer an opportunity for a unique cultural experience and to sleep "under the stars". Two Star Bed camps, Kiboko and Koija, each have two raised platforms with 4-poster double beds that are rolled out from under a thatched roof at night for a magnificent star-gazing experience. This is a joint project run by the Maasai from the local community. I felt the cultural experience was one of the best I have ever had with Maasai, and highly recommend it!

Koija Group Ranch

A community owned group ranch, Koija is located on the Northern edge of the Laikipia region.

ACCOMMODATION — Class A/B:
• **Lemarti's Camp**, is a luxury camp located on the banks of the Ewaso Nyiru in Laikipia. Each of the 5 tents has bucket showers, long drop toilets. The tents and main lounge are built on raised platforms with private

Lemarti's Camp

verandahs. Lemarti's is a joint-venture with the local community. Activities include walking safaris, mountain biking, sundowners and local village visits.

The Sanctuary at Ol Lentille

Ol Lentille is located on 14,500-acres (6,000-hectare) in the extreme northern escarpment of the Laikipia plateau.

This property is an example of cutting edge conservation tourism and joint-partnership with the Maasai community and owners, John and Gill Elias. The concept is that you have your own villa and stay for several days to a week or more. During my latest visit with my family, we enjoyed camel rides, riding out on the quad bikes, climbing Ol Lentille Hill, riding horses along the animal trails and hanging out (plus playing soccer) at the local Maasai school.

ACCOMMODATION — CLASS A+: • **The Sanctuary at Ol Lentille** has 4 luxury houses each with their own living and dining rooms, kitchens and bedrooms. Guests enjoy the service of their own butler, valet, Maasai guide and 4wd vehicle. Activities include day and night game drives, escorted walks, Maasai village visits, horseback riding and quad biking.

Sabuk

This wilderness area, located in Northern Laikipia, has plains, valleys, acacia forest and wild olive forest. Kudu, zebra, eland, elephant, giraffe, gazelle, and, of course, the predators, leopard, lion and cheetah are found here.

ACCOMMODATION — CLASS A: • **Sabuk Lodge** has six beautiful open-fronted stone-and-thatch cottages and a family room with private verandahs overlooking the Ewaso Nyiro River Gorge below, and a swimming pool. Day and night game drives, escorted walks, and walking/camel safaris as well as fly camping with Laikipiak Maasai warriors as your guides are available.

Aerial view of Borana Ranch

Borana Ranch

Borana is a 32,000-acre (12,950-hectare) ranch located in the Laikipia area about 6,500 feet (2,000 m) above sea level. Dedicated to sharing its wealth with the surrounding communities, projects such as a mobile health clinic, ancillary program, scholarship program and job training have been set up. Elephant, lion, buffalo, greater kudu and klipspringer and a variety of antelope may be seen. The activities are day and night game drives,

Mt. Kenya provides a dramatic backdrop for Borana Ranch

escorted walks, horseback riding and camel riding.

ACCOMMODATION — CLASS A:
• **Borana Lodge** is set on the edge of the escarpment and has eight luxury chalets and a swimming pool.
• **Laragai House** is a private residence that can be rented to accommodate 12 guests with a staff to take care of any needs. There is a heated swimming pool and clay tennis courts.

Between game activities at Borana Ranch, enjoy the lodge's infinity pool

Ol Malo Ranch

Ol Malo Ranch, located along the Uaso Nyiro River on the edge of Kenya's North Eastern Province, covers 5,000-acres (2,000-hectares). Day and night game drives, escorted walks, overnight fly camping, horseback riding and camel treks are offered.

ACCOMMODATION — CLASS A: • **Ol Malo Lodge**, located on an escarpment with dramatic views of the bush below, has four beautiful chalets with large bathtubs and a swimming pool. • **Ol Malo House** is a private house that can be rented for up to 12 guests.

Ol Ari Nyiro Ranch

The ranch is a rhino sanctuary, and Mukutan Retreat is owned by Kuki Gallmann, author of *I Dreamed of Africa* (Penguin Books). The lodge is built on the edge of a gorge on the top of the Rift Valley wall, and overlooks Lakes Baringo and Bogoria.

The bush is quite thick, which makes game viewing a bit difficult. The real attraction is spending time with Kuki herself; however, she does not guarantee that she will be at the lodge. Only one group of guests is accommodated at a time.

ACCOMMODATION — CLASS A: • **Mukutan Retreat** has three stone-and-thatch cottages.

Ol Pejeta Ranch

This 110,000-acre (44,000-hectare) private game reserve of savannah and riverine forest has a variety of wildlife, including black rhino, reticulated giraffe, buffalo, Grevy's zebra, oryx, Coke's hartebeest and Thomson's gazelle. Walks, day and night game drives, boat rides and camel rides are offered. There is also a chimpanzee sanctuary/rehabilitation center. A 4wd vehicle may be necessary to reach the camp from the main road during the rains.

ACCOMMODATION — CLASS A/B: • **Serena Sweetwaters Tented Camp** has 39 large tents facing a waterhole, and a swimming pool. The camp is located 150 miles (240 km) north of Nairobi. • **Ol Pejeta Ranch House** has six luxury bedrooms and is available for private parties. • **Ol Pejeta Bush Camp**, located on the banks of the Ewaso Nyiro River, features 7 tents (including a family unit).

CLASS C: • **Porini Rhino Camp** offers six tents.

Lewa Wildlife Conservancy

Located between Mt. Kenya and Samburu National Reserve, the privately owned, scenic 45,000-acre (18,000-hectare) Lewa Wildlife Conservancy has a variety of wildlife, adapted to the semi-arid environment, including a large black and white rhino population (Lewa is a rhino sanctuary), elephant, lion, leopard, cheetah, reticulated giraffe, Grevy's zebra, buffalo, hartebeest, bushbuck, gerenuk, Gunther's dikdik and Somali ostrich. Lewa is one of the few places in Kenya where the rare, semi-aquatic sitatunga antelope is sometimes seen.

Horseback riding, hiking, camel riding, day and night game drives in open 4wd vehicles and a cultural visit to the nearby Il N'gwesi Maasai tribal community are offered.

ACCOMMODATION — CLASS A/B: • **Lewa Wilderness Lodge** accommodates up to 16 guests in 8 cottages with private verandahs and a swimming pool. • **Sirikoi** has 6 luxury tents and 2 private cottages. • **Lewa House** has 3 large cottages which accommodate up to 12 guests. There is a dining room, bar and swimming pool. • **Ngarie Niti** is a large two-bedroom stone house with two separate cottages. Horseback riding is available to guests.

CLASS B: • **Lewa Safari Camp** has 12 tents, set on elevated platforms and a swimming pool. In addition to game drives, horseback riding and camel treks are available.

Il'Ngwesi

The Il'Ngwesi Conservation Area is adjacent to Lewa Downs. Wildlife includes a variety of species that have adapted to dry conditions, including oryx, reticulated giraffe, Grevy's zebra, gerenuk and dikdik.

ACCOMMODATION — CLASS B: • **Il'Ngwesi** has 6 thatched bandas with views of the Mathews Range and a swimming pool. The lodge has a covered viewing platform and offers cultural visits and camel safaris.

Tassia

Tassia is owned and managed by the Lekurruki Community Conservation Group Ranch. Walks, Maasai cultural visits and game drives are the main activities.

Accommodation — CLASS B: • **Tassia Lodge** has 6 rooms and a plunge pool, and is booked only on an exclusive-use basis.

Nyahururu (Thompson's) Falls

Thompson's Falls was named after Joseph Thomson, a Scottish geologist commissioned by the Royal Geographical Society to explore East Africa, who was the first European to see the Falls. The Fall's are located at 7,745 feet (2,360 m) altitude about 115 miles (185 km) from Nairobi, above the Rift Valley between Nanyuki and Nakuru.

ACCOMMODATION — BASIC: • **Thompson's Falls Lodge** is a rustic country hotel.

Samburu National Reserve

This relatively small (64-sq.-mi./165-km^2) but excellent reserve of scrub desert, thornbush, riverine forest, and swamps along the Ewaso Nyiro River is situated north of Mt. Kenya and the Laikipia region.

Elephant and lion are plentiful, as are Beisa oryx, reticulated giraffe, gerenuk, the endangered Grevy's zebra and other species adapted to an arid environment. Leopard are often seen.

Bird life is strikingly colorful and abundant, with golden-breasted starling, white-headed mousebird, sulphur-breasted bushshrike and a variety of weaver birds. Larger birds include the blue-necked Somali ostrich, martial eagle, Egyptian vulture and vulturine guineafowl.

Samburu and Buffalo Springs

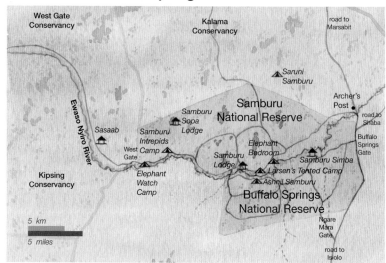

West Gate
Conservancy

Kalama
Conservancy

road to
Marsabit

*Saruni
Samburu*

Samburu
National Reserve

Archer's
Post

Ewaso Nyiro River

Sasaab

*Samburu
Sopa
Lodge*

road to
Shaba

Buffalo
Springs
Gate

*Samburu
Intrepids
Camp*

West
Gate

*Elephant
Bedroom*

*Samburu
Lodge*

Samburu Simba

Larsen's Tented Camp

*Elephant
Watch
Camp*

Ashnil Samburu

Kipsing
Conservancy

Buffalo Springs
National Reserve

5 km

Ngare
Mara
Gate

5 miles

road to
Isiolo

A game drive in Samburu National Reserve

Bush walks are a highlight during a stay at Sasaab

Samburu, probably the best-known reserve in northern Kenya, is located about 220 miles (355 km) north of Nairobi. The reserve received notoriety by Kamunyak, a lioness that adopted oryx calves. Under special arrangement, walking may be offered just outside the reserve.

ACCOMMODATION — CLASS A+:
• **Sasaab** is located on Samburu community land and was constructed using local materials with a Moroccan flair. The camp accommodates 18 guests in 9 individual rooms and private plunge pools. Activities include game drives, camel walks, cultural visits and bush walks. • **Saruni Samburu**, located on the Kalama Wildlife Conservancy, features 6 tented cottages with private decks, a large swimming pool and a fitness center. Game drives are offered in Samburu National Park and Buffalo Springs and guided walks, rock climbing and bush dinners are offered.

Sasaab's main lounge area

CLASS A: • **Elephant Watch Camp**, set on the northern bank of the Ewaso Nyiro River, has 5 spacious desert-style tents. The camp is run by Oria Douglas-Hamilton who has been working alongside her husband Iain in elephant conservation for 30 years. Activities include trailblazing elephant walks, tracking of elephant from the research camp, and visits to local Samburu projects. • **Larsen's Tented Camp**, situated on the banks of the Ewaso Nyiro River, has 20 recently refurbished spacious tents and a swimming pool.

CLASS A/B: • **Elephant Bedroom** is a small camp located on the banks of the Ewaso Nyiro River in Samburu National Reserve. The 12 tents are furnished in rustic African style. Activities include game drives and cultural visits. • **Samburu Intrepids Camp** has a swimming pool and 30 luxury tents, each with a private terrace. Game drives, astronomy, escorted walks, camel safaris and visits to neighboring Samburu communities are offered.

CLASS C: • **Samburu Sopa Lodge** has 60 cottage-style bedrooms with views overlooking the waterhole or swimming pool. Game drives, nature walks and visits to the local Samburu tribe are offered. • **Samburu Lodge**, located on the banks of the Ewaso Nyiro River, has rooms, cottages and tents (75 units) and a swimming pool. This lodge also baits for crocs and leopard.

Buffalo Springs National Reserve

Buffalo Springs is a 50-square-mile (131-km^2) reserve located south of the Ewaso Nyiro River, which serves as its northern border with Samburu National Reserve. The unusual doum palm, the only palm tree species whose trunk divides into branches, grows to over 60 feet (19 m) in height in this arid park. Wildlife is similar to what is seen in Samburu National Reserve.

ACCOMMODATION — CLASS B: • **Ashnil Samburu** is located in Buffalo Game Reserve and features 24 deluxe tents with views of the Ewaso Nyiro River, and a swimming pool. Activities include game drives, nature walks, bush breakfasts or dinners.

Shaba National Reserve

The turnoff to the entrance to Shaba National Reserve is located east of Samburu National Reserve, 2 miles (3 km) south of Archer's Post. The Ewaso Nyiro River forms the reserve's northwestern border and flows through the western part of the reserve.

This 92-square-mile (239-km^2) reserve is characterized by rocky hills and scattered thornbush. Volcanic rock is present in many areas. Mt. Shaba, a 5,320-foot- (1,622-m) high volcanic cone, which the park was named after, lies to the south of the reserve.

Shaba became famous for hosting the 2001 "Survivor" television series as well as the location of George Adamson's film *Walking with Lions*. A marsh in the center of the reserve is a good spot to look for wildlife.

Wildlife is less abundant and cannot be approached as closely as in the Samburu and Buffalo Springs National Reserves. However, there is much less traffic in this reserve.

ACCOMMODATION — CLASS A: • **Joy's Camp** offers 10 large Bedouin style tents and swimming pool. Situated at Joy Adamson's (of *Born Free* fame) original campsite, these luxury tents are set on raised platforms with great views of the surrounding hills. The camp overlooks a large natural spring and offers game drives, bush meals, massages, cultural visits and walks.

CLASS B/C: • **Shaba Sarova Lodge**, situated on the Ewaso Nyiro River, is a resort-style lodge with 85 rooms and a huge swimming pool.

Meru National Park

Meru is best known for Elsa, the lioness of Joy Adamson's *Born Free,* which was rehabituated to the wild. This 300 square-mile (870-km²) park is located 220 miles (355 km) east of Mt. Kenya, from Nairobi (via Nanayuki or Embu).

The swamps are host to most of Meru's 5,000 buffalo, sometimes seen in herds of more than 200, and a number of elephant. Oryx, eland, reticulated giraffe and Grevy's zebra are plentiful on the plains, where lion and leopard are also most likely to be seen. Lesser kudu, gerenuk and cheetah can be found along with hippo and crocs within the Tana River area. There is a good chance to see rhino as a number of them have been translocated to the park.

Over 400 species of birds have been recorded, including palm nut vulture, African finfoot, Pel's fishing owl, violet woodhoopoe, and the spectacular golden-breasted starling, which move about in small flocks.

Meru National Park *(top)*, Spectacular views from Elsa's Kopje *(bottom)*

ACCOMMODATION — CLASS A: • **Elsa's Kopje** is built on Mughwango Hill, the site of George Adamson's first camp in Meru. There are eight open-faced stone cottages and one three-tiered Honeymoon Suite, each with open verandahs overlooking the plains, and a swimming pool. There is also a family unit called the "Private House" with 2 bedrooms, living room, private garden and pool. Game drives are taken in open 4wd vehicles. Walks, massages, and bush meals are offered.

CLASS B: • **Leopard Rock** is a 60-bed lodge and swimming pool. Guests are offered game drives, walks and fishing.

Mathews Range

Located northwest of Samburu National Reserve, this remote wilderness area with lush green vegetation rises above the surrounding semi-desert lowlands. Elephant, lion, buffalo, greater kudu, waterbuck and other game may be seen, and over 100 bird species have been recorded. The real attraction of this area is its stark beauty, remoteness and opportunity for a cultural interaction with the Samburu. Camel safaris are operated in the area. Access to the region is by air charter or 4wd vehicles, which are necessary in this region.

ACCOMMODATION — CLASS A/B: • **Sarara Camp**, located on the Namunyak Conservancy, has 6 tents with private terraces and views of the Mathews Range. There is a rock swimming pool near the watering hole for guests' enjoyment. This is one of the best bird-watching areas in Kenya. • **Desert Rose**, perched on a cliff high up on the remote Mt. Nyiru, has 5 houses with open-air bathrooms. The camp offers remote cultural interactions, forest walks up Mt. Nyiru and exciting camel treks. Easiest access to the camp is by an approximately 100-minute charter flight from Nairobi.

CLASS B • **Kitich Camp** is situated on a private concession of more than 150,000-acres (60,000-hectares) in the southern part of the Mathews Range at an altitude of 4,300 feet (1,300 m). It has 6 tents overlooking the gorge of the Ngeng River. Walks in the forests with local Samburu tribesmen, game tracking, swimming in nearby natural rock pools and visits to Samburu villages are offered.

Gabra women in colorful textiles

Chalbi Desert

The Chalbi Desert is home to 30,000 nomadic Gabra tribesmen, who are still living an unaffected lifestyle in an untouched, harsh wilderness, east of the southern part of Lake Turkana. The Gabra water their goats, oblivious of the visitors, at oases and deep wells set on the edge of the Dida Galgalu plains.

A nomadic Gabra tribesman with his camels

The Kalacha Oasis is a natural spring attracting jackals, ostrich, sandgrouse and other wildlife.

THE COAST

Mombasa

Mombasa, the second largest city in Kenya with a population of around 1 million inhabitants, is situated on an island 307 miles (495 km) from Nairobi. It is a cultural blend of the Middle East, Asia and Africa.

The **Old Harbour** is haven for dhows carrying goods for trade between Arabia and the Indian subcontinent and Africa, especially from December to April. **Kilindini**, "place of deep water," is the modern harbor and largest port on the eastern coast of Africa.

Built by the Portuguese in 1593, **Fort Jesus** now serves as a museum. The **Old Town** is Muslim and Indian in flavor, with winding, narrow streets and alleys too narrow for cars. The tall, nineteenth century buildings with hand-carved doors and overhanging balconies, and small shops of Old Town and Fort Jesus are best seen on foot.

Mombasa is the best place in Kenya for excellent Swahili food. The Tamarind Restaurant, located on the water's edge overlooking Mombasa Island and Aquamarine Restaurant at Mtwapa Creek serve excellent seafood.

The city of Mombasa has no beaches, so most international visitors stay on the beautiful white sand beaches to the south or north of the island. Nyali Beach, Mombasa Beach, Kenyatta Beach and Shanzu Beach are just to the north of Mombasa, while Diani Beach is about 20 miles (32 km) to the south.

Most beach hotels on the coast offer a variety of water sports for their guests, including sailing, wind surfing, water skiing, kite-surfing, deep-sea fishing, scuba diving and snorkeling on beautiful coral reefs.

ACCOMMODATION JUST NORTH OF MOMBASA — DELUXE: • **Mombasa Serena Beach Hotel** has 166 remodeled air-conditioned rooms, a Maisha Spa, a swimming pool and tennis, scuba diving and other water sports.

FIRST CLASS: • **Sarova Whitesands Beach Resort** has 346 air-conditioned rooms, 3 swimming pools, tennis and water sports.

TOURIST CLASS: • **Nyali Beach Hotel** has 235 air-conditioned rooms with mini-bars, a small nightclub, 2 swimming pools, 2 tennis courts, shops and a very popular kite surfing center. • **Voyager Beach Resort**, located on Nyali Beach, has 236 spacious ship-themed rooms, 3 restaurants, 4 bars, 3 swimming pools, tennis courts, dive center, watersports and children's Adventurer Club • **Mombasa Beach Hotel** has 150 air-conditioned rooms, a swimming pool and tennis courts.

ACCOMMODATION JUST SOUTH OF MOMBASA — DELUXE: • **AfroChic**, located directly on the sands of Diani beach, is a stylish hotel offering 10 luxurious rooms and suites, all with private terraces. It is located five minutes from shopping, a gym, 18-hole golf course and beachside casino. A concierge can arrange excursions, scuba diving, fishing, horse riding, spa treatments and nightclub visits. The executive chef offers private dining in the suites, on the beach, by the pool or in the elegant dining room. • **Almanara Resort**, located directly on Diani Beach, features 6 fully serviced luxury villas. Each villa has a dedicated chef and maid guaranteeing an exclusive experience. There is a centrally located swimming pool, sunken bar, water sports center and massage services. • **Kinondo Kwetu**, built on a private stretch of Galu Beach, is an intimate all-inclusive, luxury resort. Each room and cottage has wooden verandahs, ceiling fans and garden or sea views. Activities include snorkeling, sailing, scuba diving, tennis and horseback riding. • **Alfajiri** consists of 3 of the finest villas on the Kenya coast. Cliff Villa accommodates 8 guests in

AfroChic is ideal for those seeking tranquility

4 bedrooms, dining room, kitchen, lounge, large verandah and private pool overlooking the Indian Ocean. The Beach Villa and Garden Villas share a pool and can accommodate 4 and 8 people respectively. • **Leopard Beach Resort & Spa**, located on 30 acres along Diani Beach, has 160 rooms and suites, 4 restaurants, bar, swimming pool, business center, floodlit tennis courts, scuba diving and water sports center and spa. • **Diani Reef Hotel** has 304 air-conditioned rooms, a swimming pool, dive school and tennis courts.

FIRST CLASS: • **Baobab Beach Resort & Spa** is located on Diani Beach and features 3 separate resorts, The Baobab, Maridadi and Kole Kole. Within the 80-acre garden there are 3 swimming pools and a variety of restaurants and bars. • **Diani House**, set on 12-acres (5-hectares) of forested garden along 820 feet (250 m) of beachfront, has 4 rooms with private verandahs (a single room has shared facilities). Snorkeling, fishing, windsurfing, visits to the local market and walks in the Kaya Kinondon and the Jadini Forest are available. • **Indian Ocean Beach Club**, set on a beautiful beach, has 100 air-conditioned rooms, a swimming pool, tennis, scuba diving and water sports.

South Of Mombasa

Shimba Hills National Park

This 74-square-mile (192-km^2) reserve of rolling hills and forests is located an hour's drive south of Mombasa and 10 miles (16 km) inland. At 1,500 feet (460 m) above sea level, this is a good place to cool off from the heat of the coast. From the park there are magnificent views of the Indian Ocean, and Mt. Kilimanjaro can even be seen on exceptionally clear days.

Wildlife includes elephant and buffalo and occasional sightings of genet, civet, serval, leopard and roan antelope. Sheldrick Falls is a great wildlife attraction.

The parks records 350 species of birds that include the Fischer's turaco, Narina trogon, red-tailed ant-thrush and East-coast akalat, African Fish eagle and the Palmnut vulture. This is the only park in Kenya with sable antelope.

Shimba Hills has tremendous biodiversity with many rare plants including endangered species of cycad and orchids.

ACCOMMODATION — CLASS B: • **Shimba Hills Lodge** is a three-story "tree hotel" with 80 beds, overlooking a floodlit waterhole.

ACCOMMODATION NEAR THE RESERVE — CLASS B: • **Sable Valley Tree Houses** is remotely located on the southern coast within the Sable Sanctuary. The 2 tree houses feature 4-poster beds that can be rolled out onto the deck for sleeping under the stars, a full-service butler and guided bush walks.

Kisite Mpunguti Marine Reserve

Kisite Mpunguti Marine Reserve is situated near the small fishing village of Shimoni ("place of the caves"), where slaves were held before shipment, near the Tanzanian border far from the mainstream of tourism. Delightful boat excursions to Wasini Island, an ancient Arab settlement across a channel from Shimoni, and snorkeling excursions are available.

The **Pemba Channel**, just off of Shimoni, is one of the world's finest marlin fishing grounds.

ACCOMMODATION — CLASS C: • **Pemba Channel Lodge** accommodates up to 14 guests in bungalows. Boats are available for hire for deep-sea fishing. The lodge is closed from April 1 to July 31. • **Shimoni Reef Lodge** has 10 basic thatched cottages, a swimming pool and a PADI Dive Center.

North Of Mombasa

Malindi-Watamu Marine National Reserve

Malindi-Watamu Marine National Reserve encompasses the area south of Malindi to south of Watamu, from 100 feet to 3 nautical miles (30 m to 5 km) offshore, and it has very good diving and snorkeling.

ACCOMMODATION IN WATAMU — FIRST CLASS: • **Hemingway's** is a 175-bed hotel, swimming pool and charter boats for deep-sea fishing and diving. • **Turtle Bay Beach Club** has 154 air-conditioned rooms.

Malindi

Malindi, located 75 miles (120 km) north of Mombasa (2 hours by car), has numerous beach hotels, nightclubs and shops. The **Vasco Da Gama** pillar symbolizes the Portuguese explorer's visit before journeying on to India. The International **Bill Fishing Competition** is held here every January. On our last visit we went out for a fun day of fishing and caught 10 wahoo weighing over 40 pounds each!

The **Sokoke Arabuko Forest** is Africa's northernmost brachystegia forest and Kenya's last remaining area of extensive lowland forest. The forest contains a variety of endemic flora and fauna, including Adder's duiker, bushy-tailed mongoose, golden-rumped elephant shrew, the Sokoke scops owl, the Sokoke pipit and Clarke's weaver.

The **Gedi Ruins**, last inhabited in the thirteenth century by about 2,500 people, is a mystery in that there are no Arabic or Swahili records of its existence.

DELUXE: • **Diamonds Dream of Africa**, located near the Malindi town center on a stretch of white sand beach, features 35 suites, a free-form swimming pool, full service spa and Mediterranean inspired restaurant. • **Diamonds Malindi Beach** is an intimate retreat with 23 garden or seaview rooms, 2 swimming pools, a restaurant and 2 bars. Guests are invited to use the spa at neighboring Diamonds Dream of Africa resort.

TOURIST CLASS: • **Driftwood Beach Club** has 27 cottages (some air-conditioned) and a swimming pool.

Lamu

Swahili culture has changed little in the past few hundred years on the island of Lamu. There are only a few motorized vehicles on the island that are owned by government officials, but plenty of donkey carts provide substitutes. Narrow, winding streets and a maze of alleyways add to the timeless atmosphere of this cultural heritage site. Many travelers have compared Lamu to a mini-Katmandu.

The **Lamu Museum** has exhibits of Swahili craftwork. Of the more than 30 mosques on Lamu, only a few are open to visitors. The best beaches are at **Shela**, a 45-minute walk or short boat ride from the town of Lamu to the Peponi Beach Hotel. **Matondoni** is a fishing village where dhows, fishing nets and traps are made. Numerous attractions are also found on nearby islands.

The best way to reach the island is to fly. Driving is not recommended because the road from Malindi is very rough and may be impassable in the rainy season.

ACCOMMODATION — DELUXE: • **Kizingoni Beach House**, built to take advantage of the sunsets and sea breezes, is a private villa with 4 bedrooms each with private balconies. Ideal for outdoor living, there is a large swimming pool, dining pavilion and shaded living room. • **Kipungani Explorer Lamu**, set on the southern end of Lamu Island, is a perfect "Robinson Crusoe hideaway" and has 13 beach bandas, hanging moon-beds, butler service and a swimming pool. Water-skiing, sailing, deep-sea fishing and snorkeling are offered.

FIRST CLASS: • **Peponi Beach Hotel**, a pleasant beach resort, is located about 1 mile (2 km) from the town of Lamu. All 24 rooms are fan-cooled.

TOURIST CLASS: • **Lamu Palace Hotel** has air-conditioned rooms (50 beds) and is located 200 yards (200 m) from the jetty. • **Petley's Inn** has been a landmark since the nineteenth century. The hotel has a rustic atmosphere. • **Kizingo Hotel** has 6 beach front bandas and offers shaded balconies and ocean views. Beyond the spectacular beach, guests can fish, snorkel and even swim with wild dolphins.

ACCOMMODATION IN THE REGION OF LAMU — DELUXE: • **Manda Bay** is located on the north western tip of **Manda Island** and has 16 cottages, 11 are set right on the seafront and 5 are slightly behind on higher ground. All the cottages have private verandahs overlooking the Indian Ocean. Deep-sea fishing, windsurfing, sailing, snorkeling, water skiing and several other options are available. The property also features dhow excursions, spa and massage, cultural visits and a swimming pool. • **The Majlis** is a boutique hotel decorated with Arab-African furnishings and features 25 rooms and suites divided into 3 villas. Each villa has a private verandah opening out onto the beach. Guests enjoy the ocean-facing pool and bar, open-air restaurants and a full-service excursion desk which can arrange snorkeling, scuba diving and deep sea fishing (additional fees apply).

The island paradise of Manda Bay

Uganda

Uganda

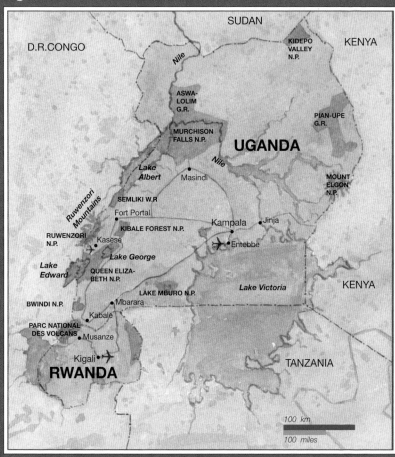

Straddling the equator, Uganda is a verdant country once referred to as the "Pearl of the British Empire in East Africa." Most of Uganda is an upland plateau averaging 3,000 feet (1,000m) above sea level. With the enormous Lake Victoria occupying the southeastern part of the country, and numerous other Rift Valley lakes as well as the mighty Nile River, one-sixth of Uganda is fresh water. Approximately the size of Oregon (or Great Britain), Uganda covers 93,000-square-miles (240,000-km²). Almost all of the 27 million population are either subsistence farmers or employed in agriculture. Kampala is the capital city with over 1.2 million inhabitants. KiSwahili and English are the main languages. Currency is the Ugandan Shilling.

Uganda
Country Highlights

- A safari to Uganda is like visiting your own Garden of Eden. The parks have few tourists, and hotels and lodges give you the personal attention rarely found in this day of international travel.

- Bwindi Impenetrable Forest is known the world over for gorilla trekking. A visit to this park will reveal a unique African adventure with one of the most fascinating primates!

- Trek into Kibale Forest National Park for the ultimate chimpanzee experience as well as the opportunity to see black-and-white colobus monkey, red colobus, gray-cheeked mangabey and red-tailed monkey.

- Experience Queen Elizabeth National Park with a varied wildlife population, extraordinary boat cruise on the Kazinga Channel and an astonishing 547 bird species — one of the highest figures for any single protected area in the world.

- Visit Murchison Falls and game view by boat on the Victoria Nile, view the dramatic waterfall, lush foliage and the largest concentration of crocodiles on the continent.

When's the Best Time to Go for Game Viewing

■ Excellent ■ Good □ Fair ■ Poor ■ Closed

Country	Park/Reserve	JAN	FEB	MAR	APR	MAY	JUN	JUL	AUG	SEP	OCT	NOV	DEC
Uganda	Bwindi												
	Queen Elizabeth												
	Kibale												
	Murchison												

Best Safari Experience
Nile Safari Lodge (Murchison Falls), Ndali Lodge (Kibale), Clouds Mountain Gorilla Lodge, Gorilla Forest Camp (Bwindi), Mihingo Lodge (Lake Mburo)

UGANDA

Uganda, once the "Pearl of the British Empire in East Africa," is one of the most beautiful countries on the continent. One-sixth of its area is covered by water. Along its western boundary lie the Ruwenzori Mountains, Africa's highest mountain range, and Ptolemy's fabled "Mountains of the Moon." The

Ugandans claim the source of the Nile is at Jinja, where it leaves Lake Victoria.

The climate in Uganda is similar to Kenya except that Uganda is wetter. The driest times of the year are December to February and June to July, and the wettest is from mid-March to mid-May, with lighter rains October to November.

English is spoken as widely here as in Kenya or Tanzania. The main religions are Christianity and Islam.

In the eighteenth century, the Kingdom of Buganda became the most powerful in the region. Together with three other kingdoms, and several native communities, it was made a British Protectorate in 1893 and achieved independence in 1962.

Over 90% of the population is employed in agriculture, with coffee as the major export.

🐾 WILDLIFE AND WILDLIFE AREAS

Uganda's tremendous diversity of wildlife is due to its situation at the junction of the East African savannahs, the West African rainforests and the semiarid Sahelian zone of North Africa. There are 10 national parks and 15 wildlife reserves, but most are smaller than those in Tanzania or Kenya. Clever planning

of the parks and reserves has, however, resulted in most of the different habitats being conserved, enabling visitors to enjoy a wide variety of wildlife and nature experiences.

Primates, including gorillas, large numbers of chimpanzees and an array of smaller monkeys are a major attraction. This is the best single country to visit for both chimpanzee (Kibale Forest National Park) and gorilla trekking (Bwindi

Impenetrable Forest National Park). The endemic Uganda kob (a beautiful antelope), as well as lion, leopard, elephant and giraffe inhabit the savannahs while the great wetlands are home to large numbers of hippo and crocodile.

Gorillas remain the greatest international attraction, and there is nothing comparable to the thrill of a close encounter with these magnificent, peaceful apes, in their native environment. Gorilla trekking is so popular that I suggest you book your safari 6 months to a year or so in advance if possible, as permits are limited.

Relative to its size, Uganda is the richest country for birds in Africa, with over 1,000 species in an area the size of Great Britain. A wealth of hornbills, turacos, barbets, sunbirds, kingfishers, weavers and storks are present, as well as the bizarre and much sought-after shoebill.

A real advantage of parks in Uganda is that they are not anywhere near as crowded as those in Kenya or Tanzania. You meet very few other vehicles on game drives — in some cases, you even have the parks almost to yourself!

NORTHERN AND WESTERN

Kidepo Valley National Park
Isolated from the Ugandan mainstream by the harsh plains to the north of Mount Elgon, Kidepo Valley National Park is Uganda's second largest national park. Kidepo is one of Africa's last great wilderness areas, a tract of rugged savannah dominated by Mt. Morungole and transected by the Kidepo and Narus Rivers. Perennial running water in the Narus River makes Kidepo an oasis in this semidesert.

While the game viewing is excellent, it is the sense of supreme isolation that distinguishes this rare slice of wild Africa — as yet undiscovered by the mass safari market. Wildlife includes elephant, giraffe, buffalo, lion, cheetah, ostrich, Jackson's hartebeest, waterbuck, zebra, Guenther's dikdik, kudu, lesser kudu, eland, aardwolf, bat-eared fox and Patas monkeys. Occasionally African wild dogs are spotted near Kanantarok Hot Springs close to the border of Sudan.

Uganda is a top bird-watching destination *(left)*, a canopied bed at Apoka Lodge *(right)*

Game viewing continues from your balcony at Apoka Lodge

Bird watchers will relish their time spent in Kidepo as it boasts 475 species, some not found anywhere else in Uganda. Birds such as the black-breasted barbet, Karamoja apalis and the rose-ringed parakeet are just some of the rarer birds to see (and hear).

The park can be explored by traditional vehicle game drives as well as tracking game on foot. You may also take a cultural excursion to nearby villages. Ask your lodge to pack a picnic lunch as there are some spectacular spots to enjoy the scenery and solitude.

Getting to Kidepo can take up to 2 days driving from Entebbe on extremely rough roads. The recommended mode of transportation is private charter flight from Entebbe.

ACCOMMODATION — CLASS A: • **Apoka Lodge** has 10 roomy cottages, built of wood, canvas and thatch, a swimming pool carved out of rock, and private balconies. The lodge has a waterhole and fantastic views down the Narus Valley. Game drives in 4wd vehicles and escorted walks are offered.

Murchison (Kabalega) Falls National Park

This park is named after the famous falls where the Victoria Nile rushes with tremendous force through a narrow, 20-foot-wide (6-m) rock gorge to crash onto the rocks 150 feet (45 m) below. Fish dazed by this fall are easy prey to one of the largest concentrations of crocodile on the continent.

Located in northwestern Uganda, this park covers approximately 1,500-square-miles (3,885-km^2) of predominantly grassy plains and savannah woodlands, with altitudes ranging from 1,650 to 4,240 feet (500 to 1,292 m). Riverine forest with giant tamarind trees lines some parts of the Victoria Nile, which traverses the park from east to west.

In addition to Murchison Falls, a highlight of the park is the three-hour, 7-mile (11 km) boat trip from the Paraa Safari Lodge to the foot of the falls. Numerous crocodile and hippo inhabit the river and along its banks, as well as buffalo, elephant, and prolific bird life (over 400 species) including red-throated bee-eater, piapiac, silverbird and black-headed gonolek.

Another great excursion is a 6-hour launch trip from the Paraa Safari Lodge to the delta where the Victoria Nile flows into Lake Albert. Shoebills (whale-headed storks) are often spotted, and are a popular feature of this trip.

Murchison Falls National Park

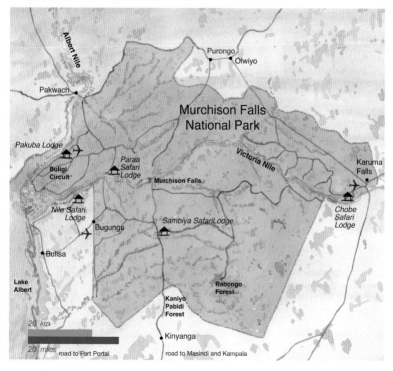

The intensity of the Nile River at Murchison Falls

The park is also home to Rothchild's giraffe, Defassa waterbuck, oribi, hartebeest, Uganda kob and Patas monkey. Record Nile perch over 200 pounds (90 kg) have been caught in the Nile. Some of the best fishing is just below Karuma Falls and Murchison Falls.

The easiest time to spot animals is January to February and the short dry season from June to July. Game viewing August to December is also good. From March to May, the landscape is more attractive, but the wildlife is less concentrated.

Park headquarters and the most extensive road system for game viewing are near the Paraa Lodge. The Buligi Circuit is located near the confluence of the Albert Nile and Victoria Nile. Waterfowl are especially abundant, along with a variety of game.

You may want to arrange a visit to the nearby **Kaniyo Pabidi Forest** for a trek to visit the habituated, resident chimpanzee family.

ACCOMMODATION — CLASS A/B: • **Paraa Safari Lodge,** located on the north side of the river, has 54 rooms with views of the Nile, equipped with ceiling fans and private verandahs. Lodge amenities include a swimming pool with a swim-up bar, souvenir shop, conference room, Captain's Table Restaurant and Explorer's Bar. • **Chobe Safari Lodge,** located on the eastern side of the park on the Nile River, features 36 guest rooms. The dining room, lounge and pool all overlook the river with sounds of the rapids.

CLASS B: • **Nile Safari Lodge** is nestled on the southern bank of the Nile River and offers exclusive accommodation in 5 wooden chalets and 5 luxury tents, each with private verandahs and views of the Nile River. The lodge has a swimming pool, lounge and restaurant. Boat trips to the base of Murchison Falls, game drives and nature walks are offered.

CLASS C: • **Sambiya River Lodge** is located in the southern section of the park on the Sambiya River and 23 miles (20 km) from the falls (a 25 minute drive). The lodge offers 25 cottages with private verandahs, a restaurant, swimming pool and a telescope.

Semliki Game Reserve

Formerly called the *Toro Game Reserve,* this 85-square-mile (220-km^2) reserve of grassland, savannah, forest and wetland habitats is bordered by Lake Albert to the north and the Ruwenzori Mountains to the southwest.

The tropical lowland forest conserved in this park is ecologically linked to the Congo basin and provides a very different Ugandan wildlife experience. The giant hardwood trees and tangled undergrowth of the forest are home to many fascinating mammals such as Africa's smallest ungulate—the tiny pygmy antelope, which is hardly bigger than a hare. Chimpanzees in the area are becoming habituated and sightings are now quite good. Other primates including the gray-cheeked mangabey, red-tailed monkey and De Brazza's monkey may also be seen.

Other wildlife includes elephant, the Uganda Kob (the most common large mammal) and warthog as well as infrequently seen buffalo, leopard, lion, hyena, bushbuck, waterbuck, reedbuck, duiker and forest hog.

The reserve is an absolute paradise for birdwatchers, with 35 of the 385 species occurring nowhere else in East Africa. Specials such as the chestnut owlet, white-crested hornbill, African piculet and fiery-breasted bushshrike attract enthusiastic observers from far and wide.

The park has an airstrip and is about a 6-hour drive from Kampala,

Game viewing in Semliki Game Reserve

A shoebill stork is also known as a whale-headed stork

a 3-hour drive from Queen Elizabeth National Park and a 2-hour drive from Kibale Forest National Park.

ACCOMMODATION — CLASS B: • **Semliki Safari Lodge** features 8 tents and a swimming pool. Activities include night game drives, chimpanzee tracking, boat trips on Lake Albert, fishing for Nile perch, tilapia and tiger fish, and visits to Nkusi Waterfalls.

Ruwenzori Mountains National Park

The third highest mountains in Africa (after Mts. Kilimanjaro and Kenya), the "Mountains of the Moon" are, in fact, the highest mountain chain on the continent. They rise 13,000 feet (3,963 m) above the western arm of the Rift Valley to 16,762 feet (5,109 m) above sea level, just north of the equator, and are usually covered in mist.

The mountain chain is approximately 60 miles (100 km) long and 30 miles (50 km) wide, with Margherita as the highest peak. A number of permanent glaciers and peaks challenge mountaineers. However, mountaineering skills are not needed for the hike itself — only for climbing the glaciers or peaks.

Unlike Mt. Kilimanjaro and many other mountains in east and central Africa, the Ruwenzoris are not volcanic in origin. The range forms part of the border with the D.R. Congo and can be climbed from either the D.R. Congo or Ugandan side. The trail on the D.R. Congo side of the Ruwenzoris is much steeper than the Ugandan side.

The Afro-alpine vegetation zones and Afro-alpine heathlands you pass through on the Ruwenzoris are the most amazing I have seen in the world. The nectar-filled flowers of massive lobelias and giant senecios attract jewel-like sunbirds while "Spanish moss" and ephiphytic orchids adorn gnarled tree branches. Several plants that are commonly small in other parts of the world grow to gigantic proportions in the Ruwenzoris.

Hikers in good condition can enjoy walking a strenuous circuit for 6 or 7 days that rises to over 13,000 feet (3,963 m) in altitude through some of the most amazing vegetation in the world. Walking routes trace the lower slopes and it is a region of great biological beauty. Successive zones of distinct vegetation ring the 6 major massifs of the Ruwenzori with woodland, evergreen forest, bamboo, boggy heathland and Afro-alpine moorland in a sequence up the slopes. Large mammals are few, but the Ruwenzori colobus, giant forest hog and yellow-backed duiker may be encountered. The exquisite Ruwenzori turaco is fairly common, while the Ruwenzori batis and bamboo warbler are found nowhere else in Uganda.

Ruwenzori Mountains – The "Mountains of the Moon"

The main trailhead begins near Ibanda. Drive 6 miles (10 km) north from Kasese on the Fort Portal road, then turn left (west) for 8 miles (13 km). The mountain huts take up to 15 people. It is best to use a tour operator for the climb, otherwise, bring all your own gear as all the equipment you need may not be available for hire.

The **Central Circuit** is the most popular route on the mountain. On Day 1, a dirt road from Ibanda runs 3 miles (5 km) to the Park Headquarters at Nyakalengija (5,400 ft./1,646 m). There is a 5-hour hike past village huts, into the park and onward to Nyabitaba Hut (8,700 ft./2,652 m). You may be lucky enough to see black-and-white colobus monkeys or the Ruwenzori turaco. Many climbers prefer staying in a nearby rock shelter instead of the hut. Water and firewood are not available near the hut. Tent spaces are located nearby.

Day 2 is the most grueling of the circuit. Climbers hike 5 or 6 hours past a bamboo forest to Nyamileju Hut (10,900 ft./3,322 m) and a nearby rock shelter. Time and energy permitting, you may continue hiking through a bog in the giant heather, lobelia and groundsel zone for about an hour to John Mate Hut (11,200 ft./3,414 m).

On Day 3, hikers must traverse a muddy bog to Bigo Hut (11,300 ft./3,444 m). A rest is recommended before continuing through Upper Bigo Bog to Bujuku Lake, where there are views of Mt. Baker, Mt. Stanley and Mt. Speke, to Bujuku Hut (13,000 ft./3,962 m). From John Mate Hut to Bujuku Hut should take about 5 to 6 hours. Technical climbers attempting Mt. Speke often use this hut as a base.

On Day 4, the hike crosses Groundsel Gully toward Scott Elliot Pass to Elena Hut (14,700 ft./ 4,372 m). Elena is the base camp for climbing Margherita Peak, which requires 2 more days, previous permission from National Parks and the proper equipment (crampons, ice axe, ropes, etc.). As you hike over Scott Elliot Pass you enter the alpine zone of limited vegetation, but with fabulous views of Margherita Peak, Mt. Baker, Elena and Savoia Glaciers. From there, the trail continues to Lake Kitandara and Kitandara Hut (13,200 ft./4,023 m) and then goes on to Kabamba Rock Shelter (12,400 ft./3,779 m). The hike from Bujuku Hut takes about 5 hours.

On Day 5, hike to Freshfield Pass and then descend past the rock shelters at Bujongolo and Kabamba (an optional overnight stop) onward to Guy Yeoman Hut (10,700 ft./3,261 m). The hike to Guy Yeoman Hut takes 6 to 7 hours.

On Day 6, there is a 5-hour hike down to Nyabitaba Hut, with an optional overnight stop, or you may choose to finish the journey with a 3-hour hike to the park gate.

The Ruwenzori Mountains have 2 rainy seasons, from March to May and September to mid-December. The best time to climb is mid-December through February and June through August during the dry season. However, no matter when you climb, you will still get wet. Wood fires are prohibited, so be prepared to use paraffin or gas stoves.

ACCOMMODATION NEAR THE RESERVE — See "Kasese" on pages 477–478.

Kibale Forest National Park

This 296-square-mile (766-km²) park consists of lowland tropical rain forest, tropical deciduous forest, marshes, grasslands and crater lakes, and is the best place in Uganda for chimpanzee trekking. It is considered by some experts to have the largest and most diverse population of primates in the world.

Kibale Forest National Park

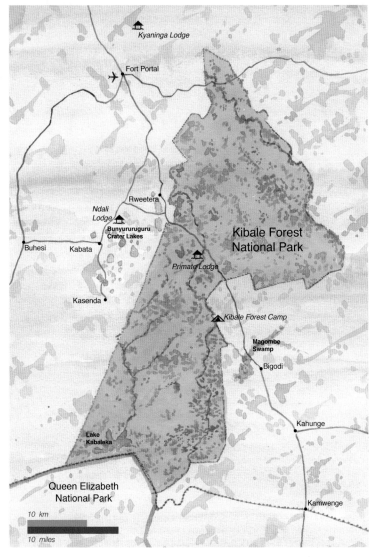

Chimps are the highlight during your visit to Kibale Forest

In addition to escorted walks, the park offers a Chimpanzee Experience. The program starts at 6:00 a.m., from the time the chimpanzees leave their nests until slightly before dark, which allows guests to observe the chimps de-nesting and nesting as well as their other daily activities. The Chimpanzee Experience needs to be booked well in advance.

Kibale is home to 12 other species of primates including black-and-white colobus monkey, red colobus, gray-cheeked mangabey and red-tailed monkey. Some of the other wildlife species include blue duiker, Harvey's red duiker, bushbuck, bushpig and over 100 species of butterflies.

Over 300 species of birds have been recorded, and experienced local guides — with their knowledge of calls and behavior — are invaluable in this challenging bird watching environment. Green-breasted pitta, black bee-eater, white-headed woodhoopoe and the tiny chestnut wattle-eye are among the possible delights for keen observers.

The park is located northeast of Queen Elizabeth National Park, 22 miles (35 km) south of Fort Portal.

ACCOMMODATION — CLASS A/B: • **Ndali Lodge** is perched on a hillside above Nyinambunga Crater Lake, in the heart of Uganda's crater lake region (a 45-minute drive from the park). The lodge has 8 cottages with private verandahs, lounge, dining room, and swimming pool. Boating, nature walks and cultural farm walks are offered. • **Kyaninga Lodge** is set against the backdrop of Lake Kyaninga, near Kibale Forest. There are 8 cottages built on platforms with an indoor sitting area and private deck. The main lodge features a double fireplace, dining room and large swimming pool.

CLASS B: • **Primate Lodge**, located adjacent to Park Headquarters, has 7 large tents that are privately located along a pathway in the forest. The main building houses the reception, bar and dining room.

CLASS C: • **Kibale Forest Camp** is a permanently based mobile camp with 7 tents with bush shower (hot water) and long-drop toilet, located 2 miles (3 km) from the park.

Queen Elizabeth National Park

A thatched cottage at Ndali Lodge

This is the best park in Uganda for big game (other than primates), and contains about 770-square-miles (1,995-km²) of tremendous scenic variety, including volcanic craters and crater lakes, grassy plains, swamps, rivers, lakes and tropical forest. The snowcapped Ruwenzori Mountains lie to the north and are not part of the park itself. The park has been extended to give migratory species more protection as they move to and from Kibale Forest.

A 2-hour launch trip on the **Kazinga Channel**, which joins Lakes Edward (Lake Rwitanzige) and George, affords excellent opportunities for viewing hippo and a great variety of waterfowl at close range. Truly marvelous photographic opportunities present themselves from the boat. The launch trip departs from just below Mweya Lodge and should not be missed!

The Katwe-Kikorongo area in the north of the park has several saline lakes. The **Chambura Gorge**, located on the northeast boundary of the park, has a population of chimpanzees. Trekkers descend from the savannah into a tropical rain forest within the gorge where turacos, hornbills and flycatchers abound.

South of the Kazinga Channel, the **Maramagambo Forest** is home for chimpanzees, black-and-white colobus monkeys, red colobus monkeys, blue monkeys, red-tailed monkeys and baboons. The **Ishasha** region in the south of the park is famous for its tree-climbing lions.

Elephant are present, as well as buffalo, leopard, sitatunga, giant forest hog, Uganda kob, topi and, Defassa waterbuck, and crocodile in the Kazinga Channel. Interestingly enough, there are no giraffe, zebra, impala or rhino.

Queen Elizabeth National Park

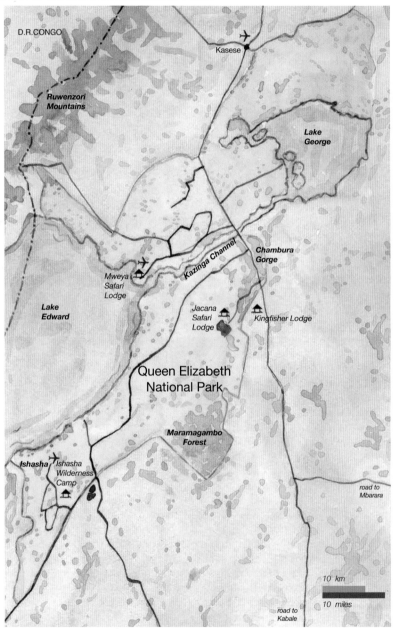

An astonishing total of 547 bird species have been recorded here, one of the highest figures for any single protected area in the world. Twelve species of kingfisher, including the giant (the world's largest) and the dwarf (the world's smallest) may be seen on waterways, in forest, and in the open savannah. There are 17 varieties of nectar-feeding sunbirds, flocks of red-throated bee-eaters, gangs of crow-like piapiacs, families of spectacular Ross's turacos in fruiting trees, and

Queen Elizabeth National Park has become a prime game destination

Tree-climbing lions are spotted in QENP *(top)*, Red throated bee-eaters *(middle, left)*, Woodland king fisher *(middle, right)*, The view from Mweya Lodge and Lake Edward *(bottom)*

the rare, prehistoric-looking shoe-bill, which may be sighted along the shores of Lake George and in the Ishasha region.

From Kampala, the park is 260 miles (420 km) via Mbarara and 285 miles (460 km) via Fort Portal. A landing strip is located at Mweya for light aircraft; larger planes can land at Kasese.

ACCOMMODATION — CLASS A & A/B:
• **Mweya Safari Lodge**, scenically situated on a high bluff overlooking the Kazinga Channel and Lake Edward, has 32 standard fan-cooled rooms (Class A/B), 12 deluxe rooms and 2 suites with air-conditioning (Class A) with private verandahs, a swimming pool, Kazinga Restaurant and Tembo Safari Bar, and a souvenir shop.

CLASS A/B: • **Jacana Safari Lodge**, located on the edge of the Maramagambo Forest on the banks of Lake Nyamusingire, has 7 luxury wooden chalets and 1 family cottage, swimming pool, restaurant, 2 bars and the Captain's Table (a pontoon boat serving as a floating restaurant). Game drives, boating and nature walks are offered. The lodge is located on the butterfly migration route. • **Kyambura Game Lodge**, built using local materials and community workmanship, features 7 grass-thatched cottages

Mweya Lodge *(top)*, Kazinga Channel boat trip *(bottom)*

each with private balconies. The swimming pool, restaurant, lounge and bar overlook the park. • **Kyambura Gorge Lodge**, a new lodge built on the escarpment overlooking the park, has 4 spacious bandas with private balconies. Game drives, boating and nature walks are offered.

CLASS B: • **Ishasha Wilderness Camp**, a permanent tented camp located on the banks of the Ntungwe River in the southern sector of the park, features 10 tents. The central lounge area has a dining room and bar under canvas and evening fire pit next to the river.

Kasese

Kasese is the largest town situated near Queen Elizabeth National Park and Ruwenzori National Park, and it is a good place to purchase supplies. Near here you have an opportunity to take photos of yourself crossing the Equator.

ACCOMMODATION — TOURIST CLASS: • **Margherita Hotel** has 36 simple rooms and suites, and is located 2 miles (3 km) out of town.

SOUTHERN

Bwindi Impenetrable Forest National Park

The major attraction of the 127-square-mile (330-km²) Bwindi Impenetrable Forest is the population of over 300 gorillas known to inhabit the park, that are in fact a different sub-species (yet to be named) from the mountain gorillas of Rwanda.

Bwindi is a forest of enormous hardwood trees, giant ferns, tangled undergrowth and hanging vines — the quintessential equatorial jungle. The size and altitudinal range of montane and lowland forests at Bwindi support more species of trees, ferns, birds and butterflies than any other forest in East Africa. It is also the only one inhabited by both chimpanzees and gorillas.

As of this writing, there are 5 groups that may be visited by up to 8 tourists per day that are accessed by accommodations in Buhoma in the northern part of the park, and 4 from the southern (Kisoro) side of the park. And as of this writing, the group makeups were as follows — but keep in mind that changes occur on a regular basis.

Northern Section of Bwindi — Buhoma Area:
Mubare Group (Group M) – 5 members, including 1 silverback.
Rushegura Group (Group R) – 21 members, including 1 silverback.
Habinyanja Group (Group H) – 17 members, including 1 silverback.

Northern Section of Bwindi — Ruhija Area (a 1-hour drive from Buhoma):
Bitukura Group (Group B) has about 13 members, including 1 silverback and 3 sub-silverbacks.
Oruzogo Group (Group O) has about 23 members, including 1 silverback and 1 sub-silverback.

Southern Section of Bwindi (near Kisoro town):
Nkuringo Group (Group Nku) has about 17 members, including 1 silverback and 3 sub-silverbacks.
Nshongi Group (Group Nhs) has about 21 members, including 1 silverback and 2 sub-silverbacks.
Mishaya Group (Group Mis) has about 7 members, including 1 silverback
Kahungye (Group K) has about 24 members, including 1 silverback and 2 sub-silverbacks.

Gorillas form themselves into fairly stable groups of 3 to 40. They are active by day and sleep in nests at night.

Bwindi Impenetrable Forest National Park

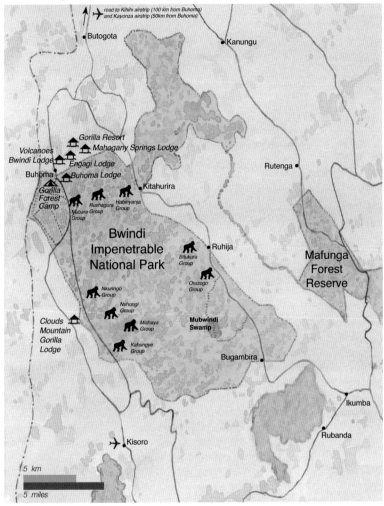

Gorillas eat leaves, buds and tubers (like wild celery), and are continuously on the move, foraging for their favorite foods. They eat morning and afternoon, interspacing their dining habits with a midday nap.

Finding gorillas can almost be guaranteed for those willing to hike 1 to 4 hours or more in search of them. Scouts locate each group early in the morning and advise the warden of their locations — indicating the length and difficulty of the hikes to reach them.

Bwindi Impenetrable Forest

Each group of visitors is usually led by a park ranger, two trackers and two armed personnel. Porters may be hired (for US $20.00 as of this writing) to carry lunch, drinks, etc., and to assist anyone who may wish to return early.

The search often involves climbing down into gullies, then pulling yourself up steep hills by holding onto vines and bamboo. Even though the pace is slow, you must be in good condition to keep up; the search may take you to altitudes of 3,800 to over 6,500 feet (1,160 to 1,982 m) or more. While this sounds difficult, almost anyone in good physical condition can do it.

The guide looks for nests used the night before, and then tracks them from that spot. Once the gorilla group has been located, he then calms them by making low grunting sounds and imitates them by picking and chewing bits of foliage. Juvenile gorillas are often found playing and tend to approach their human guests. The guide will do his best to keep you the required distance (primarily to help ensure the gorillas do not catch any communicable human diseases) of 22 feet (7 m). For the Ugandan Wildlife Authority's "Gorilla rules" brochure, visit *www.igcp.org/pdf/gorillarulesbrochure.pdf*.

Adult females are a little more cautious than the juveniles. The dominant male, called a silverback because of the silvery-grey hair on his back, usually keeps a bit further from his human visitors.

In terms of sensitivity toward the great primates and to afford you the best chances of a close and relaxed encounter, simple gorilla-viewing "etiquette" is critical. Never make eye contact with a silverback. If a silverback begins to act aggressively, look down immediately and take a submissive posture by squatting or sitting, or he may take your staring as aggression and charge. The key is to follow the directions of your well-trained guide. Gorillas are herbivores (vegetarians) and will generally not attack a human unless provoked. Your guides will instruct you not to touch the gorillas because they are susceptible to catching human colds and diseases.

For photography, bring a camera that either does not have a flash or one that can be turned off, as flash photography is not allowed. Videos and digital cameras are excellent for photography as gorillas are often found in the shadow of the forest in low-light conditions. If you are using film, use 800 ASA or higher to get enough light. Bring extra data cards or several rolls of film on the trek — you very well may need them! Be sure you do not spend all your time looking through your camera lens as you will miss most of the experience. After spending up to 60 minutes visiting with these magnificent animals, visitors descend to a more open area for a picnic lunch.

Mornings are almost always cool and misty; even if it doesn't rain, you will undoubtedly get wet from hiking and crawling around wet vegetation. Wear a waterproof jacket

The lushness of Bwindi

Guests prepare for their gorilla trek

Timeless moments during a gorilla trek

or poncho (preferably of a fabric like Gortex that "breathes"), leather gloves to protect your hands from stinging nettles, waterproof light- or medium-weight hiking boots, to give you traction on muddy slopes and to keep your feet dry, and a hat. Bring a waterproof pouch for your camera, water bottles and snacks. Do not wear bright clothes, perfumes, colognes or jewelry, because these distractions may excite the gorillas.

Visiting the gorillas is one of the most rewarding safaris in Africa. The park fees ($500.00 per trek, as of this writing), which are among the highest in Africa, go toward the preservation of these magnificent, endangered creatures.

Other primates resident in the Bwindi forest include chimpanzee, black-and-white colobus monkey, red colobus monkey, gray-cheeked mangabey, L'Hoest's monkey and blue monkey. Elephant, giant forest hog and duiker can also be found. Among the 345 species of birds recorded are the great blue turaco, yellow-eyed black flycatcher, Lühder's bushshrike, vanga flycatcher, black-faced rufous-warbler, black-throated apalis, and elusive green broadbill.

Park Headquarters are based at Buhoma, a 3-hour drive (67 mi./108 km) from Kabale, and at Nkuringo, a 1.5 hour drive (22 mi./35 km) from Kisoro and a 2-hour drive (28 mi./45 km) from the Rwanda border at Cyanika.

Due to Bwindi's location near the Rwandan border, travelers should consider also trekking in Volcanoes National Park as well.

Because trekkers must be at the park by 8:30 am, it is necessary to overnight near National Park Headquarters.

Neither children under 15 years of age nor contagiously ill adults are allowed near the gorillas.

Young gorillas are agile, whether clinging to their mother or hanging from a vine

ACCOMMODATION NEAR THE NORTHERN GROUPS AT BUHOMA — CLASS A: • **Gorilla Forest Camp** is a luxury permanent tented camp situated 5 minutes from the base station at Buhoma. The camp features 8 large tents set on raised wooden platforms, each with a bathtub — great for soaking sore muscles after a long trek. There is also a restaurant and lounge.

CLASS A/B: • **Buhoma Lodge**, located near Park Headquarters, offers 8 raised wooden cottages. The elevated lounge has a fireplace, bar and dining room. • **Mahogany Springs Lodge**, a new property in Bwindi, is located next to the river and features 6 bandas with private verandahs. The main lounge area has a bar, dining room, library, fireplace and wrap around deck.

CLASS B: • **Gorilla Resort** is located in walking distance from Park Headquarters with 2 cottages and 4 tents with bathtubs, raised on platforms, bar, lounge, dining room and

Gorilla Forest Camp

Gorilla Forest Camp's main lounge *(top)*,
Clouds Mountain Gorilla Lodge *(bottom)*

elevated campfire deck overlooking the forest. • **Engagi Lodge** is a permanent tented camp with 8 tents.

CLASS C: • **Volcanoes Bwindi Lodge**, located about half a mile (1 km) from Park Headquarters, has 8 tents, each with bush showers and short-drop toilets.

ACCOMMODATION NEAR THE SOUTHERN GROUPS NEAR KISORO — CLASS A: • **Clouds Mountain Gorilla Lodge**, a luxury lodge located on the Nteko Ridge on the edge of Bwindi Forest, is within walking distance to the Park Headquarters. Accommodations include 10 stone cottages with private decks. The main lounge is a welcome respite from a day of trekking and has comfortable sofas, a bar and dining room.

Mgahinga Gorilla National Park

Mgahinga Gorilla National Park is situated on the slopes of Mt. Muhabura and Mt. Gahinga in the southwestern corner of Uganda, bordering Rwanda and the D.R. Congo.

A joint commission has been set up by Uganda, Rwanda and the Congo to protect the mountain gorilla in the Virunga Mountains where the borders of the three countries meet.

One gorilla group has been habituated for tourism, however, as its natural range lies across political borders, gorilla viewing at Mgahinga cannot be guaranteed by any means, and therefore the reserve is not recommended for international travelers with limited time.

While gorilla trekking is the main activity in this 12-square-mile (34-km²) reserve, other mammals such as the rare golden monkey (a sub-species of the blue monkey), buffalo, black-fronted duiker, leopard, golden cat and serval may be encountered.

Bird life is not prolific, however, gems such as the red-tufted malachite sunbird, white-starred robin and Ruwenzori turaco may be observed in this highland region.

ACCOMMODATION — CLASS B/C: • **Mount Gahinga Rest Camp** has 4 rondavels and 3 tents with private facilities.

Kabale

Kabale is Uganda's highest town, situated in a beautiful area called "The Little Switzerland of Africa" in southwestern Uganda.

ACCOMMODATION — TOURIST CLASS: • **White Horse Inn** has clean rooms, bar and a restaurant.

Lake Mburo National Park

Lake Mburo National Park is located in southwestern Uganda between Masaka and Mbarara. This approximately 200-square-mile (520-km^2) park is named after the largest of the park's 14 lakes.

Located in the rain shadow between Lake Victoria and the Ruwenzori Mountains, the park is characterized by open plains in the north, acacia grassland in the center and lakes and marshes in the south. It is bounded by the Kampala-Mbarara road on the north, Lake Kachera on the east and the Ruizi River on the west.

Herds of zebra, impala (found nowhere else in Uganda) and buffalo enjoy this habitat, and the wetland system around the lake is home to the aquatic sitatunga antelope and hippo. Other game includes leopard, eland, reedbuck, topi, bushbuck and klipspringer.

Birds more typical of dryer Tanzanian savannah such as emerald-spotted dove and bare-faced go-away bird occur alongside the lilac-breasted roller and pennant-winged nightjar. The lake's edge is busy with the feeding activities of herons, storks, cormorants, ducks and pelicans.

The park offers bush walks and boating on the lake, and is a good place to overnight when driving between Bwindi and Kampala.

Mihingo Lodge, perched in the distance, has spectacular views

ACCOMMODATION — CLASS A/B: • **Mihingo Lodge** offers 10 spacious tents with thatched roofs and private verandahs. There is an infinity pool and thatched dining room. Massages and game walks are offered.

CLASS B: • **Mantana Tented Camp** has 8 tents built on wooden platforms. Game drives and escorted bush walks are offered.

CLASS C: • **Mburo Safari Lodge** features 20 cottages and suites each with private balconies, and a bar/dining area with fireplace.

Kampala and Entebbe

Kampala, the capital of Uganda, is built on seven hills. Points of interest include the **Uganda Museum** and the **Kasubi Tombs of the Kabakas** — a shrine to the former Baganda kings and a fine example of Baganda craftsmanship.

The international airport is at Entebbe, about an hour's drive from Kampala. There are several hotels located here, near the shores of Lake Victoria and the botanical gardens.

For thrill seekers wanting a close encounter with the mighty River Nile, enthralling **white-water rafting** adventures operate from near the town of Jinja, east of Kampala.

ACCOMMODATION — DELUXE: • **Emin Pasha,** located in Kampala, is Uganda's only "boutique" hotel. This colonial country house features 20 air-conditioned rooms, most with private balconies or terraces. The restaurant, bar and swimming pool are set in a tropical garden. • **Kampala Serena Hotel** is an oasis of lush gardens and extensive water features including fountains and pools. Accommodations include 152 air-conditioned rooms and suites, 24-hour room service, 3 restaurants, a lounge, a large swimming pool and gym. There is a full health club and spa with a full range of treatments.

FIRST CLASS: • **Lake Victoria Serena Resort** is located on the shores of Lake Victoria near the Entebbe airport. The design of the resort is reminiscent of a Roman villa and features 124 rooms and suites. There are several dining options, lounges, swimming pool, health club and full-service spa. • **Imperial Resort Beach Hotel** with its 181 rooms is located in Entebbe, only a short drive from the airport. The hotel offers a 24-hour restaurant, swimming pool and a half mile (1 km) private stretch of beach on Lake Victoria. • **Kampala Sheraton Hotel**, situated in an attractive park setting, has 218 rooms and suites (most with air-conditioning) with private facilities and balconies, a health club, several restaurants, 2 bars and a swimming pool. • **Golf Course Hotel** has 115 air-conditioned rooms, 2 bars, 2 restaurants (1 revolves with views of the city), Olympic-size swimming pool and complementary golf and health club membership. • **Grand Imperial Hotel** is located in the center of town and has 80 air-conditioned rooms, a swimming pool, health club, shops and restaurants. • **Mamba Point Guesthouse**, located in the suburb of Nakisero, has 6 rooms with mini-bars, gym, sauna, bar and restaurant.

TOURIST CLASS: • **Protea Hotel,** located in the suburb of Kololo (Kampala), has 70 rooms, bar and restaurant. • **Hotel Equatorial** is located in Kampala and has 275 rooms (most of them are air-conditioned). • **Hotel Africana** is a standard 3-star hotel only 3 minutes from Kampala's city center and 40 minutes from Entebbe. • **Fang Fang Hotel** is located in the hub of Kampala's business district and offers air-conditioned rooms and a restaurant on site. • **Imperial Botanical Hotel** overlooks Lake Victoria in Entebbe and has a restaurant and swimming pool for guests' enjoyment.

Ngamba Island (Chimp Island)

Ngamba Island Chimpanzee Sanctuary is situated in Lake Victoria, 90 minutes by boat transfer from Entebbe Pier. The tropical 100-acre (40-hectare) island is home to approximately 42 orphaned chimpanzees, which are free to roam the forest during the day and return to the holding facility at night. Chimpanzee viewing is the main activity. There are 2 daily viewing times during which you can watch the chimps being fed. A raised viewing platform allows you to view the chimps very closely and provides great photographic opportunities.

Day visits and overnight stays are allowed but must be booked in advance. Overnight stays require a long list of vaccinations before arrival. Swimming, kayaking, bird watching, sunset cruises and fishing are other optional activities. The Chimpanzee Sanctuary is managed by the Jane Goodall Institute.

ACCOMMODATION — CLASS B/C: • **Ngamba Island Camp** is available for overnight stay on the island. Accommodations include 4 canvas tents set on raised wooden platforms with eco-toilets and bush showers. Meals are served in the covered dining room or open dining area beside the lake.

Chimpanzee communicate like humans by touching, kissing and patting on the back

Rwanda

Rwanda

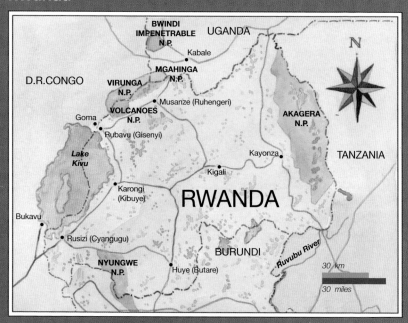

Rwanda is characterized by rolling hills and volcanic peaks with altitudes varying from 3,960 feet (1,207m) to 14,786 feet (4,507m) above sea level. Mt. Karisimbi in the Virunga range is the highest peak. Both Rwanda and Burundi are former Belgian colonies, previously united as Ruanda-Urundi. Although the country covers only 10,160 square miles (26,638-km²) it has a population of close to 10 million, making these fertile landscapes among the most densely populated in the world. Kinyarwanda is the predominant language, while French and English are widely spoken. The currency used is the Franc.

Rwanda
Country Highlights

- Gorilla Trekking is rated by many African experts as one of the greatest (if not *the* greatest) experience one can have on safari. It will take your breath away!
- As there are only a few hundred of these endangered mountain gorillas remaining, the time to visit them is NOW!
- Travel to Nyungwe Forest to see 13 species of primates including habituated chimpanzees in a beautiful forest.
- Enjoying a sundowner cruise on Lake Kivu, one of the most
- beautiful lakes on the continent.
- Visit Kigali's Genocide Museum and Women for Women Organization.
- The Rwandan government has created a very safe and inviting environment for international tourists, who are warmly welcomed by its people.
- Rwanda is one of the highest populated yet cleanest countries in the world. Rwandans are proud of their country — and it shows!

When's the Best Time to Go for Game Viewing

█ Excellent █ Good ☐ Fair █ Poor █ Closed

Country	Park/Reserve	JAN	FEB	MAR	APR	MAY	JUN	JUL	AUG	SEP	OCT	NOV	DEC
Rwanda	Volcanoes/Nyungwe												

Best Safari Experience
Sabyinyo Silverback Lodge, Jack Hanna's House, Nyungwe Forest Lodge

RWANDA

Appropriately called "The Land of a Thousand Hills," Rwanda is predominantly grassy highlands and hills, with altitudes above sea level varying from a low of 3,960 feet (1,207 m) to Mt. Karisimbi, the highest of a range of extinct volcanoes in the northwest, which reaches 14,786 feet (4,507 m). Lake Kivu forms part of the border with the Congo and is one of the most beautiful lakes in Africa. In fact, most visitors are impressed by the beauty and cleanliness of the country as a whole. Also called "The Country of Perpetual Spring," Rwanda's comfortable climate is temperate and mild with an average daytime temperature of 77°F (25°C). The main rainy season is from March to mid-May, and the shorter one is from November to mid-December.

Almost all (97%) of the people live in self-contained compounds and work the adjacent land. Over half of the population is Christian (most of which are Catholic), though many people follow traditional African beliefs.

Historically, Hutu (Bahutu) and Tutsi (Batusi) tribes made up the majority of the population. The Tutsi long dominated the Hutu farmers in a feudal

Rwanda is known as the "Land of a Thousand Hills"

system analogous to that of medieval England. Their feudal system was second in size only to Ethiopia's, and was based on cattle.

Because of its physical isolation and the fearsome reputation of its people, Rwanda was not affected by the slave and ivory trade from Zanzibar during the 1800s. The area became a German protectorate in 1899 and in 1916 was occupied by the Belgians.

Following World War I, Rwanda and Burundi were mandated by the League of Nations to Belgium as the territory of Ruanda-Urundi. Full independence for Rwanda and Burundi was achieved on July 1, 1962.

In 1994, a genocide against the Tutsi by the Hutus occurred, resulting in a civil war (that actually began in 1990) with over a million deaths, and even more refugees fleeing to neighbor-

A young Rwandan girl learns to drum

ing Congo and Tanzania. The Tutsi forces were victorious, and many refugees have returned. Most of the people no longer use tribal names as they consider themselves Rwandans.

Rwanda is a remarkable country. Crime and litter are almost non-existent. Even plastic bags are banned, and on the last Saturday of the month (Umunganda Day) the entire country does communal work for public good — from street cleaning to building homes for genocide survivors. It truly amazes visitors how clean Kigali and the entire country is.

High population density is at the root of Rwanda's economic problems. Almost all arable land is under cultivation. Tourism is now the country's major foreign exchange earner after tea and coffee.

English has become the preferred language for many Rwandans and is widely spoken along with French and Kinyarwanda; Kiswahili is spoken in the major towns and regions close to the borders of Uganda and Tanzania.

🐾 WILDLIFE AND WILDLIFE AREAS

Mountain gorilla trekking in Volcanoes National Park is by far Rwanda's major international attraction. After the release of the feature film, *Gorillas in the Mist,* about the late Dian Fossey's pioneering work habituating the gorillas, and numerous documentary films, interest in gorilla trekking has reached new heights and continues to grow yearly, with available gorilla permits being sold out virtually every day of the year. Nyungwe Forest National Park is gaining popularity for trekking for chimpanzees and other primates.

THE NORTH

Volcanoes National Park
(Parc National des Volcans)

Volcanoes National Park is home to the mountain gorilla, first documented by Europeans in the early 1900s. The peaks of the Virunga Mountains, heavily forested extinct volcanoes, serve as a border with the Democratic Republic of the Congo and Uganda and are part of the watershed between the Congo and Nile river systems.

The 62-square-mile (160-km²) park supports several vegetation zones, from lush bamboo stands to luxuriant mountain forest to Afro-alpine. From 9,020 to 10,825 feet (2,750 to 3,300 m), primary forest is dominated by hagenia trees growing 30 to 60 feet (9 to 18 m) in height. Hagenia have twisted trunks and low branches covered with lichen, out of which epiphytic orchids, moss and ferns often grow.

Volcanoes National Park borders both Virunga National Park in the Congo and the Mgahinga Gorilla National Park in Uganda. The park receives a high

Gorillas favor a diet of wild celery and bamboo shoots

Volcanoes National Park

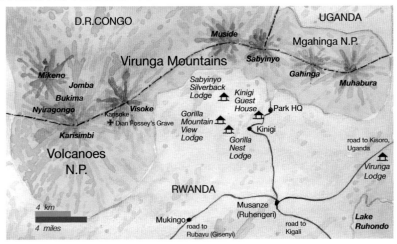

amount of rainfall, over 70 inches (1,800 mm) per year. Daytime temperatures at Park Headquarters range from 70 to 90°F (21 to 32°C).

Other wildlife in the park includes the blue monkey, golden monkey (a rare subspecies of blue monkey), black-fronted duiker (very common), bushbuck, giant forest hog, African civet, genet, and buffalo. One hundred nineteen species of birds have been recorded, including spectacular mountain turacos (the Rwenzori turaco is the most common) and forest francolin.

The mountain gorilla grows to 6 feet (1.8 m) in height and weighs up to 450 pounds (205 kg). These gentle giants are found in the Virunga Mountains (a chain of volcanoes with altitudinal ranges of 3,500 m–4,507 m). Mountain Gorillas are found in the high altitude forests surrounding these volcanoes.

Gorilla Trekking

As of this writing, there are currently 8 habituated gorilla families that can be visited. Please keep in mind that makeup of each group listed below is quite dynamic and changes on a regular basis.

> **Sabyinyo Group** – 13 members, including Guhonda, the largest known silverback in Africa
>
> **Amahoro Group** – 18 members, including 2 silverbacks
>
> **Agashya Group** (previously known as Group 13) – 25 members, including 1 silverback
>
> **Susa Group** – 30 members, including 3 silverbacks
>
> **Karisimbi Group** – 15 members, including 1 silverback
>
> **Umubano Group** – 13 members, including 1 silverback
>
> **Hirwa Group** – 16 members, including 1 silverback
>
> **Kwitonda Group** – 21 members, including 1 silverback

A maximum of 8 tourists can visit each gorilla group daily.

For an in-depth treatise on gorillas and this region beautifully presented with color photographs, I suggest *Mountain Gorillas: Biology, Conservation and Coexistence* by Gene Eckhart (University Press).

During my most recent visit, my guide drove me from Kigali to Musanze, previously called Ruhengeri. The 2.5 hour drive was on a good road through the countryside with beautifully terraced hills. During the day there are always people walking along the road, riding or pushing bicycles, many of which were laden with banana or sorgum beer. We walked around the bustling market at Kinigi — a microcosm of Rwandan country life loaded with photographic opportunities. There were many bicycle taxis and motorcycle taxis taking clients short distances at reasonable prices.

Travelers that have stayed the previous night at lodges close to the park are usually picked up around 6:30 am. Check in/registration is at 7:00 am at the RDB/ORTPN Park Headquarters at Kinigi, approximately 10 miles (15 km) from Musanze. Do not be late as they will leave without you. You will need to

Author Mark Nolting gorilla trekking in Volcanoes National Park

present your passport and fill out a form that includes your age. The trekker's driver/guides will then have a short briefing with the chief warden who will assign all the trekkers to gorilla groups. By this time, the warden would have received reports as to the location of all of the gorilla groups, along with the approximate time it should take from the departure points to the group, and the difficulty of the hikes.

This is where booking your safari with a top safari company becomes of paramount importance. Safari companies and their guides who have very good relationships with national parks have a better chance of getting their guests assigned to gorilla groups their clients prefer, or groups that require a short, medium or long hike — depending on the preference of the trekker. This provides a wonderful "comfort zone" for people who have concerns as to whether or not they feel they can handle the hiking. On the other hand, those who like to hike may want to choose a group that will involve a longer trek as the area is so beautiful.

Most travelers in good condition can trek the close groups. The guides set the pace to that of the slowest walker, and take many rest breaks enroute. There is generally no rush to find the gorillas as you will have 1 hour with them regardless. The only exception is if a group is a very long way from the departure point (i.e. the Susa Group), there may not be a lot of time to rest as you need to complete the trek before dark.

Trekkers are then separated according to the gorilla groups they will be visiting and given a briefing by their respective national park guides that lasts about 15 minutes. Trekkers then return to their vehicles and are driven to the departure points by their guides.

Departure points can be a 30- to 90-minute drive from Headquarters and difficult to find if you are not with a knowledgeable driver. Before departing Park Headquarters, make sure that you or your guide has the necessary vouchers.

As there is no public transportation from Musanze to the Park Headquarters or to the trek departure points, you need to either book your safari with a tour operator or self-drive in a 4wd vehicle (not recommended). In other words, if you do not have pre-arranged transportation, you will probably not trek.

Once at the departure point, each trekker is given a walking stick, and assigned a porter, if they choose to have one, currently at a cost $20.00. I highly recommend hiring a porter, not only to make the trek less strenuous and to have some assistance up some steep hills, but to support the local ecotourism in the area.

The hike normally begins with an uphill walk through villages and farmlands for a wonderful snapshot of rural life in Rwanda. You hike to the stone wall marking the border of the park, which is designed to keep the buffalo and elephant in the park and to mark a clear border of the park for the people not to cross. After a gorilla etiquette briefing, you begin trekking. When you get close to the gorillas you leave your hiking sticks and backpacks behind with your porters and bring only your cameras.

Young gorillas will stay with their mother for up to 3–4 years

The first trek on my last visit was to the Kwitonda Group. It was a beautiful hike through cultivated fields. The guide stopped frequently to talk about the crops and other plants along the way. This gave the slower trekkers time to catch their breath and rest. Our guide was very entertaining, and would, for instance, demonstrate what the gorillas eat by eating it himself. I tried the bamboo, which they say can make the gorillas a bit drunk, and it was quite sweet.

We were fortunate to encounter the group in fairly open areas with scattered sunlight. The group was made up of 17 individuals including one silverback. At one point I lay down on the forest floor and a baby approached very closely. Our guide said it was curious about my camera, and he kept having to keep the baby from approaching too closely. The whole experience was exhilarating and was over in a flash!

The following morning we hiked to the Sabyinyo Group, which includes the largest silverback in the park — Guhonda. He was a magnificent sight, however, as he is getting quite old, he was not too active. In contrast, the rest of the group was active indeed! This trek was longer than the first one, mostly through bamboo forests that were sometimes so dense we had to crawl through sections. Our efforts were highly rewarded as we were entertained by these amazing primates for an hour before hiking back.

In order to minimize behavioral disturbances to the gorillas, only 8 people are allowed to visit each of the families. This means that only 64 people are allowed to trek daily. The limits serve to protect gorillas from the risk of exposure to human-borne diseases.

Please note that children under 15 years of age or anyone having the flu or other sickness that might be transmitted to the gorillas are not allowed to visit the gorillas. Children of all ages are allowed into the park for other activities such as nature walks and visiting Dian Fossey's grave, if accompanied by an adult.

Each gorilla visit will be limited to a maximum of only 1 hour, once a day. One must be prepared for a strenuous hike of 1 to 6 hours each way but 2 to 3 hours is more usual. Bring plenty of water.

When visiting the gorillas, please ensure that you carry with you rain protection gear and wear good hiking boots. Boots with a good grip really do make all the difference. An extra set of dry clothes left behind in the vehicle can also be helpful. Gloves are recommended as protection from the stinging nettles (a bush). For this same reason, wear long pants and a long-sleeve shirt for the hikes.

For camera equipment we suggest a zoom lens 70 or 80 — 200 or 210 mm and a standard 50 mm lens, or lenses with similar powers. Fast lenses (F1.8–F2.8) and video cameras are best as gorillas are often found in deep shade. Please use water proof bags (NO plastic) to keep equipment dry. Mist is encountered year-round

Gorillas are the largest living primate and endangered due to poaching and destruction of habitat

and rain must be expected from November to May, so ensure your camera is protected accordingly in a waterproof container. Video is highly recommended, as long as you limit your time looking through the camera, otherwise you will miss a lot of the experience! No flash photography of any kind is allowed.

A National Parks guide will accompany all groups to the gorillas and on entry to the National Park will advise you of the rules for observing the gorillas. The main rules are total silence, no smoking or eating, and no pointing at the gorillas. Do not stand above the height of the guide so if he kneels, you need to also kneel. Follow the guide's actions at all times. Move slowly and be calm at all times. If a silverback should charge, do not run. Keep behind the guide at all times.

Porters are available at the National Park entry point to help carry bags, heavy cameras, etc. They are most definitely recommended. Please, however, do NOT leave any valuables inside the bags they will be carrying.

Tipping is not included in your park fees or tour price. Please obtain tipping instructions from your tour operator. The "head" gorilla guide will split all of his tips with his assistant guides — so there is no need to tip individual guides. Some Rwandan army personnel will accompany you into the forests. They are there for your protection. Please do not photograph them. They will not ask but please do not tip them.

Gorillas have a full range of emotion including fear, greed, joy and love

Permits must be purchased in advance through an international tour operator, or in Kigali where a copy of the first 3 pages of a visitor's passport must be presented at the time of purchase. As there are only up to 64 people allowed to gorilla trek each day, permits are very limited and should be purchased 6 months to a year or more in advance if possible.

The most popular time to visit the gorillas is during the dry seasons, which occur June to October and December to March.

Golden Monkey Trekking

In addition to gorilla trekking, a golden monkey trek is well worth considering. The golden monkey (Cercopithecus mitis kandti), a subspecies of the blue monkey, is found only in the bamboo forests of the Virunga Mountains of Rwanda, Uganda, and the Democratic Republic of the Congo. It weighs from 10 to 25 pounds and has a golden body with black limbs.

Trekking these monkeys is certainly complimentary to trekking gorillas. They are extremely playful and entertaining to watch!

Some guests trek the golden monkeys on a day between gorilla visits, as these hikes are most often less demanding than the gorilla treks. It is a perfect option for visitors 12 or older but under the 15 year age limit required for gorilla trekking.

You check in at the park gate at 6:30 am where you will meet your tracker. Once the monkeys are found, your viewing will be limited to a maximum of one hour.

The **Iby'Iwachu Cultural Village** is located near Volcanoes National Park, and is a community-based initiative that includes a walk through the village of traditional huts, meeting a local healer, see how bananas are brewed into local banana and sorghum beer (and "enjoy" a taste), watch and participate in traditional dances.

There are also local schools that are happy to have visitors; consider bringing some pens and pencils, etc., as a donation.

Dian Fossey's grave may also be visited, however it needs an extra day.

For those interested in also trekking gorillas in Uganda, Bwindi

Golden monkeys live on a diet of leaves, fruit and insects

Cultural shows are offered between gorilla treks and touring

Market day at Musanze

Impenetrable Forest National Park is less than a day's drive from Volcanoes National Park. Trekking gorillas in both reserves is highly recommended!

Mountain Climbing

Hiking in the beautiful Virunga Mountains is an adventure in itself. Trails lead to the craters or peaks of the park's 5 volcanoes, upward through the unique high vegetation zones of bamboo, hagenia-hypericum forests, giant lobelia and senecio, and finally to alpine meadows. Views from the top, which overlook the lush Rwandan valleys and into the Congo and Uganda, are spectacular.

A proud Rwandan mom and son wrapped in colorful fabric

Some travelers spend a day or 2 of gorilla trekking interspersed with hikes to one or more of the volcanoes.

Karisimbi (14,786 ft./4,507 m), which is occasionally snowcapped, is Rwanda's highest mountain. It is the most arduous ascent, requiring 2 days from the Visoke departure point. The night may be spent in a metal hut at about 12,000 feet (3,660 m).

Visoke (12,175 ft./3,711 m) has a beautiful crater lake and requires 4 hours of hiking up a steep trail from the Visoke departure point, to reach the summit. The walk around the crater rim is highly recommended. Allow 7 hours for the entire trip.

Lake Ngezi (9,843 ft./3,000 m), a small, shallow crater lake, is the easiest hike in the park; it takes only 3 to 4 hours round-trip from the Visoke departure point.

Sabyinyo (11,922 ft./3,634 m) can be climbed in 5 to 6 hours, starting at Park Headquarters near Kinigi. A metal hut is located just before you reach the lava beds. The final section is along a narrow, rocky ridge with steep drops on both sides.

Gahinga (11,398 ft./3,474 m) and **Muhabura** (13,540 ft./4127 m) are both reached from the departure point at Gasiza. The trail rises to a hut in poor condition on the saddle between the 2 mountains. Gahinga's summit can be reached in 4 hours, while 2 days are recommended to reach the summit of Muhabura.

A park guide must accompany each group, but porters are optional. Should you encounter gorillas on your hike, you may not leave the path to follow them. You may only track gorillas if you have previously purchased the proper permits.

Sabyinyo Silverback Lodge

ACCOMMODATION — CLASS A:
• **Sabyinyo Silverback Lodge** is adjacent to the Parc National des Volcans and is comprised of a central building with bar, dining room, library/games room, community awareness center and shop. There are 5 rooms, 1 family cottage and 2 suite cottages, each with a private verandah, a sitting room with fireplace, bedroom, dressing room and a large modern bathroom. The family suite has an extra bedroom and bathroom incorporated. The lodge is an innovative conservation project conceived and constructed by the African Wildlife Foundation in which the local community receives economic benefits as a result of visiting tourists. • **Jack Hanna's Guesthouse** is a comfortable ranch-style home with 2 bedrooms and 2 bathrooms. There is a separate unit that can house 2 additional people. The property is booked on an exclusive basis.

CLASS A/B: • **Virunga Lodge** is an eco-lodge, set on a hillside with views of the Virunga volcanoes and Lakes Ruhondo and Bulera. The lodge consists of 8 bandas, a bar with fireplace and dining room. The "downside" is that it is located over an hour's drive from Park Headquarters, requiring very early departures and later returns from the treks.

CLASS B: • **Gorilla Mountain View Lodge** is a 15-minute drive from the Park Headquarters and features 25 standard rooms each with a small sitting area, fireplace and private verandah. • **Gorilla Nest Lodge** is about 1.5 miles (2 kms) from the Park Headquarters. It currently has 45 standard rooms (with shower) and 2 suites with bath and shower. Renovations are scheduled, and the property may be upgraded in the near future.

BASIC: • **Gorillas Volcanoes Hotel**, located in Musanze town, has 31 rooms, a restaurant and bar, a swimming pool, conference hall, and a fitness center. • **ASOFERWA Guest House** has 15 simple rooms. • **Hotel Muhabura** is a very rustic hotel with 10 rooms and 2 pavilions, a bar and dining room. The hotel is located in Musanze about 10 miles (16 km) from Park Headquarters. • **La Palme Hotel**, also located in Musanze, has 12 rooms.

Rubavu (Gisenyi) — Lake Kivu

Rubavu (previously called Gisenyi) is a picturesque resort town on the northern shores of beautiful Lake Kivu. Lake Kivu has some nice, white beaches and is believed to have little or no bilharzias (a disease). Crocodiles are absent from the lake due to volcanic action, eons ago, that wiped them out. Beware, however, of rising sulpher gas, which can be fatal. Rubavu is a 75-minute drive from Volcanoes National Park and a 4-hour drive from Kigali, and is worth a visit if time permits.

ACCOMMODATION — DELUXE: • **Lake Kivu Serena Hotel** is located on the shores of Lake Kivu, the sixth largest lake in Africa. Accommodations are comprised of

66 air-conditioned rooms, including 6 luxury suites and 23 family rooms. The restaurant offers a stunning view of the lake. The hotel also has a gym, outdoor swimming pool, two tennis courts and volley ball. Fishing can be arranged.

FIRST CLASS: • **Gorillas Lake Kivu Hotel,** located near the beach, has 35 rooms, a restaurant, swimming pool and fitness center. • **Stipp Hotel** is popular for its charming courtyard garden and pool area. The hotel offers 25 rooms, restaurant and massage facilities.

TOURIST CLASS: • **Ubumwe Hotel** features 15 rooms.

Lake Kivu – "Kivu" means "lake" in the Bantu language

Karongi (Kibuye)

Karongi (Kibuye), located on Lake Kivu midway between Rubavu (Gisenyi) and Rusizi (Cyangugu), is a small town with an attractive beach. Be sure not to miss the over 330 foot (100 m) high **Ndaba Waterfall** (Les Chutes des Ndaba), not far from Kibuye.

ACCOMMODATION — CLASS B: • **Cormoran Lodge,** a boutique lodge, features 7 rooms with small terraces and lake views, a restaurant and bar.

THE SOUTHWEST

Nyungwe Forest National Park
Le Parc National de Nyungwe

The Nyungwe Forest is one of the most biologically diverse, high-altitude rain forests in Africa. Located in southwestern Rwanda and bordering the country of Burundi, this 375-square-mile (970-km²) reserve is home for 13 species of primates including a rare subspecies of black-and-white colobus monkey (documented in groups of several hundred), L'Hoest's monkey, blue monkey, gray-cheeked mangabey and habituated chimpanzees.

The lush Nyungwe Forest National Park

Colobus monkeys rarely descend trees to come down to the ground

Chimpanzee trekking is gaining popularity as visitors now have a very good chance of seeing them on a day's trek.

In addition to a variety of butterflies and more than 100 different species of orchids, more than 275 species of birds have been recorded. Some of the over 250 species of trees and shrubs grow to over 165 feet (50 m) in height. This mountainous national park has a variety of habitats, including wetlands, forested valleys and bamboo zones. Elevation ranges from 5,250 to 9,680 feet (1,600 to 2,950 m).

Although Nyungwe Forest National Park is situated at a lower altitude and receives less rain than Volcanoes National Park, hiking is more difficult in Nyungwe. The vegetation at Nyungwe is much thicker and many slopes are steeper.

Nyungwe Forest Lodge

ACCOMMODATION — CLASS A: • **Nyungwe Forest Lodge,** built in a tea plantation on the edge of the Nyungwe Forest, has 24 luxurious rooms and suites with private fireplace, air conditioning and balconies with forest views. The lodge features a heated outdoor swimming pool, boma for outdoor dining, fitness center, a small spa, restaurant and lounge.

CLASS B: • **Nyungwe Top View Hill Hotel** is positioned with sweeping views of the Nyungwe National Park, Kahuzi Biega National Park (Congo), tea plantation and Lake Kivu. The lodge has 12 self-contained rooms with fireplaces and private balconies.

Huye (Butare)

Located in southern Rwanda, not far from the border with Burundi, Huye is the intellectual capital of Rwanda. There you will find the **National Museum** (good archaeology and ethnology exhibits), **National University** and the **National Institute of Scientific Research** (ask about folklore dances). Several craft centers are located in villages within 10 miles (16 km) of Butare. **The Ballet National du Rwanda** is located in Nyanza, 22 miles (35 km) from Butare.

ACCOMMODATION — BASIC: • **Hotel Credo** has 25 rooms, tennis court and swimming pool. • **Hotel Faucon** has 13 rooms. • **Hotel Ibis** has 15 rooms.

CENTRAL AND EAST

Kigali

The capital of Rwanda, Kigali is the commercial center of the country. A number of very good restaurants are located in the first class hotels. The **Genocide Museum** and **Women for Women** Organization are well worth visiting.

Kigali must be the cleanest city in Africa. On my most recent visit, there was no litter to be seen at all. I found the Genocide Museum very moving.

The Women for Women Organization in Kigali *(top)*, Kigali Serena Hotel *(bottom)*

ACCOMMODATION — DELUXE: • **Kigali Serena Hotel** is located a few miles outside the city center. It has recently undergone a complete refurbishment and has 148 rooms and suites with air-conditioning. Facilities include 2 restaurants, a lounge and bar, fitness center, spa and a swimming pool. • **The Manor Hotel,** located in an upscale residential area in Kigali, features 24 rooms, 3 restaurants, a bar, 2 terraces, swimming pool and gym.

FIRST CLASS: • **Hotel des Mille Collines** has 112 rooms and suites and a swimming pool. • **Lemigo Hotel** is 10 minutes from the airport and offers

97 modern rooms and suites. There are 2 restaurants and bars, swimming pool and fully equipped gym. • **Stip Hotel** has 50 rooms, a restaurant, swimming pool and gym.

TOURIST CLASS: • **Hotel Chez Lando,** located 2 miles (3 km) from the airport, has 42 rooms. • **Hotel Gorillas,** centrally located in town, has 31 rooms, a restaurant and bar for guests. • **Ninzi Hill** is 10 minutes from the airport and offers 15 rooms, restaurant and business center. • **Hotel Okapi,** located in the center of Kigali, has 24 rooms. • **Hotel Isimbi,** located in the center of Kigali, has 26 rooms.

Akagera National Park

Akagera National Park is located about a 2-hour drive from Kigali in northeastern Rwanda along the Akagera River (a Nile affluent) bordering Tanzania. This 348-square-mile (900-km²) park is a scenic combination of savannah, woodland and wetlands comprised of a dozen lakes linked by small channels and papyrus swamps.

Wildlife includes the world's largest antelope, the Cape Eland, and some of the largest buffalo in Africa. Other wildlife includes zebra, giraffe, hippo, crocodile, lion, leopard, impala, Defassa waterbuck, eland, sable antelope, bushbuck, oribi, roan antelope and black-backed jackal. Unfortunately much of the wildlife

Akagera National Park

was killed during the civil war in the '90s, but it is slowly coming back. Birdlife is excellent with over 525 different species of birds recorded — including the papyrus gonolek and the rare shoebill.

The best time to visit the park is during the dry season July to September, while February, June and October are also good.

ACCOMMODATION — CLASS B: • **Akagera Game Lodge,** located inside the park overlooking beautiful Lake Ihema, has 60 standard rooms and 2 suites, restaurant, bar and swimming pool.

A "journey" of giraffe in Akagera National Park

Republic of
the Congo

Republic of the Congo

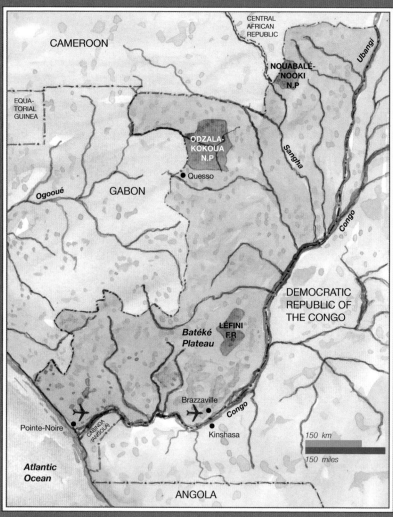

The Republic of Congo, more commonly known as Congo (Brazzaville), is located in West Central Africa, and is sometimes confused with its far larger neighbor, the Democratic Republic of Congo, or DRC. This former French colony covers 132,000-square-miles (342,000 km²) from its Atlantic Ocean in the west, up along the western bank of the mighty Congo River, across a grassy plateau and into dense lowland tropical rainforest straddling the equator. Of the 4 million people, approximately 65% live in urban areas, leaving huge areas of the country as pristine forest systems. The official language is French while Lingala and Monkutuba are the lingua franca. The currency used is the Cooperation Financiere en Africa Central (CFA) or Central African Franc.

Republic of the Congo Country Highlights

- Tracking habituated western lowland gorilla groups in pristine primary rainforest.

- Possibly the most accessible viewing in west central Africa of a host of lowland forest mammals such as forest elephant, forest buffalo, red river hog, bongo and a host of forest duiker species.

- Primate-rich environment with chimpanzee, western guereza, gray-cheeked and agile mangabeys, crowned and moustached monkeys, de Brazza's monkey, putty-nosed monkey and more.

- Salt-rich forest bais that attract a host of forest wildlife out into the open where they can be viewed as they drink, socialize and forage for minerals.

- Night walks in the forest in search of nocturnal primates such as potto and Demidoff's galago.

- Trips along majestic forested rivers in huge wooden dug pirogues.

When's the Best Time to Go for Game Viewing

■ Excellent ■ Good □ Fair ■ Poor ■ Closed

Country	Park/Reserve	JAN	FEB	MAR	APR	MAY	JUN	JUL	AUG	SEP	OCT	NOV	DEC
Congo Rep.	Odzala-Kokoua												

Best Safari Experience

Lango Camp and Ngaga Camp (Odzala-Kokoua NP)

REPUBLIC OF THE CONGO

Not to be confused with the volatile Democratic Republic of the Congo, the sparsely populated Republic of the Congo is a Central African country with seemingly endless pristine tropical forest and fingers of moist savannah covering its interior. Tourism to the Congo is at a fledgling stage with an aura of exploration and discovery enhancing every journey into its interior.

This little known former French colony holds approximately 4 million people, 65% of which live in the southwest in the urban centers of Brazzaville (the capital) and Pointe-Noire (the major port). This leaves the northern rainforest very sparsely populated and largely pristine. This is the heart of the Congo Basin, the world's second largest expanse of tropical rainforest, and, along with great forest biodiversity, holds by far the majority of the world population of western lowland gorillas.

Rivers such as the Sangha, Mambili and the mighty Congo drain this basin and provide a means of exploration through dense forests, and access to remote national parks such as Odzala-Kokoua, Nouabale-Ndoki and Conkouati-Douli.

A male forest elephant is smaller than its cousin, the African savanna elephant

Western lowland gorillas can be observed in Odzala-Kokoua and Nouabale-Ndoki National Parks

It is in these areas that endemic wildlife flourishes alongside traditional Pygmy cultures.

Following independence from the French in 1960, the Congo adopted a Marxist ideology with a one party state until 1990, which was succeeded by a period of democracy. Civil war broke out in 1997 and peace agreements were signed a few years later.

The economy is based largely on oil, followed by forestry and mining of lead, zinc, uranium, copper, gold, and magnesium. Exports, predominantly of oil, the earnings of which constitute 65% of GDP, are mostly to the USA and China. Subsistence agriculture composed primarily of cassava, rice, corn and peanuts is the primary economy of the rural areas. Cash crops consist of sugar, coffee and cocoa.

Of the 4 million inhabitants, the major ethnic groups are the Kongo (48%), the Sangha (20%), Teke (17%) and Mbochi (12%). Around half of the population are Christian, while 48% regard themselves as animist and the remaining 2% follow Islam.

WILDLIFE AND WILDLIFE AREAS

The Congo wildlife experience is about more than just western lowland gorilla viewing. Three primary national parks, Odzala-Kokoua and Nouabale-Ndoki in the north and Conkouati-Douli in the south along the coast, protect no less than 7% of the country's land area on their own (there are a number of other game and forest reserves as well). These parks provide shelter for a huge variety of lowland rainforest mammals with dozens of primate and duiker species, as well as large forest mega fauna such as western lowland gorillas, forest elephant, forest buffalo, lowland bongo, leopard and spotted hyena. Charismatic species such as the very colorful mandrill may be seen in Conkouati-Douli National Park, and the beach also provides nesting grounds for enormous leatherback turtles.

Presently, only Odzala-Kokoua National Park has accommodations and the infrastructure to cater for international tourists. Rustic accommodation is, however, available through the Wildlife Conservation Society (WCS) in both Nouabale-Ndoki and Conkouati-Douli National Parks.

Odzala-Kokoua National Park

Odzala-Kokoua, in the north of Congo and on the Gabon border, is one of Africa's oldest national parks, having been proclaimed by the French adminis-

tration in 1935. It covers primarily pristine equatorial rainforest typical of the Congo Basin, but is unique for protecting a large area of savannah as well. It is one of the "gems" of West Central Africa.

Within its 3,360,000 acres (1,360,000 hectares), the park holds globally significant populations of western lowland gorilla, forest elephant and forest buffalo, as well as a wide array of other species, and is renowned as the richest forest area in central Africa for primate species. Eleven diurnal

A western lowland gorilla has a diet of fruit, roots and tree bark primates have been recorded. The putty-nosed monkey, moustached monkey, gray-cheeked mangabey and crowned monkey are perhaps the most common primates, however, the black-and-white Colobus monkey, De Brazza's monkey and even chimpanzees are also all regularly seen. Nocturnal species such as the central potto and Demidoff's galago can be seen on night walks. Other species include the lowland bongo, harnessed bushbuck, hippopotamus, red river hogs, and an array of forest duiker species from the very large yellow-backed duiker to the diminutive blue duiker.

Gorilla trekking is the primary reason to venture here, western lowland gorillas can be observed in two different ways in Odzala-Kokoua and Nouabale-Ndoki national parks, either through tracking habituated groups or by patiently waiting at hides, platforms, on the edge of forest bais for family groups to forage.

Tracking of western lowland gorillas is quite different from the process of tracking mountain gorillas in Rwanda and Uganda. The most obvious differences are the terrain and vegetation. Although there are some relatively steep stream valleys in northern Congo, the terrain varies between undulating and flat, and

Game in the Congo varies from gorillas to forest buffalo *(top)*, Boating on the Lekoli River *(bottom)*

is not mountainous. Vegetation can also be incredibly thick, especially in areas of marantaceae (a plant on which gorillas like to feed) where gorilla densities are at their highest. Another difference is that gorilla viewing in Congo takes place in wilderness areas with very low densities of people, and as a result, other forest wildlife that can be seen exceeds that in gorilla tracking locations in Rwanda and Uganda, where human population densities are very high.

Gorilla viewing rules in Congo are based on the guidelines issued by the IUCN and is very similar to that of Rwanda and Uganda, although viewing is

The dense vegetation surrounding Odzala-Kokoua

usually limited to 6 or less people as opposed to groups of 8 allowed in Volcanoes National Park or Bwindi. The rules are designed specifically to limit behavioral impact and also potential disease transmission from humans to gorillas. Viewing is limited to one hour per day, the minimum age to trek is 15, visitors are not allowed closer that 22 feet (7 m) to the gorillas, and are not allowed to trek if they are ill (ie. with a cold or flu).

ACCOMMODATIONS — CLASS A/B: • **Ngaga Camp**, built in the forest canopy (12 feet above the ground), features 6 solar-powered rooms, a dining room and lounge all with spectacular views. Activities include tracking western lowland gorillas, birding, forest walks during the day, and night walks in search of nocturnal primates. • **Lango Camp**, architecturally inspired by a Pygmy design and building material, includes 6 rooms with views overlooking the Lango Bai. Guests gather at the main area, dining room and fire pit. Forest buffalo, elephant, western sitatunga, and large flocks of green pigeon and grey parrot are frequently seen from the deck. The camp is entirely solar powered. Activities include boating and canoeing along the Lekoli River, walking safaris through the Lango Bai system, and night and day game drives in the nearby savannah.

A forest walk through Odzala-Kokoua National Park

Brazzaville

Brazzaville is the capital city with a population of over 1 million inhabitants. It lies along the western banks of the massive Congo River just downstream from Stanley Pool and upstream of the cataracts or rapids of the Congo River. Kinshasha, the capital of the Democratic Republic of the Congo, lies across the 2 mile (3 km) wide river. Some of the city's architecture and design with many large, wide boulevards reflects its French colonial heritage. The newly built Maya Maya Airport is located only 15 minutes from the city center.

Consider having "sundowners" and/or dinner at Mami Wata (good local and western food), situated on the edge of the Congo River with views across to Kinshasha in DRC. It is popular in the ex-pat community and offers good western and local food in pleasant surroundings.

ACCOMMODATIONS — FIRST CLASS: • **Hotel Mikhael** is centrally located in Brazzaville and only 10 minutes from the airport. The modern hotel features a swimming pool and restaurant.

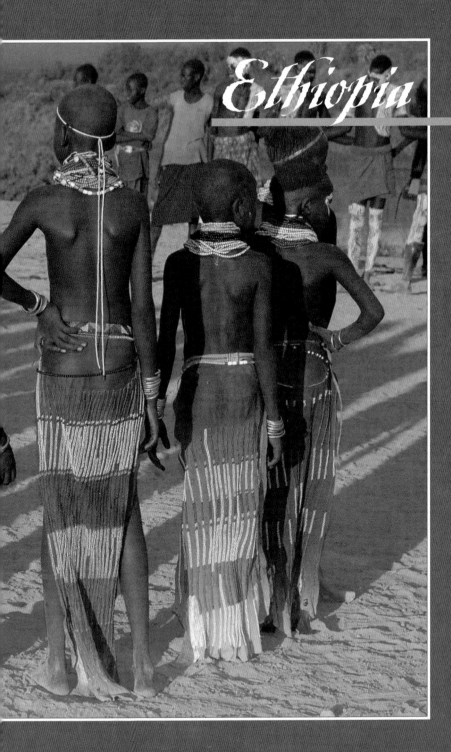

Ethiopia

Ethiopia

Ethiopia is a mountainous country situated in the Horn of Africa, covering some 435,070-square-miles (1,127,127-km²) about twice the size of Texas. It has three distinct climate zones relative to topography. The highest peaks in the Simien mountains rise above 14,400 feet (4,400 m), while those in the Bale mountains are just slightly lower. These cool temperate uplands are in stark contrast to the low-lying Danakil and Ogaden deserts which are among the hottest places on Earth. A number of endemic mammals, birds and other species are confined to Ethiopia. There are 84 indigenous languages, but English is widely used. Currency is the Birr.

Ethiopia
Country Highlights

- Visit the post-harvest festivities among the Suri people in western Omo, in July and August.
- See Bull Jumping — a right of passage ceremony for young men — among the Hamer people in the Omo Valley.
- Visit the famous Bati market, where highlanders and lowlanders meet for trade, on any Monday.
- Take part in the Orthodox Christian Festivals, such as Timket (Epiphany, 19 January), Meskal (Finding of the True Cross, 26–27 September), Genna (Christmas, 06–07 September), Easter (in April).
- Take part in a pilgrimage to a church, such as St. Mary of Zion in Axum (at the end of November) or one of the small pilgrimages that occur throughout the year.
- Travel to the Simien Mountains to witness the antics of the geladas.
- Spend the night on the volcano at Erta Ale, and watch the lava bubble away.
- Watch the sun set over Lake Tana, and see the reed boats returning to shore.

When's the Best Time to Go for Game Viewing

■ Excellent ■ Good □ Fair ■ Poor ■ Closed

Country	Park/Reserve	JAN	FEB	MAR	APR	MAY	JUN	JUL	AUG	SEP	OCT	NOV	DEC
Ethiopia	Omo												
	Historic Route												
	Simien Mountains												
	Bale Mountains												

Best Wildlife and Cultural Experience

Lumale Camp (Omo), Simiens Lodge (Simien Mountains), Mountain View Hotel (Lalibela)

ETHIOPIA

The Federal Democratic Republic of Ethiopia is one of the oldest nations in the world and stands out as the country with the richest history and culture in all of sub-Saharan Africa.

Geographically, Ethiopia is a land-locked country located in the Horn of Africa, dominated by highland plateaus with semi-deserts and deserts in the east and rain forest near the Sudanese border near Gambella on the west. It is bordered by Kenya to the south, Somalia, and Djibouti to the east, Eritrea to the north and Sudan to the west. Altitudes range from 380 feet (116 m) below sea level in the Danakil Depression in the east to 15,155 feet (4,620 m) Ras Dashen in the beautiful Simien Mountains in the north. Major rivers include the Blue Nile that flows from Lake Tana in the northwest of the country into and the Omo River that flows south and eventually empties into Lake Turkana.

The highlands and the lowlands have distinctly different rainy patterns. The highlands usually experience the main rains July to September and short, light rains April to June. The lowlands main rains usually occur April and May, with the short rains falling in November and December.

Ethiopia may have been the cradle of mankind. The world's oldest known nearly complete hominid skeleton, Lucy, is 3.3 million years old. According to legend, Menelik I, the son of King Solomon and the Queen of Sheba, brought the Ark of the Covenant to Axum from Jerusalem. From about 1000 B.C., the reign of Emperor Menelik I began what became one of the longest known uninterrupted monarchial dynasties in the world.

After the decline of the Axumite Empire, Ethiopia's rulers retreated with their Christian followers to the high escarpment of the central plateau. There, protected by mountains, they were able to repel Muslim invaders. From approximately the

The tribes of the Omo River Valley provide a rich cultural experience for travelers

seventh to the sixteenth centuries A.D. the Ethiopians were surrounded by their enemies and in effect lived in isolation for 1,000 years. This cut them off from the evolving mainstream of Christian culture and helped preserve the values of their Christian Ethiopian culture. What resulted was an isolationist society suspicious of strangers and fearful of invasions.

Parts of the country were occupied by Italy from 1936 until 1941 when the country was liberated by the British and the Ethiopian patriotic forces. Haile Selassie I became emperor in 1930 and ruled until 1974 when he was deposed by a group of soldiers, who later became known as the *Derg*. For seventeen years Ethiopia suffered from civil war and state sponsored famines, until the military regime was overthrown by a coalition of rebel groups which still dominate contemporary politics.

There are 70 languages from a variety of linguistic groups spoken in Ethiopia. The national language is Amharic which descended from Ge'ez, the language of Ancient Axum, and still used by the Ethiopian Orthodox Church today.

The economy is predominately agricultural. Approximately 25% of the population is occupied with the production of coffee, which accounts for 50% of all Ethiopia's exports. Ethiopia in fact is celebrated as the birthplace of coffee. Mining and horticultural projects are becoming more important contributors, as is the export of hydroelectric power to neighboring countries. It has the third highest population of any country in Africa.

🐾 WILDLIFE AND WILDLIFE AREAS

Wildlife enthusiasts looking for endemic species should consider visiting the Bale Mountains to see the Simien wolf and Menelik's bushbuck, and the Simien Mountains for the elusive Walia ibex and to enjoy the entertaining antics of the

The dramatic Simien Mountains – often included in a "Historic Route" tour

gelada. For big game it is necessary to go to the Omo and Mago parks in the south, or to Gambella, and even here sightings cannot be guaranteed.

More than 800 bird species are found in Ethiopia, of which 16 are endemic. Ethiopia's diverse habitats, highlands, lowlands, forests, lakes, wetlands and riverine systems provide sites for migrants. For butterfly enthusiasts there are eight families, 93 genera and 324 species to be found in the country.

Addis Ababa

Addis Ababa is a bustling, seemingly chaotic city of nearly 5 million people of many ethnic backgrounds. Addis grew like an expanding village, with modern hotels, open markets, slums, nineteenth century Armenian- and Indian-style buildings, churches, parks and malls are all mixed together. This was, in fact, still a city of tents just over 100 years ago. Founded in 1887 by Emperor Menelik I, Addis is the political, economic and social capital of Ethiopia. At between 7,545 to 8,200 feet (2,300 to 2,500 m) above sea level, it is the third highest capital in the world.

The **National Archaeological Museum** is located in the center of town and houses a replica of **Lucy**, the 3.3 million year old hominid skeleton along with a number of other hominid specimens over 1 million years old. The museum also has artifacts and relics from the Axumite and Gondorene periods up to the rule of Menelik II. This is probably the museum of greatest interest to tourists.

The **Institute of Ethiopian Studies** and the **National Anthropological Museum** displays provide insight into the cultural crossroads that is modern day Ethiopia, with its elaborate festivals and immense spiritualism amongst many different faiths. This building was once the Genete Palace of Emperor Haile Selassie I, and visitors can see his bedroom.

A trip up **Mount Entoto** to see the expanse of Addis and to visit a church dedicated to the Holy Virgin (Maryam) and another dedicated to "Saint Raguel" is recommended if time allows.

The **Menelik Mausoleum** was constructed in 1911 in the old Baata church and it serves as a tomb for Emperor Menelik II, princes and martyrs of freedom. **St. George's Cathedral** was built in 1896 in the traditional octagonal shape by the Emperor Menelik II to commemorate his victory at Adwa; it is dedicated to the national saint of Ethiopia. The museum houses a wide collection of important religious paintings, crosses of many designs, historic books and parchments, and beautiful handicrafts. There are also fine examples of modern paintings by the famous Ethiopian artist Afewerke Tekle. The **Trinity Cathedral** was built in 1941 in commemoration of Ethiopia's liberation from Italian occupation, and is where Haile Selassie was buried.

The **Jubilee Palace** is a modern palace completed to commemorate the Silver Jubilee of the coronation of Emperor Haile Selassie I. The park is home to a collection of rare indigenous wildlife.

A variety of cuisines are available in Addis, including Italian (try Castelli's, in Piassa), Greek, Armenian, Korean, Chinese, Arabic, Indian and Georgian. I highly recommend dining in one or more of the traditional Ethiopian restaurants, many of which have floor shows, such as Habesha Restaurant, Dashen Restaurant, Yod Abyssinia or the Crown Hotel.

There are some good **shopping opportunities** in Addis — whereas it's relatively poor outside the city. In general one is presented with traditional clothes and textiles, weavings, carvings, ethnic artifacts, spices/coffee, silver and gold jewelry and paintings with both modern and religious influences.

If you buy any souvenir that is worth more than US$500.00 you need to have a certificate confirming that the goods you have purchased are exportable and that they are not classified as irremovable heritage items. This is easy to obtain during normal office hours from the Ethiopian National Museum.

Churchill Road is the main souvenir shopping area of Addis. Close to the main post office are a number of souvenir shops selling silver jewelry, ethnic artifacts and carpets. Farther up the road are several shops selling cotton weavings (tablecloths, embroidered shirts and dresses, scarves). Another good place for Ethiopian fabrics that are made into traditional dresses, scarves, shawls and purses is Mesfin Tesfa's on Bole Road. The lobby and pool level of the Hilton Hotel has some extensive and good shopping opportunities. One of the best gold shops is Teclu Desta on Adwa Avenue.

Ethiopian art is another popular item, St. George Gallery behind the Sheraton has international quality handmade furniture, fabrics, paintings and jewelry, and the nearby Asni Gallery features modern art by young Ethiopian artists, as does the Makush Gallery on Bole Road, which is inside a reasonably good restaurant if you get hungry.

For export-quality fabrics, visit Muya, near Sidist Kilo by the Egyptian Embassy.

Be sure to visit the **Mercato**, the largest market area on the continent, where you can bargain for Ethiopian crafts and virtually everything else under the sun.

Nightlife in Addis is exciting and gets moving around 10:30 p.m. In addition to modern discos, there are a large number of *azmari bait* (traditional music houses) where singers and musicians perform using traditional instruments such as the *kirar* (a kind of lyre) and the *masinqo* (a single stringed violin).

ACCOMMODATION — DELUXE: • **Sheraton Luxury Collection Hotel** is the most luxurious accommodation in Ethiopia with spacious rooms and magnificent suites set in beautifully landscaped gardens. There are several restaurants, two bars, a large heated lap swimming pool, full spa, business center and conference facilities. The hotel is located about a 25 minute drive from the Bole International Airport.

FIRST CLASS: • **Intercontinental Addis Ababa Hotel** features air-conditioned rooms, rooftop swimming pool, 3 restaurants and 3 bars (please note — this is not a member of the Intercontinental hotel chain). • **Hilton Hotel** has 356 rooms with private balconies, four restaurants, swimming pool, tennis courts, health club, jogging track and shopping mall, set on 15 acres. This is one of the older style Hiltons as it was built in 1969.

TOURIST CLASS: • **Jupiter Hotel** has 2 locations, one near the airport and the other in Casanchis, each with 142 large rooms. • **Churchill Hotel** offers 53 guest rooms, lobby bar, lounge and well-equipped fitness center. • **Ghion Hotel**, government owned and centrally located, features 60 rooms and four suites with a restaurant, lush grounds and an olympic size swimming pool.

THE NORTH

The **Historic Route** and dramatic mountain scenery, particularly around the Simien Mountains is found in the north of the country.

Unlike most other African countries, Ethiopia was never colonized. This allowed them to develop relatively unaffected — resulting in unique cultures and an amazing wealth of historic sights. The best known historic sites on the Historic Route are Axum, Lalibela, Gondar and Bahir Dar.

The easiest and fastest way to get around is by scheduled flights or private air charter. In order not to miss some of the stunning scenery and other interesting, though less well-known sites, a combination of road and air travel is recommended.

If it is done by road, others sites and activities can easily be added, such as the rock hewn churches of Tigray, the markets of Senbete and Bati (where the highlanders and lowlanders meet for trade) and the beautiful Simien Mountains. Ideally, two days in each place should be allowed for Axum, Lalibela, Gondar and Bahir Dar. Two weeks plus should be allowed for doing the Historic Route by road.

Travelers can experience and even participate in ancient religious festivals (some with over 100,000 pilgrims) in this and other regions of the country. Some of the more prominent festivals include Timket (Ethiopian Epiphany), Fasika (Easter), Genna (Christmas) and Meskal (the finding of the true cross), and the special feast days of individual churches.

Every day of the month is named after a patron saint, and subsequently there is a festival somewhere in the country every day celebrating that saint. Therefore travelers really do not need to get too preoccupied with timing their visits around "festivals." In fact, travelers can get overwhelmed by millions of Ethiopians during the major festivals. I'd encourage people to avoid these big festivals as there can be real chaos, and it is much nicer and more authentic to hit one of the "living museums" (local churches) on the day of a saint.

Timket (Ethiopian Epiphany) is one of the most colorful festivals and occurs on the 19th of January, when the church Tabots are paraded to a body of water in order to commemorate Christ's baptism.

Meskal is celebrated in memory of the Finding of the True Cross by Empress Eleni and coincides with the mass blooming of the golden Maskal daisies. **Genna (Christmas)** is celebrated by church services on the 7th of January throughout the night, with worshipers moving from one church to another.

Ethiopia has a number of pilgrimage sites, Christian and Muslim, visited on certain days by thousands (in some places, tens of thousands) of pilgrims. The most important sites include the **Mariamtsion Church** in Axum, **Debre Damo Monastery**, **Hamad al-Negash** (site of the first Muslim settlement in the world), **Gabriel Kolubi** near Dire Dawa and **Sheikh Hussain** near Bale.

Axum

Axum was the capital of an Empire which even included parts of Arabia across the Red Sea. It was rated as one of the four greatest powers of the ancient world (along with China, Persia and Rome) by fourth century Persian philosopher Mani. Axum had its own alphabet and notational system, constructed dams and traded with partners as far away as India and China.

Highlights in the area include **stelae**, the largest single pieces of stone erected anywhere in the world (one of which was returned from Italy in 2005 after being in Rome for 68 years), **Axum Museum**, the castles and tombs of the kings, and **Mariamtsion Church** that was built on the site of Ethiopia's first church. A chapel within the church compound is believed by Ethiopian Orthodox Christians to house the **Ark of the Covenant** (see Graham Hancock's *The Sign and the Seal*).

Other sites in the area include the **pre-Axumite temple** built in 800 B.C. at Yeha, 34 miles (55 km) east of Axum, and the seventh century monastery at **Debre Damo**, where the only access is by rope and women are not allowed).

ACCOMMODATION — CLASS B: • **Geralta Lodge** is located in the northern region of Ethiopia, a half-day drive from Axum, and features 5 bungalows, a restaurant and lounge.

BASIC: • **Yeha Hotel** has 60 rooms and three suites, bar and restaurant.

Gondar

Gondar was the capital of the Ethiopian Empire from the seventeenth to mid-nineteenth centuries and is distinguished by its castles and imperial compound and by its churches. Debre Berhan Selassie is one of the most spectacularly painted churches in the country with its walls completely covered in murals and its ceiling covered with murals of angels' faces — each slightly different that the others. The Palace of Emperor Fasilidas is the most impressive of the castles and well worth a visit.

The ruins of the Palace of Emperor Fasilidas

Gondar is located 464 miles (748 km) by road from Addis Ababa, and is best accessed by scheduled flights.

ACCOMMODATION — TOURIST CLASS: • **Taye Hotel** is located downtown and offers 79 rooms, 2 restaurants, 2 bars, gym and swimming pool.

BASIC: • **Goha Hotel** has 60 rooms and four suites, two bars and a restaurant.

Simien Mountains

The Simien Mountains present perhaps the most dramatic mountain scenery in Africa, and are certainly one of the most beautiful mountainous regions in the world. Huge volcanic plugs formed 40 million years ago have eroded into fabulous pinnacle peaks (many over 13,100 feet/4,000 m) and river valleys. **Ras Dashen** at 15,155 feet (4,620 m) is in fact the fourth highest peak in Africa; if you wish to climb it allow eight days.

Wildlife enthusiasts venture here to see endemic species including the entertaining gelada (similar to baboons), the Walia ibex (a member of the goat family) and the Simien wolf. Simien wolves are in fact seldom seen here as there may be less than 20 individuals in the park, and are better viewed in Bale Mountains National Park.

Endemic birds in the region include wattled ibis, white-billed starling, thick-billed raven, back-headed siskin, white-collared pigeon, and white-backed black tit. Lammergeyers may also be seen.

The Simien Mountains can easily be combined with a tour on the Historic Route, as the park entrance at Debark is only about 60 miles (100 km) from Gondar.

Gelada are endemic to Ethiopia

ACCOMMODATION — CLASS B: • **Simiens Lodge** offers twenty rooms and a main lodge that has a fireplace, restaurant and bar.

Lalibela

Lalibela means "the bees recognized his sovereignty" (in the Agnew language) and is one of the most amazing historical sites on earth. At the end of the twelfth and beginning of the thirteenth centuries King Lalibela of the Zaghwe dynasty built a series of rock hewn churches. The **New Jerusalem** is in fact rightly categorized as one of the wonders of the world. The excavations were dug deep in order to enable the churches to reach three stories below ground level. All of the churches were decorated with fine carvings, which have been well preserved.

The churches are naturally divided into the Eastern and Western groups by the dry riverbed of the Yordanus River (River Jordan). There are 11 churches within the town, all of which are still in use today. There are also a number of outlying churches that can be visited if you stay for a few days. This must have been a wealthy kingdom, as it is estimated that the churches in Lalibela took 25 years to construct, and there must have been economic surpluses to pay for the large work force required for the construction.

These are indeed "living museums" used daily by the local people. Approximately 5,000 monks and priests live here, working in the churches and performing the annual Ethiopian Christian ceremonies year round.

During a festival celebrating a patron saint, the churches are full of worshipers, with priests burning incense, chanting and beating drums — making you feel as if you have been taken 800 years back in time!

Lalibela is located 398 miles (642 km) from Addis, and is most easily accessed by air.

A priest in Lalibela

ACCOMMODATION — FIRST CLASS: • **Mountain View Hotel Lalibela** is located on the edge of the Lasta Mountain chain and built at an altitude of 8,800 feet (2680 m). The bedrooms and restaurant feature panoramic views, and the hotel architecture resembles the rockhewn churches.

BASIC: • **Jerusalem Guesthouse** has 22 rooms and a restaurant. • **Seven Olives Hotel** is located close to the main entrances of the churches and has a restaurant. • **Roha Hotel** offers 60 rooms and four suites, a restaurant and bar.

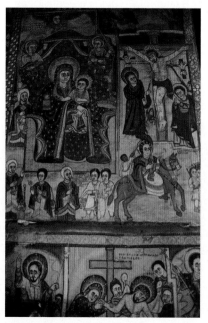

An intricate mural in Bahir Dar

Bahir Dar

Bahir Dar is situated on **Lake Tana**, which has many island monasteries and churches — many of which are closed to women. However, the churches on the **Zeghie Peninsula** are open to all. Be sure to visit the medieval church of **Debre Sina Mariam**.

Visitors can cross the lake, which is the source of the Blue Nile, from Bahir Dar to Gorgora, and vice versa. The **Blue Nile Falls** are only worth seeing when the dam gates are open.

White water rafting is generally done on the Blue Nile near Bahir Dar (a few days), along the Omo River (the whole stretch can take up to a month) and on the Awash River (one or two days). Rafting can only be done at certain times of the year, after the rains, and needs to be set up well in advance.

ACCOMMODATION — FIRST CLASS: • **Kuriftu Resort and Spa** is located on Lake Tana and offers 28 rooms in individual bungalows with lake or gardens views. There is a bar, restaurant and spa.

BASIC: • **Tana Hotel**, set on the shores of Lake Tana, has 64 rooms and suites, bar and restaurant. • **Abayminch Lodge** is located a 10-minute drive from the lake shore and features 40 rooms on attractive grounds.

THE SOUTH

Rift Lakes

South of Addis Ababa there is a string of seven lakes along the floor of the Rift Valley— Lakes Zwai, Langano, Abiata, Shalla, Awassa, Abaya and Chamo— each with a character of its own.

ACCOMMODATION — CLASS B: • **Bishangari Lodge** is located on the eastern bank of Lake Langano and has eight chalets and one suite, a bar and restaurant. Guests are taken with their luggage from reception to their chalets via donkey carts. Over 300 bird species have been recorded in the area. The lodge is located 155 miles (250 km) from Addis, and is a good overnight option if you are driving from Bale Mountains National Park to Addis. • **Paradise Lodge Arbaminch** overlooks the forest of Netch Sar National Park and Chamo and Abaya Lakes. The lodge has 8 rooms, restaurant, bar and limited spa services.

Bale Mountains National Park

Bale Mountains National Park is situated on the southern plateau approximately 8,200 feet (2,500 m) above sea level, rising up to 14,360 feet (4,377 m). This is the largest alpine area in Africa covering over 386-square-miles (1,000-km²). It also has the highest all-weather road in Africa running through it.

Bale encompasses a high altitude plateau with volcanic crags and lakes, forests, alpine moor land, trout filled streams and a great variety of fauna and flora. The main draw to the park is that it contains over half of the world's population of Semien wolves *(Canis simensis),* which is listed as critical endangered by the World Conservation Union (IUCN).

Other endemic mammals include the mountain nyala and Menelik's bushbuck. Mountain nyalas have longer hair than common species of nyala due to the cold climate in its high altitude habitat. Menelik's bushbuck is a sub-species in which the male is much darker than the common bushbuck. Sixteen endemic bird species have been also been recorded. Plant life includes giant lobelia, St. John's Wort and thistle flowers.

The park can be explored by vehicle, on foot and on horseback. The underwater river and caves of **Sof Omar** can be visited in a day trip from Goba.

The park is a two day's drive from Addis, and is best reached by taking a 1 hour 20 minute charter flight to the nearby town of Goba.

ACCOMMODATION — BASIC: • **Goba Wabe Shabelle Hotel** has very basic rooms and a restaurant.

Omo River Valley

The Omo River Valley and Omo River Delta are one of the few great tribal lands of vanishing cultures left in the world today. As the world becomes more modernized, the opportunity to go "back in time" is becoming rarer by the day.

Some of the different ethnic groups situated along the Omo River include the Karo, the Dus, the Nyangatom, the Hamar, the Kwegu (Mogudji) and the Mursi. Except for the past few decades, these tribes have lived in isolation from the modern world. Marvelous scenery, birdlife (over 300 species recorded) and limited wildlife provide an added bonus to visiting this region.

The Omo River flows for close to 620 miles (1,000 km) from the highlands southwest of Addis Ababa to Lake Turkana (Kenya). The east side of the Omo

Juvenile Karo boys paint their bodies for celebrations *(top)*, Karo elders on the edge of the Omo River *(bottom)*

is accessible by a long two day drive from Addis. The west side of the river is currently accessible only for guests booked on boat-based safaris, or for those willing to take several days and drive from Addis Ababa to Jimma, Mizan Teferi, Tum, Tulgit and Kibish, or by taking a private air charter to Tulgit where the Suri (Surma) people can be visited. A bridge is planned to be built across the Omo at Omo Rate, and once completed will make access to the west bank and the Omo National Park easier.

Visitors should allow at least five days to explore the Omo River Valley and another three days if you wish to visit the Omo River Delta.

To take photos of the people, a fee of usually 5 Ethiopian Birr (about 30 cents) per photo is paid directly to the individuals being photographed. In this way the local people benefit economically from the presence of tourists — providing a way for the villages to make additional income out of retaining their culture.

The **Karo**, who number only about 3,000 people, mainly practice flood retreat cultivation on the banks of the Omo River, as do many of the tribes. When the level of the Omo drops (usually in September or October), they cultivate the river banks — and continue to cultivate more of the river bank as the river level continues to drop. Their women make clay pots for trading with other tribes. The Karo are exceptional in their face and body painting for their dances and ceremonies. Karo women scarify their chests to beautify themselves. The scars are cut

Members of the Nyagatom tribe *(top)*, A painted Hamar man *(middle)*, The "bullah," a Hamar ceremony *(bottom)*

with a knife and ash is rubbed in the wound to produce a raised welt. Their traditional evening dances are exceptional and a thrill— especially if you are asked to join in!

The **Nyagatom** tribe is quite warlike, and has settled primarily on the western side of the river. This is a great tribe to visit as they are less visited than most of the tribes on the eastern side of the river.

The **Hamar Koke** is a large agro-pastoralist tribe with a population of around 20,000 members who are known for their practice of body adornment. The women are classically beautiful with long braided hair, and wear heavy polished iron jewelry around their necks.

The most important Hamar ceremony is the "**bullah**" or "jumping of the bulls," when a boy becomes engaged and is about to pass into adulthood. This is a complicated ceremony witnessed by several hundred invited guests in which the *"Maz,"* or recently initiated men, must take a running leap onto the back of the first bull, then run across the backs of some 15 or more lined up in a row, without falling, back and forth, 4 times. While he is running, his young female cousins and sisters are ritualistically whipped by the *Maz* to encourage him. They don't show the pain they must feel and they say they're proud of the huge scars that result. Successfully done, the initiate is then allowed to join the *Maz*. If he falls, he is considered completely unworthy and the embarrassment of failure

The Mursi tribe are famous for their lip plates

will stay with him for the rest of his life. At the end of the leap, he is blessed and sent off with the *Maz* who shave his head and make him one of their number. His kinsmen and neighbors decamp for a huge dance which is also a chance for large-scale flirting. The girls get to choose who they want to dance with and indicate their chosen partner by kicking him on the leg.

The **Hamar Market** in **Dimika** is held every Saturday. Hundreds of Hamar traders display their goods including honey, tobacco, sorghum, coffee substitute, gourds, jewelry, bananas, sorghum beer, rust colored dust used to dye their hair, and much more.

The **Kwegu** or **Mogudji** live on banks of the Omo River at its junction with the Mago River, and number only a few hundred people. They are good fishermen and also trap small game and collect honey and wild fruits. These are the poorest of the poor on the Omo. They have no cattle and no land, and have some sort of a serfdom arrangement with the Nyagatom (previously it was with the Mursi).

Many Mursi and Surma women have clay plates up to seven inched diameter inserted in their lower lips. The Mursi and Surma men practice a single-combat sport of physical skill known as "**Donga**," or "stick fighting." This has evolved into something of an art form that allows young men to take part in competitions of strength and masculinity, earn honor among their peers and win the hands of girls in marriage without serious risk of death. Often as many as 50 unmarried men will compete from two age sets between 16 and 32 years of age. The ultimate winner is borne away on a platform of poles to a group of girls who will decide among themselves which one of them will ask for his hand in marriage. Donga stick fights take place at the end of the rainy season and continue for a 3-month period. Each week, chosen villages come together and the top fighters from each village challenge each other.

The Mursi number about 5,000 members and have a war-like culture, predominantly fighting to control large tracts of land for grazing. The men practice light scarification on their shoulders after killing an enemy, and paint most of their bodies with white chalk paint during dances and ceremonies. The Mursi are in general more "commercial" than the other tribes as they are more easily visited by tourists in vehicles.

A dam is being constructed on the Omo River. A bridge across the Omo is also planned — allowing easier access to the tribes on the west bank. The government is beginning to crack down on tribal practices of which they do not approve. Therefore, if this type of travel interests you, my advice is to go as soon as possible!

Mago National Park

Mago National Park was established in 1978 and covers an area of 8,348-square-miles (21,620-km^2). The Mago Mountains form the northern border and the Mago River and Mursi Hill Range form the western border. Unfortunately, most of the wildlife has been poached.

The Mursi inhabit the park — just as many of Ethiopia's parks are inhabited by people. Physical features of the park include part of the Lake Turkana Basin to the south, the Great Rift Valley and the Ethiopian Highland massif.

All visitors need to check in at the Mago National Park offices at Neri and pick up an armed national parks ranger to ride with them to see the Mursi. From wherever you enter the park you must first drive to Neri, pay park fees and take a park ranger with you.

ACCOMMODATION IN THE OMO REGION — CLASS B: • **Lamule Camp** is a seasonal mobile camp set on the banks of the Omo River within the southern edge of Mago National Park. The camp consists of eight large standup sized tents (about 10 feet ×

13 feet/ 3 m × 4 m) with a private shower and toilet tent set back from each of the sleeping tents, and a large dining tent. At the time of this writing, the camp offers the only boat-based exploration of the Omo — giving access to more remote tribes not easily accessible (if at all) by vehicle. Lamule Camp and the Omo River are best accessed by a two-hour private charter flight from Addis Ababa to a nearby airstrip, or by a two-hour private charter flight from Nairobi to Illeret, the Kenyan town closest to the Ethiopian border with an airstrip, followed by a road transfer across the border to the camp. It takes two to three days to drive from Addis Ababa.

A tent at Lamule Camp

• **Buska Lodge**, overlooking the Buska Mountain in Turmi, has 20 standard rooms with private sun terraces, 2 restaurants serving European and Ethiopean cuisine, a bar and limited spa services.

CLASS C: • **Turmi Lodge** has 24 rooms with plans to build 24 additional rooms, restaurant and bar. • **Murulle Omo Explorer's Lodge** has eight basic chalets with cold showers and flush toilets. The camp is used for hunting as well as photographic guests. • **Jinka Resort Hotel** is located east of the town center and features basic but comfortable rooms and a restaurant serving regional cuisine. • **Eco-Omo Lodge** is located 22 miles (35 km) from Mago National Park on the outskirts of Jinka town across the Neri River. The thatched bungalows have high ceilings and private terraces.

Omo River Delta

The Omo River Delta is about 22 miles (35 km) across and covers about 230-square-miles (600-km²). The Omo empties into Lake Turkana in northern Kenya.

There are about 13,000 **Dassenech** living on islands throughout the Delta, as well as in Kenya along the northeastern side of Lake Turkana. They are primarily pastoralists who also practice flood retreat cultivation. Their cultural practices are similar to those of the Samburu and Rendille tribes in Kenya, with whom they share the custom of male and female circumcision.

You can boat all the way to Lake Turkana through a myriad of channels — some as narrow as 33 feet (10 m) apart. Birdlife includes huge flocks of white pelicans along with hammerkops, white-faced whistling tree ducks, European barn owls, African skimmers, fish eagles, yellow-billed storks, maribu storks, white-faced whistling ducks, pied kingfishers and malachite kingfishers. The Delta is best reached by motor boat from Lamule Camp.

Omo National Park

Ethiopia's largest nature reserve, Omo National Park, covers 1,570-square-miles (4,068-km^2) and is located north of Mago National Park on the west side of the Omo River. Although wildlife is sparse compared to parks in Kenya and Tanzania, visitors may see buffalo, elephant, eland, Burchell's zebra, and perhaps lion and leopard.

Due to its relative inaccessibility, the park is seldom visited. Access is by ferry across the Omo River at Omarate (about a three day drive from Addis) or by air charter to an airstrip near Park Headquarters.

ACCOMMODATION — None.

THE EAST

Danakil Depression

Located in the northeast of the country, the Danakil Depression is one of the hottest places on earth with summer temperatures exceeding 122°F (50°C). **Dalol**, at over 330 feet (100m) below sea level, is in fact the lowest point below sea level on earth. Travelers interested in geology will especially find **Mount Erta Ale** fascinating as it the only volcano in the world with a permanent lava lake. Mount Erta Ale can be accessed by road, with the ascent being made on foot with camels carrying the supplies, or by a helicopter flight from Mekele.

Harar

Harar is a walled, Muslim city considered to be the fourth most holy Islamic city after Mecca, Medina and the Dome of the Rock in Jerusalem. The city was extremely religious and in fact was closed to visitors until 1887. The most impressive of its 99 mosques is the sixteenth century **Grand Mosque** with its twin towers and minaret (women are not permitted to enter). Other attractions include the nineteenth century **Medhane Alem Church** housing examples of traditional regional art, the **Community Museum** depicting the earlier ways of life in the area and the markets — rated as some of the most colorful in the country. The **Hyena Men** Harar feed bones to wild hyenas from about 7:00 p.m. to 8:00 p.m. just outside the Fallana Gate of the old city.

Harar is located 325 miles (523 km) east of Addis Ababa.

ACCOMMODATION — BASIC: • **Ras Hotel** has very basic rooms. • Several old houses within the walled city (or "jegol") have been converted into guest rentals. These authentic Harari homes feature a courtyard but not all rooms are en suite. They can be rented as a private facility for 4 to 5 people. Rowda Waber Harari Cultural Guest House is one example.

Seychelles

Seychelles

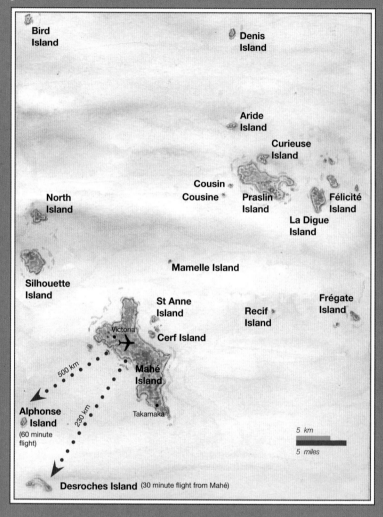

Bird
Island

Denis
Island

Aride
Island

Curieuse
Island

Cousin
Cousine

Praslin
Island

Félicité
Island

North
Island

La Digue
Island

Mamelle Island

Silhouette
Island

St Anne
Island

Recif
Island

Frégate
Island

Victoria

Cerf Island

Mahé
Island

500 km

230 km

Alphonse
Island
(60 minute
flight)

Takamaka

5 km

5 miles

Desroches Island (30 minute flight from Mahé)

The Seychelles comprise 115 islands which cover a collective land area of just 171 square miles (433 km²) in the western Indian Ocean. Mahé, the largest of the islands is located 4 degrees south of the equator. The islands are made of either granite or coral, with the former having peaks rising up to 2,970 feet (905 m). Most of the coraline or "outer" islands are just a few feet above sea level. Due to its geographic isolation, most of the flora and fauna is unique, but plants and animals introduced by man have greatly altered the landscape and endangered many species. The resident population is less than 100,000 with Creole, French and English widely spoken.

Seychelles
Country Highlights

- Exploring the powder-soft sands, turquoise waters and pristine beaches that are some of the best in the world!
- Visit Vallée de Mai, on the island of Praslin and see the world's largest seed from the Coco-de-mer tree and endangered black parrots.
- Snorkel in Sainte Anne Marine National Park, where hawksbill turtles and bottlenose dolphin frequent.
- Dine on delicious Creole dishes and practice your French language-speaking skills with the friendly locals.
- Experience a "Robinson Crusoe" vacation on the private island paradises of Cousine Island, Denis Island, Desroche or North Island.

When's the Best Time to Go

■ Excellent ■ Good □ Fair ■ Poor ■ Closed

Country	Activities	JAN	FEB	MAR	APR	MAY	JUN	JUL	AUG	SEP	OCT	NOV	DEC
Seychelles	Bird-watching												
	Diving/Snorkeling												
	Sailing												
	Fishing												
	Sunbathing												

Best Island Experience

Banyan Tree, Four Seasons (Mahe), Sainte Anne Resort (Sainte Anne), Cousine Island Eco Lodge (Cousine Island), Desroches Island Lodge (Desroches), Denis Private Island Lodge (Denis Island), North Island Lodge (North Island)

SEYCHELLES

The Seychelles are unspoiled islands that have a charm all their own, complimented by the genuine friendliness of the people. The beauty and variety of the islands make the Seychelles a vacation in itself or an excellent add-on to any safari. With numerous scheduled flights and inter-island boats, it's easy to hop from island to island. The Seychelles is certainly a fabulous place for a honeymoon!

The Seychelles are comprised of 115 islands spread over an Exclusive Economic Zone (EEZ) of no less than 500,000-square-miles (1.3 million-km^2) in the Western Indian Ocean, situated northeast of Madagascar and approximately 1,100 miles (1,800 km) east of Kenya. Mahé, the largest of the islands, is located 4 degrees south of the equator.

Forty granitic and 75 coraline islands make up the Seychelles. The granitic group are mountainous islands with peaks rising up to 2,970 feet (905 m) and surrounded by narrow coastal strips. These include the three main and most visited islands of Mahé, Praslin and La Digue. Félicité, Frégate, Silhouette and North Island are smaller granite islands with only one resort on each island. Many of the islands in the coraline group, or "outer islands," are only about 3 feet (1 m) above sea level. Visitors should consider including at least one granite and one coral island in their stay.

The people of the Seychelles are a mixture of African, Asian and European cultures. About 85% of the population resides on Mahé, the largest and the most economically important island in the Seychelles archipelago. About 89% of the population is Roman Catholic, 7% belongs to the Church of England, and the balance divided among Pentecostal, Seventh-Day Adventists, Jehovah's Witnesses, Hindus and Muslims.

Sunset is always magical in the Seychelles (Cousine Island)

Water sports abound in the crystal clear water of the Seychelles

Creole cuisine, like the origins of the racially mixed backgrounds, brings together a concoction of interesting recipes from the far corners of the world. Delicate local touches, such as varieties of curries with wonderful spices from India, stir fries and rice from Asia, and garlic-flavored dishes from France, are all enjoyed on the Seychelles. Locally brewed beers are Seybrew and Eku.

The Seychelles is very diverse, with something to suit a great variety of travelers. Accommodations vary from luxurious five-star hotels and island resorts to the less expensive family-owned guest houses, most with fewer than 20 rooms.

The islands have a tropical climate, which is generally warm and humid year-round. There are two tradewinds: The Southeast Tradewinds blow from May to September, during which it is relatively dry (although possibility of rain is year-round), and the Northwest Tradewinds blow from November to March. The rainy season starts at the beginning of December and continues until the end of January. The temperature throughout the year varies between 75° to 90° F (24° to 32° C). The average monthly rainfall in January is 15.2 inches (386 mm) and in July is 3.3 inches (84 mm). Fortunately, the Seychelles lies outside the cyclone belt.

There is much speculation about the early discovery of the Seychelles by Arab traders but no documentary evidence exists. Vasco de Gama visited part of the archipelago, the islands known as the Amirantes, in 1502. In 1756, the French were the first to colonize the islands, on which they established spice plantations. The English conquered the islands in 1794 and abolished slavery in 1835. In 1903 it became a British Crown Colony and claimed it's independence in 1976. Tourism is the major foreign exchange earner.

🐾 WILDLIFE AND WILDLIFE AREAS

Seychelles exhibits unique flora and fauna, due to its geographic isolation. Nearly 50% of the land area has been set aside for national parks, nature reserves and World Heritage sites. The Aldabra Atoll is a World Heritage site, boasting a population of 150,000 giant land tortoises—more than can be found on the Galapagos. Though the giant Aldabran tortoise *(Geochelone gigantea)* originated in the Aldabran Islands, a small breeding colony was set up in the Seychelles islands to ensure its chance of survival.

Giant Aldabran tortoises can grow a carapace as long as 56 inches (140 cm). They can live to be 150 years of age. The tortoises found on mainland Africa are smaller than these island giants and are found mostly in tropical areas. They are primarily herbivores.

Giant Aldabran tortoise

The raised shell of terrestrial tortoises, such as the Aldabran, probably evolved from the flatter shell of their aquatic ancestry for two reasons: 1) as a defense against predators, who otherwise might have been able to crush the reptile in their jaws, and 2) to provide for increased lung capacity, since they have proportionately larger lungs than do turtles.

The Seychelles has five species of frogs (four are endemic), including the smallest frog in the world, which rarely reaches 1 inch (2 cm) at maturity. Marine life is prolific, and places like Alphonse and Desroches provide some of the best diving in the world.

The flora is as exotic and unique as the islands themselves. The most exotic and strangest palm in the world is the famous "coco-de-mer," which has the largest and heaviest seed in the world.

There are seven established walking trails in the Seychelles — six on Mahé Island and one on La Digue Island. These walks offer great opportunities to enjoy the flora and fauna unique to these beautiful islands.

Bird Life

The Seychelles are the "Galapagos" of the Indian Ocean. Many tropical species of birds are not afraid of man and can be approached within a few feet (less than a meter). Colonies of over 200,000 sooty terns can be found nesting on some of the islands.

For twitchers (keen birders), these islands offer an opportunity to add several species to their lists. Birdwatchers will be well entertained by 10 endemic species and 17 endemic sub-species, which are found on the granitic islands, plus 3 endemic ones found on the coraline islands. The rare black parrot is found only on Praslin and the Seychelles black paradise flycatcher is found only on La Digue. Other rarities include magpie robins and the Seychelles fody. The best places for bird watching are the Vallee de Mai on Praslin, Denis Island and Bird Island.

Fly Fishing

The Seychelles Islands are a superb saltwater fly-fishing destination for both "flats" and blue water species. The coral islands to the south of Mahé is the region where most of the flats are to be found. St. Josephs, Poivre, Farquhar and Cosmeledo groups all offer excellent fishing for bonefish and giant trevally. St. Francois is rated by experts as one of the best bonefish destinations in the world. The area's potential has only recently been recognized, and a reasonable fisherman can expect to catch in excess of 20 of these elusive fish per day. Desroches Island and Denis Island are also great spots for fly fishing. Deeper water fishing on the drop-off, using heavier, faster-sinking lines, is productive. Several species of trevally are to be found in one spot off of Alphonse. Other species to be found are bonito, rainbow runner, dogtooth tuna, dorado, wahoo, sailfish, milkfish and triggerfish.

Access to the best areas is not easy. Places like Alphonse have a lodge where fishermen can be based and from which all the different types of fishing are available. To reach the rest of the areas, live-aboard sailing or motor yachts are the answer. The distances are formidable but the rewards are great.

Mahé Island

Mahé is the largest and most developed island, and it is the economic and political center of the Seychelles. The island covers 59-square-miles (152-km²) and is 17 miles (27 km) long and 8 miles (12 km) wide. It offers a variety of hotels and guesthouses and many lovely beaches. Both the international airport and major harbor (Victoria) are found on Mahé.

The interior of the island is mountainous, rising to 2,668 feet (905 m) at Morne Seychellois. One of the most scenic drives on the island is from Victoria through the highlands, south of Morne Seychellois National Park, to Port Glaud on the west coast.

There are 75 white sandy beaches, the most popular of which is Beau Vallon Beach, a 2-mile (3-km), crescent-shaped beach on the northwest coast. Grand' Anse is a good beach for surfing, under proper conditions. Anse Royale is a 2-mile (3-km) beach protected by a coral reef and located on the southeast coast of the island. There is a better opportunity to find deserted beaches on the south side of the island than on the more developed north side.

Victoria

Victoria is the smallest capital city in the world and the major port of the Seychelles. Places of interest include the market, the **Capuchin House**, built in colonial Portuguese style, the **State House**, a fine example of Seychelles architecture, the **Cathedral of the Immaculate Conception**, the **National Museum** and the **Botanical Gardens**. The "Pirates Arms" bar and restaurant is a popular meeting point.

Morne Seychellois National Park

This 11-square-mile (30-km²) park covers much of northwest Mahé, with altitudes ranging from sea level to 2,969 feet (905 m). There are hiking trails from Sans Souci Road to Copolia (1,630 ft./497 m), Morne Blanc (2,188 ft./667 m) and Trois Freres (2,293 ft./699 m).

Bird life includes the blue pigeon, Seychelles bulbul, Seychelles kestrel, cave swiftlet and Seychelles white-eye.

Flora in the park includes five different species of palm trees, the vanilla orchid *(Vanilla phalaenopsis)*, the extremely rare jellyfish tree *(Medusagyne oppositifolia)* and the bwa-d-fer *(Vateria seychellarum)*.

A villa at Banyan Tree *(top)*, Understated elegance at the Four Seasons *(bottom)*

ACCOMMODATION ON MAHÉ — DELUXE:
• **Banyan Tree**, located on the southwest coast overlooking Anse Intendance, has 60 air-conditioned 1- and 2-bedroom villas with private swimming pools and sundecks, gym, spa, 3 restaurants and a communal swimming pool. The Beach Villas are more spacious, and have an outdoor jacuzzi, steam shower room and feature larger private swimming pools than the Hillside Villas. • **Four Seasons Resort Seychelles** features 67 villas and suites stretching from the hillside to the beach. Each villa has a large deck, private plunge pool, daybed, expansive bedroom with sunken tub and outdoor shower. There are 2 restaurants, 2 lounges and a full service spa. • **Maia Resort** offers 30 spacious villas scattered throughout the lush hills and beach. The resort has a luxury spa, restaurant, and swimming pool. Water activities can be arranged on site. • **Hilton Seychelles Northolme Resort & Spa**, surrounded by white sand beaches and lush mountains, offers ocean view villa rooms and suites. There are 2 restaurants, 1 bar, a gym and a spa. There is a water activities desk to arrange scuba diving and snorkeling excursions.

FIRST CLASS: • **Le Meridien Fisherman's Cove**, located on Beau Vallon Bay in the northwest part of Mahé Island, has 68 air-conditioned rooms and suites with their own private balcony or terrace. The hotel offers 2 restaurants, 2 bars overlooking the bay, swimming pool, spa, tennis court and many other recreational activities. • **Sunset Beach Hotel**, situated on Mahé's northwest coast, offers a good standard of accommodation, particularly in the junior suites. The hotel is set on a rocky promontory with a pathway that leads down to a secluded sandy cove. It has 28 air-conditioned rooms with baths, and the junior suites have sitting areas. Facilities include a restaurant, bar, boutique and swimming pool. • **The Wharf Hotel and Marina** is conveniently located 5 minutes from the airport. It offers 15 air-conditioned rooms and a penthouse, 40 berth marina, pool, up-market restaurant and bar.

TOURIST CLASS: • **Sun Resort** is a short stroll from Beau Vallon Beach. It has 20 air-conditioned rooms with shower, sitting area, and a balcony or patio overlooking the swimming pool. The restaurant serves Creole cuisine, and there is a small bar and coffee shop. • **Lazare Picault** overlooks Baie Lazare on the southwest coast and has 14 rooms perched on the hillside.

Sainte Anne Marine National Park

Located east of Victoria, Sainte Anne Marine National Park includes 6 small islands and the waters that surround them. Île Ronde (Round Island), Île au Cerf and Île Moyenne islands have lovely coral beds and are excellent for snorkeling or exploring in glass-bottom boats. Among the granite islands, Sainte Anne Island is the most important nesting site for hawksbill turtles.

ACCOMMODATION ON SAINTE ANNE ISLAND — DELUXE: • **Sainte Anne Resort and Spa** is located on Sainte Anne Island, a 494-acre (200-hectare) private island and nature reserve in the Marine National Park. The resort is 10 minutes away by private launch from Mahé. The 87 luxurious sea-facing villas, some with private pools, are spread along the island's pristine beaches. Five restaurants serve a variety of cuisine including gourmet Mediterranean dishes. A Clarins Spa, and a full range of water sports are available. Daily excursions to other islands are offered.

Guests at Sainte Anne Resort enjoy private amenities

ACCOMMODATION ON ÎLE AU CERF — DELUXE: • **Cerf Island Resort** has been completely renovated and offers luxury villas with views of the tropical gardens or Indian Ocean. Each is fully equipped with air-conditioning, satellite television, mini-bar and private terrace. The resort boasts a fine dining restaurant, infinity pool, pool bar, beach-side dining, a lounge and spa. The property is located at the entrance of the Marine Park.

Praslin Island

Praslin, a granite island located 25 miles (40 km) northeast of Mahé, is the second largest island in the archipelago. Praslin is 6.5 miles (10.5 km) long and 2.3 miles (3.7 km) wide. The island is less mountainous than Mahé but still has hills over 1,150 feet (350 m) high. Beaches are less crowded than on Mahé, and Anse Lazio is considered the best beach on the island. Praslin is home to the famous Vallée de Mai National Park, which was declared a World Heritage Site by UNESCO in 1984.

Vallée de Mai National Park

The Vallée de Mai National Park contains over 4,000 coco-de-mer palm trees that grow in excess of 100 feet (30 m) in height and have a unique double-lobed coconut in the provocative shape of the human female pelvic region. At 20 pounds (9 kg), this is considered to be the world's largest fruit and takes over 10 years to ripen! Many myths and legends have arisen from the presence of this fruit, thought by some to be the original "forbidden fruit," and the island is considered the proverbial "Garden of Eden."

Allow 2 or 3 hours for your walk in this lovely park. The sale of the coco-de-mer (a unique souvenir, indeed) is strictly controlled, and a specimen may be purchased at the park or from other shops on the island.

Curieuse Marine National Park

Curieuse Marine National Park includes the waters between Curieuse Island and the northwestern coast of Praslin. The park covers 5 square-miles (14 km²) and reaches depths of 100 feet (30 m). A large colony of giant land tortoises is protected in Laraie Bay. Most visitors to the Curieuse Marine National Park disembark at Baie Laraie, where the shallow water is known for its population of large humphead parrotfish growing up to 47 inches (1.2 m) in length. At the Rangers Headquarters, giant tortoises may be seen. Sea turtles lay their eggs on the beach in front of this museum.

ACCOMMODATION ON PRASLIN — DELUXE: • **Constance Lemuria Resort** is situated in the northwest, straddling 2 beaches — Anse Kerlan and Petite Anse Kerlan. This luxury resort has 96 suites plus 8 2-bedroom villas with sea-facing balconies or patios. Facilities include a choice of 3 restaurants, bars, lounge, health spa, boutique, children's club, swimming pool, tennis courts, 18-hole championship golf course and water sports. There is a third, more private beach located nearby. • **Raffles Praslin Seychelles**, located on the northeastern tip of the island, features 86 villas with private plunge pools and an expansive outdoor pavilion. Facilities include several restaurants and bars, butler service, 24-hour in-villa dining, Kid's Club, spa, boutique and watersports.

FIRST CLASS: • **L'Archipel** is situated on the southwest coast on a lovely beach called Anse Gouvernment. The resort has 52 air-conditioned rooms and suites with private terraces, 2 restaurants, lounge, bar, swimming pool, gym, boutique, and free water sports including windsurfing, canoeing and snorkeling. • **La Réserve**, located on Anse Petite Cour, has 40 elegant air-conditioned Superior and Deluxe rooms. The hotel offers a weekly Sundown and Discovery Cruise. • **Hotel Coco de Mer**, located on Anse Takamaka, has 52 air-conditioned rooms and suites with sitting area and terrace. Facilities include 2 restaurants, 2 bars, swimming pool, tennis and water sports, including windsurfing and canoeing. The hotel's 2 catamarans are available for charter. • **Hotel Acajou**, named after the timber used in its log cabin-style accommodation, is located on the Cote d'Or Beach. It has 32 air-conditioned rooms with balconies facing the sea. Facilities include a restaurant, bar, beach snack bar, cocktail lounge, swimming pool, gym, boutique and massage room. Diving and bicycle hire can be arranged.

TOURIST CLASS: • **Le Duc de Praslin** is just a few minutes walk from Cote d'Or Beach. Each of the spacious 27 rooms and suites are air conditioned and has a veranda. Facilities include swimming pool, 2 restaurants and bar.

Cousine Island

Cousine, not to be confused with Cousin Island (next page), is a privately owned, 175-acre (70-hectare) island situated between Praslin and Mahé islands. The island has large granitic outcrops, open plains and pristine sandy-white beaches with beautiful coral reefs just offshore.

Wildlife above and below the sea is superb; many rare and endangered species, such as brush warblers and giant tortoises, may be found on and around the island.

At certain times of the year, turtles come ashore during the day and night to lay their eggs. Over 200,000 noddy terns plus a host of other interesting seabirds, such as tropicbirds and frigatebirds, roost and breed on the island.

Access to the island is only by helicopter.

The island paradise of Cousine Island

ACCOMMODATION — DELUXE: • **Cousine Island Eco Lodge** caters to a maximum of 8 guests in luxurious villas. Resident scientists conducting research on the island act as your guides. No day-trippers are allowed — which guarantees an intimate meeting with nature for guests. Activities include nature walks and lectures, beach walking, boating, fishing, snorkeling and scuba diving.

Cousin Island

Cousin is a 67-acre (27-hectare) granitic island located 2 miles (3 km) from Praslin. It became the world's first internationally-owned preserve when it was purchased in 1968 by the International Council for Bird Preservation (now called Bird International) to establish a bird sanctuary to protect endangered species, including the Seychelles fody and Seychelles brush warbler. Between May and October, thousands of seabirds can be seen nesting on the island. This island is also the most important breeding site for hawksbill turtles. The island can be visited Monday through Friday 10:00 a.m. to 12:00 p.m.

Aride Island

Aride Island is located 6 miles (10 km) due north of Praslin. It was bought in 1973 by the Cadbury Family (of chocolate fame) and donated to the Royal Society of Wildlife Trusts. Today it is managed by Seychelles Island Conservation Society.

Aride Island is probably the most natural and least touched of all the islands of Seychelles. It is the breeding ground for over 1 million sea birds, and is home to endemic species including the Fodie, Magpie robin and brush warbler. Turtles also nest on its shores. The island is uninhabited except for a handful of researchers and no overnight accommodation is available. However, day visits are allowed on the island's boats.

La Digue Island

La Digue is a granite island that has spectacular rock formations and secluded beaches. The best way to travel around this, the fourth largest island in the archipelago, is by foot, bicycle or ox cart. There are only a few vehicles on the island.

The highest point on this small 2-by-3 mile (3-by-5 km) island is 1,092 feet (333 m). A lovely walking trail from La Passe to Grand' Anse can be completed on foot or by bicycle. The island is reached by a 30-minute boat ride from Praslin.

La Domaine de l'Orangerie

ACCOMMODATION — FIRST CLASS: • **La Digue Island Lodge**, located on the west coast, has 69 air-conditioned rooms, most of which are thatched roofed A-frame chalets. Amenities include a beachfront restaurant, bar, boutique, swimming pool, windsurfing, snorkeling and a dive center.

TOURIST CLASS: • **Patatran Village**, located on the northwest coast, has 21 air-conditioned rooms and suites. It has a restaurant, bar, swimming pool and a small beach close by. • **Le Domaine de L'Orangerie**, located on the northwest part of La Digue, is comprised of 45 villas, 2 restaurants, bar and a spa.

Bird Island (Ile Aux Vaches)

Bird Island is a small coral island (1.5-by-0.5 mi./2.5-by-1 km) that is located about 70 miles (110 km) north of Mahé — about a 30-minute flight. A leisurely walk around this pristine island, with stops for an occasional swim and snorkel, takes about 2 to 3 hours. Several million sooty terns nest on the island, an event that usually occurs May through October.

ACCOMMODATION — FIRST CLASS: • **Bird Island Lodge**, the only property on the island, has 24 fan-cooled, spacious and comfortable bungalows. Facilities include a restaurant, bar, lounge, boutique and the use of snorkeling equipment.

Desroches Island

Desroches, a coral island 6 miles long and 1.5 miles wide (10-by-2 km), is the largest island in the Amirantes group. It is situated 30 minutes by air from Mahé with a scheduled flight every day. This is an excellent island for those who enjoy water sports. Scuba diving, big game fishing and fly-fishing are excellent.

ACCOMMODATION — DELUXE: • **Desroches Island Lodge**, the only lodge on the island, has 20 air-conditioned Beach Suites, 23 Beach Villas and 1 Presidential Villa. Facilities include a restaurant, lounge, swimming pool, boutique, and Conservation Society Research Center. Water sports include hobie cat sailing, snorkeling, scuba diving, windsurfing and deep-sea fishing.

Denis Island

This small (350-acre/140-hectare) coral island is only 25 minutes by air north of Mahé, and is often thought of as the "perfect desert island." Denis is located on the edge of the Seychelles Bank, where water depths quickly reach over 6,500 feet (2,000 m). Deep-sea fishing for barracuda, dog-tooth tuna, marlin and sailfish is excellent. There is only one exclusive lodge on the island.

A luxury suite on Desroche Island *(top)*, Denis Island has expansive suites *(bottom)*

ACCOMMODATION — FIRST CLASS: • **Denis Private Island** has 25 large, spacious, air-conditioned villas with expansive living spaces, open-air bathroom and an outdoor shower secluded in a private garden. The villas are separated from each other by lush gardens and hedges. Facilities include a restaurant, lounge, bar, wine cellar, swimming pool and PADI Dive Center.

Frégate Island

Frégate Island, historically a haven for pirates, is a granite island that is 1.5 miles long and a quarter-mile wide (2.5-by-0.4 km). It is situated about 20 minutes east of Mahé by air. The island has magnificent beaches and a variety of flora and bird life, including the Seychelles magpie robin and Seychelles blue pigeon.

ACCOMMODATION — DELUXE: • **Frégate Island Private**, the only accommodation on the island, has 17 air-conditioned villas. Each Indonesian-style villa overlooks the sea and consists of a separate bedroom and lounge divided by a foyer. The sun deck includes a private pool and sunbeds. Activities include scuba diving, snorkeling and guided nature walks.

A deserted beach at the Labriz Resort

Silhouette Island

Located 15 minutes northwest of Mahé by helicopter, this unspoiled granite island is the third largest island in the Seychelles and can be seen from the north coast of Mahé. Mountains rise to 2,427 feet (740 m) on this thickly forested, round island, which is approximately 3 miles (5 km) in diameter.

ACCOMMODATION — FIRST CLASS: • **Hilton Seychelles Labriz Resort and Spa** is a resort featuring 110 air-conditioned villas and pavilions with outdoor showers, terraces and courtyard gardens. Some beach villas and pavilions have a private plunge pool. Labriz features 7 restaurants and bars, a spa and wellness center, and numerous water activities such as diving, snorkeling and fishing.

Alphonse Island

Alphonse Island is located in the Amirantes Group some 300 miles (500 km) and an hour by plane from Mahé. It boasts 2 miles (3 km) of reef-protected coastline and a tranquil lagoon.

ACCOMMODATION — TOURIST CLASS • **Alphonse Island Lodge** is used October to April for small private groups of fly-fishing anglers.

North Island

North Island is a privately owned island consisting of over 497-acres (201-hectares) in size, with 4 wonderful white sand beaches, mountains and freshwater lakes. Great snorkeling and scuba diving is a specialty.

For the fisherman, blue water fishing is excellent. Due to environmental conservation, trawling on a short line is used. Working from a boat is the most productive method of fishing and the drop off is a 2-hour boat ride from the island. Trevally, dorado, bonito, tuna and sailfish are all found in the area.

ACCOMMODATION — DELUXE: • **North Island Lodge**, the only property on the island, has 10 presidential villas (approximately 4,500 sq. ft./420-m²) and 1 larger villa, #11 (approximately 7,000 sq. ft/650-m²) — providing a "Robinson Crusoe," barefoot luxury experience for guests. Each luxurious villa has a sunken bath, indoor-outdoor shower, bidet, private rock pool, study, sala and butler service. Dining is a sumptuous affair with custom designed meals based around a guest's desires and preferences. Exploring the island can be done on foot, mountain bike or by your private Island Buggie (electric powered golf cart). Activities include snorkeling, scuba diving, health spa treatments and interactions with the scientists on the island.

North Island is the ultimate island paradise *(top)*,
A villa on North Island guarantees privacy and sublime accommodations *(bottom)*

Mauritius

Mauritius

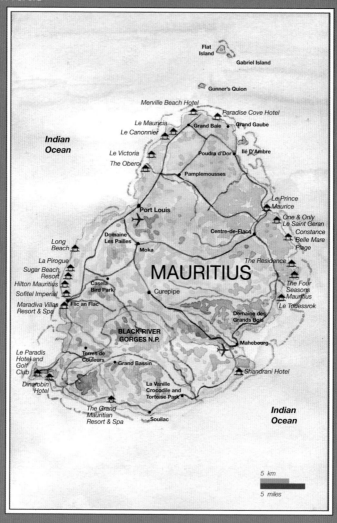

Mauritius is a volcanic island in the southwestern Indian Ocean, 520 miles (840 km) east of Madagascar. The island extends over 720-square-miles (1,865-km²), which is about the size of Rhode Island (or Luxembourg). The terrain of Mauritius is hilly with some small but spectacular mountains, the highest of which rise to some 2,700 feet (824 m). The 125 mile (200 km) coastline is fringed by coral reef, although much of this is not in a pristine state. The island was previously forested but — along with much of the native fauna — has been lost to development. The dodo is the most famous victim of colonization by humans. The resident population is estimated at 1.2 million. Creole, French and English are predominate languages. The currency is the Mauritius Rupee.

Mauritius
Country Highlights

- World class resort and hotels!
- Fantastic food, with a mix of Chinese, Indian, and French making up the 'creole' flavor.
- Soak up the sun on one of Mauritius gorgeous beaches.
- Visit Curepipe for the beautiful botanical gardens, housing the rarest palm tree in the world (single surviving specimen), and stop at the miniature ship building factories.
- Mauritius is a friendly and welcoming island, making it an ideal destination for all — from honeymooners to families.

When's the Best Time to Go

■ Excellent ■ Good □ Fair ■ Poor ■ Closed

Country	Activities	JAN	FEB	MAR	APR	MAY	JUN	JUL	AUG	SEP	OCT	NOV	DEC
Mauritius	Scuba/snorkel												
	Deep sea fishing (marlin)												
	Sunbathing												

Best Island Experience

Four Seasons Mauritius, One&Only Le Saint Géran, Le Touessrok, Constance Belle Mare Plage

MAURITIUS

Mauritius lies east off the coast of southern Africa and is visited by international travelers looking for a fabulous beach holiday. The combination of a cosmopolitan atmosphere, virgin-white beaches, crystal-clear waters, chic hotels with service to match — along with exquisite Creole, Indian, Chinese and European cuisine — is difficult to beat.

The beaches, water sports, fabulous holiday hotels and exquisite dining are by far the major attractions of the island. Most visitors come for four days to a week or more and base themselves in one of the island's beach hotels for their entire stay.

This mountainous island paradise lies in the middle of the Indian Ocean in the tropics about 1,200 miles (1,935 km) east of Durban (South Africa), 1,100 miles (1,775 km) southeast of Mombasa (Kenya), 2,900 miles (4,675 km) southwest of Bombay (India) and 3,700 miles (5,970 km) west of Perth (Australia). Combining a visit to this remote island with a safari on the African mainland or an around-the-world vacation should be considered.

The 720-square-mile (1,865-km^2) island features a central plateau, with the south more mountainous than the north.

The population of just over one million consists of Indians, Creoles, French and Chinese. Religious faiths include Hindu, Muslim, and Christian. Festivals are frequent. English is the official language, and French is widely spoken, but most of the native people prefer to speak Creole. Creole cooking, which emphasizes the use of curries, fresh seafood and tropical fruits, is often served. Mauritian beer and rum are popular.

The island is known for the awkward dodo, which, living on an island free of large predators, never needed to evolve the ability to fly. This evolutionary trait ironically contributed to its demise; the dodo was easily hunted to extinction during Dutch rule in the 1800s.

Mauritius has a tropical, oceanic climate. The best time to visit for a beach holiday is from September through mid-December and from April through June, when the days are sunny and the temperatures are warm. From mid-December through March is the cyclone season, which brings occasional tropical rains. June to August (winter) nights are cool and the temperatures along the coastline are pleasant. The average daily maximum temperature in January is 86°F (30°C) and in July is 75°F (24°C). Surf temperatures around the reefs average 74°F (23°C) in winter and 81°F (27°C) in summer.

The first known discovery of Mauritius was by colonizers from Iran in 975 A.D., but they chose not to settle. They moved on to what is now Mombasa

Mauritius is surrounded by extensive barrier reefs

and Pemba Island. In the sixteenth century, the Portuguese used the island as a staging post along their trade route to India.

The Dutch came in 1598, led by Wybrandt van Warwyck, who named the island Mauritius after Prince Maurice of Nassau. However, the Dutch did not settle on the island until 1638. In 1710 they left the island to be replaced by the French in 1715, and the French renamed it Isle de France. The island then became a "legal" haven for pirates who preyed on British cargo ships during the war between Britain and France. In fact, this type of pirating was viewed by many at the time as a respectable business.

After 95 years of French control and influence, the British took over Mauritius in 1810. Slavery was abolished in 1835. As the emancipated slaves no longer wished to work on the sugar plantations, thousands of indentured Chinese and Indian workers were brought in to fill their places.

Mauritius became an independent member of the British Commonwealth in 1968. Mauritius has a parliamentary democracy, holding elections every five years. Republic Day was proclaimed on March 12, 1992.

Industrial products and sugar are the country's major exports.

🐾 WILDLIFE AND WILDLIFE AREAS

Mauritius's major wildlife attractions are found both on land and below the surface of the Indian Ocean.

Mauritius has a number of endemic species of birds — many of which are found nowhere else in the world. Ornithologists or keen birders who wish to add unique species to their lists will find the long journey to this birder's paradise well worthwhile.

The pic-pic (Mauritian grey white-eye) is the only commonly seen bird of the island's 9 known remaining endemic species. The pink pigeon is thought to be the rarest pigeon in the world, and the echo parakeet is the world's rarest parrot, with approximately 40 birds alive. The Mauritius kestrel is also one of the rarest birds in the world; only 4 were known to exist in 1974. Fortunately, due to conservation efforts, populations of all the rare bird species are increasing. Other endemic species include the flycatcher, parakeet, Mauritius fody, olive white-eye, the merle and the cuckoo shrike. In total, about 45 species are found on the island.

Scuba Diving/Snorkeling

The 205 mile (330 km) coastline of Mauritius is almost completely surrounded by coral reefs, making it a good destination for snorkeling and scuba diving. You can dive on the colorful coral reefs and over 50 wrecks, which harbor a great variety of sea life.

The best conditions for scuba diving and sailing are during the period from October through March. Most of the larger beach hotels offer dive excursions and lessons, and they rent equipment. Spearfishing while snorkeling or diving with scuba equipment is prohibited.

Big-Game Fishing

Big-game fish, including blue marlin (plentiful), black marlin, yellowfin tuna, skipjack tuna, jackfish, wahoo, barracuda, sea bass and many species of shark can be caught. Fishing is excellent only a few miles offshore; the ocean drops to over 2,300 feet (700 m) in depth just one mile from shore! The best fishing is from November to April and is sometimes good as late as May. An international fishing tournament is held every year in December.

The largest fleets of deep-sea fishing boats are based at the Centre de Pêche at Rivière Noire (Black River) and at the Organization de Pêche du Nord at Trou-aux-Biches. Boats can be hired through your hotel or through travel agencies and should be booked well in advance during the prime fishing season. Fishing in the lagoons during this same period is also very good.

Port Louis

Port Louis, the chief harbor and capital city, is partially surrounded by mountains and is multifaceted in character. The city has a large **market** where indigenous fruits and vegetables, spices, pareos (colorful cloth wraps) and other clothing and souvenirs are sold. Just off the main square along Place d'Armes are some eighteenth century buildings, including the **Government House** and **Municipal Theatre**. The **Caudan Waterfront** and the **Port Louis Waterfront** are good areas for shopping. There are also a few movie houses and numerous eateries.

Curepipe

Curepipe, a large town located on the central plateau, is a good place to shop and cool off from the warm coast. Garment manufacturing is one of the principal industries in Mauritius and there are several international designer outlet shops located in Curepipe. An extinct volcano, **Trou aux Cerfs**, may be visited nearby.

Other Attractions on the Island

Peaceful **Casela Bird Park** covers 25 acres (10 hectares) and harbors over 140 varieties of birds from 5 continents, including the Mauritian pink pigeon. Black River Gorges National Park, proclaimed as the country's first national

The white sand beaches of Mauritius attract vacationers from around the world

Golf is a popular activity when you have tired of the beach

park in 1994, is 25-square-miles (65-km²) in size (3.5% of the island) and protects much of its remaining native forests. Nine endemic bird species, including the pink pigeon and Mauritius kestrel, are present. The Black River Gorges are located in the highest mountain chain on the island and offer splendid views of the countryside. There are several scenic hiking trails, including a 4 mile (7 km) hike to the Macchabee Forest and a 9 mile (15 km) hike through the gorges to the Black River.

Domaine Des Grands Bois is a 2,000 acre (800 hectare), forested park located north of Mahebourg on the east coast. Wildlife includes introduced stags, deer, wild boar and African monkeys.

La Vanille Crocodile & Tortoise Park, located in the south, breeds around 1,000 Nile crocodiles from Madagascar. There is a small zoo featuring the wild animals found on Mauritius, as well as guided nature walks through lush gardens with a variety of endemic plants and trees.

Domaine Les Pailles, situated south of Port Louis, covers over 3,000 acres (1,200 hectares) at the base of the Moka Mountain Range that can be explored by horse-drawn carriage, 4wd vehicle or by train. Other attractions include a spice garden and an ancient sugarmill.

The world-renowned botanical gardens of **Pamplemousses** have dozens of bizarre plants and trees including the talipot palm — at age 60 it blooms only once, then it dies. Giant water lilies imported from Brazil are also found here.

On sunny days, the land takes on the colors of the rainbow at **Terres de Couleurs** (the colored earth), located in the southwestern mountains near Chamarel.

Grand Bassin is a lake in an extinct volcano's caldera; it is the holy lake of the Hindus, who celebrate the Maha Shivaratree, an exotic festival held yearly in February or March.

Accommodation — Beach Hotels

Hotels are spread out, so visitors spend most of their time enjoying the many activities and sports their particular hotel has to offer. In many of the top hotels, most water and land sports, with the exception of scuba diving, horseback riding and big-game fishing, are free, including wind surfing, water skiing, sailing, snorkeling, volleyball, golf and tennis. Small sailboats are available at most resorts. Casinos are operated at the Trou aux Biches, as well as at the Casino of Domaine Les Pailles in Pailles and the Casino de Maurice. If you wish to visit the island during the high season (December to February and July to August) and Easter, I suggest that you book your trip several months in advance. Demand for accommodation in the top hotels is high year-round.

ACCOMMODATION — DELUXE: • **The Four Seasons Mauritius** at Anahita offers 123 luxurious villas and residences each with a private landscaped terrace, plunge pool, open-air bathroom with deep soaking tub and outdoor shower. The resort has a world-class spa, 18-hole golf course and 4 restaurants. • **Le Prince Maurice**, set in 60 acres (24 hectares) of private land, tropical gardens and sheltered beaches on the northeast coast of the island, has 89 air-conditioned junior and senior suites. The hotel has two à la carte restaurants — one of which is a "floating" restaurant — 2 bars, health and fitness centers, and water sports. • **The Oberoi**, located at Baie of Tortues on the northwest coast, has luxuriously furnished villas with sunken baths in private walled gardens. Facilities include 2 restaurants, bar, an ocean-front swimming pool, gym, health spa, tennis courts and water sports. • **One&Only Le Saint Géran**, located on Pointe de Flacq on the east coast of the island, has 3 restaurants, Givenchy Spa, 9-hole golf course, sailing and scuba diving. All 163 junior and ocean suites are air-conditioned with 24-hour butler service and a private terrace or balcony. • **Le Touessrok**, situated

The Four Seasons villas have private plunge pools

on the east coast at Trou d'Eau Douce, offers air-conditioned rooms and suites each with ocean views, spa, swimming pools, restaurants, shops, Ilot Mangenie (a private "Robinson Crusoe"-style island retreat), and Ile de Cerfs — an offshore water-sport playground that also offers secluded coves for sunbathing and an 18-hole golf course. • **Le Paradis Hotel and Golf Club** is located in the southwest of the island on a lagoon at the foot of the dramatic Le Morne Mountain. The hotel has 299 air-conditioned rooms and villas, 4 restaurants, swimming pools, 18-hole golf course, spa, casino, disco, nightly entertainment, scuba diving, water sports and a fleet of deep-sea fishing boats. • **Dinarobin Hotel Golf** comprises 174 suites, 4 restaurants, swimming pools and a spa. It is located adjacent to Le Paradis on a private peninsula, and the two hotels share all their facilities.

• **Shandrani Hotel** is conveniently located 4 miles (6 km) from the international airport on Blue Bay on the southeastern coast. This 327-room hotel has 3 separate beaches, all the usual water sports and tennis. All rooms are air-conditioned. • **Maradiva Villas Resort and Spa** (formerly the *The Taj Exotica*), located on the west coast of Mauritius, is spread over 27 acres and overlooks tranquil Tamarin Bay. Sixty-five spacious villas, each with a private pool and garden, exude an intimate ambiance for guests combined with all the modern day luxuries. There is a spa, lounge, 2 restaurants serving international dishes and local cuisine, and a variety of water sports are offered. • **Constance Belle Mare Plage**, located on one of the most beautiful beaches on Mauritius' east coast, has 92 sea-facing rooms and suites. The resort features two 18-hole golf courses, 7 restaurants, 6 bars, a spa and fitness center and variety of watersports.

FIRST CLASS: • **The Residence**, set on a lovely stretch of beach on the east coast of the island, has 135 luxury air-conditioned rooms and 28 suites with balconies or terraces and butler service. Facilities include 2 restaurants, snack bar, health center, beauty salon and water sports. • **The Hilton Mauritius**, located on the island's western coast, has 193 richly decorated rooms. The hotel has 4 restaurants, fitness club, jacuzzi and sauna, hairdressing salon, water sports and an 18-hole golf course nearby. • **Le Mauricia** offers 234 rooms and is located close to Grand Baie. The property is ideal for families and there is evening entertainment and discos. • **Le Victoria**, located between Grand Baie and Port Louis, has 254 extra large rooms and suites (all sea facing) and is ideal for

One&Only Le Saint Géran's oceanfront restaurant *(top)*, Constance Belle Mare Plage *(bottom)*

One&Only Le Saint Géran has an idyllic location on Mauritius

families. • **Paradise Cove Hotel**, located at Anse La Raie on the north coast, has 67 air-conditioned rooms, 2 restaurants, bars, swimming pool and water sports. • **Sugar Beach Resort** is a plantation-style resort, set on the west coast of the island, with a total of 238 air-conditioned rooms located in the Manor House and 16 Creole-style beach villas. Guests may enjoy a variety of water sports and the island's largest landscaped swimming pool, and they may also use the amenities of the nearby sister hotel, La Pirogue. • **Long Beach**, a new property on the east coast of Mauritius, features 255 ocean-view rooms. The resort offers several restaurants, bars, a full service spa and a variety of watersports. • **La Pirogue** is located on a fine, white beach at Flic-en-Flac on the island's west coast. Thatched cottages spread out from the main building that features a distinctive, sail-like roof. All 248 air-conditioned rooms are located on the ground floor and open out on the palm grove. • **Le Canonnier** has 284 rooms and duplexes. The property is ideal for families and there is evening entertainment and discos. • **The Grand Mauritian Resort and Spa** is spread over 25 acres and is bordered by the reef, an oceanic nature park and sugar cane fields. The resort features 193 rooms and suites and has several restaurants, bars, 2 swimming pools, spa and water sports facility.

TOURIST CLASS: • **The Merville Beach Hotel** is a comfortable hotel situated on Grand Bay near the northern tip of the island, with 169 air-conditioned rooms, a swimming pool and the usual water sports. • **Sofitel Imperial**, located at Flic-en-Flac on the island's west coast, has 191 air-conditioned rooms, 3 restaurants, a piano bar and the usual water sports.

Safari Resource Directory

We have endeavored to make the information that follows as current as possible. However, Africa is undergoing constant change. My reason for including the following information, much of which is likely to change, is to give you an idea of the right questions to ask — not to give you information that should be relied on as gospel. Wherever possible, a resource has been given to assist you in obtaining the most current information.

AIRPORT DEPARTURE TAXES

Ask your Africa tour operator, go online or call an airline that serves your destination, or the tourist office, embassy or consulate of the country(ies) in question, for current international and domestic airport taxes that are not included in your air ticket and must be paid with cash before departure. International airport departure taxes often must be paid in U.S. dollars or other hard currency, such as the Euro or British pounds. Be sure to have the exact amount required — often change will not be given. Domestic airport departure taxes may be required to be paid in hard currency as well, or in some cases may be payable in the local currency.

At the time of this writing, international airport departure taxes for the countries in this guide are listed below.

International Airport Departure Taxes

Country	Taxes due	Country	Taxes due
Botswana	*	Rwanda	* / **
Congo, Rep. of the	* / **	Seychelles	*
Ethiopia	*	South Africa	*
Kenya	*	Tanzania	*
Malawi	* / **	Uganda	*
Mauritius	*	Zambia	* / **
Mozambique	* / **	Zimbabwe	* / **
Namibia	*		

* Included in price of air ticket.
**Exceptions apply for charter flights.

BANKS

Barclays and Standard Chartered Banks are located in most of these countries. Banks are usually open Monday through Friday mornings and early afternoons, sometimes on Saturday mornings, and closed on Sundays and holidays. Most hotels, lodges and camps are licensed to exchange foreign currency. Quite often, the best place to exchange money is at the airport upon arrival.

CREDIT CARDS/ATMS/TRAVELER'S CHECKS/CASH

Major international **credit cards** are accepted by most top hotels, restaurants, lodges, permanent safari camps and shops. Visa and MasterCard are most widely accepted. American Express and Diner's Club are also accepted by most first-class hotels and many businesses. However, American Express is not often taken in more remote areas and camps.

ATMs are in many locations in South Africa, but are found in few other countries (except some major cities) covered in this book. Visa is the most reliable card to use at ATMs. MasterCard might not be accepted as well as other international ATM/credit cards. Only local currency can be withdrawn at an ATM and in limited amounts.

It is advisable to contact your bank before you travel and let them know that you will be using your ATM card/credit card in a foreign country so your card is not blocked while attempting to withdraw money. Confirm that the card will work in ATMs in the countries you will be visiting. ATM fraud is a common occurance, so keep your card and PIN safe.

American Express, Thomas Cook's, MasterCard and Visa **traveler's checks** are accepted at most banks and currency exchanges in international airports but in few other locations and therefore are not as useful as cash in hard currencies (U.S. Dollar, British Pound, Euro, etc.).

One way to obtain additional funds is to have money sent by telegraph **international money order** (Western Union), telexed through a bank or sent via international courier (i.e., DHL).

CURRENCIES

Current rates for many African countries can usually be found on the Internet.

For U.S. dollars, bring only the newer "big faced" bills as the older bills are generally not accepted. Traveler's checks are *not* widely accepted.

The currency of Namibia is on par with the South African Rand. The South African Rand may be accepted in Namibia, however, the currency of Namibia is not accepted in South Africa.

The currencies used by the countries included in this guide are as follows:

Botswana	1 Pula	=	100 thebe
Congo, Rep.	1 Central African Franc	=	100 centimes
Ethiopia	1 Birr	=	100 cents
Kenya	1 Kenya Shilling	=	100 cents
Malawi	1 Kwacha	=	100 tambala
Mauritius	1 Mauritius Rupee	=	100 cents
Mozambique	1 Metical	=	100 centavos
Namibia	1 Namibian Dollar	=	100 cents
Rwanda	1 Rwanda Franc	=	100 centimes
Seychelles	1 Seychelles Rupee	=	100 cents
South Africa	1 Rand	=	100 cents
Tanzania	1 Tanzania Shilling	=	100 cents
Uganda	1 Uganda Shilling	=	100 cents
Zambia	1 Kwacha	=	100 ngwee
Zimbabwe	1 U.S. Dollar	=	100 cents

CURRENCY RESTRICTIONS

A few African countries require visitors to complete currency declaration forms upon arrival; all foreign currency, traveler's checks and other negotiable instruments must be recorded. These forms must be surrendered on departure. When you leave the country, the amount of currency you have with you must equal the amount with which you entered the country less the amount exchanged and recorded on your currency declaration form.

For some countries in Africa, the maximum amount of local currency that may be imported or exported is strictly enforced. Check for current restrictions by contacting the tourist offices, embassies or consulates of the countries you wish to visit.

In some countries, it is difficult (if not impossible) to exchange unused local currency back to foreign exchange (i.e., U.S. Dollars). Therefore, it is best not to exchange more than you feel you will need.

DUTY-FREE ALLOWANCES
Contact the nearest tourist office or embassy for current, duty-free import allowances for the country(ies) that you intend to visit. The duty-free allowances vary; however, the following may be used as a general guideline: 1 to 2 liters (approximately 1 to 2 qt./33.8 to 67.4 fl. oz.) of spirits, one carton (200) of cigarettes or 100 cigars.

ELECTRICITY
Electric current is 220- to 240-volt AC 50 Hz. Adapters: Three-prong square or round plugs are most commonly used (plugs not drawn to size).

Plug 1 (top) – Used in South Africa, Botswana, Zambia, Namibia

Plug 2 (middle) – used in Kenya, Tanzania, Uganda, Malawi, Seychelles

Plug 3 (bottom) – used in Ethiopia, Rwanda, Congo, Mozambique

Zimbabwe and Mauritius utilize both Plug 2 and 3

GETTING TO AFRICA
By Air:
Most travelers from North America flying to the countries listed in this guide must pass through Europe, with the exceptions of South African Airways, which flies New York-JFK and Washington-Dulles to Johannesburg, South Africa, Delta Air Lines from Atlanta to Johannesburg, EgyptAir from New York to Cairo, Egypt, Royal Air Maroc to Casablanca, Morocco and Ethiopian Airlines from Washington-Dulles to Addis Ababa, Ethiopia. Major European carriers such as British Airways, Iberia, KLM, Air France, Swiss, Lufthansa and Brussels Airlines offer extensive service throughout Africa. African carriers including South African Airways, Kenya Airways, Ethiopian Airlines, EgyptAir, Air Seychelles, Air Madagascar, Air Mauritius and Air Namibia offer regularly scheduled service via Europe in cooperation with partner carriers from North America. Several other carriers such as Emirates, Qatar, Etihad and Turkish Airlines have greatly expanded their services to various destinations in Africa and are offering interesting and often financially competitive options worth consideration.

Frequent flyer programs offer a great option to reduce the cost of travel to Africa. I suggest booking frequent flyer award travel as far in advance as possible (usually just less than a year in advance) as seats for award travel are limited. Airlines usually work with several partners so if you are unable to obtain a reservation on your preferred airline be certain to inquire about alternatives that may be available on a partner airline. Also be aware of alternate cities served in Africa that may still work for your safari itinerary (i.e. for East Africa safaris consider checking availability for Nairobi, Addis Ababa, Entebbe, Kigali, Kilimanjaro and Dar es Salaam or for Southern Africa safaris consider checking availability for Johannesburg, Cape Town, Lusaka, etc.).

Availability changes continuously so if you are not successful on your first attempt it is wise to continue to check back online or by telephone for current availability of award travel seats. Once booked, ask the issuing carrier to advise of restrictions/fees associated with changes once your tickets are issued in the event that a more preferable option becomes available.

I strongly suggest you book your air with the tour operator with which you are booking your land arrangements; if there is an air schedule change or cancellation it will appear on their airline computer screens and they can work to get you back on track and adjust your land arrangements accordingly — otherwise you may show up at an airport only to find there is no flight!

By Road:

From Egypt to Sudan and Ethiopia to Kenya and southward; trans-Sahara through Algeria, Niger, Nigeria or Chad, Cameroon, Central Africa Republic, Democratic Republic of the Congo, Rwanda or Uganda and eastern and southern Africa. Allow several months because the roads are very bad.

By Ship:

Some cruise ships stop along the coasts of Kenya, Tanzania and South Africa and at Mauritius and the Seychelles.

GETTING AROUND AFRICA

See each country's map for details on major roads, railroad lines and waterways.

By Air:

Capitals and major tourist centers are served by air. There is regularly scheduled commercial air service to the following destinations within Africa (there is also scheduled air charter service to most parks and reserves):

Botswana: Gaborone, Maun, Francistown and Kasane.

Congo, Republic of: Brazzaville.

Kenya: Kisumu, Malindi, Mombasa, Lamu and Nairobi.

Malawi: Blantyre, Lilongwe, Mzuzu.

Mauritius: Plaisance International Airport.

Mozambique: Maputo, Vilanculos, Inhambane, Benguerra Island, Pemba, Beira.

Namibia: Windhoek, Lüderitz, Swakopmund and Walvis Bay.

Rwanda: Kigali.

Seychelles: Mahe and Praslin.

South Africa: Bloemfontein, Cape Town, Durban, Eastgate (Hoedspruit), East London, George, Johannesburg, Kimberley, Nelspruit, Port Elizabeth, Richards Bay, Mpumalanga (replaced Nelspruit), Umtata and Upington.

Tanzania: Kilimanjaro International, Dar es Salaam and Zanzibar.

Uganda: Entebbe.

Zambia: Lusaka, Livingstone (Victoria Falls), Mfuwe (South Luangwa National Park) and Ndola.

Zimbabwe: Bulawayo, Harare and Victoria Falls.

By Road:

Major roads are tarmac (paved) and are excellent in Namibia, South Africa, Botswana and Rwanda. Most major roads are tarmac in fair condition in Kenya, Tanzania, Uganda, Zambia, Malawi and Mozambique. The Republic of the Congo has very few tarmac roads. Many dirt roads (except in Namibia) are difficult and many are impassable in the rainy season (especially the Republic of the Congo), often requiring 4wd vehicles.

Taxis are available in the larger cities and at international airports. Service taxis travel when all seats are taken and are an inexpensive but uncomfortable means of long-distance travel. Local buses are very crowded, uncomfortable and are recommended for only the hardiest of overland travelers. Pickup trucks (matatus in East Africa) often crammed with 20 passengers, luggage, produce, chickens, etc., are used throughout the continent. Be sure to agree on the price before setting off.

By Rail:

The Blue Train and Rovos Rail rate as two of the most luxurious trains in the world. The Blue Train runs from Cape Town to Pretoria (and vice versa) and occasionally to Durban. Rovos Rail runs from Pretoria to Cape Town, Victoria Falls, Durban, Windhoek and Swakopmund (Namibia) and Dar es Salaam (Tanzania). Please see the chapter on South Africa for further details. With the exception of South Africa, regular train travel is slow and not recommended except for those who are on an extremely low budget or who have plenty of time to spare. Train travel is possible from Arusha (Tanzania) through Zambia, Zimbabwe and Botswana to Cape Town, South Africa.

By Boat:

Steamer service on Lake Tanganyika serves Bujumbura (Burundi), Kigoma (Tanzania), Mpulungu (Zambia) and Kalemie (D.R. Congo) about once a week; steamers on Lake Victoria service Kisumu (Kenya), Musoma and Mwanza (Tanzania) and Kampala-Port Bell (Uganda); steamers circumnavigate Lake Malawi. These steamers are extremely basic and are used primarily by the local people and not tourists.

HEALTH

Malarial risk exists in all of the countries included in this guidebook (except for Lesotho and much of South Africa), so be sure to take your malaria pills (unless advised by your doctor not to take them) as prescribed before, during and after your trip. Contact your doctor, an immunologist or the Centers for Disease Control and Prevention in Atlanta (toll-free tel. 1-888-232-3228, toll-free fax 1-888-232-3299, Website: www.cdc.gov) or the appropriate source in your own country for the best prophylaxis for your itinerary. Use an insect repellent. Wear long-sleeve shirts and slacks for further protection, especially at sunset and during the evening.

Bilharzia is a disease that infests most lakes and rivers on the continent but can be easily cured. Do not walk barefoot along the shore or wade or swim in a stream, river or lake unless you know for certain it is free of bilharzia. Bilharzia does not exist in salt water or in fast flowing rivers or along shorelines that have waves. A species of snail is involved in the reproductive cycle of bilharzia, and the snails are more often found near reeds and in slow-moving water. If you feel you may have contracted the disease, go to your doctor for a blood test. If diagnosed in its early stages, it is easily cured.

Wear a hat and bring sun-block to protect yourself from the tropical sun. Drink plenty of fluids and limit alcohol consumption at high altitudes. In hot weather, do not drink alcohol and limit the consumption of coffee and tea unless you drink plenty of water.

For further information, U.S. citizens can obtain a copy of "Health Information for International Travel" from the U.S. Government Printing Office, Washington, DC 20402.

INOCULATIONS

See "Visa and Inoculations Requirements" on page 577.

INSURANCE

Travel insurance packages often include a combination of emergency evacuation, medical, baggage, and trip cancellation. I feel that it is *imperative* that all travelers to Africa cover themselves fully with an insurance package from a reputable provider. Many tour operators require guests to be fully insured, or to at least have emergency evacuation insurance as a requirement for joining a safari. The peace of mind afforded by such insurance far outweighs the cost. Ask your Africa travel specialist for information on relatively inexpensive group-rate insurance.

MAPS

Before going on safari, obtain good maps for each country you intend to visit. This will increase your awareness of the areas you want to see and enhance your enjoyment of the trip. For a selection of resource books, field guides and maps I suggest you go to www.AfricanAdventure.com and view our products. It is best to purchase maps before arriving in Africa, because they may not be readily available upon your arrival.

METRIC SYSTEM OF WEIGHTS AND MEASURES

The metric system is used in Africa. The U.S. equivalents are listed in the following conversion chart.

MEASUREMENT CONVERSIONS

1 inch	=	2.54 centimeters (cm)
1 foot	=	0.305 meter (m)
1 mile	=	1.60 kilometers (km)
1 square mile	=	2.59 square kilometers (km²)
1 quart liquid	=	0.946 liter (l)
1 ounce	=	28 grams (g)
1 pound	=	0.454 kilogram (kg)
1 cm	=	0.39 inch (in.)
1 m	=	3.28 feet (ft.)
1 km	=	0.62 mile (mi.)
1 acre	=	0.4 hectares
1 km²	=	0.3861 square mile (sq. mi.)
1 l	=	1.057 quarts (qt.)
1 g	=	0.035 ounce (oz.)
1 kg	=	2.2 pounds (lb.)

TEMPERATURE CONVERSIONS

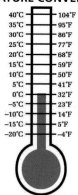

TEMPERATURE CONVERSION FORMULAS

To convert degrees Centigrade into degrees Fahrenheit:
Multiply Centigrade by 1.8 and add 32.
To convert degrees Fahrenheit into degrees Centigrade:
Subtract 32 from Fahrenheit and divide by 1.8.

PASSPORT OFFICES

To obtain a passport in the United States, contact your local post office for the passport office nearest you. Then call the passport office to be sure you will have everything on hand that will be required (www.travel.state.gov/).

PHONES

International Dialing Country Codes:
(from the USA, dial 011 + code + number)

Botswana	267	Mauritius	230	South Africa	27
Rep. of the Congo	242	Mozambique	258	Tanzania	255
Ethiopia	251	Namibia	264	Uganda	256
Kenya	254	Rwanda	250	Zambia	260
Malawi	265	Seychelles	248	Zimbabwe	263

Cell phones:

Your cell phone provider will be able to assist you with the possibility of using your own phone while in Africa; however obtaining international roaming service can be expensive. You will need to have your phone unlocked by your cell phone company in order to use it abroad. In most major cities you will be able to purchase a SIM card and air time which may be exchanged for your normal SIM card. Remember though that reception in the bush may not be possible. Satellite phones are only available to rent in the Johannesburg Airport in South Africa, so if you feel you need one, you may want to rent one for your trip prior to leaving home. A quad band phone that is programmed for worldwide use is considered best.

SHOPPING IDEAS

Botswana: Baskets, wood carvings, pottery, tapestries and rugs. There are curio shops in many safari camps, hotels and lodges.

Congo, Republic of: Wood carvings, malachite, copper goods, semiprecious stones and baskets.

Ethiopia: Traditional clothes and textiles, weavings, carvings, ethnic artifacts, wooden headrests, spices/coffee, silver and gold jewelry and paintings with both modern and religious influences.

Kenya: Makonde and Akomba ebony wood carvings, soapstone carvings, colorful kangas and kikois (cloth wraps) and beaded belts. In Mombasa, Zanzibar chests, gold and silverwork, brasswork, Arab jewelry and antiques.

Malawi: Wood carvings, woven baskets.

Mauritius: Intricately detailed, handmade model sailing ships of camphor or teak, pareos (colorful light cotton wraps), knitwear, textiles, T-shirts, Mauritian dolls, tea, rum, and spices.

Mozambique: Wood carvings, colorful paintings, silverware and island sarongs.

Namibia: Semiprecious stones and jewelry, karakul wool products, wood carvings, ostrich eggshell necklaces and beadwork.

Rwanda: Woven baskets, placemats, tablecloths, jewelry, wooden sculptures including gorilla sculptures, drums, colorful bags and purses, and coffee.

Seychelles: Coco-de-mer nuts (may be purchased with a government permit that is not difficult to obtain), batik prints, spices for Creole cooking and locally produced jewelry, weavings and basketry.

South Africa: Diamonds, gold, wood carvings, dried flowers, wire art, wildlife paintings and sculpture, and wine.

Tanzania: Makonde carvings, meerschaum pipes and tanzanite.

Uganda: Wood carvings.

Zambia: Wood carvings, statuettes, semiprecious stones and copper souvenirs.

Zimbabwe: Carvings in wood, stone and Zimbabwe's unique verdite, intricate baskets, wildlife paintings and sculpture, ceramic ware, and crocheted garments.

SHOPPING HOURS

Shops are usually open Monday through Friday from 8:00 or 9:00 a.m. until 5:00 to 6:00 p.m. and from 9:00 a.m. until 1:00 p.m. on Saturdays. Shops in the coastal cities of Kenya and Tanzania often close midday for siesta. Use the shopping hours given above as a general guideline; exact times can vary within the respective country.

THEFT

The number one rule in preventing theft on vacation is to leave all unnecessary valuables at home. What you must bring, keep on your person or lock in room safes or safety deposit boxes when not in use. Carry all valuables in your carry-on luggage — do not put any valuables in your checked luggage. Consider leaving showy gold watches and jewelry at home. Theft in Africa is generally no worse than in Europe or the United States. One difference is that Africans are poorer and may steal things that most American or European thieves would consider worthless. Be careful in all African cities (like most large cities in North America) and do not go walking around the streets at night.

TIME ZONES

EST = Eastern Standard Time (east coast of the United States)
GMT = Greenwich Mean Time (Greenwich, England)
* Time difference could vary 1 hour depending on daylight savings time

EST + 6/GMT + 1
Congo

EST + 7/GMT + 2

Botswana	South Africa
Malawi	Zambia
Mozambique	Zimbabwe
Namibia	
Rwanda	

EST + 8/GMT + 3
Ethiopia
Kenya
Tanzania
Uganda

EST + 9/GMT + 4
Mauritius
Seychelles

TIPPING

A 10% tip is recommended at restaurants for good service where a service charge is not included in the bill. For advice on what tips are appropriate for guides, safari camps and lodges, ask the Africa specialist booking your safari.

VACCINATIONS

Check with the tourist offices or embassies of the countries you wish to visit for current requirements. If you plan to visit one or more countries in endemic zones (i.e., in Africa, South America, Central America or Asia), be sure to mention this when requesting vaccination requirements. Many countries do not require any vaccinations if you are only visiting the country directly from the United States, Canada or Western Europe; but, if you are also visiting countries in endemic zones, there may very well be additional requirements.

Then check with your doctor, and preferably an immunologist, or call your local health department or the Centers for Disease Control in Atlanta, GA (toll-free tel. 1-888-232-3228, toll-free fax 1-888-232-3299, Website: www.cdc.gov) for information. They will probably recommend some vaccinations in addition to those required by the country you will be visiting.

Make sure you carry with you the International Certificate of Vaccinations showing the vaccinations you have received.

Malarial prophylaxis (pills) is highly recommended for all the countries included in this guide, except for parts of South Africa.

VISA AND INOCULATION REQUIREMENTS

Travelers from most countries must obtain visas to enter some of the countries included in this guide. You may apply for visas with the closest diplomatic representative or through a visa service well in advance (but not so early that the visas will expire before or soon after your journey ends) and check for all current requirements. Travelers must obtain visas (either before travel or on arrival) and have proof that they have received certain inoculations for entry into some African countries.

	VISA REQUIREMENTS			INOCULATIONS
COUNTRY	U.S.	CANADA	U.K.	
Botswana	No	No	No	*see notes
Congo, Rep of	Yes	Yes	Yes	Yellow fever
Ethiopia**	Yes	Yes	Yes	Yellow fever
Kenya**	Yes	Yes	Yes	*see notes
Malawi	No	No	No	*see notes
Mauritius	No	No	No	*see notes
Mozambique	Yes	Yes	Yes	*see notes
Namibia	No	No	No	*see notes
Rwanda	No	Yes	No	Yellow fever
Seychelles	No	No	No	*see notes
South Africa	No	No	No	*/***see notes
Tanzania**	Yes	Yes	Yes	*see notes
Zanzibar (Tanzania)				*see notes
Uganda**	Yes	Yes	Yes	Yellow fever
Zambia**	Yes	Yes	Yes	*see notes
Zimbabwe**	Yes	Yes	Yes	*see notes

Notes:

1. Some optional vaccinations include: (a) hepatitis A, (b) hepatitis B, (c) typhoid, (d) tetanus, (e) meningitis, (f) oral polio.

2. Anti-malaria: It is not mandatory but is strongly urged. Anti-malaria is a tablet, not an inoculation. Malaria exists in almost all of the countries listed above.

3. Cholera: The cholera vaccination is not a guaranteed inoculation against infection, and most countries do not require a cholera vaccination for direct travel from the United States. Check with your local doctor and with embassies of the respective countries. Some require proof of a cholera vaccination even if you are arriving directly from the United States.

4. *: Yellow fever: Only if arriving from an infected area (i.e., Rwanda).

5. **: Visa may be obtained on arrival by paying a visa fee.

6. Complete necessary visa forms and return with your valid passport (valid for at least six months after travel dates) to the embassy or consulate concerned or use a visa service.

7. ***: South Africa: Yellow fever vaccination is also required if arriving from Kenya, Tanzania or Zambia. Visitors must have at least two consecutive blank pages in their passport.

WILDLIFE ASSOCIATIONS

African Wildlife Foundation, 1400 16th St. NW, Suite 120, Washington, DC 20036; tel. (202) 939-3333. Headquartered in Nairobi, Kenya, African Wildlife Foundation (AWF) is a leading international conservation organization focused solely on Africa. Since its inception in 1961, AWF has protected endangered species and land, promoted conservation enterprises that benefit local African communities, and trained hundreds of African nationals in conservation — all to ensure the survival of Africa's unparalleled wildlife heritage. AWF is a nonprofit organization and registered as a 501(c)(3) in the United States. Website: www.awf.org.

David Sheldrick Wildlife Trust was established in 1977 in Kenya and has been involved in a variety of activities to conserve wildlife; most notable is its work with elephant and rhino orphans. USA Representative: US Friends of the David Sheldrick Wildlife Trust, 201 N Illinois Street, 16th Floor, South Tower, Indianapolis, IN 46204; website: www.sheldrickwildlifetrust.org.

The **Dian Fossey Gorilla Fund International**, 800 Cherokee Avenue, S.E., Atlanta, GA 30315; tel. (404) 624-5881 or 1 (800) 851 0203; website: www.gorillafund.org.

Maasailand Preservation Trust works in conjunction with ol Donyo Lodge and 4,500 Maasai shareholders. Lions are regularly killed by the locals for preying on their livestock. The outreach program pays compensation for cattle losses due to predators and positive results are the rise in the lion population. Website: www.maasailand preservationtrust.com.

The **Mother Africa Trust** was established in 2011 and, in addition to hosting volunteers on purpose driven safaris, undertakes a wide variety of research, conservation and humanitarian development projects. The Trust works in the Matobo Hills, Hwange wildlife area and the city of Bulawayo, all in Zimbabwe. Focus activities include a children's home, Southern Ground Hornbill breeding research, a home for abused women and children in addition to supporting several rural schools. Address: The Bulawayo Club, Cnr 8th Ave/Fort Street, Bulawayo, Zimbabwe, Africa. Website: www.mother-africa.org.

Save the Rhino Trust, The Save the Rhino Trust (SRT) mission is to "serve as a leader in conservation efforts in the Kunene, including monitoring, training and research focused on desert-adapted black rhino, in order to ensure security for these and other wildlife species, responsible tourism development, and a sustainable future for local communities." P.O. Box 2159, Swakopmund, Namibia; tel. +264 (64) 403829; Website: www.savetherhinotrust.org.

Wildlife Conservation Network is dedicated to protecting endangered species and preserving their natural habitats. By supporting innovative conservationists and their projects, they are able to develop new approaches that work with the local communities. Current wildlife projects in Africa include African wild dog, cheetah, lion and elephant. Website: www.wildlifeconservationnetwork.org

The **Wilderness Safaris Wildlife Trust** seeks to make a difference in Africa, to its wildlife and its people. These projects address the needs of existing wildlife populations, seek solutions to save threatened species and provide education and training for local people and their communities. Financial and educational empowerment of local communities so that they benefit from the wildlife on their doorsteps is vital, and as such, broad-based and comprehensive initiatives are the bedrock of the Trust, providing skills, knowledge and education necessary to communities to value and manage their wildlife populations. A portion of each guest's fare while staying in Wilderness Safaris camps and lodges is allocated to this Trust, and 100% of these funds go to Trust-approved projects.

Donations to the Trust can be tax-deductible through a 501(c)(3) facility. Please email Laura Mass of the Resources First Foundation at lmass@resourcesfirstfoundation.org. For more details about the Trust or donations, please call Trust Secretary Mari dos Santos in Johannesburg, South Africa, tel: +27 11 807 1800.

Safari Glossary

4wd — Abbreviated term standing for 4-wheel drive vehicle.

Acacia: Common, dry-country trees and shrubs armed with spines or curved thorns; they also have tiny, feathery leaflets.

Adaptation: The ability, through structural or functional characteristics, to improve the survival rate of an animal or plant in a particular habitat.

Aloe: A succulent plant of the lily family with thick, pointed leaves and spikes of red or yellow flowers.

Arboreal: Living in trees.

Avifauna: The birdlife of a region.

Bais: A large open area surrounded by Equitorial rain forest.

Banda: A basic shelter or hut, often constructed of reeds, bamboo, grass, etc.

Bathroom, open-air: A bathroom attached to a chalet or permanent tent that is enclosed on all sides, and does not have a roof.

Boma: A place of shelter, a fortified place, enclosure, community (East Africa).

Browse: To feed on leaves.

Bum crawl: To move while sitting on the ground by using you're arms for propulsion — used primarily to approach wildlife more closely while on a walk.

Calving season: A period during which the young of a particular species are born. Not all species have calving seasons. Most calving seasons occur shortly after the rainy season begins. Calving seasons can also differ for the same species from one park or reserve to another.

Camp: Camping sites; also refers to lodging in chalets, bungalows or tents in a remote location.

Canopy: The uppermost layer of a tree.

Caravan: A camping trailer.

Carnivore: An animal that lives by consuming the flesh of other animals.

Carrion: The remains of dead animals.

Charter flight (private): An air charter booked from one point to another for a private party. The plane is not available for the guests for the entire day — only for the route for which they have paid.

Charter flight (scheduled): An air charter that is used by different parties of guests. Most scheduled air charters make multiple stops on a route, picking up and dropping off passangers. Travelers preferring not having stops should consider booking a private charter.

Crepuscular: Active at dusk or dawn.

Diurnal: Active during the day.

Dung: Feces, or "droppings" of animals.

Dung midden: A pile of animal droppings, usually in connection with scent marking/marking of territories.

En suite: Refers to a bathroom that is within a room, chalet or tent.

Endangered: An animal that is threatened with extinction.

Endemic: Native and restricted to a particular area.

Estrus: A state of sexual readiness in a female mammal when she is capable of conceiving.

Fixed tented camp: (also known as "permanent" tented camp) Applies to a safari camp that is not moved.

Fly Camp: A mobile tented camp, generally with small tents and separate shower and toilet tents that can easily be transported to remote areas. Fly camps can also be of a "luxury" standard.

Game: Wildlife.

Gestation: The duration of pregnancy.

Grazer: An animal that eats grass.

G.R.: An abbreviation for "Game Reserve."

Habitat: An animal's or plant's surroundings that offers everything it needs to live.

Habituated: An animal that has been introduced to and has accepted the presence of human beings.

Herbivore: An animal that consumes plant matter for food.

Hide: A camouflaged structure from which one can view wildlife without being seen.

Home range: An area familiar to (utilized by) an adult animal but not marked or defended as a territory.

Kopje (pronounced kopee): Rock formations that protrude from the savannah, usually caused by wind erosion (southern Africa).

Koppie: Same as kopje (East Africa).

Kraal: Same as boma (southern Africa).

Mammal: A warm-blooded animal that produces milk for its young.

Migratory: A species or population that moves seasonally to an area with predictably better food/grazing or water.

Midden: Usually, an accumulation of dung deposited in the same spot as a scent-marking behavior.

Mokoro: A traditional-style canoe, which is used for exploring the shallow waters of the Okavango Delta.

Nocturnal: Active during the night.

N.P.: An abbreviation for "National Park."

N.R.: An abbreviation for "Nature Reserve."

Omnivore: An animal that eats both plant and animal matter.

Pan: A shallow depression that seasonally fills with rainwater.

Permanent tented camp: Safari camps that are not moved. The tents are normally very large with en suite bathrooms, and often set on raised decks.

Predator: An animal that hunts and kills other animals for food.

Prey: An animal hunted by a predator for food.

Pride: A group or family of lions.

Rondavel: An African-style structure for accommodation.

Ruminant: A mammal with a complex stomach which therefore chews the cud.

Rutting: The behavioral pattern exhibited by the male of the species during a time period when mating is most prevalent, e.g., impala, wildebeest.

Sala: An additional private lounge area located off a tent's deck and features comfortable seating or a bed for relaxing.

Savannah: An open, grassy landscape with widely scattered trees.

Scavenger: An animal that lives off of carrion or the remains of animals killed by predators or that is dead from other causes.

Shower, bush, bucket or safari: (Usually associated with a mobile tented camp) Upon request by the guest, water is heated by a campfire and then placed in a raised container over a shower tent.

Species: A group of plants or animals with specific characteristics in common, including the ability to reproduce among themselves.

Spoor: A track (i.e., footprint) or trail made by animals.

Symbiosis: An association of two different organisms in a relationship that may benefit one or both partners.

Tarmac: An asphalt-paved road.

Termitarium: A mound constructed by termite colonies.

Territory: An area occupied, scent-marked and defended from rivals of the same species.

Toilet, long-drop: A permanent bush toilet or "outhouse" in which a toilet seat has been placed over a hole that is dug about 6 feet (2 m) deep.

Toilet, safari or short-drop: A temporary bush toilet, usually a toilet tent used on mobile tented safaris in which a toilet seat is placed over a hole that has been dug about 3 feet (1 m) deep.

Tracking: Following and observing animal spoor by foot.

Tribe: A group of people united by traditional ties.

Troop: A group of apes or monkeys.

Ungulate: A hooved animal.

Veld: Southern African term for open land.

Vlei: An open grassy area, usually along a drainage line and with trees along the edge.

Wallow: The art of keeping cool and wet, usually in a muddy pool (i.e., rhinoceros, buffalo and hippopotamus).

Suggested Reading

GENERAL/WILDLIFE/AFRICA

African Elephants, Daryl and Sharna Balfour, 1997 (South Africa: Struik)
Africa's Top Wildlife Countries, Mark Nolting, 2012 (USA: Global Travel)
Behaviour Guide to African Animals, Richard Estes, 1995 (USA: University California Press)
Birds of Africa, Sinclair and Ryan, 2003 (South Africa: Struik)
Birds of the Indian Ocean Islands, I. Sinclair and O. Langrand, 1998 (South Africa: Struik)
Blue Nile, The, Alan Moorehead, 1983 (U.K.: Penguin)
Elephant Memories, Cynthia Moss, 1999 (USA: Chicago University Press)
Eyes Over Africa, Michael Poliza, 2007 (USA: teNeues Publishing Company)
Field Guide to the Reptiles of East Africa, S. Spawls, K. Howell, R. Drews and J. Ashe, 2002 (U.K.: Academic Press)
I Dreamed of Africa, K. Gallman, 1991 (USA: Penguin Books)
Kingdon Field Guide to African Mammals, The Jonathan Kingdon, 1997 (U.K.: Harcourt Brace)
Mountain Gorillas–Biology, Conservation, and Coexistence, Gene Eckhart and Annette Lanjouw, 2008 (USA: University Press)
Night of the Lions, K. Gallman, 2000 (U.K.: Penguin Books)
North of South, Shiva Naipaul, 1994 (U.K.: Penguin)
Roberts Birds of Southern Africa, Gordon Maclean, 1993 (South Africa: Voelcker Trust)
Running Wild, John McNutt and Lesley Boggs, 1996 (South Africa: Southern Books Publishers)
Safari Companion, A Guide to Watching African Mammals, Richard D. Estes, 2001 (South Africa: USA: Chelsea Green Publishing)
Through a Window, J. Goodall, 2000 (U.K.: Phoenix Press)
Tree Where Man Was Born, The Peter Matthiessen, 1997 (USA: Dutton)
The White Nile, Alan Moorehead, 1973 (U.K.: Penguin)
Vanishing Africa, Kate Klippensteen, 2002 (USA: Abbeville Press)
Whatever You Do, Don't Run, Chris Roche, 2006 (South Africa: Tafelberg Publishers)

SOUTHERN AFRICA

Guide to Nests & Eggs of Southern African Birds, Warwick Tarboton, 2001 (South Africa: Struik)
Illustrated Guide to Game Parks and Nature Reserves of Southern Africa, 1999 (South Africa: Readers Digest)
Long Walk to Freedom, Nelson Mandela, 1995 (U.K.: Abacus, Little Brown)
Lost World of the Kalahari, Laurens van der Post, 2001 (U.K.: Vintage)
Newman's Birds of Southern Africa, Kenneth Newman, 2010 (South Africa: Struik)
Sasol Birds of Southern Africa, Ian Sinclair, 2002 (South Africa: Struik)
Trees of Southern Africa, Keith Coates Palgrave, 1977 (South Africa: Struik)
Walk with a White Bushman, Laurens van der Post, 2002 (U.K.: Vintage)
Wildlife of Southern Africa: A Field Guide, V. Carruthers, 1997 (South Africa: Southern Books)

BOTSWANA

Chobe, Africa's Untamed Wilderness, Daryl and Sharna Balfour, 1999 (South Africa: Struik)

Cry of the Kalahari, Mark and Delia Owens, 1984 (USA: Houghton Mifflin)
Hunting with Moon, The Lions of Savuti, Dereck and Beverley Joubert, 1998 (USA: National Geographic)
Miracle Rivers, The Chobe & Okavango Rivers of Botswana, Peter and Beverly Pickford, 1999 (South Africa: Struik)
Running Wild, John McNutt and Lesley Boggs, 1996 (South Africa: Southern Book Publishers)
The Africa Diaries, Derek and Beverley Joubert, 2000 (USA: National Geographic)
The Heart of the Hunter, Laurens van der Post, 2002 (U.K.: Vintage)
The No. 1 Ladies Detective Agency, Alexander McCall Smith (USA: Random House)
Wildlife of the Okavango: Common Animals and Plants, D. Butchart, 2000 (South Africa: Struik)

ZAMBIA and ZIMBABWE
African Laughter, Doris Lessing, 1992 (U.K.: Harper Collins)
Bibliography of Zimbabwean Archaeology to 2005, Paul Hubbard, 2007 (African Heritage and Archaeology)
Bitter Harvest, Ian Smith, 2001 (U.K.: Collins)
Don't Let's Go to the Dogs Tonight, An African Childhood, Alexander Fuller, 2001 (USA: Random House)
Eye of the Elephant, Mark and Delia Owens, 1992 (USA: Houghton Mifflin)
Hwange, Retreat of the Elephants, Nick Greaves, 1996 (South Africa: Struik)
Kakuli, Norman Carr, 1995 (U.K.: Corporate Brochure Company) (O/P)
Madzimbahwe of the Southwest: A Guide to Khami, DhloDhlo & Naletale, P. Hubbard & R.S. Burrett, 2011 (Bulawayo: Khami Press)
The Last Resort, Douglas Rogers, 2010 (USA: Random House)
The Leopard Hunts in Darkness (and other series), Wilbur Smith, 1992 (U.K.: Macmillan)
The Matopos: A Guide and Short History, P. Hubbard & R.S. Burrett, 2011 (Bulawayo: Khami Press)
Zambezi, L. Watermeyer, J. Dabbs and Y. Christian, 1988 (Zimbabwe: Albida Samara Pvt. Ltd.)

SOUTH AFRICA
Long Walk to Freedom, Nelson Mandela, 1995 (U.K.: Abacus, Little Brown)
The Covenant, James A. Michener, 1980 (USA: Random House)
The Heart of the Hunter (series), Laurens van der Post, 1987 (U.K.: Vintage)
The Washing of the Spears: The Rise and Fall of the Zulu Nation, Donald R. Morris, 1995 (U.K.: Pimlico)
When the Lion Feeds (series), Wilbur Smith, 1986 (U.K.: Macmillan)
World That Made Mandela, L. Callinicos, 2001 (South Africa: STE Publishers)

EAST AFRICA
Among the Man-eaters, Stalking the Mysterious Lions of Tsavo, Philip Caputo, 2002 (USA: National Geographic)
Birds of Kenya & Tanzania, Zimmerman, Turner and Pearson, 1999 (U.K.: A & C Black, USA: Princeton University Press)

KENYA
Wildflower, Mark Seal, 2009 (Random House)
Born Free Trilogy, Joy Adamson, 2000 (U.K.: Macmillan)
Elephant Memories, Portraits in the Wild, Cynthia Moss, 1999 (USA: Chicago University Press)
Flame Trees of Thika: Memories of an African Childhood, Elspeth Huxley, 1998

(U.K.: Pimlico)
I Dreamed of Africa, Kuki Gallman, 1991 (U.K.: Penguin)
Out in the Midday Sun, Elspeth Huxley, 2000 (U.K.: Pimlico)
Out of Africa, Isak Dinesen, 1989 (U.K.: Penguin Books)
Wildlife Wars, Battle to Save Africa's Elephants, Richard Leakey, 2001 (U.K.: Macmillan)

TANZANIA
Golden Shadows, Flying Hooves, George B. Schaller, 1989 (USA: University of Chicago Press)
Journal of Discovery of the Source of the Nile, John Hanning Speke, 1996 (USA: Dover Publications)
Serengeti Shall Not Die, Bernard and Michael Grzimek, 1960 (U.K.: Hamish Hamilton)
Snows of Kilimanjaro, Ernest Hemingway, 1994 (U.K.: Arrow)
The Chimpanzees of Gombe, Patterns of Behavior, Jane Goodall, 1986 (USA: Harvard University Press) Chimpanzee research.

RWANDA
Gorillas in the Mist, Dian Fossey, 2001 (U.K.: Phoenix Press)
Mountain Gorillas–Biology, Conservation, and Coexistence, Gene Eckhart and Annette Lanjouw, 2008 (USA: University Press)

ARTS AND CRAFTS
Hands-On Africa: Art Activities for All Ages Featuring Sub-Saharan Africa, Yvonne Merrill, 2006 (USA: Kits Publishing)

DVDs
Duma (2006) Warner Bros Ent; Director: Carroll Ballard
Explore the Wildlife Kingdom Series: Wildebeest — the Great African Migration (2006) Reel Productions
Explore the Wildlife Kingdom Series: Lions — Kings of Africa (2005)
I Dreamed of Africa (2000) Director: Hugh Hudson
Out of Africa (1985) Director: Sydney Pollack
As Close As You Dare — Africa; Documentary (2007) Crowe World Media
As Close As You Dare — Africa was shot on location in Zimbabwe, Botswana, and Namibia. This film immerses you in startlingly close encounters with wildlife and a rare opportunity to interact with a disappearing culture, the San Bushmen. Strongly recommended for anyone interested in walking safaris and African cultures. List price $19.95. Available from the Africa Adventure Company for $9.95, www.AfricanAdventure.com; 800-882-9453, 954-491-8877.

Bush Tails

Dear Alison and all the staff at AAC who were involved in making our trip to Africa so wonderful and memorable.

This was our 3rd trip to that beautiful continent that you, AAC, arranged. We were hard pressed to believe, in advance, that it would surpass our prior trips...each of which were so unbelievable in themselves.

...In every place we stayed, we received special "50th" anniversary treatment. From candle lit champagne dinners, to sundowners with camp staff, including more champagne, to the special dinner we had our last night in the Nairobi hotel, which you all so graciously must have arranged.

Little Makalolo...(elephants/giraffe and zebra greeted us for lunch at the watering hole just off the dining area our day of arrival and during our first early morning breakfast we were greeted by 17 lions in the same spot)...

Vundu (we butt/crab walked within 20 ft of two male lions on our first walking safari. Bob could virtually touch a young bull elephant from his canoe on the first canoe trip). Both places were just awesome...the camp staffs so very attentive, gracious and friendly, the food was great and the wildlife was unforgettable...

The gorilla trekking in **Uganda** and **Rwanda** was everything we had hoped for... and MORE!

...We could go on and on in talking about our total experiences but this is already too verbose. Suffice it to say, you all planned an excellent trip for us and we can't thank you enough.

Our sincerest best wishes and thanks to you all, we will return...

— *Bob and Ardythe McCracken, Nevada*

Dear Alison:

A note to say thanks for the July **Tanzania** safari arrangements. Needless to say, we had an amazing time...

Where do I start? We had a fascinating cultural experience and thoroughly enjoyed all the game viewing that the parks provided! Let's start with our private guide, Ephata. He was the BEST! He was knowledgeable, sensitive to our family needs and a perfect ambassador for Tanzania and for our family. Our visits with the **Maasai**, **Hadzape** and **Datoga** tribes providing priceless experiences into the lives of local Africans. My kids especially enjoyed our visit to the school near **Mto Wa Mbu**. Our hunting with the Hadzape was also quite an experience...

...We would love to do it all over again, tomorrow, next year and even many years from now.

What an incredible visit! Thanks for all of your help and guidance.

— *Anne, Shawn, Kelly, Shawn and*
Karen Brosko, Connecticut

Dear Alison,

Congratulations on your 25th anniversary — Karen and I wish we had started our Africa safari-ing with you back in 1986.

Nic Polenakis **(Specialist Zimbabwe guide)** was once again the highlight of our safari, just like our previous trips with him. His contagious enthusiasm and sincere kindness and empathy, coupled with an apparently infinite reservoir of wildlife knowledge makes time with him such a pleasure. We're already thinking about our next trip.

Somalisa was our favorite camp with its combination of great game viewing, authentic bush camp atmosphere and excellent food and staff. We loved the front porch waterhole and one day watched an elephant family dote on an hour-old elephant baby...

Our **mobile camp in northern Hwange** near Shumba was delightful — more excellent meals and service...We enjoyed seeing literally hundreds of elephants, plus a big herd of buffalo coming to water, along with roan, kudu, hippo, honey badger...

At **Vundu Camp in Mana Pools** our dreams came true one morning when we got in the midst of seventeen wild dogs on the hunt. It was so exciting seeing them run and split up into pairs and singles and then regroup and go again....

At **Camp Amalinda** we were in the care of guide Paul Hubbard...a virtual encyclopedia of all things Matabo and especially cave paintings. Paul made our stay there so fulfilling and enjoyable — not to forget our visit to the Children's Home, which we would not miss and hope to return.

All the travel arrangements, connections and transfers went perfectly. The small plane flights were reassuringly professional and delightful.

A genuine Thank You!! from both of us,

Sincerely,

— *Fred & Karen Peters, Arizona*

Hi Ian, well, our trip was great!! The **Rwanda** gorilla experience is really unmatched and not adequately described with words. I had to step back so a 500 lb. silverback could lumber by only two feet away. I could smell him!!!

The chimp trekking was not so great. The chimps are way up high in the trees but it was still good. The sounds they make are something...can hear them way before you see them...

Zanzibar was absolutely beautiful! Matemwe Retreat is probably one of the nicest places we have ever stayed. The food was great, the service tremendous, and all in all a really wonderful place...

We swam with dolphins in the open Indian Ocean and that almost rivaled the gorilla experience. It was truly a magical thing...

— *Ed Rahal, Florida*

"Trip of a lifetime," seems like a cliché but our recent safari to **Botswana** and **Zimbabwe** was truly an adventure of a lifetime. Having been on incredible trips to Alaska and

Costa Rica, our group of three families (6 adults, 8 children ages 11–17) had sky high expectations before our African safari and those expectations were blown away. From the awe-inspiring wildlife, to fantastic accommodations and seamless travel transitions, our trip was truly unbelievable, primal, exciting and at times a little scary.

Our **mobile camp at Moremi** was such a warm place to return each day and to wake up to in the "winter like" mornings. The staff was incredible and the accommodations/food left us wondering — how did they pull it off? The sounds at night were distractingly beautiful, with the hyenas, lions and hippos providing a constant chorus of reminders that were not back home...

Vundu Camp in Mana Pools is a spectacular destination. The setting is very dramatic along side the Zambezi River with a wonderful view across the river of the mountains in Zambia...

...Nick Murray was a special and unique guide...He has a commanding presence which instilled confidence in the kids and parents. We quickly understood that if we followed his lead, we could have amazing and safe animal encounters. Nick also slipped in a prankster fun-loving side that kept a great balance...

...Mana Pools is a special and unspoiled place. While perhaps not as well known as other African destinations, it would be hard to imagine any place offering a better adventure or a more genuine African safari.

— *The Klockenbrink and Carlson Families, Virginia and California*

THANKS Kyle. It really was a wonderful and memorable safari to **Tanzania**. Our guide Mkenda was one person who made it extra special. He is incredibly knowledgeable and very friendly. He was quite patient and willing to wait while Lana got "just the right" picture. We are already talking about going back. We really liked all of the places we stayed. I think our favorites were **Migration Camp, Gibb's Farm** and **Lemala**. Everyone made us feel welcome, and two weeks seemed like barely enough time!

Thanks for all your help. You did a great job planning our trip and your recommendations were great!!

Sincerely,

— *Vikki Canfield, Oklahoma*

Hi Lynne,

First and foremost, I want to say how totally impressed we were with the ease of the trip...

I can't say enough good things about our arrival at **Mashatu**...Mashatu really was a perfect first taste of safari for us all, especially the boys...

Thank you so much for arranging this wonderful trip for us. Although it was the farthest we've ever traveled, it really was the easiest. What an amazing experience... I will always remember the sights, sounds and even smells (I miss the wild sage especially) of this first safari. And we will look forward to the day when you can plan another adventure for us.

Warm regards,

— *MARGARET, BOB, ANDREW AND MATTHEW FISHMAN, FLORIDA*

FANTASTIC!!!!!!! When can we go again?

Szilvia, Thank you so much for planning such a wonderful trip for us — actually, I keep telling everyone, it was not a trip, it was an "experience" — we absolutely loved it and did not want to come home...Your advice to have a private guide in all the camps was right on.

MalaMala (Rattray's) — our absolute favorite!!!!!! We loved everything there — every day saw something new and exciting. On our very first safari experience — saw

all of the Big 5...Superb accommodations and food and a great staff and excellent guide — Donald. We almost cried when we left.

Victoria Falls — great visit. We loved everything we did — elephant safari was fun — Esther is a sweetheart and gave us a great tour of the falls...

Little Mombo...Loved that there were only 3 cabins in our section. We arrived at our room to find an elephant with his trunk on our porch — nice greeting, great accommodations and staff and we had an excellent guide, Lebo...

Cape Town...We loved the Radisson — very clean and sleek looking with a great view of the marina and Table Mountain. Walked in Cape Grace Hotel — just to see it — we liked the Radisson better.

...It was absolutely the best experience ever! THANKS FOR EVERYTHING!!!!!

— *SALLY STALKER AND CAROLINE DAVIS, ATLANTA*

Hello Africa Adventure team,

We are writing to report on our trip to **Kenya** which is no easy task because it was all fantastic! People keep asking our kids what their favorite part of the trip was and they can't answer because every part of it was a favorite...

...Our trip was just one highlight after another. We feel like we had the BEST guide who was suited perfectly for our family.

We had requested from you that we see different topographical areas. You did an excellent job. It was really fun to see the different animals in the different regions and we were amazed with all the animals we got to see...

...We loved all of the places we stayed! Our youngest, a boy, made friends with one of the **Samburu** warriors who worked at the lodge keeping monkeys out of the restaurant. The warrior gave our son a slingshot and our son gave him an American bracelet...

It was a fabulous trip and we appreciate all of the work you put into it to make it so incredible.

THANK YOU —

— *THE SEAN AND JOANNE MURPHY FAMILY, CALIFORNIA*

Hi Mark,

My wife and I want to personally thank you for the outstanding Photo Safari you and your staff arranged for us in Botswana to the **Okavango Delta** and **The Kalahari Desert**.

– We were at Wilderness Camps for this trip and they all were excellent experiences. Your good judgment for us in this regard was much appreciated.

– We had the privilege of seeing leopard, a pack of 10 wild dog shortly after a kill at Little Vumbura as well as a 6 hour experience following a lengthy hunt by lioness's at Duba Plains...

– Our private guides really knew their stuff. They knew what areas to check for the species we had identified as wanting to see and were very good a positioning for photography...

– The desert is more than worth a trip this time of year as it is lush and full. We saw black mane lions, cheetah a few feet from the vehicle and honey badgers, which can be hard to locate.

...This was our 8th trip to Africa. Our expectations were high and they were exceeded! Thanks!

Regards,

— *BRUCE AND PATTI SCHADOW, MINNESOTA*

Hi Kyle,

I am not sure how to thank you and the Africa Adventure Company for the most amazing trip ever! What I am most amazed about was that there was not one single glitch during the entire **Tanzanian** safari...

Thank you for providing us with a guide who had to endure my son's countless (and repetitive) questions. Ephata rocks! Beyond being extremely knowledgeable, he is a kind, patient, wonderful man. My kids simply adored him!...

Of course the animals were amazing! I expected them to be!...What I guess I didn't expect was how much of an impact the cultural aspect of the trip would make upon myself and my family...

I have to admit that I thought the "day with the Bushmen" was going to be hokey, and yet it ended up being the most memorable aspect of the trip...We were blown away by how they live! The experience still seems surreal...

Kyle, I am so grateful to have found you and your wonderful company. You really understood, probably more than I did, what I was looking for. As a result, my family had the most incredible experience. I have a feeling that this is the first of many trips we will be booking with you.

Thanks,

— *Julie, Steven, Lindsay and Benjamin Reich, New Jersey*

Oh my goodness! **Little Makalolo** is magic, isn't it? We had Charles for a guide, and he was wonderful! Actually, he greeted us wearing an Africa Adventure hat because he had shown Mark Nolting (author and owner of AAC) and his family around. We went to the hide to see elephants, spent one whole morning tracking rhinos on foot, and saw so many different animals...

...We have so many great memories and the trip was truly something we had been hoping to do for the last several years. Best yet, you listened to what we wanted to do, and this was exactly it!...

Coming back to Johannesburg, we had our two Africa Adventure bags and were getting our boarding passes. A gentleman asked if we'd had a good time, and it was Mark Nolting! We got to meet his family and hear about their trip too. How nice of him to take the time to do that...

Thanks so much for working with us and making the safari just what we'd hoped it would be!

Sincerely,

— *Luann and Bill Moth, Illinois*

Mark:
  Thank you for a fantastic trip. It was everything that was advertised and more. Seeing the **mountain gorillas** is a magical experience we will never forget. The sunsets in the **Serengeti** and baobab trees in **Tarangire** were stunning. We saw the migration, the big five, cheetah, lions stalking prey, lions in trees, lions mating, lions feasting on a kill, and much more.

  Our guides were outstanding. Both Theo and Rasul were experts in the art of flexibility with meals, game drives, sightseeing, etc, taking the best advantage of the situations on the ground. Both were also great ambassadors for their countries and their people. Rasul lived up to his reputation as guide of the year. He knew when and where to find the animals and reacted quickly to sightings by other guides...
  The Bushtops camp was over-the-top luxury. Soaking in the outdoor hot tub after a game drive was sublime. There was only one other family in camp for most of the time that we were there, so we practically had the camp and staff to ourselves. The food was the best of the trip....
  ...After Mark's honeymoon and now this experience, it's clear why the Africa Adventure Company is regarded as the best in the field.
  Thank you for the "trip of a lifetime."

— *MIKE AND MARK NICKELSBURG, VIRGINIA*

Hi Lynne!
  Well, where can I begin? Thanks you so much for arranging this fantastic trip — I have fallen in love with Africa — the trip exceeded our expectations in so many ways — the sights were so incredible...

  ...We had great variety in game viewing — at **Simbambili** it was necessary to track the animals to find them — but we saw everything except lions — including wild dogs...We also saw cheetahs there — we had no idea the animals would be right next to our landrover!! We thought we would need binoculars to see them.
  MalaMala did not need trackers because all of the animals were right there — right away when we got there we saw a pride of lions...
  I have to say that for the total experience — I loved **Chobe Chilwero** and I have to say I am glad we had the best for last — the lodge was beautiful...the scenery looking out over the Chobe River was incredible and I actually loved the game drives the best there...
  ...I will definitely have you arrange our next trip to Africa if we are lucky enough to be able to go again! In the meantime — I am already singing your praises to people I know.
  ...Thank you, thank you, thank you for a fabulous trip —

— *MICHELLE AND ED ROSS, GEORGIA*

Hi Mark,

Finally taking time out to write and tell you about another fabulous trip courtesy of the Africa Adventure Company. Armed with my new backpack that carried my most precious items, I was excited to embark on another adventure.

After another great stay at the House of Waine and a fun day in Nairobi...I was off on our flight to the **Omo River Valley**. It was wonderful seeing Joseph again...I

hadn't seen him since my first visit...The Kara were in their farms tending their sorghum crops thus the villages were pretty empty — so we went there. I spent a day at the market with "the girls" which is always fun. This Omo trip was all about seeing friends and renewing friendships... The Omo experience was relaxing and heart warming — I felt like I was visiting family and I WAS!

My adventure continued to the **Maasai Mara**...within 45 minutes we had seen all of the "Big Five" as well as many other species. The best thing about the

Mara is that you never know what is on the other side of the bush or tree...it's always an extraordinary, awe-inspiring surprise...

Many times we'd sit for a very long time watching — it's amazing what you can observe if you do more than snap a few photos and move on...

Again Mark, Bill, Szilvia and all staff members...thank you so much for your part in planning this memorable trip for me. I look forward to the next one.

Much love and appreciative hugs to you all,

— *Abby Lazar, New York*

Alison and Mark,

First, Chris was excellent in Cape Town. Don't know what we would have done without him. Excellent knowledge and knew just what do to in terms of weather appropriate activities.

What a piece of heaven we experienced. I could write a book on just our visit to **Botswana** between the animals, the high water (not a problem except for the staff and guides), and each camp being more spectacular than the last. The "Living with the Elephants," we all felt was an experience no one should

miss. Brooks for the first 6 days was a treasure...great sense of humor, serious when he needed to be, and excellent guide skills to get us to the game we wanted to see. Reuben at Duba, Carter at Stanley were also very, very good. Pete at Mombo was another excellent guide with excellent skills and information. We have so many stories and unfortunately not enough time to tell...

Can't thank you all enough for such a terrific "trip of a lifetime."

Fondly,

— *Anne Vallotton, Pennsylvania*

About Mark Nolting, Author and Africa Expert

Mark Nolting heads up the Africa Adventure Company, Ft. Lauderdale, Florida. He is the author of two award-winning books, *Africa's Top Wildlife Countries* and the *African Safari Journal*.

Known as the "Travel Expert of Africa" in the industry, Nolting and his experienced staff arrange safaris for travelers who want to experience the beauty and drama of Africa in exciting ways.

"One morning," said Nolting, "I just woke up and realized I wanted to travel around the world. And I decided, if I don't go, I'll always regret it, and if I don't go now, I never will."

Two weeks later, he departed for Luxembourg. During the 1976 Winter Olympics in Innsbruck, Austria, he worked for ABC Sports. Next he found a job in middle management with the world's third-largest mail order catalog house, located in Germany.

But Nolting wasn't trying to become a European businessman. He was out to see the world. He took a six-month detour through Africa and traveled across the Sahara Desert and on through central and east Africa. He toured several parks and reserves and fell in love with the "safari experience."

Then he found his way to the Mideast and was fast-tracked through a program for oil-drilling engineers. He eventually came back to the United States, yet the yearning for more in-depth travel through Africa was still with him. He couldn't shake the memory of the wildlife and the spectacular terrain he had seen there. And so, once again, he was off, heading for Africa with a purpose in mind.

He returned to Africa and traveled for two years through 16 countries, from Cairo to Cape Town, gathering material for his books and establishing contacts with safari companies and tour guides. On his return to the United States in 1985, he wrote his books and established the Africa Adventure Company.

In July 1992 he married Alison Wright, whom he had met a few years previously at a safari camp she was running in Zimbabwe. In July 1993, they had their first child, Miles William Nolting, and in 1996, their second child, Nicholas Hamilton Nolting.

His many visits have included touring the antiquities of Egypt and scuba diving off the Sinai Peninsula; crossing Lake Nasser and the deserts of Sudan; experiencing the multitude of lodge safaris and authentic African mobile tented safaris in the wildlife reserves of Kenya and Tanzania; climbing Mt. Kenya, Mt. Kilimanjaro in Tanzania and the Ruwenzoris in the Democratic Republic of the Congo; visiting the beautiful Kenyan coast; gorilla trekking and mountain climbing in Rwanda; hunting with Pygmies, gorilla trekking and game viewing in the Democratic Republic of the Congo; and visiting some of the most primitive tribes in the world in the Omo River Valley along with castles and fourteenth century rock-hewn churches in Ethiopia.

In southern Africa his adventures have included walking safaris from bush camp to bush camp and day and night game drives in Zambia; 1- and 7-day, white-water, rafting safaris (Class 5) on the Zambezi River; viewing Victoria Falls at different times of the year; kayak safaris upstream of Victoria Falls; several canoeing safaris on the lower Zambezi River; walking with top professional guides and game viewing by boat and open vehicle on day and night game drives in Zimbabwe; flying safaris to the major reserves of Botswana; mokoro safaris in the Okavango Delta; flying safaris to the Skeleton Coast, Etosha, Ongava, Damaraland, Kaokoland, Namib-Naukluft, Namib-Rand, Swakopmund, Lüderitz and the Fish River Canyon in Namibia; driving the Garden Route, sightseeing in Cape Town and visiting the private reserves and parks and shark diving in South Africa; holidaying in the beautiful island countries of Mauritius and the Seychelles.

Mark continues to travel to Africa yearly to update information and explore new areas, and especially enjoys taking his family with him on safari. Hard-to-find information on Africa is always at his fingertips, and he loves to take the time to talk to people about the many adventures that can be found on the continent.

— The Publishers

Acknowledgments

The completion and accuracy of this guide would not have been possible without the assistance of many people. Many thanks to all who have contributed to this project, including the following:

To all the guides in the field that have shared their in depth knowledge of wildlife in Africa, and to our clients who have provided us with comprehensive trip reports on their African adventures.

Special thanks to Dawn Scheepmaker, Colin Bell, Dave van Smeerdijck, Kim Nixon, Chris Badger, Tessa Redman, Dave and Linda Bennett, Birigit Bekker, Edna Mohrmann, Chris Roche, Map Ives, Phil Ward, Yvonne Christian, David Evans, Duncan Butchart, John Coppinger, Nick Murray, Desiree Murray, Paul Hubbard, Sharon Stead, Grant Cummings, Craig Sholley, Jason Turner, Steve Turner, Joseph Birori, Tony Hickey, Jos Janisch, Gary Balfour, Taqi and Abbas Moledina for their assistance; to Sarah Taylor for her many hours of work on this update; to my staff at The Africa Adventure Company; and especially to my wife, Alison, for her assistance on the entire project.

Index

Index

Map Index

Photo Credits

Thanks to all the Africa camps and companies, guides and Africa Adventure Company travelers.

Cover
Front Cover
African Continent
Cheetahs - Barry Hamann
Elephants – Beverly Joubert
Vehicle with lion – Dana Allen
Giraffe - Linda Moskowitz
Zebras – Michael Poliza

Spine — Peter Gordon

Back Cover — Desiree Murray

Call of the Wild
14 + 15 – Susan Stribling
17 – Dana Allen – Wilderness Safaris
18 – Beth Tetterton
20 – Colin Bell
21 – Colin Bell
23 – Shenton Safaris
24 – Colin Bell
26 – (top) – Dana Allen – Wilderness Safaris
26 – (bottom) – Asilia
28 – Singita
29 – Beth Tetterton
30 – Dana Allen – Wilderness Safaris
32 – Ranger Safaris
34 – Desiree Murray
36 – Desiree Murray
37 – Malloon family
39 – Abby Lazar
41 – Ranger Safaris
42 – Chiawa Camp
43 – Art Meyer
45 – Beth Tetterton
46 – Joe Lyle
48 – Marci Blicher
49 – Eric Gurwin
50 – (top) – Wild Horizons
50 – (middle) – Heidi Brown
50 – (bottom) – Colin Bell
51 – Ian Flores
54 – Eric Gurwin
56 – Daniel Firestone
57 – Lynne Glasgow
59 – Dave Carson
61 – Chris Swindal
63 – Chris Swindal
64 – Dana Allen – Wilderness Safaris
68 – Kyle Witten

72 – Margaret Maxwell
80 – Ed Rahal

Botswana
84 + 85 – Chris Swindal
88 – (top) – Steve Dennis
88 – (bottom) – Dana Allen – Wilderness Safaris
89 – Eric Gurwin
91 – Colin Bell
96 – Kristin Provost
97– (top) – Capture Africa
97 – (middle) – Mike Myers – Wilderness Safaris
97 – (bottom) – Mike Myers – Wilderness Safaris
100 – (top) – Dana Allen – Wilderness Safaris
100 – (bottom) – Chris Swindal
101 – Dana Allen – Wilderness Safaris
102 – Dana Allen – Wilderness Safaris
103 – Dana Allen – Wilderness Safaris
104 – (top) – Dana Allen – Wilderness Safaris
104 – (middle) – Wilderness Safaris
104 – (bottom) – Wilderness Safaris
105 – (top) – Dana Allen – Wilderness Safaris
105 – (bottom) – Dana Allen – Wilderness Safaris
106 – Desert & Delta
108 – Capture Africa
109 – Jennifer Mullen
110 – (top) – Chris Swindal
110 – (bottom) – Eric Gurwin
112 – (top left) – Great Plains
112 – (top right) – Great Plains
112 – (middle) – Desert & Delta
112 – (bottom) – Mike Myers – Wilderness Safaris
115 – (top) – Sanctuary Lodges
115 – (bottom) – Larry Pinsky
116 – (top) – Sanctuary Lodges
116 – (bottom) – Mantis Collection
119 – Evan Chu
120 – (top) – Uncharted Africa
120 – (bottom) – Mike Myers – Wilderness Safaris
122 – (top) – Cindi Maudlin

122 – (bottom) – Wilderness Safaris
123 – Mashatu Game Reserve
124 – (top) – Mashatu Game Reserve
124 – (bottom) – Mashatu Game Reserve
125 – Mashatu Game Reserve

Zimbabwe
126 + 127 – Beth Tetterton
130 – Paul Klockenbrink
131 – Beth Tetterton
133 – Bushlife Safaris
136 – Woody Stone
137 – John Howard
138 – Wild Horizons
139 – (top) – Mark Nolting
139 – (bottom) – Elephant Camp
142 – (top) – Alison Nolting
142 – (bottom) – Nic Polenakis
143 – Dana Allen – Wilderness Safaris
144 – Dana Allen – Wilderness Safaris
146 – (top left) – Dana Allen – Wilderness Safaris
146 – (top right) – Kazuma Trails
146 – (middle left) – Dana Allen – Wilderness Safaris
146 – (middle right) – African Bush Camps
146 – (bottom left) – Amalinda Collection
146 – (bottom right) – Dave Carson
149 – Krysanthe Dawes
150 – (top) – Krysanthe Dawes
150 – (bottom) – Cathy Wright
152 – Beth Tetterton
153 – Alison Nolting
154 – Desiree Murray
155 – Dana Allen – Wilderness Safaris
156 – Paul Hubbard
157 – Amalinda Collection
158 – Paul Hubbard
159 – Paul Hubbard
160 – (top) – Mother Africa
160 – (middle) – Tracy Hinkemeyer
160 – (bottom) – Tracy Hinkemeyer
161 – Amalinda Collection
162 – Alison Nolting
163 – (top) – Singita
163 – (bottom) – Singita

Photo Credits

164 – Singita

Zambia

166 + 167 – Chiawa
170 – Chongwe
171 – Chiawa
174 – (top) – Sanctuary Lodges
174 – (bottom) – Sanctuary Lodges
175 – Robin Pope Safaris
176 – (top) – Remote Africa
176 – (middle left) – Shenton Safaris
176 – (middle right) – Shenton Safaris
176 – (bottom) – Remote Africa
180 – Remote Africa
181 – (top) – Chiawa
181 – (bottom) – Chiawa
182 – (top) – Chiawa
182 – (middle) – Chiawa
182 – (bottom) – Chongwe
183 – Dana Allen – Wilderness Safaris
185 – Dana Allen – Wilderness Safaris
186 – Dana Allen – Wilderness Safaris
187 – (top) – Dana Allen – Wilderness Safaris
187 – (bottom) – Dana Allen – Wilderness Safaris
189 – Rahn Huffstutler
190 – (top) – Sanctuary Lodges
190 – (bottom) – Mike Myers – Wilderness Safaris
191 – (top) – Dana Allen – Wilderness Safaris
191 – (middle) – Tongabezi Safari Lodge
191 – (bottom) – Tongabezi Safari Lodge

Namibia

192 + 193 – Dana Allen – Wilderness Safaris
196 – (top) – Pietro Bianchi
196 – (bottom) – Wilderness Safaris
197 – Pietro Bianchi
199 – Olive Exclusive
201 – Pietro Bianchi
202 – Dana Allen – Wilderness Safaris
203 – (top) – Wilderness Safaris
203 – (middle) – Dana Allen – Wilderness Safaris
203 – (bottom) – Dana Allen – Wilderness Safaris
204 – (top) – Dana Allen – Wilderness Safaris
204 – (bottom) – Wolwedans

205 – (top) – Pietro Bianchi
205 – (bottom) – Namibia Tracks & Trails
206 – Wilderness Safaris
207 – (top) – Natasha Zapata
207 – (bottom) – Pietro Bianchi
208 – Pietro Bianchi
209 – Pietro Bianchi
211 – Dana Allen – Wilderness Safaris
212 – (top) – Dana Allen – Wilderness Safaris
212 – (bottom) – Dana Allen – Wilderness Safaris
213 – (top) – Dana Allen – Wilderness Safaris
213 – (bottom) – Dana Allen – Wilderness Safaris
215 – (top) – Michael Poliza
215 – (middle) – Dana Allen – Wilderness Safaris
215 – (bottom) – Dana Allen – Wilderness Safaris
216 – Caroline Culbert – Wilderness Safaris
219 – (top) – Dana Allen – Wilderness Safaris
219 – (middle) – Michael Poliza
219 – (bottom) – Dana Allen – Wilderness Safaris
220 – Nhoma Camp
221 – Pietro Bianchi
222 – (top) – Pietro Bianchi
222 – (bottom) – Lüderitz Nest Hotel

South Africa

224 + 225 – Tswalu Kalahari Reserve
228 – Tanda Tula
229 – Beth Tetterton
230 – Brenda Dittmore
232 – (top) – Saxon Hotel
232 – (middle) – Intercontinental Johannesburg Airport Sun
232 – (bottom) – African Rock
233 – Blue Train
234 – Rovos Rail
235 – Rovos Rail
238 – Dana Allen – Wilderness Safaris
239 – Beth Tetterton
240 – (top) – Singita
240 – (bottom) – Dana Allen – Wilderness Safaris
242 – (top) – Camp Jabulani
242 – (bottom) – Singita
243 – MalaMala Game Reserve
244 – (top) – Singita
244 – (middle, left) – Lion Sands

244 – (middle, right) – MalaMala Game Reserve
244 – (bottom) – Singita
245 – Cheetah Plains
247 – (top) – Tanda Tula
247 – (bottom) – Camp Jabulani
248 – Camp Jabulani
249 – Cybele Forest
252 – Paul Brown
255 – (top) – Tswalu Kalahari Reserve
255 – (bottom) – Tswalu Kalahari Reserve
256 – Eric Gurwin
258 – Kenneth Covelman
259 – Lorraine Lutgen
260 – Cape Grace
261 – (top) – Radisson Blu
261 – (middle) – Cape Grace
261 – (bottom, left) – Kensington Place
261 – (bottom, right) – Ellerman House
262 – (top) – Twelve Apostles
262 – (far left) – Welgelegen
262 – (middle right) – Steenberg Hotel
262 – (bottom right) – O on Kloof
265 – (top) – La Residence
265 – (bottom) – Lanzerac Manor
266 – (top) – Majeka House
266 – (middle) – Le Quartier Francais
266 – (bottom) – Delaire
267 – La Petit Ferme
269 – Bushmans Kloof
270 – (top) – Bushmans Kloof
270 – (bottom) – Bushmans Kloof
272 – (top) – The Marine
272 – (bottom) – Auberge Burgundy
273 – Grootbos
274 – (top) – Grootbos
274 – (bottom) – Steve Murdock
275 – (top) – The Plettenberg
275 – (bottom) – The Plettenberg
281 – Bill Powell
281 – (middle) – &Beyond
281 – (bottom) – &Beyond
286 – (top, middle + bottom) – &Beyond
287 – Caroline Culbert – Wilderness Safaris
288 – (top) – Anthony Grote – Wilderness Safaris
288 – (bottom) – Martin Benadie – Wilderness Safaris

Mozambique

290 + 291 – Vamizi Island, Mozambique

434 – Serena Lodges
436 – Becci Crowe
437 – (top + bottom) Becci Crowe
440 – Cheli & Peacock
442 – Safari Collection
443 – (top) – Safari Collection
443 – (bottom) – Safari Conservation and Company (SCC)
444 – Safari Conservation and Company (SCC)
445 – (top + bottom) – Safari Conservation and Company (SCC)
448 – Safari Collection
449 – (top + bottom) – Safari Collection
451 – (top + bottom) – Cheli & Peacock
452 – Becci Crowe
453 – Becci Crowe
454 – (top + bottom) – Elewana
457 – (top + bottom) – Safari Conservation and Company (SCC)

Uganda
458 + 459 – Eric Gurwin
462 – (top) – Alison Nolting
462 – (bottom) – Michael Levine
463 – (left) – Chet Stein
463 – (right) – Classic Africa Safaris
464 – Classic Africa Safaris
466 – Ron Magill
467 – Classic Africa Safaris
468 – Chet Stein
469 – Classic Africa Safaris
472 – Eric Gurwin
473 – Alison Nolting
475 – (top, left) – Classic Africa
475 – (top, right) – Chet Stein
475 – (bottom) – Chet Stein
476 – (top) – Chet Stein
476 – (middle, left) – Chet Stein
476 – (middle, right) – Chet Stein
476 – (bottom) – Alison Nolting
477 – (top) – Mweya Lodge
477 – (bottom) – Classic Africa Safaris

480 – Classic Africa Safaris
481 – (top) – Sanctuary Lodges
481 – (bottom) – Sanctuary Lodges
482 – (top) – Alison Nolting
482 – (middle) – Gene Covey
482 – (bottom) – Eric Gurwin
483 – (top left) – Eric Gurwin
483 – (top right) – Eric Gurwin
483 – (bottom) – Sanctuary Lodges
484 – (top) – Alison Nolting
484 – (bottom) – Alison Nolting
485 – Alison Nolting
487 – (top + bottom) – Abby Lazar

Rwanda
488 + 489 – Danielle Moriarty
492 – (top) – Danielle Moriarty
492 – (bottom) – Steve Turner
493 – Alan Leshner
494 – Gene Covey
496 – Mark Nolting
498 – Danielle Moriarty
499 – Ed Rahal
500 – Mickey Koplove
501 – Primate Safaris
502 – (top) – Gene Covey
502 – (bottom) – Ed Rahal
503 – Ardythe McCracken
504 – Michael Poliza
505 – (top) – Primate Safaris
505 – (bottom) – Classic Africa
506 – (top, left) – Lynne Crawford
506 – (top, right) – Lynne Crawford
506 – (bottom) – Classic Africa
507 – (top) – Women for Women International
507 – (bottom) Kigali Serena Hotel
508 – Primate Safaris
508 – Primate Safaris

Congo
510 + 511 – Wilderness Safaris
514 – Wilderness Safaris
515 – Mike Myers – Wilderness Safaris
516 – Wilderness Safaris
517 – (top) – Wilderness Safaris
517 – (bottom) – Wilderness Safaris
518 – Wilderness Safaris
519 – Wilderness Safaris

Ethiopia
520 + 521 – Cover – Tom Trainer
524 – Tom Trainer
525 – Steve Turner
529 – Steve Turner
530 – Steve Turner
531 – Abby Lazar
532 – Steve Turner
534 – (top) – Abby Lazar
534 – (bottom) – Tom Trainer
535 – (top) – Mark Nolting
535 – (middle) – Abby Lazar
535 – (bottom) – Mark Nolting
536 – Steve Turner
538 – Tom Trainer

Seychelles
540 + 541 – Ricardo Maitsch
544 – Cousine Island
545 – Mike Myers – Wilderness Safaris
546 – Cousine Island
548 – (top) – Creole Travel – Banyan Tree
548 – (bottom) – Creole Travel – Four Seasons
549 – Creole Travel – Sainte Anne
551 – Cousine Island
552 – Creole Travel – La Domaine de l'Orangerie
553 – (top) – Creole Travel – Desroche Island
553 – (bottom) – Creole Travel – Denis Island
554 – Creole Travel – Labriz Resort
555 – (top) – Mike Myers – Wilderness Safaris
555 – (bottom) – Dana Allen – Wilderness Safaris

Mauritius
556 + 557 – One&Only – Barbara Kraft
560 – One&Only
561 – Unusual Destinations
563 – Belle Mare Plage
564 – Belle Mare Plage
565 – Four Seasons
566 – (top) – One&Only
566 – (bottom) – Belle Mare Plage
567 – One&Only

Praise for
African Safari Journal

As someone who has visited Africa over 40 times, I can say without hesitation that the *African Safari Journal* is the best single resource one can have with them on what is sure to be an adventure of a lifetime. Its easy-to-read style and wide variety of information make it a "must have" for anyone on safari!

— RON MAGILL – COMMUNICATIONS & MEDIA MIAMI METROZOO

Mark Nolting has done it again! Clearing out the clutter from the safari experience, making sense of what is good and what is bad, getting prepared once you have decided are all often overlooked and sometimes overwhelming aspects of the safari. Thanks to *African Safari Journal* it's all done for you, and all that is left is to engulf yourself in our continent's pleasures.

— DERECK JOUBERT – EXPLORER IN RESIDENCE AT THE
NATIONAL GEOGRAPHIC SOCIETY, CONSERVATIONIST, FILMMAKER

If *Africa's Top Wildlife Countries* is the first book to grab when planning your safari, then the *African Safari Journal* is the first book to grab when you're headed to the airport to go on your safari! Nolting has got you covered from planning your safari, to living it, and reliving it again through the notes in your own personal safari journal. Packed full of information, maps, hundreds of color illustrations, and space for your own notes, it's the only book you'll ever need while on safari!

— GENE ECKHART – PROFESSIONAL PHOTOGRAPHER AND AUTHOR OF
"MOUNTAIN GORILLAS – BIOLOGY, CONSERVATION AND COEXISTENCE"

Mark Nolting's *African Safari Journal* has accompanied our family on each of our sojourns to Africa. Incorporating an abbreviated guide to the African bush, a planner and a personal journal in a compact format, the *African Safari Journal* has been an indispensable tool accompanying us on our travels. Upon return, it remains a keepsake of treasured memories and mementos secreted within its pages.

— TERRI WILLIAMS – JAKWAY WHITE BEAR LAKE, MN

African Safari Journal, 5th Edition

by Mark W. Nolting

A wildlife guide, trip organizer, map directory, safari directory, phrase book, safari diary, and wildlife checklist—all-in-one and now with 168 pages in color!

As many safariers have strict baggage limits, this **seven-books-in-one** journal becomes all the more valuable as it is packed with all the information a traveler to Africa is going to need.

With the valuable **African Safari Journal** contents you can become an instant authority on safari!

* **311 COLOR illustrations** and detailed descriptions of mammals, reptiles, birds, insects and trees for easy identification

* **Checklists** for recording sightings in reserves

* **60 COLOR maps** detailing regions, countries and major wildlife reserves

* **Swahili, Tswana, Shona, Zulu and French** words, phrases, and mammal names (with phonetics)

* **Constellation Map** of the Southern Hemisphere – and star gazers guide

* **Safari and Photographic tips**

* **Suggested shopping list** with "gifts and trades" ideas

* **Contact information** for US Embassies and Canadian and British High Commissions in Africa

* **Over 50 journal pages** to record your personal safari experiences

AFRICAN SAFARI JOURNAL
Fifth Edition
$19.95 ISBN 978-0-939895-11-3
328 pp, 311 Color Illustrations,
60 Color Maps, 5x8

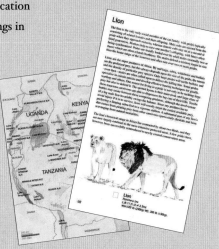

Global Travel Publishers
5353 N. Federal Highway, Suite 300
Ft. Lauderdale, FL 33308 USA
Tel: 800-882-9453 or 954-491-8877
info@globaltravelpublishers.com
www.globaltravelpublishers.com

Volume Discounts Available

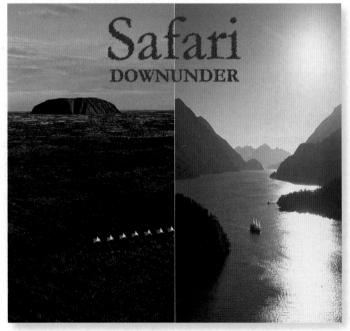

The
Africa Adventure
Company

Dear Adventurer:

The Africa Adventure Company is your passport to the safari of your dreams. Our team is managed and directed by Mark and Alison Nolting, two people whose combined experience and knowledge of Africa is unsurpassed in the safari business.

Mark is the author of *Africa's Top Wildlife Countries,* an award-winning guide book that is considered by the travel industry as the quintessential guide for planning a safari, and the *African Safari Journal,* a diary, phrase book and wildlife guide, all in one. He has received the **Conde Nast Traveler** magazine award as one of the World's Top African Travel Specialists for the past 9 years, has been listed on **Travel & Leisure's** A-List for several years. In addtion, the Africa Adventure Company has been acclaimed by **National Geographic Adventurer** as one of the greatest safari companies on earth. Born and raised in Zimbabwe, Alison managed a safari camp for several years hosting guests in the bush and worked in the Africa travel industry in England before joining Mark in 1991.

So how do you know which safari is right for you? Private or group? East Africa or Southern Africa? A luxury itinerary with premier camps and lodges or camping out in the bush with mobile tents? This is where our passionate staff and years of experience set us apart. We are here to guide you through all the choices.

We offer a refreshing assortment of over 100 unique and exciting itineraries that can only beckon your travel spirit to Africa. Many can be adapted to your personal specifications. Taking into consideration your needs and desires, we take your dream of the "perfect day on safari" and make it a reality.

As we constantly receive reports from our guides and operators on the ground, receive trip reports from thousands of returning clients and visit Africa often ourselves, *we keep very current as to where the best wildlife is being seen and which safari camps and lodges are providing the best wildlife experience, accommodations, food and service NOW* — allowing us to present the absolute best safari options for you. No amount of research on the Internet can provide this information.

We encourage you to contact us so that we may send you our easy-to-use SAFARI PLANNER and assist you in planning your African journey. Our personalized service will exceed your expectations!

Cordially,

Mark and Alison Nolting

The Africa Adventure Company • 5353 N. Federal Hwy., Suite 300, Ft. Lauderdale, FL 33308
Tel: 800.882.9453 or 954.491.8877; Fax: 954.491.9060 • Email: safari@AfricanAdventure.com
Website: www.AfricanAdventure.com

Botswana	Madagscar	Seychelles
Congo, Republic of	Malawi	South Africa
Egypt	Mauritius	Tanzania
Ethiopia	Morocco	Uganda
Kenya	Mozambique	Zambia
Jordan	Namibia	Zimbabwe
	Rwanda